THE FRENCH COOKIE BOOK

THE FRENCH COOKIE BOOK

CLASSIC AND
CONTEMPORARY
RECIPES FOR
EASY AND ELEGANT
COOKIES

BRUCE HEALY
WITH PAUL BUGAT

ILLUSTRATIONS BY PAUL BUGAT
PHOTOGRAPHY BY PIERRE GINET
DESIGN BY STEPHANIE TEVONIAN

WILLIAM MORROW AND COMPANY, INC.
NEW YORK

Library of Congress Cataloging-in-Publication Data

Healy, Bruce.
    The French cookie book : classic and contemporary recipes for easy and elegant cookies / Bruce Healy with Paul Bugat.
        p.   cm.
    Includes bibliographical references and indexes.
    ISBN 0-688-08833-3
    1. Cookies.   2. Cookery, French.
    I. Bugat, Paul.   II. Title.
TX772.H397   1994
641.8'654—dc20   94-18567
                                               CIP

Printed in the United States of America
First Edition

1   2   3   4   5   6   7   8   9   10

FOR CHARLOTTE

ACKNOWLEDGMENTS

When I began working on this book, longer ago than I care to admit, I was familiar with a couple of dozen French cookies. I knew they were easy to make, and so naturally I assumed that assembling a book on classic and contemporary French cookies would be a project I could complete quickly. I was, shall we say, naive. Nearly all of the cookies are indeed easy—once you know how to make them. Unfortunately, the subject was a morass of little tricks and subtleties. And while the repertoire of cookies made in France at the end of the nineteenth century was truly vast, by the late twentieth century it had dwindled to barely more than those I knew at the outset. What's more, the cookbook writers of that golden age of French cookies were addressing a market of professional pastry chefs, people who were familiar with the subject and needed a compendium of aides de mémoire. Today, their ''recipes'' are little more than clues—typically vague, occasionally contradictory or misleading—to an enormous body of knowledge that seems distant to even the most knowledgeable modern pastry chefs.

So researching this book has been a project of detective work, assembling bits and pieces of information from the past with the concrete knowledge of the present, developing and perfecting recipes in seemingly endless succession, until the parts fit together in a coherent way, like solving a giant jigsaw puzzle. In the process, I have been indebted, on the one hand, to those pastry chefs who laid out the trail of clues, and on the other hand to the friends and colleagues who, through their generous consultation, encouragement, and support, have helped me to find in the morass the intrinsic logic, beauty, and simplicity of the subject. Among those friends and colleagues, I wish to thank especially:

My wife, Alice Healy, for her unfailing love and support, for reading the manuscript and contributing a wealth of indispensable comments and suggestions, and for her critical assessment of every cookie.

My daughter, Charlotte Alexandra Healy, for her unconditional affection and for the inspiration of her vivacious spirit and boundless enthusiasm.

My parents, James and Margaret Healy, for their enlightened upbringing, selfless generosity, and enduring support.

Peter and Nancy Kranz for their friendship and encouragement; to Peter for innumerable discussions on all aspects of gastronomy; and to Nancy for helping me expand my library.

André Neveu for introducing me to Paul Bugat many years ago, thereby making our collaboration possible.

Shirley Corriher for many discussions on the science of baking and for her encouragement.

Harold McGee for sharing his broad understanding of food science, for his help in taking some of the mystery out of whipping eggs and preparing macaroons, for a critical reading of Chapters 2 and 3, and for arranging an invitation for me to the International Workshop on Molecular and Physical Gastronomy in Erice during August 1992.

Peter Barham for valuable discussions on the science of baking, for clarifying my understanding of the physics behind the creation of egg foams, for his collaboration in the development of a theoretical explanation of the process that transforms whipped egg whites into a meringue, and for a careful reading of all of the scientific sections of the book.

Nicholas Kurti for arranging funds for my transportation to the International Workshop on Molecular and Physical Gastronomy. Nicholas Kurti, Hervé This, and Harold McGee for organizing this remarkable workshop. And the Ettore Majorana Center for Scientific Culture for its hospitality in Erice.

Richard Hopkins for his capable and dependable assistance in the kitchen during much of the time when I was developing the recipes, and for many helpful practical suggestions.

Robert Howell for testing the recipes in Chapter 1 and for his valuable comments.

Rose Beranbaum for introducing me to our publisher, William Morrow and Company.

Maria Guarnaschelli for accepting the proposal for our book at Morrow six years ago, for valuable discussions, for entrusting the line editing to Maureen Haviland, for suggesting Stephanie Tevonian to design the book, and, upon her departure from Morrow, for seeing that the editing of the book was transferred to the capable hands of Megan Newman.

Maureen Haviland for her perceptive advice and suggestions on revising the text and improving the headnotes and for carefully testing the recipes.

Megan Newman for taking on the enormous task of completing the editing of this book, for her attention to every detail, for her insightful guidance in resolving numerous dilemmas that had accumulated over the years, for her gentle hand in shaping the final product, and for accepting my input on every aspect of the book.

Stephanie Tevonian for listening to my aesthetic preferences and transforming them into a sophisticated modern design that is in exquisite harmony with the text.

Pierre Ginet for his stylish and sensual photography. And Christine Drin for her elegant and creative prop styling.

Bob Berkeley for his discerning consultation on the photography.

Bruce Healy
Boulder

It is a pleasure to express my gratitude to my family and colleagues, in particular to:

My wife Danielle Bugat for her patient support and for taking on an extra share of the responsibility of running our pâtisserie while I was working on the drawings.

Danielle and our children, Isabelle, Nathalie, and Marc Bugat, for their unwavering love and encouragement.

Isabelle and Nathalie for their help with the drawings.

Pierre Ginet and Christine Drin for the pleasure of collaborating with them in styling the photographs, and for Pierre's consummate artistry.

Michael Hentges for his sage advice on simplifying the drawings.

Paul Bugat
Paris

CONTENTS

INTRODUCTION

Every book about cookies will tell you that cookie making is fun, easy, and gratifying. We add a new twist. French cookies are fun, easy, gratifying, and beautiful. Not only is the perfume of the baking cookies heavenly, not only do the cookies taste wonderful, not only do you get the soul-satisfying feeling of creating a home-baked product that tastes better and fresher than its store-bought counterpart. On top of all that, French cookies look exquisite—like edible jewels that you would think only a professional pastry chef could produce.

At this point you are perhaps a bit skeptical. After all, you say, French pastry is a complex art. Each dessert is built of components: flaky pastry doughs, airy cake layers, creamy fillings, and glistening glazes. For the average home cook, the creation of these delights seems as formidable as the finished products are delectable.

In our first book, *Mastering the Art of French Pastry,* we set out to demystify pastry making, organizing its intricacies to reveal the systematic underlying structure so that fabulous French pastries can be prepared in the American home kitchen. Still, elegant desserts do take time and patience, and for most home cooks they must be reserved for special occasions.

French cookies are another story. They are simple, fast to make, and don't require advance preparation of a battery of components. You whip up a batter or dough, shape it, bake it, and *voilà*—in a matter of minutes you have a cookie jar full of delicious treats to enjoy every day. The equipment required is minimal and the list of ingredients is short. Decoration is usually supplied by the shapes of the cookies themselves, sometimes accented with chocolate, sugar glaze, or glacé fruit.

It is surprising that we Americans, who are so enamored with cookies, doting on the humble chocolate chip and collecting a staggering array of recipes from around the world, have neglected all but a tiny handful from the vast repertory of truly extraordinary French cookies. To be sure, we are familiar with Madeleines and Ladyfingers, Cats' Tongues and Almond Tiles, Florentines and Palm Leaves. But Friands and Gerbet Macaroons, Vietnamese Hats and Field Marshal's Batons, Russian Lace and Nero's Ears are still unknown to us.

French cookies certainly are different from their American counterparts. Most American cookies are large and homey, even when made by professionals. They group naturally—according to how they are shaped—into bar cookies, drop cookies, rolled cookies, icebox cookies, and hand-formed cookies. In contrast, French cookies tend to be relatively small and elegant. Nearly all are made from batters that are piped from a pastry bag (the analog of drop cookies) or from pastry doughs (including both rolled cookies and icebox cookies). As you will soon learn, it makes more sense to organize them by the method of preparing the batter or dough rather than by how they are shaped.

While the French love cookies, for them the American concept of a cookie does not really exist. Their *petits fours* include miniature baked goods of every conceivable variety. In particular, *petits fours secs* are what we would call small cookies. But if the same cookies are made in a larger size, they are no longer *petits fours* at all but instead *petits gâteaux*—literally "small cakes." And naturally, *petits gâteaux* also include serving-size cakes and pastries of every description. We can only speculate what the average Frenchman would think of a monster chocolate chip cookie.

In *Mastering the Art of French Pastry,* we included a few *petits gâteaux,* but no *petits fours* at all. Now, in *The French Cookie Book,* we explore the full range of *petits fours secs,* as well as the larger cookies that are made as *petits gâteaux.* We have divided it into three parts. The first part encompasses the cookies that are made from batters. We differentiate five types, with a chapter devoted to each; batters based on creamed butter and sugar; meringue batters; almond paste batters; sponge cake batters; and miscellaneous nut batters. The second part covers cookies made from pastry doughs. Here there are only two chapters, based on sweet pastry doughs of the *sablé* type and on the flaky pastry dough called *feuilletage,* respectively. The third part includes sections on equipment, ingredients, product sources, and measurement and equivalences, as well as detailed explanations of how to use a pastry bag and some basic preparations and procedures.

You are probably still thinking that, despite our assurances, you will find French cookies more tricky, time-consuming, and difficult than the American cookies you have been making for years. In fact, French pastry chefs have refined their techniques through decades of hard work and careful thought, to the point where the recipes are straightforward and efficient. Most of the recipes call for a pastry bag or rolling pin because these tools are easy to use and make shaping the cookies a breeze. You will find that our cookies are some of the easiest and least time consuming you have ever made.

Now that you know what is in this book, you can start baking. Pick a recipe, try it, enjoy the cookies. And most of all, have fun in the kitchen because that is what *The French Cookie Book* is all about.

COOKIES MADE FROM BATTERS

CHAPTER 1
BATTERS BASED ON CREAMED BUTTER AND SUGAR

Start with creamed butter and sugar, beat in eggs (whole eggs, yolks, or whites) and flavorings, and mix in flour. Then pipe or spoon the resulting batter onto a baking sheet and bake. This simple procedure is the basis for an enormous variety of cookies. Let me give you an idea of the possibilities.

The proportions of butter, sugar, eggs, and flour in the batter determine its consistency. With equal weights of these four basic ingredients the batter will be soft and easy to pipe with a pastry bag, and it will spread moderately during baking. These batters are almost always piped in finger or dome shapes with a plain pastry tube. The resulting cookies, such as Ladies' Wafers and Cats' Tongues, are thin and crisp, delicate buttery morsels that are as easy to prepare as they are to enjoy.

For cookies with more complicated shapes you need a much drier and firmer batter with a higher proportion of flour. Some shapes—such as flowers, grape clusters, and spirals—are piped with a plain pastry tube. Fingers, rosettes, teardrops, Ss, and wreaths, on the other hand, are piped with a fluted pastry tube. You must apply more pressure on the pastry bag to pipe these batters. The cookies spread very little during baking and hold their shape well. Cookies of this type, such as Piped Sablés, Tea Cookies, and Viennese Cookies, are thick and buttery, with an appealing sandy texture similar to cookies made from sweet pastry doughs.

In the opposite direction are very thin, soft batters that contain a lower proportion of flour than the batters made from equal weights of the four basic ingredients. These are also piped onto baking sheets with a plain pastry tube, and they spread quite a bit during baking. Cookies of this type are crisp and light. After baking, some of them are hand-formed into traditional shapes; for example, Russian Cigarettes are rolled into cylinders.

Other factors besides the proportions of the basic ingredients can affect the texture of the finished cookies. Confectioners' sugar produces crisper cookies, whereas with superfine sugar more air is beaten into the batter, yielding lighter cookies. Compared to whole eggs, egg whites alone make the cookies crisper, and yolks alone make them richer and softer. Introducing ground almonds into the batter not only adds flavor but also enriches the cookies and produces a finely grained texture.

The possibilities multiply when these textures and shapes are coupled with an assortment of flavorings, fillings, glazes, and decorations. Vanilla, citrus zests, rum, orange liqueurs, nuts, and cocoa are the most popular choices for flavoring the batters. The baked cookies can be filled with jam, buttercream, praliné butter, almond paste, or chocolate. They can be glazed with chocolate or with apricot jam followed by a confectioners' sugar and water glaze. Or they can be decorated with glacé fruits or with a sprinkling of crystal sugar or confectioners' sugar.

PREPARING THE BATTER

①

Remove the butter from the refrigerator and let it rest at room temperature until it warms to between 59 and 63° F (15–17° C) and begins to soften. Place the butter in a small stainless-steel bowl and beat it with a wooden spatula to make it soft and smooth. (Or see the following section for using an electric mixer.) As you beat the butter ①, gently warm it over low direct heat as needed to soften it, but do not let it become runny and liquid. It must not get warmer than 68° F (20° C), which is the melting point of butterfat. Continue beating the butter vigorously until it is white, soft, and creamy—the French call it butter *en pommade*.

②

Beat the sugar (confectioners' sugar should be sifted first) into the creamed butter ② with the wooden spatula. If the quantity of sugar is less than or approximately equal to the amount of butter, add the sugar all at once. If there is much more sugar than butter, beat in half the sugar at a time in order to incorporate the sugar quickly without knocking it out of the bowl as you beat the butter. For batters that include ground nuts (always in the form of a nut and sugar powder), these are added with or immediately after the sugar. Continue beating vigorously until smooth and light.

③

Next beat in the first egg (whether whole egg, white, or yolk) with the wooden spatula. Then beat in the remaining eggs ③ (if there are any) one at a time with a stiff wire whisk. Be sure that each egg is incorporated before adding more. Any additional liquids and most flavorings are whisked in right after the eggs. Do not whisk any longer than necessary to mix or you may incorporate too much air in the batter, making it bubble too much when baked. Note that in some batters there is not enough sugar to absorb all the liquid in the eggs, and the batter may look curdled at this stage. Don't worry; the batter will become smooth again when the flour is added.

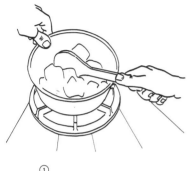

④

Finally, sift the flour ④ over the batter and then mix it in quickly with the wooden spatula. Stop mixing as soon as the batter is smooth. It isn't necessary to use a folding motion, but don't overwork the batter. Continuing to stir the batter after it is mixed could activate the gluten in the flour and make the cookies tough. This is particularly important for cookies that are low in butter. For cookies with a high butter content, the butterfat coats the gluten strands in the batter, making the cookies more tender.

While there are occasional exceptions (notably the batter for Russian

Cigarettes, which needs to firm in the refrigerator before piping and baking), most of the creamed butter and sugar batters can be piped and baked right away. Or you can store the batter in the refrigerator and bake it later (see Storage section later in this chapter).

USING AN ELECTRIC MIXER

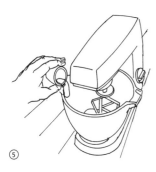

For the small quantities in our recipes, it is easiest to prepare the creamed butter and sugar batters by hand. However, if you want to multiply our recipes and make large batches of batter at once, then you will find it advantageous to prepare the batters in a heavy-duty electric mixer. Cream the softened butter and beat in the sugar using the flat beater of your mixer. You will not have to warm the butter because the machine will warm it as it works. Beat in the first egg with the flat beater ⑤, then switch to the wire whip attachment and beat in the remaining eggs (if any) one at a time, followed by any additional liquids and the flavorings. Beat only long enough to mix, otherwise you will incorporate too much air and the batter will bubble when baked. Then sift the flour over the batter and mix it in with a wooden spatula.

⑤

PREPARING THE BAKING SHEETS

Most of the soft batters in this chapter are baked on buttered and floured baking sheets so that the cookies will hold a nice shape. For glazed cookies, such as Brussels Rum Cookies and Lemon Wafers, we often prefer parchment lined baking sheets. On the other hand, cookies that must spread and become very thin, such as Buttery Almond Tiles and Russian Cigarettes, should be baked on buttered (but not floured) baking sheets.

For thicker batters that hold more complicated shapes, the cookies are usually baked on buttered baking sheets. For several of these, including Piped Sables and Viennese Cookies, there should be only a thin film of butter on the baking sheet so that the batter will stick to the baking sheet as you pipe it. For these, first brush a light coating of melted butter on the baking sheet, and then wipe off the excess with a clean paper towel.

PASTRY BAG, ICE CREAM SCOOP, OR COOKIE PRESS

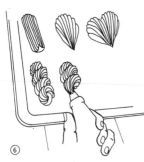

Depositing the batter on the baking sheet by piping with a pastry bag is the easiest way to make cookies of uniform size and shape, which is essential for even baking and is aesthetically pleasing. A pastry bag also allows you to produce decorative fluting and many shapes ⑥ that would otherwise be nearly impossible. Once you master the piping techniques (explained in "How to Use a Pastry Bag"; see page 474), this method is easy and efficient.

Alternatively, for many of the cookies in this chapter you can spoon the

⑥

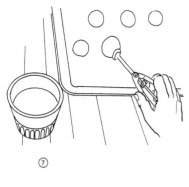

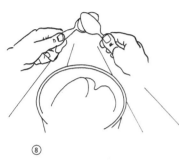

7

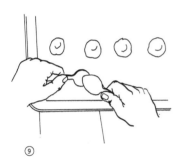

9

batter onto the baking sheet using a small ice cream scoop 7. (Obviously the ice cream scoop is suitable only for round cookies with no fluting.) For most small cookies either a #100 portion-control ice cream scoop (1¾-teaspoon or 9 ml capacity) or a "midget" ice cream scoop (1-teaspoon or ½ cl capacity) is the perfect size. A #70 ice cream scoop (2¾-teaspoon or 1.4 cl capacity) is good for some larger cookies. (See the reference section on Equipment, page 411, for details and sources.) If too much batter sticks to the scoop, dip it in cold water after every two or three cookies. Lacking an ice cream scoop, you can drop the batter onto the baking sheets with a teaspoon or tablespoon (depending upon the size of the cookies). Scoop up a lump of batter. Then use a second spoon or your fingertip (moistened with cold water as needed) to shape the batter 8 into a ball, push it off the first spoon 9, and deposit it on the baking sheet in a symmetrical dome.

As another alternative, the very firm batters (such as Piped Sablés, Tea Cookies, and Viennese Cookies) can be piped from a cookie press or cookie gun. In fact, many old-fashioned French cookies were piped from a syringe-type cookie press fitted with a variety of pastry tubes because this method requires less physical effort than piping firm batters from a pastry bag. Most of the cookie presses sold in the United States today are equipped with a selection of plates through which the dough is pressed, but they are not designed for use with pastry tubes. This makes it difficult or impossible to produce some of the classic shapes, but very easy to produce others. By experimenting you will learn which ones work best with your cookie press. Don't be afraid to deviate from the classic shapes for each cookie. They will be just as delicious in the shapes that are easiest for you.

STORAGE

All of the cookies in this chapter are at their best when freshly made. If kept at room temperature, covered airtight in a cookie jar or a tin cookie box, most will last for up to one week. The cookies with a high proportion of flour, such as Piped Sablés, Tea Cookies, and Viennese Cookies, will keep for up to two weeks. On the other hand, softer cookies, such as Lemon Wafers, Turkish Batons, Raisin Boulders, and Cornmeal Cookies, will last only three or four days.

Cookies filled with buttercream or praliné butter (Praliné-Filled Wafers and Ladies' Muffs) are very perishable. They can be kept in a cool place—below 60° F (15° C)—for up to twelve hours. Otherwise they must be refrigerated (always tightly covered) and will last at most a day or two after filling. Before filling they can be kept at room temperature in a cookie jar or tin cookie box for up to a week.

Cookies that are glazed or filled with chocolate must be kept cool—

below 70° F (20° C)—to prevent fat bloom from forming on the chocolate. Also, since the chocolate melts easily, avoid serving them in hot weather.

In very humid weather any of the crisp cookies can become soft and limp in less than a day. If they are not filled or glazed, they can be dried and crisped by laying them out on a baking sheet in a low 250° F (120° C) oven for a few minutes.

Most of the creamed butter and sugar batters can be stored in the refrigerator, tightly covered, for up to one week before baking. In this case the batter will become much firmer. If it is too firm to pipe with a pastry bag, take the batter out of the refrigerator and let it warm up, then stir it with a wooden spatula, warming it over low direct heat as needed to make it smooth and soft enough to pipe easily. This procedure does not work so well for batters with a high proportion of flour, however. Because of their high flour content, these batters become very firm when chilled, and in the process of softening them you can easily overwork the batter.

Batters that are suitable for storage in the refrigerator can also be frozen, tightly covered, for up to one month. Before using, defrost the batter overnight in the refrigerator and then proceed as for a refrigerated batter.

Refrigerating and/or freezing the batter are primarily of interest when you want to make a large quantity of batter and then bake it in several small batches as the need or desire for fresh cookies arises. For the small quantities in our recipes, preparing the batter is so fast and easy that the extra effort required to refrigerate, then warm and soften the batter usually makes these options impractical.

LADIES' WAFERS
PALETS DE DAMES

This simple cookie is the prototype for many of the fancier cookies in this chapter. Palets de dames *is the French name for the game ringtoss, and the cookies are thin, round disks with browned rims that, with a soupçon of imagination, recall the rope rings used in that game. Unfortunately, the poetry of the French gets lost in the translation, and ''rope rings'' just isn't an appealing name for a cookie. So we refer to them by the conventional (if prosaic) name Ladies' Wafers.*

EQUIPMENT

3 or 4 large, heavy baking sheets
• Brush with melted butter.
• Dust with flour.
A large pastry bag fitted with
• a ½-inch (12 mm) plain pastry tube (Ateco #6),
or a #100 ice cream scoop

BATTER

3½ ounces (100 g), or 7 tablespoons,
    unsalted butter, softened
3½ ounces (100 g), or ¾ cup plus 4 teaspoons,
    confectioners' sugar
2 large eggs
1 teaspoon (½ cl) vanilla extract
3½ ounces (100 g), or ⅔ cup plus 1 tablespoon,
    all-purpose flour

For about 55 to 60 cookies

Preheat the oven to 400° F (200° C).

1. Place the butter in a small stainless-steel bowl and beat with a wooden spatula, warming it over low heat as needed to make it smooth, white, and creamy. Sift the sugar over the butter and beat it in. Beat in 1 egg with the wooden spatula. Beat in the remaining egg with a wire whisk. Whisk in the vanilla. Sift the flour over the batter and mix it in with the wooden spatula.

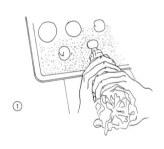

①

2. Scoop the batter into the pastry bag, and pipe the batter ① in domes 1¼ inches (3 cm) wide, arranging them on the baking sheets in staggered rows and separating them by 1½ inches (4 cm). Or, spoon the batter in 1½-teaspoon (¾ cl) domes using the ice cream scoop.

3. Bake, 1 sheet at a time, until the cookies are lightly browned around the edges but still pale in the center, about 6 to 10 minutes.

4. Slide the cookies onto a wire rack using a metal spatula and let cool to room temperature.

STORAGE: Covered airtight in a cookie jar or tin cookie box for up to 1 week.

CATS' TONGUES
LANGUES DE CHAT

Cats' Tongues are finger-shaped cookies closely related to
Ladies' Wafers (page 9). In fact the two can be made from the same batter, which includes
whole eggs. Or, Cats' Tongues can be made with just egg whites instead of the whole eggs
to make a lighter, crisper, and slightly less rich cookie. We give both alternatives. Either
way, their crisp texture, subtle flavor of vanilla and butter, and stark elegance make them
irresistible and versatile, equally good to eat on their own or as an accompaniment to a
dish of ice cream.

The name is pure French whimsy. The shape of langues de chat *is vaguely suggestive
of a cat's tongue.*

EQUIPMENT

3 or 4 large, heavy baking sheets
- Brush with melted butter.
- Dust with flour.

A large pastry bag fitted with
- a ⁵⁄₁₆-inch (8 mm) plain pastry tube (Ateco #3)

BATTER

3½ ounces (100 g), or 7 tablespoons, unsalted butter, softened

3½ ounces (100 g), or ¾ cup plus 4 teaspoons, confectioners' sugar

3 large egg whites or 2 large eggs

1 teaspoon (½ cl) vanilla extract

3½ ounces (100 g), or ⅔ cup plus 1 tablespoon, all-purpose flour

For about 55 to 60 cookies

Preheat the oven to 400° F (200° C).

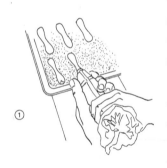

1. Place the butter in a small stainless-steel bowl and beat with a
wooden spatula, warming it over low heat as needed to make it smooth,
white, and creamy. Sift the sugar over the butter and beat it in. Beat in 1
egg or egg white with the wooden spatula. Beat in the remaining egg or
whites, 1 at a time, with a wire whisk. Whisk in the vanilla. Sift the flour
over the batter and mix it in with the wooden spatula.

2. Scoop the batter into the pastry bag, and pipe the batter ① on the
diagonal in fingers 2½ inches (6 cm) long and ⅜ inch (1 cm) wide at the
center, arranging them on the baking sheets in staggered rows and separating them by 1½ inches (4 cm). The ends of each finger should be fatter
than the center, like a dumbbell.

3. Bake, 1 sheet at a time, until the cookies are lightly browned
around the edges but still pale in the center, about 6 to 10 minutes.

4. Slide the cookies onto a wire rack using a metal spatula and let
cool to room temperature.

STORAGE: Covered airtight in a cookie jar or tin cookie box for up
to 1 week.

BRUSSELS RUM COOKIES
BRUXELLOIS

~~~~~~~~

These oval cookies, rich in butter and flavored with rum, are brushed with apricot jam followed by a glaze of rum and confectioners' sugar. The shiny, golden cookies remind me of the glittering, gilded façades facing the Grand Place, the great public square in Brussels (Bruxelles in French), the capital of Belgium. Cookies made from the same batter piped in rounds instead of ovals are called Glazed Wafers (palets glacés).

EQUIPMENT

2 large, heavy baking sheets
- Brush edges and diagonals with melted butter.
- Line with kitchen parchment.

A large pastry bag fitted with
- a ⁷⁄₁₆-inch (11 mm) plain pastry tube (Ateco #5)

BATTER

3½ ounces (100 g), or 7 tablespoons, unsalted
     butter, softened
2⅓ ounces (65 g), or ½ cup plus 2 teaspoons,
     confectioners' sugar
1 large egg

2 teaspoons (1 cl) dark Jamaican rum
2 ounces (60 g), or ¼ cup plus 3 tablespoons,
     all-purpose flour

GLAZE

2 to 2½ tablespoons (40–50 g) strained apricot jam
     [*Basic Preparation*, page 484]
1¾ ounces (50 g), or ⅓ cup plus 4 teaspoons,
     confectioners' sugar
2 teaspoons (1 cl) dark Jamaican rum

For about 30 to 35 cookies

Preheat the oven to 400° F (200° C).

1. Place the butter in a small stainless-steel bowl and beat with a wooden spatula, warming it over low heat as needed to make it smooth, white, and creamy. Sift the sugar over the butter and beat it in. Beat in the egg. Beat the batter briskly with a wire whisk, and whisk in the rum. Sift the flour over the batter and mix it in with the wooden spatula.

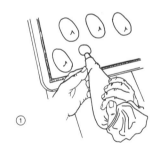

2. Scoop the batter into the pastry bag, and pipe the batter ① on the diagonal in ovals 2 inches (5 cm) long and ¾ inch (2 cm) wide, arranging them on the baking sheets in staggered rows and separating them by 2 inches (5 cm).

3. Bake, 1 sheet at a time, until the cookies are lightly browned around the edges but still pale cream color in the center, about 7 to 10 minutes.

4. Place the baking sheet on a wire rack and let the cookies cool to room temperature.

Raise the oven temperature to 450° F (230° C).

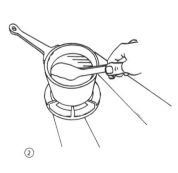

5. Warm the apricot jam over low heat, stirring occasionally ② until melted. Brush each cookie with jam ③ until lightly coated and glistening.

6. Sift the confectioners' sugar into a small bowl and stir in the rum. Then stir in enough cold water to make a smooth, creamy paste that is just fluid enough to spread easily with a pastry brush. Lightly brush this sugar glaze over the jam on top of each cookie. Return the cookies to the oven,

(continued)

1 baking sheet at a time, until the glaze turns from opaque white to translucent, about 1 minute. If the glaze starts to bubble, remove the cookies from the oven immediately.

7. Let the cookies cool on the baking sheets.

STORAGE: Covered airtight in a cookie jar or tin cookie box for up to 1 week.

③

LEMON WAFERS
PALETS AU CITRON

~~~~~~~~~~

This variant of Ladies' Wafers (page 9) has lemon zest in the batter and lemon juice in the shiny sugar glaze on top. Flavoring both batter and glaze results in an emphatically lemony cookie that is perfect with a cup of tea.

EQUIPMENT

2 or 3 large, heavy baking sheets
• Brush edges and diagonals with melted butter.
• Line with kitchen parchment.
A large pastry bag fitted with
• a ½-inch (12 mm) plain pastry tube (Ateco #6),
or a #100 ice cream scoop

BATTER

4½ ounces (125 g), or ½ cup plus 1 tablespoon,
    unsalted butter, softened
4½ ounces (125 g), or 1 cup plus 2 teaspoons,
    confectioners' sugar

4½ ounces (125 g), or ¾ cup plus 2 tablespoons,
    all-purpose flour
1 large egg yolk
Finely grated zest of 1 lemon
½ cup (12 cl) milk

GLAZE

3 tablespoons (60 g) strained apricot jam
    [*Basic Preparation*, page 484]
2½ ounces (70 g), or ½ cup plus 4 teaspoons,
    confectioners' sugar
2 teaspoons (1 cl) strained fresh lemon juice

For about 50 cookies

Preheat the oven to 350° F (175° C).

1. Place the butter in a small stainless-steel bowl and beat with a wooden spatula, warming it over low heat as needed to make it smooth, white, and creamy. Sift the sugar with 1½ ounces (45 g), or ⅓ cup, of the flour, and beat them into the butter. Then beat in the egg yolk and lemon zest. Whisk in the milk very gradually so that it doesn't splatter. Sift the remaining flour over the batter and mix it in with the whisk.

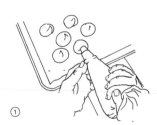

①

2. Scoop the batter into the pastry bag, and pipe the batter ① in domes. 1¼ inches (3 cm) wide, arranging them on the baking sheets in staggered rows and separating them by 1½ inches (4 cm). Or, spoon the batter in 1½-teaspoon (¾ cl) domes using the ice cream scoop.

3. Bake, 1 sheet at a time, until the cookies are browned around the edges but still pale cream color in the center, about 16 to 20 minutes.

4. Place the baking sheet on a wire rack and let the cookies cool to room temperature.

Raise the oven temperature to 450° F (230° C).

5. Warm the apricot jam ② over low heat, stirring occasionally until melted. Brush each cookie with jam ③ until lightly coated and glistening.

6. Sift the confectioners' sugar into a small bowl, and stir in the lemon juice. Then stir in enough cold water to make a smooth, creamy paste that is just fluid enough to spread easily with a pastry brush. Lightly brush this sugar glaze over the jam on top of each cookie. Return the cookies to the oven, 1 baking sheet at a time, until the glaze turns from opaque white to translucent, about 1 minute. If the glaze starts to bubble, remove the cookies from the oven immediately.

7. Let the cookies cool on the baking sheets.

➤ **HOWS & WHYS:** The batter contains milk, which gives the cookies a softer texture. The milk has a tendency to splatter as it is whisked into the creamed butter and sugar. Adding part of the flour with the sugar helps absorb the milk more quickly to minimize splattering.

STORAGE: Covered airtight in a cookie jar or tin cookie box for up to 3 days.

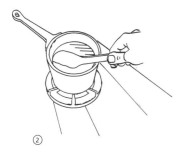

②

③

VISCONTIS
VISCONTIS

~~~~~~~

The Visconti family ruled Milan and Lombardy from the thirteenth to fifteenth centuries. Perhaps the chef who adopted their name for these cookies spent some time in northern Italy.

The batter you will use here is similar to the basic Ladies' Wafers batter (page 9), but it is richer, sweeter, and more substantial and is enhanced with the complementary flavors of orange zest and curaçao liqueur. The batter is then piped into rounds, just as for Ladies' Wafers. The big difference is a sprinkling of chopped almonds on top of the cookies that transforms the somewhat austere prototype by adding an appealing crunch and visual depth.

EQUIPMENT

2 large, heavy baking sheets
• Brush with melted butter.
• Dust with flour.
A large pastry bag fitted with
• a ½-inch (12 mm) plain pastry tube (Ateco #6), or a #100 ice cream scoop

BATTER

2¼ ounces (65 g), or 4½ tablespoons, unsalted butter, softened
2 ounces (60 g), or ½ cup, confectioners' sugar
1 large egg
1 tablespoon (1½ cl) curaçao liqueur
Finely grated zest of 1 orange
2 ounces (60 g), or ¼ cup plus 3 tablespoons, all-purpose flour

DECORATION

2 ounces (60 g), or ⅓ cup plus 1 tablespoon, blanched almonds, chopped
Confectioners' sugar

For about 30 cookies

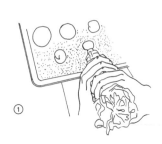
①

②

Preheat the oven to 400° F (200° C).

1. Place the butter in a small stainless-steel bowl and beat with a wooden spatula, warming it over low heat as needed to make it smooth, white, and creamy. Sift the sugar over the butter and beat it in. Beat in the egg. Beat the batter briskly with a wire whisk, and whisk in the curaçao and orange zest. Sift the flour over the batter and mix it in with the wooden spatula.

2. Scoop the batter into the pastry bag, and pipe the batter ① in domes 1¼ inches (3 cm) wide, arranging them on the baking sheets in staggered rows and separating them by 1½ inches (4 cm). Or, spoon the batter in 1½-teaspoon (¾ cl) domes using the ice cream scoop.

3. Dust chopped almonds ② over the piped batter. Turn each baking sheet upside down and tap it with a wooden spatula ③ to remove the excess almonds, then quickly turn the baking sheet right side up again. Dust the piped batter with confectioners' sugar.

4. Bake, 1 sheet at a time, until the cookies are lightly browned around the edges but still pale in the center, about 7 to 10 minutes.

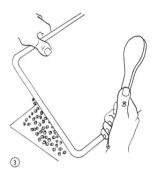

5. Slide the cookies onto a wire rack using a metal spatula and let them cool to room temperature.

➤ **HOWS & WHYS:** The confectioners' sugar dusting on these cookies helps the tops of the cookies brown, giving them a richer color.

VARIATION: To vary the shape, you can also pipe this batter in fingers, like Cats' Tongues, and call the cookies Almond Tongues (*langues aux amandes*). Use a ⅜-inch (1 cm) plain pastry tube (Ateco #4). In step 2, pipe the batter on the diagonal in fingers 2½ inches (6 cm) long and ⅜ inch (1 cm) wide at the center, arranging them on the baking sheets in staggered rows and separating them by 1½ inches (4 cm). The ends of each finger should be fatter than the center, like a dumbbell. Then proceed with steps 3–5.

STORAGE: Covered airtight in a cookie jar or tin cookie box for up to 1 week.

BUTTERY ALMOND TILES
TUILES AU BEURRE

T*he classic Almond Tiles (see page 257) have the curved shape of Spanish roof tiles; they contain sliced almonds and practically no butter. In comparison, our Buttery Almond Tiles have the same curved shape but are based on a butter-rich batter studded with chopped almonds. Thanks to their bold shape and buttery crispness, they are always a hit.*

EQUIPMENT

4 large, heavy baking sheets
• Brush with melted butter.
A large pastry bag fitted with
• an 11/16-inch (18 mm) plain pastry tube (Ateco #9), or a #70 ice cream scoop
A narrow (about 2 inches or 5 cm wide) trough-shaped mold
• Either a special *tuiles* mold with multiple troughs
• Or a yule log mold, *pain de mie* mold, or ring mold

BATTER

4½ ounces (125 g), or ½ cup plus 1 tablespoon, unsalted butter, softened
4½ ounces (125 g), or ½ cup plus 2 tablespoons, superfine sugar
2 large egg whites
Finely grated zest of 1 lemon
4½ ounces (125 g), or ¾ cup plus 4 teaspoons, blanched almonds, coarsely chopped
3½ ounces (100 g), or ⅔ cup plus 1 tablespoon, all-purpose flour

For about 40 to 45 cookies

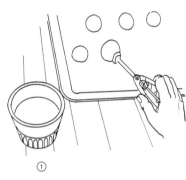

①

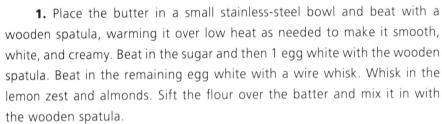

②

③

Preheat the oven to 400° F (200° C).

1. Place the butter in a small stainless-steel bowl and beat with a wooden spatula, warming it over low heat as needed to make it smooth, white, and creamy. Beat in the sugar and then 1 egg white with the wooden spatula. Beat in the remaining egg white with a wire whisk. Whisk in the lemon zest and almonds. Sift the flour over the batter and mix it in with the wooden spatula.

2. Scoop the batter into the pastry bag, and pipe the batter in 2½-teaspoon (1¼ cl) mounds, arranging them on the baking sheets in staggered rows and separating them by at least 2 inches (5 cm). Or, spoon the batter in 2½-teaspoon (1¼ cl) mounds using the ice cream scoop ①.

3. Flatten each mound ② of batter with the back of a fork (dipped in cold water as needed to prevent sticking) to distribute the almonds evenly.

4. Bake, 1 sheet at a time, until the cookies have spread and are browned around the edges but still pale in the center, about 7 to 11 minutes.

5. Remove the baked cookies from the oven. One at a time, lift each cookie with a metal spatula and press it upside down into a narrow, trough-shaped mold ③ to give the cookie the curved shape of a Spanish roof tile. Once the cookies are cool enough to hold their shape, they can be unmolded and more cookies pressed into the mold.

STORAGE: Covered airtight in a tin cookie box for up to 1 week. The cookies are fragile, so be careful not to break them.

ALMOND LACE COOKIES
CRÉPINETTES

The name of these delectable almond cookies derives from a small, flat French sausage that is encased in lacy caul fat. Almond Lace Cookies are similar to Buttery Almond Tiles (page 16), but are even more buttery, and they are flat rather than curved. They are extremely easy to prepare. When baked, the very soft batter spreads to produce a thin, crunchy cookie with the requisite lacy appearance. The almond and butter flavor is enhanced with a hint of orange zest.

EQUIPMENT

3 large, heavy baking sheets
- Brush edges and diagonals with melted butter.
- Line with kitchen parchment.

A #70 ice cream scoop, or a tablespoon

1 large egg
Finely grated zest of 1 orange
3½ ounces (100 g), or 1 cup, sliced almonds
2 ounces (60 g), or ¼ cup plus 3 tablespoons,
    all-purpose flour

BATTER

4½ ounces (125 g), or ½ cup plus 1 tablespoon,
    unsalted butter, softened
4½ ounces (125 g), or 1 cup plus 2 teaspoons,
    confectioners' sugar

For about 25 to 30 cookies

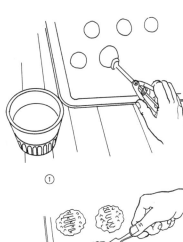

Preheat the oven to 400° F (200° C).

1. Place the butter in a small stainless-steel bowl and beat with a wooden spatula, warming it over low heat as needed to make it smooth, white, and creamy. Sift the sugar over the butter and beat it in. Beat in the egg with the wooden spatula. Beat the batter with a wire whisk, then whisk in the orange zest. Mix in the sliced almonds with the wooden spatula. Sift the flour over the batter and mix it in with the wooden spatula.

2. Spoon the batter in 2½-teaspoon (1¼ cl) mounds with the ice cream scoop ① or a tablespoon, arranging them on the baking sheets in staggered rows and separating them by at least 2 inches (5 cm).

3. Flatten each mound ② of batter with the back of a fork (dipped in cold water as needed to prevent sticking) to distribute the almonds evenly.

4. Bake, 1 sheet at a time, until the cookies have spread and are browned around the edges but still golden yellow in the center, about 7 to 11 minutes.

5. Remove from the oven, place the baking sheet on a wire rack, and let the cookies cool on the baking sheet.

STORAGE: Covered airtight in a cookie jar or tin cookie box for up to 1 week.

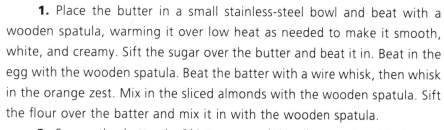

RAISIN WAFERS
PALETS AUX RAISINS

For these handsome cookies, a batter similar to that for Ladies' Wafers (page 9) is piped in domes and topped with a couple of raisins. After baking, the cookies are glazed with apricot jam and a brushing of rum and confectioners' sugar. The flavor harmony of rum, raisins, and butter—along with the contrast in textures between the soft, plump raisins and the crisp, buttery cookie—makes Raisin Wafers one of our favorites. The raisins and glaze on top give them great visual appeal, and their unique appearance has made Raisin Wafers a staple among the cookie assortments at many elegant restaurants and pastry shops in France.

EQUIPMENT

2 or 3 large, heavy baking sheets
- Brush edges and diagonals with melted butter.
- Line with kitchen parchment.

A large pastry bag fitted with
- a ½-inch (12 mm) plain pastry tube (Ateco #6),

or a #100 ice cream scoop

BATTER

4 ounces (115 g), or ½ cup, unsalted butter, softened
4 ounces (115 g), or ¾ cup plus 3 tablespoons, confectioners' sugar

2 large eggs
4 teaspoons (2 cl) dark Jamaican rum
4 ounces (115 g), or ¾ cup plus 1 tablespoon, all-purpose flour
2 to 3 ounces (60–85 g), or ¼ cup plus 2 to 4 tablespoons, seedless golden raisins

GLAZE

3 to 4 tablespoons (60–80 g) strained apricot jam [*Basic Preparation*, page 484]
2½ ounces (70 g), or ½ cup plus 4 teaspoons, confectioners' sugar
2 teaspoons (1 cl) dark Jamaican rum

For about 50 cookies

Preheat the oven to 400° F (200° C).

1. Place the butter in a small stainless-steel bowl and beat with a wooden spatula, warming it over low heat as needed to make it smooth, white, and creamy. Sift the sugar over the butter and beat it in. Beat in 1 egg with the wooden spatula. Then beat in the remaining egg with a wire whisk. Whisk in the rum. Sift the flour over the batter and mix it in with the wooden spatula.

2. Scoop the batter into the pastry bag, and pipe the batter ① in domes 1¼ inches (3 cm) wide, arranging them on the baking sheets in staggered rows and separating them by 1½ to 2 inches (4–5 cm). Or, spoon the batter in 1½-teaspoon (¾ cl) domes using the ice cream scoop.

3. Press 3 raisins on top of each mound ②.

4. Bake, 1 sheet at a time, until the cookies are lightly browned around the edges but still pale cream color in the center, about 7 to 10 minutes.

5. Place the baking sheet on a wire rack and let the cookies cool to room temperature.

Raise the oven temperature to 450° F (230° C).

③

6. Warm the apricot jam over low heat, stirring occasionally until melted. Brush each cookie with jam ③ until lightly coated and glistening.

7. Sift the confectioners' sugar into a small bowl, and stir in the rum. Then stir in enough cold water to make a smooth, creamy paste that is just fluid enough to spread easily with a pastry brush. Lightly brush this sugar glaze over the jam on top of each cookie. Return the cookies to the oven, 1 sheet at a time, until the glaze turns from opaque white to translucent, about 1 minute. If the glaze starts to bubble, remove the cookies from the oven immediately.

8. Let the cookies cool on the baking sheets.

➤ **HOWS & WHYS:** The raisins are softened by steam escaping from the batter as it bakes.

STORAGE: Covered airtight in a cookie jar or tin cookie box for up to 1 week.

TURKISH BATONS
BÂTONS DE SMYRNE

Smyrna (now called Izmir), in Turkey, has been one of the most important cities of Asia Minor since ancient times, and it was a principal port of the Ottoman Empire. Raisins made from sultanina grapes originated in Turkey. Since most of the golden raisins exported to Western Europe were shipped from Smyrna, they became known as Smyrna raisins (raisins de Smyrne in French) to distinguish them from the smaller, darker raisins from Corinth, called currants (raisins de Corinthe in French). Today, most of the seedless raisins sold in the United States are from California and are made from Thompson seedless grapes.

The batter for these cookies includes raisins pureed with rum. Stripped of their distinctive texture, the familiar taste of the raisins becomes slightly mysterious. Cloaking one end of each cookie in chocolate makes the raisin flavor even more elusive, and the unexpected combination of rum, raisins, and chocolate will disarm even the most sophisticated flavor sleuth.

EQUIPMENT

3 or 4 large, heavy baking sheets
- Brush edges and diagonals with melted butter.
- Line with kitchen parchment.

A large pastry bag fitted with
- a ⅜-inch (1 cm) plain pastry tube (Ateco #4)

BATTER

1½ ounces (45 g), or ¼ cup, seedless golden raisins
2 tablespoons (3 cl) white Jamaican rum

6 ounces (170 g), or ½ cup plus 4 tablespoons, unsalted butter, softened
6 ounces (170 g), or 1¼ cups plus 3 tablespoons, confectioners' sugar
1 large egg
6 ounces (170 g), or 1 cup plus 3½ tablespoons, all-purpose flour

GLAZE

9 ounces (250 g) European bittersweet chocolate (such as Lindt Surfin)
1¼ teaspoons (6 ml) almond oil (preferably) or neutral vegetable oil

For about 75 to 85 cookies

1. Puree the raisins with the rum in your electric blender. Set aside. Preheat the oven to 350° F (175° C).

2. Place the butter in a small stainless-steel bowl and beat with a wooden spatula, warming it over low heat as needed to make it smooth, white, and creamy. Sift the sugar over the butter and beat it in. Beat in the egg with the wooden spatula, then beat in the pureed raisins and rum with a wire whisk. Sift the flour over the batter and mix it in with the wooden spatula.

3. Scoop the batter into the pastry bag, and pipe the batter ① on the diagonal in fingers 2½ inches (6 cm) long and ⅜ inch (1 cm) wide at the center, arranging them on the baking sheets in staggered rows and separating them by 1½ inches (4 cm). Both ends of each finger should be fatter than the center, like a dumbbell.

4. Bake, 1 sheet at a time, until the cookies are lightly browned around the edges but still pale beige in the center, about 12 to 15 minutes.

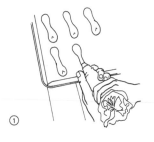

①

②

③

5. Place the baking sheet on a wire rack and let the cookies cool to room temperature.

6. Temper the chocolate with the almond oil as follows: Gently melt the chocolate ② and stir in the almond oil. Dip the bottom of the pot of chocolate in a bowl of cold water and stir the chocolate until it begins to thicken. Immediately remove from the cold water and dip the bottom of the pot of chocolate in a bowl of hot water. Stir over the hot water just long enough to make the chocolate fluid again, then remove from the hot water.

7. Dip one end ③ of each cookie diagonally into the chocolate to glaze it, clean off the excess on the edge of the pot, and place the cookies on a sheet of wax paper. Let the chocolate set.

STORAGE: Covered airtight in a cookie jar or tin cookie box for up to 3 days in a cool place (below 70° F or 20° C).

RAISIN BOULDERS
ROCHERS AUX RAISINS

*T*he classic Almond Boulders (page 116), made from Swiss meringue with sliced almonds, are shaped like rocks or boulders. Prepared from a totally different batter, Raisin Boulders are not really tall and rocklike in appearance like Almond Boulders, but they are thicker and softer than the other cookies in this chapter. Rarely seen in France today, their bumpy shapes and soft, almost chewy texture make them seem more like American cookies than French ones. In order for the batter to hold those thick, bumpy shapes without spreading it must be refrigerated overnight. The batter for these cookies is best shaped with an ice cream scoop. If you have children who enjoy helping in the kitchen, let them spoon this batter onto the baking sheets.

EQUIPMENT

2 or 3 large, heavy baking sheets
- Brush with melted butter.
- Dust with flour.
A #70 ice cream scoop, or a tablespoon

BATTER

3 ounces (85 g), or 6 tablespoons, unsalted butter, softened

5⅓ ounces (150 g), or ¾ cup, superfine sugar
3 large egg whites
1 teaspoon (½ cl) vanilla extract
3 ounces (85 g), or ½ cup plus 1 tablespoon, seedless raisins
3½ ounces (100 g), or ⅔ cup plus 1 tablespoon, all-purpose flour

For about 35 cookies

1. Place the butter in a small stainless-steel bowl and beat with a wooden spatula, warming it over low heat as needed to make it smooth, white, and creamy. Beat in half the sugar. When smooth, beat in the remaining sugar, followed by 1 egg white. Beat in the remaining egg whites 1 at a time with a wire whisk. Then whisk in the vanilla. Mix in the raisins with the wooden spatula. Sift the flour over the batter and mix it in with the wooden spatula. Cover the batter and let it rest in the refrigerator overnight, or for up to 1 week.

Preheat the oven to 400° F (200° C).

2. Spoon a half or a third of the batter onto 1 baking sheet in 2½-teaspoon (1¼ cl) mounds with the ice cream scoop or a tablespoon ①, arranging them in staggered rows and separating them by 1½ to 2 inches (4–5 cm). Keep the remaining batter in the refrigerator until you are ready to bake it.

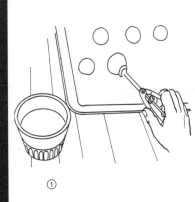

①

3. Bake, 1 sheet at a time, until the cookies are just beginning to brown around the edges but still pale in the center, about 5 to 8 minutes.

4. Slide the cookies onto a wire rack and let them cool to room temperature. If you have not yet baked all of the batter, return to step 2.

STORAGE: Covered airtight in a cookie jar or tin cookie box for up to 3 days.

PARLIAMENT COOKIES
PARLEMENTS

*T*hese *are a gentleman's palets de dames (page 9). The two cookies are similar in appearance, but Parliament Cookies have a deeper, more masculine coloring and a less sweet taste. Powdered almonds in the batter bestow a quiet elegance. Like a good statesman, Parliament Cookies are appropriate in every situation—simple and tasty enough for the cookie jar, yet with a refinement suitable to the most formal dinner.*

EQUIPMENT

2 or 3 large, heavy baking sheets
- Brush with melted butter.
- Dust with flour.

A large pastry bag fitted with
- a ⁷⁄₁₆-inch (11 mm) plain pastry tube (Ateco #5)

or a #100 ice cream scoop

BATTER

2 ounces (60 g), or 4 tablespoons, unsalted butter, softened

1 ounce (25 g), or 2 tablespoons, superfine sugar

4 ounces (120 g), or ¾ cup plus 2 tablespoons, almond and sugar powder

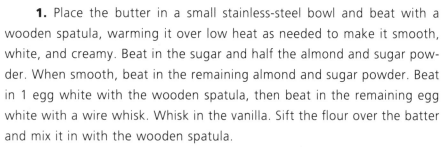

} *Basic Preparation, page 482:*
2 ounces (60 g), or ⅓ cup plus 1 tablespoon, blanched almonds
2 ounces (60 g), or ½ cup, confectioners' sugar

2 large egg whites

¾ teaspoon (4 ml) vanilla extract

1½ ounces (40 g), or ¼ cup plus 2 teaspoons, all-purpose flour

For about 35 cookies

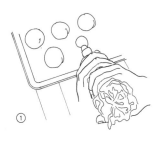

①

Preheat the oven to 400° F (200° C).

1. Place the butter in a small stainless-steel bowl and beat with a wooden spatula, warming it over low heat as needed to make it smooth, white, and creamy. Beat in the sugar and half the almond and sugar powder. When smooth, beat in the remaining almond and sugar powder. Beat in 1 egg white with the wooden spatula, then beat in the remaining egg white with a wire whisk. Whisk in the vanilla. Sift the flour over the batter and mix it in with the wooden spatula.

2. Scoop the batter into the pastry bag, and pipe the batter ① in domes 1¼ inches (3 cm) wide, arranging them on the baking sheets in staggered rows and separating them by at least 2 inches (5 cm). Or, spoon the batter in 1½-teaspoon (¾ cl) domes using the ice cream scoop.

3. Bake, 1 sheet at a time, until the cookies are lightly browned around the edges but still pale cream color in the center, about 7 to 11 minutes.

4. Slide the cookies onto a wire rack using a metal spatula and let them cool to room temperature.

STORAGE: Covered airtight in a cookie jar or tin cookie box for up to 1 week.

VIETNAMESE HATS
ANNAMITES

A tiny pyramid of sweet pastry dough props up the center of this cookie to give it the familiar shape of the wide, almost flat straw hats traditionally worn in Vietnam. (Annam *is the name for the central region of Vietnam.) A glistening glaze of apricot jam and sugar highlights the graceful form.*

EQUIPMENT

3 or 4 large, heavy baking sheets
- Brush all but one of them lightly with melted butter.

A large pastry bag fitted with
- a ⅝-inch (16 mm) plain pastry tube (Ateco #8), or a #100 ice cream scoop

PASTRY DOUGH PROPS

1½ ounces (40 g) sweet pastry dough (see Note)
Flour for dusting countertop

BATTER

3 ounces (85 g), or 6 tablespoons, unsalted butter, softened
1¼ ounces (35 g), or 3 tablespoons, superfine sugar

6 ounces (170 g), or 1¼ cups, almond and sugar powder

Basic Preparation, page 482:
3 ounces (85 g), or ½ cup plus 1 tablespoon, blanched almonds
3 ounces (85 g), or ⅔ cup plus 2 teaspoons, confectioners' sugar

2 large egg whites
1 teaspoon (½ cl) vanilla extract
3 ounces (85 g), or ½ cup plus 2 tablespoons, all-purpose flour

GLAZE

4 tablespoons (80 g) strained apricot jam [*Basic Preparation*, page 484]
3 ounces (85 g), or ⅔ cup plus 2 teaspoons, confectioners' sugar
1 tablespoon (1½ cl) dark Jamaican rum

For about 40 cookies

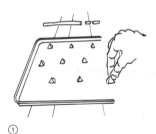
①

1. On a lightly floured counter, roll the pastry dough under your palms into a rope about 20 inches (50 cm) long. Cut the rope into ½-inch (12 mm) lengths to get 40 small lumps of dough. Arrange the lumps of dough on the baking sheets in staggered rows, separating them by 3 inches (7 cm) and shaping each into a pyramid ⅜ to ½ inch (1–1½ cm) high as you press it firmly onto the baking sheet with your fingertips ①. Let rest in the refrigerator for 30 to 60 minutes.

Preheat the oven to 400° F (200° C).

2. Place the butter in a small stainless-steel bowl and beat with a wooden spatula, warming it over low heat as needed to make it smooth, white, and creamy. Beat in the sugar and half the almond and sugar powder. When smooth, beat in the remaining almond and sugar powder. Beat in 1 egg white with the wooden spatula, then beat in the remaining egg white with a wire whisk. Whisk in the vanilla. Sift the flour over the batter and mix it in with the wooden spatula. If the pyramids of pastry dough on the baking sheet have not chilled sufficiently, then refrigerate the batter until the pyramids are firm.

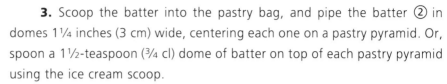

3. Scoop the batter into the pastry bag, and pipe the batter ② in domes 1¼ inches (3 cm) wide, centering each one on a pastry pyramid. Or, spoon a 1½-teaspoon (¾ cl) dome of batter on top of each pastry pyramid using the ice cream scoop.

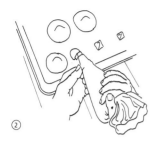

②

4. When you finish piping, tap the baking sheets firmly on the counter to spread the batter evenly.

5. Bake, 1 sheet at a time, until the edges and bottoms of the cookies just begin to color, about 4 to 6 minutes. Then place an empty baking sheet underneath the sheet of cookies (or, lacking an empty baking sheet, raise the baking sheet to the top shelf of the oven and reduce the oven temperature to 300° F or 150° C) to protect the bottoms from burning, and continue baking until the bottoms of the cookies are lightly colored and the tops are a pale cream color in the center with a golden brown crown around the edges. The total baking time will be about 9 to 14 minutes.

6. Place the baking sheet on a wire rack and let the cookies cool to room temperature.

Raise the oven temperature to 450° F (230° C).

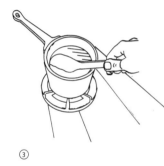

③

7. Warm the apricot jam ③ over low heat, stirring occasionally until melted. Brush each cookie with jam ④ until lightly coated and glistening.

8. Sift the confectioners' sugar into a small bowl and stir in the rum. Then stir in enough cold water to make a smooth creamy paste that is just fluid enough to spread easily with a pastry brush. Lightly brush this sugar glaze over the jam on top of each cookie. Return the cookies to the oven, 1 baking sheet at a time, until the glaze turns from opaque white to translucent, about 1 minute. If the glaze starts to bubble, remove the cookies from the oven immediately.

④

9. Slide the cookies onto a wire rack using a metal spatula and let cool to room temperature.

NOTE: Trimmings left over from rolling out and cutting many of the sweet pastry doughs in Chapter 6 can be used to make the pastry dough props for Vietnamese Hats. The sweet pastry doughs that we recommend are: Tea Sablés (page 286), Rum Punch Cookies (page 288), Italian Crowns (page 290), Spectacles (page 310), Souvaroffs (page 312), Valois (page 316), Three-Cornered Hats (page 319), Little Neapolitan Cakes (page 340), Small Sandwich Sablés (page 336), or Siamese Twins (page 338).

STORAGE: Covered airtight in a cookie jar or tin cookie box for up to 1 week.

LITTLE MARQUIS
PETITS MARQUIS

These cookies are made from a light Cats' Tongues (page 10) batter, piped in rounds rather than fingers. The baked wafers are sandwiched with a filling of bittersweet chocolate and chopped, toasted hazelnuts. The thin, firm chocolate provides a rich and flavorful counterpoint to the light, crisp wafers—just the combination (elegant but not fragile) to satisfy the appetite of a pampered little marquis.

EQUIPMENT

3 or 4 large, heavy baking sheets
- Brush with melted butter.
- Dust with flour.

A large pastry bag fitted with
- a ½-inch (12 mm) plain pastry tube (Ateco #6),

or a "midget" ice cream scoop

BATTER

3½ ounces (100 g), or 7 tablespoons, unsalted butter, softened

3½ ounces (100 g), or ¾ cup plus 4 teaspoons, confectioners' sugar

3 large egg whites

1 teaspoon (½ cl) vanilla extract

3½ ounces (100 g), or ⅔ cup plus 1 tablespoon, all-purpose flour

FILLING

1½ ounces (40 g), or ¼ cup plus ½ tablespoon, hazelnuts

3½ ounces (100 g) European bittersweet chocolate (such as Lindt Surfin)

½ teaspoon (¼ cl) almond oil (preferably) or neutral vegetable oil

For about 30 to 35 cookies

Preheat the oven to 400° F (200° C).

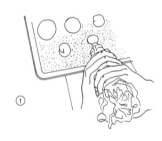

1. Place the butter in a small stainless-steel bowl and beat with a wooden spatula, warming it over low heat as needed to make it smooth, white, and creamy. Sift the sugar over the butter and beat it in. Beat in 1 egg white with the wooden spatula. Then beat in the remaining whites, 1 at a time, with a wire whisk. Whisk in the vanilla. Sift the flour over the batter and mix it in with the wooden spatula.

2. Scoop the batter into the pastry bag, and pipe the batter ① in domes 1 inch (2½ cm) wide, arranging them on the baking sheets in staggered rows and separating them by 1½ inches (4 cm). Or, spoon the batter in 1-teaspoon (½ cl) domes using the ice cream scoop.

3. Bake, 1 sheet at a time, until the cookies are lightly browned around the edges but still pale cream color in the center, about 6 to 10 minutes.

4. Slide the cookies onto a wire rack using a metal spatula and let them cool to room temperature.

Reduce the oven temperature to 350° F (175° C).

5. Spread out the hazelnuts on a baking sheet and toast them in the oven, stirring occasionally to prevent the nuts nearest the edge from burning, until light brown in the center, 15 to 25 minutes. (Test by cutting one in half.) Transfer the hazelnuts to a large sieve, and rub the hot nuts against

②

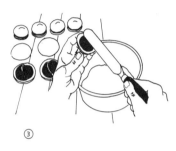

③

the mesh, using a towel to protect your hand, to remove most of their skins. Let the nuts cool, then chop them very finely with your chef's knife.

6. Temper the chocolate with the almond oil as follows: Gently melt the chocolate ② and stir in the almond oil. Dip the bottom of the pot of chocolate in a bowl of cold water and stir the chocolate until it begins to thicken. Immediately remove from the cold water and dip the bottom of the pot of chocolate in a bowl of hot water. Stir over the hot water just long enough to make the chocolate fluid again, then remove from the hot water.

7. Stir the chopped hazelnuts into the tempered chocolate. Using a palette knife, spread a dab of this filling on the back of one cookie ③ and sandwich it back to back with a second cookie. Gently press the 2 cookies together. Repeat with the remaining cookies, and allow the chocolate to set.

STORAGE: Covered airtight in a cookie jar or tin cookie box for up to 3 days in a cool place (below 70° F or 20° C). Before filling, the cookies can be kept in a cookie jar or tin cookie box for up to 1 week.

PRALINÉ-FILLED WAFERS
GALETTES PRALINÉES

Avery sexy cookie made by sandwiching praliné butter between two light, crisp wafers. The luxurious flavor and sensual contrast of textures make this cookie irresistible.

EQUIPMENT
2 large, heavy baking sheets
- Brush with melted butter.
- Dust with flour.

A large pastry bag fitted with
- a ½-inch (12 mm) plain pastry tube (Ateco #6),

or a "midget" ice cream scoop
A small pastry bag fitted with
- a ⅜-inch (1 cm) plain pastry tube (Ateco #4),

or a small palette knife

BATTER
3½ ounces (100 g), or 7 tablespoons, unsalted butter, softened
3½ ounces (100 g), or ½ cup, superfine sugar

2 large egg whites
⅛ teaspoon (½ ml) cream of tartar (optional)
3½ ounces (100 g), or ⅔ cup plus 1 tablespoon, all-purpose flour

DECORATION
1½ ounces (40 g), or ¼ cup plus ½ tablespoon, hazelnuts

FILLING
2 ounces (60 g), or 4 tablespoons, unsalted butter, softened
2 ounces (60 g) praliné
[*Basic Preparation*, page 485]

For 25 to 30 cookies

Preheat the oven to 350°F (175°C).

1. Spread out the hazelnuts on a baking sheet and toast them in the oven, stirring occasionally to prevent the nuts nearest the edge from burning, until light brown in the center, 15 to 25 minutes. (Test by cutting one in half.) Transfer the hazelnuts to a large sieve, and rub the hot nuts against the mesh, using a towel to protect your hand, to remove most of their skins. Let the nuts cool, then chop them finely with your chef's knife.

2. Place the butter in a small stainless-steel bowl and beat with a wooden spatula, warming it over low heat as needed to make it smooth, white, and creamy. Beat in 3 ounces (85 g), or ¼ cup plus 3 tablespoons, of the sugar.

3. Whip the egg whites in an electric mixer at low speed until they start to froth. If you are not whipping the whites in a copper bowl, add the cream of tartar at this point. Gradually increase the whipping speed to medium-high, and continue whipping until the whites form very stiff peaks and just begin to slip and streak around the side of the bowl. Add the remaining superfine sugar ① and continue whipping at high speed for a few seconds longer to make the meringue smooth and shiny.

4. Quickly stir about half the meringue into the creamed butter and sugar. Gently fold in the remaining meringue. When almost completely

①

mixed, sift the flour over the batter and continue folding until the batter is smooth and homogeneous.

5. Scoop the batter into the large pastry bag, and pipe the batter ② in domes 1 inch (2½ cm) wide, arranging them on the baking sheets in staggered rows and separating them by 1½ inches (4 cm). Or, spoon the batter in 1-teaspoon (½ cl) domes using the ice cream scoop.

②

6. Dust the domes with chopped hazelnuts ③. Turn the baking sheet upside down and tap it firmly with a wooden spatula to dislodge the excess hazelnuts, then quickly turn the baking sheet right side up again.

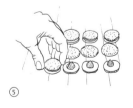

③

7. Bake, 1 sheet at a time, until the cookies are lightly browned around the edges but still pale cream color in the center, about 9 to 14 minutes.

8. Slide the cookies onto a wire rack using a metal spatula and let them cool to room temperature.

9. Place the butter for the filling in a small stainless-steel bowl and beat with a wooden spatula, warming it over low heat as needed to make it smooth, white, and creamy. Gradually beat the butter into the praliné. When all of the butter has been added, beat the praliné butter vigorously with a wire whisk to make it light and smooth. As you beat air into the praliné butter, the color of the filling will also lighten noticeably. (However, if the filling is too warm it will not become light in texture or in color and will remain runny. Chill it briefly, and then whisk again.)

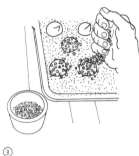

④

10. Turn half the cookies upside down. Scoop the praliné butter into the small pastry bag, and pipe about 1 teaspoon (½ cl) of praliné butter on the center ④ of each upside-down cookie. (Or, spread the praliné butter using a small palette knife.) Then place a second cookie right side up on top of each ⑤ and press gently to make a sandwich. Chill the cookies to firm the praliné butter.

⑤

➤ **HOWS & WHYS:** The batter for this cookie is unusual in that the egg whites are whipped before they are added to the creamed butter and sugar. This makes the batter hold its shape better and produces a slightly lighter cookie. Also, because the batter contains meringue, it cannot be stored for later use.

STORAGE: Covered airtight in a cookie jar or tin cookie box for up to 1 day in a cool place (below 60° F or 15° C). Before filling, the cookies can be kept in a cookie jar or tin cookie box for up to 1 week.

RUSSIAN CIGARETTES
CIGARETTES RUSSES

One of the French cookies most familiar to Americans, light and crisp Russian Cigarettes make a stylish accompaniment to a dish of ice cream, and they are equally enjoyable by themselves. They can also have their centers filled with almond paste and their ends dipped in chocolate (see Filled Cigarettes, page 32). While many chefs use an austere and inexpensive batter (sugar, butter, egg whites, and flour) for their cigarettes, we prefer the luxury of a batter enriched with powdered almonds. The batter is runny and must be refrigerated overnight to be firm enough to pipe; then as it bakes, it becomes runny again and spreads to produce very thin cookies that you can roll up easily.

Years ago, Russian Cigarettes were sold with long cardboard tips styled after the elegant cigarette holders popular with the beau monde during the 1920s. At the time, many Russian aristocrats who had fled the revolution were enjoying the good life in Paris and were an integral part of café society.

EQUIPMENT

4 large, heavy baking sheets
• Brush heavily with melted butter.
A large pastry bag fitted with
• a ⅝-inch (16 mm) plain pastry tube (Ateco #8),
or a "midget" ice cream scoop
A wooden dowel or metal tube, ⅜ inch (1 cm) in diameter and about 12 inches (30 cm) long (see Note)

BATTER

2½ ounces (70 g), or 5 tablespoons, unsalted butter, softened
2⅔ ounces (75 g), or 6 tablespoons, superfine sugar

1 ounce (30 g), or about 3½ tablespoons, almond and sugar powder
  Basic Preparation, page 482:
  ½ ounce (15 g), or 1 tablespoon plus 2 teaspoons, blanched almonds
  ½ ounce (15 g), or 2 tablespoons, confectioners' sugar
3 large egg whites
¼ teaspoon (1 ml) vanilla extract
1¾ ounces (50 g), or ⅓ cup plus 1 teaspoon, all-purpose flour

For about 50 cookies

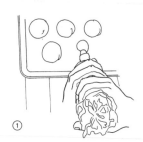

1. Place the butter in a small stainless-steel bowl and beat with a wooden spatula, warming it over low heat as needed to make it smooth, white, and creamy. Beat in the sugar. When smooth, beat in the almond and sugar powder. Beat in 1 egg white with the wooden spatula. Then beat in the remaining egg whites, one at a time, with a wire whisk. Whisk in the vanilla. Sift the flour over the batter and mix it in with the wooden spatula. Cover the batter airtight and refrigerate overnight or for up to 1 week.

Preheat the oven to 425°F (220°C).

2. Scoop the batter into the pastry bag, and pipe the batter ① in domes 1 inch (2½ cm) wide, arranging them on the baking sheets in staggered rows and separating them by 2 to 3 inches (5–7 cm). (Do not pipe more than 12 or 13 cookies on each baking sheet or you won't be able to roll them before they cool.) Or, spoon the batter in 1-teaspoon (½ cl) domes using the ice cream scoop.

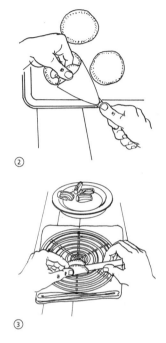

②

③

3. Let rest at room temperature for about 5 minutes before baking.

4. Bake, 1 sheet at a time, until the cookies are golden brown around the edges but still pale in the center, about 4 to 7 minutes.

5. While the cookies are baking, place a folded kitchen towel (a smooth, untextured towel, not terry cloth) on your countertop. One at a time, lift each cookie ② off the baking sheet using a metal spatula and place it upside down on the towel. Roll it around the wooden dowel or metal rod to form a cigarette ③. As you finish rolling the cigarette, press down firmly on the dowel to prevent the cigarette from unrolling, then slide it off the dowel onto a plate. Work quickly because if the cookies cool they will become brittle. If they do cool and start to crack as you roll them, return the baking sheet to the oven briefly to reheat them.

NOTE: Precut brass tubes are available in hobby shops.

STORAGE: Covered airtight in a cookie jar or tin cookie box for up to 1 week.

FILLED CIGARETTES
CIGARETTES FOURRÉES

For a truly sumptuous cookie, fill Russian Cigarettes (page 30) with liqueur-flavored almond paste (marzipan), then dip the ends in chocolate. Fancy and extremely rich, Filled Cigarettes are perfect for a holiday dessert buffet.

You can purchase imported Danish marzipan in supermarkets. However, it is easy enough to make this type of cooked almond paste at home using a food processor, and the result is much fresher and more reliable than the packaged variety.

EQUIPMENT
A small or medium pastry bag fitted with
• a ¼-inch (6 mm) plain pastry tube (Ateco #2)

---

50 Russian Cigarettes (page 30)
FILLING
5¼ ounces (150 g), or ¾ cup, granulated sugar
1 ounce (25 g), or 1 tablespoon plus 1 teaspoon, light corn syrup
3 ounces (85 g), or ½ cup plus 1 tablespoon, blanched almonds

1¾ ounces (50 g), or ⅓ cup plus 4 teaspoons, confectioners' sugar
Kirsch, dark Jamaican rum, or curaçao
Green food coloring
GLAZE
5¼ ounces (150 g) European bittersweet chocolate (such as Lindt Surfin)
¾ teaspoon (4 ml) almond oil (preferably) or neutral vegetable oil

For 50 cookies

1. Combine the granulated sugar and 3 tablespoons (4½ cl) of water in a small saucepan or caramel pot and stir to thoroughly moisten the sugar. Bring to a boil over medium heat. Wash down the walls of the pot with a moistened pastry brush to dissolve any sugar crystals that form there. Then continue boiling until the sugar reaches the firm-ball stage, or about 245° F (118° C).

2. Meanwhile, combine the almonds and confectioners' sugar in your food processor. When the syrup is ready, turn on the food processor and pour in the syrup. Continue processing until the almond paste is completely smooth. It will be hot.

3. Transfer the almond paste to a stainless-steel bowl, cover it with a damp kitchen towel to prevent it from drying out, and let cool to room temperature.

4. Place the almond paste on your countertop and gradually work in the liqueur by kneading it with the heel of your hand. Add sufficient liqueur to make the almond paste soft enough to pipe from a pastry bag, but not runny. Tint the almond paste a pale green by kneading in a drop or two of green food coloring.

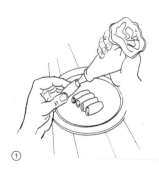
①

5. Scoop the filling into the pastry bag, and pipe it into both ends of each cigarette ① to fill the entire length.

②

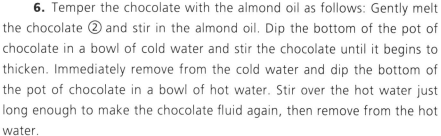

6. Temper the chocolate with the almond oil as follows: Gently melt the chocolate ② and stir in the almond oil. Dip the bottom of the pot of chocolate in a bowl of cold water and stir the chocolate until it begins to thicken. Immediately remove from the cold water and dip the bottom of the pot of chocolate in a bowl of hot water. Stir over the hot water just long enough to make the chocolate fluid again, then remove from the hot water.

7. Dip one end of each cigarette in the chocolate, clean off the excess on the edge of the pot, and place the cigarette on a sheet of wax paper until the chocolate sets. Then dip the other end of each cigarette in the chocolate, clean off the excess on the edge of the pot, and return to the sheet of wax paper until the chocolate on both ends has set ③.

STORAGE: Covered airtight in a cookie jar or tin cookie box for up to 1 day in a cool place (below 70° F or 20° C).

③

LADIES' MUFFS
MANCHONS

〰〰

These cookies are named for their resemblance to an old-fashioned lady's muff. A variety of cigarette batter is piped in rectangles, then rolled up lengthwise after baking to make short cylinders. When cool, they are filled with luscious praliné butter and the ends are dipped in chopped pistachios. We have used a cigarette batter less rich than our recipe for Russian Cigarettes (page 30) because of the richness of the filling. For chocolate lovers, omit the pistachios and instead dip the ends in melted chocolate (compare Filled Cigarettes, page 32).

EQUIPMENT

3 or 4 large, heavy baking sheets
- Brush lightly with melted butter.
- Then wipe with a paper towel to leave only a thin film of butter.

A large pastry bag fitted with
- a ¾-inch (2 cm) ribbon tube (Ateco #47ST)

A small pastry bag fitted with
- a ¼-inch (6 mm) plain pastry tube (Ateco #2)

A wooden dowel or metal tube, ⅜ inch (1 cm) in diameter and about 12 inches (30 cm) long (see Note)

BATTER

2½ ounces (70 g), or 5 tablespoons, unsalted butter, softened
3½ ounces (100 g), or ¾ cup plus 4 teaspoons, confectioners' sugar

2 large egg whites
½ teaspoon (¼ cl) vanilla extract
2¼ ounces (65 g), or ¼ cup plus 3½ tablespoons, all-purpose flour

FILLING

3 ounces (85 g), or 6 tablespoons, unsalted butter, softened
3 ounces (85 g), or ¼ cup plus 1 tablespoon, praliné
[*Basic Preparation*, page 485]

DECORATION

1½ ounces (45 g), or ¼ cup plus 1 tablespoon, chopped pistachios

For about 40 cookies

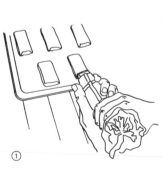

①

Preheat the oven to 400° F (200° C).

1. Place the butter in a small stainless-steel bowl and beat with a wooden spatula, warming it over low heat as needed to make it smooth, white, and creamy. Sift the sugar over the butter and beat it in. Beat in 1 egg white with the wooden spatula. Then beat in the remaining egg white with a wire whisk. Whisk in the vanilla. Sift the flour over the batter and mix it in with the wooden spatula.

2. Scoop the batter into the large pastry bag. Holding the fluted side of the tube against the baking sheet, pipe the batter ① on the diagonal in thin rectangular strips 2 inches (5 cm) long, arranging them on the baking sheets in staggered rows and separating them by 2 to 3 inches (5–7 cm). (Do not pipe more than 13 or 14 cookies on each baking sheet or you won't be able to roll them before they cool.)

3. Bake, 1 sheet at a time, until the cookies are browned around the edges but still pale in the center, about 6 to 10 minutes.

4. While the cookies are baking, place a folded kitchen towel (a smooth, untextured towel, not terry cloth) on your countertop. One at a time, lift each cookie off the baking sheet using a metal spatula and place it upside down on the towel. Roll it lengthwise around the wooden dowel or metal rod to form a short cylinder ②. As you finish rolling the cylinder, press down firmly ③ on the dowel to prevent the cylinder from unrolling, then slide it off the dowel onto a plate. Work quickly because as the cookies cool they will become brittle. If they do cool and start to crack as you roll them, return the baking sheet to the oven briefly to reheat them.

5. Place the butter for the filling in a small stainless-steel bowl and beat with a wooden spatula, warming it over low heat as needed to make it smooth, white, and creamy. Gradually beat the butter into the praliné. When all of the butter has been added, beat the praliné butter vigorously with a wire whisk to make it light and smooth. As you beat air into the praliné butter, the color of the filling will also lighten noticeably. (However, if the filling is too warm it will not become light in texture or in color and will remain runny. Chill it briefly, and then whisk again.)

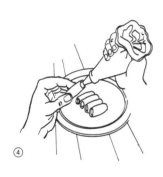

6. Scoop the praliné butter into the small pastry bag, and pipe it into both ends ④ of each cylinder to fill the entire length. Dip the ends in the chopped pistachios ⑤.

NOTE: Precut brass tubes are available in hobby shops.

➤ **HOWS & WHYS:** When you roll up the cookies in step 6, the cylinders should be about 2 inches (5 cm) long. If they are much longer, then the creamed butter in the batter was too soft, or there was too much butter on the baking sheet, or you piped the batter too thick.

STORAGE: Covered airtight in a cookie jar or tin cookie box for up to 1 day in a cool place (below 60° F or 15° C). Before filling, the cookies can be kept in a cookie jar or tin cookie box for up to 1 week.

PIPED SABLÉS
SABLÉS À LA POCHE

The sandy, shortbreadlike texture of these cookies resembles that of sablés cookies made from sweet pastry dough (see Chapter 6—for example, Tea Sablés, page 286), but here the cookies are prepared by piping a batter in fanciful forms with a pastry bag (poche in French) rather than by rolling out a pastry dough with a rolling pin. In this recipe we include three shapes: Ss glazed on one end with chocolate, spirals glazed on the back with chocolate, and wreaths filled with a button of cocoa-flavored batter. For other ideas, see the recipes for Tea Cookies (page 38) and Viennese Cookies (page 46). The cookies can also be formed with a cookie press.

EQUIPMENT

4 large, heavy baking sheets
- Brush all but one of them lightly with melted butter.
- Then wipe with a paper towel to leave only a thin film of butter.

A large pastry bag fitted with
- a medium-small fluted pastry tube (Ateco #3) for Ss and wreaths
- a ¼-inch (6 mm) plain pastry tube (Ateco #2) for spirals

For wreaths only, a small pastry bag fitted with
- a ⁵⁄₁₆-inch (8 mm) plain pastry tube (Ateco #3)

BATTER

4 ounces (115 g), or ½ cup, unsalted butter, softened
3½ ounces (100 g), or ½ cup, superfine sugar

1 large egg
5 teaspoons (2½ cl) milk
1 teaspoon (½ cl) vanilla extract
7 ounces (200 g), or 1¼ cups plus 3 tablespoons, all-purpose flour
¾ teaspoon (3 g) baking powder

DECORATION FOR WREATHS

2 teaspoons (4 g) unsweetened Dutch-processed cocoa powder

GLAZE FOR Ss AND SPIRALS

7 ounces (200 g) European bittersweet chocolate (such as Lindt Surfin)
1 teaspoon (½ cl) almond oil (preferably) or neutral vegetable oil

For about 50 to 55 cookies

Preheat the oven to 400° F (200° C).

1. Place the butter in a small stainless-steel bowl and beat with a wooden spatula, warming it over low heat as needed to make it smooth, white, and creamy. Beat in the sugar and then the egg with the wooden spatula. Beat in the milk and vanilla with a wire whisk. Sift the flour and baking powder over the batter and mix them in with the wooden spatula.

2. FOR Ss: Scoop the batter into the pastry bag, and pipe the batter ① in scrolly S shapes 2 inches (5 cm) high and 1¼ inches (3 cm) wide.

FOR SPIRALS: Scoop the batter into the pastry bag, and pipe the batter ② on the diagonal in finger-shaped spirals 2 inches (5 cm) long and ⅝ inch (1½ cm) wide.

FOR WREATHS: Take out 6 tablespoons (100 g) of the batter and mix in the cocoa powder to flavor and color it. Scoop the plain batter into the

①

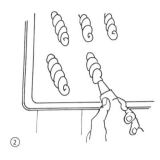

large pastry bag, and pipe this batter ③ in rings 1½ inches (4 cm) wide, with a ⅜- to ½-inch (10–12 mm) hole in the center. Scoop the cocoa-flavored batter into the small pastry bag, and pipe a button of it in the center ④ of each wreath to fill the hole.

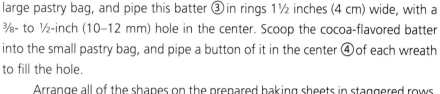

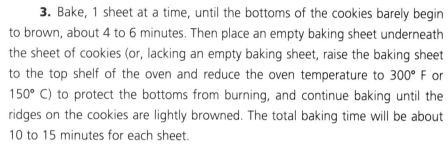

Arrange all of the shapes on the prepared baking sheets in staggered rows, separating them by 1½ inches (4 cm).

3. Bake, 1 sheet at a time, until the bottoms of the cookies barely begin to brown, about 4 to 6 minutes. Then place an empty baking sheet underneath the sheet of cookies (or, lacking an empty baking sheet, raise the baking sheet to the top shelf of the oven and reduce the oven temperature to 300° F or 150° C) to protect the bottoms from burning, and continue baking until the ridges on the cookies are lightly browned. The total baking time will be about 10 to 15 minutes for each sheet.

4. Slide the cookies onto a wire rack using a metal spatula and let them cool to room temperature.

5. For spirals and *S*s, temper the chocolate with the almond oil as follows: Gently melt the chocolate and stir in the almond oil. Dip the bottom of the pot of chocolate in a bowl of cold water and stir the chocolate until it begins to thicken. Immediately remove from the cold water and dip the bottom of the pot of chocolate in a bowl of hot water. Stir over the hot water just long enough to make the chocolate fluid again, then remove from the hot water.

6. Dip one end of each *S* in the chocolate ⑤, clean off the excess on the edge of the pot, and place the cookies on a sheet of wax paper.

Spread the back of each spiral with chocolate ⑥ and smooth it with a palette knife, then place the cookies chocolate side up on your countertop.

Let the chocolate set.

STORAGE: Covered airtight in a cookie jar or tin cookie box for up to 2 weeks, in a cool place (below 70° F or 20° C) for cookies glazed with chocolate.

TEA COOKIES
FOURS À THÉ

The name of these cookies is typical of the convenient shorthand employed by French pastry chefs. It is an abbreviation of the more cumbersome petits fours à thé, which translates loosely as "tea cookies." These Tea Cookies are similar to Piped Sablés (page 36), but they are less sweet and are flavored with lemon rather than vanilla, making them particularly appropriate with tea. Piping the batter in decorative shapes is de rigueur, and we offer four suggestions—wreaths, bow ties, flowers, and grape clusters. This batter can also be shaped with a cookie press.

EQUIPMENT

4 large, heavy baking sheets
- Brush all but one of them with melted butter.

A large pastry bag fitted with
- a medium-small fluted pastry tube (Ateco #3) for wreaths and bow ties
- a ⁵/₁₆-inch (8 mm) plain pastry tube (Ateco #3) for flowers and grape clusters

BATTER

4 ounces (115 g), or ½ cup, unsalted butter, softened

2⅔ ounces (75 g), or 6 tablespoons, superfine sugar

1 large egg white

Finely grated zest of 1 lemon

6 ounces (170 g), or 1 cup plus 3½ tablespoons, all-purpose flour

DECORATION

Glacé cherries and pineapple

For about 40 to 45 cookies

Preheat the oven to 400° F (200° C).

1. Place the butter in a small stainless-steel bowl and beat with a wooden spatula, warming it over low heat as needed to make it smooth, white, and creamy. Beat in the sugar and then the egg white, followed by the lemon zest. Sift the flour over the batter and mix it in with the wooden spatula.

2. Scoop the batter into the pastry bag.

①

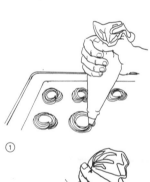

②

FOR WREATHS: Pipe the batter ① in rings 1¾ inches (4½ cm) wide with a ½-inch (12 mm) hole in the center. Cut some glacé pineapple into wedges ⅛ inch (3 mm) thick and ½ inch (12 mm) high. Place a wedge on one side of each wreath.

FOR BOW TIES: Pipe a teardrop 1¼ inches (3 cm) long and 1 inch (2½ cm) wide. Then pipe a second teardrop ② pointing in the opposite direction and joining the first one at the tip. Repeat with the remaining batter. Place a quarter of a glacé cherry on the center of each bow tie.

FOR GRAPE CLUSTERS: Pipe six ½-inch (12 mm) domes of batter adjacent to each other in a triangle (like bowling pins). Cut some green glacé pineapple into "stems" about ⅛ inch (3 mm) thick, ³/₁₆ inch (4½ mm) wide, and ½ inch (12 mm) long, and insert a stem in the center of one side of each grape cluster.

FOR FLOWERS: Pipe five ½- to ⅝-inch (12–14 mm) domes of batter

③

arranged adjacent to each other in a circle ③. Repeat with the remaining batter. Place half of a glacé cherry (preferably yellow or green) in the center of each flower.

Arrange all of the shapes on the prepared baking sheets in staggered rows, separating them by 1½ inches (4 cm).

3. Bake, 1 sheet at a time, until the bottoms of the cookies barely begin to brown, about 4 to 6 minutes. Then place an empty baking sheet underneath the sheet of cookies (or, lacking an empty baking sheet, raise the baking sheet to the top shelf of the oven and reduce the oven temperature to 300° F or 150° C) to protect the bottoms from burning, and continue baking until the ridges on the cookies are lightly browned. The total baking time will be about 10 to 15 minutes for each sheet.

4. Slide the cookies onto a wire rack using a metal spatula and let them cool to room temperature.

STORAGE: Covered airtight in a cookie jar or tin cookie box for up to 2 weeks.

CHOCOLATE TEARDROP SABLÉS
SABLÉS À LA POCHE AU CHOCOLAT

Surprisingly few pastry chefs in France today make chocolate sablés cookies, and these cookies are also very rare historically. But our Chocolate Teardrop Sablés are no esoteric curiosity. We flavor our basic Piped Sablés batter (page 36) with cocoa and pipe it in teardrops, then we sandwich the baked teardrops with raspberry jam and dip the tips in chocolate. With their appealing balance of flavors and textures, these cookies are good enough to start a new trend.

EQUIPMENT

4 large, heavy baking sheets
- Brush 3 of them lightly with melted butter.
- Then wipe with a paper towel to leave only a thin film of butter.

A large pastry bag fitted with
- a medium-small fluted pastry tube (Ateco #3)

BATTER

4 ounces (115 g), or ½ cup, unsalted butter, softened

3½ ounces (100 g), or ½ cup, superfine sugar

1 large egg

2 tablespoons (3 cl) milk

6½ ounces (185 g), or 1¼ cups plus 1 tablespoon, all-purpose flour

1 teaspoon (4 g) baking powder

½ ounce (12 g), or about 2 tablespoons, unsweetened Dutch-processed cocoa powder

FILLING

5 tablespoons (100 g) raspberry jam

GLAZE

5¼ ounces (150 g) European bittersweet chocolate (such as Lindt Surfin)

¾ teaspoon (4 ml) almond oil (preferably) or neutral vegetable oil

For about 35 to 40 cookies

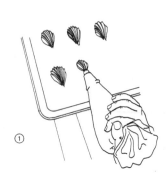
①

Preheat the oven to 400° F (200° C).

1. Place the butter in a small stainless-steel bowl and beat with a wooden spatula, warming it over low heat as needed to make it smooth, white, and creamy. Beat in the sugar and then the egg with the wooden spatula. Beat in the milk with a wire whisk. Sift the flour, baking powder, and cocoa powder over the batter and mix them in with the wooden spatula.

2. Scoop the batter into the pastry bag, and pipe the batter ① on the diagonal in teardrops 1½ inches (4 cm) long and 1 inch (2½ cm) wide, arranging them on the prepared baking sheets in staggered rows and separating them by 1 to 1½ inches (2½–4 cm).

3. Bake, 1 sheet at a time, for 5 minutes. Then place an empty baking sheet underneath the sheet of cookies (or, lacking an empty baking sheet, raise the baking sheet to the top shelf of the oven and reduce the oven temperature to 300° F or 150° C) to protect the bottoms from burning, and continue baking until the edges and bottoms of the cookies just begin to brown. The total baking time will be about 10 to 15 minutes for each sheet.

②

③

4. Slide the cookies onto a wire rack using a metal spatula and let them cool to room temperature.

5. If the raspberry jam is at all runny, simmer it gently to reduce the excess liquid and then cool before using. Spread about ⅜ teaspoon (2 ml) of jam on the back of one teardrop ② with a palette knife, and sandwich it back to back with a second teardrop. Repeat with the remaining teardrops.

6. Temper the chocolate with the almond oil as follows: Gently melt the chocolate and stir in the almond oil. Dip the bottom of the pot of chocolate in a bowl of cold water and stir the chocolate until it begins to thicken. Immediately remove from the cold water and dip the bottom of the pot of chocolate in a bowl of hot water. Stir over the hot water just long enough to make the chocolate fluid again, then remove from the hot water.

7. Dip the tip of each teardrop in the chocolate, clean off the excess on the edge of the pot, and place the cookies on a sheet of wax paper ③. Let the chocolate set.

STORAGE: Covered airtight in a cookie jar or tin cookie box for up to 2 weeks in a cool place (below 70° F or 20° C).

RAILROAD TRACKS
CHEMINS DE FER

~~~~~~~~

Chemins de fer—*literally "paths of iron"*—means *"railroads" in French, and the shape of these sweet, crisp, lemon-flavored cookies is reminiscent of rail-road tracks. To create this effect we pipe thin bands of batter with a fluted ribbon tube. After baking, we brush the hot cookies with a mixture of confectioners' sugar and water, which sets immediately to form a shiny glaze. Children especially enjoy the vivid imagery of railroad travel evoked by these delightful cookies.*

EQUIPMENT

3 large, heavy baking sheets
• Brush 2 of them lightly with melted butter.
A large pastry bag fitted with
• a ¾-inch (2 cm) fluted ribbon tube (Ateco #47ST)

BATTER

2 ounces (60 g), or 4 tablespoons, unsalted
    butter, softened
2½ ounces (70 g), or ½ cup plus 4 teaspoons,
    confectioners' sugar

1 large egg yolk
5 teaspoons (2½ cl) lightly beaten egg
Finely grated zest of 1 lemon
4½ ounces (125 g), or ¾ cup plus 2 tablespoons,
    all-purpose flour

GLAZE

2½ ounces (70 g), or ½ cup plus 4 teaspoons,
    confectioners' sugar
1 tablespoon water

For about 60 cookies

Preheat the oven to 450° F (230° C).

1. Place the butter in a small stainless-steel bowl and beat with a wooden spatula, warming it over low heat as needed to make it smooth, white, and creamy. Sift the sugar over the creamed butter and beat it in. Beat in the egg yolk. Beat in the beaten egg and then the lemon zest with a wire whisk. Sift the flour over the batter and mix it in with the wooden spatula.

2. Scoop the batter into the pastry bag, and pipe the batter in fluted strips ① the length of the prepared baking sheets, separating them by 1 to 1½ inches (2½–4 cm). Score each strip ② crosswise at 2-inch (5 cm) intervals by pressing through the batter with a small palette knife or the back edge of a paring knife. Wipe off the blade after every 3 or 4 cuts to remove any batter that sticks to it.

3. Bake on the top oven shelf, 1 sheet at a time, until the cookies just begin to brown on the bottoms, about 4 minutes. Then place an empty baking sheet underneath the sheet of cookies (or, lacking an empty baking sheet, reduce the oven temperature to 300° F, or 150° C) to prevent the bottoms from burning, and continue baking until the ridges on the cookies are very lightly browned. The total baking time will be about 7 to 10 minutes for each sheet. Remove from the oven immediately, and place the baking sheet on a cooling rack. Let the cookies cool on the baking sheet for 1 minute.

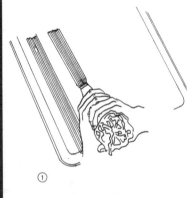

①

②

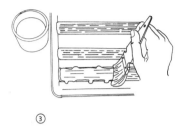

③

4. While the cookies are baking, stir together the confectioners' sugar and water to make a smooth, creamy paste that is just fluid enough to spread easily with a pastry brush. If necessary, add a little more cold water to get the right consistency. When the cookies have been out of the oven for 1 minute (but are still hot), brush them well with this sugar glaze ③. Then let them continue cooling on the baking sheet. Break the strips into lengths at the scored marks and slide them off the baking sheet while they are still warm.

STORAGE: Covered airtight in a cookie jar or tin cookie box for up to 1 week.

CORNMEAL COOKIES
MAÏS

Here is a very rare French cookie, made with cornmeal (maïs is the French word for corn). It probably originated in the Bresse region of southern Burgundy, where corn is an important crop and is used more in cooking than in other regions of France. In fact, the people of Bresse are nicknamed ventre jaune (yellow belly) because they have the reputation of eating so much corn.

Our Cornmeal Cookies are tender, with a texture reminiscent of corn bread, and they are shaped like tiny ears of corn.

EQUIPMENT

1 or 2 large, heavy baking sheets
- Brush edges and diagonals with melted butter.
- Line with kitchen parchment.

A large pastry bag fitted with
- a medium, fluted "French style" pastry tube (Ateco #4B)

BATTER

1¾ ounces (50 g), or 3½ tablespoons, unsalted butter, softened

2 ounces (60 g), or about ½ cup, confectioners' sugar

2 large egg yolks

Finely grated zest of 1 lemon

2⅔ ounces (75 g), or ½ cup plus 2 teaspoons, all-purpose flour

2 ounces (60 g), or 7 tablespoons plus 1 teaspoon, yellow cornmeal

For about 40 cookies

①

②

Preheat the oven to 475° F (245° C).

1. Place the butter in a small stainless-steel bowl and beat with a wooden spatula, warming it over low heat as needed to make it smooth, white, and creamy. Sift the sugar over the creamed butter and beat it in. Beat in 1 egg yolk with the wooden spatula. Then beat in the remaining yolk with a wire whisk. Whisk in the lemon zest. Sift the flour and cornmeal over the batter and mix them in with the wooden spatula.

2. Scoop the batter into the pastry bag, and pipe the batter in ½-inch-(12 mm) wide fluted strips ① the length of the baking sheets, separating them by 1 to 1½ inches (2½–4 cm). Score each strip ② crosswise at 2½-inch (6 cm) intervals by pressing through the batter with a small palette knife or the back edge of a paring knife. Wipe off the blade after every 3 or 4 cuts to remove any batter that sticks to it.

3. Bake, 1 sheet at a time, until the cookies begin to brown on the bottoms but are still pale yellow on the tops, about 5 minutes.

4. Transfer the baking sheet to a wire rack and let the cookies cool to room temperature.

5. When the cookies are cool, separate them at the scored intervals.

STORAGE: Covered airtight in a cookie jar or tin cookie box for up to 3 days.

LITTLE JACKS
PETITS JACKS

These finger-shaped cookies have a tender texture and a vibrant flavor of hazelnuts accented with vanilla and apricot jam. As with many great wines, the taste sensation can be described best as mouth-filling. We think Little Jacks are especially good with chocolate ice cream or a cup of potent, aromatic coffee such as espresso or café filtré. The word jacks isn't really French; our best guess is that petits jacks may derive from someone's nickname.

EQUIPMENT

3 large, heavy baking sheets
- Brush lightly with melted butter.
- Then wipe with a paper towel to leave only a thin film of butter.

A large pastry bag fitted with
- a ⅜-inch (1 cm) plain pastry tube (Ateco #4)

BATTER

3½ ounces (100 g), or 7 tablespoons, unsalted butter, softened

7 ounces (200 g), or about 1½ cups, hazelnut and sugar powder

} *Basic Preparation, page 482:*
3¾ ounces (105 g), or ¾ cup, hazelnuts
3½ ounces (100 g), or ¾ cup plus 4 teaspoons, confectioners' sugar

1 large egg

1 teaspoon (½ cl) vanilla extract

1 tablespoon (20 g) strained apricot jam
    [*Basic Preparation, page 484*]

5 ounces (140 g), or 1 cup, all-purpose flour

GLAZE

1 large egg, lightly beaten

For about 75 Cookies

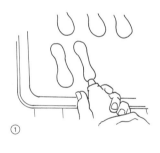

Preheat the oven to 325° F (160° C).

1. Place the butter in a small stainless-steel bowl and beat with a wooden spatula, warming it over low heat as needed to make it smooth, white, and creamy. Beat in the hazelnut and sugar powder and then the egg, followed by the vanilla and the apricot jam. Sift the flour over the batter and mix it in with the wooden spatula.

2. Scoop the batter into the pastry bag, and pipe the batter ① on the diagonal in fingers 2½ inches (6 cm) long and ⅜ inch (1 cm) wide at the center, arranging them on the baking sheets in staggered rows and separating them by 1 inch (2½ cm). Both ends of each finger should be fatter than the center, like a dumbbell.

3. Lightly brush each finger with beaten egg.

4. Bake, 1 sheet at a time, until the cookies are browned on the bottoms and the egg glaze on the tops turns golden brown, about 14 to 18 minutes.

5. Slide the cookies onto a wire rack using a metal spatula and let them cool to room temperature.

STORAGE: Covered airtight in a cookie jar or tin cookie box for up to 1 week.

VIENNESE COOKIES
VIENNOIS

Many pastry chefs refer to all cookies of the Piped Sablés type as viennois, because such cookies are popular in Viennese pastry. We use viennois, or Viennese Cookies, in a more restrictive sense for a luxurious variation that contains ground almonds, and we offer four traditional shapes that are reminiscent of old Europe. Fingers with one end dipped in chocolate are called simply Viennese Cookies. Teardrops sandwiched back to back with jam and the tips dipped in chocolate are Jam-Filled Viennese Cookies. Rosettes with a glacé cherry on the center are Sultanas. And hearts with a raw almond on the center and the back side glazed with chocolate are Almond Hearts. From a single batter you can easily create an enticing assortment of cookies to serve on a special occasion or to package in a beautiful cookie tin as an extravagant gift. Like Piped Sablés and Tea Cookies, the Viennese Cookie batter can also be formed with a cookie press.

EQUIPMENT
3 or 4 large, heavy baking sheets
- Brush all but one of them lightly with melted butter.
- Then wipe with a paper towel to leave only a thin film of butter.

A large pastry bag fitted with
- a medium-small fluted pastry tube (Ateco #3)

BATTER
2½ ounces (70 g), or 5 tablespoons, unsalted butter, softened
1¾ ounces (50 g), or ¼ cup, superfine sugar
1¾ ounces (50 g), or ¼ cup plus 2 tablespoons, almond and sugar powder
Basic Preparation, page 482:
1 ounce (25 g), or 2 tablespoons plus 2 teaspoons, blanched almonds
1 ounce (25 g), or 3 tablespoons plus 1 teaspoon, confectioners' sugar

1 large egg
½ teaspoon (¼ cl) vanilla extract
4½ ounces (125 g), or ¾ cup plus 2 tablespoons, all-purpose flour

DECORATION FOR SULTANAS
About 20 glacé cherries, cut in halves

DECORATION FOR ALMOND HEARTS
About 40 raw almonds

FILLING FOR JAM-FILLED VIENNESE COOKIES
5 tablespoons (100 g) strained apricot jam
[Basic Preparation, page 484]
or raspberry jam

GLAZE FOR VIENNESE COOKIES, JAM-FILLED VIENNESE COOKIES, AND ALMOND HEARTS
7 ounces (200 g) European bittersweet chocolate (such as Lindt Surfin)
1 teaspoon (½ cl) almond oil (preferably) or neutral vegetable oil

For about 40 cookies

Preheat the oven to 400°F (200°C).

1. Place the butter in a small stainless-steel bowl and beat with a wooden spatula, warming it over low heat as needed to make it smooth, white, and creamy. Sift the sugar over the butter and beat it in. Beat in the almond and sugar powder, and then the egg and the vanilla. Sift the flour over the batter and mix it in with the wooden spatula.

2. Scoop the batter into the pastry bag.

FOR VIENNESE COOKIES: Pipe the batter ① on the diagonal in fingers 2½ inches (6 cm) long and ½ to ⅝ inch (12–16 mm) wide. To form each

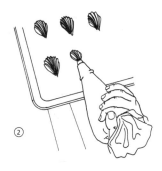

finger, first press on the pastry bag and start moving the pastry tube away from you, then quickly reverse direction and pull the pastry tube toward you in a straight line. Terminate by reversing direction once again and flicking the tip of the pastry tube horizontally over the end of the finger and up.

FOR JAM-FILLED VIENNESE COOKIES: Pipe the batter ② on the diagonal in teardrops 1½ inches (4 cm) long and 1 inch (2½ cm) wide.

FOR SULTANAS: Pipe the batter in rosettes 1¼ inches (3 cm) wide using a tight circular movement with the tip of the pastry tube. Press half of a glacé cherry on the center of each rosette.

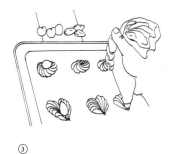

FOR ALMOND HEARTS: Pipe a teardrop 1½ inches (4 cm) long and 1 inch (2½ cm) wide. Then pipe a second teardrop ③ adjacent to the first one to form a heart. Repeat with the remaining batter. Press a raw almond in the center of each heart.

Arrange all of the shapes on the prepared baking sheets in staggered rows and separate them by 1 to 1½ inches (2½–4 cm).

3. Bake, 1 sheet at a time, until the bottoms of the cookies barely begin to brown, about 4 to 6 minutes. Then place an empty baking sheet underneath the sheet of cookies (or, lacking an empty baking sheet, raise the baking sheet to the top shelf of the oven and reduce the oven temperature to 300° F or 150° C) to protect the bottoms from burning, and continue baking until the ridges on the cookies are lightly browned. The total baking time will be about 10 to 15 minutes for each sheet.

4. Slide the cookies onto a wire rack using a metal spatula and let them cool to room temperature.

5. For Jam-Filled Viennese Cookies, if the raspberry jam is at all runny, simmer it gently to reduce the excess liquid and then cool before using. Spread about ⅜ teaspoon (2 ml) of jam on the back of one teardrop with a palette knife, and sandwich it back to back with a second teardrop ④. Repeat with the remaining teardrops.

6. For Viennese Cookies, Jam-Filled Viennese Cookies, and Almond Hearts, temper the chocolate with the almond oil as follows: Gently melt the chocolate and stir in the almond oil ⑤. Dip the bottom of the pot of chocolate in a bowl of cold water and stir the chocolate until it begins to thicken. Immediately remove from the cold water and dip the bottom of the pot of chocolate in a bowl of hot water. Stir over the hot water just long enough to make the chocolate fluid again, then remove from the hot water.

(continued)

7. Dip one end of each Viennese Cookie or the tip of each Jam-Filled Viennese Cookie in the chocolate, clean off the excess on the edge of the pot, and place the cookies on a sheet of wax paper ⑥.

Spread the back of each Almond Heart with chocolate and smooth it with a palette knife, then place the cookies chocolate side up on your countertop.

Let the chocolate set.

STORAGE: Covered airtight in a cookie jar or tin cookie box for up to 2 weeks, in a cool place (below 70° F or 20° C) for cookies glazed with chocolate.

HAZELNUT INDEX CARDS
FICHES

Named *for their resemblance to index cards (fiches in French), these thin cookies are redolent of roasted hazelnuts. After baking, the hot cookies are glazed with a mixture of confectioners' sugar and pungent Jamaican rum. We especially like them with a bowl of ripe, juicy berries.*

EQUIPMENT

3 or 4 large, heavy baking sheets
- Brush all but one of them lightly with melted butter.

A large pastry bag fitted with
- a ¾-inch (2 cm) fluted ribbon tube (Ateco #47ST)

BATTER

2½ ounces (70 g), or 5 tablespoons, unsalted butter, softened

4 ounces (120 g), or ¾ cup plus 2 tablespoons, hazelnut and sugar powder

Basic Preparation, page 482:
2¼ ounces (65 g), or ¼ cup plus 3½ tablespoons, hazelnuts
2 ounces (60 g), or ½ cup, confectioners' sugar

1 large egg

1 teaspoon (½ cl) vanilla extract

3½ ounces (100 g), or ⅔ cup plus 1 tablespoon, all-purpose flour

GLAZE

2½ ounces (70 g), or ½ cup plus 4 teaspoons, confectioners' sugar

1 tablespoon (1½ cl) dark Jamaican rum

For about 75 to 80 cookies   *Preheat the oven to 425° F (220° C).*

1. Place the butter in a small stainless-steel bowl and beat with a wooden spatula, warming it over low heat as needed to make it smooth, white, and creamy. Beat in the hazelnut and sugar powder and then the

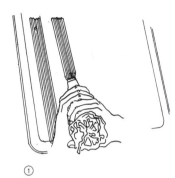

①

②

③

egg, followed by the vanilla. Sift the flour over the batter and mix it in with the wooden spatula.

2. Scoop the batter into the pastry bag, and pipe the batter in fluted strips ① the length of the prepared baking sheets, separating them by 1 to 1½ inches (2½–4 cm). Score each strip ② crosswise at 2-inch (5 cm) intervals by pressing through the batter with a small palette knife or the back edge of a paring knife. Wipe off the blade after every 3 or 4 cuts to remove any batter that sticks to it.

3. Bake, 1 sheet at a time, for 4 minutes. Then place an empty baking sheet underneath the sheet of cookies (or, lacking an empty baking sheet, raise the baking sheet to the top shelf of the oven and reduce the oven temperature to 300° F or 150° C) to prevent the bottoms from burning, and continue baking until the tops of the cookies are pale beige with the edges lightly browned. The total baking time will be about 7 to 11 minutes for each sheet. Remove from the oven, and place the baking sheet on a cooling rack. Let the cookies cool on the baking sheet for 2 minutes.

4. While the cookies are baking, stir together the confectioners' sugar and rum to make a smooth, creamy paste that is just fluid enough to spread easily with a pastry brush. If necessary, add a little more cold water to get the right consistency. When the cookies have been out of the oven for 2 minutes (but are still hot), brush them well with this sugar glaze ③. Then let them continue cooling on the baking sheet. Break the strips into lengths at the scored marks and slide them off the baking sheet using a metal spatula while they are still warm.

STORAGE: Covered airtight in a cookie jar or tin cookie box for up to 1 week.

CHAPTER 2
MERINGUE
BATTERS

A meringue is simply a mixture of stiffly whipped egg whites and sugar. There are three distinct methods of preparing meringue batters, called French, Italian, and Swiss, depending on how the sugar is incorporated. For French (or "ordinary") meringue, sugar is beaten into the whipped whites, while for Italian meringue hot sugar syrup is used instead of dry sugar. For Swiss meringue, egg whites and sugar are combined at the outset and whipped over low heat. We explain these methods more fully later.

All three basic meringue batters are very light and quite sweet. They can be flavored and used directly to make some delightful cookies such as Meringue Squiggles and Meringue Ladies' Fingers, but the variety is limited. The exciting thing about meringue is that these batters will accommodate large additions of powdered nuts or chocolate and still retain some of their characteristic lightness. The fascinating array of meringue-based cookies includes crisp, chocolate-glazed Biarritz; the rich, luxurious macaroons called Gerbet; soft and tender Blidas; and the exotic, meltingly chocolaty Madagascans, to name just a few of our favorites. Ordinary meringue is also used in the preparation of some sponge cake batters, which are the subject of Chapter 4.

The word *meringue* is thought to derive from Mieringen (or Mehrinyghen), a small town south of Luzern in the Swiss Alps. A Swiss pastry chef of Italian descent named Gasparini, who worked in that town, has been credited with the invention of the meringue around 1720. However, some culinary historians believe that meringues were first created even earlier.

Meringues were introduced into France a little later in the eighteenth century by Stanislaus Leszczynski, the deposed king of Poland who got the dukedom of Lorraine as a consolation prize after losing the Polish war of succession in 1735. King Stanislaus was the father-in-law of King Louis XV of France, and he was a noted gourmet who also had a role in the development of rum babas. Meringues quickly became the rage among royalty after Stanislaus began serving them to his entourage at the court in Luneville. Toward the end of the century they were a favorite of Queen Marie Antoinette, who prepared them herself at the Petit Trianon, her retreat on the grounds of Versailles.

It is easy to envisage elaborately piped, scrolly shapes when thinking of meringues in the context of eighteenth-century French royalty. However, the pastry bag was not invented until the nineteenth century. Prior to that, meringues were shaped with spoons. So the eighteenth-century enchantment with meringues must have been based more on their seemingly miraculous lightness than on their visual beauty.

Whipping egg whites properly is essential to making any kind of meringue. The delicate stability of the whipped egg whites depends on several factors. By understanding and controlling these factors, you can make whipping egg whites a trouble-free procedure.

WHIPPING EGG WHITES: A BRIEF SCIENTIFIC EXPLANATION

The egg white, or albumen, is a solution of several proteins in water. When you whip the egg whites, you disperse air in the liquid albumen, producing a mass of bubbles that we call a foam. At the same time, whipping stablizes the foam by altering the physical configuration of the proteins and linking them to each other and to water molecules.

At the outset, the albumen has a cohesiveness that is a result of a layered structure of its component molecules in the solution. Beating the whites quickly breaks up this structure and makes the whites more fluid.

The albumen proteins are long, chainlike molecules, each molecule tightly folded onto itself in a compact ball. They are held in this compact ball by loose physical bonds (called hydrogen bonds) as well as stronger chemical bonds between adjacent folds of the chain. Because the protein molecules are large, the albumen is thick and viscous (the fluid resists forces that tend to make it flow). The mechanical action of whipping produces an extensional force on each protein molecule that is directly proportional to the fluid's viscosity and (at least approximately) to the whipping speed. When this force becomes great enough, the hydrogen bonds that help keep the molecules folded begin to break, and the molecules get stretched out like long strings. We say the protein molecules are "denatured" because we have altered their natural physical configuration without breaking the strong chemical (covalent) bonds that keep each molecule in one piece. Denaturing the proteins increases the viscosity of the albumen first because the stretched-out molecules are more likely to run into each other, and second because the denatured proteins can now cross-link with each other and with water molecules by forming hydrogen bonds between adjacent molecules. These bonds are not permanent. They are constantly forming, breaking, and reforming, but they introduce a quasi-stable structure into the fluid albumen.

In the early stages of whipping, air is dragged into the albumen by the whisk, producing bubbles. But the albumen quickly flows out of the bubble walls, allowing the air to escape. As the albumen becomes more viscous, it flows more slowly and the bubbles remain trapped longer. Parts of the unfolded proteins in the bubble walls are hydrophobic (they avoid water), and these parts stick up into the air bubbles, thus avoiding the water in the albumen. At the same time, other parts of the molecules are hydrophilic (they like water), and these parts form hydrogen bonds with water molecules, as well as with each other. Since this configuration of the molecules is energetically favorable, the bubbles acquire a lower surface energy (and their walls acquire an elasticity) that keeps the air trapped in the bubbles.

Continued whipping incorporates more air in the foam and divides large bubbles into smaller ones. It also denatures more proteins and brings the proteins into closer contact with each other so they can form more temporary physical cross-links. Gradually this process builds up a fragile network of protein and water molecules that stabilizes the foam.

When the whipped whites are baked, the air in the bubbles expands. At the same time, the heat breaks some of the remaining bonds still holding folds in the protein molecules, and the denatured protein molecules cross-link in a more permanent fashion by coagulating, forming chemical, covalent bonds between the parts of the molecules that have been held close together by the physical, hydrogen bonds. The result is a more solid structure that doesn't collapse when the bubbles in the foam burst and the air escapes.

The critical force required to initiate denaturing the albumen proteins is different for each protein. As a result, the different albumen proteins will begin to unfold sequentially as the viscosity of the albumen and the speed of whipping increase. One of the albumen proteins, called ovalbumin, is much more difficult to denature than the others. It turns out that this protein is primarily responsible for providing the solid structure that survives when the foam is baked. We propose that in order to denature enough ovalbumin molecules, it is necessary to increase dramatically the extensional force on the molecules at the end of the whipping, when most of the other proteins are already unfolded. This goal is accomplished by adding sugar (which abruptly increases the viscosity of the fluid in the foam walls) and by simultaneously increasing the whipping speed. The high whipping speed quickly supplies the energy needed to bring ovalbumin molecules close together so they can form hydrogen bonds with each other. The trick is to denature and cross-link enough ovalbumin proteins for stability, without forming so many cross-links that the baked meringue becomes tough.

When sugar is added to the whipped whites, it dissolves in the water in the bubble walls, making the bubble walls thicker and more elastic. As a result, bubbles slide past each other rather than breaking and coalescing, and the foam holds together rather than separating into fluffy, semisolid masses. When the foam bakes, the greater elasticity of the bubbles helps prevent them from expanding too much and bursting too early. The sugar also contributes to the foam's stability during baking by delaying the evaporation of water from the foam, giving the proteins more time to coagulate.

WHIPPING EGG WHITES: PRELIMINARY PRECAUTIONS

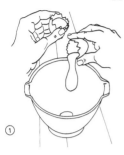

First, the eggs should be separated carefully, so that no yolk gets in the whites ①. Fats, particularly egg yolks (which contain emulsifiers as well as fats), interfere with the development of the egg white foam. The presence of even a speck of egg yolk will drastically increase the amount of energy required to produce the foam and will reduce its stability. For this reason, you should always use a very clean bowl and whisk (or beater) to whip egg whites. (Never use plastic bowls because the plastic retains traces of fat on its surface.) After the whites have been whipped, ingredients containing fats can be added without damaging the foam.

(From the scientific standpoint, the hydrophobic parts of the albumen proteins that like to stick up into the air bubbles and help stablize the foam are even more likely to avoid the water in the albumen by sticking in fat globules, which is more energetically favorable. Also, fat globules collect at the air-water interface, reducing the surface area available to albumen proteins. So when fat is present, more albumen proteins must be denatured to have enough of them to stabilize the foam. Denaturing these additional proteins requires more energy and more prolonged beating. When fat is present during the whipping, bubbles will be constantly coalescing as protein molecules migrate from the air-water interface to the fat-water interface and bubble walls break down. If too much fat is present, it will not be possible to denature proteins fast enough to compensate for this migration, and the result will be a coarser foam with larger bubbles.)

The fresher the eggs, the more viscous the albumen. Because of their slightly lower viscosity, the whites of eggs that are at least three days old can actually be whipped to slightly greater volume than those of very fresh eggs. This is an advantage for making soufflés, where maximum volume is desirable. In pastry making, stability is more important than maximum volume, and the higher viscosity of fresh whites makes the foam more stable. (Some chefs suggest adding a tiny amount of salt to very fresh whites to reduce their viscosity so they can be whipped to greater volume. We advise against this procedure because it reduces the stability of the foam and, for desserts, risks producing a salty taste unless executed with extreme caution.)

While it is easiest to separate eggs when they are cold, it is easier to whip air into warm whites (because the thermal vibrations of the molecules facilitate denaturing the proteins). For this reason the egg whites should be allowed to warm to room temperature before whipping.

It is best to whip the whites using a flexible wire whisk or the wire whip of a planetary-action electric mixer (see page 6). The whisk gives you tremendous control, but whisking even two or three egg whites for a meringue takes a lot of energy. We strongly recommend using the planetary-action electric mixer. An eggbeater-type electric mixer is very efficient for the early stages of whipping the whites, but when the whites become thick, it whips them unevenly. If you have this type of mixer, you can use it to whip the whites until they start to become thick, and then finish with a wire whisk.

Use a copper, stainless-steel, glass, or glazed ceramic bowl to whip egg whites. Do not use aluminum, which discolors the whites. A good rule of thumb is that the bowl should have a volume at least sixteen times that of the initial volume of the whites. Since the volume of eight large egg whites is about 1 cup (2.4 dl), you will need a bowl with a capacity of at least 1 quart (1 L) for every two large whites. We recommend whipping a minimum of two large egg whites when making a meringue. The volume of one large egg white is only 2 tablespoons (3 cl) before whipping, and most whisks and beaters are too large to whip air into so small a quantity of albumen effectively.

The advantage of a copper mixing bowl is that atoms of copper bind with molecules of one of the albumen proteins (specifically conalbumen), producing a complex that requires more energy to denature than the original protein itself and promotes cross-linking between the protein molecules. The result is an egg white foam that is creamier and less easy to overwhip than one whipped in a stainless-steel bowl. To keep the copper bowl absolutely free of fats or detergents, follow these steps: After each use, wash the bowl thoroughly with hot water; clean the surface with a mixture of coarse salt (such as coarse kosher salt) and distilled white vinegar (or other inexpensive white vinegar), which removes oxidation as well as fats and detergents; rinse it out with cold water; and leave it upside down to drain and air-dry.

If you do not have a copper bowl, add some cream of tartar to the whites shortly after you begin whipping them. The cream of tartar, which lowers the initially alkaline pH of the whites (and thereby reduces the electrical repulsion between protein molecules), also reduces the risk of overwhipping the whites. While the mechanism is totally different (and not well understood), the end result is similar to that produced by whipping in a copper bowl.

WHIPPING EGG WHITES: THE PRACTICAL PROCEDURE

Now you are ready to whip the whites. Start at low speed to break up the whites. At the beginning, the albumen is so cohesive that there is a tendency to whip large bubbles into the whites. By starting slowly, you get smaller bubbles and a finer texture.

If you are whipping by hand with a wire whisk, tilt the bowl and move the whisk in a rhythmic circular motion ②. Sweeping the whisk around the

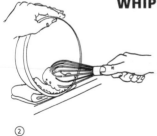
②

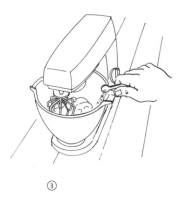

③

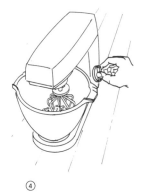

④

bottom of the bowl, in and out of the mass of egg white (which will actually lift with each stroke of the whisk at the beginning) is the most efficient way to break up the whites and drag the maximum amount of air into them.

If you are whipping with an eggbeater-type electric mixer, constantly move it around the bowl to beat the whites evenly.

Soon the whites will begin to froth. If you are not whipping the whites in a copper bowl, add a little cream of tartar ③ at this point. The amount of cream of tartar required is about ⅛ teaspoon (½ ml) for three large egg whites. (If you use much more than that, it will be impossible to determine when the whites have been beaten to the optimal degree.)

Now gradually increase the whipping speed ④. We find that medium-high speed works best in a planetary-action electric mixer. If you are whipping by hand using a wire whisk, do most of the beating at medium speed so you can save your energy for a burst of high-speed whipping at the end.

As progressively more air is whipped into the albumen, large air bubbles are divided into progressively finer ones, and more proteins are denatured and cross-linked. The whites will increase in volume and change from a slightly yellowish, clear liquid to an opaque white foam that soon becomes thick enough to hold soft, bending peaks as you lift the whisk. When you tilt the bowl at this ''soft-peak'' stage, the mass of egg white will slide around in it and will not cling to the side of the bowl. If you are whipping with an eggbeater-type mixer, quickly switch to a wire whisk when you reach the soft-peak stage. (If you were to stop whipping at the soft-peak stage, the foam would not be light, firm, or fine enough, and there would not be enough proteins denatured and cross-linked to support it. The result would have low volume and be unstable.)

Continue whipping. The whites will become stiffer and will begin to cling to the side of the bowl so that the mass of whites will not slip when the bowl is tipped. Lifting the whip will produce stiff, unbending peaks, and the whites will still be moist and shiny. This is the ''stiff-but-not-dry'' stage. For soufflés you will get the best results (maximum expansion and optimal moisture inside when baked) by whipping the whites to this point. However, for pastry making most batters will be too soft and will spread too much when baked if you stop at this point.

As you whip the whites still more, the surface of the whites will become a little duller, and the whites around the side of the bowl (where whipping applies the greatest force on the albumen) will just begin to release a little moisture. The moisture allows the mass of egg white to slip on the side of the bowl, forming streaks as the whisk drags it around. This behavior gives a sharp, well-defined test for the point at which the optimal texture is reached. We refer to it as the ''slip-and-streak'' stage.

⑤

If you whip the whites past the slip-and-streak stage, the albumen proteins will continue to be denatured and form physical cross-links. They will gradually lose their ability to hold water (as the proteins form progressively more hydrogen bonds with each other rather than with water molecules). The foam will release liquid, become grainy, and lose volume. The whites are overwhipped. They cannot be rescued, but fortunately egg whites are cheap. Discard the overwhipped whites and start again.

So far you have only whipped egg whites. They do not become a meringue until the sugar is added. In both French and Italian meringues you add the sugar at the end of the whipping ⑤, usually at the slip-and-streak stage. You then whip the whites at maximum speed for a few seconds to incorporate the sugar and "tighten" the meringue. The sugar makes the foam smoother and more cohesive almost instantly. The extent of the change depends on the quantity of sugar used. Tightening the meringue by whipping it briefly at high speed after adding the sugar helps prevent the meringue from expanding too much in the oven and then deflating, which would cause the cookies to be too dry inside and tacky on the surface.

(Adding the sugar to the egg whites at the beginning instead of the end of the whipping would have at least two negative consequences: First, by increasing the surface energy of the liquid, it would make it much more difficult to create new air bubbles. Second, by surrounding the protein molecules, it would slow cross-linking of the albumen proteins.)

FRENCH MERINGUE

French (or ordinary) meringue is the simplest type of meringue to prepare. It is always baked, and it is the most widely used meringue in cookies, as well as in cake making. When used alone (as in Meringue Squiggles), it is almost always baked crisp and dry. The texture is very fine, crumbly, and fragile. When eaten, it is tender and melting.

On the average it is also the least sweet type of meringue. For plain meringue cookies the amount of sugar used ranges from 4½ to 9 ounces (125–250 g) for three large egg whites. The more sugar, the firmer the batter and the crisper the baked cookies. For almond meringues, the French meringue is mixed with an almond and sugar powder. Here, the ratio of sugar to egg whites can be much lower, depending on the desired texture of the finished product. Caracas Wafers, for example, contain only 2¾ ounces (80 g) of sugar for three whites, and the cookies are crisp and light. On the other hand, almond meringue cookies with a higher proportion of sugar also typically contain a high proportion of almonds, which makes them much richer. The batter for Gerbet Macaroons contains 8 ounces (225 g) of sugar and 4½ ounces (125 g) of almonds for three whites, producing a moist, soft, and rich cookie.

The whites are usually whipped to the slip-and-streak stage and then "meringued" by whipping in part of the sugar called for in the recipe. The remaining sugar, as well as other ingredients, are folded in after the completion of the whipping. Whipping in too much sugar, or whipping for too long after adding the sugar, would make the finished cookies tough and chewy (because it would form too many cross-links between ovalbumin proteins). Folding in part of the sugar produces more tender cookies.

The sugar used to tighten the meringue is always superfine or confectioners' because these fine-textured sugars dissolve quickly. Superfine is easier to use because it doesn't require sifting and mixes in readily without clinging to the side of the bowl or forming dust in the air, as confectioners' sugar is prone to do. But confectioners' sugar is preferable in some cookies because it dissolves even more quickly and can make the surface of the cookies shinier. The sugar that is folded in after the whites are meringued is most often confectioners'.

The proportion of the sugar whipped in depends partly on how the cookies are baked, and partly on the other ingredients included in the recipe. For plain meringues, typically half of the sugar is whipped in. This makes the whipped whites very shiny, smooth, firm, and cohesive, enabling you to pipe very precise forms that hold their shape. Since the cookies are normally baked crisp, the result is a desirable brittleness rather than an undesirable chewiness. These meringues are tolerant of slight overwhipping before adding the sugar because the high amount of sugar used to tighten the meringue can bind water released by the proteins. However, it is especially important that after adding the sugar they be whipped only the minimum necessary to incorporate the sugar and make the meringue smooth and shiny. Otherwise the baked cookies will be tough.

In contrast, for almond meringues only a small amount of sugar—typically ½ to 1 ounce (15–30 g) for three large whites—is whipped into the whites. The idea is to use the minimum quantity of sugar needed to tighten and stabilize the whites so that the texture of the cookies will be as tender as possible. In this case the meringue will be light and smooth, but still delicate, fluffy, and not very cohesive after tightening with the sugar. Since there is less sugar to bind with water released by the albumen proteins, you must be especially careful not to overwhip the whites for such meringues. (In a few recipes where we use the absolute minimum amount of sugar to tighten the meringue, we find it best to whip the whites only to the stiff-but-not-dry stage.)

Because the meringues tightened with a small amount of sugar are so delicate and sensitive to overwhipping, we offer an alternative procedure that can be used to reduce the risk of overwhipping for these meringues: As the whites form soft peaks, start adding the sugar allotted for tightening the whites, and continue adding it gradually while you continue whipping. The sugar will keep the whipped whites smooth and shiny, and the meringue will become very stiff without forming jagged peaks or slipping and streaking around the side of the bowl. When the meringue is very stiff but still moist and shiny, tighten it by whipping for a few seconds at maximum speed and then stop. It must not be allowed to become even slightly grainy because no more sugar will be whipped in to tighten it. The advantage of this procedure is that it slows physical cross-linking of the albumen proteins so that it takes longer to overwhip them. Its disadvantage is that the point at which you should stop whipping is less sharply defined than when the whites are whipped alone to the slip-and-streak stage. We recommend this alternative procedure only if you are using an electric mixer to whip extremely fresh whites, which, as mentioned earlier, have very high viscosity and are therefore easier to overwhip than are whites a few days old.

ITALIAN MERINGUE

Italian meringue is the lightest, and on average the sweetest, of all the meringues. Unlike French meringue, it does not have to be baked. Because it is partly cooked by the hot sugar syrup used to meringue the whites, it has great stability and is partly sterilized. It is frequently used like whipped cream to lighten fillings or frozen desserts, or to stabilize sorbets. There is even a buttercream made by whipping softened butter into Italian meringue. This meringue can also be used to mask and decorate the surfaces of large desserts including cakes, pies, and frozen desserts such as Norwegian omelette (baked Alaska). For these purposes it is usually browned quickly in a hot oven to color the surface while keeping the inside of the meringue soft and creamy.

When Italian meringue is used for cookie batters, the result can be similar to that produced with French meringue, but there are also important differences. If baked dry (for example, in Meringue Ladies' Fingers), the Italian meringue is also quite crisp but not as fragile. However, Italian meringue bakes faster than ordinary meringue, and it can be baked crisp on the outside but still soft and creamy inside (as in Madagascans), whereas plain French meringue does not normally produce a successful result unless crisp throughout. Italian meringue is most often flavored with chocolate or coffee to offset its sweetness. Almond meringue cookies based on Italian meringue are unusual, but not unheard of, and we have included in this chapter a very intriguing one called Khedives.

The amount of sugar used in Italian meringue is typically 6 to 9 ounces (175–250 g) for three large egg whites. The sugar is moistened with water and cooked to the upper firm-ball stage (about 248° F or 120° C). Then the hot syrup is added to egg whites that have been whipped to the slip-and-streak stage. The syrup and whites must be ready simultaneously, so these meringues can be a little tricky to prepare.

To prepare the syrup, combine the granulated sugar with a little water in a small saucepan or caramel pot. Ideally the pot should have a spout for pouring the syrup in a thin stream, and the level of the sugar syrup in the pot should be high enough so that you can easily measure its temperature. Use about ¼ cup (6 cl) of water for each 7 ounces (200 g), or 1 cup, of sugar. Stir to thoroughly moisten the sugar, then bring to a boil over medium heat. Do not stir while you are cooking the sugar because syrup splashed on the walls of the pot dries and produces unwanted sugar crystals.

Right after the syrup comes to a boil, some sugar crystals will form on the walls of the pot. Dissolve these crystals by washing down the pot with a moistened pastry brush, using as little water as possible so that you don't slow the cooking.

Start whipping the egg whites after the syrup comes to a boil. We strongly recommend using a planetary-action electric mixer to prepare Italian meringue. It is almost impossible to whisk the egg whites by hand (or even to whip them with a hand-held electric mixer) while you assess the progress of the sugar syrup. Also, pouring hot sugar syrup with one hand while you whisk it into the whites with the other is dangerous, even for an experienced professional. If you must whisk the whites by hand, then have a second person cook the syrup and pour it into the whites.

As you continue to boil the syrup, you will evaporate water and raise the temperature of the syrup, making it more viscous. You can check the temperature of the syrup either with a candy thermometer or by testing its viscosity.

To test the viscosity of the syrup, pluck out a little syrup (professionals use their moistened fingertips, but most amateurs prefer a spoon) and plunge it into a bowl of cold water. Feel the cooled syrup between your thumb and index finger. At the beginning it will dissolve immediately in the water, but then as it becomes more viscous it will dissolve more slowly. When it reaches the soft-ball stage, or 234 to 239° F (113–115° C), you will be able to roll it between your fingertips into a small, very soft and sticky ball that will flatten as you lift it. Then as you continue to raise the temperature you will be able to form the cooled syrup into a larger, firmer ball that will hold its shape. When you reach the upper firm-ball stage—about 248° F (120° C)—the ball will be a little larger than a pea and will no longer stick to your moistened fingertips, but it will still be firm and malleable rather than hard. This is the temperature you need for the Italian meringue. (If you are cooking a sugar syrup at high altitude, adjust the temperature to compensate for the change in the boiling point of water. For all stages of sugar cooking up to and including the soft-crack stage, reduce the temperature specified by 1.8° F [1° C] for each 1,000 feet [300 m] above sea level.)

Gradually increase the speed at which you whip the whites as the temperature of the syrup increases, so that the whites reach the slip-and-streak stage at the same time as the sugar reaches the upper firm-ball stage. If you find that the whites are progressing too rapidly, then reduce the whipping speed. Or if the syrup is heating too rapidly, lower the heat.

When the sugar reaches the upper firm-ball stage, immediately plunge the bottom of the pot of syrup into a large bowl of cold water to prevent the temperature from continuing to rise. Then quickly remove it from the cold water so you don't lower the temperature of the syrup.

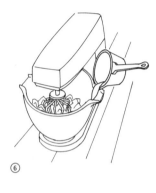

Now pour the hot syrup into the whites in a thin stream while you whip the whites at high speed. The meringue will rise and become very light. Avoid pouring the syrup onto the wire whip or it will splatter around the sides of the bowl. Try to pour the syrup directly into the whites ⑥. The problem is that in a planetary-action mixer the bowl has very steep sides that make this impossible unless you are whipping a large volume of meringue. For the small volume of meringue in our cookie recipes, you will probably need to pour the syrup down the side of the bowl in order to avoid pouring it onto the whip.

After all of the syrup has been added, continue whipping for a few seconds at high speed to make the meringue smooth and shiny. Quickly reduce the mixer to the lowest speed and continue stirring to prevent a crust from forming on top of the meringue while you finish any final mixing of the remaining ingredients in the recipe. Then turn off the machine and remove any syrup that has solidified on the side of the bowl using a bowl scraper. For baking, the meringue must be used while it is still hot.

SWISS MERINGUE

This was the original meringue. It was once widely used to mask and decorate the outsides of desserts, to pipe into decorations like meringue mushrooms, and to make cookies. Today, Swiss meringue has been almost completely superseded by French and Italian meringues.

Like French meringue, Swiss meringue is always baked. It is heavier and more solid and crunchy than ordinary meringue, but not as fragile. Its sturdiness is one reason why some chefs still like to use it for making decorations.

Despite its general lack of finesse, there is one very popular and famous cookie for which Swiss meringue is everyone's first choice. This is Almond Boulders, and it is the only cookie in this book made with Swiss meringue.

The whipping procedure for Swiss meringue is altogether different from that described above. Here, the egg whites and sugar are combined ⑦ at the

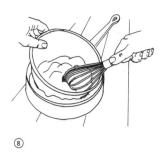

outset, which already limits the volume and lightness of the meringue. You whip the whites and sugar over low heat using a wire whisk ⑧ until they reach a temperature of about 130° F (55° C). This should be done in a stainless-steel or copper bowl (which conduct heat quickly) set over a saucepan of hot water, or equivalently in a double boiler. As for other meringues, start whipping at low speed, and then steadily increase the pace. The mixture will thicken and become white and shiny. (If you whip it vigorously enough, it will become light and thick enough to form soft, bending peaks. However, this is not necessary. At this point, it is sufficient to have the whites just thick enough to heavily coat a wooden spoon.) As soon as the whites have warmed to the required temperature, remove them from the heat and whip the meringue with an electric mixer ⑨ until it is cool, light, and very thick. (Don't even think about doing this part of the whipping by hand unless you have the strength and endurance of an Olympic athlete.) If you have a planetary-action electric mixer, whip the meringue at medium-high speed. If not, you can use an eggbeater-type electric mixer provided you circulate the beaters around the bowl constantly. When the meringue is finished, it will be firm enough to hold stiff peaks, and while quite light, it will be heavier and more substantial than either French or Italian meringue.

(Warming the Swiss meringue as it is whipped increases the vibration of the albumen molecules, making the proteins easier to denature. At the same time, the sugar raises the viscosity of the whites, and energy supplied by the heat encourages sugar, water, and protein molecules to get into closer proximity and form hydrogen bonds with each other. These factors partly compensate for the difficulties connected with adding the sugar to the whites at the outset.)

Swiss meringue is very thick and stable, and overwhipping is rarely a problem. So whipping in a copper bowl, or adding cream of tartar in lieu of a copper bowl, is not nearly as important as it is for other meringues. Some chefs like to add a little acid (usually lemon juice or vinegar) to make the meringue whiter.

Since the Swiss meringue is partly cooked, like Italian meringue it bakes more quickly than ordinary meringue. It is at its best when crisp outside but still soft inside. What makes Almond Boulders so appealing is that the batter is laden with sliced almonds, giving a nutty contrast to the soft, chewy interior of the meringue.

ADDING OTHER INGREDIENTS

Regardless of the type of meringue you have made, other ingredients can be incorporated in two ways. For recipes that contain no significant amount of liquid, dry ingredients are gently and gradually folded into the

meringue ⑩. Flavoring liquids are usually added after part of the dry ingredients have been folded in to minimize deflating the batter. Food colorings are usually whipped into the whites ⑪ immediately before they are meringued by whipping in the sugar, in order to give a uniform color without overfolding and deflating the batter.

If the recipe does contain a significant amount of liquid, such as milk or unwhipped whites, then the liquid is mixed with the dry ingredients to form a paste. Part (usually about one-third) of the meringue is "sacrificed" by quickly stirring it into the paste to soften and lighten the paste so that the remaining meringue can be incorporated without too much deflating. Finally, the remaining meringue is gently folded into the softened paste.

ABOUT MACAROONS

The majority of macaroons are made from almond-paste batters and are included in Chapter 3. However, a few macaroons are made with an almond meringue. Such cookies can be dry and crisp (as are the Italian amaretti) or soft and moist.

In France, the meringue-based macaroons are almost exclusively of the soft and moist variety. They are very different from the other almond-meringue cookies. First, the quantity of almonds is typically much greater than for other almond-meringue cookies, and the texture much moister, softer, and more tender. Second, they have a very smooth, shiny surface.

These macaroons can be made by two distinct methods, depending on whether all or half of the egg whites in the recipe are made into a meringue:

▪ If half the whites are used for the meringue, then the other half of the whites are mixed with the almond and sugar powder to make a paste. The meringue is folded into the paste just as for other almond meringues. However, since such a high fraction of the whites is not whipped, the resulting batter is softer and shinier than most other almond-meringue batters. This produces the shiny surface of the baked cookies.

▪ On the other hand, if all the egg whites in the recipe are made into a meringue, then after the almond and sugar powder is folded into the meringue it will still be firm and dull. It must then be folded a little longer to deflate the batter slightly and make it shiny. Of course, when you fold such a high quantity of dry ingredients into the meringue, you must be very gentle in order to keep it firm and not deflate it. But if you have been careful, the last step will be necessary to give the batter the correct texture and give the surface of the baked cookies the requisite shine.

▪ Remarkably, these two very different procedures produce almost identical macaroons.

Like other macaroons (and unlike other meringue-based cookies), the meringue-based macaroons are baked on baking sheets lined with newsprint (the paper on which newspapers are printed, see page 423). The macaroons are steamed off the newsprint after baking. (These procedures are explained in detail in Chapter 3, see page 126.) Then they are sandwiched back to back in pairs to keep them fresh and prevent the insides from drying too quickly. We usually include some brown sugar in the batter to help keep them soft and moist. The macaroons can also be filled with a simple buttercream to make some of the richest, most luxurious cookies imaginable.

PIPING VERSUS SPOONING

Nearly all meringues can be shaped most quickly and uniformly by piping with a pastry bag. As with the creamed butter and sugar cookies in Chapter 1, this produces cookies that bake more evenly and look better. The batter is most often piped on a buttered and floured baking sheet, or on a baking sheet lined with kitchen parchment. As mentioned above, the macaroons are baked on newsprint. A few very rare meringues (such as Chocolate Meringue Walnuts) are baked on a moistened sheet of plywood covered with newsprint to produce cookies with a moist, custardy interior. There is also a group of meringue cookies called "soufflés" that are baked in pleated bonbon cups.

Spooning the batter onto the baking sheet with a small ice cream scoop is not a good alternative for most meringues. Unlike many of the creamed butter and sugar cookies, nearly all of the meringue cookies hold their shape and do not spread and flatten out as they bake. If they are poorly shaped to start out with, they will stay that way. Plain meringue batters are quite sticky, which makes using an ice cream scoop exasperating, and most of them are piped in specialized shapes that are difficult to produce with a round scoop.

The only round almond meringues that spread sufficiently to make the ice cream scoop a good alternative to piping are Biarritz and Duchesses. You can also use an ice cream scoop for any of the cookies baked in pleated bonbon cups, though the small size of the bonbon cups makes this quite cumbersome and slow.

BAKING

Batters based on French meringue should be baked as soon as possible after they are prepared. If they are allowed to wait too long before baking, they begin to deflate. Also, sugar syrup can separate from the batter, drip onto the baking sheet, and make it difficult to remove the meringues after baking. Most chefs recommend baking these meringues immediately, but this may be impossible given the space limitations of a home oven. If you cannot bake all of the cookies at once, it is best to pipe out only as much as you can bake at one time, and keep the remaining batter in the pastry bag until the first batch of cookies is baked. Be sure the back end of the bag is closed securely, and prop the pastry bag, tube end up, on your countertop, using a bowl, the wall, or whatever else is convenient to keep it upright.

While Italian and Swiss meringues are more stable than French meringue, they also deteriorate with time. We recommend the same precautions be followed as for French meringue. The exceptions are cookies, such as Madagascans and Khedives, which must rest to form a crust before baking.

Plain meringues are most often baked at a low oven temperature—250 to 325° F (120–160° C). If the oven temperature is too high, the meringues expand too much and the outsides color too quickly while the insides become tough and chewy. But if the oven temperature is too low, the meringues don't expand enough and are dry, hard, and heavy.

Almond meringues are normally baked at a low to moderate oven temperature, usually 300 to 350° F (150–175° C), to avoid drying them too much and to brown them lightly. Because of their thickness, those in pleated bonbon cups should be baked in a low 275 to 300° F (135–150° C) oven to prevent the bottoms from browning excessively before the insides are done.

If the baking temperature is low, it is possible to bake two sheets of meringues on two oven racks simultaneously. Place one sheet on the bottom oven rack and the other on an upper oven rack, being sure there is plenty of space between them. Then reverse the positions of the two sheets about halfway through the baking period. A good rule of thumb is that this will always work if the oven temperature is 300° F (150° C) or lower. If the oven temperature is 350° F (175° C) or higher, then bottom heat is too important a factor for this procedure to be successful. At 325° F (160° C), it will work well for cookies in which the tops and bottoms brown uniformly (indicating that bottom heat is not a major factor), but not for those where the tops have a gradation of browning between center and edge or the browning of the tops is distinctly different from the browning of the bottoms.

Many meringue cookies are baked with the oven door ajar. In some cases this allows them to dry out more quickly. In others, it helps prevent the surface of the cookies from cracking.

Some of the meringue-based macaroons are baked, like other almond meringues, at a low to moderate oven temperature. The oven door must be ajar so that steam can escape and the tops of the cookies won't crack. However, it is more common to start the macaroons in a hot 450° F (230° C) oven for a minute or two with the oven door closed, then reduce the oven temperature to 375 to 400° F (190–200° C) and finish them with the oven door ajar and a second baking sheet underneath to protect the bottoms. This special treatment helps give the macaroons their unique moist, soft interior.

STORAGE

Meringue cookies should be kept covered airtight in a tin cookie box or a cookie jar, and they should not be exposed to high humidity. In fact, meringues are so adversely affected by high humidity that it is better not to make them at all in humid weather. Unless the meringues are coated with chocolate or filled with something other than jam, they should be kept at room temperature.

Crisp meringues can last for up to one or two weeks. Italian and Swiss meringues with soft centers are better kept for no more than two or three days so they don't dry out too much, and meringues that are steamed on a moistened plank will last only for a day or two.

Almond meringues that are crisp will usually last for at least four to six days, while those that are soft inside and the macaroons are better eaten within two or three days. However, if soft almond meringues are filled with jam, the jam will keep the insides soft and they can last for as long as the crisp almond meringues.

If the cookies are coated with chocolate, then they must be stored in a cool place—below 70° F (20° C)—to prevent bloom from forming on the chocolate. Cookies filled with buttercream or *ganache* (chocolate cream) can be kept in a very cool place—below 60° F (15° C)—for up to twelve hours. Otherwise they must be refrigerated and will last at most a few days. After that they can acquire a noticeable refrigerator taste.

MERINGUE SQUIGGLES
MERINGUETTES

French meringue can be piped in an infinite variety of shapes. Meringue kisses and fluted meringue fingers are certainly familiar to everyone. Our Meringue Squiggles have a more intriguing appearance: The batter is piped in broad fingers using a serpentine movement of the pastry tube.

These crisp, sweet cookies can accommodate many different flavorings. Two of our favorites are vanilla and raspberry brandy, and we suggest dividing the batter in half and flavoring one half with each. The light, brittle texture of Meringue Squiggles makes them a particularly fine accompaniment to a dish of ice cream or fresh berries with whipped cream.

EQUIPMENT

2 large, heavy baking sheets
- Brush with melted butter.
- Dust with flour.

A large pastry bag fitted with
- a medium-small fluted pastry tube (Ateco #3)

⅛ teaspoon (½ ml) cream of tartar (optional)
3½ ounces (100 g), or ½ cup, superfine sugar
¼ teaspoon (1 ml) vanilla extract
1 teaspoon (½ cl) *eau-de-vie de framboise* (raspberry brandy)
Red food coloring

BATTER

4 ounces (115 g), or ¾ cup plus 3 tablespoons, confectioners' sugar
⅓ ounce (10 g), or 1 tablespoon plus ½ teaspoon, all-purpose flour
3 large egg whites, at room temperature

For about 30 to 35 cookies

Preheat the oven to 250° F (120° C).

1. Mix the confectioners' sugar and flour and sift them together. Divide the mixture in half.

2. Whip the egg whites in an electric mixer at low speed until they start to froth. If you are not whipping the whites in a copper bowl, then add the cream of tartar at this point. Gradually increase the whipping speed to medium-high, and continue whipping until the whites form very stiff peaks and just begin to slip and streak around the side of the bowl. Add the superfine sugar and continue whipping at high speed for a few seconds longer to make the meringue smooth and shiny.

3. Transfer half the meringue to another bowl. Gently fold half the confectioners' sugar and flour into half the meringue ①. When almost incorporated, add the vanilla and continue folding until completely mixed and smooth.

4. Stir about 2 tablespoons (12 g) of the remaining confectioners' sugar and flour into the framboise brandy and mix in a drop of red food coloring. Start folding the rest of the confectioners' sugar and flour into

②

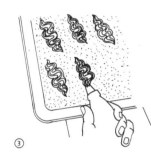

③

the second half of the meringue. When about half has been folded in, add the framboise mixture ② and continue folding in the confectioners' sugar and flour until completely mixed and smooth.

5. Scoop the vanilla meringue into the pastry bag, and pipe this meringue on one of the baking sheets in fingers 2½ inches (6½ cm) long and 1⅜ inches (3½ cm) wide, arranging them on the diagonal in staggered rows and separating them by about 1 inch (2½ cm). To form each finger ③, use a serpentine back-and-forth motion with the tip of the pastry tube. Start with a small amplitude, gradually increase until you reach the center, then gradually decrease the amplitude until the end. Terminate by a quick semicircular flick of the tip of the pastry tube at the end of the last sidewise stroke. It should take about 4 back-and-forth strokes, or 8 sidewise movements altogether, to form each finger. Try to establish a smooth, rhythmical motion.

6. Scoop the framboise meringue into the same pastry bag, and pipe it onto the second baking sheet in the same serpentine fingers as you did with the vanilla meringue.

7. Place one baking sheet on a lower oven rack and one on an upper oven rack, and bake for 30 minutes, using a wooden spatula to hold the oven door ajar. Reverse the positions of the 2 baking sheets, and continue baking with the oven door ajar until the meringues barely begin to color and are dry inside, about 30 to 40 minutes longer.

8. Place each baking sheet on a wire rack and let the cookies cool to room temperature.

➤ **HOWS & WHYS:** Thickening the framboise with a little confectioners' sugar makes it easier to mix in without deflating and softening the meringue. It is essential that the meringue remain firm in order to hold the fluted, serpentine shape.

STORAGE: Covered airtight in a tin cookie box or a cookie jar, for up to 2 weeks if they are not exposed to high humidity.

FIELD MARSHAL'S BATONS
BÂTONS DE MARÉCHAL

These cookies, made from a meringue batter containing powdered raw almonds, are baked crisp and glazed on the flat side with chocolate—quite masculine and dignified. Some chefs call them rothschilds, a name that we find a bit too luxurious for this very refined cookie.

EQUIPMENT

2 large, heavy baking sheets
- Brush with melted butter.
- Dust with flour.

A large pastry bag fitted with
- a ⅜-inch (1 cm) plain pastry tube (Ateco #4)

BATTER

⅔ ounce (18 g), or 2 tablespoons, all-purpose flour
5⅓ ounces (150 g), or 1 cup plus 2 tablespoons, raw-almond and sugar powder

} *Basic Preparation, page 482:*
2⅔ *ounces (75 g), or ½ cup, raw almonds*
2⅔ *ounces (75 g), or ½ cup plus 2 tablespoons, confectioners' sugar*

3 large egg whites, at room temperature
⅛ teaspoon (½ ml) cream of tartar (optional)
1 ounce (25 g), or 2 tablespoons, superfine sugar

DECORATION

3 ounces (85 g), or ½ cup plus 1 tablespoon, blanched almonds, finely chopped

GLAZE

3½ ounces (100 g) European bittersweet chocolate (such as Lindt Surfin)
½ teaspoon (¼ cl) almond oil (preferably) or neutral vegetable oil

For about 55 to 60 cookies

Preheat the oven to 325° F (160° C).

1. Sift the flour and toss it with the raw-almond and sugar powder.

2. Whip the egg whites in an electric mixer at low speed until they start to froth. If you are not whipping the whites in a copper bowl, then add the cream of tartar at this point. Gradually increase the whipping speed to medium-high, and continue whipping until the whites form very stiff peaks and just begin to slip and streak around the side of the bowl. Add the superfine sugar and continue whipping at high speed for a few seconds longer to incorporate the sugar and tighten the meringue.

3. Gently fold in the raw-almond and sugar powder and flour.

4. Scoop the batter into the pastry bag, and pipe the batter ① on the diagonal in batons 2½ inches (6½ cm) long and ½ to ⅝ inch (12–16 mm) wide, arranging them on the baking sheets in staggered rows and separating them by about 1 inch (2½ cm). Unless you have 2 ovens, pipe only 1 sheet of cookies at a time, and keep the remaining batter in the pastry bag until the first sheet is baked.

5. Dust chopped almonds ② over the piped batter. Turn the baking sheet upside down and tap it with a wooden spatula to dislodge the excess almonds, then quickly turn the baking sheet right side up again.

①

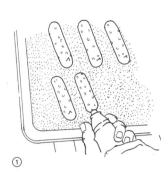

②

6. Bake, 1 sheet at a time, until the cookies are browned on the bottoms, dry on top, and the chopped almonds begin to brown lightly, about 19 to 21 minutes.

7. Place the baking sheet on a wire rack and let the cookies cool. While they are still warm and before the butter sets, slide them off the baking sheet and onto a wire rack with a metal spatula. Then let them finish cooling on the wire rack.

③

8. Temper the chocolate with the almond oil as follows: Melt the chocolate ③ and stir in the almond oil. Dip the bottom of the pot of chocolate in a bowl of cold water and stir the chocolate until it begins to thicken. Immediately remove from the cold water and dip the bottom of the pot of chocolate in a bowl of hot water. Stir over the hot water just long enough to make the chocolate fluid again, then remove from the hot water.

④

9. Spread the back of each cookie with chocolate ④ and smooth it with a small palette knife. Place the batons chocolate side up on your countertop, and let the chocolate set.

STORAGE: Covered airtight in a tin cookie box or a cookie jar for up to 4 or 6 days in a cool place (below 70° F or 20° C).

SNOWBALLS
BOULES DE NEIGE

*T*hese cookies are made from the same batter as Field Marshal's Batons (page 70), but there the similarity ends. For Snowballs, the batter is piped in domes, then baked at a higher temperature than Field Marshal's Batons and for a shorter time so they will be soft inside. The baked domes are sandwiched with raspberry jam, and dusted with confectioners' sugar so they look like snowballs. Both texture and presentation are softer and more tender than the slightly austere (but equally delicious) Batons.

EQUIPMENT

2 large, heavy baking sheets
- Brush with melted butter.
- Dust with flour.

A large pastry bag fitted with
- a ⅜-inch (1 cm) plain pastry tube (Ateco #4)

___

BATTER

⅔ ounce (18 g), or 2 tablespoons, all-purpose flour

5⅓ ounces (150 g), or 1 cup plus 2 tablespoons, raw-almond and sugar powder

Basic Preparation, page 482:

2⅔ ounces (75 g), or ½ cup, raw almonds

2⅔ ounces (75 g), or ½ cup plus 2 tablespoons, confectioners' sugar

3 large egg whites, at room temperature

⅛ teaspoon (½ ml) cream of tartar (optional)

1 ounce (25 g), or 2 tablespoons, superfine sugar

DECORATION

3 ounces (85 g), or ½ cup plus 1 tablespoon, blanched almonds, finely chopped

Confectioners' sugar

FILLING

7 tablespoons (140 g) raspberry jam

For about 40 cookies

Preheat the oven to 350° F (175° C).

1. Sift the flour and toss it with the raw-almond and sugar powder.

2. Whip the egg whites in an electric mixer at low speed until they start to froth. If you are not whipping the whites in a copper bowl, then add the cream of tartar at this point. Gradually increase the whipping speed to medium-high, and continue whipping until the whites form very stiff peaks and just begin to slip and streak around the side of the bowl. Add the superfine sugar and continue whipping at high speed for a few seconds longer to incorporate the sugar and tighten the meringue.

3. Gently fold in the raw-almond and sugar powder and flour.

①

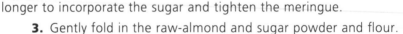

②

4. Scoop the batter into the pastry bag, and pipe the batter ① in domes 1 inch (2½ cm) wide, arranging them on the baking sheets in staggered rows and separating them by about 1 inch (2½ cm). Unless you have 2 ovens, pipe only 1 sheet of cookies at a time, and keep the remaining batter in the pastry bag until the first sheet is baked.

5. Dust chopped almonds ② over the piped batter. Turn the baking sheet upside down and tap it with a wooden spatula to dislodge the excess almonds, then quickly turn the baking sheet right side up again.

6. Bake, 1 sheet at a time, until the cookies are lightly browned on the bottoms, the tops are dry, barely beginning to brown around the edge, and don't collapse when touched gently, about 15 to 18 minutes.

7. Place the baking sheet on a wire rack and let the cookies cool. While they are still warm and before the butter sets, slide them off the baking sheet and onto a wire rack with a metal spatula. Then let them finish cooling on the wire rack.

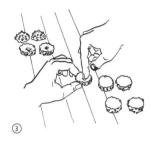

③

8. If the raspberry jam is at all runny, simmer it gently to reduce the excess liquid and then cool before using. Press the center of each dome on the flat side with your fingertip ③ to make a slight depression. Turn half of the domes upside down and spoon about ½ teaspoon (¼ cl) of raspberry jam on the center ④ of each. Then place a second dome right side up on top of each to make a sandwich. Dust the balls with confectioners' sugar, then turn them upside down and dust the other side as well ⑤.

④

STORAGE: Covered airtight in a tin cookie box or a cookie jar for up to 4 or 6 days. Snowballs look best if they are dusted with confectioners' sugar shortly before serving.

⑤

MIRRORS
MIRROIRS

~~~

This pretty cookie calls for two simple batters. The first, an almond meringue similar to that used for Field Marshal's Batons (page 70) and Snowballs (page 72) is piped in oval rings and dusted with chopped almonds. Then the centers are filled with an uncooked almond pastry cream. After baking, the centers are brushed with apricot jam and a rum and confectioners' sugar glaze to make the cookies look like dainty oval mirrors.

EQUIPMENT
2 large, heavy baking sheets
- Brush with melted butter.
- Dust with flour.
A plain oval cookie cutter (see Note),
2⅝ inches (6½ cm) long
and 1¾ inches (4½ cm) wide
A large pastry bag fitted with
- a ⅜-inch (1 cm) plain pastry tube (Ateco #4)
A small or medium pastry bag fitted with
- a ⅜-inch (1 cm) plain pastry tube (Ateco #4)

BATTER
1 ounce (30 g), or 3½ tablespoons,
    all-purpose flour
9½ ounces (270 g), or 2 cups, almond and sugar
    powder

Basic Preparation, page 482:
} 4¾ ounces (135 g), or ¾ cup plus 2½ tablespoons,
    blanched almonds
} 4¾ ounces (135 g), or 1 cup plus 2 tablespoons,
    confectioners' sugar
3 large eggs, separated, at room temperature
1 ounce (30 g), or 2 tablespoons, unsalted butter,
    barely melted
1 tablespoon (1½ cl) dark Jamaican rum
⅛ teaspoon (½ ml) cream of tartar (optional)
1 ounce (25 g), or 2 tablespoons, superfine sugar

DECORATION
3½ ounces (100 g), or ⅔ cup, blanched almonds,
    finely chopped

GLAZE
3 tablespoons (60 g) strained apricot jam
    [*Basic Preparation,* page 484]
1¾ ounces (50 g), or ⅓ cup plus 4 teaspoons,
    confectioners' sugar
2 teaspoons (1 cl) dark Jamaican rum

For about 30 cookies

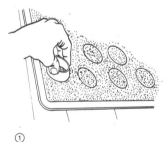

①

1. Mark about 15 ovals in the flour on each baking sheet using the oval cookie cutter ①. Arrange the ovals in staggered rows and separate them by at least 1 inch (2½ cm).

Preheat the oven to 325° F (160° C).

2. Sift 4 teaspoons (12 g) of the flour and toss it with 4¼ ounces (120 g), or ¾ cup plus 2½ tablespoons, of the almond and sugar powder. Combine with the egg yolks, melted butter, and rum in a small bowl and stir to mix. This is the almond pastry cream batter for the centers of the mirrors.

3. Sift the remaining flour and toss it with the remaining almond and sugar powder.

4. Whip the egg whites in an electric mixer at low speed until they start to froth. If you are not whipping the whites in a copper bowl, then add the cream of tartar at this point. Gradually increase the whipping speed to medium-high, and continue whipping until the whites form very stiff peaks and just begin to slip and streak around the side of the bowl. Add the superfine sugar and continue whipping at high speed for a few seconds longer to incorporate the sugar and tighten the meringue.

5. Gently fold in the almond and sugar powder and flour to make the meringue batter for the rims of the mirrors.

6. Scoop the meringue batter into the large pastry bag, and pipe a ring of batter ② just inside each oval marked on the baking sheets, leaving a 1½ by ¾-inch (2 by 4 cm) oval hole in the center. Unless you have 2 ovens, pipe only 1 batch of cookies at a time, keeping the remaining batter in the pastry bag.

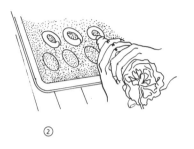

7. Dust chopped almonds ③ over the piped batter. Turn the baking sheet upside down and tap it with a wooden spatula to dislodge the excess almonds, then quickly turn the baking sheet right side up again.

8. Scoop the almond pastry cream into the small pastry bag and pipe it into the center ④ of each ring to form an oval mound about ⅜ inch (1 cm) thick.

9. Bake, 1 sheet at a time, until the cookies are browned on the bottoms, dry on top of the rim, and the chopped almonds begin to brown lightly, about 19 to 21 minutes. The centers should be dry but soft.

10. Meanwhile, warm the apricot jam over low heat, stirring occasionally until melted. When the cookies have finished baking, brush the almond cream center of each with jam ⑤ until the jam fills the pores in the surface and the tops of the cookies glisten.

11. Slide the cookies onto a wire rack using a metal spatula and let cool to room temperature.

12. Sift the confectioners' sugar into a small bowl, and stir in the rum. Then stir in enough cold water to make a smooth, creamy paste that is just fluid enough to spread easily in a thin coat with a pastry brush. Lightly brush this sugar glaze over the jam on the center of each cookie. It should go on translucent. If it looks white and opaque, then thin it a little more by stirring in cold water, a few drops at a time, before proceeding. Let the glaze set.

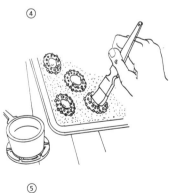

NOTE: You can make the oval cookie cutter from a round cutter 2¼ inches (5¾ cm) in diameter by carefully bending it into shape.

➤ **HOWS & WHYS:** This cookie is not returned to the oven to finish dissolving the sugar in the glaze. As a result, if the glaze is not thinned sufficiently before brushing, it will be opaque white and dull after it sets.

STORAGE: Covered airtight in a tin cookie box or a cookie jar for up to 3 or 4 days.

BLIDAS
BLIDAHS

~~~~~~~~~~~~

Blida is a city in Algeria, southwest of Algiers, that was established in the sixteenth century. The old city was destroyed by an earthquake in 1825, and the current city was completely rebuilt about a mile from the original site. Blida was under French control from 1838 until Algeria became independent in 1962, and as a result the city has a very French character.

These cookies are sometimes called *éponges* (Sponges) because they have a soft, spongelike texture. They are dusted with chopped almonds, and after baking they are sandwiched with apricot jam.

EQUIPMENT
2 large, heavy baking sheets
- Brush with melted butter.
- Dust with flour.

A large pastry bag fitted with
- a ⅜-inch (1 cm) plain pastry tube (Ateco #4)

BATTER
⅔ ounce (18 g), or 2 tablespoons, all-purpose flour
7 ounces (200 g), or 1½ cups, almond and sugar powder

> *Basic Preparation, page 482:*
> *3½ ounces (100 g), or ⅔ cup, blanched almonds*
> *3½ ounces (100 g), or ¾ cup plus 4 teaspoons, confectioners' sugar*

For about 30 cookies

3 large egg whites, at room temperature
⅛ teaspoon (½ ml) cream of tartar (optional)
½ ounce (15 g), or 1 tablespoon plus ½ teaspoon, superfine sugar

DECORATION
3 ounces (85 g), or ½ cup plus 1 tablespoon, blanched almonds, finely chopped
Confectioners' sugar

FILLING
5 tablespoons (100 g) strained apricot jam
[*Basic Preparation*, page 484]

Preheat the oven to 325° F (160° C).

1. Sift the flour and toss it with the almond and sugar powder.

2. Whip the egg whites in an electric mixer at low speed until they start to froth. If you are not whipping the whites in a copper bowl, then add the cream of tartar at this point. Gradually increase the whipping speed to medium-high, and continue whipping until the whites form very stiff peaks and just begin to slip and streak around the side of the bowl. Add the superfine sugar and continue whipping at high speed for a few seconds longer to incorporate the sugar and tighten the meringue.

3. Gently fold in the almond and sugar powder and flour.

4. Scoop the batter into the pastry bag, and pipe the batter ① in domes 1 inch (2½ cm) wide, arranging them on the baking sheets in staggered rows and separating them by about 1 inch (2½ cm). Unless you have 2 ovens, pipe only 1 sheet of cookies at a time, and keep the remaining batter in the pastry bag until the first sheet is baked.

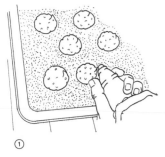

①

②

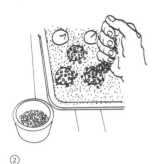

③

④

⑤

5. Dust chopped almonds ② over the piped batter. Turn the baking sheet upside down and tap it with a wooden spatula to dislodge the excess almonds, then quickly turn the baking sheet right side up again. Dust with confectioners' sugar. Let rest for about 1 minute to allow some of the confectioners' sugar to dissolve.

6. Bake, 1 sheet at a time, until the cookies are lightly browned on the bottom and dry and crusty on top, but still soft inside, about 15 to 18 minutes.

7. Place the baking sheet on a wire rack and let the cookies cool. While they are still warm and before the butter sets, carefully transfer them to a wire rack with a metal spatula. Then let them finish cooling on the wire rack.

8. Press the center of each dome on the flat side with your fingertip to make a slight depression ③. Turn half the domes upside down and spoon about ½ teaspoon (¼ cl) of apricot jam on the center ④ of each. Then place a second dome right side up on top of each to make a sandwich. Lightly dust the balls with confectioners' sugar ⑤, then turn them upside down and dust the other side as well.

STORAGE: Covered airtight in a tin cookie box or a cookie jar for up to 4 to 6 days. They look best if they are dusted with confectioners' sugar shortly before serving.

ORANGE BLIDAS
BLIDAHS ORANGES

~~~~~~~

Blida is famous for its orange groves, and in April the scent of orange blossoms perfumes the air for miles around. This variation on ordinary Blidas (page 76) is flavored with orange zest, piped in large ovals, and dusted with confectioners' sugar. The cookies are served as is, not sandwiched with jam. They would be an ideal choice to include in a cookie assortment for a spring garden party.

EQUIPMENT

1 or 2 large, heavy baking sheets
- Brush with melted butter.
- Dust with flour.
A plain oval cookie cutter (see Note),
2⅛ inches (5½ cm) long
and 1⅜ inches (3½ cm) wide
A large pastry bag fitted with
- a ½-inch (12 mm) plain pastry tube (Ateco #6)

BATTER

⅔ ounce (18 g), or about 2 tablespoons, all-purpose flour
7 ounces (200 g), or about 1½ cups, almond and sugar powder
{ *Basic Preparation, page 482:*
3½ ounces (100 g), or ⅔ cup, blanched almonds
3½ ounces (100 g), or ¾ cup plus 4 teaspoons, confectioners' sugar
Finely grated zest of 1 orange
3 large egg whites, at room temperature
⅛ teaspoon (½ ml) cream of tartar (optional)
Red food coloring
½ ounce (15 g), or 1 tablespoon plus ½ teaspoon, superfine sugar

DECORATION

Confectioners' sugar

For about 30 cookies

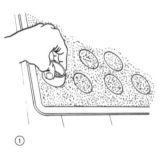
①

②

1. Mark about 30 ovals in the flour ① using the cookie cutter. Arrange the ovals in staggered rows and separate them by at least 1 inch (2½ cm). *Preheat the oven to 325° F (160° C).*

2. Sift the flour and toss it with the almond and sugar powder and the orange zest.

3. Whip the egg whites in an electric mixer at low speed until they start to froth. If you are not whipping the whites in a copper bowl, then add the cream of tartar at this point. Gradually increase the whipping speed to medium-high, and continue whipping until the whites form very stiff peaks and just begin to slip and streak around the side of the bowl. Add 2 drops of red food coloring. Then add the superfine sugar and continue whipping at high speed for a few seconds longer to incorporate the sugar and tighten the meringue.

4. Gently fold in the almond and sugar powder, flour, and orange zest.

5. Scoop the batter into the pastry bag, and pipe the batter in oval domes about ½ inch (12 mm) thick at the center ②, using the marks on

the baking sheet as a guide for size and shape. Unless you have 2 ovens, pipe only 1 sheet of cookies at a time, and keep the remaining batter in the pastry bag until the first sheet is baked.

6. Dust the ovals heavily with confectioners' sugar ③. Let rest for about 1 minute to allow some of the confectioners' sugar to dissolve.

7. Bake, 1 sheet at a time, until the cookies are very lightly browned on the bottoms and dry and crusty on top, but the insides are still soft and the tops are still pink with at most a hint of beige, about 20 to 23 minutes.

8. Place the baking sheet on a wire rack and let the cookies cool. While they are still warm, and before the butter sets, carefully transfer them to a wire rack with a metal spatula. Then let them finish cooling on the wire rack.

NOTE: You can make the oval cookie cutter from a round cutter 1¾ inches (4½ cm) in diameter by carefully bending it into shape.

VARIATION: If you prefer, you can dust Orange Blidas with sliced almonds instead of confectioners' sugar.

STORAGE: Covered airtight in a tin cookie box or a cookie jar for up to 2 or 3 days.

MERINGUE BATTERS

79

DUCHESSES
DUCHESSES

The almond meringue used to make Duchesses is very different from those in Field Marshal's Batons (page 70), Snowballs (page 72), and Blidas (page 76). Because it contains a little milk and melted butter, it is slightly richer and spreads more than the others so that these cookies come out thin and crisp. Like Snowballs, the batter is piped in small domes, but here the domes spread to become flat disks that are sandwiched with praliné butter after baking.

EQUIPMENT

2 or 3 large, heavy baking sheets
- Brush heavily with melted butter.
- Dust with flour.

A large pastry bag fitted with
- a ⅜-inch (1 cm) plain pastry tube (Ateco #4),
or a "midget" ice cream scoop

A small pastry bag fitted with
- a ⅜-inch (1 cm) plain pastry tube (Ateco #4),
or a small palette knife

BATTER

1½ ounces (40 g), or ¼ cup plus 1¾ teaspoons, all-purpose flour

5⅓ ounces (150 g), or 1 cup plus 2 tablespoons, raw-almond and sugar powder

} *Basic Preparation, page 482:*
2⅔ ounces (75 g), or ½ cup, raw almonds
2⅔ ounces (75 g), or ½ cup plus 2 tablespoons, confectioners' sugar

For about 50 cookies

3 large egg whites, at room temperature

⅛ teaspoon (½ ml) cream of tartar (optional)

½ ounce (15 g), or 1 tablespoon plus ½ teaspoon, superfine sugar

¼ cup (6 cl) milk

1¾ ounces (50 g), or 3½ tablespoons, unsalted butter, melted

FILLING

1¾ ounces (50 g), or 3½ tablespoons, unsalted butter, softened

1¾ ounces (50 g), or 3 tablespoons, praliné [*Basic Preparation*, page 485]

Preheat the oven to 325° F (160° C).

1. Sift the flour and toss it with the raw-almond and sugar powder.

2. Whip the egg whites in an electric mixer at low speed until they start to froth. If you are not whipping the whites in a copper bowl, then add the cream of tartar at this point. Gradually increase the whipping speed to medium-high, and continue whipping until the whites form very stiff peaks and just begin to slip and streak around the side of the bowl. Add the superfine sugar and continue whipping at high speed for a few seconds longer to incorporate the sugar and tighten the meringue.

3. Stir together the raw-almond and sugar powder and flour with the milk and melted butter. Quickly mix in about one-third of the meringue. Then gently fold in the remaining meringue.

4. Scoop the batter into the large pastry bag, and pipe the batter  in domes 1 inch (2½ cm) wide, arranging them on the baking sheets in

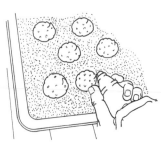

①

staggered rows and separating them by at least 1⅜ inches (3½ cm). Or, spoon the batter in 1-teaspoon (½ cl) domes using the ice cream scoop. Unless you have 2 ovens, pipe only 1 sheet of cookies at a time, and keep the remaining batter in the pastry bag until the first sheet is baked.

5. Tap the baking sheet on the counter to spread the batter a little.

6. Bake, 1 sheet at a time, until the cookies are dry and firm to the touch and lightly browned around the rim, but still pale in the center, about 18 to 23 minutes.

7. Tap the baking sheet firmly on the countertop to loosen the cookies. Then carefully transfer them to a wire rack with a metal spatula and let them cool to room temperature.

②

8. Place the butter in a small stainless-steel bowl and beat with a wooden spatula, warming it over low heat as needed to make it smooth, white, and creamy. Gradually beat the butter into the praliné. When all of the butter has been added, beat the praliné butter vigorously with a wire whisk to make it light and smooth. As you beat air into the praliné butter, the color of the filling will also lighten noticeably. (However, if the filling is too warm it will not become light in texture or in color and will remain runny. Chill it briefly, and then whisk again.) Scoop the praliné butter into the small pastry bag, and pipe about ½ teaspoon (¼ cl) of praliné butter on the center ② of each upside down cookie. (Or, spread the praliné butter using a small palette knife.) Then place a second cookie right side up on top of each and press gently to make a sandwich ③. Chill the cookies to firm the praliné butter.

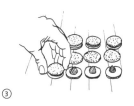

③

STORAGE: Covered airtight in a tin cookie box or a cookie jar for up to 12 hours at a cool temperature (below 60° F or 15° C); or in the refrigerator for a few days. Before filling, the cookies can be kept covered airtight for up to 1 week at room temperature, provided they are not exposed to high humidity.

BIARRITZ
BIARRITZ

~~~~~~

These cookies are made from the same batter as Duchesses (page 80), and like Duchesses, they are piped in domes that spread and flatten during baking to become thin, crisp disks. However, for Biarritz the domes are piped larger, and after baking the disks have a layer of bittersweet chocolate spread on the back rather than being sandwiched with praliné butter.

Biarritz are named for the resort city on the Bay of Biscay. At the beginning of the nineteenth century, it was just a small fishing village with only a few hundred inhabitants. But its mild climate and beautiful beaches began to attract aristocratic vacationers year-round—the English in winter and the French, Russians, and Spaniards in summer. Biarritz became a favorite resort of the emperor Napoléon III and the empress Eugénie, who had a villa overlooking La Grande Plage (the beach that extends for a half mile on the northeast of the city). Under their patronage it became an important watering hole, with casinos, baths, and elegant hotels to keep the beau monde entertained. Perhaps we shouldn't be surprised that the cookies Duchesses and Biarritz are so closely associated.

EQUIPMENT
2 or 3 large, heavy baking sheets
- Brush heavily with melted butter.
- Dust with flour.
A large pastry bag fitted with
- a ³⁄₈-inch (1 cm) plain pastry tube (Ateco #4),
or #100 ice cream scoop

BATTER
1½ ounces (40 g), or ¼ cup plus 1¾ teaspoons,
    all-purpose flour
5⅓ ounces (150 g), or 1 cup plus 2 tablespoons,
    raw-almond and sugar powder
{ *Basic Preparation, page 482:*
2⅔ ounces (75 g), or ½ cup, raw almonds
2⅔ ounces (75 g), or ½ cup plus 2 tablespoons,
    confectioners' sugar

3 large egg whites, at room temperature
⅛ teaspoon (½ ml) cream of tartar (optional)
½ ounce (15 g), or 1 tablespoon plus ½ teaspoon,
    superfine sugar
¼ cup (6 cl) milk
1¾ ounces (50 g), or 3½ tablespoons, unsalted
    butter, melted

GLAZE
7 ounces (200 g) European bittersweet chocolate,
    (such as Lindt Surfin)
1 teaspoon (½ cl) almond oil (preferably) or neutral
    vegetable oil

For about 60 cookies

Preheat the oven to 325° F (160° C).

1. Sift the flour and toss it with the raw-almond and sugar powder.

2. Whip the egg whites in an electric mixer at low speed until they start to froth. If you are not whipping the whites in a copper bowl, then add the cream of tartar at this point. Gradually increase the whipping speed to medium-high, and continue whipping until the whites form very stiff peaks and just begin to slip and streak around the side of the bowl. Add the superfine sugar and continue whipping at high speed for a few seconds longer to incorporate the sugar and tighten the meringue.

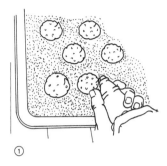
①

②

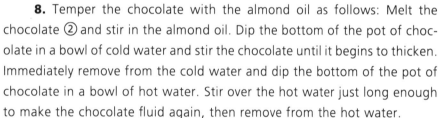
③

④

3. Stir together the raw-almond and sugar powder and flour with the milk and melted butter. Quickly mix in about one-third of the meringue. Then gently fold in the remaining meringue.

4. Scoop the batter into the large pastry bag, and pipe the batter ① in domes 1¼ inches (3 cm) wide, arranging them in staggered rows and separating them by at least 1⅜ inches (3½ cm). Or, spoon the batter in 1¾-teaspoon (9 ml) domes using the ice cream scoop. Unless you have 2 ovens, pipe only 1 sheet of cookies at a time, and keep the remaining batter in the pastry bag until the first sheet is baked.

5. Tap the baking sheet on the counter to spread the batter a little.

6. Bake, 1 sheet at a time, until the cookies are dry and firm to the touch and lightly browned around the rim, but still pale in the center, about 18 to 23 minutes.

7. Tap the baking sheet firmly on the countertop to loosen the cookies. Then carefully transfer them to a wire rack with a metal spatula and let them cool to room temperature.

8. Temper the chocolate with the almond oil as follows: Melt the chocolate ② and stir in the almond oil. Dip the bottom of the pot of chocolate in a bowl of cold water and stir the chocolate until it begins to thicken. Immediately remove from the cold water and dip the bottom of the pot of chocolate in a bowl of hot water. Stir over the hot water just long enough to make the chocolate fluid again, then remove from the hot water.

9. Spread the back of each cookie with a thin layer of chocolate ③ and smooth it with a small palette knife. Place the cookies chocolate side up on your countertop, and let the chocolate set.

VARIATION: For a fancier presentation, increase the amount of glaze to 12 ounces (350 g) bittersweet chocolate plus 1¾ teaspoons (9 ml) almond oil. Spread a thin layer of chocolate glaze on the back of each cookie and let the chocolate set, as in step 9 above. Keep the pot of chocolate warm so that it doesn't set. Spread the back of each cookie with chocolate a second time using the palette knife, and make a sweeping curve or a wavy pattern ④ across it with a scalloped bread knife or a cake decorating comb; then place the cookie on the counter chocolate side up until the chocolate sets.

STORAGE: Covered airtight in a tin cookie box or a cookie jar for up to 1 week in a cool place (below 70° F or 20° C) or in the refrigerator for a few days. Before filling, the cookies can be kept covered airtight for up to 1 week at room temperature, provided they are not exposed to high humidity.

MERINGUE BATTERS

CARACAS WAFERS
PALETS CARAQUES

〰〰〰

Light, crisp oval domes of almond and hazelnut meringue sandwiched with bittersweet chocolate and praliné provide a beguiling combination of flavor harmonies and textural contrasts. Some of the finest cocoa in the world is grown in Venezuela, and the cocoa from around Caracas is noted for its exceptionally fine aroma.

EQUIPMENT

2 large, heavy baking sheets
- Brush edges and diagonals with melted butter.
- Line with kitchen parchment.

A large pastry bag fitted with
- a ⅜-inch (1 cm) plain pastry tube (Ateco #4)

BATTER

⅓ ounce (9 g), or about 1 tablespoon, all-purpose flour

4½ ounces (130 g), or ¾ cup plus 3½ tablespoons, hazelnut, raw-almond, and sugar powder

Basic Preparation, page 482:

1¼ ounces (35 g), or ¼ cup, hazelnuts

1 ounce (30 g), or 3½ tablespoons, raw almonds

2¼ ounces (65 g), or ½ cup plus 2 teaspoons, confectioners' sugar

3 large egg whites, at room temperature

⅛ teaspoon (½ ml) cream of tartar (optional)

½ ounce (15 g), or 1 tablespoon plus ½ teaspoon, superfine sugar

1 teaspoon (½ cl) vanilla extract

FILLING

1¾ ounces (50 g) European bittersweet chocolate (such as Lindt Excellence), melted

1¾ ounces (50 g) praliné

[*Basic Preparation,* page 485]

For about 30 cookies

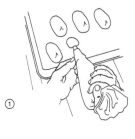

①

Preheat the oven to 300° F (150° C).

1. Sift the flour and toss it with the nut and sugar powder.

2. Whip the egg whites in an electric mixer at low speed until they start to froth. If you are not whipping the whites in a copper bowl, then add the cream of tartar at this point. Gradually increase the whipping speed to medium-high, and continue whipping until the whites form very stiff peaks and just begin to slip and streak around the side of the bowl. Add the superfine sugar and continue whipping at high speed for a few seconds longer to incorporate the sugar and tighten the meringue.

3. Gently fold in the nut and sugar powder and flour. When almost completely incorporated, add the vanilla and continue folding until mixed.

4. Scoop the batter into the pastry bag, and pipe ① in oval domes 1½ inches (4 cm) long and 1 inch (2½ cm) wide, arranging them on the baking sheets in staggered rows and separating them by about ¾ inch (2 cm).

5. Place 1 baking sheet on a lower oven rack and 1 on an upper oven rack, and bake for 20 minutes. Reverse the positions of the 2 baking sheets, and continue baking until the cookies are lightly browned on top and bottom and dry to the touch, about 20 to 25 minutes longer.

6. Place each baking sheet on a wire rack and let the cookies cool to room temperature.

7. Stir the chocolate into the praliné with a wooden spatula. Place the bowl of chocolate and praliné over a bowl of cold water and stir until the mixture thickens lightly, then remove it immediately. The mixture sets quickly and if it does set while you are working with it, then simply melt it again and return it to a good spreading consistency.

②

8. Turn half the ovals upside down and spread about ½ teaspoon (¼ cl) of filling on the back ② of each using a small palette knife. Then place a second oval right side up on top of each and press gently to sandwich them together.

STORAGE: Covered airtight in a tin cookie box or a cookie jar for up to 1 week in a cool place (below 70° F or 20° C).

ALMOND SOUFFLÉS
SOUFFLÉS AUX AMANDES

*T*hese are light, moist almond meringue cookies baked in pleated bonbon cups. The bonbon cups contain the batter so that the cookies puff up like little soufflés when baked. Bonbon cups are available in a variety of fancifully printed papers that children—particularly little girls—adore.

EQUIPMENT
2 large, heavy baking sheets
About 55 pleated bonbon cups, ⅝-inch (16 mm) deep and about 1 inch (2½ cm) wide across the bottom
A large pastry bag fitted with
• a ⅜-inch (1 cm) plain pastry tube (Ateco #4)

⅛ teaspoon (½ ml) cream of tartar (optional)
⅔ ounce (18 g), or 1½ tablespoons, superfine sugar
1½ teaspoons (¾ cl) vanilla extract
DECORATION
Confectioners' sugar
Sliced almonds

BATTER
1¾ ounces (50 g), or 2½ tablespoons, peach jam
4 large egg whites, at room temperature
6 ounces (170 g), or 1¼ cups, almond and sugar powder

   Basic Preparation, page 482:
   3 ounces (85 g), or ½ cup plus 1 tablespoon, blanched almonds
   3 ounces (85 g), or ⅔ cup plus 2 teaspoons, confectioners' sugar

For about 55 cookies

①

②

Preheat the oven to 275° F (135° C).

1. Warm the peach jam over low heat to melt it. Force the jam through a fine sieve ① with a wooden pestle to puree the pieces of fruit. Work as much of the fruit through the sieve as you can. Discard any dry, fibrous bits that won't go through the sieve. Return the jam to the heat, stir with a wooden spatula to make it homogeneous, and cook it over low heat to evaporate the excess liquid and reduce it to about 1 tablespoon plus 2 teaspoons (2½ cl). Then remove from the heat and let cool to luke-warm.

2. Stir 2 of the egg whites into the peach jam, and mix with the almond and sugar powder in a 2-quart (2 L) stainless-steel bowl. Set the bowl over a saucepan of barely simmering water, and beat the mixture with a wire whisk ② until it warms to about 130° F (55° C). Then remove from the heat, but keep it warm.

3. Whip the remaining 2 egg whites in an electric mixer at low speed until they start to froth. If you are not whipping the whites in a copper bowl, then add the cream of tartar at this point. Gradually increase the whipping speed to medium-high, and continue whipping until the whites form very stiff peaks and just begin to slip and streak around the side of the bowl. Add the superfine sugar and continue whipping at high speed for a few seconds longer to incorporate the sugar and tighten the meringue.

4. Stir the vanilla into the warm jam mixture, then stir in about one-third of the meringue. Gently fold in the remaining meringue.

5. Arrange the bonbon cups adjacent to each other on your counter-top. Scoop the batter into the pastry bag, and pipe the batter into the bonbon cups ③, filling them to three-quarters of their height. Lightly dust with confectioners' sugar ④, and lest rest for about 2 minutes to allow some of the sugar to dissolve.

③

6. Scatter a few almond slices on the top of each soufflé. Carefully transfer the soufflés to a baking sheet, arranging them in staggered rows and separating them by at least ⅜ inch (1 cm). Place an empty baking sheet underneath the sheet of soufflés to protect the bottoms.

7. Bake, using a wooden spatula to hold the oven door ajar, until the soufflés are lightly browned on the bottoms, pale beige and crusty on top, and spring back when pressed gently with your fingertip, about 50 to 55 minutes.

④

8. Slide the soufflés onto a wire rack and let them cool to room temperature.

➤ **HOWS & WHYS:** The peach jam in this recipe helps keep the soufflés moist inside. Traditionally, French pastry chefs use an apple jam (made by mixing applesauce with sugar and reducing it to a jam consistency) in this recipe. However, the quantity of jam required is very small and we find that peach jam, which is readily available in the United States, produces the same results.

STORAGE: Covered airtight in a tin cookie box or a cookie jar for up to 2 or 3 days.

PINEAPPLE SOUFFLÉS
BEIGNETS ANANAS

~~~~~~~~~~

The most familiar culinary preparations called beignets *include a diverse assortment of light, deep-fried fritters and doughnuts. However, this odd French name, which derives from the Celtic word for ''swelling,'' is also used for several petits fours that are closely related to Almond Soufflés (page 86). The distinctive flavor of our moist, fragrant Pineapple Soufflés comes from a triple dose of pineapple—diced pineapple and pineapple jam in the meringue, and a garnish of glacé pineapple.*

EQUIPMENT
2 large, heavy baking sheets
About 40 pleated bonbon cups, ⅝-inch (16 mm) deep and about 1 inch (2½ cm) wide across the bottom
A large pastry bag fitted with
• a ⅜-inch (1 cm) plain pastry tube (Ateco #4)

BATTER
5⅓ ounces (150 g), or 1 cup plus 2 tablespoons, almond and sugar powder
Basic Preparation, page 482:
  2⅔ ounces (75 g), or ½ cup, blanched almonds
  2⅔ ounces (75 g), or ½ cup plus 2 tablespoons, confectioners' sugar

8½-ounce (234 g) can pineapple chunks in heavy syrup
1 tablespoon (20 g) pineapple jam
1 tablespoon lightly beaten egg white
1 tablespoon (1½ cl) kirsch
Yellow food coloring
⅓ ounce (9 g), or 1 tablespoon, all-purpose flour
2 large egg whites, at room temperature
⅛ teaspoon (½ ml) cream of tartar (optional)
⅔ ounce (18 g), or 1½ tablespoons, superfine sugar

DECORATION
Confectioners' sugar
Glacé pineapple, cut into about 40 ¼-inch (6 mm) dice

For about 40 cookies

Preheat the oven to 275° F (135° C).

1. Drain the pineapple chunks thoroughly, then press the pineapple between paper towels to extract as much of the liquid as possible. This will require a few changes of paper towels, and in the end you should have only about 1¾ ounces (50 g) of pressed pineapple flesh.

2. Warm the pineapple jam over low heat to melt it. Force the jam through a fine sieve with a wooden pestle to puree the pieces of fruit ①. Work as much of the fruit through the sieve as you can. Combine any dry, fibrous bits that won't go through the sieve with the pressed pineapple flesh. Stir the jam with a wooden spatula to make it homogeneous.

3. Finely chop the pineapple flesh. In a 1-quart (1 L) bowl, mix the pineapple flesh with the pineapple jam, lightly beaten egg white, kirsch, and 2 drops of yellow food coloring.

4. Sift the flour and toss it with the almond and sugar powder. Stir it into the pineapple mixture.

①

5. Whip the remaining 2 egg whites in an electric mixer at low speed until they start to froth. If you are not whipping the whites in a copper bowl, then add the cream of tartar at this point. Gradually increase the whipping speed to medium-high, and continue whipping until the whites form very stiff peaks and just begin to slip and streak around the side of the bowl. Add the superfine sugar and continue whipping at high speed for a few seconds longer to incorporate the sugar and tighten the meringue.

6. Stir about one-third of the meringue into the almond and pineapple mixture. Then gently fold in the remaining meringue.

②

7. Arrange the bonbon cups adjacent to each other on your countertop. Scoop the batter into the pastry bag, and pipe the batter into the bonbon cups ②, filling them to three-quarters of their height. Lightly dust with confectioners' sugar, and lest rest for about 1 minute to allow the sugar to dissolve.

8. Place a piece of glacé pineapple on the center ③ of each soufflé. Carefully transfer them to a baking sheet, arranging them in staggered rows and separating them by at least ⅜ inch (1 cm). Place an empty baking sheet underneath the sheet of soufflés to protect the bottoms.

③

9. Bake, using a wooden spatula to hold the oven door ajar, until the bottoms of the soufflés are very lightly browned and the tops are dry, spring back when pressed gently with your fingertip, and are still pale yellow, with at most a hint of beige, about 50 to 55 minutes.

10. Slide the soufflés onto a wire rack and let them cool to room temperature.

STORAGE: Covered airtight in a tin cookie box or a cookie jar for up to 2 or 3 days.

HAZELNUT SOUFFLÉS
SOUFFLÉS AUX AVELINES

~~~~~~

The nuts of the city Avella, in the Campania region of southern Italy, were highly esteemed by the ancient Romans, and Pliny referred to hazelnuts as avellana. The French originally used the word avelines for the very large, elongated, early-ripening St. John filberts cultivated in the surrounding province of Avellino. Gradually the meaning of the word was generalized to include all filberts, but today both filberts and hazelnuts are more commonly referred to as noisettes.

Like the other soufflé cookies, Hazelnut Soufflés are baked in pleated bonbon cups. Compared with Almond Soufflés (page 86), their texture is a bit drier, with a nicely crusty exterior to contrast with their soft, chewy centers. The taste of hazelnuts, accented with vanilla, is overwhelming and addictive, and they are heavenly paired with vanilla ice cream.

EQUIPMENT
2 large, heavy baking sheets
About 50 pleated bonbon cups, ⅝ inch (16 mm) deep and about 1 inch (2½ cm) wide across the bottom
A large pastry bag fitted with
• a ⅜-inch (1 cm) plain pastry tube (Ateco #4)

BATTER
1¼ ounces (35 g), or ¼ cup plus 2 teaspoons, confectioners' sugar
⅔ ounce (18 g), or about 2 tablespoons, all-purpose flour

8 ounces (225 g), or 1½ cups plus 3 tablespoons, hazelnut and sugar powder
Basic Preparation, page 482:
4 ounces (115 g), or ¾ cup plus 1 tablespoon, hazelnuts
4 ounces (115 g), or ¾ cup plus 3 tablespoons, confectioners' sugar
3 large egg whites, at room temperature
⅛ teaspoon (½ ml) cream of tartar (optional)
½ ounce (15 g), or 1 tablespoon plus ½ teaspoon, superfine sugar
¾ teaspoon (4 ml) vanilla extract

DECORATION
Confectioners' sugar

For about 50 cookies

Preheat the oven to 300° F (150° C).

1. Sift the confectioners' sugar with the flour and toss with the hazelnut and sugar powder.

2. Whip the egg whites in an electric mixer at low speed until they start to froth. If you are not whipping the whites in a copper bowl, then add the cream of tartar at this point. Gradually increase the whipping speed to medium-high, and continue whipping until the whites form very stiff peaks and just begin to slip and streak around the side of the bowl. Add the superfine sugar and continue whipping at high speed for a few seconds longer to incorporate the sugar and tighten the meringue.

3. Gently fold the hazelnut and sugar mixture into the whipped whites. When almost completely incorporated, add the vanilla and continue folding until mixed.

4. Arrange the bonbon cups adjacent to each other on your counter-top. Scoop the batter into the pastry bag, and pipe the batter into the

bonbon cups ①, filling them to three-quarters of their height. Lightly dust with confectioners' sugar, and lest rest for about 2 minutes to allow some of the sugar to dissolve.

5. Carefully transfer the soufflés to a baking sheet, arranging them in staggered rows and separating them by at least ⅜ inch (1 cm). Place an empty baking sheet underneath the sheet of soufflés to protect the bottoms.

6. Bake until the bottoms of the soufflés are lightly browned and the tops are shiny, cracked, and dry and firm to the touch, but the soufflés are still soft inside, about 35 to 40 minutes.

7. Slide the soufflés onto a wire rack and let them cool to room temperature.

STORAGE: Covered airtight in a tin cookie box or a cookie jar for up to 2 or 3 days.

TENDER MACAROONS
MACARONS MOELLEUX

〰〰〰〰

This type of macaroon is very popular in France today. They have a soft, moist interior and a smooth, shiny surface. Though made by a different method, they are closely related to Gerbet Macaroons (page 96). The adjective moelleux is frequently used in connection with wine, where it refers to the round, mellow quality that is particularly evident in great red burgundies. In our context it characterizes the soft, tender texture of these cookies. The same macaroons made with a slightly lower proportion of almonds are called Princess Macaroons (macarons princesse), and if you find macarons moelleux too daunting to pronounce, you can equally well use this alternative name.

EQUIPMENT

4 large, heavy baking sheets
• Newsprint cut to fit 3 of them
A large pastry bag fitted with
• a ⅜-inch (1 cm) plain pastry tube (Ateco #4)

10¼ ounces (290 g), or 2⅓ cups plus 4 teaspoons, confectioners' sugar
4 large egg whites, at room temperature
⅛ teaspoon (½ ml) cream of tartar (optional)
1 teaspoon (½ cl) vanilla extract

BATTER

6 ounces (170 g), or 1 cup plus 2 tablespoons, blanched almonds
1½ ounces (40 g), or 3 tablespoons, light brown sugar

For about 70 cookies

Preheat the oven to 450° F (230° C).

1. Grind the almonds with the brown sugar and 1½ ounces (45 g), or ¼ cup plus 2 tablespoons, of the confectioners' sugar in your food processor, stopping to break up any caking as needed, until finely ground but not at all oily. Sift through a medium sieve. Grind the almonds that don't pass through the sieve with another 3 ounces (85 g), or ⅔ cup plus 2 teaspoons, of the confectioners' sugar until reduced to a fine powder. Transfer all of the almond and sugar powder to a bowl, break up any caking with your fingertips, and mix thoroughly.

2. Sift 3½ ounces (100 g), or ¾ cup plus 4 teaspoons, of the remaining confectioners' sugar and toss it with the almond and sugar powder.

3. Sift the rest of the confectioners' sugar onto a sheet of wax paper.

4. Whip 2 egg whites in an electric mixer at low speed until they start to froth. If you are not whipping the whites in a copper bowl, then add the cream of tartar at this point. Gradually increase the whipping speed to medium-high, and continue whipping until the whites form very stiff peaks and just begin to slip and streak around the side of the bowl. Add the confectioners' sugar and continue whipping at high speed for a few seconds longer to make the meringue smooth and shiny.

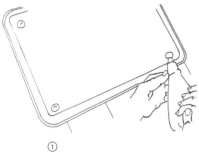

①

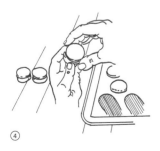

②

③

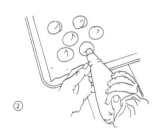

④

5. Add the remaining 2 egg whites and the vanilla to the almond and sugar mixture and mix with a wooden spatula, stirring only the minimum necessary. Stir in about one-third of the meringue. Then gently fold in the remaining meringue.

6. Scoop the batter into the pastry bag. Pipe a small dab of batter in each corner ① of 3 baking sheets, and line them with newsprint, pressing the corners of the newsprint on the dabs of batter to hold it in place. Pipe the batter ② in domes 1 inch (2½ cm) wide, arranging them on the news-print in staggered rows and separating them by about 1 inch (2½ cm). Unless you have 2 ovens, pipe only 1 sheet of cookies at a time, and keep the remaining batter in the pastry bag until the first sheet is baked.

7. Bake 1 sheet at a time. After 2 minutes at 450° F (230° C), reduce the temperature to 400° F (200° C), place an empty baking sheet underneath the sheet of cookies, and continue baking, using a wooden spatula to hold the oven door ajar, until the tops of the cookies are lightly browned and crusty while the insides are still soft and the bottoms still pale, about 5 to 8 minutes longer.

8. Lift the baking sheet of cookies off the empty baking sheet and take it to the sink. Pour cold water (about ½ cup, or 1 dl, per baking sheet) between the paper and the baking sheet ③ (tilting the baking sheet so that the water runs over the entire surface and drains thoroughly into the sink) to steam the cookies off the paper. Then place the baking sheet on a wire rack and cool.

9. Carefully slide (don't lift) the cookies off the paper before the paper dries, and sandwich them ④ back to back in pairs.

STORAGE: Covered airtight in a tin cookie box or a cookie jar for up to 3 days.

HONEY MACAROONS
MACARONS AU MIEL

~~~~~~~~

This is a variation on Tender Macaroons (page 92) made with a smaller proportion of almonds and flavored with honey. Here again the tops should be smooth and shiny, the insides moist and tender.

Before the seventeenth century, when refined cane sugar first became widely available in Europe, all macaroons would have been made with honey as the sweetener. Today it is used only rarely, and in small doses because its flavor can be overpowering. In this very modern macaroon, just 1 ounce (25 g) of honey in the batter is enough to permeate the cookies with its distinctive flavor.

EQUIPMENT

3 or 4 large, heavy baking sheets
• Newsprint cut to fit all but one of them
A large pastry bag fitted with
• a ⅜-inch (1 cm) plain pastry tube (Ateco #4)

1 ounce (25 g), or 1 tablespoon plus 1 teaspoon, honey
4 large egg whites, at room temperature
⅛ teaspoon (½ ml) cream of tartar (optional)

BATTER

4½ ounces (130 g), or 1 cup plus 4 teaspoons, confectioners' sugar
10 ounces (280 g), or 2 cups plus 1½ tablespoons, almond and sugar powder
Basic Preparation, page 482:
5 ounces (140 g), or ¾ cup plus 3 tablespoons, blanched almonds
5 ounces (140 g), or 1 cup plus 2½ tablespoons, confectioners' sugar

For about 60 cookies

Preheat the oven to 325° F (165° C).

1. Sift 2½ ounces (70 g), or ½ cup plus 4 teaspoons, of the confectioners' sugar and toss it with the almond and sugar powder. Stir the honey and 2 of the egg whites into the almond and sugar mixture using a wooden spatula. Let rest for 10 minutes while you prepare the meringue.

2. Sift the rest of the confectioners' sugar onto a sheet of wax paper.

3. Whip the remaining 2 egg whites in an electric mixer at low speed until they start to froth. If you are not whipping the whites in a copper bowl, then add the cream of tartar at this point. Gradually increase the whipping speed to medium-high, and continue whipping until the whites form very stiff peaks and just begin to slip and streak around the side of the bowl. Whip a few seconds longer until the slipping and streaking is very clear. Add the confectioners' sugar and continue whipping at high speed for a few seconds longer to make the meringue smooth and shiny.

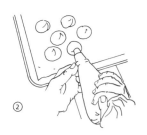

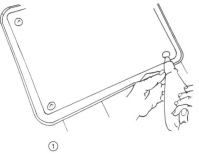

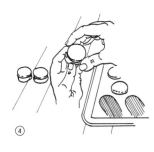

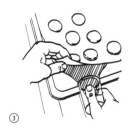

4. Stir about one-third of the meringue into the almond mixture. Then gently fold in the remaining meringue.

5. Scoop the batter into the pastry bag. Pipe a small dab of batter in each corner ① of all but one baking sheet, and line them with newsprint, pressing the corners of the newsprint on the dabs of batter to hold it in place. Pipe the batter ② in domes 1 inch (2½ cm) wide, arranging them on the newsprint in staggered rows and separating them by about 1 inch (2½ cm). Unless you have 2 ovens, pipe only 1 sheet of cookies at a time, and keep the remaining batter in the pastry bag until the first sheet is baked.

6. One at a time, place each sheet of cookies on an empty baking sheet and bake, using a wooden spatula to hold the oven door ajar, until the tops of the cookies are pale golden brown and crusty while the insides are still soft and the bottoms still pale, about 17 to 20 minutes.

7. Lift the baking sheet of cookies off the empty baking sheet and take it to the sink. Pour cold water (about ½ cup, or 1 dl, per baking sheet) between the paper and the baking sheet ③ (tilting the baking sheet so that the water runs over the entire surface and drains thoroughly into the sink) to steam the cookies off the paper. Then place the baking sheet on a wire rack and cool.

8. Carefully slide (don't lift) the cookies off the paper before the paper dries, and sandwich them ④ back to back in pairs.

➤ **HOWS & WHYS:** The egg whites for this cookie should be slightly overwhipped. If they are at all underwhipped, the cookies spread too much and deflate and the tops crack.

In addition to contributing its distinctive flavor, the honey in these cookies helps keep them soft and moist longer.

STORAGE: Covered airtight in a tin cookie box or a cookie jar for up to 3 days.

GERBET MACAROONS
MACARONS GERBET

‿‿‿‿‿

Gerbet was a nineteenth-century pastry chef who worked in Chartres. The cookies named for him are not well known outside of France, but in the world of Parisian pastry they are the king of modern macaroons. They are very smooth and glossy, with a soft, tender interior. In their most sumptuous form they are filled with a very simple buttercream, but they can also be left unfilled. We offer three flavor alternatives here—vanilla, coffee, and lemon. Chocolate and Raspberry Gerbet Macaroons are in the following recipes. Whatever the flavor, my appetite for these supremely elegant morsels is insatiable.

EQUIPMENT

3 large, heavy baking sheets
• Newsprint cut to fit 2 of them
A large pastry bag fitted with
• a ⅜-inch (1 cm) plain pastry tube (Ateco #4)
A small pastry bag fitted with
• a ⅜-inch (1 cm) plain pastry tube (Ateco #4),
or a small palette knife

BATTER AND FILLING

5½ ounces (150 g), or 1 cup, blanched almonds
1¼ ounces (35 g), or 2 tablespoons plus 2 teaspoons, light brown sugar
7½ ounces (215 g), or 1¾ cups plus 2 teaspoons, confectioners' sugar

3 large egg whites, at room temperature
⅛ teaspoon (½ ml) cream of tartar (optional)
1¾ ounces (50 g), or 3½ tablespoons, unsalted butter, softened
Flavorings
  1 teaspoon (½ cl) vanilla extract
                   or
  1 tablespoon (1½ cl) freeze-dried coffee, dissolved in 2 teaspoons (1 cl) boiling water
                   or
  Finely grated zest of 1 large lemon
  1 teaspoon fresh lemon juice
  Yellow food coloring

For about 40 to 45 cookies

Preheat the oven to 450° F (230° C).

1. Grind the almonds with the brown sugar and 1½ ounces (40 g), or ⅓ cup, of the confectioners' sugar in your food processor, stopping to break up any caking as needed, until finely ground but not at all oily. Sift through a medium sieve. Grind the almonds that don't pass through the sieve with another 2⅔ ounces (75 g), or ½ cup plus 2 tablespoons, of the confectioners' sugar until reduced to a fine powder. Transfer all of the almond and sugar powder to a bowl, break up any caking with your fingertips, and mix thoroughly.

2. Sift 2½ ounces (70 g), or ½ cup plus 4 teaspoons, of the remaining confectioners' sugar and toss it with 9 ounces (250 g), or 1¾ cups plus 2 tablespoons, of the almond and sugar powder; for lemon macaroons, add half the lemon zest at the same time. Reserve the remaining almond and sugar powder for the filling.

3. Sift the rest of the confectioners' sugar onto a sheet of wax paper.

4. Whip the egg whites in an electric mixer at low speed until they start to froth. If you are not whipping the whites in a copper bowl, then add the cream of tartar at this point. Gradually increase the whipping speed to medium-high, and continue whipping until the whites form very stiff peaks and just begin to slip and streak around the side of the bowl. For lemon macaroons, add 4 drops of yellow food coloring. Add the confectioners' sugar and continue whipping at high speed for a few seconds longer to incorporate the sugar and tighten the meringue.

5. Gently fold the almond mixture into the meringue. When almost completely incorporated, add ¾ teaspoon (4 ml) of the vanilla for vanilla macaroons or 2 teaspoons (1 cl) of the coffee for coffee macaroons and continue folding until mixed. The batter must be smooth and shiny, and it should spread easily without being at all runny. If it is dull and firm, fold it a little longer to deflate it slightly and get the required consistency. But do not deflate it too much or the batter will spread too much and the tops of the cookies will crack when baked.

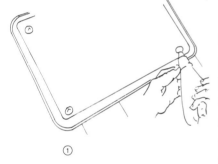

①

6. Scoop the batter into the large pastry bag. Pipe a small dab of batter in each corner of 2 baking sheets ①, and line them with newsprint, pressing the corners of the newsprint on the dabs of batter to hold it in place. Pipe the batter ② in domes 1 inch (2½ cm) wide, arranging them on the newsprint in staggered rows and separating them by about 1 inch (2½ cm). Unless you have 2 ovens, pipe only 1 sheet of cookies at a time, and keep the remaining batter in the pastry bag until the first sheet is baked.

②

7. Bake 1 sheet at a time. After 1 minute at 450° F (230° C), reduce the temperature to 375° F (190° C), place an empty baking sheet underneath the sheet of cookies, and continue baking, using a wooden spatula to hold the oven door ajar, until the tops of the cookies are very lightly browned and dry to the touch while the insides are still soft and the bottoms still pale, about 8 to 10 minutes longer.

8. Lift the baking sheet of cookies off the empty baking sheet and take it to the sink. Pour cold water (about ½ cup, or 1 dl, per baking sheet) between the paper and the baking sheet ③ (tilting the baking sheet so that the water runs over the entire surface and drains thoroughly into the sink) to steam the cookies off the paper. Then place the baking sheet on a wire rack and cool.

③

9. To make the filling, place the butter in a small stainless-steel bowl and beat with a wooden spatula, warming it over low heat as needed to

(continued)

make it smooth, white, and creamy. Gradually beat the remaining almond and sugar powder into the butter. Then stir in the rest of the flavoring and, for lemon macaroons, 2 drops of yellow food coloring. Beat this buttercream vigorously with a wire whisk to make it light and smooth. As you beat air into the buttercream, the color of the filling will also lighten noticeably. (However, if the filling is too warm it will not become light in texture or in color and will remain runny. Chill it briefly, and then whisk again.)

10. Carefully slide (don't lift) the cookies off the paper before the paper dries, and arrange them upside down on your countertop. Scoop the filling into the small pastry bag, and pipe about ½ teaspoon (¼ cl) of filling on the center ④ of half of the cookies. (Or, spread the buttercream using a small palette knife.) Then place a second cookie right side up on top of each and press gently to make a sandwich ⑤. Chill the cookies to firm the buttercream.

④

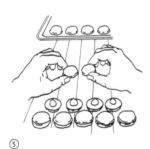

VARIATION: For a simpler, and less rich, version of these cookies, omit the filling and sandwich them back to back in pairs as soon as you remove them from the newsprint.

STORAGE: Covered airtight in a tin cookie box or a cookie jar for up to 2 or 3 days in the refrigerator.

⑤

CHOCOLATE GERBET MACAROONS
GERBETS CHOCOLAT

*C*hocolate Gerbet Macaroons are flavored with cocoa powder and filled with ganache (chocolate cream). They are very rich and chocolaty, and at the same time moist and tender. We give Chocolate Gerbet Macaroons our vote for the chocolate cookies closest to perfection, and my wife Alice ranks them as without equal in the entire cookie domain.

EQUIPMENT
3 large, heavy baking sheets
• Newsprint cut to fit 2 of them
A large pastry bag fitted with
• a ⅜-inch (1 cm) plain pastry tube (Ateco #4)
A small pastry bag fitted with
• a ⅜-inch (1 cm) plain pastry tube (Ateco #4),
or a small palette knife

BATTER
4½ ounces (125 g), or ¾ cup plus 4 teaspoons, blanched almonds
1 ounce (30 g), or 2 tablespoons plus 1 teaspoon, light brown sugar

6½ ounces (185 g), or 1½ cups plus 2 teaspoons, confectioners' sugar
⅓ ounce (10 g), or 1½ tablespoons, unsweetened Dutch-processed cocoa powder
3 large egg whites, at room temperature
⅛ teaspoon (½ ml) cream of tartar (optional)
Red food coloring

FILLING
2¼ ounces (65 g) European bittersweet chocolate (such as Lindt Excellence)
3 tablespoons plus 1 teaspoon (5 cl) heavy cream

For about 40 to 45 cookies

Preheat the oven to 450° F (230° C).

1. Grind the almonds with the brown sugar and 1¼ ounces (35 g), or ¼ cup plus 2 teaspoons, of the confectioners' sugar in your food processor, stopping to break up any caking as needed, until finely ground but not at all oily. Sift through a medium sieve. Grind the almonds that don't pass through the sieve with another 2 ounces (60 g), or ½ cup, of the confectioners' sugar until reduced to a fine powder. Transfer all of the almond and sugar powder to a bowl, break up any caking with your fingertips, and mix thoroughly.

2. Sift 2 ounces (60 g), or about ½ cup, of the remaining confectioners' sugar with the cocoa powder and toss it with the almond and sugar powder.

3. Sift the rest of the confectioners' sugar onto a sheet of wax paper.

4. Whip the egg whites in an electric mixer at low speed until they start to froth. If you are not whipping the whites in a copper bowl, then add the cream of tartar at this point. Gradually increase the whipping speed to medium-high, and continue whipping until the whites form very stiff peaks and just begin to slip and streak around the side of the bowl. Add a

(continued)

drop of red food coloring. Then add the confectioners' sugar and continue whipping at high speed for a few seconds longer to incorporate the sugar and tighten the meringue.

5. Gently fold the almond mixture into the meringue. The batter must be smooth and shiny, and it should spread easily without being at all runny. If it is dull and firm, fold it a little longer to deflate it slightly and get the required consistency. But do not deflate it too much or the batter will spread too much and the tops of the cookies will crack when baked.

6. Scoop the batter into the large pastry bag. Pipe a small dab of batter in each corner of 2 baking sheets ①, and line them with newsprint, pressing the corners of the newsprint on the dabs of batter to hold it in place. Pipe the batter ② in domes 1 inch (2½ cm) wide, arranging them on the newsprint in staggered rows and separating them by about 1 inch (2½ cm). Unless you have 2 ovens, pipe only 1 sheet of cookies at a time, and keep the remaining batter in the pastry bag until the first sheet is baked.

7. Bake 1 sheet at a time. After 1 minute at 450° F (230° C), reduce the temperature to 375° F (190° C), place an empty baking sheet underneath the sheet of cookies, and continue baking, using a wooden spatula to hold the oven door ajar, until the tops of the cookies are glossy and dry to the touch while the insides are still soft, about 8 to 10 minutes longer.

8. Lift the baking sheet of cookies off the empty baking sheet and take it to the sink. Pour cold water (about ½ cup, or 1 dl, per baking sheet) between the paper and the baking sheet ③ (tilting the baking sheet so that the water runs over the entire surface and drains thoroughly into the sink) to steam the cookies off the paper. Then place the baking sheet on a wire rack and cool.

9. To make the *ganache* filling, chop the chocolate and put it in a small stainless-steel bowl. Bring the cream just to a boil, then reduce the heat and simmer for 2 minutes, stirring constantly with a wire whisk, to sterilize the cream. Gradually stir the cream into the chocolate ④ with the whisk, and continue stirring until the chocolate is completely melted. (If some of the chocolate still doesn't melt, dip the bottom of the bowl of *ganache* in a bowl of hot water and stir a little longer.) Then allow it to cool, stirring occasionally with a wooden spatula, until it starts to thicken. Fill the cookies right away, before the *ganache* sets. If the *ganache* does set before you finish using it, dip the bottom of the bowl of *ganache* in a

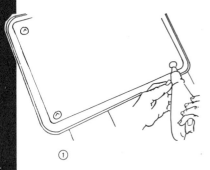

①

②

③

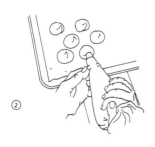

④

THE FRENCH COOKIE BOOK

⑤

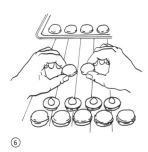

⑥

bowl of hot water and stir it with a wooden spatula until it is soft and smooth (but not runny) again.

10. Carefully slide (don't lift) the cookies off the paper before the paper dries, and arrange them upside down on your countertop. Scoop the *ganache* into the small pastry bag, and pipe about ½ teaspoon (¼ cl) of *ganache* on the center ⑤ of half the cookies. (Or, spread the *ganache* using a small palette knife.) Then place a second cookie right side up on top of each and press gently to make a sandwich ⑥.

VARIATION: For a simpler, and less rich, version of these cookies, omit the filling and sandwich them back to back in pairs as soon as you remove them from the newsprint.

STORAGE: Covered airtight in a tin cookie box or a cookie jar for up to 2 or 3 days in the refrigerator.

RASPBERRY GERBET MACAROONS
GERBETS FRAMBOISE

~~~~

Raspberry Gerbet Macaroons are flavored with eau-de-vie de framboise, a colorless raspberry brandy with a heady perfume. The filling is a simple butter-cream made by whipping raspberry jam into an equal amount of creamed butter, and it too is enhanced with a little framboise brandy. Like all of the other Gerbet Macaroons, these are soft, rich, and luscious, and the raspberry taste is almost overpowering.

EQUIPMENT

3 large, heavy baking sheets
- Newsprint cut to fit 2 of them

A large pastry bag fitted with
- a ⅜-inch (1 cm) plain pastry tube (Ateco #4)

A small pastry bag fitted with
- a ⅜-inch (1 cm) plain pastry tube (Ateco #4), or a small palette knife

BATTER

4½ ounces (125 g), or ¾ cup plus 4 teaspoons, blanched almonds
1 ounce (30 g), or 2 tablespoons plus 1 teaspoon, light brown sugar
7 ounces (200 g), or about 1⅔ cups, confectioners' sugar

3 large egg whites, at room temperature
⅛ teaspoon (½ ml) cream of tartar (optional)
Red food coloring
½ teaspoon (¼ cl) *eau-de-vie de framboise* (raspberry brandy)

FILLING

2 ounces (55 g), or 4 tablespoons, unsalted butter, softened
2 tablespoons plus 2 teaspoons (55 g) raspberry jam (with seeds)
1 teaspoon (½ cl) *eau-de-vie de framboise* (raspberry brandy)
Red food coloring

For about 40 to 45 cookies

Preheat the oven to 450° F (230° C).

1. Grind the almonds with the brown sugar and 1½ ounces (40 g), or ⅓ cup, of the confectioners' sugar in your food processor, stopping to break up any caking as needed, until finely ground but not at all oily. Sift through a medium sieve. Grind the almonds that don't pass through the sieve with another 2 ounces (60 g), or ½ cup, of the confectioners' sugar until reduced to a fine powder. Transfer all of the almond and sugar powder to a bowl, break up any caking with your fingertips, and mix thoroughly.

2. Sift 2½ ounces (70 g), or ½ cup plus 4 teaspoons, of the remaining confectioners' sugar and toss it with the almond and sugar powder.

3. Sift the rest of the confectioners' sugar onto a sheet of wax paper.

4. Whip the egg whites in an electric mixer at low speed until they start to froth. If you are not whipping the whites in a copper bowl, then add the cream of tartar at this point. Gradually increase the whipping speed to medium-high, and continue whipping until the whites form very stiff peaks and just begin to slip and streak around the side of the bowl. Add 2 drops of red food coloring. Then add the confectioners' sugar and continue whipping at high speed for a few seconds longer to incorporate the sugar and tighten the meringue.

5. Gently fold the almond mixture into the meringue. When almost completely incorporated, add the framboise brandy and continue folding until mixed. The batter must be smooth and shiny, and it should spread easily without being at all runny. If it is dull and firm, fold it a little longer to deflate it slightly and get the required consistency. But do not deflate it too much or the batter will spread too much and the tops of the cookies will crack when baked.

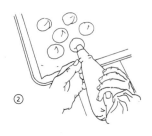

6. Scoop the batter into the large pastry bag. Pipe a small dab of batter in each corner of 2 baking sheets ①, and line them with newsprint, pressing the corners of the newsprint on the dabs of batter to hold it in place. Pipe the batter ② in domes 1 inch (2½ cm) wide, arranging them on the newsprint in staggered rows and separating them by about 1 inch (2½ cm). Unless you have 2 ovens, pipe only 1 sheet of cookies at a time, and keep the remaining batter in the pastry bag until the first sheet is baked.

7. Bake 1 sheet at a time. After 1 minute at 450° F (230° C), reduce the temperature to 375° F (190° C), place an empty baking sheet underneath the sheet of cookies, and continue baking, using a wooden spatula to hold the oven door ajar, until the tops of the cookies are dry to the touch but still pink with at most a hint of browning, while the insides are soft and the bottoms still pale, about 8 to 10 minutes longer.

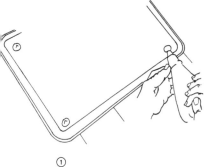

8. Lift the baking sheet of cookies off the empty baking sheet and take it to the sink. Pour cold water (about ½ cup, or 1 dl, per baking sheet) between the paper and the baking sheet ③ (tilting the baking sheet so that the water runs over the entire surface and drains thoroughly into the sink) to steam the cookies off the paper. Then place the baking sheet on a wire rack and cool.

9. To make the filling, place the butter in a small stainless-steel bowl and beat with a wooden spatula, warming it over low heat as needed to make it smooth, white, and creamy. Gradually beat the raspberry jam into the butter. Then stir in the framboise brandy and a drop of red food coloring. Beat this buttercream vigorously with a wire whisk to make it light and smooth. As you beat air into the buttercream, the color of the filling

(continued)

will also lighten noticeably. (However, if the filling is too warm it will not become light in texture or in color and will remain runny. Chill it briefly, and then whisk again.)

10. Carefully slide (don't lift) the cookies off the paper before the paper dries, and arrange them upside down on your countertop. Scoop the filling into the small pastry bag, and pipe about ½ teaspoon (¼ cl) of filling on the center ④ of half the cookies. (Or, spread the buttercream using a small palette knife.) Then place a second cookie right side up on top of each and press gently to make a sandwich ⑤. Chill the cookies to firm the buttercream.

VARIATION: For a simpler, and less rich, version of these cookies, omit the filling and sandwich them back to back in pairs as soon as you remove them from the newsprint. Or fill them with a little raspberry jam alone.

STORAGE: Covered airtight in a tin cookie box or a cookie jar for up to 2 or 3 days in the refrigerator.

④

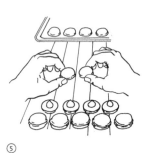

⑤

WALNUT MACAROONS
MACARONS AUX NOIX

~~~~

The French use walnuts in chocolate bonbons, but only rarely in cookies. These Walnut Macaroons are made from the same recipe as Gerbet Macaroons (page 96), with half of the almonds replaced by walnuts. Forty years ago they would have been sandwiched with a filling based on walnut marzipan. We prefer a ganache (chocolate cream) filling because the chocolate cream provides a richer counterpoint to the assertive taste of the walnuts. Walnut Macaroons are sensual and sophisticated cookies that will stimulate the appetite of even the most jaded connoisseur.

EQUIPMENT

3 large, heavy baking sheets
• Newsprint cut to fit 2 of them
A large pastry bag fitted with
• a ⅜-inch (1 cm) plain pastry tube (Ateco #4)
A small pastry bag fitted with
• a ⅜-inch (1 cm) plain pastry tube (Ateco #4),
or a small palette knife

BATTER

2 ounces (60 g), or ½ cup plus 1 tablespoon, English walnuts
2 ounces (60 g), or ⅓ cup plus 1 tablespoon, blanched almonds

For about 40 to 45 cookies

1 ounce (30 g), or 2 tablespoons plus 1 teaspoon, light brown sugar
7 ounces (200 g), or about 1⅔ cups, confectioners' sugar
3 large egg whites, at room temperature
⅛ teaspoon (½ ml) cream of tartar (optional)

FILLING

2¼ ounces (65 g) European bittersweet chocolate (such as Lindt Excellence)
3 tablespoons plus 1 teaspoon (5 cl) heavy cream

Preheat the oven to 450° F (230° C).

1. Grind the walnuts and almonds with the brown sugar and 1 ounce (30 g), or ¼ cup, of the confectioners' sugar in your food processor, stopping to break up any caking as needed, until finely ground but not at all oily. Sift through a medium sieve. Grind the nuts that don't pass through the sieve with another 2 ounces (60 g), or ½ cup, of the confectioners' sugar until reduced to a fine powder. Transfer all of the nut and sugar powder to a bowl, break up any caking with your fingertips, and mix thoroughly.

2. Sift 2½ ounces (70 g), or ½ cup plus 4 teaspoons, of the remaining confectioners' sugar and toss it with the nut and sugar powder.

3. Sift the rest of the confectioners' sugar onto a sheet of wax paper.

4. Whip the egg whites in an electric mixer at low speed until they start to froth. If you are not whipping the whites in a copper bowl, then add the cream of tartar at this point. Gradually increase the whipping speed to medium-high, and continue whipping until the whites form very stiff peaks and just begin to slip and streak around the side of the bowl. Add the confectioners' sugar and continue whipping at high speed for a few seconds longer to incorporate the sugar and tighten the meringue.

(continued)

5. Gently fold the nut mixture into the meringue. The batter must be smooth and shiny, and it should spread easily without being at all runny. If it is dull and firm, fold it a little longer to deflate it slightly and get the required consistency. But do not deflate it too much or the batter will spread too much and the tops of the cookies will crack when baked.

6. Scoop the batter into the large pastry bag. Pipe a small dab of batter in each corner of 2 baking sheets ①, and line them with newsprint, pressing the corners of the newsprint on the dabs of batter to hold it in place. Pipe the batter ② in domes 1 inch (2½ cm) wide, arranging them on the newsprint in staggered rows and separating them by about 1 inch (2½ cm). Unless you have 2 ovens, pipe only 1 sheet of cookies at a time, and keep the remaining batter in the pastry bag until the first sheet is baked.

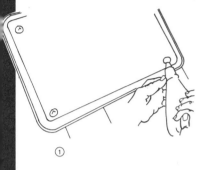

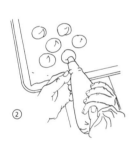

7. Bake 1 sheet at a time. After 1 minute at 450° F (230° C), reduce the temperature to 375° F (190° C), place an empty baking sheet underneath the sheet of cookies, and continue baking, using a wooden spatula to hold the oven door ajar, until the tops of the cookies are very lightly browned and dry to the touch while the insides are still soft and the bottoms still pale, about 8 to 10 minutes longer.

8. Lift the baking sheet of cookies off the empty baking sheet and take it to the sink. Pour cold water (about ½ cup, or 1 dl, per baking sheet) between the paper and the baking sheet ③ (tilting the baking sheet so that the water runs over the entire surface and drains thoroughly into the sink) to steam the cookies off the paper. Then place the baking sheet on a wire rack and cool.

9. To make the *ganache* filling, chop the chocolate and put it in a small stainless-steel bowl. Bring the cream just to a boil, then reduce the heat and simmer for 2 minutes, stirring constantly with a wire whisk, to sterilize the cream. Gradually stir the cream into the chocolate ④ with the whisk, and continue stirring until the chocolate is completely melted. (If some of the chocolate still doesn't melt, dip the bottom of the bowl of *ganache* in a bowl of hot water and stir a little longer.) Then allow it to cool, stirring occasionally with a wooden spatula, until it starts to thicken. Fill the cookies right away, before the *ganache* sets. If the *ganache* does set before you finish using it, dip the bottom of the bowl of *ganache* in a bowl of hot water and stir it with a wooden spatula until it is soft and smooth (but not runny) again.

10. Carefully slide (don't lift) the cookies off the paper before the paper dries, and arrange them upside down on your countertop. Scoop the *ganache* into the small pastry bag, and pipe about ½ teaspoon (¼ cl) of *ganache* on the center ⑤ of half the cookies. (Or, spread the *ganache* using a small palette knife.) Then place a second cookie right side up on top of each and press gently to make a sandwich ⑥.

STORAGE: Covered airtight in a tin cookie box or a cookie jar for up to 2 or 3 days in the refrigerator.

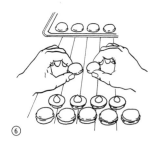

MERINGUE LADIES' FINGERS
DOIGTS DE DAMES

~~~~~~

*T*hese are the simplest cookies made from Italian meringue. The batter is flavored with chocolate or coffee, then piped with a plain pastry tube in large batons. If the same batter is piped in very small batons, the cookies are called Fairy Fingers (doigts de fées). Either way, the meringues are very light, sweet, and crisp. Typically they crack around the base as they bake. Meringue Ladies' Fingers would be a good choice to serve with a cup of coffee at the end of a filling dinner, and included in a buffet cookie assortment their shape and texture provide a nice contrast to most other cookies.

EQUIPMENT

2 large, heavy baking sheets
• Brush with melted butter.
• Dust with flour.
A large pastry bag fitted with
• a ½-inch (12 mm) plain pastry tube (Ateco #6)

BATTER

3½ ounces (100 g), or ¾ cup plus 4 teaspoons, confectioners' sugar
7 ounces (200 g), or 1 cup, granulated sugar

3 large egg whites, at room temperature
⅛ teaspoon (½ ml) cream of tartar (optional)
Flavorings
   2 tablespoons (3 cl) freeze-dried coffee,
      dissolved in 4 teaspoons (2 cl) boiling water
         or
1 large egg white, at room temperature
Red food coloring
1½ ounces (40 g) unsweetened chocolate, melted

For about 55 to 60 cookies

Preheat the oven to 275° F (135° C).

1. Sift the confectioners' sugar.

2. Combine the granulated sugar and ¼ cup (6 cl) of water in a small saucepan or caramel pot and stir to thoroughly moisten the sugar. Bring to a boil over medium heat. Wash down the walls of the pot with a moistened pastry brush to dissolve any sugar crystals that form there. Then continue boiling until the sugar reaches the high end of the firm-ball stage, or about 248° F (120° C).

3. After the sugar has come to a boil, start whipping the egg whites in an electric mixer. Whip them at low speed until they start to froth. If you are not whipping the whites in a copper bowl, then add the cream of tartar at this point. Gradually increase the whipping speed to medium-high, and continue whipping until the whites form very stiff peaks and just begin to slip and streak around the side of the bowl. Adjust the speed at which you whip the whites and the rate at which you cook the sugar so that they are ready simultaneously.

4. Pour the syrup into the egg whites ① in a thin stream while you whip the whites at high speed. The meringue will rise and become very light. Do not pour the syrup on the wire whip or it will splatter around the sides of the bowl. Try to pour the syrup directly into the whites, but in an

①

electric mixer with a steep-sided bowl you will probably need to pour the syrup down the side of the bowl in order to avoid pouring it onto the whip.

5. After all of the syrup has been added, continue whipping for a few seconds at high speed to make the meringue smooth and shiny. Reduce the mixer to the lowest speed to stir the meringue and prevent a crust from forming on top while you get the flavorings ready. Then turn off the machine and remove any sugar syrup that has solidified on the side of the bowl using a bowl scraper.

6. For coffee, mix half the confectioners' sugar with the coffee.

For chocolate, mix half the confectioners' sugar with the egg white and a drop of red food coloring using a wooden spatula. Then stir this mixture into the melted chocolate all at once.

7. Gently fold the remaining confectioners' sugar into the meringue. Stir a little of the meringue into the coffee or chocolate mixture. Then gently fold this back into the rest of the meringue.

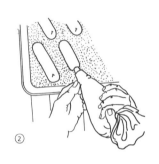

②

8. Scoop the meringue into the pastry bag, and pipe the meringue in batons 3¼ inches (8 cm) long and ¾ inches (2 cm) wide ②, arranging them on the baking sheets on the diagonal in staggered rows and separating them by about ¾ inch (2 cm). If you cannot bake all of the cookies at once, pipe only as much as you can bake and leave the remaining batter in the pastry bag until the first batch is finished.

9. Place 1 baking sheet on a lower oven rack and 1 on an upper oven rack, and bake for 25 minutes. Reverse the positions of the 2 baking sheets, and continue baking until the meringues are set, dry, firm to the touch, and almost dry inside, about 15 to 25 minutes longer.

10. Place each baking sheet on a wire rack and let the cookies cool to room temperature.

➤ **HOWS & WHYS:** The cracking around the base of these cookies is due to the high sugar content of the meringue batter. There is a slight imbalance between the sugar and egg whites, which allows some of the sugar syrup to melt and bubble during the baking. Since the high sugar content is also the source of the unique crisp yet tender texture of these cookies, the cracking is regarded as normal rather than as a defect.

STORAGE: Covered airtight in a tin cookie box or a cookie jar for up to 1 week, provided they are not in a humid place.

CHOCOLATE MERINGUE WALNUTS
NOIX CHOCOLAT

*T*he batter for this cookie is very similar to that for chocolate Meringue Ladies' Fingers (page 108). In fact, you can use the same Italian meringue (either the one in our Meringue Ladies' Fingers recipe or the one below) for both cookies, and you can make Coffee Meringue Walnuts using our coffee-flavored Meringue Ladies' Fingers batter. But unlike Meringue Ladies' Fingers, Chocolate Meringue Walnuts are baked on a moistened sheet of plywood so that the insides of the meringues are steamed and remain soft and creamy while the outsides become crisp. These cookies have an oval shape that resembles a walnut shell; and because they are made with Italian meringue, their interiors are luscious and velvety.

EQUIPMENT

2 large, heavy baking sheets
2 sheets of ⅜-inch (1 cm) plywood, cut to fit on your baking sheets
• Newsprint cut to fit the plywood
A large pastry bag fitted with
• a ⅜-inch (1 cm) plain pastry tube (Ateco #4)

BATTER

3½ ounces (100 g), or ¾ cup plus 4 teaspoons, confectioners' sugar
6 ounces (175 g), or ¾ cup plus 2 tablespoons, granulated sugar
3 large egg whites, at room temperature
⅛ teaspoon (½ ml) cream of tartar (optional)
Red food coloring
3½ ounces European bittersweet chocolate (such as Lindt Excellence), finely grated

For about 45 to 50 cookies

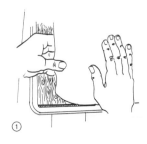
①

1. Soak the sheets of plywood in cold water until thoroughly moistened. Then drain them. Place each sheet of plywood on a baking sheet and cover it with a sheet of newsprint ①.

Preheat the oven to 300° F (150° C).

2. Sift the confectioners' sugar.

3. Combine the granulated sugar and ¼ cup (6 cl) of water in a small saucepan or caramel pot and stir to thoroughly moisten the sugar. Bring to a boil over medium heat. Wash down the walls of the pot with a moistened pastry brush to dissolve any sugar crystals that form there. Then continue boiling until the sugar reaches the high end of the firm-ball stage, or about 248° F (120° C).

4. After the sugar has come to a boil, start whipping the egg whites in an electric mixer. Whip them at low speed until they start to froth. If you are not whipping the whites in a copper bowl, then add the cream of tartar at this point. Gradually increase the whipping speed to medium-high, and continue whipping until the whites form very stiff peaks and just begin to slip and streak around the side of the bowl. Adjust the speed at which you

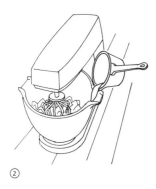

②

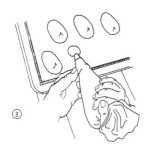

③

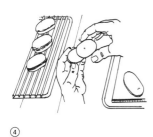

④

whip the whites and the rate at which you cook the sugar so that they are ready simultaneously.

5. Pour the syrup into the egg whites ② in a thin stream while you whip the whites at high speed. The meringue will rise and become very light. Do not pour the syrup on the wire whip or it will splatter around the sides of the bowl. Try to pour the syrup directly into the whites, but in an electric mixer with a steep-sided bowl you will probably need to pour the syrup down the side of the bowl in order to avoid pouring it onto the whip.

6. After all of the syrup has been added, add 2 drops of red food coloring and continue whipping for a few seconds at high speed to make the meringue smooth and shiny. Turn off the machine and remove any sugar syrup that has solidified on the side of the bowl using a bowl scraper.

7. Gently fold the remaining confectioners' sugar into the meringue. When almost completely incorporated, gently fold in the grated chocolate.

8. Scoop the batter into the pastry bag, and pipe the batter ③ in oval domes 1⅜ inches (3½ cm) long and 1 inch (2½ cm) wide, arranging them on the baking sheets in staggered rows and separating them by about ¾ inch (2 cm).

9. Place 1 baking sheet on a lower oven rack and 1 on an upper oven rack, and bake for 15 minutes. Reverse the positions of the 2 baking sheets, and continue baking until the meringues are dry and crusty outside and still soft (but no longer runny) inside, about 15 minutes longer. The base of the meringues will bubble up during baking, and when they are ready the surface will just begin to become crusty at the base. Do not overbake or the insides of the meringues will shrink.

10. Place each baking sheet on a wire rack and let the meringues cool until they can be moved without breaking. Then carefully slide (don't lift) each warm oval dome off the paper and sandwich it back to back with a second one ④. The bottoms of the ovals will be soft and sticky and they will stick together. Place the meringue walnuts on a wire rack and let finish cooling to room temperature.

STORAGE: Covered airtight in a tin cookie box or a cookie jar for up to 1 or 2 days.

MADAGASCANS
MALGACHES

~~~~~

Madagascar, in the Indian Ocean, is the third largest island in the world. It was a French colony from 1896 to 1960, and the French introduced the cultivation of vanilla to the island.

The name of this chocolate cookie is puzzling since, while Madagascar is today the leading producer of vanilla, it is not one of the countries where chocolate is grown. Madagascans are dome-shaped Italian meringues that bake with a "foot" around the bottom and a smooth, satiny top. The outside is crisp, the inside tender and melting. The piped batter must be allowed to rest and form a crust before baking, so don't try to make them in humid weather.

EQUIPMENT
2 large, heavy baking sheets
• Brush with melted butter.
A large pastry bag fitted with
• a ⅜-inch (1 cm) plain pastry tube
(Ateco #4)

BATTER
7 ounces (200 g), or 1 cup, granulated sugar
4 large egg whites, at room temperature
⅛ teaspoon (½ ml) cream of tartar (optional)
6 ounces (170 g) European bittersweet chocolate
(such as Lindt Surfin), melted and cooled but
still fluid

For about 60 cookies

1. Combine the granulated sugar and ¼ cup (6 cl) of water in a small saucepan or caramel pot and stir to thoroughly moisten the sugar. Bring to a boil over medium heat. Wash down the walls of the pot with a moistened pastry brush to dissolve any sugar crystals that form there. Then continue boiling until the sugar reaches the high end of the firm-ball stage, or about 248° F (120° C).

2. After the sugar has come to a boil, start whipping 2 of the egg whites in an electric mixer. Whip them at low speed until they start to froth. If you are not whipping the whites in a copper bowl, then add the cream of tartar at this point. Gradually increase the whipping speed to medium-high, and continue whipping until the whites form very stiff peaks and just begin to slip and streak around the side of the bowl. Adjust the speed at which you whip the whites and the rate at which you cook the sugar so that they are ready simultaneously.

3. Pour the syrup into the egg whites ① in a thin stream while you whip the whites at high speed. The meringue will rise and become light. Do not pour the syrup on the wire whip or it will splatter around the sides of the bowl. Try to pour the syrup directly into the whites, but in an electric mixer with a steep-sided bowl you will probably need to pour the syrup down the side of the bowl in order to avoid pouring it onto the whip.

4. After all of the syrup has been added, continue whipping for a few seconds at high speed to make the meringue smooth and shiny. Reduce the

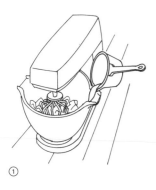

①

mixer to the lowest speed to stir the meringue and prevent a crust from forming on top while you get the chocolate ready. Then turn off the machine and remove any sugar syrup that has solidified on the side of the bowl using a bowl scraper.

5. Stir the remaining 2 egg whites into the chocolate all at once using a wooden spatula. Stir until the mixture is just smooth and still has some of the characteristic viscosity of the egg whites. Then gently fold this mixture into the meringue. Stop folding when the batter is still marbled with varying shades of brown, but there is no white meringue left uncolored by the chocolate.

②

6. Scoop the meringue into the pastry bag, and pipe the meringue in domes 1⅜ inches (3½ cm) wide ②, arranging them on the baking sheets in staggered rows and separating them by about 1 inch (2½ cm).

7. Let the piped batter rest in a dry place until the tops of the domes have dried and formed a crust that will crack and shatter when pressed with your fingertip. This may take as little as 3 or 4 hours, but it is more likely to require an overnight rest.

Preheat the oven to 325° F (160° C).

8. Bake, 1 sheet at a time, until the outsides of the cookies are dry, set, and firm to the touch, but the insides are still soft, about 14 to 16 minutes.

9. Slide the cookies onto a wire rack using a metal spatula and let cool to room temperature.

➤ **HOWS & WHYS:** It is essential that the egg whites not be overwhipped for this cookie. Otherwise the tops, which are smooth before baking, will become scarred when baked. If the cookies do not puff up and form a foot when baked or the tops crack, then either the batter was mixed too much with the chocolate, or the piped batter was not allowed to rest long enough to form a crust before baking.

STORAGE: Covered airtight in a tin cookie box or a cookie jar for up to 3 days, provided they are not exposed to high humidity.

KHEDIVES
KHÉDIVES

~~~~~~~~~~~~~~~~~

The Persian word khedive *means "prince" or "sovereign." It was the title granted by the sultan of Turkey to his viceroys in Egypt from 1867 to 1914. One of the khedives had an opulent mansion on the Bosporus in Istanbul. Today it is a beautiful restaurant called the Kasr of the Khedive.*

These cookies are similar to Madagascans (page 112) in several ways: They are made with Italian meringue and flavored with chocolate; the batter is piped in domes that must rest to form a crust before baking; and a "foot" forms around the base when they are baked. But in contrast to Madagascans, the batter for Khedives is enriched with powdered raw almonds and the tops are dusted with chopped almonds, producing a more complex cookie.

EQUIPMENT

2 large, heavy baking sheets
- Brush edges and diagonals with melted butter.
- Line with kitchen parchment.

A large pastry bag fitted with
- a ⅜-inch (1 cm) plain pastry tube (Ateco #4)

DECORATION

4 ounces (115 g), or ¾ cup plus 1 teaspoon,
    blanched almonds

BATTER

1 ounce (25 g), or 3 tablespoons plus 1 teaspoon,
    confectioners' sugar

4 ounces (120 g), or ¾ cup plus 2⅓ tablespoons,
    raw-almond and sugar powder
  Basic Preparation, page 482:
  *2 ounces (60 g), or ⅓ cup plus 1 tablespoon,
    raw almonds*
  2 ounces (60 g), or ½ cup, confectioners' sugar
5¼ ounces (150 g), or ¾ cup, granulated sugar
4 large egg whites, at room temperature
⅛ teaspoon (½ ml) cream of tartar (optional)
1¼ ounces (35 g) unsweetened chocolate, melted
½ teaspoon (¼ cl) vanilla extract

For about 60 to 70 cookies

Preheat the oven to 350° F (175° C).

1. Spread out the blanched almonds for decoration on a baking sheet and roast them in the oven, stirring occasionally, until they are lightly browned in the center, about 15 to 20 minutes. (Test 1 by cutting it in half.) Transfer the almonds to your countertop and allow them to cool. Then chop them finely.

2. Sift the confectioners' sugar and toss it with the raw-almond and sugar powder.

3. Combine the granulated sugar and ¼ cup (6 cl) of water in a small saucepan or caramel pot and stir to thoroughly moisten the sugar. Bring to a boil over medium heat. Wash down the walls of the pot with a moistened pastry brush to dissolve any sugar crystals that form there. Then continue boiling until the sugar reaches the high end of the firm-ball stage, or about 248° F (120° C).

4. After the sugar has come to a boil, start whipping 3 of the egg whites in an electric mixer. Whip them at low speed until they start to froth.

If you are not whipping the whites in a copper bowl, then add the cream of tartar at this point. Gradually increase the whipping speed to medium-high, and continue whipping until the whites form very stiff peaks and just begin to slip and streak around the side of the bowl. Adjust the speed at which you whip the whites and the rate at which you cook the sugar so that they are ready simultaneously.

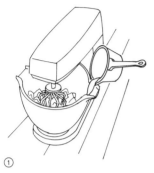

5. Pour the syrup into the egg whites ① in a thin stream while you whip the whites at high speed. The meringue will rise and become very light. Do not pour the syrup on the wire whip or it will splatter around the side of the bowl. Try to pour the syrup directly into the whites, but in an electric mixer with a steep-sided bowl you will probably need to pour the syrup down the side of the bowl in order to avoid pouring it onto the whip.

6. After all the syrup has been added, continue whipping for a few seconds at high speed to make the meringue smooth and shiny. Reduce the mixer to the lowest speed to stir the meringue and prevent a crust from forming on top while you get the chocolate ready. Then turn off the machine and remove any sugar syrup that has solidified on the side of the bowl using a bowl scraper.

7. Stir the remaining egg white into the chocolate all at once using a wooden spatula. Mix it with the raw-almond and sugar powder and the vanilla. When smooth, stir in about one-third of the meringue. Then gently fold in the remaining meringue.

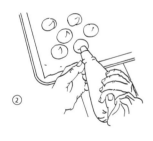

8. Scoop the meringue into the pastry bag, and pipe the meringue in domes 1⅜ inches (3½ cm) wide ②, arranging them on the baking sheets in staggered rows and separating them by about 1 inch (2½ cm).

9. Dust the chopped almonds ③ over the domes. Turn each baking sheet upside down and tap it with a wooden spatula to dislodge the excess almonds, then quickly turn the baking sheet right side up again.

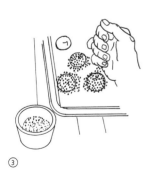

10. Let the piped batter rest overnight in a dry place until the tops of the domes have dried and formed a crust that will crack when pressed with your fingertip.

Preheat the oven to 300° F (150° C).

11. Bake, 1 sheet at a time, until the cookies are set, firm to the touch, and dry inside, about 35 minutes.

12. Place the baking sheet on a wire rack and let the cookies cool to room temperature.

STORAGE: Covered airtight in a tin cookie box or a cookie jar for up to 1 week, provided they are not in a humid place.

ALMOND BOULDERS
ROCHERS AUX AMANDES

~~~~~~~~~~~~

This is one of the only cookies still made with Swiss meringue. The insides of the cookies are soft and chewy and laden with roasted sliced almonds, while the outsides are crisp. We suggest three flavors—vanilla, coffee, and raspberry. The batter is dressed in irregular rock shapes, and you can, if you wish, spoon it onto the baking sheet. However, we recommend using a pastry bag with no pastry tube to produce more interesting and exaggerated shapes. The pastry bag is also much faster and easier. On the other hand, these cookies are fun to make with kids (after the batter is prepared), and for children the spoon is the tool of choice.

EQUIPMENT

2 large, heavy baking sheets
- Brush with melted butter.
- Dust with flour.

A large pastry bag
- with a ¾ to 1-inch (2–3 cm) diameter opening and no pastry tube, or a pair of spoons

BATTER

6½ ounces (185 g), or 1¾ cups plus 1½ tablespoons, sliced almonds

6½ ounces (185 g), or 1½ cups plus 2 teaspoons, confectioners' sugar

3 large egg whites, at room temperature

Flavorings
    1 teaspoon (½ cl) vanilla extract
                      or
    1 tablespoon (1½ cl) instant coffee, dissolved in
        2 teaspoons (1 cl) of boiling water
                      or
    1 tablespoon (1½ cl) *eau-de-vie de framboise*
        (raspberry brandy)
Red food coloring

For about 60 cookies

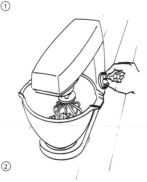

①

②

Preheat the oven to 350° F (175° C).

1. Break up the sliced almonds very roughly with your fingertips, just to reduce the size of the slices so they won't clog the tip of the pastry bag.

2. Spread out the almonds on a baking sheet and roast them in the oven, stirring occasionally, until they are very lightly browned, about 10 minutes. Transfer the almonds to your countertop and allow them to cool.

Raise the oven temperature to 400° F (200° C).

3. Sift the confectioners' sugar.

4. Combine the sugar and egg whites in a 2-quart (2 L) copper or stainless-steel bowl and stir with a wire whisk to break up the whites. Set the bowl over a saucepan of barely simmering water. (Or use a double boiler.) Beat the egg whites with a wire whisk ① (or a portable electric mixer), starting at low speed and increasing speed as the egg whites warm. The mixture will become smooth and shiny and will thicken. When the temperature reaches about 130° F (55° C), remove the bowl from the heat. Transfer the mixture to a planetary-action electric mixer and whip ② the meringue at medium-high speed until it is cool and light and holds stiff, unbending peaks. (If you must whip the meringue with an egg-beater type electric mixer, circulate the beaters around the bowl constantly.) For raspberry, whip in a few drops of red food coloring to tint the batter pink.

5. Whip in the vanilla, coffee, or framboise brandy, then turn off the mixer.

6. Gently fold the sliced almonds into the meringue.

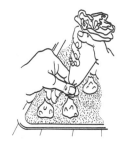

③

7. Scoop the batter into the pastry bag, and pipe the batter in peaked rock shapes about 1¼ inches (3 cm) wide and 1¼ to 1½ inches (3–4 cm) tall, arranging them on the baking sheets in staggered rows and separating them by about 1 inch (2½ cm). To form each rock, hold the tip of the pastry bag between the thumb and index finger of one hand to control the flow of batter. Start with the tip of the pastry bag just above the baking sheet and press firmly on the bag with the other hand to force out some batter. When the batter starts to spread around the tip of the pastry bag, lift the bag up from the baking sheet and squeeze closed the tip of the pastry bag to terminate the mound of meringue in a sharp peak ③. (Alternatively, use a pair of spoons to deposit the batter. Scoop up the batter with one spoon, and scrape it off the spoon and onto the baking sheet with the second spoon.)

8. Place 1 baking sheet on a lower oven rack and 1 on an upper oven rack. Reduce the oven thermostat to 325° F (160° C) and bake for 10 minutes, using a wooden spatula to hold the oven door ajar. Reverse the positions of the 2 baking sheets, and continue baking with the oven door ajar until the meringues are dry and crisp outside, but still soft inside and not yet browned, about 5 to 10 minutes longer.

9. Place each baking sheet on a wire rack and let the cookies cool to room temperature.

➤ **HOWS & WHYS:** Like Meringue Ladies' Fingers (page 108), the surfaces of these meringues crack because of their high sugar content.

STORAGE: Covered airtight in a tin cookie box or a cookie jar for up to 2 or 3 days, provided they are not in a humid place. However, right after baking, when they have barely cooled, they have a creamy tenderness that is as incomparable as it is evanescent.

CHAPTER 3
ALMOND PASTE
BATTERS

Once upon a time, preparing the cookies in this chapter required hard physical work. The only tool available for making almond paste was the mortar and pestle, and pounding almonds to a paste by hand with this primitive tool ranks near the top in terms of kitchen drudgery. Today, these cookies are a snap to prepare using the food processor.

Almond paste cookies are extremely popular in France because of their rich nut flavors and soft, chewy textures, ranging from moist and dense to light and delicate. In the United States they are much less well known since few recipes for almond paste cookies appear in American cookbooks and few pastry shops outside of major cities sell them.

In our modern, food processor approach to almond (and other nut) paste cookies, the starting point is always a powder made from equal proportions of nuts and sugar. Our method for preparing this almond and sugar powder produces a very fine texture while extracting the minimum amount of oil from the almonds. If you have a supply of almond and sugar powder in your pantry, baking a batch of these cookies is as easy as making brownies from a mix.

The basic batter for all of the cookies in this chapter is an uncooked almond paste prepared by moistening the almond and sugar powder with egg whites. By varying the proportions of almonds, sugar, and egg whites and the way in which you incorporate the egg whites, you can prepare batters with a wide range of consistencies. The consistency of the batter determines whether it is piped with a plain or a fluted pastry tube, shaped by hand, or rolled out into a sheet with a rolling pin. The flavor of the almonds in the batter can stand on its own, as in the rich, dense Cherry Rosettes and the more delicate Parisian Macaroons. It can be enhanced by vanilla (for example, in the very decorative Niçois Suns and the ethereal Nancy Macaroons) or by citrus zest (orange zest in Mandarins, lemon zest in Reichembergs). Or it can be totally transformed with cocoa (in the whimsical Dominoes), with coffee (in the potent, glazed Martinique Rectangles), or with glacé fruit (in the robust Provençal Crescents). Pineapple jam is added to the batter to give Pineapple Crowns their tropical flavor, and a filling of raspberry jam balances the lemon flavor of Reichembergs. Finally, replacing the almonds with other nuts brings in an entirely different dimension—pistachios in Pistachio Hearts and Pistachio Macaroons and hazelnuts or filberts in Snowballs and Filbert Macaroons.

There are actually two broad categories of cookies within the almond paste family. The French call them *petits four aux amandes* and *macarons*.

While this distinction is less common in English, we find it invaluable; and a direct translation of the terminology as "almond petits fours" and "macaroons" serves quite well.

ALMOND PETITS FOURS

For these cookies the almonds and sugar are combined in equal proportions by weight. The proportion of egg white in the batter determines how it is shaped and the texture of the finished cookies. Usually a small amount of apricot jam is added with the egg whites to make the baked cookies stay fresh longer. You stir the egg white into the jam and then stir this mixture into the almond and sugar powder using either a wooden spatula or the flat beater of an electric mixer ①. The resulting batters are thick and heavy, but soft. To avoid making the cookies too chewy, stir only long enough to mix. When necessary, you can adjust the consistency by adding either more almond and sugar powder or more egg whites.

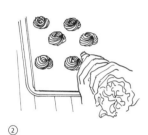

The most familiar cookies of this type are piped from a pastry bag with a fluted pastry tube to form rosettes, fingers, or other shapes with sharp ridges ②. The batters for these cookies must be soft enough to pipe, but firm enough to hold the ridges when baked. As a benchmark, for these batters we use one large egg white plus 1 tablespoon (20 g) of strained apricot jam to moisten 9 ounces (250 g) of almond and sugar powder.

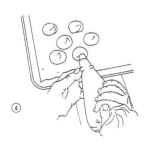

If a smaller proportion of egg white is used, then the batter will be too firm to pipe and must be either shaped by hand (for example, in crescents or balls) or rolled out into a sheet with a rolling pin. The rolled sheets of almond paste are coated with royal icing and then cut into shapes with a knife before baking. To prepare these very firm batters, first make a batter similar to that for the piped cookies using most of the almond and sugar powder called for in the recipe. Then place the batter on your countertop and work in the remaining almond and sugar powder with the heel of your hand ③.

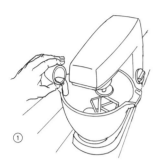

In the opposite direction, moistening the almond and sugar powder with more egg white produces a much softer batter that will not hold ridges and is piped with a plain pastry tube in smooth domes ④, or occasionally into molds. For these batters, you beat the egg whites into the almond and sugar powder gradually to keep the consistency from becoming runny and to incorporate some air. This procedure gives the batter a thicker and lighter consistency than it would have if the whites were mixed in all at once. As a result, the batter doesn't spread excessively and the finished cookies are lighter than those containing less egg white. (The scientific reason is that when the batter is thicker, the mechanical action of beating is more effective in unfolding, or denaturing, the albumen proteins. The unfolded proteins form physical bonds with each other, making it possible to continue adding egg whites while keeping the batter thick. The combination of batter thickness and the denaturing and cross-linking of albumen proteins then enhances foam formation and stability.)

If the batter is piped with a fluted pastry tube or formed by hand, then after piping it must be allowed to rest overnight at room temperature to form a crust on the surface of the cookies. This crust helps the cookies hold their shape in the oven. The cookies are baked at a high oven temperature to give color to the outsides without drying the insides. When the piped cookies and some of the hand-formed cookies (particularly those coated with sliced almonds) come out of the oven, you brush them  ⑤ with a sugar and milk syrup. The heat of the cookies dries the syrup, making a shiny glaze. (Professionals use a gum arabic solution instead of the sugar and milk syrup because it isn't as perishable and can be prepared in advance.)

⑤

The cookies that have been rolled out in a sheet and coated with royal icing ⑥ need to rest before baking only long enough for the icing to dry and form a crust on top, about 30 minutes. Then they are baked at a low oven temperature to prevent the royal icing from browning.

The cookies piped with a plain pastry tube are not allowed to rest and are baked right away in a moderately hot oven. They must color lightly on top but remain soft inside, and they are the most tender and delicate of the almond petits fours.

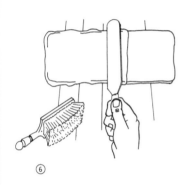

⑥

For all of the piped batters the baking sheets are lined with newsprint, which is the type of paper on which newspapers are printed (see page 423). After baking, the hot cookies are loosened by moistening the paper (see page 126 for details). The very firm batters that are formed by hand or rolled out with a rolling pin are baked on kitchen parchment. For these, the baking sheet of cookies should be placed on a wire rack to cool after baking. Then the cookies can be lifted off easily because the parchment prevents sticking. (In a pinch, if you don't have any newsprint, you can use parchment for the cookies piped from a fluted pastry tube, cooling and removing them from the parchment in the same way as the hand-formed cookies. However, parchment is not an acceptable alternative to newsprint for the cookies piped from a plain pastry tube.)

For all of the almond petits fours, an empty baking sheet is placed underneath the sheet of cookies, either at the start of the baking period or, for cookies piped from a fluted pastry tube, after about three minutes in the oven. The second sheet protects the bottoms of the cookies from drying too much or burning. The baking time is always short. If the cookies are baked too long they will crack open and lose their shape, and they will be dry inside.

MACAROONS

Macaroons are among the most ancient types of cookies. The English word derives from the French *macarons,* which in turn comes from the Italian *maccarone* for a small cake or biscuit containing ground almonds. (The root is the same as for the pasta we call macaroni.) The records of the French court show that the royal chefs were already preparing macaroons in 1553. They may have been introduced into France by Catherine de Médicis, the great-granddaughter of Lorenzo the Magnificent. In 1533, the fourteen-year-old Catherine married Henry, duke of Orléans and son of François I, who became King Henry II in 1547.

Recipes for macaroons can be found in French cookbooks dating from the beginning of the eighteenth century, and by the middle of the eighteenth century the nuns in many French convents were making macaroons to serve to visitors. Those made by the sisters of the Benedictine order in Nancy were particularly famous. A few macaroons are referred to as *massepains.* This old-fashioned term came from the Italian *marzapane,* which originally meant a sugar-candy box and derived from the Arabic word *mautaban* for a glazed vessel. (*Massepain* can also mean a cooked almond paste, or marzipan, prepared by grinding almonds with hot sugar syrup.)

There are many types of macaroons, but they all have in common three characteristics: the primary ingredients are almonds (or other nuts), sugar, and egg whites; they are round or oval with a smooth (rather than fluted) surface; and they are sandwiched back to back in pairs (usually with no filling).

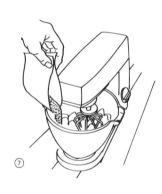

In order for the macaroons to hold their shape in the oven, the batter must have sufficient "body." This body can be developed in two ways: First, the egg whites can be whipped ⑦ and made into a meringue with a little sugar before mixing with the almond and sugar powder. Recipes of this type are included in Chapter 2 with the meringue cookies. The resulting cookies may be either soft and tender or dry and crunchy, but in France today the norm is soft and tender.

Alternatively, unwhipped egg whites can be mixed with the almonds and sugar to make a paste that is worked (traditionally in the mortar and pestle, but today in the food processor) to denature some of the egg white proteins (which then form physical bonds with each other as well as with water molecules, giving body and cohesion to the batter), incorporate a little air, and extract just enough oil from the almonds to provide a batter of the right consistency. The oil is broken up into fine droplets, which are kept separated and dispersed by clinging to the almond particles and by associating with the hydrophobic (water-avoiding) parts of the albumen proteins to form an emulsion with the water from the egg whites. These batters are true almond pastes, and the macaroons based on them are included in this chapter. Typically these macaroons are lighter, finer in texture, and often sweeter than the almond petits fours.

The ratio of sugar to almonds is the variable that determines the texture of the macaroons. It can be as low as 1 to 1 or as high as 3 to 1. With equal proportions of sugar and almonds, the macaroons will be moist and rich. A higher proportion of sugar makes the macaroons lighter and drier. Regardless of the proportions, all of our macaroons are soft and chewy rather than crunchy. Some famous macaroons that illustrate the effect of the sugar-to-almond ratio are Amiens Macaroons (dense, heavy macaroons with 1 part sugar to 1 part almonds), Nancy Macaroons (lighter, but still quite moist with 2.4 parts sugar to 1 part almonds), and Dutch Macaroons (light and relatively dry, but still soft inside, with 3 parts sugar to 1 part almonds).

The proportion of egg whites is determined by the requirement that the batter be piped from a plain pastry tube into round or oval domes that will hold their shape when baked. Too much egg white, and the batter will be runny and spread excessively, then puff up and become hollow when baked. Too little egg white, and the surface of the macaroons will crack irregularly in the oven. As a result, most macaroon batters have similar consistencies, and the ratio of almonds plus sugar to egg white is usually close to 4 to 1.

The macaroons made from almond paste batters have, until now, been regarded as tricky and difficult to prepare. If the egg white proteins aren't denatured and cross-linked enough, the batter won't hold together; but if too much air is incorporated into the batter, there will be insufficient structure to support its expansion and the cookies will bake hollow or collapse. Also, if too much oil is extracted from the almonds the macaroons will have an unpleasant, pasty texture when baked. The traditional method for making these macaroon batters was to pound whole almonds with a little egg white in a mortar and pestle and then gradually work (the word *work* is used here advisedly and emphatically) in more egg whites and the sugar, still using the mortar and pestle. As recently as 1982 the *Cookies and Crackers* book in Time-Life's Good Cook series recommended pounding the almonds in the mortar and pestle for thirty minutes. Fortunately, we have developed a food processor method that eliminates this tedious chore.

To make the batter for macaroons of this type, combine the almond and sugar powder in the food processor with the additional sugar and part of the egg white called for in the recipe. Turn on the processor and check the consistency. Ideally, the mixture should form a soft paste around the side of the bowl, with part of the mass moving around the inside in a soft lump

⑧

that continually mixes with the rest of the paste. If necessary, add more egg white, a little at a time, to get this consistency ⑧. Do not add too much egg white or the almond paste will be runny and the processor will swirl it around without cutting the almonds finer to extract more oil or denaturing sufficient proteins to develop the required body.

At the beginning the almond paste will look dull and slightly grainy. For most macaroons you should continue processing, with the feed tube open to let moisture escape ⑨, until it becomes soft and satiny and warms to between 105 and 115° F (40–45° C). This will take about four minutes.

When you have finished processing the almond paste, transfer it to a bowl and beat in the remaining egg white ⑩, a little at a time, with a wooden spatula. Then beat in any flavorings. Occasionally, the batter can be made lighter by folding in a little meringue (as in Parisian Macaroons).

There are two notable exceptions to the procedure outlined above. One is Amiens Macaroons, which contain a much lower proportion of egg whites than the other macaroons. For these very rich macaroons, only part of the almond and sugar powder is combined with the egg whites in the food processor, and the paste is processed for a shorter time. Then the remaining almond and sugar powder is kneaded into the paste by hand on your countertop. The other exception is our Delicate Macaroons, for which half of the egg whites are replaced with crème fraîche. These macaroons are very light and are prepared, like the almond petits fours, with a high egg white content, by gradually beating the egg whites into the almond and sugar powder with the flat beater ⑪ of the electric mixer.

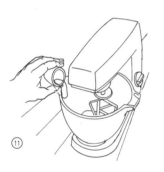

We recommend letting nearly all macaroon batters rest overnight in the refrigerator before piping them. The batter will be less runny and easier to pipe, and the sugar will dissolve more completely, giving the baked macaroons a more beautiful appearance. The exceptions are the batters for macaroons (such as Delicate Macaroons and Parisian Macaroons) that are lightened either by beating in the electric mixer or by the addition of a small amount of meringue. These batters should be piped right away to take fullest advantage of the air beaten into them.

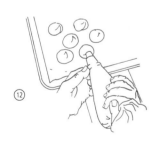

Most macaroon batters are piped in small domes ⑫ (or occasionally ovals) using a plain pastry tube. When you take the batter out of the refrigerator, transfer it to a bowl and beat it with a wooden spatula to soften and smooth it so that it will be easy to pipe.

A few macaroon batters are too firm to pipe and are shaped into balls by hand ⑬. The most famous macaroons of this type are Amiens Macaroons.

Macaroons are always baked on baking sheets lined with newsprint, with an empty baking sheet underneath the sheet of cookies to prevent the bottoms from burning. The oven temperature is typically moderate, and the macaroons must remain soft inside. After baking, the hot cookies are loosened by moistening the paper, and then they are sandwiched back to back in pairs.

LINING BAKING SHEETS WITH NEWSPRINT AND STEAMING COOKIES OFF THE NEWSPRINT

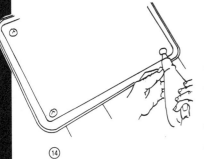

For all of the piped batters in this chapter, both almond petits fours and macaroons, the baking sheets are lined with newsprint (the paper on which newspapers are printed—see page 423). Pipe a small dab of batter in each corner ⑭ of the baking sheets. Place the newsprint on top and press the corners of the newsprint on the dabs of batter ⑮ to hold it in place.

⑭

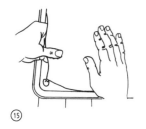

When the cookies come out of the oven they must be loosened from the newsprint by moistening the paper with steam. To accomplish this, lift the baking sheet of cookies off the empty baking sheet underneath and take it to the sink. Place one end of the baking sheet on the bottom of the sink and hold the other end with a pot holder, so that the surface of the baking sheet slopes down into the sink. Carefully fold back the edge of the newsprint nearest you, and pour ½ (1 dl) cup cold water ⑯ between the newsprint and the baking sheet. Tilt the baking sheet as needed to make the water run over the entire surface and drain the excess water into the sink. The heat of the baking sheet will convert some of the water into steam, moistening the newsprint and the bottoms of the cookies. The cookies will still be hot and fragile. Place the baking sheet on a wire rack and let the cookies cool on the baking sheet.

⑮

Most macaroons should be removed from the paper when lukewarm. A few are too fragile to move until completely cool, but they should be removed from the paper before it dries. In either case, sandwich the macaroons back to back ⑰ in pairs; this keeps them fresh longer. The bottoms will be damp and will stick together easily.

⑯

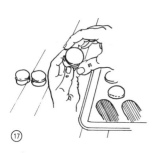

The almond petits fours piped with a pastry tube should be allowed to cool completely on the baking sheet. After cooling, those piped with a plain tube are removed from the paper and sandwiched back to back with jam. Those piped with a fluted pastry tube are not sandwiched. If the bottoms are still damp when you remove them from the paper, lay the cookies on a wire rack to finish drying.

⑰

STORAGE

Nearly all of the cookies in this chapter can be kept at room temperature, covered airtight in a tin cookie box or a cookie jar, for up to three days. They are soft inside and dry out quickly, so they should be put in the cookie box as soon as they cool. To help keep them soft, we frequently include a little apricot jam in the batter. The jam contains invert sugar, which retains moisture. Occasionally we use honey or a cooked sugar syrup instead of apricot jam; glucose, reduced apple compote, or brown sugar can also be used for this purpose.

If the cookies are coated with chocolate, then they must be stored in a cool place—below 70° F (20° C)—to prevent bloom from forming on the chocolate.

A few cookies (such as Snowballs) made from almond paste batters are cooked until dry inside. Typically these have a high sugar-to-almond ratio. They can be kept for up to one week.

CHERRY ROSETTES
ROSACES AUX CERISES

When you see these cookies (as well as Mandarins, page 130) at a pastry shop in France, they are almost invariably labeled with the rather prosaic name fours poche. This is the pastry chef's shorthand for the more cumbersome petits fours aux amandes à la poche, which translates as "almond petits fours piped with a pastry bag." Not what you would call a catchy name. But then, unlike the typical American consumer, the French are more interested in how their foods look and taste than in the gimmicky names used to merchandise them. Fours poche have been selling quite nicely, thank you, for well over a hundred years.

These rosettes of almond paste are topped with half of a glacé cherry. Many American cookbooks refer to them as macaroons, which they are not because they have a fluted (rather than smooth) surface and are not sandwiched back to back. They are also much heavier than most macaroons, but what they lack in finesse they make up for in their luxurious density and rich almond flavor.

EQUIPMENT

2 or 3 large, heavy baking sheets
• Newsprint cut to fit all but one of them
A large pastry bag fitted with
• a medium fluted pastry tube (Ateco #5)

BATTER

1 large egg white
1 tablespoon (20 g) strained apricot jam
[*Basic Preparation*, page 484]

9 ounces (250 g), or 1¾ cups plus 2 tablespoons, almond and sugar powder
Basic Preparation, page 482:
4½ ounces (125 g), or ¾ cup plus 4 teaspoons, blanched almonds
4½ ounces (125 g), or 1 cup plus 2 teaspoons, confectioners' sugar

DECORATION

About 12 glacé cherries, cut in half

GLAZE

⅓ ounce (8 g), or 2 teaspoons, superfine sugar
2 teaspoons (1 cl) milk

For about 24 cookies

①

1. Stir the egg white into the apricot jam. Stir this mixture into the almond and sugar powder, using a wooden spatula or the flat beater of your electric mixer, to make the almond paste.

2. Scoop the almond paste into the pastry bag. Pipe a small dab of almond paste in each corner of all but one baking sheet, and line the baking sheets with newsprint, pressing the corners of the newsprint on the dabs of almond paste to hold it in place. Pipe the almond paste in rosettes 1¼ inches (3 cm) wide ① using a tight circular movement with the tip of the pastry tube. Arrange the rosettes on the newsprint in staggered rows and separate them by about 1 inch (2½ cm). Place half of a glacé cherry on the center of each.

3. Let rest at room temperature for 24 hours to form a crust on the almond paste.

Preheat the oven to 425° F (220° C).

4. Bake 1 sheet at a time. After 3 minutes, place an empty baking sheet underneath the sheet of cookies to protect the bottoms from burning, and continue baking until the ridges on the cookies are beige, about 3 to 6 minutes longer.

5. While the cookies are baking, mix the superfine sugar with the milk and warm over low heat, stirring until the sugar dissolves. When the cookies are finished baking, brush the tops very lightly with this sugar and milk syrup ② to make them shiny.

6. Lift the baking sheet of cookies off the empty baking sheet and take it to the sink. Pour cold water ③ (about ½ cup, or 1 dl, per baking sheet) between the paper and the baking sheet (tilting the baking sheet so that the water runs over the entire surface and drains thoroughly into the sink) to steam the cookies off the paper. Then place the baking sheet on a wire rack and let cool. Remove the cookies from the paper. If the bottoms of the cookies are slightly damp, lay the cookies on a wire rack to let them finish drying.

STORAGE: Covered airtight in a tin cookie box or a cookie jar for up to 3 days.

MANDARINS
MANDARINES

~~~~

In the Chinese Empire, public officials were called kwan by the Chinese and were known to foreigners as mandarins. The name derives through Portuguese from the Malay word mantri for a counselor or minister of state. It is ultimately based on the Sanskrit root man-, which means "to think" and from which our man and mind are also derived.

The mandarin orange (actually a tangerine) is the fruit of the Chinese citrus tree Citrus nobilis, and is so-called not because it is Chinese but rather because of the connotation of superiority conveyed by the title "mandarin." Our Mandarins are fluted fingers of almond paste, scented with orange zest and decorated with diamonds or squares of candied orange peel.

EQUIPMENT
2 or 3 large, heavy baking sheets
- Newsprint cut to fit all but one of them
A large pastry bag fitted with
- a medium fluted pastry tube (Ateco #5)

___

BATTER
1 large egg white
1 tablespoon (20 g) strained apricot jam
    [*Basic Preparation*, page 484]
    or substitute strained orange marmalade

9 ounces (250 g), or 1¾ cups plus 2 tablespoons, almond and sugar powder
  Basic Preparation, page 482:
  4½ ounces (125 g), or ¾ cup plus 4 teaspoons, blanched almonds
  4½ ounces (125 g), or 1 cup plus 2 teaspoons, confectioners' sugar
Finely grated zest of ½ orange

DECORATION
About 24 small diamonds or squares of candied orange peel (just select nicely shaped pieces of diced candied orange peel)

GLAZE
⅓ ounce (8 g), or 2 teaspoons, superfine sugar
2 teaspoons (1 cl) milk

For about 24 cookies

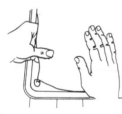

1. Stir the egg white into the apricot jam. Stir this mixture into the almond and sugar powder, using a wooden spatula or the flat beater of your electric mixer, to make the almond paste. Stir in the orange zest to flavor it.

2. Scoop the almond paste into the pastry bag. Pipe a small dab of almond paste in each corner of all but one baking sheet, and line the baking sheets with newsprint ①, pressing the corners of the newsprint on the dabs of almond paste to hold it in place. Pipe the almond paste on the diagonal in fingers 2 inches (5 cm) long and ¾ inch (2 cm) wide ②. To form each finger, first press on the pastry bag and start moving the pastry tube away from you, then quickly reverse direction and pull the pastry tube toward you in a straight line. Terminate by reversing direction once again and flicking the tip of the pastry tube horizontally over the end of the finger and up. Arrange the fingers on the newsprint in staggerered rows and separate them by about 1 inch (2½ cm). Place a diamond or square of orange peel on the center of each finger.

3. Let rest at room temperature for 24 hours to form a crust on the almond paste.

Preheat the oven to 425° F (220° C).

4. Bake 1 sheet at a time. After 3 minutes, place an empty baking sheet underneath the sheet of cookies to protect the bottoms from burning, and continue baking until the ridges on the cookies are beige, about 3 to 6 minutes longer.

5. While the cookies are baking, mix the superfine sugar with the milk and warm over low heat, stirring until the sugar dissolves. When the cookies are finished baking, brush the tops very lightly with this sugar and milk syrup to make them shiny.

6. Lift the baking sheet of cookies off the empty baking sheet and take it to the sink. Pour cold water ③ (about ½ cup, or 1.2 dl, per baking sheet) between the paper and the baking sheet (tilting the baking sheet so that the water runs over the entire surface and drains thoroughly into the sink) to steam the cookies off the paper. Then place the baking sheet on a wire rack and let cool. Remove the cookies from the paper. If the bottoms of the cookies are slightly damp, lay the cookies on a wire rack to let them finish drying.

STORAGE: Covered airtight in a tin cookie box or a cookie jar for up to 3 days.

PISTACHIO HEARTS
COEURS PISTACHE

Pistachios are much more expensive than almonds in France (and in the United States as well). This is undoubtedly the main reason why pistachio cookies are so rare, particularly among the almond paste cookies where the proportion of nuts is very high. Given the extravagant nature of pistachios, when we do use them for this type of cookie, we like to make a shape that is more distinctive and unusual than the ubiquitous rosettes and fingers we use for Cherry Rosettes (page 128) and Mandarins (page 130). Hearts fill the bill nicely. Because the pistachio taste is so strong, a nut paste made by combining a small proportion of pistachios with almonds yields a cookie with a luxurious pistachio taste coupled with the rich, dense texture shared by all cookies of this type. We hope Pistachio Hearts will be as dear to your hearts as they are to ours.

EQUIPMENT

2 or 3 large, heavy baking sheets
• Newsprint cut to fit all but one of them
A large pastry bag fitted with
• a medium fluted pastry tube (Ateco #5)

BATTER

1 ounce (25 g), or 3 tablespoons, unsalted pistachios
3½ ounces (100 g), or ⅔ cup, blanched almonds
4½ ounces (125 g), or 1 cup plus 2 teaspoons, confectioners' sugar

For about 24 cookies

1 large egg white
1 tablespoon (20 g) strained apricot jam
  [*Basic Preparation*, page 484]
Green and yellow food colorings

DECORATION

About 24 blanched almonds

GLAZE

⅓ ounce (8 g), or 2 teaspoons, superfine sugar
2 teaspoons (1 cl) milk

1. Grind the pistachios and almonds with half the confectioners' sugar in your food processor, stopping to break up any caking as needed, until finely ground but not at all oily. Sift through a medium sieve. Grind the nuts that don't pass through the sieve with the remaining confectioners' sugar until reduced to a fine powder. Transfer all of the nut and sugar powder to a bowl, break up any caking with your fingertips, and mix thoroughly.

2. Stir the egg white into the apricot jam. Stir this mixture into the nut and sugar powder, using a wooden spatula or the flat beater of your electric mixer, to make the nut paste. Stir in a drop each of green and yellow food coloring to tint it a stronger pistachio color.

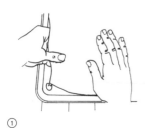
①

3. Scoop the nut paste into the pastry bag. Pipe a small dab of nut paste in each corner of all but one baking sheet, and line the baking sheets with newsprint ①, pressing the corners of the newsprint on the dabs of nut paste to hold it in place. Pipe a teardrop 1¾ inches (4 cm) long and ¾ to 1 inch (2–2½ cm) wide. Then pipe a second teardrop adjacent to the first one to form a heart ②. Repeat with the remaining batter, arranging the hearts on the newsprint in staggered rows and separating them by about 1 inch (2½ cm). Place a blanched almond on the center of each heart.

②

4. Let rest at room temperature for 24 hours to form a crust on the nut paste.

Preheat the oven to 425° F (220° C).

5. Bake 1 sheet at a time. After 3 minutes, place an empty baking sheet underneath the sheet of cookies to protect the bottoms from burning, and continue baking until the ridges on the cookies are beige but the grooves are still green, about 3 to 5 minutes longer.

6. While the cookies are baking, mix the superfine sugar with the milk and warm over low heat, stirring until the sugar dissolves. When the cookies are finished baking, brush the tops very lightly with this sugar and milk syrup to make them shiny.

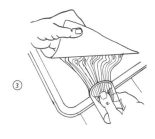

7. Lift the baking sheet of cookies off the empty baking sheet and take it to the sink. Pour cold water ③ (about ½ cup, or 1.2 dl, per baking sheet) between the paper and the baking sheet (tilting the baking sheet so that the water runs over the entire surface and drains thoroughly into the sink) to steam the cookies off the paper. Then place the baking sheet on a wire rack and let cool. Remove the cookies from the paper. If the bottoms of the cookies are slightly damp, lay the cookies on a wire rack to let them finish drying.

STORAGE: Covered airtight in a tin cookie box or a cookie jar for up to 3 days.

PINEAPPLE CROWNS
COURONNES ANANAS

~~~~~~

Adding pineapple jam to the almond paste batter gives it tropi-
cal allure. The batter is piped in rings and decorated with a wedge of glacé pineapple on
one side to produce golden crowns, each set with a single glittering jewel.

EQUIPMENT

2 or 3 large, heavy baking sheets
- Newsprint cut to fit all but one of them

A large pastry bag fitted with
- a medium fluted pastry tube (Ateco #5)

BATTER

2½ tablespoons (50 g) pineapple jam

1 large egg white

9 ounces (250 g), or 1¾ cups plus 2 tablespoons,
    almond and sugar powder

> *Basic Preparation, page 482:*
> *4½ ounces (125 g), or ¾ cup plus 4 teaspoons,*
>   *blanched almonds*
> *4½ ounces (125 g), or 1 cup plus 2 teaspoons,*
>   *confectioners' sugar*

Yellow food coloring

For about 24 cookies

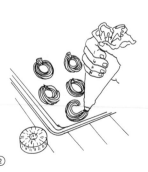

DECORATION

About 24 wedges of glacé pineapple, each ⅛ inch
    (3 mm) thick and ½ inch (12 mm) high

GLAZE

⅓ ounce (8 g), or 2 teaspoons, superfine sugar

2 teaspoons (1 cl) milk

1. Warm the pineapple jam over low heat to melt it. Force the jam
through a fine sieve with a wooden pestle to puree the pieces of fruit ①.
Work as much of the fruit through the sieve as you can. Discard any dry,
fibrous bits that won't go through the sieve. Stir the jam with a wooden
spatula to make it homogeneous.

2. Stir the egg white into the strained pineapple jam. Stir this mixture
into the almond and sugar powder, using a wooden spatula or the flat
beater of your electric mixer, to make the almond paste. Stir in a drop of
yellow food coloring.

3. Scoop the almond paste into the pastry bag. Pipe a small dab of
almond paste in each corner of all but one baking sheet, and line the baking
sheets with newsprint, pressing the corners of the newsprint on the dabs
of almond paste to hold it in place. Pipe the almond paste in rings 2 inches
(5 cm) wide with a ½-inch (12 mm) hole in the center ②, arranging them
on the newsprint in staggered rows and separating them by 1 inch (2½
cm). Place a wedge of glacé pineapple on one side of each ring.

4. Let rest at room temperature for 24 hours to form a crust on the
almond paste.

Preheat the oven to 425° F (220° C).

5. Bake 1 sheet at a time. After 3 minutes, place an empty baking sheet underneath the sheet of cookies to protect the bottoms from burning, and continue baking until the ridges on the cookies are beige, about 3 to 4 minutes longer.

6. While the cookies are baking, mix the superfine sugar with the milk and warm over low heat, stirring until the sugar dissolves. When the cookies are finished baking, brush the tops very lightly with this sugar and milk syrup to make them shiny.

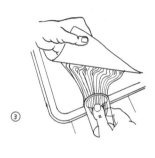

7. Lift the baking sheet of cookies off the empty baking sheet and take it to the sink. Pour cold water ③ (about ½ cup, or 1.2 dl, per baking sheet) between the paper and the baking sheet (tilting the baking sheet so that the water runs over the entire surface and drains thoroughly into the sink) to steam the cookies off the paper. Then place the baking sheet on a wire rack and let cool. Remove the cookies from the paper. If the bottoms of the cookies are slightly damp, lay the cookies on a wire rack to let them finish drying.

➤ **HOWS & WHYS:** Since strained pineapple jam is used in only a few cookies, we recommend preparing only as much of it as you need for the recipe.

STORAGE: Covered airtight in a tin cookie box or a cookie jar for up to 3 days.

NIÇOIS SUNS
SOLEILS DE NICE

While cookies similar to these have been made since at least the nineteenth century, they probably got the name *soleils de nice* in the early years of the twentieth century. In those days the fashionable summer resorts were Deauville and Biarritz, and wealthy French people vacationed on the Côte d'Azur in winter, when the warm Provençal sun was a welcome relief to the gray skies of Paris. Nice was particularly popular because it is sheltered by mountains from the mistral—the cold, dry wind that blows down the Rhone valley to Provence for much of the winter.

For this pretty cookie, a ball of almond paste is coated with chopped almonds, then pressed in the center with a fingertip to make a depression. After baking, the depression is filled with apricot jam and this ''sun'' is surrounded with a few slivers of pistachio to form its rays. The crunchy chopped almonds and smooth, viscous jam make Niçois Suns a fascinating study in textural contrast, and the apricot accent enhances their almond flavor. For a simpler, but still quite elegant, presentation, omit the pistachios.

EQUIPMENT

3 large, heavy baking sheets
- Brush edges and diagonals of 2 of them with melted butter.
- Line these 2 with kitchen parchment.

A small pastry bag fitted with
- a ⅜-inch (1 cm) plain pastry tube (Ateco #4)

BATTER AND FILLING

1 large egg white
8 tablespoons (160 g) strained apricot jam
[*Basic Preparation*, page 484]

14 ounces (400 g), or 3 cups, almond and sugar powder

    Basic Preparation, page 482:
    7 ounces (200 g), or 1⅓ cups, blanched almonds
    7 ounces (200 g), or 1⅔ cups, confectioners' sugar

2 teaspoons (1 cl) vanilla extract

COUNTERTOP DUSTING

Confectioners' sugar

DECORATION

1 large egg white, lightly beaten
5½ ounces (150 g), or 1 cup, blanched almonds, chopped
A few unsalted pistachios, cut into slivers or slices

For 40 cookies

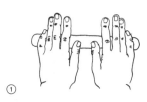

①

②

1. Stir the egg white into 1 tablespoon (20 g) apricot jam. Stir in about 2 cups (270 g) of almond and sugar powder, using a wooden spatula or the flat beater of your electric mixer, to make the almond paste. Stir in the vanilla extract. Transfer the almond paste to your countertop and work in the remaining almond and sugar powder with the heel of your hand.

2. Dust the countertop with confectioners' sugar and place the almond paste on it. Dust with confectioners' sugar and roll the almond paste back and forth under your palms into a cylinder ①. Cut it into 4 equal pieces. Roll each piece under your palms into a rope 10 inches (25 cm) long. Cut each rope into 10 equal pieces ②. Dip each piece of almond paste in the beaten egg white to coat it, then place on the countertop. Place the chopped almonds on a sheet of wax paper. Drop a few of the pieces of almond paste in the almonds. One at a time, take each piece of almond

paste and some chopped almonds in your hands and roll the almond paste between your palms to form it into a ball ③ and coat it with almonds. Repeat with the remaining pieces of almond paste.

3. Place each ball on the prepared baking sheets and press the tip of your index finger on the center ④ to make a deep indentation, flattening and widening the ball to about 1¾ inches (4 cm) wide, with a ½-inch-(12 mm) thick rim. Lightly moisten your fingertip with cold water as needed to prevent sticking. Separate them by about 1 inch (2½ cm).

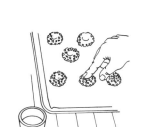

4. Let rest at room temperature for 24 hours to form a crust so that the Suns will hold their shape in the oven.

Preheat the oven to 450° F (230° C).

5. One at a time, place each baking sheet of cookies on an empty baking sheet to protect the bottoms, and bake until the rims of the cookies just begin to color, about 4 to 6 minutes. Do not cook them too long or they will crack open and loose their shape.

6. Place the baking sheet on a wire rack and let cool. Then remove the cookies from the paper.

7. Spoon the remaining apricot jam into the pastry bag, and fill the center of each cookie ⑤ with about ½ teaspoon (¼ cl) of jam. Then arrange a few pistachio slivers or slices on top of each cookie, radiating out from the jam like the rays of the sun.

STORAGE: Covered airtight in a tin cookie box or a cookie jar for up to 3 days. Let the jam filling dry thoroughly before stacking the cookies one on top of the other.

PROVENÇAL CRESCENTS
CROISSANTS DE PROVENCE

Provence, in the south of France, is famous for both almonds and glacé fruits. Provençal Crescents combine a hefty dose of both in a very firm almond paste batter that is shaped by hand into crescents, then coated with sliced almonds. The sliced almonds toast as the cookies bake, while the interiors remain especially moist and luxurious.

EQUIPMENT

3 large, heavy baking sheets
- Brush edges and diagonals of 2 of them with melted butter.
- Line these 2 with kitchen parchment.

BATTER

1 large egg white
1 tablespoon (20 g) strained apricot jam
[*Basic Preparation*, page 484]
14 ounces (400 g), or 3 cups, almond and sugar powder
Basic Preparation, page 482:
   7 ounces (200 g), or 1⅓ cups, blanched almonds
   7 ounces (200 g), or 1⅔ cups, confectioners' sugar
6 ounces (170 g) glacé cherries and pineapple, chopped

COUNTERTOP DUSTING

Confectioners' sugar

DECORATION

1 large egg white, lightly beaten
6 ounces (170 g), or 1½ cups plus 3 tablespoons, sliced almonds

GLAZE

½ ounce (13 g), or 1 tablespoon, superfine sugar
1 tablespoon (1½ cl) milk

For 48 cookies

②

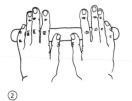

①

1. Stir the egg white into the apricot jam. Stir in about 2 cups (270 g) of almond and sugar powder, using a wooden spatula or the flat beater of your electric mixer, to make the almond paste. Transfer the almond paste to your countertop and work in the remaining almond and sugar powder ① with the heel of your hand. Mix in the chopped glacé fruits.

2. Dust the countertop with confectioners' sugar and place the almond paste on it. Dust with confectioners' sugar and roll the almond paste back and forth under your palms into a cylinder ②. Cut it into 4 equal pieces. Roll each piece under your palms into a rope about 12 inches (30 cm) long. Cut each rope into 12 equal pieces ③. Dip each piece of almond paste in the beaten egg white to coat it, then place on the countertop. Place the sliced almonds on a sheet of wax paper. Drop a few of the pieces of almond paste in the almonds. One at a time, take each of these pieces and some sliced almonds in your hands and roll the almond paste between your palms to form it into a ball and coat it with almonds. Repeat with the remaining pieces of almond paste.

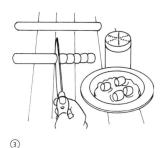

③

④

3. Form each ball into an orange-segment-shaped crescent ④ about 2 inches (5 cm) long and ⅝ inch (1½ cm) high by pressing it between your fingers and onto the prepared baking sheet. Separate them by about 1 inch (2½ cm).

4. Let rest at room temperature for 24 hours to form a crust so that the crescents will hold their shape in the oven.

Preheat the oven to 425° F (220° C).

5. One at a time, place each baking sheet of crescents on an empty baking sheet to protect the bottoms, and bake until the crescents just begin to color, about 5 to 8 minutes. Do not cook them too long or they will crack open and loose their shape.

6. While the cookies are baking, mix the superfine sugar with the milk and warm over low heat, stirring until the sugar dissolves. When the cookies are finished baking, brush the tops very lightly with this sugar and milk syrup to make them shiny.

7. Place the baking sheet on a wire rack and let cool. Then remove the crescents from the paper.

STORAGE: Covered airtight in a tin cookie box or a cookie jar for up to 3 days.

CHERRY BALLS
BOULES AUX CERISES

~~~~~~~

Liqueur-soaked glacé cherries are wrapped in almond paste, then rolled in sliced almonds and baked. Cherry Balls are so rich and succulent that they approach the boundary between cookies and candies.

EQUIPMENT

3 large, heavy baking sheets
- Brush edges and diagonals of 2 of them with melted butter.
- Line these 2 with kitchen parchment.

CENTERS

40 glacé cherries soaked in maraschino liqueur, kirsch, or brandy to cover for at least several days

BATTER

1 large egg white
1 tablespoon (20 g) strained apricot jam [*Basic Preparation*, page 484]

For 40 cookies

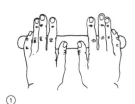

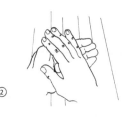

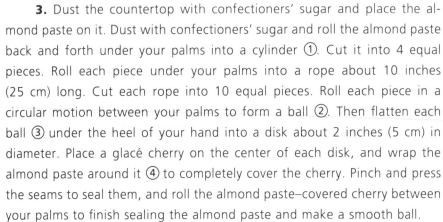

14 ounces (400 g), or 3 cups, almond and sugar powder

} *Basic Preparation*, page 482:
7 ounces (200 g), or 1⅓ cups, blanched almonds
7 ounces (200 g), or 1⅔ cups, confectioners' sugar

COUNTERTOP DUSTING

Confectioners' sugar

DECORATION

1 large egg white, lightly beaten
6 ounces (170 g), or 1½ cups plus 3 tablespoons, sliced almonds

GLAZE

½ ounce (13 g), or 1 tablespoon, superfine sugar
1 tablespoon (1½ cl) milk

1. Drain the cherries thoroughly.

2. Stir the egg white into the apricot jam. Stir in about 2 cups (270 g) of almond and sugar powder, using a wooden spatula or the flat beater of your electric mixer, to make the almond paste. Transfer the almond paste to your countertop and work in the remaining almond and sugar powder with the heel of your hand.

3. Dust the countertop with confectioners' sugar and place the almond paste on it. Dust with confectioners' sugar and roll the almond paste back and forth under your palms into a cylinder ①. Cut it into 4 equal pieces. Roll each piece under your palms into a rope about 10 inches (25 cm) long. Cut each rope into 10 equal pieces. Roll each piece in a circular motion between your palms to form a ball ②. Then flatten each ball ③ under the heel of your hand into a disk about 2 inches (5 cm) in diameter. Place a glacé cherry on the center of each disk, and wrap the almond paste around it ④ to completely cover the cherry. Pinch and press the seams to seal them, and roll the almond paste–covered cherry between your palms to finish sealing the almond paste and make a smooth ball.

4. Dip each ball in the egg white to coat it, then place on the countertop. Roughly break up the sliced almonds by crushing them between your palms so that the slices won't be quite so large. Place the sliced almonds on a sheet of wax paper. Drop a few of the balls in the almonds. One at a

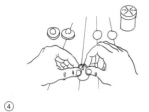

④

⑤

time, take each of these balls and some sliced almonds in your hands and roll the ball between your palms ⑤ to coat it with almonds. Repeat with the remaining balls. Arrange the balls on the prepared baking sheets, separating them by about 1 inch (2½ cm).

5. Let rest at room temperature for 24 hours to form a crust so that the Cherry Balls will hold their shape in the oven.

Preheat the oven to 425° F (220° C).

6. One at a time, place each baking sheet of balls on an empty baking sheet to protect the bottoms, and bake until the balls just begin to color on top, about 5 to 8 minutes. Do not cook them too long or the almond paste will sag around the bottoms of the balls and then they will crack open.

7. While the cookies are baking, mix the superfine sugar with the milk and warm over low heat, stirring until the sugar dissolves. When the cookies are finished baking, brush them very lightly with this sugar and milk syrup to make them shiny.

8. Place the baking sheet on a wire rack and let cool. Then remove the balls from the paper.

STORAGE: Covered airtight in a tin cookie box or a cookie jar for up to 3 days.

SNOWBALLS
BOULES DE NEIGE

Perhaps because snowy winters are not the norm in most of France, snowballs have a certain fascination for the French and are a recurrent theme in pâtisserie—from frozen desserts to meringues to petits fours. This almond paste version is shaped in balls, rolled in confectioners' sugar, and then baked in pleated bonbon cups. Some chefs like to flavor them with coffee or cocoa powder, but our preference is to replace half the almonds with hazelnuts. The result is a firm, dry, and sweet cookie, less chewy and more melting than is typical of almond paste cookies, and permeated with the seductive flavor of hazelnuts. With their winter theme and their unusual appearance, texture, and taste, these Snowballs should become a staple in your Christmas cookie assortments.

EQUIPMENT

1 large, heavy baking sheet

24 pleated bonbon cups, ⅝ inch (16 mm) deep and about 1 inch (2½ cm) wide across the bottom

BATTER

1 large egg white

8½ ounces (240 g), or 1¾ cups plus 1 tablespoon, hazelnut, almond, and sugar powder

{ *Basic Preparation, page 482:*

2 ounces (60 g), or ¼ cup plus 3 tablespoons, hazelnuts

2 ounces (60 g), or ⅓ cup plus 1 tablespoon, blanched almonds

4 ounces (120 g), or 1 cup, confectioners' sugar

1 teaspoon (½ cl) vanilla extract

3⅓ ounces (95 g), or ¾ cup plus 2 teaspoons, confectioners' sugar

COUNTERTOP DUSTING

Confectioners' sugar

DECORATION

1 large egg white, lightly beaten

Confectioners' sugar

For 24 cookies

Preheat the oven to 375° F (190° C).

1. Stir the egg white into the nut and sugar powder, using a wooden spatula or the flat beater of your electric mixer, to make the nut paste. Stir in the vanilla extract. Transfer the nut paste to your countertop and work in the confectioners' sugar with the heel of your hand.

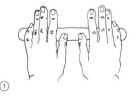
①

2. Dust the countertop with confectioners' sugar and place the nut paste on it. Dust with confectioners' sugar and roll the nut paste back and forth under your palms into a cylinder ①. Cut it into 2 equal pieces. Roll each piece under your palms into a rope about 12 inches (30 cm) long. Cut each rope into 12 equal pieces. Roll each piece in a circular motion between your palms to form a ball.

3. Dip each ball in beaten egg white and then lay it on a paper towel to drain the excess. Place a pile of confectioners' sugar on a sheet of wax paper. Drop a few balls of nut paste in the confectioners' sugar. One at a

(2)

(3)

time, take each of these balls and some confectioners' sugar in your hands and roll the ball between your palms ② to coat it with the sugar, then carefully drop it into a bonbon cup ③. Repeat with the remaining balls. Arrange the filled bonbon cups on the baking sheet.

4. Bake until the balls puff up and begin to crack, about 5 to 6 minutes.

5. Place the baking sheet on a wire rack and let cool. Serve the Snowballs in the bonbon cups.

STORAGE: Covered airtight in a tin cookie box or a cookie jar for up to 1 week.

ACORNS
GLANDS

To make Acorns, almond paste is tinted green and shaped by hand into oval balls. After baking, one end is dipped in chocolate and then in chocolate sprinkles. This is an ideal cookie to make with children. The evocative shape and irresistible taste make them a favorite with children of all ages, and shaping the cookies is particularly easy. As for the chocolate dipping (and concomitant finger licking), my daughter Charlotte assures me that this is her idea of paradise.

EQUIPMENT

3 large, heavy baking sheets
- Brush edges and diagonals of 2 of them with melted butter.
- Line these 2 with kitchen parchment.

BATTER

1 large egg white
1 tablespoon (20 g) strained apricot jam
   [*Basic Preparation*, page 484]
14 ounces (400 g), or 3 cups, almond and sugar powder
   Basic Preparation, page 482:
   7 ounces (200 g), or 1⅓ cups, blanched almonds
   7 ounces (200 g), or 1⅔ cups, confectioners' sugar
Green food coloring

COUNTERTOP DUSTING

Confectioners' sugar

DECORATION

3½ ounces (100 g) European bittersweet chocolate (such as Lindt Surfin)
½ teaspoon (¼ cl) almond oil (preferably) or neutral vegetable oil
2 ounces (50 g), or ¼ cup plus 1 tablespoon, chocolate sprinkles

For 48 cookies

①

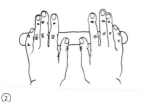
②

1. Stir the egg white into the apricot jam. Stir in about 2 cups (270 g) of almond and sugar powder, using a wooden spatula or the flat beater of your electric mixer, to make the almond paste. Tint the almond paste a pale green with 2 drops of food coloring. Transfer the almond paste to your countertop and work in the remaining almond and sugar powder with the heel of your hand ①.

2. Dust the countertop with confectioners' sugar and place the almond paste on it. Dust with confectioners' sugar and roll the almond paste back and forth under your palms into a cylinder ②. Cut it into 4 equal pieces. Roll each piece under your palms into a rope about 12 inches (30 cm) long. Cut each rope into 12 equal pieces. One at a time, take each piece of almond paste in your hands and roll it in a circular motion between your palms ③ to form a ball. Then roll it back and forth between your palms to stretch the ball into an elongated egg shape, about 1½ inches (4 cm) long. Arrange the pieces of almond paste on the prepared baking sheets, separating them by about 1 inch (2½ cm).

③

④

⑤

3. Let rest at room temperature for 24 hours to form a crust so that the Acorns will hold their shape in the oven.

Preheat the oven to 425° F (220° C).

4. One at a time, place each baking sheet of Acorns on an empty baking sheet to protect the bottoms, and bake until the Acorns just begin to brown, 6 to 8 minutes. Do not bake them too long or they will crack open and loose their shape.

5. Place the baking sheet on a wire rack and let cool. Then remove the Acorns from the paper.

6. Temper the chocolate with the almond oil as follows: Melt the chocolate ④ and stir in the almond oil. Dip the bottom of the pot of chocolate in a bowl of cold water and stir the chocolate until it begins to thicken. Immediately remove from the cold water and dip the bottom of the pot of chocolate in a bowl of hot water. Stir over the hot water just long enough to make the chocolate fluid again, then remove from the hot water.

7. Place the chocolate sprinkles in a small bowl. Dip one end of each Acorn in the tempered chocolate, wipe off the excess on the edge of the pot of chocolate, and then dip it in the chocolate sprinkles ⑤. Place the Acorns on a sheet of wax paper until the chocolate sets.

VARIATION: If you like pistachios, you can substitute 1¾ ounces (50g), or ⅓ cup, of unsalted pistachios for an equal weight of blanched almonds when you prepare the almond and sugar powder

STORAGE: Covered airtight in a tin cookie box or a cookie jar for up to 3 days in a cool place (below 70° F, or 20° C).

BOURBONS
BOURBONS

The noble family of Bourbon derived its name from the town of Bourbon l'Archambault in the Bourbonnais region of central France. The first known Bourbon was Adhemar, a ninth-century baron of the region, and the descendants of his line included kings not only of France but also of Spain, Naples, and Sicily, as well as princes, dukes, counts, and lesser nobility too numerous to mention. Greatest of all in this noblest of noble families was Louis XIV of France, the Sun King.

Many members of the Bourbon family were distinguished soldiers, so perhaps it is the baton shape of this rich, coffee-flavored cookie that inspired the name. The almond paste batons are formed by hand, then rolled in chopped almonds and dusted with confectioners' sugar, giving a crunchy contrast to their firm, smooth interiors.

EQUIPMENT
3 large, heavy baking sheets
- Brush edges and diagonals of 2 of them with melted butter.
- Line these 2 with kitchen parchment.

BATTER
1 large egg white
1 tablespoon (20 g) strained apricot jam
  [*Basic Preparation*, page 484]

14 ounces (400 g), or 3 cups, almond and sugar powder
Basic Preparation, page 482:
  7 ounces (200 g), or 1⅓ cups, blanched almonds
  7 ounces (200 g), or 1⅔ cups, confectioners' sugar
1 tablespoon (1½ cl) instant coffee, dissolved in
  2 teaspoons (1 cl) boiling water

COUNTERTOP DUSTING
Confectioners' sugar

DECORATION
1 large egg white, lightly beaten
7 ounces (200 g), or 1⅓ cups, blanched almonds, chopped
Confectioners' sugar

For 48 cookies

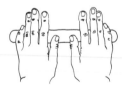
①

②

1. Stir the egg white into the apricot jam. Stir in about 2 cups (270 g) of almond and sugar powder, using a wooden spatula or the flat beater of your electric mixer, to make the almond paste. Flavor it with the coffee. Transfer the almond paste to your countertop and work in the remaining almond and sugar powder with the heel of your hand.

2. Dust the countertop with confectioners' sugar and place the almond paste on it. Dust with confectioners' sugar and roll the almond paste back and forth under your palms into a cylinder ①. Cut it into 8 equal pieces. Roll each piece under your palms into a cylinder about 9 inches (24 cm) long. One at a time, lightly brush all sides of each cylinder with egg white ②. Place the chopped almonds on your countertop and roll the cylinder back and forth under your palms on the almonds ③ to coat it and elongate it into a rope 18 inches (48 cm) long. Cut the rope into six 3-inch (8 cm) batons. Arrange the batons on the baking sheets, separating them by about 1 inch (2½ cm).

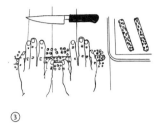

③

3. Let rest at room temperature for 24 hours to form a crust so that the batons will hold their shape in the oven.

Preheat the oven to 475° F (250° C).

4. One at a time, place each baking sheet of batons on an empty baking sheet to protect the bottoms, and bake until the chopped almonds barely begin to brown, about 3 to 4 minutes. If any of the cookies start to crack, remove all of them from the oven immediately.

5. Place the baking sheet on a wire rack and let cool. Then remove the batons from the paper and lightly dust with confectioners' sugar.

STORAGE: Covered airtight in a tin cookie box or a cookie jar for up to 3 days.

VANILLA BATONS
BÂTONS VANILLE

While these are called ''batons,'' actually they are flat strips shaped more like the ivories on a piano. The firm almond paste is rolled out into a sheet and covered with a thin layer of royal icing, making an almond paste version of the flaky pastry Matchsticks in Chapter 7 (page 384). The light, brittle icing offers a nice counterpoint to the dense almond paste, and their textures and vanilla flavor make Vanilla Batons an admirable accompaniment to fresh pears.

EQUIPMENT

3 large, heavy baking sheets
- Brush edges and diagonals of 2 of them with melted butter.
- Line these 2 with kitchen parchment.

BATTER

1 large egg white
1 tablespoon (20 g) strained apricot jam
  [*Basic Preparation*, page 484]

14 ounces (400 g), or 3 cups, almond and sugar powder
  Basic Preparation, page 482:
  7 ounces (200 g), or 1⅓ cups, blanched almonds
  7 ounces (200 g), or 1⅔ cups, confectioners' sugar
1 teaspoon (½ cl) vanilla extract

ROYAL ICING

1 large egg white, at room temperature
4 ounces (115 g), or ¾ cup plus 2 tablespoons, confectioners' sugar
⅛ teaspoon (½ ml) distilled white vinegar

COUNTERTOP DUSTING

Confectioners' sugar

For 40 cookies

①

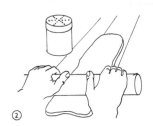
②

1. Stir the egg white into the apricot jam. Stir in about 2 cups (270 g) of almond and sugar powder, using a wooden spatula or the flat beater of your electric mixer, to make the almond paste. Flavor it with the vanilla. Transfer the almond paste to your countertop and work in the remaining almond and sugar powder ① with the heel of your hand.

2. Place the egg white for the royal icing in your electric mixer. Sift the confectioners' sugar and gradually stir it into the egg white. When all of the sugar has been added, beat at medium speed with the flat beater for 15 minutes to make the mixture light and thick, like a meringue. It will form soft peaks when you lift the beater. Add the vinegar and continue beating a little longer.

3. Dust your countertop with confectioners' sugar and place the almond paste on it. Dust with confectioners' sugar and roll out the almond paste with your rolling pin into a sheet ② about 6 by 15 inches (15 by 40 cm). Brush the top of the sheet to remove any confectioners' sugar. Spread the top with a thin layer of royal icing ③ (you will need less than half of it). Then smooth it with your palette knife by sweeping in one long, even motion over the length of the sheet, slowly rotating the blade of the palette knife as you go to remove the excess icing.

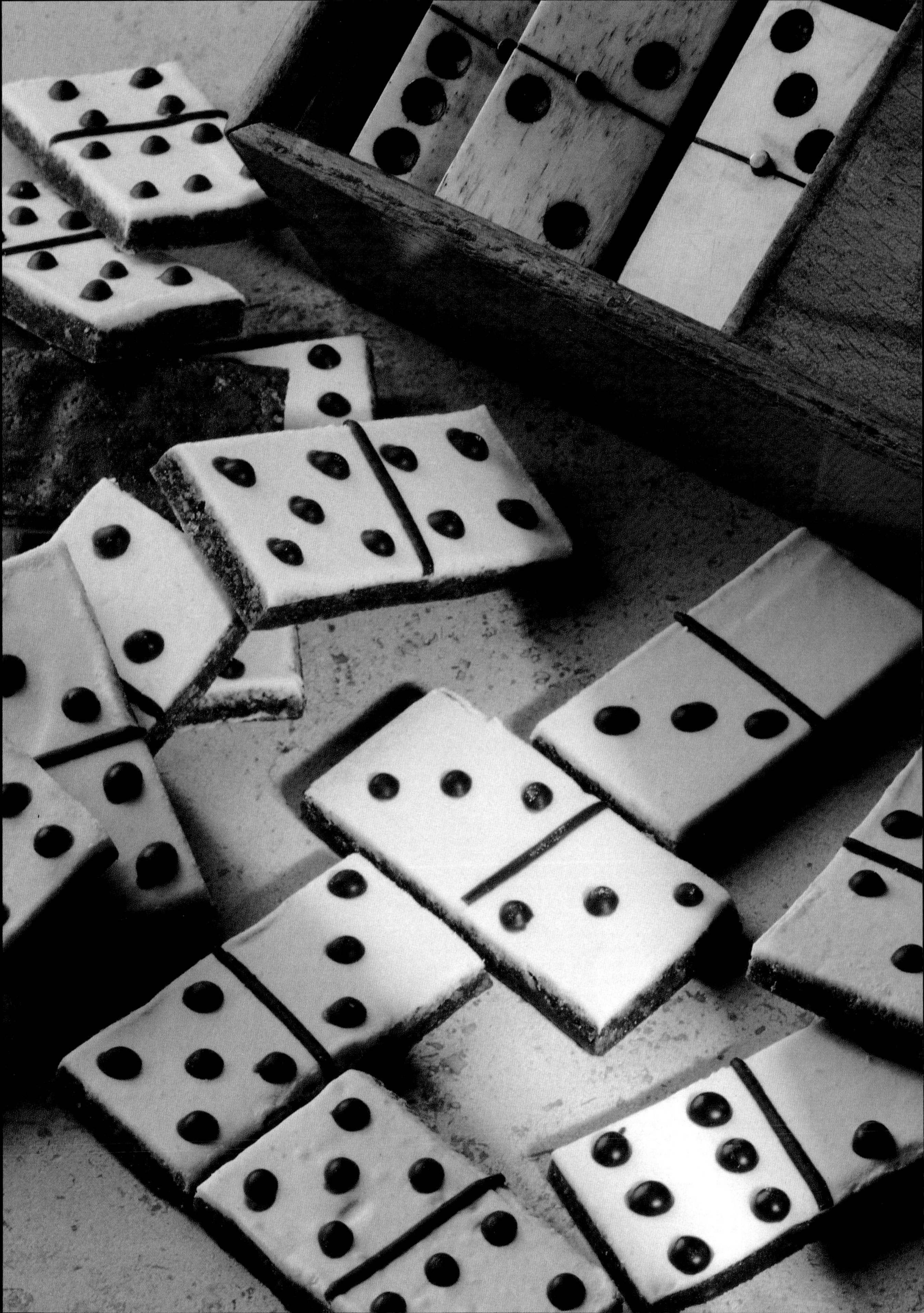

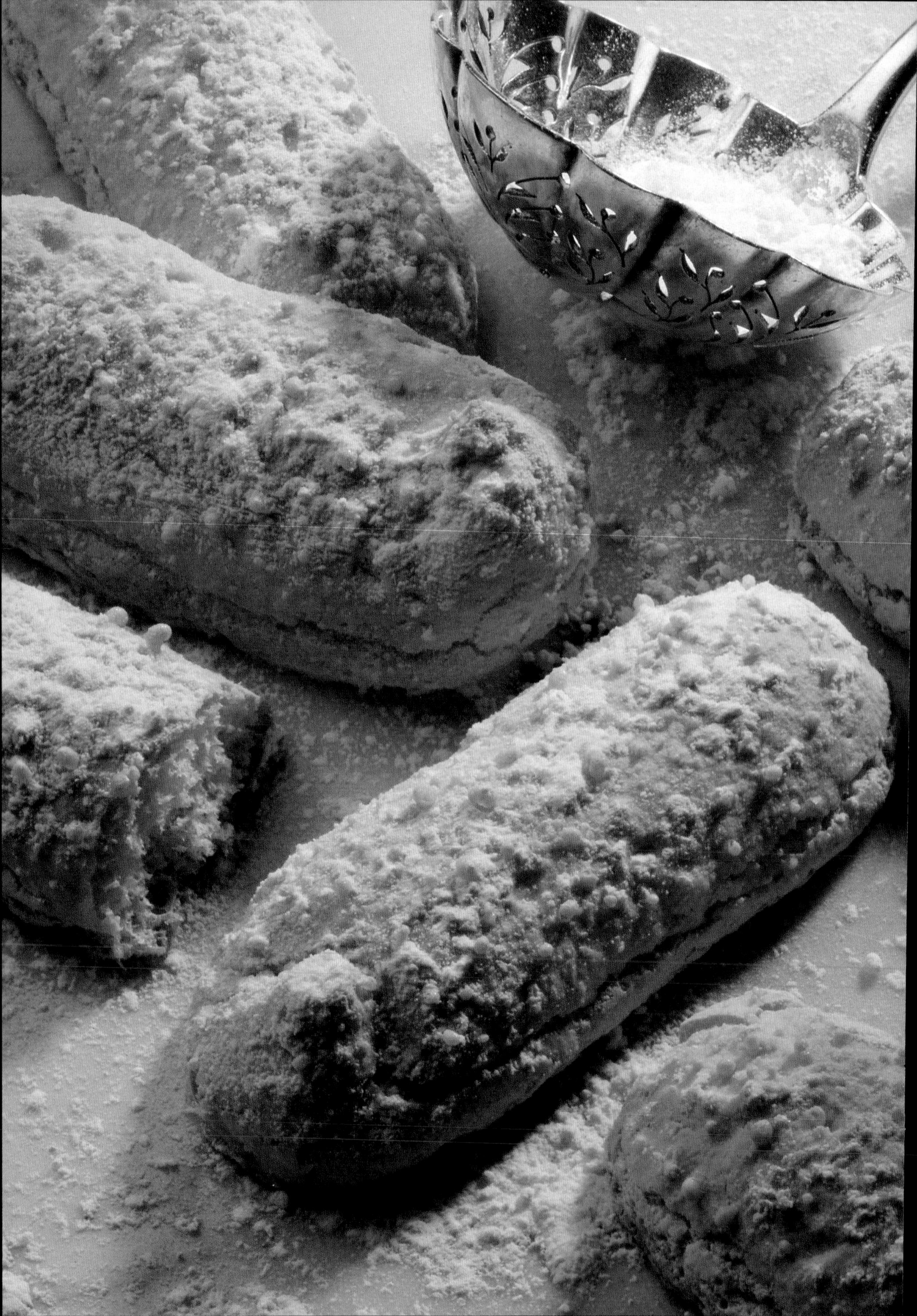

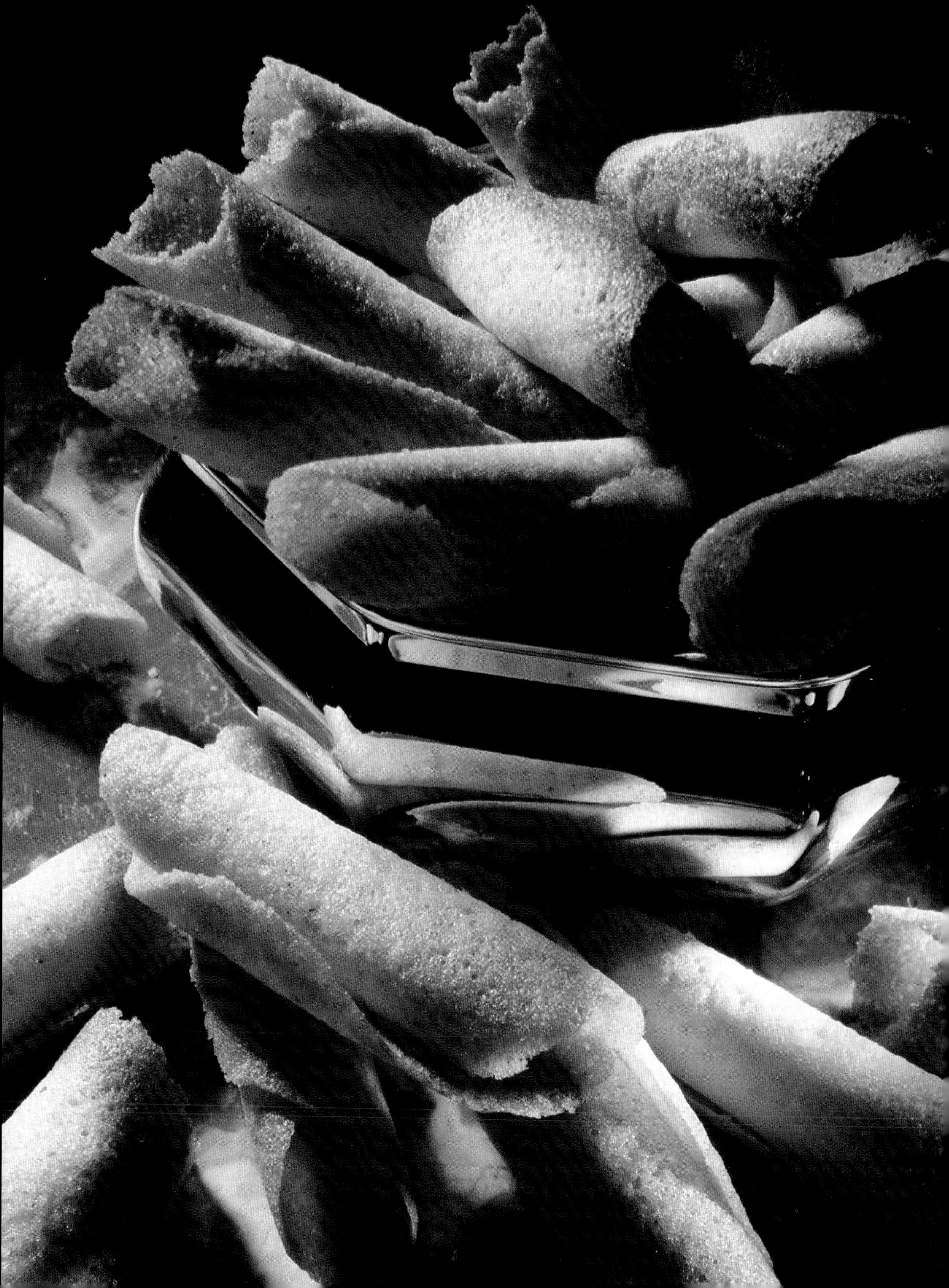

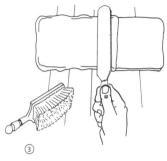

③

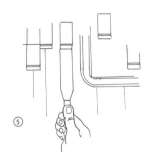

④

⑤

4. Trim the edges of the sheet with your chef's knife, dipping it in flour between cuts to prevent sticking. Then cut the sheet in half lengthwise and cut each half crosswise into ¾ by 3-inch (2 by 7½ cm) strips ④, dipping the blade of your chef's knife in flour between each cut. Carefully lift the strips, one at a time, with a metal spatula ⑤, and arrange them on the prepared baking sheets, separating them by about 1 inch (2½ cm).

5. Let rest until the royal icing forms a crust on top, at least 30 minutes.

Preheat the oven to 300° F (150° C).

6. One at a time, place each baking sheet of batons on an empty baking sheet to protect the bottoms, and bake for about 5 to 8 minutes to dry the outsides of the cookies. Remove them from the oven as soon as the edges of 1 or 2 cookies begin to expand.

7. Place the baking sheet on a wire rack and let cool. Then remove the batons from the paper.

VARIATIONS: These can be made in a variety of shapes. The simplest are triangles and rectangles (for Vanilla Dominoes, decorate them with dots of chocolate).

➤ **HOWS & WHYS:** Allowing the royal icing to form a crust on top before baking gives it a nice shiny appearance when baked. Since the minimum recipe for royal icing makes more than double the amount needed for these cookies, you might want to make another cookie (such as Martinique Rectangles [page 150] or Dominoes [page 152]) glazed with royal icing on the same day to use up the icing. Be sure to keep the container of icing covered so that the surface doesn't dry and form a crust.

STORAGE: Covered airtight in a tin cookie box or a cookie jar for up to 3 days.

MARTINIQUE RECTANGLES
FONDANTS MARTINIQUE

*T*he West Indian island Martinique, in the Lesser Antilles, was discovered by Columbus, probably in 1502, and colonized by the French beginning in 1635.
To this day it is a département of France, and it has become a favorite vacation spot for
many French people. While the main crop of the island is sugar, coffee has been grown
there since 1723, and the name ''martinique'' is often used in French pastry for desserts
that contain coffee.

Fondants martinique *are prepared in the same way as Vanilla Batons (page 148), but
the shape is different and they are dominated by the assertive flavor of coffee. Fondant
means ''melting'' and refers to the luscious quality of these cookies as they dissolve addic-
tively in your mouth.*

EQUIPMENT

3 large, heavy baking sheets
- Brush edges and diagonals of 2 of them with
  melted butter.
- Line these 2 with kitchen parchment.

BATTER

1 large egg white
1 tablespoon (20 g) strained apricot jam
  [*Basic Preparation, page 484*]
14 ounces (400 g), or 3 cups, almond and sugar
    powder
{ *Basic Preparation, page 482:*
  7 ounces (200 g), or 1⅓ cups, blanched almonds
  7 ounces (200 g), or 1⅔ cups, confectioners' sugar
4 teaspoons (2 cl) freeze-dried coffee, dissolved in
    1 tablespoon (1½ cl) boiling water

ROYAL ICING

1 large egg white, at room temperature
4 ounces (115 g), or ¾ cup plus 2 tablespoons,
    confectioners' sugar
⅛ teaspoon (½ ml) distilled white vinegar

COUNTERTOP DUSTING

Confectioners' sugar

For 40 cookies

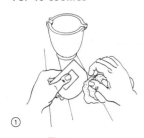

①

1. Stir the egg white into the apricot jam. Stir in about 2 cups
(270 g) of almond and sugar powder, using a wooden spatula or the flat
beater of your electric mixer, to make the almond paste. Flavor it with 2
teaspoons (1 cl) of the coffee. Transfer the almond paste to your countertop
and work in the remaining almond and sugar powder with the heel of your
hand ①.

2. Place the egg white for the royal icing in your electric mixer. Sift
the confectioners' sugar and gradually stir it into the egg white. When all
of the sugar has been added, beat at medium speed with the flat beater
for 15 minutes to make the mixture light and thick, like a meringue. It will
form soft peaks when you lift the beater. Add the vinegar and continue
beating a little longer. Stir in 1 teaspoon (½ cl) of the coffee.

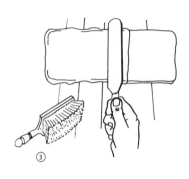

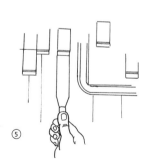

3. Dust your countertop with confectioners' sugar and place the almond paste on it. Dust with confectioners' sugar and roll out the almond paste with your rolling pin into a sheet ② about 6¼ by 16 inches (15 by 40 cm). Brush the top of the sheet to remove any confectioners' sugar. Spread the top with a thin layer of royal icing ③ (you will need less than half of it). Then smooth it with your palette knife by sweeping in one long, even motion over the length of the sheet, slowly rotating the blade of the palette knife as you go to remove the excess icing.

4. Trim the edges of the sheet with your chef's knife, dipping it in flour between cuts to prevent sticking. Cut the sheet lengthwise into five 1¼-inch- (3 cm) wide bands, and then cut it crosswise into 1¼ by 2-inch (3 by 5 cm) rectangles ④, dipping the blade of your chef's knife in flour between each cut. Carefully lift the rectangles, one at a time, with a metal spatula ⑤, and arrange them on the prepared baking sheets, separating them by about 1 inch (2½ cm).

5. Let rest until the royal icing forms a crust on top, at least 30 minutes.

Preheat the oven to 300° F (150° C).

6. One at a time, place each baking sheet of cookies on an empty baking sheet to protect the bottoms, and bake for about 5 to 8 minutes to dry the outsides of the cookies. Remove them from the oven as soon as the edges of 1 or 2 cookies begin to expand.

7. Place the baking sheet on a wire rack and let cool. Then remove the cookies from the paper.

VARIATIONS: These can be made in a variety of shapes. For example, Coffee Batons are cut into strips, just like Vanilla Batons (page 148).

➤ **HOWS & WHYS:** Allowing the royal icing to form a crust on top before baking gives it a nice shiny appearance when baked. Since the minimum recipe for royal icing makes more than double the amount needed for these cookies, you might want to make another cookie (such as Vanilla Batons, page 148, or Dominoes page 152) glazed with royal icing on the same day to use up the icing. Be sure to keep the container of icing covered so that the surface doesn't dry and form a crust.

STORAGE: Covered airtight in a tin cookie box or a cookie jar for up to 3 days.

DOMINOES
DOMINOES

The game of dominoes first became popular in Italy during the eighteenth century. Then, as now, the game was played with twenty-eight oblong pieces—the dominoes—which originally had ivory faces backed with ebony. Both ends of each domino were marked (like dice) with zero to six black dots, called pips. The name is believed to derive from the black hooded cloak, called a domino, worn with a small half mask to a costume ball or masquerade by guests not dressed in character.

Our Dominoes are made from cocoa-flavored almond paste, rolled out into a thin sheet and glazed with royal icing. After baking, the crisp white icing is decorated with pips of melted chocolate. Dominoes are an enchanting cookie for children's parties, and they would be a truly urbane selection to serve at your next masquerade.

EQUIPMENT

3 large, heavy baking sheets
- Brush edges and diagonals of 2 of them with melted butter.
- Line these 2 with kitchen parchment.

A parchment decorating cone (see page 426)

BATTER

1 large egg white
1 tablespoon (20 g) strained apricot jam
    [*Basic Preparation*, page 484]
14 ounces (400 g), or 3 cups, almond and sugar
    powder
    } *Basic Preparation, page 482:*
    7 ounces (200 g), or 1⅓ cups, blanched almonds
    7 ounces (200 g), or 1⅔ cups, confectioners' sugar
1½ tablespoons (10 g) unsweetened
    Dutch-processed cocoa powder

ROYAL ICING

1 large egg white, at room temperature
4 ounces (115 g), or ¾ cup plus 2 tablespoons,
    confectioners' sugar
⅛ teaspoon (½ ml) distilled white vinegar

COUNTERTOP DUSTING

Confectioners' sugar

DECORATION

⅔ ounce (18 g) European bittersweet chocolate
    (such as Lindt Surfin), barely melted

For 40 cookies

①

1. Stir the egg white into the apricot jam. Mix about 2 cups (270 g) of almond and sugar powder with the cocoa powder and stir it into the egg white mixture, using a wooden spatula or the flat beater of your electric mixer, to make the almond paste. Transfer the almond paste to your countertop and work in the remaining almond and sugar powder with the heel of your hand ①.

2. Place the egg white for the royal icing in your electric mixer. Sift the confectioners' sugar and gradually stir it into the egg white. When all of the sugar has been added, beat at medium speed with the flat beater for 15 minutes to make the mixture light and thick, like a meringue. It will form soft peaks when you lift the beater. Add the vinegar and continue beating a little longer.

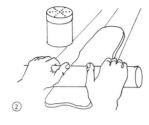

②

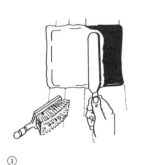

③

④

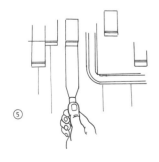

⑤

3. Dust the countertop with confectioners' sugar and place the almond paste on it. Dust with confectioners' sugar and roll out the almond paste with your rolling pin into a sheet ② about 8 by 10 inches (20 by 25 cm). Brush the top of the sheet to remove any confectioners' sugar. Spread the top with a thin layer of royal icing ③ (you will need less than half of it). Then smooth it with your palette knife by sweeping in one long, even motion over the length of the sheet, slowly rotating the blade of the palette knife as you go to remove the excess icing.

4. Trim the edges of the sheet with your chef's knife, dipping it in flour between cuts to prevent sticking. Cut the sheet lengthwise into 8 strips 1 inch (2½ cm) wide; then cut the strips crosswise into 1 by 2-inch (2½ by 5 cm) rectangles ④. Always dip the blade of your chef's knife in flour between each cut. Carefully lift the rectangles, one at a time, with a metal spatula ⑤, and arrange them on the prepared baking sheets, separating them by about 1 inch (2½ cm).

5. Let rest until the royal icing forms a crust on top, at least 30 minutes.

Preheat the oven to 300° F (150° C).

6. One at a time, place each baking sheet of cookies on an empty baking sheet to protect the bottoms, and bake for about 5 to 8 minutes to dry the outsides of the cookies. Remove them from the oven as soon as the edges of 1 or 2 cookies begin to expand.

7. Place the baking sheet on a wire rack and let cool.

8. Transfer the melted chocolate to the parchment decorating cone ⑥. Cut the tip of the cone and decorate the tops of the rectangles like dominoes ⑦. Pipe a line crosswise on the center of each rectangle to divide it into 2 squares. Then pipe 0 to 6 pips on each square. You will have duplicates, but be sure to pipe 1 complete set of 28 dominoes.

9. Remove the dominoes from the paper.

VARIATIONS: These cookies can also be made in other shapes, such as triangles, in which case the domino decoration is omitted.

➤ **HOWS & WHYS:** Allowing the royal icing to form a crust on top before baking gives it a nice shiny appearance when baked. Since the minimum recipe for royal icing makes more than double the amount needed for these cookies, you might want to make another cookie (such as Vanilla Batons, page 148, or Martinique Rectangles, page 150), glazed with royal icing on

(continued)

⑥

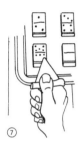

⑦

the same day to use up the icing. Be sure to keep the container of icing covered so that the surface doesn't dry and form a crust.

The chocolate does not need to be tempered for decorating these cookies. As long as the chocolate is barely melted, so that it is not too thin, the small dots of chocolate will set quickly. Chilling in the refrigerator while the dots set is an extra precaution you can take to ensure that no bloom forms on the chocolate.

STORAGE: Covered airtight in a tin cookie box or a cookie jar for up to 3 days.

LAVOISIERS
LAVOISIERS

Named for the great eighteenth-century French chemist Antoine-Laurent Lavoisier, these almond paste cookies are flavored with chopped walnuts and coffee and baked in rectangular *petits fours* molds. Their texture is much more cakelike than the other cookies in this chapter.

EQUIPMENT

36 rectangular *petits fours* molds, 2 inches (5 cm) long, 1 inch (1½ cm) wide, and ⅜ inch (1 cm) deep
• Clarified butter, melted
1 large, heavy baking sheet
A large pastry bag fitted with
• a ⁷⁄₁₆-inch (11 mm) plain pastry tube (Ateco #5)

1½ ounces (45 g), or ¼ cup plus 3 tablespoons, walnuts, chopped
1 teaspoon (½ cl) instant coffee, dissolved in ¾ teaspoon (4 ml) boiling water

DECORATION

About 1 ounce (25 g), or ¼ cup, sliced almonds

BATTER

2 large egg whites, lightly beaten, at room temperature
7 ounces (200 g), or 1½ cups, almond and sugar powder

{ *Basic Preparation, page 482:*
3½ ounces (100 g), or ⅔ cup, blanched almonds
3½ ounces (100 g), or ¾ cup plus 4 teaspoons, confectioners' sugar

For 36 cookies

①

②

1. Brush the *petits fours* molds ① with clarified butter and arrange them on the baking sheet.

Preheat the oven to 300° F (150° C).

2. Gradually stir the egg whites into the almond and sugar powder, either in your electric mixer using the flat beater at low to medium speed, or by hand using a wooden spatula and beating vigorously. Stir in the walnuts and coffee.

3. Scoop the batter into the pastry bag. Pipe the batter into the molds, filling them about two-thirds ②. Scatter a few almond slices on top of each.

4. Bake until the cookies puff up, turn pale beige on top, barely begin to brown around the edges, and shrink from the sides of the molds, about 5 to 6 minutes.

5. Slide the molds onto a wire rack and let cool to lukewarm. Then loosen the cookies by sliding the tip of a small palette knife or a paring knife around the edges, and carefully lift the cookies out of the molds.

STORAGE: Covered airtight in a tin cookie box or a cookie jar for up to 3 days.

ABRICOTINES
ABRICOTINES

~~~~~~~~~~

Abricot *is the French word for apricot. The name* abricotine *is used frequently in classical French pastry for desserts (from large* gâteaux *to frozen desserts to cookies) in which the flavor of apricot plays an essential role.*

The almond is the pit of a stone fruit in the same family as the apricot, so there is a certain naturalness in the flavor affinity of apricots and almonds. In our Abricotines, almond paste is moistened (and lightened) with egg white, piped in small domes, and dusted with chopped almonds. After baking, the domes are sandwiched with a filling of apricot jam. The amount of jam is quite small, yet the apricot is assertive enough to provide a depth of flavor that belies the delicacy of these tender morsels.

EQUIPMENT

2 or 3 large, heavy baking sheets
- Newsprint cut to fit all but one of them

A large pastry bag fitted with
- a 7/16-inch (11 mm) plain pastry tube (Ateco #5)

BATTER

2 large egg whites, lightly beaten, at room
 temperature
9 ounces (250 g), or 1¾ cups plus 2 tablespoons,
 almond and sugar powder

Basic Preparation, page 482:
4½ ounces (125 g), or ¾ cup plus 4 teaspoons,
* blanched almonds*
4½ ounces (125 g), or 1 cup plus 2 teaspoons,
* confectioners' sugar*
1 teaspoon (½ cl) vanilla extract

DECORATION

About 2⅔ ounces (75 g), or ½ cup, blanched
 almonds, chopped

FILLING

4 tablespoons (80 g) strained apricot jam
 [*Basic Preparation, page 484*]

For about 30 cookies

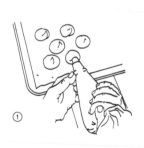

Preheat the oven to 400° F (200° C).

1. Stir about one-third of the egg whites into the almond and sugar powder. Beat the mixture at medium speed in your electric mixer using the flat beater. Add the remaining egg whites 1 teaspoon (½ cl) at a time, beating thoroughly after each addition. Then gradually beat in the vanilla.

2. Scoop the batter into the pastry bag. Pipe a small dab of batter in each corner of all but one baking sheet and line the baking sheets with newsprint, pressing the corners of the newsprint on the dabs of batter to hold it in place. Pipe the batter in domes ¾ inch (2 cm) wide ①, arranging them on the newsprint in staggered rows and separating them by 1 inch (2½ cm).

3. Dust the chopped almonds ② over the domes. Turn each baking sheet upside down and tap it with a wooden spoon to dislodge the excess almonds, then quickly turn the baking sheet right side up again.

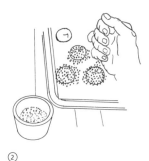

②

③

④

4. One at a time, place each baking sheet of cookies on an empty baking sheet to protect the bottoms, and bake until the cookies turn pale beige on top and the chopped almonds begin to toast lightly, about 9 to 12 minutes.

5. Lift the baking sheet of cookies off the empty baking sheet and take it to the sink. Pour cold water (about ½ cup, or 1.2 dl, per baking sheet) between the paper and the baking sheet (tilting the baking sheet so that the water runs over the entire surface and drains thoroughly into the sink) to steam the cookies off the paper. Then place the baking sheet on a wire rack and let cool.

6. Remove the cookies from the paper before the paper dries. Make a small indentation in the center ③ of the back of each cookie using the tip of your little finger. Turn half of them upside down and spread about ⅜ teaspoon (2½ g) of jam over the depression ④ on the back of each using a small palette knife. Then place a second dome right side up on top of each to make a sandwich.

STORAGE: Covered airtight in a tin cookie box or a cookie jar for up to 3 days.

REICHEMBERGS

REICHEMBERGS

~~~~~~~~~~

Presumably, the odd name for this cookie is a misspelling of Rei-chenberg, the German name for the Czech city Liberec. We have also seen the cookie name spelled as "rechembergs," which is even more peculiar. Whatever the spelling, the Germanic-sounding name is especially incongruous because these cookies are among the lightest and most delicate of the almond petits fours. Lemon-flavored domes are sand-wiched together with raspberry jam and decorated with a sprinkling of sanding sugar. The melodic lemon and raspberry flavor duet, combined with the harmonic underlying taste and texture of the almond cookies, make Reichembergs a graceful complement to afternoon tea or the end of an elegant dinner party.

EQUIPMENT

3 large, heavy baking sheets
- Newsprint cut to fit 2 of them
A large pastry bag fitted with
- a ⁷⁄₁₆-inch (11 mm) plain pastry tube (Ateco #5)

BATTER

2 large egg whites, lightly beaten, at room
    temperature
10 ounces (280 g), or 2 cups plus 1½ tablespoons,
    almond and sugar powder
   Basic Preparation, page 482:
    5 ounces (140 g), or ¾ cup plus 3 tablespoons,
     blanched almonds
    5 ounces (140 g), or 1 cup plus 2½ tablespoons,
     confectioners' sugar

2 teaspoons (1 cl) egg yolk
Finely grated zest of ½ lemon

DECORATION

Sanding sugar (see page 463)

FILLING

5½ tablespoons (110 g) raspberry jam

For about 40 cookies

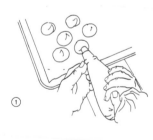
①

1. If the raspberry jam for the filling is at all runny, simmer it gently to reduce the excess liquid. Then cool before using.

Preheat the oven to 400° F (200° C).

2. Stir about half the egg whites into the almond and sugar powder. Beat the mixture at medium speed in your electric mixer using the flat beater. Add the remaining egg whites 1 teaspoon (½ cl) at a time, beating thoroughly after each addition. Then beat in the egg yolk, followed by the lemon zest.

3. Scoop the batter into the pastry bag. Pipe a small dab of batter in each corner of two baking sheets, and line the baking sheets with news-print, pressing the corners of the newsprint on the dabs of batter to hold it in place. Pipe the batter in domes ¾ inch (2 cm) wide ①, arranging them on the newsprint in staggered rows and separating them by 1 inch (2½ cm).

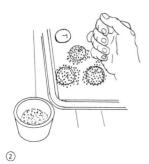

②

③

④

4. Dust the sanding sugar ② over the domes. Turn each baking sheet upside down and tap it with a wooden spoon to dislodge the excess sugar, then quickly turn the baking sheet right side up again.

5. One at a time, place each baking sheet of cookies on an empty baking sheet to protect the bottoms, and bake until the cookies puff up and turn pale beige on top, about 10 to 12 minutes.

6. Lift the baking sheet of cookies off the empty baking sheet and take it to the sink. Pour cold water (about ½ cup, or 1.2 dl, per baking sheet) between the paper and the baking sheet (tilting the baking sheet so that the water runs over the entire surface and drains thoroughly into the sink) to steam the cookies off the paper. Then place the baking sheet on a wire rack and let cool.

7. Remove the cookies from the paper before the paper dries. Make a small indentation ③ in the center of the back of each cookie using the tip of your little finger. Turn half of them upside down and spread about ⅜ teaspoon (2½ g) of jam over the depression ④ on the back of each using a small palette knife. Then place a second dome right side up on top of each to make a sandwich.

➤ **HOWS & WHYS:** Adding a little egg yolk to the batter softens the cookies and makes them dry out less quickly.

STORAGE: Covered airtight in a tin cookie box or a cookie jar for up to 3 days.

AMIENS MACAROONS
MACARONS D'AMIENS

*T*he city of Amiens, in Picardy, is famous for its spectacular thirteenth-century cathedral, considered by many the finest gothic cathedral in France, and for its old-fashioned macaroons. While the nave of the cathedral soars to a height of nearly 140 feet (43 m), Amiens Macaroons are among the richest and heaviest of all macaroons. It is traditional to wrap them individually in foil paper.

EQUIPMENT

2 or 3 large, heavy baking sheets
• Newsprint cut to fit all but one of them

BATTER

10 ounces (280 g), or 2 cups plus 1½ tablespoons, almond and sugar powder

} *Basic Preparation, page 482:*
5 ounces (140 g), or ¾ cup plus 3 tablespoons, blanched almonds
5 ounces (140 g), or 1 cup plus 2½ tablespoons, confectioners' sugar

2 large egg whites
1 tablespoon (20 g) strained apricot jam
  [*Basic Preparation,* page 484]
1 teaspoon (½ cl) vanilla extract

OPTIONAL DECORATION:

16 foil paper wrappers (see page 418), each 5 inches (13 cm) square

For about 16 cookies

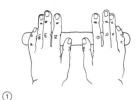
①

②

1. Combine 8 ounces (225 g), or 1½ cups plus 3 tablespoons, of the almond and sugar powder with 1 egg white, the jam, and the vanilla in your food processor, and process (with the feed tube open to let moisture escape) until the almond paste changes from slightly grainy to smooth but still a little dull and warms to between 90 and 100° F (about 35° C), about 2 minutes. It must not be processed too fine. Transfer the almond paste to your countertop and work in the remaining almond and sugar powder with the heel of your hand. Then place it in a storage container, cover airtight, and let rest overnight in the refrigerator.

Preheat the oven to 450° F (230° C).

2. Lightly beat the second egg white. Take out about 2 teaspoons of the almond paste and add just enough of the egg white to form a soft, sticky paste. Put a dab of this paste in each corner of all but one baking sheet, and line the baking sheets with newsprint, pressing the corners of the newsprint on the dabs of almond paste to hold it in place.

3. Place the remaining almond paste on your countertop and roll it under your palms into a cylinder ①. Cut the cylinder in half, and roll each half under your palms into a rope 16 inches (40 cm) long. Cut each rope into 1-inch (2½ cm) lengths. Roll each piece between your palms to shape it into a ball ②, and lay the balls on the prepared baking sheets. Arrange them in staggered rows and separate them by about 1¼ inches (3 cm).

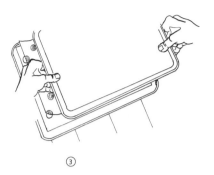

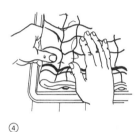

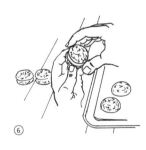

4. Lay a piece of wax paper over the balls on each baking sheet. Place a second baking sheet on top ③ and press gently to flatten the balls to about ⅜ inch (1 cm) thick. Then lift off the second baking sheet and carefully peel off the wax paper.

5. Immediately before baking, lightly moisten the top and sides of each cookie with cold water, either by brushing with a pastry brush or by draping a damp towel ④ over the cookies.

6. One at a time, place each baking sheet of cookies on an empty baking sheet to protect the bottoms, and bake on the top oven rack until the tops of the cookies just begin to brown lightly, about 7 to 9 minutes. (Check at 30-second intervals because these cookies overcook quickly.)

7. Lift the baking sheet of cookies off the empty baking sheet and take it to the sink. Pour cold water (about ½ cup, or 1.2 dl, per baking sheet) between the paper and the baking sheet ⑤ (tilting the baking sheet so that the water runs over the entire surface and drains thoroughly into the sink) to steam the cookies off the paper. Then place the baking sheet on a wire rack and let rest until lukewarm.

8. While the cookies are still warm, remove them from the paper and sandwich them back to back in pairs ⑥.

➤ **HOWS & WHYS:** These macaroons contain sugar and almonds in equal proportions. This makes them very rich. The batter is very dry and can be shaped by hand without using any confectioners' sugar or water to prevent sticking. The cookies are moistened with cold water before baking to prevent the tops from drying too quickly and forming hollow bubbles, and they are baked on the top oven rack to prevent the bottoms from browning and becoming too dry to stick together.

STORAGE: Covered airtight in a tin cookie box or a cookie jar for up to 3 days.

DELICATE MACAROONS
MACARONS FINS

For these macaroons, the proportions of ingredients are identical to those for Abricotines (page 156), except that half the egg whites are replaced by crème fraîche. As for Abricotines, the batter is prepared in the electric mixer, and Delicate Macaroons are quite light for macaroons so rich in nuts. However, despite their similarities, Abricotines are almond petits fours and these are macaroons. Thanks to the butterfat in the crème fraîche, Delicate Macaroons are a little more moist than Abricotines and are sandwiched directly back to back without being filled with apricot jam. When baked, they bubble up around the edges while the top surface remains smooth and shiny—unadorned, as is typical of macaroons—whereas Abricotines are dusted with chopped almonds. The crème fraîche also gives Delicate Macaroons an especially soft and delicate texture.

EQUIPMENT

2 or 3 large, heavy baking sheets
• Newsprint cut to fit all but one of them
A large pastry bag fitted with
• a ½-inch (12 mm) plain pastry tube (Ateco #6)

BATTER

1 large egg white, at room temperature
9 ounces (250 g), or 1¾ cups plus 2 tablespoons, almond and sugar powder
  Basic Preparation, page 482:
  4½ ounces (125 g), or ¾ cup plus 4 teaspoons, blanched almonds
  4½ ounces (125 g), or 1 cup plus 2 teaspoons, confectioners' sugar
2 tablespoons (3 cl) crème fraîche (see Note)
1 teaspoon (½ cl) vanilla extract

For about 25 cookies

Preheat the oven to 425° F (220° C).

1. Stir the egg white into the almond and sugar powder. Beat the mixture at medium speed in your electric mixer using the flat beater. Add the crème fraîche, 1 teaspoon (½ cl) at a time, beating thoroughly after each addition ①. Then beat in the vanilla.

2. Scoop the batter into the pastry bag. Pipe a small dab of batter in each corner of all but one baking sheet, and line the baking sheets with newsprint, pressing the corners of the newsprint on the dabs of batter to hold it in place. Pipe the batter in domes 1 inch (2½ cm) wide ②, arranging them on the newsprint in staggered rows and separating them by 1 inch (2½ cm).

3. Let rest at room temperature for 10 to 15 minutes before baking.

4. One at a time, place each baking sheet of cookies on an empty baking sheet to protect the bottoms, and bake, using a wooden spatula to hold the oven door ajar, until the cookies puff up and the tops are smooth and shiny and have begun to brown lightly, about 8 to 11 minutes.

5. Lift the baking sheet of cookies off the empty baking sheet and take it to the sink. Pour cold water (about ½ cup, or 1.2 dl, per baking

③

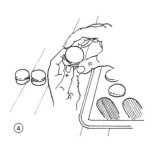

④

sheet) between the paper and the baking sheet ③ (tilting the baking sheet so that the water runs over the entire surface and drains thoroughly into the sink) to steam the cookies off the paper. Then place the baking sheet on a wire rack and let cool.

6. Remove the cookies from the paper before the paper dries, and sandwich them back to back in pairs ④.

➤ **HOWS & WHYS:** Letting the piped batter rest before baking, and leaving the oven door ajar, both help prevent the tops of the cookies from being too soft and fragile.

Using crème fraîche (instead of an equivalent amount of egg white) as part of the liquid in the recipe contributes to the smooth, shiny surface of these macaroons by lowering the water content of the batter (about one-third of the crème fraîche is butterfat) and thus reducing the shrinkage of the surface of the cookies due to evaporation as they bake.

NOTE: The crème fraîche for this recipe can be made at home (see page 491) or be store bought, but it must have a butterfat content close to that of ordinary heavy cream. If it has a very high butterfat content (over 40 percent), it must be thinned with milk in order to provide enough moisture for the batter.

STORAGE: Covered airtight in a tin cookie box or a cookie jar for up to 3 days.

FILBERT MACAROONS
MACARONS AUX AVELINES

ike Amiens Macaroons (page 160) and Delicate Macaroons (page 162), these filbert macaroons have a sugar-to-nut ratio of 1 to 1. However, while Amiens Macaroons are inordinately rich (because of the combination of high almond and low egg white contents), and Delicate Macaroons are unusually light (thanks to replacing half of the egg whites with crème fraîche and beating the batter in the electric mixer), our Filbert Macaroons occupy a middle ground. They are rich and moist, with a hint of cakeyness, and they have a fine-grained, matte surface. With such a high nut content, the filbert taste would be too intense if we used filberts (or hazelnuts) alone. With a mixture of half almonds and half filberts, the filberts still dominate, but the flavor is more refined. A dash of vanilla in the batter brings it into perfect balance.

EQUIPMENT

2 or 3 large, heavy baking sheets
• Newsprint cut to fit all but one of them
A large pastry bag fitted with
• a 7/16-inch (11 mm) plain pastry tube (Ateco #5)

2 large egg whites, 1 of them lightly beaten, at
    room temperature
1 teaspoon (7 g) strained apricot jam
    [*Basic Preparation*, page 484]
½ teaspoon (¼ cl) vanilla extract

BATTER

7¾ ounces (220 g), or 1⅔ cups, hazelnut, almond,
    and sugar powder

Basic Preparation, page 482:
2 ounces (55 g), or ⅓ cup plus 1 tablespoon,
    hazelnuts or filberts
2 ounces (55 g), or ⅓ cup plus ½ tablespoon,
    blanched almonds
3¾ ounces (110 g), or ¾ cup plus 2½ tablespoons,
    confectioners' sugar

For about 25 cookies

①

1. Combine the nut and sugar powder with 1 egg white and the jam in your food processor, and process with the feed tube open to let moisture escape. The mixture should form a soft paste around the side of the bowl, with part of the mass moving around the inside in a soft lump that continually mixes with the rest of the paste. Add part of the second egg white, 1 teaspoon (½ cl) at a time, to get this consistency ①. Then continue processing until the paste changes from dull and slightly grainy to smooth and satiny and warms to between 105 and 115° F (40–45° C), about 4 minutes. Transfer to a bowl and beat in the remaining egg white 1 teaspoon (½ cl) at a time with a wooden spatula. Then beat in the vanilla.

2. Cover the batter airtight and let rest overnight in the refrigerator. *Preheat the oven to 325° F (160° C).*

3. Place the batter in a bowl and beat it with a wooden spatula to soften and smooth it. Scoop the batter into the pastry bag. Pipe a small dab of batter in each corner of all but one baking sheet, and line the baking sheets with newsprint, pressing the corners of the newsprint on the dabs of batter to hold it in place. Pipe the batter in domes 1 inch (2½ cm) wide , arranging them on the newsprint in staggered rows and separating them by 1 inch (2½ cm).

4. One at a time, place each baking sheet of cookies on an empty baking sheet to protect the bottoms, and bake until the tops of the cookies are dry to the touch and spring back when pressed gently with your fingertip, about 15 to 18 minutes. These cookies bake very pale and should show at most a hint of browning on top.

5. Lift the baking sheet of cookies off the empty baking sheet and take it to the sink. Pour cold water  (about ½ cup, or 1.2 dl, per baking sheet) between the paper and the baking sheet (tilting the baking sheet so that the water runs over the entire surface and drains thoroughly into the sink) to steam the cookies off the paper. Then place the baking sheet on a wire rack and let cool.

6. Remove the cookies from the paper before the paper dries, and sandwich them back to back in pairs 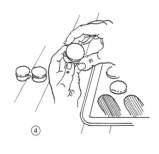.

VARIATION: For a rather different taste, substitute ⅛ teaspoon (a pinch) of ground cinnamon for the vanilla. The filbert-and-cinnamon combination is a classic that has been all but forgotten in France today—so old that it seems new and innovative.

STORAGE: Covered airtight in a tin cookie box or a cookie jar for up to 3 days.

CRACKLED MACAROONS
MACARONS CRAQUELÉS

〰〰〰

The shiny surface of these macaroons is broken up by many fine, irregular cracks. This crackling is typical of a number of macaroons, but here it is emphasized and refined for decorative effect.

Some cookbooks offer this recipe, or one very similar to it, as a shortcut version of Nancy Macaroons (page 174). In fact, the two are quite different in both texture and appearance. Crackled Macaroons have a sugar-to-almond ratio of 1.5 to 1, compared with 2.4 to 1 for Nancy Macaroons, and the batter here includes a little apricot jam rather than the substantial amount of sugar syrup used in Nancy Macaroons. The resulting cookies are richer and chewier than Nancy Macaroons (which have a smooth and shiny surface), and they are regarded as one of the classic macaroons by French pastry chefs.

EQUIPMENT

2 or 3 large, heavy baking sheets
• Newsprint cut to fit all but one of them
A large pastry bag fitted with
• a ½-inch (12 mm) plain pastry tube (Ateco #6)

1¾ ounces (50 g), or ¼ cup, superfine sugar
2 large egg whites, 1 of them lightly beaten at room
    temperature
1 teaspoon (7 g) strained apricot jam
    [*Basic Preparation*, page 484]

BATTER

7 ounces (200 g), or 1½ cups, almond and sugar
    powder
    Basic Preparation, page 482:
    3½ ounces (100 g), or ⅔ cup, blanched almonds
    3½ ounces (100 g), or ¾ cup plus 4 teaspoons,
    confectioners' sugar

For about 16 cookies

1. Combine the almond and sugar powder and the superfine sugar with 1 egg white and the jam in your food processor, and process with the feed tube open to let moisture escape. The mixture should form a soft paste around the side of the bowl, with part of the mass moving around the inside in a soft lump that continually mixes with the rest of the paste. Add part of the second egg white, 1 teaspoon (½ cl) at a time, to get this consistency. Then continue processing until the paste changes from dull and slightly grainy to smooth and satiny and warms to between 105 and 115° F (40–45° C), about 4 minutes. Transfer to a bowl and beat in the remaining egg white 1 teaspoon (½ cl) at a time with a wooden spatula.

2. Cover the batter airtight and let rest overnight in the refrigerator.

3. Place the batter in a bowl and beat it with a wooden spatula to soften and smooth it. Scoop the batter into the pastry bag. Pipe a small dab of batter in each corner ① of all but one baking sheet, and line the baking sheets with newsprint, pressing the corners of the newsprint on the

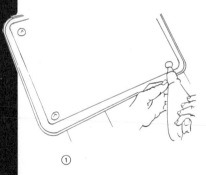

①

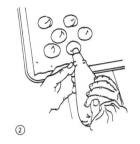
②

③

④

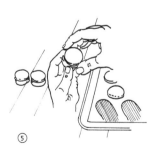
⑤

dabs of batter to hold it in place. Pipe the batter in domes 1½ inch (3½ cm) wide ②, arranging them on the newsprint in staggered rows and separating them by 1¼ inches (3 cm).

4. Let rest at room temperature for about 1 hour before baking. *Preheat the oven to 325° F (160° C).*

5. Immediately before baking, lightly moisten the top and sides of each cookie with cold water, either by brushing with a pastry brush ③ or by draping a damp towel over the cookies.

6. One at a time, place each baking sheet of cookies on an empty baking sheet to protect the bottoms, and bake, using a wooden spatula to hold the oven door ajar, until the cookies are puffed up and the tops are crackled and barely beginning to brown, about 17 to 20 minutes.

7. Lift the baking sheet of cookies off the empty baking sheet and take it to the sink. Pour cold water ④ (about ½ cup, or 1.2 dl, per baking sheet) between the paper and the baking sheet (tilting the baking sheet so that the water runs over the entire surface and drains thoroughly into the sink) to steam the cookies off the paper. Then place the baking sheet on a wire rack and let rest until lukewarm.

8. While the cookies are still warm, remove them from the paper and sandwich them back to back in pairs ⑤.

➤ **HOWS & WHYS:** Moistening the surface of the cookies with cold water and then baking with the oven door ajar produce the characteristic crackled surface of these macaroons.

STORAGE: Covered airtight in a tin cookie box or a cookie jar for up to 3 days.

PISTACHIO MACAROONS
MACARONS AUX PISTACHES

For our taste, these are the most exquisite of all pistachio cookies. They contain a larger proportion of pistachios than do Pistachio Hearts (page 132) and so have a more intense flavor, but at the same time they are lighter and more delicate. The surface is smooth and shiny, domed with a hint of dimpling and a "foot" around the base where the smooth surface lifts off the baking sheet as the cookies rise during baking. Their pale pistachio green color is unmistakable and guaranteed to elicit the classic Pavlovian response in those of us addicted to the slightly erotic flavor of these luxurious nuts.

EQUIPMENT

2 or 3 large, heavy baking sheets
• Newsprint cut to fit all but one of them
A large pastry bag fitted with
• a ½-inch (12 mm) plain pastry tube (Ateco #6)

BATTER

1½ ounces (40 g), or ¼ cup plus ½ tablespoon, unsalted pistachios
2 ounces (60 g), or ⅓ cup plus 1 tablespoon, blanched almonds
5⅔ ounces (160 g), or 1⅓ cups, confectioners' sugar
2 large egg whites, 1 of them lightly beaten, at room temperature
¼ teaspoon (1 ml) vanilla extract

For about 24 cookies

1. Grind the pistachios and almonds with 1¾ ounces (50 g), or ⅓ cup plus 4 teaspoons, of the confectioners' sugar in your food processor, stopping to break up any caking as needed, until finely ground but not at all oily. Sift through a medium sieve. Grind the nuts that don't pass through the sieve with another 1¾ ounces (50 g), or ⅓ cup plus 4 teaspoons, of the confectioners' sugar until reduced to a fine powder. Transfer all of the nut and sugar powder to a bowl, break up any caking with your fingertips, and mix thoroughly.

2. Combine the nut and sugar powder and the confectioners' sugar with 1 egg white in your food processor, and process with the feed tube open to let moisture escape. The mixture should form a soft paste around the side of the bowl, with part of the mass moving around the inside in a soft lump that continually mixes with the rest of the paste. Add part of the second egg white, 1 teaspoon (½ cl) at a time, to get this consistency. Then continue processing ① until the paste changes from dull and slightly grainy to smooth and satiny and warms to between 105 and 115° F (40–45° C), about 4 minutes. Transfer to a bowl and beat in the remaining egg white 1 teaspoon (½ cl) at a time with a wooden spatula. Then beat in the vanilla.

3. Place the batter in a storage container, cover airtight, and let rest overnight in the refrigerator.

Preheat the oven to 325° F (160° C).

①

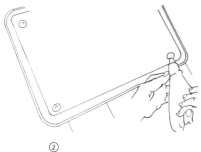

②

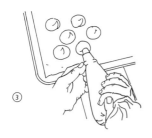

③

④

4. Place the batter in a bowl and beat it with a wooden spatula to soften and smooth it. Scoop the batter into the pastry bag. Pipe a small dab of batter in each corner ② of all but one baking sheet, and line the baking sheets with newsprint, pressing the corners of the newsprint on the dabs of batter to hold it in place. Pipe the batter in domes 1 inch (2½ cm) wide ③, arranging them on the newsprint in staggered rows and separating them by 1 inch (2½ cm).

5. One at a time, place each baking sheet of cookies on an empty baking sheet to protect the bottoms, and bake until the cookies are puffed up and cracked around the base, the tops are smooth, shiny, and still pale green, and the bottoms are barely beginning to brown, about 16 to 18 minutes. The tops of the cookies should spring back when pressed gently with your fingertip.

6. Lift the baking sheet of cookies off the empty baking sheet and take it to the sink. Pour cold water ④ (about ½ cup, or 1.2 dl, per baking sheet) between the paper and the baking sheet (tilting the baking sheet so that the water runs over the entire surface and drains thoroughly into the sink) to steam the cookies off the paper. Then place the baking sheet on a wire rack and let rest until lukewarm.

7. While the cookies are still warm, remove them from the paper and sandwich them back to back in pairs ⑤.

➤ **HOWS & WHYS:** These macaroons are baked at a low temperature to preserve their distinctive green color.

STORAGE: Covered airtight in a tin cookie box or a cookie jar for up to 3 days.

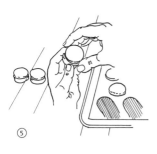

⑤

PARISIAN MACAROONS
MACARONS DE PARIS

~~~

At the turn of the century, these macaroons were ubiquitous in Paris. They are sometimes called macarons mous (Soft Macaroons). Parisian Macaroons have very similar proportions of ingredients to Crackled Macaroons (page 166), but here one-third of the egg whites is made into a meringue, whereas for Crackled Macaroons none of the whites is whipped. As a result, Parisian Macaroons are lighter, more tender, and a little more soft and cakey than Crackled Macaroons. Also, in contrast to the shiny crackled surface of Crackled Macaroons, Parisian Macaroons have a smooth, matte surface, beautifully domed with a little bubbling around the edges.

EQUIPMENT

3 or 4 large, heavy baking sheets
• Newsprint cut to fit all but one of them
A large pastry bag fitted with
• a ⅜-inch (1 cm) plain pastry tube (Ateco #4)

3 large egg whites, 1 of them lightly beaten, at
    room temperature
⅛ teaspoon (½ ml) cream of tartar (optional)

DECORATION

Confectioners' sugar

BATTER

3 ounces (85 g), or ¼ cup plus 3 tablespoons,
    superfine sugar
9½ ounces (270 g), or 2 cups, almond and sugar
    powder

Basic Preparation, page 482:
4¾ ounces (135 g), or ¾ cup plus 2½ tablespoons,
    blanched almonds
4¾ ounces (135 g), or 1 cup plus 2 tablespoons,
    confectioners' sugar

For about 45 cookies

Preheat the oven to 375° F (190° C).

1. Set aside 1 tablespoon (12 g) of the superfine sugar. Combine the almond and sugar powder and the rest of the superfine sugar with 1 egg white in your food processor, and process with the feed tube open to let moisture escape. The mixture should form a soft paste around the side of the bowl, with part of the mass moving around the inside in a soft lump that continually mixes with the rest of the paste. Add part of the second egg white, 1 teaspoon (½ cl) at a time, to get this consistency ①. Then continue processing until the paste changes from dull and slightly grainy to smooth and satiny and warms to between 105 and 115° F (40–45° C), about 4 minutes. Transfer to a bowl and beat in the rest of the second egg white 1 teaspoon (½ cl) at a time with a wooden spatula. Cover the bowl with plastic wrap to prevent drying.

2. Whip the third egg white in an electric mixer at low speed until it starts to froth. If you are not whipping the egg white in a copper bowl, then add the cream of tartar at this point. Gradually increase the whipping

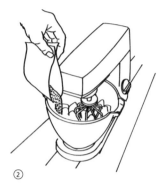

②

③

④

⑤

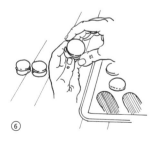

⑥

speed to medium-high, and continue whipping until the white forms very stiff peaks and just begins to slip and streak around the side of the bowl. Add the reserved superfine sugar ② and continue whipping at high speed for a few seconds longer to incorporate the sugar and tighten the meringue.

3. Fold the meringue into the almond paste.

4. Scoop the batter into the pastry bag. Pipe a small dab of batter in each corner of all but one baking sheet, and line the baking sheets with newsprint, pressing the corners of the newsprint on the dabs of batter to hold it in place. Pipe the batter in domes 1 inch (2½ cm) wide ③, arranging them on the newsprint in staggered rows and separating them by 1 inch (2½ cm). Unless you have 2 ovens, pipe only 1 sheet of cookies at a time, and keep the remaining batter in the pastry bag until the first sheet is baked.

5. Dust confectioners' sugar ④ heavily over the cookies. Let them rest for 2 minutes to absorb some of the sugar. Turn the baking sheet upside down and tap the back sharply with a wooden spatula to dislodge the excess sugar, then quickly turn the baking sheet right side up again.

6. One at a time, place each baking sheet of cookies on an empty baking sheet to protect the bottoms, and bake on the top oven rack, using a wooden spatula to hold the oven door ajar, about 10 to 12 minutes. The cookies are done when the bottoms bubble up but the tops are still pale beige and dull, with some white specks of undissolved confectioners' sugar.

7. Lift the baking sheet of cookies off the empty baking sheet and take it to the sink. Pour cold water ⑤ (about ½ cup, or 1.2 dl, per baking sheet) between the paper and the baking sheet (tilting the baking sheet so that the water runs over the entire surface and drains thoroughly into the sink) to steam the cookies off the paper. Then place the baking sheet on a wire rack.

8. Remove the cookies from the paper while they are still warm, and sandwich them back to back in pairs ⑥.

➤ **HOWS & WHYS:** If you find it difficult to meringue 1 egg white, then add an extra egg white and 1 tablespoon (12 g) of superfine sugar to the recipe. Meringue 2 whites with 2 tablespoons (25 g) of sugar, and then add only half of the meringue to the almond paste. Use the remaining meringue for another purpose or discard it.

STORAGE: Covered airtight in a tin cookie box or a cookie jar for up to 3 days.

ORANGE MACAROONS
MACARONS À L'ORANGE

⌇⌇⌇⌇⌇⌇⌇

Finely chopped candied orange peel, which the French call oran-geat, *gives these macaroons a distinctive orange taste and also helps keep them soft and fresh longer. Orange Macaroons are quite different in flavor and texture from the almond petits fours called Mandarins (page 130). While Mandarins are flavored with fresh orange zest and are less sweet, the macaroons contain more egg white and are lighter and more delicate.*

These macaroons can also be made with candied angelica instead of orange peel. In this case they should be dusted with sanding sugar (page 463) and called Niort Macaroons, for the city in western France that claims them as a specialty.

EQUIPMENT

2 or 3 large, heavy baking sheets
• Newsprint cut to fit all but one of them
A large pastry bag fitted with
• a 7/16-inch (11 mm) plain pastry tube (Ateco #5)

2 large egg whites, 1 of them lightly beaten, at
    room temperature
1½ ounces (40 g), or 3½ tablespoons, candied
    orange peel, finely chopped
1½ ounces (40 g), or 3 tablespoons, superfine sugar

BATTER

8 ounces (230 g), or 1½ cups plus 3½ tablespoons,
    almond and sugar powder
{
  Basic Preparation, page 482:
  4 ounces (115 g), or ¾ cup plus 1 teaspoon,
    blanched almonds
  4 ounces (115 g), or ¾ cup plus 3½ tablespoons,
    confectioners' sugar
}

For about 30 cookies

1. Combine the almond and sugar powder with 1 egg white in your food processor, and process with the feed tube open to let moisture escape. The mixture should form a soft paste around the side of the bowl, with part of the mass moving around the inside in a soft lump that continually mixes with the rest of the paste. Add part of the second egg white, 1 teaspoon (½ cl) at a time, to get this consistency. Then continue processing until the paste changes from dull and slightly grainy to smooth and satiny and warms to between 105 and 115° F (40–45° C), about 4 minutes. Add the candied orange peel and process a little longer, scraping down the side of the pro-cessor bowl if necessary, to puree the orange peel. Transfer to a bowl and gradually beat in the remaining egg white 1 teaspoon (½ cl) at a time, alternating with the superfine sugar, using a wooden spatula.

2. Cover the batter airtight and let rest overnight in the refrigerator. *Preheat the oven to 375° F (190° C).*

3. Place the batter in a bowl and beat it with a wooden spatula to soften and smooth it. Scoop the batter into the pastry bag. Pipe a small

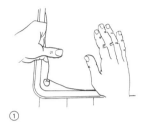

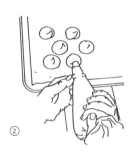

dab of batter in each corner of all but one baking sheet, and line the baking sheets with newsprint ①, pressing the corners of the newsprint on the dabs of batter to hold it in place. Pipe the batter in domes 1 inch (2½ cm) wide ②, arranging them on the newsprint in staggered rows and separating them by 1 inch (2½ cm).

4. One at a time, place each baking sheet of cookies on an empty baking sheet to protect the bottoms, and bake until the cookies are puffed up and the tops are crackled and dry and spring back when pressed gently with your fingertip, about 11 to 13 minutes. They will be very pale, not browned at all.

5. Lift the baking sheet of cookies off the empty baking sheet and take it to the sink. Pour cold water ③ (about ½ cup, or 1.2 dl, per baking sheet) between the paper and the baking sheet (tilting the baking sheet so that the water runs over the entire surface and drains thoroughly into the sink) to steam the cookies off the paper. Then place the baking sheet on a wire rack and let rest until lukewarm.

6. While the cookies are still warm, remove them from the paper and sandwich them back to back in pairs ④.

➤ **HOWS & WHYS:** Pureeing the orange peel with the almond paste gives the macaroons a smoother texture than if the orange peel were just chopped with a chef's knife.

STORAGE: Covered airtight in a tin cookie box or a cookie jar for up to 3 days.

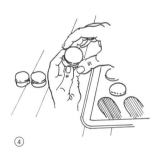

NANCY MACAROONS
MACARONS DE NANCY

~~~~~~

These are the most famous of all macaroons. Whether by stealth or divine intervention, the sisters of the Benedictine order in Nancy, the capital of the dukes of Lorraine, learned the secret of preparing macaroons from the French court in Paris. The convent became well known throughout France for these cookies, and the nuns even devised a windmill for grinding the almonds. When the convents were closed by the revolutionaries in 1793, two of the nuns, Sister Marguerite-Suzanne Gaillot and Sister Elisabeth Morlot, found asylum with the family of a Doctor Gormand at 10 rue de la Hache. To repay the doctor's generosity, they set up a business making macaroons according to the old recipe. Sister Suzanne died, and Sister Elisabeth passed on the recipe to her niece and nephew-in-law, whose name was Muller de Savigny. The Mullers became pastry chefs, and two succeeding generations of Mullers continued baking the cookies at the same address. In 1952, Nancy changed the name of the rue de la Hache to the rue des Soeurs-Macarons (the street of the macaroon sisters).

While the original recipe for Nancy Macaroons remained a closely guarded secret, many pastry chefs have tried to duplicate the result. At the turn of the century, the two great pastry compendiums, Pierre Lacam's Mémorial de la pâtisserie and Darenne and Duval's Traité de pâtisserie moderne, both included recipes which, while differing in the details, were in fairly close agreement on the proportions of ingredients and general method of preparation. The unique feature common to these recipes is the inclusion in the batter of some sugar syrup cooked to the soufflé stage. Our modern method is based on their detective work.

EQUIPMENT

3 or 4 large, heavy baking sheets
- Newsprint cut to fit all but one of them
A large pastry bag fitted with
- a ⁷⁄₁₆-inch (11 mm) plain pastry tube (Ateco #5)

BATTER

9 ounces (250 g), or 1¾ cups plus 2 tablespoons, almond and sugar powder

Basic Preparation, page 482:
 4½ ounces (125 g), or ¾ cup plus 4 teaspoons, blanched almonds
 4½ ounces (125 g), or 1 cups plus 2 teaspoons, confectioners' sugar

2⅔ ounces (75 g), or ½ cup plus 2 tablespoons, confectioners' sugar

3 large egg whites, 2 of them lightly beaten, at room temperature

3½ ounces (100 g), or ½ cup, granulated sugar, moistened with 2 tablespoons (3 cl) water

1 teaspoon (½ cl) vanilla extract

For about 40 cookies

1. Combine the almond and sugar powder and the confectioners' sugar with 1 egg white in your food processor, and process with the feed tube open to let moisture escape. Add some of the remaining egg whites, 1 teaspoon (½ cl) at a time (and about 1 tablespoon, or 1½ cl, altogether), to make the mixture form a soft paste around the side of the bowl, with part of the mass moving around the inside in a soft lump that continually

mixes with the rest of the paste. Continue processing until the paste changes from dull and slightly grainy to smooth and satiny and warms to between 105 and 115° F (40–45° C), about 4 minutes. Pour in the remaining egg whites in a thin stream, then stop the machine. Scrape down the sides of the bowl and pulse the machine a few times to finish mixing. Let rest briefly while you prepare the sugar syrup.

2. Cook the moistened sugar in a small, heavy saucepan or caramel pot to the soufflé stage (230° F or 110° C). Turn on the food processor and pour in the hot syrup ① in a thin stream, then add the vanilla. Stop the machine. Scrape down the sides of the bowl and pulse the machine several times to finish mixing.

3. Transfer the batter to a bowl, cover airtight, and let rest at room temperature for 2 to 3 hours to cool.

Preheat the oven to 375° F (190° C).

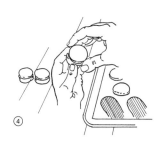

4. Beat the batter with a wooden spatula. Scoop the batter into the pastry bag. Pipe a small dab of batter in each corner of all but one baking sheet, and line the baking sheets with newsprint, pressing the corners of the newsprint on the dabs of batter to hold it in place. Pipe the batter in domes 1 inch (2½ cm) wide ②, arranging them on the newsprint in staggered rows and separating them by 1 inch (2½ cm).

5. One at a time, place each baking sheet of cookies on an empty baking sheet to protect the bottoms, and bake on the top oven rack until the cookies have bubbled up around the edges and the tops are puffed up, smooth, shiny, and very lightly browned, about 10 to 12 minutes.

6. Lift the baking sheet of cookies off the empty baking sheet and take it to the sink. Pour cold water ③ (about ½ cup, or 1.2 dl, per baking sheet) between the paper and the baking sheet (tilting the baking sheet so that the water runs over the entire surface and drains thoroughly into the sink) to steam the cookies off the paper. Then place the baking sheet on a wire rack and let rest until lukewarm.

7. While the cookies are still warm, remove them from the paper and sandwich them back to back in pairs ④.

➤ **HOWS & WHYS:** Adding cooked sugar to the almond paste in this recipe gives the macaroons a smooth, shiny surface and helps keep them soft and fresh.

STORAGE: Covered airtight in a tin cookie box or a cookie jar for up to 3 days.

CHOCOLATE MACAROONS
MACARONS CHOCOLAT

*T*here are many ways to make chocolate macaroons. This recipe is the simplest and at the same time gives delicious, almost fudgy macaroons. Many French pastry chefs like to sprinkle their chocolate macaroons with sanding sugar before baking, and we offer this as an option you may wish to try.

My daughter Charlotte enjoys eating Chocolate Macaroons (preferably sugar dusted) with a glass of cold milk, and truth be told, this combination is equally irresistible to adults.

EQUIPMENT

2 or 3 large, heavy baking sheets
- Newsprint cut to fit all but one of them

A large pastry bag fitted with
- a ½-inch (12 mm) plain pastry tube (Ateco #6)

BATTER

5⅓ ounces (150 g), or 1 cup plus 2 tablespoons, almond and sugar powder

Basic Preparation, page 482:
} 2⅔ ounces (75 g), or ½ cup, blanched almonds
} 2⅔ ounces (75 g), or ½ cup plus 2 tablespoons, confectioners' sugar

2⅔ ounces (75 g), or ¼ cup plus 2 tablespoons, superfine sugar

2 large egg whites, 1 of them lightly beaten

1 tablespoon (20 g) strained apricot jam
   [*Basic Preparation*, page 484]

1 teaspoon (½ cl) vanilla extract

1 ounce (30 g) unsweetened chocolate, melted

OPTIONAL DECORATION

Sanding sugar (see page 463)

For about 25 cookies

1. Combine the almond and sugar powder and the superfine sugar with 1 egg white and the apricot jam in your food processor, and process with the feed tube open to let moisture escape. The mixture should form a soft paste around the side of the bowl, with part of the mass moving around the inside in a soft lump that continually mixes with the rest of the paste. If necessary, add part of the second egg white, 1 teaspoon (½ cl) at a time, to get this consistency ①. Then continue processing until the paste changes from dull and slightly grainy to smooth and satiny and warms to between 105 and 115° F (40–45° C), about 4 minutes. Transfer to a bowl and gradually beat in the the remaining egg white 1 teaspoon (½ cl) at a time with a wooden spatula. Then beat in the vanilla. Quickly stir about ½ cup (1.2 dl) of the batter into the chocolate, then stir the chocolate mixture back into the remaining batter.

2. Cover the batter airtight and let rest overnight in the refrigerator. *Preheat the oven to 400° F (200° C).*

3. Place the batter in a bowl and beat it with a wooden spatula to soften and smooth it. Scoop the batter into the pastry bag. Pipe a small dab of batter in each corner of all but one baking sheet, and line the baking sheets with newsprint, pressing the corners of the newsprint on the dabs

③

④

⑤

of batter to hold it in place. Pipe the batter in domes 1 inch (2½ cm) wide ②, arranging them on the newsprint in staggered rows and separating them by 1 inch (2½ cm).

4. If desired, dust the sanding sugar ③ over the cookies. Turn each baking sheet upside down and tap it with a wooden spatula to dislodge the excess sugar, then quickly turn the baking sheet right side up again.

5. One at a time, place each baking sheet of cookies on an empty baking sheet to protect the bottoms, and bake on the top oven rack until the tops of the cookies are crackled and dry and spring back when pressed gently with your fingertip, about 8 to 10 minutes.

6. Lift the baking sheet of cookies off the empty baking sheet and take it to the sink. Pour cold water ④ (about ½ cup, or 1.2 dl, per baking sheet) between the paper and the baking sheet (tilting the baking sheet so that the water runs over the entire surface and drains thoroughly into the sink) to steam the cookies off the paper. Then place the baking sheet on a wire rack and let rest until lukewarm.

7. While the cookies are still warm, remove them from the paper and sandwich them back to back in pairs ⑤.

➤ **HOWS & WHYS:** If the cookies are not baked on the top oven rack, the bottoms dry out too much and they won't stick together after baking.

STORAGE: Covered airtight in a tin cookie box or a cookie jar for up to 3 days.

DUTCH MACAROONS
MASSEPAINS HOLLANDAIS

Dutch Macaroons are allowed to rest after piping to form a crust, then the crust is slit so that when they bake the slit opens, allowing the batter inside to expand. Some of the batter bubbles up through the slit, and after baking looks porous and dull, while the surface on either side is smooth and shiny. This eruption gives Dutch Macaroons a distinctive appearance. They are also very light and soft inside.

Vanilla is the traditional flavoring for Dutch Macaroons. When the same cookies are flavored with coffee, a purist would call them *hollandais café*. The coffee version has the same distinctive shape with the slit down the center, but it has a richer, caramel color. We offer both the vanilla and coffee flavor options, and for simplicity we refer to them both as Dutch Macaroons.

EQUIPMENT

2 or 3 large, heavy baking sheets
• Newsprint cut to fit all but one of them
A large pastry bag fitted with
• a 7/16-inch (11 mm) plain pastry tube (Ateco #5)

BATTER

5 ounces (140 g), or 1 cup plus 2 teaspoons, almond and sugar powder
Basic Preparation, page 482:
2½ ounces (70 g), or ¼ cup plus 2½ tablespoons, blanched almonds
2½ ounces (70 g), or ½ cup plus 4 teaspoons, confectioners' sugar

5 ounces (140 g), or 1 cup plus 2½ tablespoons, confectioners' sugar
2 large egg whites, 1 of them lightly beaten, at room temperature
Flavorings
½ teaspoon (¼ cl) vanilla extract
or
1½ teaspoons (¾ cl) freeze-dried coffee, dissolved in 1 teaspoon (½ cl) boiling water

For about 18 cookies

1. Combine the almond and sugar powder and the confectioners' sugar with 1 egg white in your food processor, and process with the feed tube open to let moisture escape. Add some of the remaining egg whites, 1 teaspoon (½ cl) at a time (and about 1 tablespoon, or 1½ cl, altogether), to make the mixture form a soft paste around the side of the bowl, with part of the mass moving around the inside in a soft lump that continually mixes with the rest of the paste. Continue processing until the paste changes from dull and slightly grainy to smooth and satiny and warms to between 105 and 115° F (40–45° C), about 4 minutes. Transfer to a bowl and beat in the remaining egg white 1 teaspoon (½ cl) at a time with a wooden spatula. Then beat in the vanilla or coffee.

2. Cover the batter airtight and let rest overnight in the refrigerator.

3. Place the batter in a bowl and beat it with a wooden spatula to soften and smooth it. Scoop the batter into the pastry bag. Pipe a small dab of batter in each corner ① of all but one baking sheet, and line the

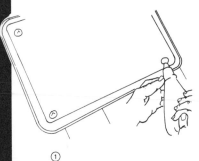

baking sheets with newsprint, pressing the corners of the newsprint on the dabs of batter to hold it in place. Pipe the batter in ovals 1⅝ inches (4 cm) long and ¾ inch (2 cm) wide ②, arranging them on the newsprint in staggered rows and separating them by 1¼ inches (3 cm).

4. Let rest at room temperature for 5 to 8 hours before baking. *Preheat the oven to 375° F (190° C)*.

5. Immediately before baking, slit the top crust of each cookie lengthwise ③ down the center from one end to the other using the tip of a very sharp paring knife (or a razor blade) dipped in cold water as needed to prevent sticking.

6. One at a time, place each baking sheet of cookies on an empty baking sheet to protect the bottoms, and bake on the top oven rack until the cookies are puffed up and a uniform beige (for vanilla) or pale caramel (for coffee) color on top, the slits are split open and the batter that has bubbled up through the slits is dull, porous, and lightly browned, about 11 to 13 minutes.

7. Lift the baking sheet of cookies off the empty baking sheet and take it to the sink. Pour cold water ④ (about ½ cup, or 1.2 dl, per baking sheet) between the paper and the baking sheet (tilting the baking sheet so that the water runs over the entire surface and drains thoroughly into the sink) to steam the cookies off the paper. Then place the baking sheet on a wire rack and let rest until cool.

8. Remove the cookies from the paper before the paper dries, and sandwich them back to back in pairs.

➤ **HOWS & WHYS:** The batter flattens out after piping, but does not spread excessively. It is important that the batter not be too firm or too much of the batter will depart through the slits, leaving the insides hollow. The high sugar content in these cookies makes them very light.

STORAGE: Covered airtight in a tin cookie box or a cookie jar for up to 3 days.

DUTCH CHOCOLATE MACAROONS
MASSEPAINS CHOCOLAT

~~~~~~~

These distinctive cookies are a chocolate version of Dutch Macaroons (page 178). To vary the presentation, Dutch Chocolate Macaroons are piped round, rather than in ovals, and the tops are slit in a cross rather than a single slit. The combination of dry crusty surface enclosing a light and meltingly tender chocolate interior is truly seductive. Don't even think about massepains chocolat if you are short on self-control.

EQUIPMENT

2 or 3 large, heavy baking sheets
• Newsprint cut to fit all but one of them
A large pastry bag fitted with
• a ½-inch (12 cm) plain pastry tube (Ateco #6)

BATTER

4 ounces (120 g), or ¾ cup plus 2½ tablespoons, almond and sugar powder

Basic Preparation, page 482:
   2 ounces (60 g), or ⅓ cup plus 1 tablespoon, blanched almonds
   2 ounces (60 g), or ½ cup, confectioners' sugar

4¼ ounces (120 g), or 1 cup, confectioners' sugar

2 large egg whites, 1 of them lightly beaten, at room temperature

¾ ounce (20 g) unsweetened chocolate, melted

For about 18 cookies

1. Combine the almond and sugar powder and the confectioners' sugar with 1 egg white in your food processor, and process with the feed tube open to let moisture escape. Add some of the remaining egg white, 1 teaspoon (½ cl) at a time (and about 1 tablespoon, or 1½ cl, altogether), to make the mixture form a soft paste around the side of the bowl, with part of the mass moving around the inside in a soft lump that continually mixes with the rest of the paste. Continue processing until the paste changes from dull and slightly grainy to smooth and satiny and warms to between 105 and 115° F (40–45° C), about 4 minutes. Transfer to a bowl and beat in the remaining egg white 1 teaspoon (½ cl) at a time with a wooden spatula. Quickly stir about ⅓ cup (8 cl) of the batter into the melted chocolate. Then stir this chocolate mixture back into the remaining batter.

2. Cover the batter airtight and let rest overnight in the refrigerator.

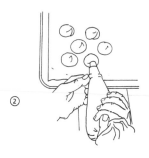

3. Place the batter in a bowl and beat it with a wooden spatula to soften and smooth it. Scoop the batter into the pastry bag. Pipe a small dab of batter in each corner of all but one baking sheet, and line the baking sheets with newsprint ①, pressing the corners of the newsprint on the dabs of batter to hold it in place. Pipe the batter in domes 1¼ inches (3 cm) wide ②, arranging them on the newsprint in staggered rows and separating them by 1¼ inches (3 cm).

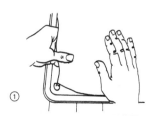

4. Let rest at room temperature for 5 to 8 hours before baking.

THE FRENCH COOKIE BOOK

③

④

Preheat the oven to 375° F (190° C).

5. Immediately before baking, slit the top crust of each cookie across the center from one side to the other using the tip of a very sharp paring knife (or a razor blade) dipped in cold water as needed to prevent sticking. Then make a second slit, perpendicular to the first slit, across the center to form a cross ③.

6. One at a time, place each baking sheet of cookies on an empty baking sheet to protect the bottoms, bake on the top oven rack until the cookies are puffed up, the slits are split open, the batter that has bubbled up through the slits is dull, porous, and dry to the touch, and the surfaces between the slits are smooth and spring back when pressed gently with your fingertip, about 10 to 12 minutes.

7. Lift the baking sheet of cookies off the empty baking sheet and take it to the sink. Pour cold water ④ (about ½ cup, or 1.2 dl, per baking sheet) between the paper and the baking sheet (tilting the baking sheet so that the water runs over the entire surface and drains thoroughly into the sink) to steam the cookies off the paper. Then place the baking sheet on a wire rack and let rest until cool.

8. Remove the cookies from the paper before the paper dries, and sandwich them back to back in pairs.

➤ **HOWS & WHYS:** The batter flattens out after piping, but does not spread excessively. It is important that the batter not be too firm or too much of the batter will depart throught the slits, leaving the insides hollow. The high sugar content in these cookies makes them very light.

STORAGE: Covered airtight in a tin cookie box or a cookie jar for up to 3 days.

CHAPTER 4
SPONGE CAKE
BATTERS

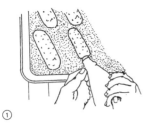

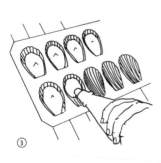

At first glance, ladyfingers, champagne biscuits, *madeleines,* and brownies seem to be a diverse group of cookies. For that matter, you might argue that, with the exception of champagne biscuits, these don't seem much like cookies at all. Ladyfingers and *madeleines* are two very different "tea cakes," and brownies are, well, just brownies. Nonetheless, these four are prototypes of four classic groups of cookies that are all made from sponge cake batters. We use the term *sponge cake* rather loosely here for any cake batter that employs eggs (yolks and whites) as its primary leavening agent. Before we examine the methods for preparing these batters in detail, we elaborate on the four groups of cookies that are related to our prototypes.

Ladyfingers (*biscuits à la cuillère* in French) are piped from a pastry bag in fat finger shapes ① and are not molded. They are light and dry, and since they contain no butter or powdered almonds, they are not at all rich. Other cookies that share these features (but are piped in different shapes) include Ladies' Biscuits, Lemon Biscuits, Milanese Cakes, and Flemish Wands. Like Ladyfingers, Ladies' Biscuits are soft and delicate, whereas most of the others contain higher proportions of sugar and flour and are crisp or crunchy. Lemon Biscuits fall in between in texture, with a crusty exterior and soft interior.

Champagne biscuits ② are always light and dry and never soft. The batters for these cookies are quite similar to those for some of the crisp or crunchy cookies in the ladyfinger family, and they almost never contain butter or powdered almonds. What distinguishes them is that they are molded in long, slender baton or finger shapes. The champagne biscuits include Classic Champagne Biscuits, Strawberry Champagne Biscuits, Langres Biscuits, Labbé Biscuits, Cossack Biscuits, Mexican Biscuits, and Palma Biscuits. There is an oddball in every crowd, and here it is Alicante Biscuits. Made from the same batter as Classic Champagne Biscuits but molded in *barquette* pans, like Lemon Biscuits they are soft inside and crusty outside.

Thanks to Marcel Proust, *madeleines* ③ are probably the most famous French cookie. Like champagne biscuits, cookies of the *madeleine* family are always molded. But unlike champagne biscuits they are always soft, moist, and butter-rich. Some are further enriched with powdered almonds. The diverse shapes used include shells (Madeleines, Commercy Madeleines, and Provençaux), turbans (Visitandines), ovals (Perfect and Saint-Cyriens), gem pans (Little Fruitcakes), *barquettes* (Little English Cakes), and an assortment

④

of *tartelettes* (Nantes Loaves, Friands, Jaconas, and Little Provençal Cakes).

Brownies ④ are the quintessential American bar cookie. They don't seem French at all, and in fact bar cookies of any type are quite uncommon in France. But as with all else gastronomic, when the French do something, they do it right. Our French Brownies (*carrés chocolat*) will hold their own against any American brownie, and the small group of related cookies (Chestnut Squares, Matildas, Success, and Algerian Almond Squares) are also exceptionally good. Obviously cookies of this type are neither piped nor molded, but rather baked in a cake pan and then cut into squares or rectangles (sometimes even diamonds or triangles). Rich in butter and nuts, they are either glazed (with chocolate or apricot jam) or dusted with confectioners' sugar before cutting.

Biscuit is the French word for sponge cake. Its origin goes back at least as far as the thirteenth century, and it derives from the fact that the baked goods to which it was originally applied were cooked (*cuit*) twice (*bis*). Biscuit batters related to the recipes we use today were first developed in France around the beginning of the seventeenth century. However, the cakes made at that time were rather heavy. It was not until the beginning of the eighteenth century, contemporary with the invention of meringue, that chefs began to beat the egg whites and yolks separately to achieve lighter cakes. At around the same time, they began to create sponge cakes enriched by the addition of melted butter. By the end of the nineteenth century, the advent of mechanical whipping machines had made it very easy to prepare a wide variety of light sponge cake batters.

BATTER PREPARATION METHODS

For nearly all sponge cake cookies we use a variation on one of three basic methods to prepare the batter. Let's call them the "separated egg method," the "whole egg method," and the "creamed butter method." For all three we recommend using an electric mixer, preferably a heavy-duty planetary-action model. You can whip the batter by hand if you like, but that is hard work even for the small quantities in our recipes.

SEPARATED EGG METHOD

This is the true sponge cake method. It is used primarily for very light batters that contain eggs, sugar, and flour but little or no butter. There are actually two different procedures that give equivalent results for most batters.

The traditional way is to whip the egg yolks with part of the sugar and to whip the whites separately, then "meringue" the whites with the remaining sugar. The two are folded together, and finally the flour is folded in. This is an unnecessarily cumbersome procedure for most batters.

⑤

⑥

⑦

⑧

⑨

The modern approach is to whip the egg whites and "meringue" them with all of the sugar, then whip in the yolks one at a time, and fold in the flour last. This produces a more consistent and stable batter with less work, so we use it whenever the separated egg method is called for unless (as in Chestnut Squares) the recipe includes a large proportion of ground nuts.

Now let's be more precise. First separate the eggs and be sure they are at room temperature. (The number of yolks used may or may not equal the number of whites.)

Place the egg whites in your electric mixer and start whipping them at low speed to break up the whites. If you have a copper bowl for your mixer, use it; if not, then when the whites start to froth add a little cream of tartar, using ⅛ teaspoon (½ ml) for every three egg whites ⑤. Gradually increase the whipping speed ⑥ to medium-high and continue whipping. When you reach the stiff-but-not-dry stage, the whites will be thick and shiny, cling to the side of the bowl, and form stiff unbending peaks if you lift the whip. As you continue whipping still more, the whites will become firmer, the surface will become a little duller, and the mass of egg whites will begin to slip on the side of the bowl, forming streaks as the wire whip drags it around. With rare exceptions, this slip-and-streak stage is the crucial one to look for. Do not continue to whip the whites after reaching this stage or they will give up too much moisture and become grainy. On the other hand, if you were to stop at the stiff-but-not-dry stage, the batter would be too soft and would spread too much when it baked. (For a more detailed explanation of whipping egg whites, see the introduction to Chapter 2 on Meringue Batters.)

As soon as the mass of egg whites starts to slip and streak around the side of the bowl, pour in the sugar ⑦ (always superfine for sponge cakes) in a steady stream and continue whipping at maximum speed for a few seconds to incorporate the sugar and tighten the meringue. The whites will become more cohesive almost immediately; and if enough sugar is whipped in, it will become shiny and totally smooth. Do not whip more than necessary to incorporate the sugar or the meringue will become too tough. Reduce the mixer to medium-high speed and add the egg yolks ⑧ one right after the other, followed by any liquids called for in the recipe. Stop as soon as the batter is smooth and homogeneous, and remove the bowl from the mixer. Sift the flour, and gently and gradually fold it into the batter ⑨.

Some recipes call for confectioners' sugar in addition to the superfine sugar used to meringue the whites. In that case the confectioners' sugar and flour are sifted and folded in together.

When a small amount of butter is required in the recipe, melt the butter and add it last, folding it in when the flour is almost completely incorporated. The butter should be barely melted and not at all hot.

WHOLE EGG METHOD

The simplest sponge cake method is to whip the whole eggs (or whatever combination of yolks and whites is called for in the recipe) with the sugar until the mixture is cream-colored, thick, and light, then fold in flour and/or cornstarch.

The texture and volume of the resulting batter depend on the proportions of ingredients. In most cases, the whipped egg and sugar mixture will not reach the volume and thickness of the ribbon stage (see later in this section), and the batter will require a larger proportion of flour than a separated egg batter if it is to be piped and hold its shape. The cookies will not be as light as those produced by the separated egg method. The reason is that the presence of fat in the egg yolks makes it more difficult to produce a light, stable foam. (See page 55 in the introduction to Chapter 2 for more details.)

In addition to its simplicity, this method offers the advantages that it can easily accommodate a wide range of proportions of butter as well as other additions such as powdered almonds, and it produces cookies with a fine, tight grain.

Now for the details: As always, the eggs should be at room temperature. Combine the eggs and sugar (it can be superfine or confectioners'), plus almond and sugar powder if any, in your electric mixer. Start beating at low speed with the wire whip, and gradually increase the whipping speed to medium ⑩. (Beating at high speed would make the texture of the cookies coarse.) The batter will become progressively paler and whiter in color and will begin to thicken. At the same time it will gain volume and become light. The color depends on the proportion of yolks as well as optional ingredients such as almond and sugar powder and, of course, food coloring. In most cases the batter will start out yellow and eventually become cream-colored. A few batters will actually become thick enough to form slowly dissolving ribbons ⑪ when dropped from the wire whip, but most will thicken only lightly.

If the recipe calls for a small amount of liquid, beat it in after the batter becomes cream-colored, thick, and light. Then stop beating and remove the bowl from the mixer. Sift the flour and/or cornstarch (occasionally with a little baking powder or ammonium carbonate), and gently and gradually fold them into the batter ⑫. On the other hand, if the recipe requires a large amount of liquid or includes butter, it is better to add the liquid last, folding it in after the flour is almost completely incorporated.

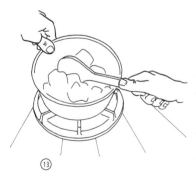

When butter is included in the recipe, it is creamed (by beating with a wooden spatula, warming it over low heat as needed, until smooth, white, and creamy ⑬) and it is added last. The flour and/or cornstarch are sifted and folded into the beaten egg and sugar mixture as usual, and when almost completely incorporated a small portion of this batter is stirred into the creamed butter with any required liquid flavorings. Then the remaining batter is gently folded in. This procedure permits incorporating a large amount of butter without deflating the batter too much.

A few recipes require variations on the whole egg method. For some champagne biscuits, such as Classic Champagne Biscuits and Alicante Biscuits, a thicker batter is required. To get it, you beat the eggs into the sugar one at a time , allowing the mixture to whiten and become thicker and fluffier before adding each succeeding egg. After adding the last egg, continue beating for 12 minutes (in our 4-egg recipe) to make the mixture light and thick enough to form slowly dissolving ribbons when dropped from the wire whip. At the beginning, the mixture of one egg with all of the sugar is quite thick and viscous, and this high viscosity makes it easier to denature the egg proteins. (Remember that the extensional force exerted on the protein molecules by whipping increases as the viscosity increases.) At the same time, whipping incorporates air and the denatured proteins form physical bonds with each other to stabilize the foam, thus increasing the viscosity. Adding the next egg temporarily lowers the viscosity, but as you continue whipping, the viscosity increases again. By keeping the viscosity high, this method makes it possible to denature and cross-link enough egg proteins to overcome the foam-inhibiting effect of the fat in the egg yolks. It produces a light, thick batter and very fine textured cookies.

For Madeleines, beating the eggs and sugar until cream-colored, thick, and light incorporates too much air in the batter and does not produce the requisite humps on the backs of the cookies. So in this case you whip the eggs and sugar only until pale yellow and lightly thickened.

CREAMED BUTTER METHOD

This is not really a sponge cake method but rather the classic pound cake method. We include it with the sponge cakes because the texture of the cookies is very similar to that of butter-rich cookies produced by the whole egg method. Compare, for example, Nantes Loaves (creamed butter method) with Little English Cakes (whole egg method). For these cookies the creamed butter method is easier than the whole egg method and produces a slightly finer and tighter grain. Unfortunately, some cookies are difficult to unmold when the batter is made by the creamed butter method, so we use it only when unmolding will not be a problem.

Before starting the eggs should be at room temperature. Ideally the butter should be softened by letting it warm up to about 60° F (15° C). However it must not be warmer than that or it will melt in the mixing process.

Since the mixer warms the butter as it works, the advantage of using softened butter is speed. If you prefer you can use butter at a cooler temperature (even directly from the refrigerator) to avoid any risk of melting it.

Place the butter in your electric mixer and beat it with the flat beater until smooth, white, and creamy. (Or you can beat the butter with a wooden spatula, warming the butter as needed.) Add the superfine sugar (along with almond and sugar powder if required) and continue beating until smooth and light. Then beat in the first egg, still using the flat beater ⑮ (or wooden spatula). When the first egg is completely incorporated, switch to the wire whip and beat in the remaining eggs ⑯ one by one at medium speed, being sure each egg is completely incorporated and the batter has lightened slightly before adding the next one. When all of the eggs have been added, beat in any flavorings. Then remove the bowl from the mixer and gently and gradually fold in the flour ⑰ (sifted, occasionally, with a little baking powder). (Sometimes if the amount of liquid flavoring is large enough, it is better to add it to the batter after folding in the flour in order not to soften the batter too much.)

(The mechanism by which air is incorporated in the creamed butter batters is somewhat devious. The creamed butter is beaten with the sugar to introduce air bubbles into the mixture. The sugar crystals break up the crystal structure of the butterfat, making way for tiny air cells between the fat crystals. Superfine sugar is preferable to ordinary granulated sugar because it has a larger number of smaller crystals and thus more sharp edges to interrupt the crystals of butterfat; it also dissolves more quickly than ordinary granulated sugar after the eggs are added. When the eggs are whipped in, the air bubbles are transferred from the butter to the liquid phase supplied by the water in the eggs. As whipping continues, still more air is whipped into the batter and egg proteins are denatured and cross-linked, stablizing the foam.)

Notice that this method is almost identical with the method used in Chapter 1 for creamed butter and sugar cookies. Here more air is beaten into the batter and a little baking powder is often included for added lightness; and since the cookies are molded, they do not flatten out and become thin and crisp as they bake. To see just how close the recipes can be, compare the recipe for Nantes Loaves (page 222) with Ladies' Wafers (page 9) in Chapter 1.

The creamed butter method lends itself to an interesting variation that produces a cake well suited to some bar cookies, such as French Brownies and Algerian Almond Squares. Separate some or all of the eggs. Beat the yolks and any remaining whole eggs into the creamed butter and sugar (or sometimes almond and sugar powder) as usual. Whip the egg whites until stiff but not dry. Add the minimum amount of superfine sugar (⅙ ounce or 5 g per egg white) needed to meringue the whites, and whip at high speed for a few seconds longer to incorporate the sugar and tighten the meringue. Sift the flour or cornstarch over the batter and add about a third of the meringue. Stir with a wooden spatula to mix quickly, then gently fold in the remaining meringue. Note that for these batters the whites are only whipped to the stiff-but-not-dry stage because, with such a small amount of sugar, the meringue would not be cohesive enough (and would be difficult to incorporate into the batter) if they were whipped to the slip-and-streak stage. This procedure gives the cookies a very moist, dense, and delicate texture.

COMPOSITE METHODS

A few sponge cake cookies are not made by one of these three general methods but fall somewhere in between. The most notable examples are Commercy Madeleines, Visitandines, and Friands.

FAT IN THE FOAM: A SCIENTIFIC NOTE

Egg foams are stabilized by the egg's protein molecules, which have hydrophobic (water-avoiding) and hydrophilic (having an affinity to water) patches along their lengths. The proteins arrange themselves in the bubble walls so that their hydrophilic parts are in the water and their hydrophobic parts are in the air bubbles. When a whole egg foam is produced either by whipping egg yolks into a meringue or by whipping whole eggs together with sugar from the start, fat globules from the yolk compete with the air bubbles for the hydrophobic parts of the protein molecules, reducing the foam's stability. In sponge cakes, this reduction of stability is offset by including flour or cornstarch in the batter. The starch granules gelatinize, absorbing water and swelling up as the batter bakes. And because the starch molecules do not dissolve in the water, they contribute a solid, structural component to the baked cookies. At the same time, fats coat the protein molecules in the flour and prevent them from combining to form gluten, which would make the cookies tough.

PREPARATION OF MOLDS AND BAKING SHEETS

For sponge cake cookies that are baked directly on the baking sheet, the baking sheet is always either buttered and floured or lined with kitchen parchment.

For molded cookies, the molds are usually buttered or buttered and floured. Always use clarified butter, which more effectively prevents the cookies from sticking to the molds. The butter must be melted but not hot. Coat the insides of the molds generously using a pastry brush ⑱. Any small natural bristle pastry brush will do. Depending on the size and shape of the molds you may prefer a flat style brush between ¾ and 1½ inches (2–4 cm)

⑱

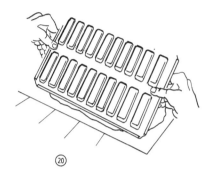

wide or a round style pastry brush about ½ to ⅝ inch (12–16 mm) in diameter.

There should be an even layer of butter on the bottoms and sides of the molds. If the butter pools on the bottoms of the molds, you have used too much or it is too warm. After brushing, allow the butter to set.

To dust individual molds with flour, spoon a little flour into each mold, shake it around to coat the bottom and sides evenly, and then turn it upside down and tap the back sharply with a wooden spatula to dislodge the excess flour ⑲.

For plaques it is often easier to sift a large mound of flour onto a sheet of wax paper on your countertop. Turn the plaque upside down and gently press the insides of the depressions into the flour to coat them ⑳. Repeat, fluffing up the flour as needed, until all the depressions are coated. Then tap the back of the plaque sharply with a wooden spatula to dislodge the excess flour.

If the flour dissolves in yellow patches on the bottoms of the molds, you did not let the butter set sufficiently.

Some molded sponge cake cookies require a different mold preparation, either to facilitate unmolding or to produce a better surface texture. These variations include dusting buttered molds with sliced or chopped almonds (Nantes Loaves and Little Provençal Cakes), brushing the molds with a mixture of browned butter and flour (Commercy Madeleines), and coating the insides of the molds with Vaseline instead of clarified butter. Vaseline is used for Classic Champagne Biscuits because it makes unmolding trivial and it produces a smoother, less porous surface than does clarified butter. Occasionally, Vaseline-coated molds are dusted with cornstarch (see Strawberry Champagne Biscuits). In either case the amount of Vaseline that ends up on the cookies is infinitesimal.

For bar cookies the cake pan is prepared either with butter and flour or with butter and newsprint (or substitute kitchen parchment). In either case, first brush the bottom and sides of the pan with melted butter ㉑ (here it may or may not be clarified) using a medium size (about 1½ to 2 inches or 4–5 cm wide) flat pastry brush.

To dust the inside of the cake pan with flour, scoop some flour into the pan and tilt and shake the pan to coat it evenly ㉒. Turn the pan upside down and tap the bottom sharply with a wooden spatula ㉓ to dislodge the excess flour.

For fragile cakes, unmolding will be easier if you line the bottom of the cake pan with newsprint (the paper on which newspapers are printed, see page 423) or kitchen parchment. Cut a piece of newsprint to size and lay it on the bottom of the buttered pan. Then brush the newsprint with melted butter until it is thoroughly permeated with butter. Newsprint, unlike parchment, absorbs and holds the butter. If you are using parchment, then brush it only lightly with butter. The sides of the cake pan are only buttered and are not lined with newsprint.

PIPING, SPOONING, AND SMOOTHING

For sponge cake cookies baked directly on the baking sheet, the best and easiest way to deposit the batter on the sheet is to pipe it with a pastry bag ㉔. Lemon Biscuits are the only cookies in this group for which an ice cream scoop is a good alternative to the pastry bag.

For molded cookies the best method for depositing the batter in the molds depends on the size and shape of the mold. For all the champagne biscuit family ㉕, which are baked in long, slender molds, and for all cookies baked in *barquettes,* we recommend using a pastry bag in order to distribute the batter evenly. For small cookies baked in *petits fours*–size *tartelette* molds, piping with a pastry bag is by far the most efficient method. But for larger cookies in shell, oval or turban molds, *tartelettes,* or gem pans, it is every bit as convenient to spoon the batter into the molds using a portion control ice cream scoop ㉖ as it is to pipe the batter. In fact, the ice cream scoops make it easier to get the same amount of batter in every mold. The sizes used here are the #50 (4-teaspoon or 2 cl), #40 (5-teaspoon or 2½ cl), and #30 (2-tablespoon or 3 cl) scoops. (See page 418 for details and sources.) Lacking an ice cream scoop, you can scoop the batter into the molds with a large spoon (such as a tablespoon), using your finger to push the batter from the spoon.

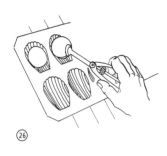

Bar cookies are the easiest. You simply pour and scrape the batter out of the mixing bowl into the cake pan, and spread it evenly. Be careful to smooth the surface so the top will be flat. The best tool for this purpose is the flat edge of a nylon bowl scraper ㉗ (see page 415).

For some sponge cake cookies, you may not have enough molds to accommodate the entire recipe at once. In this event, fill and bake only as many molds as you have. Keep the remaining batter in the pastry bag (or in the bowl, covered, if you are using an ice cream scoop) until the first baking is completed. (Be sure the back end of the pastry bag is closed securely, and prop the pastry bag, tube end up, on your countertop, using a bowl, the wall, or whatever else is convenient to keep it upright.) Then cool and clean the molds and prepare them for baking the rest of the batter.

STORAGE

The storage times for sponge cake cookies vary from a couple of hours to a couple of weeks, depending on their size, shape, texture, and composition. In general, cookies that are smaller, thinner, lighter, softer, unglazed, or contain a higher percentage of butter are more perishable. All of the sponge cake cookies should be stored in as airtight a fashion as possible without damaging their surface. For small cookies, a tin cookie box or a cookie jar with a tight-fitting lid is usually best. For bar cookies, a covered cake platter works well.

The soft sponge cake cookies are quite perishable because the cakelike structure exposes a large interior surface area to the air. They are at their best when freshly made; and, unless the outside surfaces of the cookies are well sealed, they will dry and go stale quickly. The problem is compounded because the thin and delicately crusty surface characteristic of many of these cookies quickly becomes soft and limp in a sealed storage container. Madeleines, for example, are small and poorly sealed, contain a high proportion of butter, and have an exquisitely crusty surface; they are at their peak for a couple of hours at most. (In fact, some of the best pastry shops in France do not sell *madeleines* because they got fed up with complaints that *madeleines* baked only two or three hours earlier were already stale.) Similar cookies that have the top surface sealed by glazing (such as Little English Cakes) and cookies that contain no butter (such as Ladies' Biscuits) can be good for up to two or three days. Bar cookies will also last a few days before they are cut and separated; but after they are separated, the side edges are not sealed at all and so they dry and go stale quickly.

The least perishable sponge cake cookies are those that contain no butter and are dry and crisp or crunchy. Most champagne biscuits and some of the ladyfinger family (such as Milanese Cakes and Flemish Wands) will keep easily for up to two weeks, possibly even longer. On the other hand, cookies made from the same type of batter but baked in such a way that they remain soft inside (for example, Lemon Biscuits and Alicante Biscuits) are as perishable as Madeleines because their unique and appealing soft interior becomes hard and stale very quickly.

LADYFINGERS
BISCUITS À LA CUILLÈRE

These sponge cake cookies have been around for a long time. The French call them biscuits à la cuillère *because, up until the nineteenth century, the batter was deposited on the baking sheet with a spoon (cuillère in French). Originally they were shaped in rounds. The distinguished statesman (and gastronome) Charles Maurice de Talleyrand Périgord liked to dip them in Madeira. He asked his pastry chef, who was none other than the young Carême, if he could adjust the shape to make dunking easier. In response, Carême devised a technique (still using spoons) for forming the rather stubby, unladylike shape that is traditional to this day.*

The pastry bag (which came into use only a few years after Carême's innovation) makes it possible to produce uniform fingers quickly and easily. Freshly baked, our Ladyfingers are light, soft, and delicate morsels, with a hint of orange flower water—totally unrelated to the marginally edible packaged ladyfingers we see on supermarket shelves. In France, they are often served with a glass of good wine as a restorative to the sick or elderly—a practice many healthy people indulge in as well. Paul also recommends serving them with strawberries in wine or a fruit salad as a refreshing way to soak up the liqueur, and with Snow Eggs (oeufs à la neige) for dipping in the custard. If your Ladyfingers somehow survive their ephemeral peak of freshness, you can use them to line the outside of a charlotte russe.

EQUIPMENT

2 large, heavy baking sheets
- Brush with melted butter.
- Dust with flour.

A large pastry bag fitted with
- an 1¹⁄₁₆-inch (18 mm) plain pastry tube (Ateco #9)

¼ teaspoon (1 ml) orange flower water
2⅔ ounces (75 g), or ½ cup plus 2 teaspoons, all-purpose flour

DECORATION

Confectioners' sugar

BATTER

3 large eggs, separated, at room temperature
⅛ teaspoon (½ ml) cream of tartar (optional)
2⅔ ounces (75 g), or ¼ cup plus 2 tablespoons, superfine sugar

For about 35 ladyfingers

Preheat the oven to 400° F (200° C).

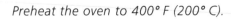

1. Whip the egg whites in an electric mixer at low speed until they start to froth. If you are not whipping the whites in a copper bowl, then add the cream of tartar at this point. Gradually increase the whipping speed to medium-high, and continue whipping until the whites form very stiff peaks and just begin to slip and streak around the side of the bowl. Add the superfine sugar and continue whipping at high speed for a few seconds longer to make the meringue smooth and shiny. Then reduce the speed to medium-high and whip in the egg yolks one at a time ①, followed by the

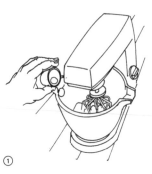

①

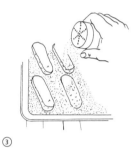

orange flower water. Stop as soon as the batter is homogeneous. Sift the flour and gently fold it into the batter.

2. Scoop the batter into the pastry bag, and pipe the batter on the diagonal in fingers 1 inch (2½ cm) wide and 3 inches (8 cm) long ②, arranging them on the baking sheets in staggered rows and separating them by 1 to 1½ inches (2½–3½ cm).

3. Dust confectioners' sugar over the Ladyfingers ③ on 1 baking sheet until the surface of the batter is white. Wait until the sugar dissolves, about 2 minutes, then dust with confectioners' sugar a second time. Turn the baking sheet upside down and tap the back sharply with a wooden spatula to dislodge the excess sugar ④, then quickly turn the baking sheet right side up again.

4. Place the baking sheet in the oven and splash some water on the oven floor. Bake until the Ladyfingers are a light beige and crusty outside, but still soft inside and not dry, about 9 to 12 minutes.

5. Place the baking sheet on a wire rack and allow the Ladyfingers to cool on the baking sheet. Meanwhile, if you have not yet baked both sheets of Ladyfingers, repeat steps 3 through 5 with the second sheet.

➤ **HOWS & WHYS:** The batter is piped with a very large pastry tube in order to get thick fingers without deflating it. Apply only gentle pressure to the pastry bag and be careful not to make the fingers too wide.

Dusting the piped batter with sugar, then splashing water on the oven floor as you begin baking, gives the tops of the Ladyfingers a pearly appearance.

STORAGE: Covered airtight in a tin cookie box, with as little air space between them as possible, for up to 2 or 3 days. Best eaten the day they are made.

LADIES' BISCUITS
PALAIS DE DAMES

With so many desserts in their collective repertoire, it is no surprise that French pastry chefs occasionally use the same name for more than one of them.
In this case, palets de dames *(page 9)* are thin, crisp cookies that are one of the prototypes
of the creamed butter and sugar cookies of Chapter 1, whereas the totally different palais
de dames *are very light, soft sponge cakes that are similar to Ladyfingers in texture but are
round and glazed on the flat side with apricot jam and a brushing of confectioners' sugar
and water.*

But wait, you say. Why do we consider the names palets de dames *and* palais de
dames *identical when, though pronounced the same, they are spelled differently? Simple.
The traditions of French pastry were handed down verbally from generation to generation
of chefs. When the recipes were finally recorded, two different words emerged depending
on what each chef assumed he had heard. We believe that the correct spelling is invariably*
palets, *except for cookies such as* palais de boeuf *("beef palates," a very rustic flaky pastry
cookie) where the meaning is obviously "palate." We have spelled this cookie as* palais de
dames *purely to avoid confusion with the classic* palets de dames *and to give us an excuse
to tell you this bit of the history of French pastry.*

EQUIPMENT

3 large, heavy baking sheets
- Brush with melted butter.
- Dust with flour.

A large pastry bag fitted with
- a ⅝-inch (16 mm) plain pastry tube (Ateco #8)

BATTER

4½ ounces (125 g), or ½ cup plus 2 tablespoons,
    superfine sugar
1 vanilla bean

3 large eggs, separated, at room temperature
⅛ teaspoon (½ ml) cream of tartar (optional)
3 ounces (85 g), or ½ cup plus 2 tablespoons,
    all-purpose flour

GLAZE

3 tablespoons (60 g) strained apricot jam
    [*Basic Preparation,* page 484]
4 ounces (115 g), or ¾ cup plus 3 tablespoons,
    confectioners' sugar
½ teaspoon (¼ cl) vanilla extract

For about 55 cookies

Preheat the oven to 325° F (160° C).

1. Mix the sugar with ¼ cup (6 cl) cold water. Slit the vanilla bean
lengthwise, scrape out the seeds, and add both seeds and pod to the sugar.
Cook to the large thread stage (217° F or 103° C). Remove the vanilla pod.

2. Meanwhile, whip the egg whites in an electric mixer at low speed
until they start to froth. If you are not whipping the whites in a copper
bowl, then add the cream of tartar at this point. Gradually increase the
whipping speed to medium-high, and continue whipping until the whites
form very stiff peaks and just begin to slip and streak around the side of
the bowl. Gradually pour in the syrup in a steady stream ① and continue
whipping at high speed just long enough to make the meringue smooth
and shiny. Then reduce the speed to medium-high and whip in the egg

①

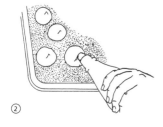

yolks one at a time. Stop as soon as the batter is homogeneous. Sift the flour and gently fold it into the batter.

3. Scoop the batter into the pastry bag, and pipe the batter in domes 1½ inches (4 cm) wide ②, arranging them on the baking sheets in staggered rows and separating them by 1 inch (2½ cm).

4. Bake, 1 sheet at a time, until the bottoms of the cookies are lightly browned and the tops are pale beige and dry to the touch, about 19 to 22 minutes.

5. Place the baking sheet on a wire rack, and let the cookies cool on the baking sheet.

6. Warm the apricot jam over low heat, stirring occasionally, until melted. Brush the flat side of each cookie with jam ③ until lightly coated and glistening, then lay the cookies flat side up on your countertop.

7. Sift the confectioners' sugar into a small bowl, and stir in the vanilla and enough cold water to make a smooth, creamy paste that is just fluid enough to spread easily with a a pastry brush. Lightly brush this sugar glaze over the jam ④ on the flat side of each cookie, then let the glaze set.

➤ **HOWS & WHYS:** Here hot sugar syrup, rather than superfine sugar, is used to meringue the egg whites. This makes the batter lighter and gives the cookies a soft, light, and slightly chewy texture.

STORAGE: Let the glaze on the cookies dry thoroughly (for several hours) so they don't stick together. Then keep covered airtight in a cookie jar or tin cookie box for up to 3 or 4 days.

LEMON BISCUITS
BISCUITS CITRON

These sponge cakes are totally different from the very soft and tender Ladyfingers (page 194). Lemon Biscuits are round, with flat tops and a dusting of confectioners' sugar. They are piped the day before baking to allow the surface to dry. After baking, they are crusty outside, but soft inside. Try them with a cup of dark, rich black coffee such as café filtré or espresso.

EQUIPMENT

2 or 3 large, heavy baking sheets
- Brush with melted butter.
- Dust with flour.
A large pastry bag fitted with
- a ⅝-inch (16 mm) plain pastry tube (Ateco #8)

BATTER

4¾ ounces (135 g), or ⅔ cup, superfine sugar
2 large eggs, at room temperature
Finely grated zest of ½ lemon
5⅔ ounces (160 g), or 1 cup plus 2½ tablespoons, all-purpose flour

DECORATION

Confectioners' sugar

For about 30 cookies

1. Combine the superfine sugar, eggs, and lemon zest in your electric mixer and beat with the wire whip, starting at low and gradually increasing to medium speed, until cream-colored, thick, and light. Sift the flour and gently fold it into the batter.

2. Scoop the batter into the pastry bag, and pipe the batter in domes 1½ inches (4 cm) wide ①, arranging them on the baking sheets in staggered rows and separating them by 1½ inches (4 cm). (Or, spoon the batter in 4-teaspoon (2 cl) domes using a #50 ice cream scoop.) Dust the domes heavily with confectioners' sugar ②. Then gently press the top of each (with the bottom of the dredge ③, if you are using one; otherwise with the bottom of a soup can) to flatten and enlarge it to about 2 inches (5 cm) in diameter.

3. Turn each baking sheet upside down and tap the back sharply with a wooden spatula to dislodge the excess sugar, then quickly turn the baking sheet right side up again. Let the piped batter rest overnight at room temperature.

Preheat the oven to 400° F (200° C).

4. Bake, 1 sheet at a time, until the bottoms of the cookies are browned and the tops are medium beige, about 7 to 10 minutes. Slide the cookies onto a wire rack using a metal spatula and let them cool to room temperature.

VARIATION: Russian Biscuits (*biscuits russes*) are made from the same batter as Lemon Biscuits, but they are piped in fingers instead of rounds, and they are dusted with crystal sugar instead of confectioners' sugar. In step 2, use a ½-inch (12 mm) plain pastry tube (Ateco #6) to pipe

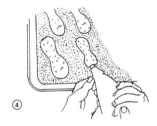

the batter ④ in fingers 3½ inches (8 cm) long and ½-inch (12 mm) wide at the center. Both ends of each finger should be fatter than the center, like a dumbbell. Dust the fingers heavily with crystal sugar ⑤. Then gently press the top of each with the bottom of a *barquette* mold ⑥ to flatten and enlarge it slightly. Proceed with steps 3 and 4 of the recipe. The cookies are finished baking when they are pale beige on top.

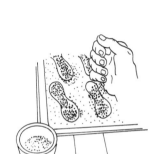

Because they are long and narrow, Russian Biscuits dry out quickly in the oven. The baked cookies are dry and crisp throughout, in contrast to Lemon Biscuits, which are round and wide and retain their soft interiors.

STORAGE: Covered airtight in a cookie jar or tin cookie box. Lemon biscuits are best eaten within 1 day; after that they dry out and become hard. Russian Biscuits will keep for up to 1 week.

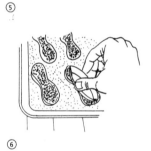

MILANESE CAKES
GÂTEAUX DE MILAN

The batter for these large, round cookies is similar to that for Lemon Biscuits (page 198). Here a little ammonium carbonate or baking powder is included, the lemon flavoring is omitted, and the piped batter is not allowed to rest overnight before baking. As a result, Milanese Cakes are lighter and more delicate. A dusting of sparkling crystal sugar on top adds to the crunch of their dry interiors. Serving them with tea would be canonical, but because their taste is relatively neutral they can equally well accompany a cup of barely sweetened hot cocoa or strong black coffee, where their sweetness and texture would be a felicitous foil to the intensity and bitterness of the beverage.

EQUIPMENT

2 or 3 large, heavy baking sheets
• Brush edges and diagonals with melted butter.
• Line with kitchen parchment.
A large pastry bag fitted with
• a ⅝-inch (16 mm) plain pastry tube (Ateco #8)

BATTER

4½ ounces (125 g), or ½ cup plus 2 tablespoons, superfine sugar
2 large eggs, at room temperature
6 ounces (170 g), or 1 cup plus 3½ tablespoons, all-purpose flour
¾ teaspoon (4 ml) ammonium carbonate, or substitute 1 teaspoon (4 g) baking powder

DECORATION

Crystal sugar

For about 30 to 35 cookies

Preheat the oven to 450° F (230° C).

1. Combine the sugar and eggs in your electric mixer and beat with the wire whip, starting at low and gradually increasing to medium speed, until cream-colored, thick, and light. Sift together the flour and ammonium carbonate or baking powder and gently fold them into the batter.

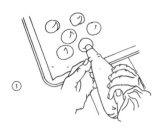

2. Scoop the batter into the pastry bag, and pipe the batter ① in domes 1½ inches (4 cm) wide, arranging them on the baking sheets in staggered rows and separating them by 1½ inches (4 cm).

3. Dust crystal sugar ② over the piped batter. Turn each baking sheet upside down and tap the back sharply with a wooden spatula to dislodge the excess sugar, then quickly turn it right side up again.

4. Bake, 1 sheet at a time, until the cookies are lightly browned, about 8 to 10 minutes.

5. Place the baking sheet on a wire rack and let the cookies cool on the baking sheet.

STORAGE: Covered airtight in a cookie jar or tin cookie box for up to 2 weeks.

FLEMISH WANDS
BAGUETTES FLAMANDES

Flavored with vanilla and topped with chopped almonds, these baton-shaped cookies are the sweetest, lightest, and crispest of the ladyfinger family. The legendary French chef Henri-Paul Pellaprat, whose teaching at Le Cordon Bleu in Paris and books on both French cuisine and pastry enlightened an entire generation of cooks, described Flemish Wands as ''excellent with tea.'' We think they are also quite nice served with a raspberry sorbet.

EQUIPMENT

2 or 3 large, heavy baking sheets
- Brush edges and diagonals with melted butter.
- Line with kitchen parchment.
A large pastry bag fitted with
- a ½-inch (12 mm) plain pastry tube (Ateco #6)

BATTER

6 ounces (175 g), or ¾ cup plus 2 tablespoons, superfine sugar
2 large eggs, at room temperature
1 teaspoon (½ cl) vanilla extract
6 ounces (170 g), or 1 cup plus 3½ tablespoons, all-purpose flour

DECORATION

5½ ounces (150 g), or 1 cup, blanched almonds, chopped

For about 35 to 40 cookies

Preheat the oven to 400° F (200° C).

1. Combine the sugar and eggs in your electric mixer and beat with the wire whip, starting at low and gradually increasing to medium speed, until cream-colored, thick, and light. Beat in the vanilla. Sift the flour and gently fold it into the batter.

2. Scoop the batter into the pastry bag, and pipe the batter ① on the diagonal in batons 4 inches (10 cm) long and ⅝ inch (16 mm) wide, arranging them on the baking sheets in staggered rows and separating them by 1 inch (2½ cm).

3. Dust chopped almonds ② over the piped batter. Turn each baking sheet upside down and tap the back sharply with a wooden spatula to dislodge the excess almonds, then quickly turn the baking sheet right side up again.

4. Bake, 1 sheet at a time, until the tops of the cookies are pale beige and dry to the touch, and the almonds are lightly browned, about 11 to 14 minutes. The cookies flatten out and crack lengthwise ③ as they bake.

5. Place the baking sheet on a wire rack and let the cookies cool on the baking sheet.

STORAGE: Covered airtight in a cookie jar or tin cookie box for up to 2 weeks.

CLASSIC CHAMPAGNE BISCUITS
BOUDOIRS

Also called biscuits de reims *(after the city in the Champagne district), these dry, baton-shaped cookies are baked in special molds and traditionally served with champagne. A* boudoir *is a lady's private sitting room where she would enter-tain (and perhaps seduce) male guests. The appropriate beverage on such occasions would be champagne, which may be the reason such a risqué name is attached to a fairly austere cookie.*

A large variety of cookies has developed around this prototype. Since they are dry and store very well, packaged versions that are produced industrially have taken over the mar-ket and few pastry shops make them fresh. Not surprisingly, the packaged varieties often leave something to be desired, so if you serve champagne (whether in the boudoir *or the dining room), making champagne biscuits at home is definitely worthwhile.*

EQUIPMENT

3 champagne biscuit plaques stamped with 20 rectangular depressions, each 4¼ inches (11 cm) long and 1 inch (2½ cm) wide
• Melted Vaseline
A large pastry bag fitted with
• a ⁷⁄₁₆-inch (11 mm) plain pastry tube (Ateco #5)
1 large, heavy baking sheet

BATTER

9 ounces (250 g), or 1¼ cups, superfine sugar
4 large eggs, at room temperature
9½ ounces (270 g), or 1¾ cups plus 3 tablespoons, all-purpose flour
1½ teaspoons (¾ cl) vanilla extract

DECORATION

Superfine sugar

For 60 cookies

①

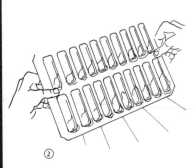

②

Preheat the oven to 350° F (175° C).

1. Heat one champagne biscuit plaque in the oven. Deposit a pool of melted Vaseline in each depression ① in the hot plaque using a pastry brush. Tilt the plaque to coat the bottom and sides of each depression ② with Vaseline. Pour out the excess, and turn the plaque upside down on a wire rack to finish draining while it cools. Repeat with the remaining plaques.

2. Combine the sugar with 1 egg in your electric mixer and beat at medium speed with the wire whip until the mixture whitens and the grain of the sugar begins to disappear. Add a second egg and continue beating until the mixture whitens and becomes fluffy. Add a third egg and beat until the mixture whitens and becomes fluffy again. (Allow 2 to 3 minutes of beating before adding each successive egg.) Add the fourth egg and beat for 12 minutes longer. When finished, the mixture will be light and fluffy and will form slowly dissolving ribbons when dropped from the wire whip. Sift the flour and gently fold it into the batter. When the flour is almost completely incorporated, add the vanilla and continue folding until completely mixed.

Meanwhile, raise the oven temperature to 400° F (200° C).

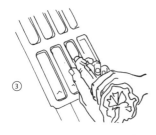

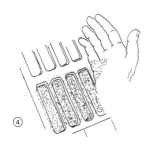

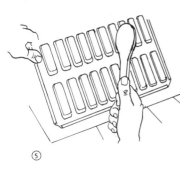

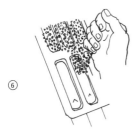

3. Scoop the batter into the pastry bag, and pipe a ½-inch (12 mm) wide band of batter down the center of each depression ③ in the plaques. Dust with superfine sugar ④ and let rest for about 1 minute. Turn each plaque upside down, tap the back sharply with a wooden spatula ⑤ to dislodge the excess sugar, then quickly turn the plaque right side up again. (If you don't have enough plaques for an entire recipe, keep the remaining batter in the pastry bag until the first baking is completed.)

4. One at a time, place each plaque on the baking sheet and bake until the biscuits turn a uniform beige on the tops and edges, about 14 to 19 minutes.

5. Slide the plaque onto a wire rack and let the cookies cool in the plaque. When cool enough to handle but still very warm, carefully lift the cookies out of the plaque and let them finish cooling on the wire rack.

VARIATION: Almond Champagne Biscuits (*biscuits aux amandes*) are identical to Classic Champagne Biscuits except for the decoration. Instead of dusting with superfine sugar in step 3, dust chopped almonds over the molded batter ⑥. Turn each plaque upside down, tap the back sharply with a wooden spatula to dislodge the excess almonds, then quickly turn the plaque right side up again. Next, lightly dust with confectioners' sugar ⑦ and let rest for about 2 minutes. Turn each plaque upside down once more, tap the back sharply with a wooden spatula to dislodge the excess sugar, then quickly turn the plaque right side up again. Bake, cool, and unmold as for Classic Champagne Biscuits.

➤ **HOWS & WHYS:** If the cookies are beige on top but still pale yellow on the edges, they are underbaked and will be pale on the bottoms and not dry inside. On the other hand, if the edges are darker than the tops, the cookies are overbaked and the bottoms will be too dark.

Dusting the biscuits with sugar before baking gives the tops a smooth, matte, nonporous surface.

STORAGE: Covered airtight in a cookie jar or tin cookie box for up to 2 weeks.

STRAWBERRY CHAMPAGNE BISCUITS
BISCUITS ROSETTE

This intriguing variation on the champagne biscuit theme has a subtle strawberry taste accented with a hint of kirsch. The flavor is elusive until you learn that it is strawberry, and then it seems so obvious that you wonder how you could fail to identify it. The strawberries give the cookies a rosy color, which accounts for their name.

EQUIPMENT

3 champagne biscuit plaques stamped with 20 rectangular depressions, each 4¼ inches (11 cm) long and 1 inch (2½ cm) wide
- Melted Vaseline
- Cornstarch

A large pastry bag fitted with
- a ⁷⁄₁₆-inch (11 mm) plain pastry tube (Ateco #5)

1 large, heavy baking sheet

BATTER

1½ ounces (40 g) fresh strawberries
1 tablespoon (1½ cl) kirsch
4½ ounces (125 g), or 1 cup plus 2 teaspoons, confectioners' sugar

2 large eggs, at room temperature
1 large egg yolk, at room temperature
1 teaspoon (½ cl) vanilla extract
Red food coloring
3½ ounces (100 g), or ⅔ cup plus 1 tablespoon, all-purpose flour
1¾ ounces (50 g), or ¼ cup plus 2 tablespoons, cornstarch
¼ teaspoon (1 ml) baking powder

DECORATION

Superfine sugar

For 50 cookies

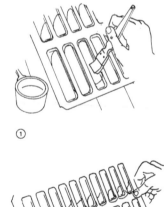
①

②

Preheat the oven to 350° F (175° C).

1. Heat one champagne biscuit plaque in the oven. Deposit a pool of melted Vaseline in each depression ① in the hot plaque using a pastry brush. Tilt the plaque to coat the bottom and sides of each depression ② with Vaseline. Pour out the excess, and turn the plaque upside down on a wire rack to finish draining while it cools. Repeat with the remaining plaques.

2. Scoop a mound of cornstarch onto a sheet of wax paper. Turn each plaque upside down and gently press the depressions in the plaque into the cornstarch ③ to coat them. (Fluff up the cornstarch as needed.) Then tap the back sharply with a wooden spatula to dislodge the excess cornstarch.

Raise the oven temperature to 400° F (200° C).

3. Brush the strawberries to remove any sand and hull them. Puree the berries with the kirsch in your electric blender, then strain through a fine sieve.

4. Sift the confectioners' sugar and combine it with the strawberry puree, eggs, yolk, and vanilla in your electric mixer. Add a drop or two of red food coloring to reinforce the strawberry color. Beat with the wire whip,

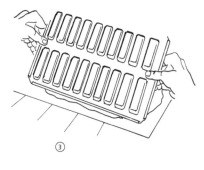

③

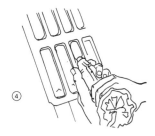

④

⑤

⑥

starting at low and gradually increasing to medium speed, until the batter is light and thick and forms slowly dissolving ribbons when dropped from the whip. Sift together the flour, cornstarch, and baking powder and gently fold them into the batter.

5. Scoop the batter into the pastry bag, and pipe a ⅝-inch (16 mm) wide band of batter down the center of each depression ④ in the plaques. Dust with superfine sugar ⑤. Let rest for 1 minute. Turn each plaque upside down and tap the back sharply with a wooden spatula ⑥ to dislodge the excess sugar, then quickly turn the plaque right side up again. (If you don't have enough plaques for an entire recipe, keep the remaining batter in the pastry bag until the first baking is completed.)

6. One at a time, place each plaque on the baking sheet and bake until the cookies are dry and firm to the touch and are a uniform rosy beige on the tops and edges, about 14 to 18 minutes.

7. Slide the plaque onto a wire rack and let the cookies cool in the plaque. When cool enough to handle, but still very warm, carefully lift the cookies out of the plaque and let them finish cooling on the wire rack.

➤ **HOWS & WHYS:** Dusting the biscuits with sugar before baking gives the tops a smooth, matte, nonporous surface.

STORAGE: Covered airtight in a cookie jar or tin cookie box for up to 1 week.

LANGRES BISCUITS
BISCUITS DE LANGRES

Located just north of Dijon and south of Champagne, Langres was the birthplace of the great eighteenth-century philosopher, critic, and encyclopedist Denis Diderot. It is situated on a high promontory (the Langres Plateau) and from the ramparts surrounding the town there is a panoramic view of the valley of the Marne, the Côte d'Or, and the Vosges mountains with (on a clear day) Mont Blanc visible 160 miles (260 km) in the distance. The source of the river Seine is only a few miles away.

Langres Biscuits are champagne biscuits flavored with finely chopped candied orange peel (which the French call orangeat) and have an exceptionally fine, tight grain. Unlike many of the other champagne biscuits, they are not dusted with sugar before baking, and as a result they have a slightly porous top surface.

EQUIPMENT

2 champagne biscuit plaques stamped with 20 rectangular depressions, each 4¼ inches (11 cm) long and 1 inch (2½ cm) wide
• Clarified butter, melted
A large pastry bag fitted with
• a ½-inch (12 mm) plain pastry tube (Ateco #6)
1 large, heavy baking sheet

BATTER

1 ounce (25 g), or 2 tablespoons, candied orange
   peel
5½ ounces (150 g), or 1 cup plus 4 teaspoons,
   all-purpose flour
1½ ounces (40 g), or ⅓ cup, confectioners' sugar
3 large eggs, separated, at room temperature
⅛ teaspoon (½ ml) cream of tartar (optional)
3½ ounces (100 g), or ½ cup, superfine sugar

For 40 cookies

①

②

1. Brush the depressions in the champagne biscuit plaques with clarified butter ①.

Preheat the oven to 350° F (175° C).

2. Combine the candied orange peel with 2 tablespoons (15 g) of the flour and chop it very fine with your chef's knife. Sift the remaining flour with the confectioners' sugar, then toss with the chopped orange peel.

3. Whip the egg whites in an electric mixer at low speed until they start to froth. If you are not whipping the whites in a copper bowl, then add the cream of tartar at this point. Gradually increase the whipping speed to medium-high, and continue whipping until the whites form very stiff peaks and just begin to slip and streak around the side of the bowl. Add the superfine sugar and whip at medium-high speed for a few seconds longer to make the meringue smooth and shiny. Then reduce the speed to medium-high and whip in the egg yolks ② one at a time. Stop as soon as the mixture is homogeneous. Gently fold in the flour, confectioners' sugar, and chopped orange peel.

4. Scoop the batter into the pastry bag, and pipe the batter in a ⅝-inch (16 mm) wide band down the center of each depression ③ in the plaques. (If you have only 1 plaque, keep the remaining batter in the pastry bag until the first baking is completed.)

THE FRENCH COOKIE BOOK

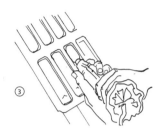

5. Bake, 1 plaque at a time, until the cookies are lightly browned on top and bottom and dry to the touch, about 24 to 30 minutes.

6. Unmold the cookies onto a wire rack and let cool to room temperature.

STORAGE: Covered airtight in a cookie jar or tin cookie box for up to 2 weeks.

LABBÉ BISCUITS
BISCUITS LABBÉ

Père Philippe Labbé was one of the great scholar-priests whose publication of original historical documents helped make the seventeenth century the "golden age of learning." The champagne biscuits named for him contain currants, which give them a slightly uneven appearance but add to their textural appeal and make them a congenial companion to a light sweet wine. While Père Philippe may have eaten these (or very similar) biscuits, if he drank champagne with them, it was still (not sparkling) champagne. Not until the end of the seventeenth century did the monk Dom Pérignon, cellarmaster at the Benedictine Abbey of Hautvillers, introduce the cork into the production of champagne, making possible the development of a marketable sparkling wine.

EQUIPMENT
2 champagne biscuit plaques stamped with 20 rectangular depressions, each 4¼ inches (11 cm) long and 1 inch (2½ cm) wide
- Clarified butter, melted
- Flour

A large pastry bag fitted with
- a ⁹⁄₁₆-inch (14 mm) plain pastry tube (Ateco #7)

1 large, heavy baking sheet

BATTER
4½ ounces (125 g), or ½ cup plus 2 tablespoons, superfine sugar

2 large eggs, at room temperature

2 large egg yolks, at room temperature

3½ ounces (100 g), or ⅔ cup plus 1 tablespoon, all-purpose flour

1¾ ounces (50 g), or ⅓ cup plus 4 teaspoons, cornstarch

3 ounces (85 g), or ½ cup plus 1 tablespoon, currants

DECORATION
Superfine sugar

For 40 cookies

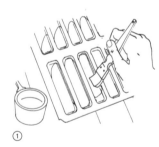

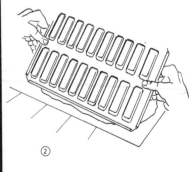

1. Brush the depressions in the champagne biscuit plaques with clarified butter ①. Scoop a mound of flour onto a sheet of wax paper. Turn each plaque upside down and gently press the depressions in the plaque into the flour ② to coat them. (Fluff up the flour as needed.) Then tap the back sharply with a wooden spatula ③ to dislodge the excess flour.

Preheat the oven to 400° F (200° C).

2. Combine the sugar with the eggs and yolks in your electric mixer. Beat with the wire whip, starting at low and gradually increasing to medium speed, until the batter is cream-colored, light, and thick and forms slowly dissolving ribbons when dropped from the whip. Sift together the flour and cornstarch and gently fold them into the batter. When almost mixed, add the currants ④ and continue folding until completely mixed.

3. Scoop the batter into the pastry bag, and pipe a ⅝- to ¾-inch (16–20 mm) wide band of batter down the center of each depression ⑤ in the plaques. Dust with superfine sugar and let rest for 1 minute. Turn each plaque upside down and tap the back sharply with a wooden spatula to dislodge the excess sugar, then quickly turn the plaque right side up again.

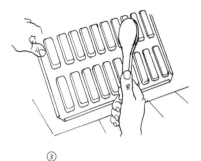

③

④

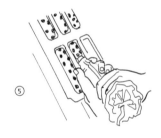

⑤

(If you have only 1 plaque, keep the remaining batter in the pastry bag until the first baking is completed.)

4. One at a time, place each plaque on the baking sheet and bake until the cookies are lightly browned on top and bottom and dry to the touch, about 15 to 18 minutes.

5. Unmold the cookies onto a wire rack and let cool to room temperature.

➤ **HOWS & WHYS:** Normally champagne biscuit batters are piped with a smaller pastry tube. However, the currants would clog a smaller tube, and the size we recommend is the smallest one that works well here. Be especially careful not to pipe too wide a band of batter in the molds, or your cookies will spread together and look sloppy.

Dusting the biscuits with sugar before baking gives the tops a smooth, matte, nonporous surface.

STORAGE: Covered airtight in a cookie jar or tin cookie box for up to 2 weeks.

COSSACK BISCUITS
BISCUITS COSAQUE

Baked in champagne biscuit molds, these cookies contain pow-
dered raw almonds and butter (but no egg yolks), which give them a luxurious taste and an
extremely tender texture. They are a bit too rich to serve with champagne, and a better
choice would be a bottle of fine Sauternes or Barsac. With or without the Sauternes, we
find it difficult to imagine Cossacks eating such elegant cookies.

EQUIPMENT

2 champagne biscuit plaques stamped with 20
rectangular depressions, each 4¼ inches (11 cm)
long and 1 inch (2½ cm) wide
• Clarified butter, melted
A large pastry bag fitted with
• a ½-inch (12 mm) plain pastry tube (Ateco #6)
1 large, heavy baking sheet

BATTER

3½ ounces (100 g), or ⅔ cup, raw almonds
3½ ounces (100 g), or ½ cup, granulated sugar
3 ounces (85 g), or 6 tablespoons, unsalted butter,
    softened
5 large egg whites
¼ teaspoon (1 ml) cream of tartar (optional)
3½ ounces (100 g), or about ⅔ cup plus
      1 tablespoon, all-purpose flour
1½ teaspoons (¾ cl) vanilla extract

For 40 cookies

①

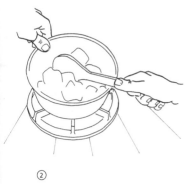

②

1. Brush the depressions in the champagne biscuit plaques with clarified butter ①.

2. Grind the almonds with the sugar in your food processor, stopping
to scrape down the sides of the processor bowl and break up any caking
as needed. Process until the almonds are finely ground, but not so long that
the mixture becomes at all oily. Transfer the almond and sugar powder to
a bowl and break up any caking with your fingertips.

Preheat the oven to 325° F (160° C).

3. Place the butter in a small stainless-steel bowl and beat with a
wooden spatula ②, warming it over low heat as needed to make it smooth,
white, and creamy.

4. Whip the egg whites in an electric mixer at low speed until they
start to froth. If you are not whipping the whites in a copper bowl, then
add the cream of tartar at this point. Gradually increase the whipping speed
to medium-high, and continue whipping until the whites form very stiff
peaks and just begin to slip and streak around the side of the bowl. Add
the almond and sugar powder ③ and whip at high speed for a few seconds
longer to make the meringue smooth and shiny.

5. Sift the flour and gently fold it into the meringue. When almost
completely incorporated, combine about ½ cup (1.2 dl) of the batter and
the vanilla with the creamed butter in a medium-size bowl and stir with
a wooden spatula to mix thoroughly. Then gently fold in the remaining
batter.

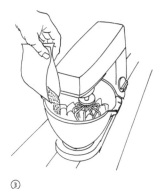

③

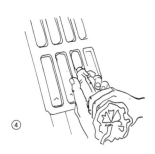

④

6. Scoop the batter into the pastry bag, and pipe a ⅝-inch (16 mm) wide band of batter down the center of each depression ④ in the champagne biscuit plaques. (If you have only 1 plaque, keep the remaining batter in the pastry bag until the first baking is completed.)

7. One at a time, place each plaque on the baking sheet and bake until the cookies are lightly browned, dry to the touch, and shrink from the sides of the depressions, about 30 to 35 minutes.

8. Unmold the cookies onto a wire rack and let them cool to room temperature.

➤ **HOWS & WHYS:** These cookies are not true biscuits, since they contain no egg yolks. Here butter supplies the fat that would normally come from the yolks. Cossack Biscuits contain much more butter than needed to replace the yolks, making them exceptionally rich for a member of the champagne biscuit family.

In this recipe the almonds are ground with granulated sugar (rather than confectioners' sugar) because the almond and sugar powder is used instead of superfine sugar to meringue the egg whites. For this reason it is especially important that the almond and sugar powder not be at all oily.

STORAGE: Covered airtight in a tin cookie box or cookie jar for up to 1 week.

MEXICAN BISCUITS
BISCUITS MEXICAINS

Chocolate was introduced into Europe by Hernando Cortés, who brought it back from Mexico in 1528. These finger-shaped champagne biscuits get their name from the grated chocolate in the batter, which gives them a speckled appearance. At the risk of being totally unconventional, we think they are an ideal complement to a dish of chocolate ice cream, and they aren't bad with a cup of steaming hot cocoa, either.

EQUIPMENT

5 *langues de chat* plaques stamped with 10 dumbbell-shaped depressions, each 3¾ inches (9½ cm) long and ⅝ inch (16 mm) wide
- Clarified butter, melted
- Flour

A large pastry bag fitted with
- a ⁷⁄₁₆-inch (11 mm) plain pastry tube (Ateco #5)

1 large, heavy baking sheet

BATTER

3½ ounces (100 g), or ¾ cup plus 4 teaspoons, confectioners' sugar

2 large eggs, at room temperature

1 large egg yolk, at room temperature

2 ounces (60 g) European bittersweet chocolate (such as Lindt Excellence), grated

1 teaspoon (½ cl) vanilla extract

2 ounces (60 g) or ¼ cup plus 3 tablespoons, all-purpose flour

2 ounces (60 g), or ¼ cup plus 3 tablespoons, cornstarch

For 50 cookies

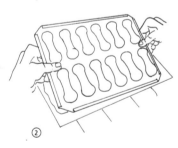

①

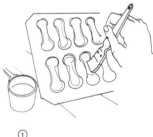

②

③

1. Brush the depressions in the *langues de chat* plaques with clarified butter ①. Scoop a mound of flour onto a sheet of wax paper. Turn each plaque upside down and gently press the depressions in the plaque into the flour ② to coat them. (Fluff up the flour as needed.) Then tap the back sharply with a wooden spatula ③ to dislodge the excess flour.

Preheat the oven to 400° F (200° C).

2. Sift the sugar and combine it with the eggs and yolk in your electric mixer. Beat with the wire whip, starting at low and gradually increasing to medium speed, until the batter is cream-colored, thick, and light and forms slowly dissolving ribbons when dropped from the whip. Stir in the chocolate and vanilla at low speed. Sift together the flour and cornstarch and gently fold them into the batter.

3. Scoop the batter into the pastry bag, and pipe a ½-inch (12 mm) wide band of batter down the center of each depression ④ in the plaques. (If you don't have enough plaques for an entire recipe, keep the remaining batter in the pastry bag until the first baking is completed.)

4. Place the plaques on the baking sheet 2 or 3 at a time, and bake until the cookies brown lightly on top and bottom and are firm to the touch, about 12 to 15 minutes.

5. Slide the plaques onto a wire rack and let the cookies cool in the plaques. When cool enough to handle, but still very warm, carefully lift the

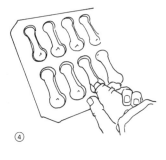

cookies out of the plaques and let them finish cooling on the wire rack.

➤ **HOWS & WHYS:** Originally Mexican Biscuits were baked in special oval champagne biscuit molds, but such molds are no longer available. We use instead *langues de chat* plaques, and ordinary champagne biscuit plaques are an equally good alternative.

STORAGE: Covered airtight in a cookie jar or tin cookie box for up to 2 weeks.

PALMA BISCUITS
BISCUITS PALMA

Palma, *the capital of the Spanish island Majorca, gives its name to these exquisite champagne biscuits flavored with fresh oranges. The most important fruit crops of Majorca are oranges and figs, and at least up to the beginning of the twentieth century, most of this produce was exported to France.*

Compared with Langres Biscuits (page 206), which are flavored with candied orange peel, Palma Biscuits are lighter and more perfumed (from the fresh orange zest), with a smooth, matte, and slightly rosy top surface contrasting against their lightly browned, porous bottoms. Nineteenth-century recipes for Palma Biscuits recommend whipping the whole eggs, sugar, and orange juice together over low heat. We find this procedure too tedious. Our modern separated egg method for preparing the batter makes it quite easy to produce the fine, uniform texture and elegant surface characteristic of these cookies.

EQUIPMENT
5 *langues de chat* plaques stamped with 10 dumbbell-shaped depressions, each 3¾ inches (9½ cm) long and ⅝ inch (16 mm) wide
- Clarified butter, melted
- Flour

A large pastry bag fitted with
- a ⁷⁄₁₆-inch (11 mm) plain pastry tube (Ateco #5)

1 large, heavy baking sheet

BATTER
2 large eggs, separated, at room temperature
⅛ teaspoon (½ ml) cream of tartar (optional)
3½ ounces (100 g), or ½ cup, superfine sugar
1 tablespoon (1½ cl) fresh orange juice
1 teaspoon (½ cl) finely grated orange zest
Red food coloring
4½ ounces (125 g), or ¾ cup plus 2 tablespoons, all-purpose flour
1 ounce (25 g), or 3 tablespoons plus 1 teaspoon, confectioners' sugar

DECORATION
Superfine sugar

For 50 cookies

①

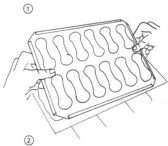

②

1. Brush the depressions in the *langues de chat* plaques with clarified butter ①. Scoop a mound of flour onto a sheet of wax paper. Turn each plaque upside down and gently press the depressions in the plaque into the flour ② to coat them. (Fluff up the flour as needed.) Then tap the back sharply with a wooden spatula to dislodge the excess flour.

Preheat the oven to 400° F (200° C).

2. Whip the egg whites in an electric mixer at low speed until they start to froth. If you are not whipping the whites in a copper bowl, then add the cream of tartar at this point. Gradually increase the whipping speed to medium-high, and continue whipping until the whites form very stiff peaks and just begin to slip and streak around the side of the bowl. Add the superfine sugar and whip at high speed for a few seconds longer to make the meringue smooth and shiny. Reduce the speed to medium-high and whip in the egg yolks one at a time. Then whip in the orange juice, orange zest, and a drop or two of red food coloring. Stop as soon as the

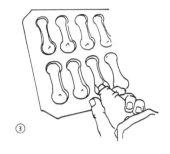

③

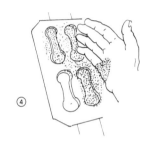

④

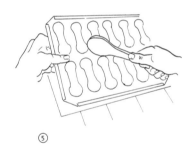

⑤

mixture is homogeneous. Sift together the flour and confectioners' sugar and gently fold them into the batter.

3. Scoop the batter into the pastry bag, and pipe the batter in a ½-inch (12 mm) wide band down the center of each depression ③ in the plaques. Dust with superfine sugar ④ and let rest for 1 minute. Turn each plaque upside down and tap the back sharply with a wooden spatula ⑤ to dislodge the excess sugar, then quickly turn the plaque right side up again. (If you don't have enough plaques for an entire recipe, keep the remaining batter in the pastry bag until the first baking is completed.)

4. Place the plaques on the baking sheet 2 or 3 at a time, and bake until the cookies are lightly browned on top and bottom and dry to the touch, about 12 to 15 minutes.

5. Unmold the cookies onto a wire rack and let cool to room temperature.

➤ **HOWS & WHYS:** Originally Palma Biscuits were baked in special fluted champagne biscuit molds, but such molds are no longer available. We use instead *langues de chat* plaques, and ordinary champagne biscuit plaques are an equally good alternative.

Dusting the biscuits with sugar before baking gives the tops a smooth, matte, nonporous surface.

STORAGE: Covered airtight in a cookie jar or tin cookie box for up to 2 weeks.

ALICANTE BISCUITS
BISCUITS ALICANTE

These cookies are made from Classic Champagne Biscuits batter (page 202) tinted red and baked in barquette molds. Like many other champagne biscuits, the bottoms are browned and a little porous, while the tops are smooth and matte. With a raw almond decorating their pink tops, they look like little filled pastry shells. In fact, they have a soft, cakey interior that contrasts nicely with their dry, crusty exterior and makes their texture quite different from the other champagne biscuits.

The boat shape and the almond probably account for the name. Alicante is a seaport on Spain's Mediterranean coast, and Spain is France's primary European source for almonds.

EQUIPMENT

36 *barquette* molds 3½ inches (9 cm) long
- Clarified butter, melted
- Flour

1 or 2 large, heavy baking sheets
A large pastry bag fitted with
- a ⅝-inch (16 mm) plain pastry tube (Ateco #8)

BATTER

9 ounces (250 g), or 1¼ cups, superfine sugar
4 large eggs, at room temperature
Red food coloring
9½ ounces (270 g), or 1¾ cups plus 3 tablespoons, all-purpose flour
2 teaspoons (1 cl) vanilla extract

DECORATION

36 raw almonds
Superfine sugar

For 36 cookies

1. Brush the *barquette* molds ① with clarified butter. Spoon some flour into each mold and shake the mold back and forth to coat it evenly. Then turn each mold upside down and tap the back sharply with a wooden spatula to dislodge the excess flour.

2. Combine the sugar with 1 egg in your electric mixer and beat at medium speed with the wire whip until the mixture whitens and the grain of the sugar begins to disappear. Add a second egg and continue beating until the mixture whitens and becomes fluffy. Add a third egg and beat until the mixture whitens and becomes fluffy again. (Allow 2 to 3 minutes of beating before adding each successive egg.) Add the fourth egg and beat for 12 minutes longer. When finished, the mixture will be light and fluffy and will form slowly dissolving ribbons when dropped from the wire whip. Beat in a couple of drops of red food coloring. Sift the flour and gently fold it into the batter. When the flour is almost completely incorporated, add the vanilla and continue folding until completely mixed.

Meanwhile, preheat the oven to 450° F (230° C).

3. Scoop the batter into the pastry bag, and pipe the batter into the molds ②, filling them by about three-quarters. Place an almond on the center of each. Dust the top of each with superfine sugar ③ and let rest 2 minutes. Turn each mold upside down and tap the back sharply with a

③

wooden spatula to dislodge the excess sugar, then turn it right side up again. (If you don't have enough molds for an entire recipe, keep the remaining batter in the pastry bag until the first baking is completed.)

4. Place the molds on baking sheets and bake, 1 sheet at a time, until the biscuits are lightly browned on the bottoms and the tops are dry to the touch, about 7 to 11 minutes.

5. Unmold the biscuits onto a wire rack and let cool to room temperature.

➤ **HOWS & WHYS:** Dusting the biscuits with sugar before baking gives the tops a smooth, matte, nonporous surface.

STORAGE: Best eaten the day they are made.

MADELEINES
MADELEINES

〜〜〜〜〜

Marcel Proust immortalized madeleines in Swann's Way by us-
ing them as the key to unlock his memories. A madeleine soaked in tea provided the prototype smell and taste that ''remains poised a long time, like souls, ready to remind us . . .
and bear unfaltering, in the tiny, almost impalpable drop of their essence, the vast structure of recollection.'' No matter that Proust hadn't eaten them since his childhood in Illiers-
Combray (though he saw them often, ''without tasting them, on the trays in pastry cooks
windows''). Or that in Proust's original manuscript, it was a biscotte dipped in tea. (Obviously there is more poetry in madeleines than in biscottes.) Even for those who have never
read a word of his seven-volume Remembrance of Things Past, the association of Proust
with madeleines and tea has become a cliché of twentieth-century gastronomy.

These mythical madeleines are shell-shaped little pound cakes, each like a dromedary
camel, with a single, disproportionate hump rising awkwardly from its oval back. They are
served hump side up, and if it seems paradoxical that the pretty fluted side should face the
plate, imagine how ridiculous they would look balancing precariously on a distended belly.
Our recipe produces exquisite cookies with a tender and tight-grained interior, a thin and
delicate crust, and a golden, pleated surface—the perfect realization of Proust's ''little
scallop shell of pastry, so richly sensual under its severe religious folds.'' Served fresh from
the oven and barely cool, they are an ethereal treat.

EQUIPMENT

2 *madeleine* plaques stamped with 12 shell-shaped
depressions, each 3 inches (8 cm) long
- Clarified butter, melted
- Flour

A #40 ice cream scoop, a tablespoon,
or a large pastry bag fitted with
- a ⁹⁄₁₆-inch (14 mm) plain pastry tube (Ateco #7)

BATTER

5⅓ ounces (150 g), or ½ cup plus 2⅔ tablespoons,
  unsalted butter, softened
5⅓ ounces (150 g), or ¾ cup, superfine sugar
3 large eggs, at room temperature
1 large egg yolk, at room temperature
4¾ ounces (135 g), or 1 cup plus 4 teaspoons,
  cake flour
½ teaspoon (2 g) baking powder
1½ teaspoons (¾ cl) vanilla extract

For 24 cookies

1. Place the butter in a small stainless-steel bowl and beat with a
wooden spatula, warming as needed, until smooth, white, and creamy.

2. Combine the sugar, eggs, and yolk in your electric mixer and beat
with the wire whip, starting at low and gradually increasing to medium
speed, until the batter is pale yellow and lightly thickened, 2 minutes. Sift
together the flour and baking powder and gently fold them into the batter.
When the flour is almost completely incorporated, add about 1 cup of the
batter and the vanilla to the butter and stir with a wooden spatula to mix
thoroughly. Then gently fold in the remaining batter. Let the batter rest in
a cool place for 30 minutes.

Meanwhile, preheat the oven to 475° F (245° C).

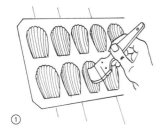

①

②

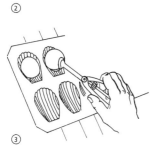

③

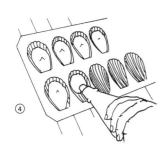

④

3. Brush the *madeleine* plaques ① with clarified butter. Spoon some flour into each mold and shake the mold back and forth ② to coat it evenly. Then turn each mold upside down and tap the back sharply with a wooden spatula to dislodge the excess flour.

4. Spoon 5 teaspoons (2½ cl) of batter into each shell ③ using the ice cream scoop or tablespoon. Or scoop the batter into the pastry bag, and pipe the batter ④ into the shells. (If you have only 1 plaque, keep the remaining batter in the bowl until the first baking is completed.)

5. Bake on the bottom oven rack until the Madeleines are golden on top and lightly browned around the edges, about 8 to 10 minutes. Then unmold them onto a wire rack, turn them hump side up, and let cool to room temperature.

➤ **HOWS & WHYS:** In order for the Madeleines to have the hump on the back, the eggs must not be beaten too much and the batter must contain only a small amount of baking powder. Baking at high temperature forms a crust on the outside before the inside sets; and the gas trapped inside then pushes up the center, forming the hump. We use cake flour because its lower gluten content makes the Madeleines more tender.

We advise against black steel *madeleine* plaques because they make the Madeleines brown excessively.

STORAGE: Madeleines are wonderful fresh from the oven, but they are noticeably less good even a couple of hours later. Don't even think about trying to keep them overnight.

COMMERCY MADELEINES
MADELEINES DE COMMERCY

Madeleines *are believed to have been invented in the town of Commercy, in Lorraine. They first became fashionable around 1730 in Versailles and Paris, thanks to Stanislaus Leszczynski, the deposed king of Poland, father-in-law of King Louis XV of France, and (after 1735) duke of Lorraine. The duke's court at Luneville saw the introduction of a dazzling succession of innovations in the art of pastry, including meringues and rum babas.*

Alexandre Dumas, in his Grand dictionnaire de cuisine, *tells the story of a friend who, on a journey to Strasbourg, arrived late at night in a small village. Exhausted and famished, he found only one building that still had a light burning, and when he knocked at the door he was greeted by the local baker. The baker "took out a little basket in which were about a dozen beautiful, golden oval cakes," and watched in delight as Dumas's friend devoured them all. The traveler then asked, " 'What do you call these succulent little cakes?'*

" 'What, you don't know the madeleines *of Commercy?'*

" 'Am I then in Commercy?'

" 'Yes, and you may be sure that you have just eaten the best cakes in the world.' "

By the end of the nineteenth century, madeleines *were popular throughout France, and many recipes for them had been developed. The version that became known as Commercy Madeleines is made with browned butter, which gives these little tea cakes a beige crumb and a slightly nutty flavor. For our taste, these are, if anything, even more delectable than our "ordinary" (but already quite extraordinary) Madeleines (page 218).*

EQUIPMENT

2 *madeleine* plaques stamped with 12 shell-shaped depressions, each 3 inches (8 cm) long
A #40 ice cream scoop, a tablespoon, or a large pastry bag fitted with
• a 9/16-inch (14 mm) plain pastry tube (Ateco #7)

BATTER

6 ounces (170 g), or ½ cup plus 4 tablespoons, unsalted butter
4⅔ ounces (130 g), or ¾ cup plus 3 tablespoons, all-purpose flour
4½ ounces (125 g), or ½ cup plus 2 tablespoons, superfine sugar
3 extra-large eggs, separated, at room temperature
⅛ teaspoon (½ ml) lemon extract

For 24 cookies

①

1. Melt the butter in a 1-quart (1 L) saucepan, and boil it. Foam will come to the top. When it collapses, stir to mix. Continue to boil. Soon bubbles will start to form on the surface, at first large bubbles and then progressively smaller ones. When the surface is covered with an opaque foam of tiny bubbles and the foam mounts ① in the saucepan, stir to deflate it. Boil the butter until a new layer of tiny bubbles forms on top, then stir to deflate it again. Pour through a fine strainer ② into a bowl. This is *beurre noisette,* or browned butter.

2. Stir 1 tablespoon (1½ cl) of the browned butter with 2 teaspoons

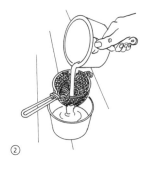

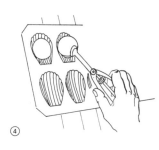

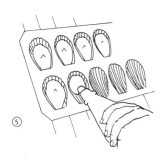

(5 g) of the flour, and brush the *madeleine* plaques ③ with it. Let the remaining browned butter cool, but do not let it thicken and begin to solidify.

Preheat the oven to 475° F (245° C).

3. Sift the flour. Combine the sugar with 1 egg white in your electric mixer and beat at medium speed with the flat beater. Add the remaining whites one by one, followed by the yolks, one by one, as soon as the previous white or yolk is incorporated. Then mix in the lemon extract. Do not overbeat. Turn the mixer down to low and gradually add the flour. When mixed, gradually add the browned butter. Transfer the batter to a small bowl and let it rest in a cool place for 30 to 60 minutes.

4. Spoon 5 teaspoons (2½ cl) of batter into each shell ④ using the ice cream scoop or tablespoon. Or scoop the batter into the pastry bag, and pipe the batter ⑤ into the shells. (If you have only 1 plaque, keep the remaining batter in the bowl until the first baking is completed.)

5. Bake on the bottom oven rack until the Madeleines are golden on top and lightly browned around the edges, about 8 to 10 minutes. Then unmold them onto a wire rack, turn them hump side up, and let cool to room temperature.

➤ **HOWS & WHYS:** In order for the Commercy Madeleines to have the hump on the back, the eggs must be beaten as little as possible. The batter will be fairly thin, but will thicken a bit as it rests and the butter in it cools. If you beat the batter too much, the batter will have more volume and be thicker, but it will not rise properly in the oven and the Madeleines will have no humps.

We advise against black steel *madeleine* plaques because they make the Madeleines brown excessively.

STORAGE: Commercy Madeleines are wonderful fresh from the oven, but they are noticeably less good even a couple of hours later. Don't even think about trying to keep them overnight.

NANTES LOAVES
PAINS NANTAIS

~~~~~~~~

These little pound cakes are perhaps the most festive looking cookies in this chapter. Baked in tartelette molds, their bottoms are embedded with sliced almonds, and a kirsch-flavored sugar glaze on top highlights the aromatic orange zest in their soft, tender interiors. A sprinkling of multicolored crystal sugar or décors non-pareils on the center of the shiny glaze adds just enough color to draw the eye of adult and child alike.

EQUIPMENT

18 *tartelette* molds 2¾ inch (7 cm) wide and ½ inch (12 mm) deep
- Clarified butter, melted
- Sliced almonds

1 or 2 large, heavy baking sheets
A #40 ice cream scoop, a tablespoon, or a large pastry bag fitted with
- an ¹¹⁄₁₆-inch (18 mm) plain pastry tube (Ateco #9)

BATTER

3½ ounces (100 g), or ¼ cup plus 3 tablespoons, unsalted butter, softened
3½ ounces (100 g), or ½ cup, superfine sugar

2 large eggs, at room temperature
Finely grated zest of 1 orange
4½ ounces (125 g), or ¾ cup plus 2 tablespoons, all-purpose flour
½ teaspoon (2 g) baking powder

GLAZE

3 tablespoons (60 g) strained apricot jam [*Basic Preparation*, page 484]
2½ ounces (70 g), or ½ cup plus 4 teaspoons, confectioners' sugar
2 teaspoons (1 cl) kirsch

DECORATION

1 teaspoon (5 g) multicolored crystal sugar or décors non-pareils

For 18 cookies

①

②

1. Brush the *tartelette* molds ① with clarified butter. Spoon some sliced almonds into each mold and shake the mold back and forth ② to coat it evenly. Then turn each mold upside down and tap the back sharply with a wooden spatula to dislodge the excess almonds.

Preheat the oven to 425° F (220° C).

2. Place the butter in your electric mixer and beat with the flat beater until smooth, white, and creamy. Beat in the sugar, and when smooth and light, beat in 1 egg. Beat in the remaining egg with the wire whip, then beat in the orange zest. Sift together the flour and baking powder and gently fold them into the batter.

3. Spoon 5 teaspoons (2½ cl) of batter into the center of each mold using the ice cream scoop or tablespoon. Or scoop the batter into the pastry bag, and pipe ③ a dome of batter 1⅝ inches (4 cm) wide in the center of each mold. (If you don't have enough molds for the entire recipe, keep the remaining batter in the bowl until the first baking is completed.)

4. Place the molds on the baking sheets and bake, 1 sheet at a time, until the cookies barely begin to brown around the edges and spring back to the touch, about 9 to 12 minutes.

③

④

⑤

⑥

5. Unmold the cookies onto a wire rack, turn them right side up, and let cool to room temperature.

6. Warm the apricot jam over low heat, stirring occasionally, until melted. Brush the top of each cookie ④ with jam until lightly coated and glistening.

7. Sift the confectioners' sugar into a small bowl, and stir in the kirsch. Stir in enough cold water to make a smooth, creamy paste that is just fluid enough to spread easily with a pastry brush. Brush an even coat of this sugar glaze over the jam on top of each cookie. Run your finger around the edge ⑤ to clean off any drips. Drop a pinch of crystal sugar ⑥ or décors non-pareils on the center of each cookie while the glaze is still moist, then let the glaze set.

STORAGE: Let the glaze on the cookies dry thoroughly (for several hours) so they don't stick together. Then keep covered in a cookie jar or tin cookie box for up to 2 or 3 days.

LITTLE ENGLISH CAKES
PETITS ANGLAIS

~~~~~

These boat-shaped little pound cakes are a diminutive version of the classic cake called gâteau anglais *(English cake)*, which is baked in a wide, shallow tarte *ring. Alexandre Dumas tells us that the* gâteau anglais *is derived from the traditional English wedding cake, and that the customs surrounding this wedding cake are described in the works of Charles Dickens.*

Little English Cakes are also similar to Nantes Loaves (page 222), but they are richer in butter, studded with currants and candied citron, and flavored with rum in both the batter and the sugar glaze on top.

EQUIPMENT

32 *barquette* molds 3½ inches (9 cm) long

• Clarified butter, melted

1 or 2 large, heavy baking sheets

A large pastry bag fitted with

• a ⅝-inch (16 mm) plain pastry tube (Ateco #8)

BATTER

4½ ounces (125 g), or ½ cup plus 1 tablespoon, unsalted butter, softened

3½ ounces (100 g), or ⅔ cup plus 1 tablespoon, all-purpose flour

1 ounce (25 g), or 3 tablespoons, cornstarch

1¾ ounces (50 g), or ¼ cup, candied citron

1¾ ounces (50 g), or ⅓ cup, currants

2 large eggs, at room temperature

4½ ounces (125 g), or ½ cup plus 2 tablespoons, superfine sugar

2 tablespoons (3 cl) dark Jamaican rum

GLAZE

3 tablespoons (60 g) strained apricot jam [*Basic Preparation*, page 484]

3½ ounces (85 g), or ⅔ cup plus 2 teaspoons, confectioners' sugar

2 teaspoons (1 cl) dark Jamaican rum

For 32 cookies

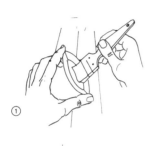

1. Brush the *barquette* molds ① with clarified butter. *Preheat the oven to 425° F (220° C).*

2. Place the butter in a small stainless-steel bowl and beat with a wooden spatula, warming it over low heat as needed, to make it smooth, white, and creamy.

3. Sift together the flour and cornstarch. Combine about 2 tablespoons (15 g) of it with the citron and chop the citron with your chef's knife. Toss the chopped citron and the currants with the flour and cornstarch.

4. Combine the eggs and sugar in your electric mixer and beat with the wire whip, starting at low and gradually increasing to medium speed, until light and cream-colored. Gently fold the flour, cornstarch, citron, and currants into the batter. When almost completely incorporated, add about ⅓ cup (8 cl) of the batter and the rum to the butter, and stir with a wooden spatula to mix thoroughly. Then gently fold in the remaining batter.

5. Scoop the batter into the pastry bag, and pipe the batter into the molds ②, filling them by about three-quarters. (If you don't have enough molds for the entire recipe, keep the remaining batter in the pastry bag until the first baking is completed.)

6. Place the molds on the baking sheets and bake, 1 sheet at a time, until the cookies barely begin to brown around the edges and spring back to the touch, about 9 to 12 minutes.

7. Unmold the cookies onto a wire rack, turn them right side up, and let cool to room temperature.

8. Warm the apricot jam over low heat, stirring occasionally, until melted. Brush the top of each cookie ③ with jam until lightly coated and glistening.

9. Sift the confectioners' sugar into a small bowl, and stir in the rum. Stir in enough cold water to make a smooth creamy paste that is just fluid enough to spread easily with a pastry brush. Lightly brush this sugar glaze over the jam on top of each cookie, then let the glaze set.

STORAGE: Let the glaze on the cookies dry thoroughly (for several hours) so they don't stick together. Then keep covered in a cookie jar or tin cookie box for up to 2 or 3 days.

LITTLE FRUITCAKES
PETITS CAKES

In English cooking there was a variety of pound cake flavored with spices, studded with prunes, and called plum cake. The English gradually modified plum cake, keeping the spices but dropping the prunes and replacing them with sultana raisins and candied fruits, and changed the name to fruitcake. Meanwhile, the French adapted the recipe by dropping the spices and prunes and replacing them with raisins and glacé fruits, but they continued to call their version plum cake. Eventually, the name plum cake was just too offbeat for the French, both plum and cake being nonexistent words in the French language. So it got shortened to le cake.

Our Little Fruitcakes are miniature versions of le cake—rich, buttery little pound cakes laden with soft golden raisins and bits of glacé fruits and soaked (imbibé, in the pastry chef's evocative jargon) with a generous sprinkling of rum. Unlike traditional American and English fruitcakes, they need no aging and last only a few days. But don't worry—these little cakes are so good that their likelihood of even getting into a storage container is remote.

EQUIPMENT

4 twelve-cup gem pans (miniature cupcakes), each cup 1¾ inches (4½ cm) wide
- Insert a crimped paper liner in each cup.
A #50 ice cream scoop, or a tablespoon

BATTER

6 ounces (170 g), or 1 cup plus 3 ½ tablespoons, all-purpose flour
1 teaspoon (4 g) baking powder
4 ounces (115 g), or ½ cup plus 2 tablespoons, glacé fruits

4 ounces (115 g), or ¾ cup, golden raisins
6 ounces (170 g), or ½ cup plus 4 tablespoons, unsalted butter, softened
5½ ounces (150 g), or ¾ cup, superfine sugar
3 large eggs, at room temperature
2 tablespoons (3 cl) dark Jamaican rum

IMBIBAGE

¼ cup plus 3 tablespoons (1 dl) dark rum

GLAZE

2½ tablespoons (50 g) strained apricot jam
[*Basic Preparation*, page 484]

For 48 cookies

1. Sift together the flour and baking powder. Add about 6 tablespoons (40 g) of the flour to the glacé fruits, and chop them finely with your chef's knife. Then toss with the remaining flour and the raisins.

Preheat the oven to 425° F (220° C).

2. Place the butter in your electric mixer and beat with the flat beater until smooth, white, and creamy. Beat in the sugar, and when smooth and light, beat in 1 egg. Beat in the remaining eggs, 1 at a time, with the wire whip. Fold the glacé fruits, raisins, flour, and baking powder into the batter, then fold in the rum.

3. Spoon 4 teaspoons (2 cl) of batter into each mold ① using the ice cream scoop or a tablespoon. (If you don't have enough gem pans for the entire recipe, keep the remaining batter in the bowl until the first baking is completed.)

①

②

③

4. Bake until the cakes are very lightly browned on top and spring back to the touch, about 11 to 14 minutes.

5. Unmold the cakes onto a wire rack and turn them right side up. While still hot, sprinkle them ② with the rum, then let cool to room temperature.

6. Warm the apricot jam over low heat, stirring occasionally, until melted. Lightly brush the tops of the cakes ③ with jam.

➤ **HOWS & WHYS:** The cakes absorb the sprinkled rum better while they are hot.

STORAGE: Covered airtight in a cookie jar or tin cookie box, in 1 layer so they don't stick together, for up to 2 or 3 days.

PERFECT
IDÉAL

*T*he combination of apricot jam, curaçao, and rum gives these small almond cakes a deep, resonant, mouth-filling taste. One bite and you'll know why they got their name.

EQUIPMENT

18 "royal" oval molds 2¾ inches (7 cm) long, 1¾ inches (4½ cm) wide, and ¹¹/₁₆ inch (18 mm) deep
- Clarified butter, melted
- Flour

2 large, heavy baking sheets
A #30 ice cream scoop, or a tablespoon

BATTER

1¾ ounces (50 g), or 3½ tablespoons, unsalted butter, softened
3 tablespoons (60 g) apricot jam
1 tablespoon plus 1 teaspoon (2 cl) curaçao liqueur

2 teaspoons (1 cl) dark Jamaican rum
7 ounces (200 g), or about 1½ cups, almond and sugar powder

Basic Preparation, page 482:
3½ ounces (100 g), or ⅔ cup, blanched almonds
3½ ounces (100 g), or ¾ cup plus 4 teaspoons, confectioners' sugar

1 ounce (25 g), or 2 tablespoons, superfine sugar
2 large eggs, at room temperature
1½ ounces (40 g), or ¼ cup plus 1½ teaspoons, all-purpose flour

For 18 cookies

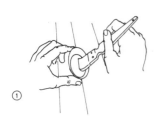

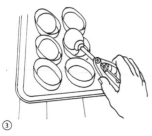

1. Brush the "royal" oval molds ① with clarified butter. Spoon some flour into each mold and shake the mold back and forth ② to coat it evenly. Then turn each mold upside down and tap the back sharply with a wooden spatula to dislodge the excess flour. Place them on the baking sheet.

Preheat the oven to 425° F (220° C).

2. Place the butter in a small stainless-steel bowl and beat with a wooden spatula, warming it over low heat as needed to make it smooth, white, and creamy.

3. If there are any large pieces of fruit in the apricot jam, break them up. Stir in the curaçao and rum.

4. Combine the almond and sugar powder, sugar, and eggs in your electric mixer and beat with the wire whip, starting at low and gradually increasing to medium speed, until cream-colored, thick, and light. Sift the flour and gently fold it into the batter. When almost completely incorporated, add the apricot jam, curaçao, rum, and about ⅓ cup (8 cl) of the batter to the creamed butter, and stir with a wooden spatula to mix thoroughly. Then gently fold in the remaining batter.

5. Place the molds on a baking sheet. Spoon 2 tablespoons (3 cl) of batter into each mold ③ using the ice cream scoop or a tablespoon. (If you don't have enough molds for the entire recipe, keep the remaining batter in the bowl until the first baking is completed.)

6. Bake for 5 minutes. Place the second baking sheet underneath the sheet of cookies, reduce the oven temperature to 350° F (175° C), and continue baking until the cookies are golden brown on top and spring back to the touch, about 18 to 22 minutes altogether.

7. Unmold the cookies onto a wire rack, turn them right side up, and let cool to room temperature.

STORAGE: Covered airtight in a cookie jar or tin cookie box for up to 2 or 3 days at room temperature.

SAINT-CYRIENS
SAINT-CYRIENS

~~~~~~

These small, oval almond cakes are flavored with orange zest and esprit d'orange *(literally "spirit of orange")*, an orange extract produced by steeping fresh orange zest in vodka. In contrast to orange liqueurs, esprit d'orange *is not sweet. If you like, you can prepare a larger quantity of this extract than needed for the recipe, and store it for use in other desserts. It provides a nice accent to the flavor of oranges in mousses, pastry creams, cake fillings, and sorbets, or simply in a dessert fruit salad.*

Saint-Cyriens are cadets at the military academy of Saint Cyr, the French equivalent of West Point or Sandhurst. But don't let the military association mislead you. These luxuriously moist, tender, and delicately scented morsels are a hedonistic delight.

EQUIPMENT

18 "royal" oval molds 2¾ inches (7 cm) long, 1¾ inches (4½ cm) wide, and ¹¹⁄₁₆ inch (18 mm) deep
- Clarified butter, melted
- Flour

1 large, heavy baking sheet

A #40 ice cream scoop, or a tablespoon

7 ounces (200 g), or 1½ cups, almond and sugar powder

    Basic Preparation, page 482:

    3½ ounces (100 g), or ⅔ cup, blanched almonds

    3½ ounces (100 g), or ¾ cup plus 4 teaspoons, confectioners' sugar

2 large eggs, at room temperature

1 ounce (25 g), or 3 tablespoons, cornstarch

BATTER

1 orange

2 tablespoons (3 cl) vodka

1½ ounces (40 g), or 3 tablespoons, unsalted butter, softened

For 18 cookies

①

②

1. Strip the zest from half the orange. Place it in a small jar and cover with the vodka. Seal airtight and let steep for at least a couple of days. Cover the orange with plastic wrap and save it in the refrigerator.

2. Brush the "royal" oval molds ① with clarified butter. Spoon some flour into each mold and shake the mold back and forth ② to coat it evenly. Then turn each mold upside down and tap the back sharply with a wooden spatula to dislodge the excess flour. Place them on a large, heavy baking sheet.

Preheat the oven to 425° F (220° C).

3. Finely grate the zest from the second half of the orange. Strain the vodka and discard the orange zest that steeped in it.

4. Place the butter in a small stainless-steel bowl and beat with a wooden spatula, warming it over low heat as needed, to make it smooth, white, and creamy.

5. Combine the almond and sugar powder with the eggs in your electric mixer and beat with the wire whip, starting at low and gradually increasing to medium speed, until cream-colored, thick, and light. Sift the cornstarch and gently fold it into the batter. When almost completely incorporated, add the grated orange zest, the orange-flavored vodka, and about ⅓ cup (8 cl) of the batter to the creamed butter, and stir with a wooden spatula to mix thoroughly. Then gently fold in the remaining batter.

6. Place the molds on the baking sheet. Spoon 5 teaspoons (2½ cl) of batter into each mold 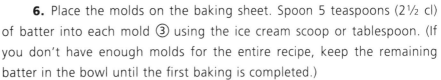 using the ice cream scoop or tablespoon. (If you don't have enough molds for the entire recipe, keep the remaining batter in the bowl until the first baking is completed.)

7. Bake until the cookies shrink from the sides of the molds and the tops are golden and spring back to the touch, about 9 to 12 minutes.

8. Unmold the cookies onto a wire rack, turn them right side up, and let cool to room temperature.

STORAGE: Covered airtight in a cookie jar or tin cookie box for up to 2 days.

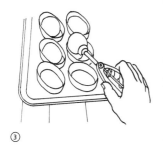

③

PROVENÇAUX
PROVENÇAUX

PROVENÇAUX

These small, rum-flavored almond cakes are shaped like scallop shells. If anything, they fit Proust's description of madeleines as ''those short, plump little cakes . . . which look as though they had been molded in the fluted scallop of a pilgrim's shell'' better than do Madeleines (page 218) themselves.

Provençaux *also have a hump on the back, but the humps are not so pronounced as those on* madeleines. *On the other hand, the flavor and texture of* Provençaux *are more sumptuous than their illustrious cousins.*

EQUIPMENT

2 *coque* plaques stamped with 8 scallop-shell depressions, each 2½ inches (6½ cm) wide
- Clarified butter, melted
- Flour

A #30 ice cream scoop, a tablespoon, or a large pastry bag fitted with
- a 9/16-inch (14 mm) plain pastry tube (Ateco #7)

BATTER

2½ ounces (70 g), or 5 tablespoons, unsalted butter, softened

7 ounces (200 g), or 1½ cups, almond and sugar powder

  Basic Preparation, page 482:
  3½ ounces (100 g), or ⅔ cup, blanched almonds
  3½ ounces (100 g), or ¾ cup plus 4 teaspoons, confectioners' sugar

2 large eggs, at room temperature

1 large egg yolk, at room temperature

1¾ ounces (50 g), or ⅓ cup plus 1 teaspoon, all-purpose flour

2 tablespoons (3 cl) dark Jamaican rum

For 16 cookies

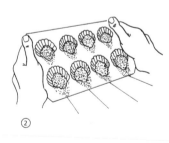

①

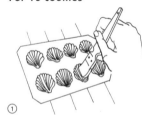

②

1. Brush the *coque* plaques ① with clarified butter. Spoon some flour into each mold and shake the mold back and forth ② to coat it evenly. Then turn each mold upside down and tap the back sharply with a wooden spatula to dislodge the excess flour.

Preheat the oven to 450° F (230° C).

2. Place the butter in a small stainless-steel bowl and beat with a wooden spatula, warming it over low heat as needed, until smooth, white, and creamy.

3. Combine the almond and sugar powder, eggs, and egg yolk in your electric mixer and beat with the wire whip, starting at low and gradually increasing to medium speed, until cream-colored, thick, and light. Sift the flour and gently fold it into the batter. When almost completely incorporated, add the rum and about ½ cup (1.2 dl) of the batter to the creamed butter, and stir with a wooden spatula to mix thoroughly. Then gently fold in the remaining batter.

4. Spoon 2 tablespoons (3 cl) of batter into each mold using the ice cream scoop or a tablespoon. Or scoop the batter into the pastry bag, and

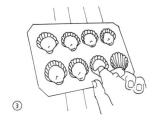

pipe the batter ③ into the shells. (If you have only 1 plaque, keep the remaining batter in the bowl until the first baking is completed.)

5. Bake until the cookies brown around the edges and spring back to the touch, about 9 to 12 minutes.

6. Unmold the cookies onto a wire rack, turn them right side up (that is, fluted side down), and let cool to room temperature.

STORAGE: Best eaten the day they are made.

VISITANDINES
VISITANDINES

The batter for these small, turban-shaped almond cakes is flavored with browned butter and is very similar to that for Friands (page 236). Visitandines were originally made by nuns of the Order of the Visitation in Nancy. They have a thin, crusty surface with a soft and rich interior, and like Madeleines (page 218) they have a distinctive hump on the back. With their high butter and almond content, they are among the most opulent of the madeleines family.

Visitandine *plaques* are an uncommon mold, and many pastry chefs use *barquette* molds instead. You might also bake them in madeleine *plaques* or even gem pans, but undoubtedly the nuns would take a dim view of such alterations.

EQUIPMENT

2 *visitandine* plaques stamped with 8 turban-shaped depressions, each 2⅜ inches (6 cm) wide
- Clarified butter, melted
- Flour

A #40 ice cream scoop, or a tablespoon

BATTER

1¾ ounces (50 g), or ⅓ cup plus 1 teaspoon, all-purpose flour

6 ounces (170 g), or 1¼ cups, almond and sugar powder

Basic Preparation, page 482:

3 ounces (85 g), or ½ cup plus 1 tablespoon, blanched almonds

3 ounces (85 g), or ⅔ cup plus 2 teaspoons, confectioners' sugar

½ ounce (15 g), or 1 tablespoon, superfine sugar

4 large egg whites, at room temperature

1 teaspoon (½ cl) vanilla extract

3½ ounces (100 g), or 7 tablespoons, unsalted butter

For 16 cookies

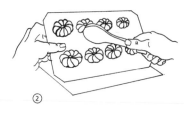

①

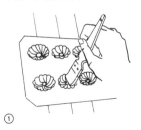

②

1. Brush the *visitandine* plaques ① with clarified butter. Spoon some flour into each mold and shake the mold back and forth to coat it evenly. Then turn each mold upside down and tap the back sharply with a wooden spatula ② to dislodge the excess flour.

Preheat the oven to 450° F (230° C).

2. Sift the flour. Combine the almond and sugar powder, flour, superfine sugar, egg whites, and vanilla in your electric mixer. Stir with the wire whip to mix thoroughly.

3. Melt the butter in a 1-quart (1 L) saucepan, and boil it. Foam will come to the top. When it collapses, stir to mix. Continue to boil. Soon bubbles will start to form on the surface, at first large bubbles and then progressively smaller ones. When the surface is covered with an opaque foam of tiny bubbles and the foam mounts ③ in the saucepan, stir to deflate it. Boil the butter until a new layer of tiny bubbles forms on top, then stir to deflate it again. Pour through a fine strainer into a bowl. This is *beurre noisette,* or browned butter.

③

④

4. Turn on the electric mixer at low speed, and pour in the hot browned butter in a steady stream. Continue to stir at low speed with the wire whip until the batter is cool. It will be a little runny. Do not overbeat.

5. Spoon 5 teaspoons (2½ cl) of batter into each mold using the ice cream scoop ④ or tablespoon. (If you have only 1 plaque, keep the remaining batter in the bowl until the first baking is completed.)

6. Bake until the cookies brown very lightly on top and spring back to the touch, about 12 to 15 minutes.

7. Unmold the cookies onto a wire rack, turn them right side up, and let cool to room temperature.

➤ **HOWS & WHYS:** The traditional method for making Visitandines batter requires whipping some of the egg whites separately, and then folding them into the rest of the batter. Our method produces a finer texture and is much easier, particularly for the small quantity needed in the home kitchen.

STORAGE: Best eaten within a few hours.

FRIANDS
FRIANDS

As an adjective applied to food, friand *means "dainty" or "tasty." In* cuisine, friands à la saucisse *(sausage friands) are small rolls of sausage meat wrapped in flaky pastry dough. But in* pâtisserie, *when* friands *is used as a noun, it is almost invariably short for* friands aux amandes *(almond friands) and refers to these little almond cakes baked in rectangular* petits fours *molds. Sometimes called* financiers, *they are made from a batter similar to* Visitandines *but have an even more pronounced nutty flavor of browned butter. True to their name, Friands are both dainty and tasty. They have been a staple at Paul Bugat's* Pâtisserie Clichy *for generations, and they are one of our personal favorites.*

EQUIPMENT
40 rectangular *petits fours* molds 2 inches (5 cm) long, 1 inch (2½ cm) wide, and ⅜ inch (1 cm) deep
• Clarified butter, melted
1 large, heavy baking sheet
A large pastry bag fitted with
• a ⁷⁄₁₆-inch (11 mm) plain pastry tube (Ateco #5)

1¾ ounces (50 g), or ¼ cup, superfine sugar
3 large egg whites, at room temperature
½ teaspoon (¼ cl) vanilla extract
3 ounces (85 g), or 6 tablespoons, unsalted butter, softened

OPTIONAL DECORATION
40 blanched almonds

BATTER
1¼ ounces (35 g), or ¼ cup, all-purpose flour
3½ ounces (100 g), or ¾ cup, almond and sugar powder
  Basic Preparation, page 482:
  { 1¾ ounces (50 g), or ⅓ cup, blanched almonds
  { 1¾ ounces (50 g), or ⅓ cup plus 4 teaspoons, confectioners' sugar

For 40 cookies

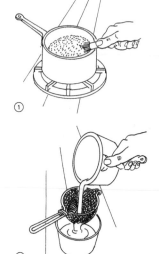

①

②

1. Sift the flour. Combine the almond and sugar powder, flour, superfine sugar, egg whites, and vanilla extract in your electric mixer and stir with the wire whip to mix thoroughly.

2. Melt the butter in a 1-quart (1 L) saucepan, and boil it. Foam will come to the top. When it collapses, stir to mix. Continue to boil. Soon bubbles will start to form on the surface, at first large bubbles and then progressively smaller ones. When the surface is covered with an opaque foam of tiny bubbles and the foam mounts ① in the saucepan, stir to deflate it. Boil the butter until a new layer of tiny bubbles forms on top, then stir to deflate it again. Pour through a fine strainer ② into a bowl. This is *beurre noisette*, or browned butter.

3. Turn on the electric mixer at low speed and pour in the hot browned butter in a steady stream. Continue to stir at low speed with the wire whip until the batter is cool. The batter will be easier to pipe into the

molds and will bake better if you first allow it to chill in the refrigerator for several hours or overnight.

Preheat the oven to 450° F (230° C).

4. Brush the *petits fours* molds ③ with clarified butter, and arrange them on the baking sheet.

5. Scoop the batter into a pastry bag, and pipe the batter ④ into the molds, filling them by about two-thirds. Place an optional blanched almond on the center of each. (If you don't have enough molds for the entire recipe, keep the remaining batter in the pastry bag until the first baking is completed.)

6. Bake until the Friands brown lightly around the edges and spring back to the touch, about 7 to 10 minutes.

7. Slide the molds onto a wire rack and let rest until cool enough to touch, but still hot. Unmold the Friands onto the rack and let cool to room temperature.

STORAGE: Best eaten the day they are baked. The uncooked batter can be kept in the refrigerator, covered airtight, for up to 1 week.

JACONAS
JACONAS
~~~~~~~~~~

The name is a total mystery, but these delightful, butter-rich cookies are simply pain de gênes *(an almond pound cake)* batter baked in round or square petits fours *molds. Simply seductive!*

EQUIPMENT
32 *tartelette* molds, either 1½-inch (4 cm) round or 1⅝-inch (4½ cm) square, or some of each
• Clarified butter, melted
1 large, heavy baking sheet
A large pastry bag fitted with
• a ⁷⁄₁₆-inch (11 mm) plain pastry tube (Ateco #5)

BATTER
4 ounces (120 g), or ¾ cup plus 2½ tablespoons, almond and sugar powder
 Basic Preparation, page 482:
 2 ounces (60 g), or ⅓ cup plus 1 tablespoon, blanched almonds
 2 ounces (60 g), or ½ cup, confectioners' sugar

1 large egg, at room temperature
⅓ ounce (10 g), or 1 tablespoon plus ½ teaspoon, all-purpose flour
⅓ ounce (10 g), or 1 tablespoon plus ½ teaspoon, cornstarch
1 tablespoon (1½ cl) maraschino liqueur
1½ ounces (45 g), or 3 tablespoons, unsalted butter, barely melted

GLAZE
2½ tablespoons (50 g) strained apricot jam
 [*Basic Preparation, page 484*]

DECORATION
8 glacé cherries, cut in quarters

For 32 cookies

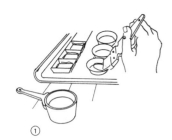
①

②

1. Brush the *petits fours* molds heavily with clarified butter ① and arrange them on the baking sheet.

2. Combine the almond and sugar powder with the egg in your electric mixer and beat with the wire whip, starting at low and gradually increasing to medium speed, until cream-colored and light. Sift the flour and cornstarch and gently fold them into the batter. When the flour is almost completely incorporated, add about ¼ cup (6 cl) of the batter and the maraschino liqueur to the butter and stir with a wooden spatula to mix thoroughly. Then gently fold in the remaining batter. Let the batter rest in the refrigerator for 30 to 60 minutes.

Preheat the oven at 450° F (230° C).

3. Scoop the batter into the pastry bag, and pipe the batter ② into the molds, filling them by about three-quarters. (If you don't have enough molds for the entire recipe, keep the remaining batter in the pastry bag until the first baking is completed.)

4. Bake until the cakes spring back to the touch and just begin to brown around the edges but are still pale in the center, about 5 to 8 minutes.

5. Slide the molds onto a wire rack and let rest until cool enough to handle, but still hot. Then unmold the cookies and let them finish cooling on the wire rack.

③

6. Warm the apricot jam over low heat, stirring occasionally, until melted. Brush the top of each cookie with jam until lightly coated and glistening. Place a quarter of a glacé cherry on the center ③ of each, then lightly brush the cherries with jam.

➤ **HOWS & WHYS:** Refrigerating the batter before piping makes it less runny, so it is easier to pipe.

STORAGE: Covered airtight in a tin cookie box or a cookie jar, in 1 layer so they don't stick together, for up to 1 or 2 days.

LITTLE PROVENÇAL CAKES
PETITS PROVENÇAUX

This is a spin-off of Madeleines (page 218), not a smaller version of the cookies we call simply Provençaux (page 232). Almonds are ground to a paste with milk, anisette liqueur, and sugar, then mixed with a madeleine batter and baked in round or square petits fours molds. The cookies are called provençaux, the plural of the adjective that means "pertaining to Provence," because anisette and almonds are popular in the south of France.

EQUIPMENT

36 *tartelette* molds, either 1½-inch (4 cm) round or 1⅝-inch (4½ cm) square, or some of each
- Clarified butter, melted
- Blanched almonds, finely chopped

1 large, heavy baking sheet
A large pastry bag fitted with
- a ⅜-inch (1 cm) plain pastry tube (Ateco #4)

BATTER

3 ounces (85 g), or ½ cup plus 1 tablespoon, blanched almonds
2 tablespoons (3 cl) anisette liqueur
3 tablespoons (4½ cl) milk
1¾ ounces (50 g), or ⅓ cup plus 4 teaspoons, confectioners' sugar
1¼ ounces (35 g), or ¼ cup, all-purpose flour
1¼ ounces (35 g), or 3 tablespoons, superfine sugar
1 large egg, separated, at room temperature
1¼ ounces (35 g), or 2½ tablespoons, unsalted butter, barely melted

For 36 cookies

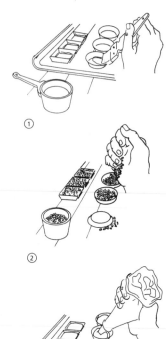

1. Brush the *petits fours* molds ① with clarified butter. Fill each mold with chopped almonds ②, then turn it upside down and tap it sharply on the countertop to dislodge the excess almonds. Arrange the molds on the baking sheet.

2. Combine the almonds, anisette, milk, and confectioners' sugar in your electric blender and puree at high speed until the mixture is a smooth paste. Transfer to a bowl.

Preheat the oven to 425° F (220° C).

3. Sift the flour. Combine the sugar with the egg white in your electric mixer and beat at medium speed with the flat beater. When the mixture is white and frothy, add the yolk and continue beating until creamy yellow and frothy. Turn the mixer down to low and gradually add the flour. When mixed, gradually add the melted butter. Finally, mix in the almond paste. Transfer the batter to a small bowl and let it rest in the refrigerator for 30 minutes.

4. Scoop the batter into the pastry bag, and pipe a 1½-teaspoon (¾ cl) mound of batter ③ into each mold. (If you don't have enough molds for the entire recipe, pipe and bake as much batter as you have molds for. Keep the remaining batter in the pastry bag until the first baking is completed.)

5. Bake until the cookies brown lightly around the edges and spring back to the touch, about 8 to 10 minutes. Slide them onto a wire rack and let rest until cool enough to handle, but still hot. Then unmold them onto a wire rack and let cool to room temperature.

➤ **HOW & WHYS:** The old-fashioned way to make the almond paste for this recipe was with a mortar and pestle. That is hard work, and a blender is much faster. A food processor does not work well with such a small quantity because most of it ends up on the side of the processor bowl.

STORAGE: Best eaten the day they are made. If necessary, can be kept covered airtight in a cookie jar or tin cookie box for a few days.

FRENCH BROWNIES
CARRÉS CHOCOLAT

~~~~~~

For our taste, this is the ultimate brownie—moist, dense, and unconscionably rich (but not heavy), with most of the flour replaced by powdered raw almonds. The old-fashioned way was to glaze carrés chocolat (literally, "chocolate squares") with chocolate fondant, but the trend today is to use a very elegant (and easy) glaze of shiny bittersweet chocolate. They could also be served as unglazed brownies, but that would not be very French. Including chunks of nuts in the brownies would be out of the question from the French point of view.

EQUIPMENT

A 9-inch (24 cm) square cake pan, about 1½ inches (3½–4 cm) deep
- Brush with melted clarified butter.
- Dust with flour.

BATTER

4½ ounces (125 g), or ½ cup plus 1 tablespoon, unsalted butter, softened

4½ ounces (130 g), or ¾ cup plus 3½ tablespoons, raw-almond and sugar powder

{ *Basic Preparation, page 482:*

2¼ ounces (65 g), or ¼ cup plus 3 tablespoons, raw almonds

2¼ ounces (65 g), or ½ cup plus 2 teaspoons, confectioners' sugar

1 ounce (25 g), or 2 tablespoons, superfine sugar

1 large egg, at room temperature

3 large eggs, separated, at room temperature

1 teaspoon (½ cl) vanilla extract

4½ ounces (125 g) European bittersweet chocolate (such as Lindt Excellence), melted

⅛ teaspoon (½ ml) cream of tartar (optional)

1 ounce (30 g), or 3½ tablespoons, all-purpose flour

GLAZE

7 ounces (200 g) European bittersweet chocolate (such as Lindt Surfin)

1 teaspoon (½ cl) almond oil (preferably) or neutral vegetable oil

For 25 cookies

Preheat the oven to 350° F (175° C).

1. Place the butter in your electric mixer and beat with the flat beater until smooth, white, and creamy. Beat in the raw-almond and sugar powder and ⅓ ounce (10 g), or 2½ teaspoons, of the superfine sugar. When smooth and light, beat in the whole egg. Beat in the egg yolks one by one with the wire whip, then beat in the vanilla and the chocolate.

2. Whip the egg whites in an electric mixer at low speed until they start to froth. If you are not whipping the whites in a copper bowl, then add the cream of tartar at this point. Gradually increase the whipping speed to medium-high, and continue whipping until the whites are stiff but not dry. Add the remaining superfine sugar and whip at high speed for a few seconds longer to incorporate the sugar and tighten the meringue.

3. Sift the flour over the chocolate mixture, add about a third of the meringue, and stir with a wooden spatula to mix quickly. Then gently fold in the remaining meringue.

4. Transfer the batter to the cake pan, spread it evenly, and smooth the surface ①.

5. Bake until the top of the cake is dry and springs back to the touch, about 25 to 32 minutes. Then unmold it onto a wire rack, turn it right side up onto a second rack, and let cool to room temperature.

6. When ready to glaze, trim any large bumps from the surface ② of the cake. Then invert it onto a cake cardboard so that you have a perfectly flat top surface to coat with chocolate.

7. Temper the chocolate with the almond oil as follows: Melt the chocolate ③ and stir in the almond oil. Dip the bottom of the pot of chocolate in a bowl of cold water and stir the chocolate until it begins to thicken. Immediately remove from the cold water and dip the bottom of the pot of chocolate in a bowl of hot water. Stir over the hot water just long enough to make the chocolate fluid again, then remove from the hot water.

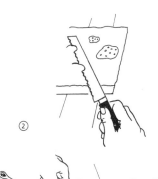

8. Pour the chocolate over the top of the cake and spread it evenly with a palette knife ④, letting the excess flow down the sides. Then let the chocolate set.

9. Carefully trim the edges from the cake and cut the rest into 1⅝-inch (4 cm) squares ⑤. You can either saw through the chocolate glaze with a bread knife, or melt through it using a slicing knife with the blade warmed before each cut. In either case, work slowly so that you don't crack the chocolate. Do not separate the squares until ready to serve, and pack the trimmings against the sides of the cake to prevent them from drying out.

➤ **HOWS & WHYS:** We advise against black steel cake pans because they make the bottom and sides of the cake cook too quickly.

STORAGE: In a covered cake platter for up to 3 or 4 days. Keep in a cool place—below 70° F (20° C)—to prevent fat bloom from forming on the chocolate glaze. If already cut, pack the trimmings against the sides of the cake to prevent the sides from drying out.

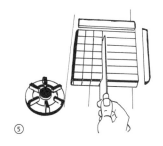

CHESTNUT SQUARES
CARRÉS AUX MARRONS

The French love chestnut desserts, so it may seem surprising that chestnut cookies are so rare. In fact, these unusual, starchy nuts don't lend themselves to many cookie preparations. But here is the exception. Our opulent Chestnut Squares are a heavenly chestnut cake glazed with bittersweet chocolate. Fifty years ago they would have been glazed with vanilla or chocolate fondant, but the modern fashion is to use less fondant and more pure chocolate glazes. The thin, meltingly firm glaze is the perfect foil for the sumptuous chestnut flavor and moist, delicate texture of this cake.

EQUIPMENT

A 9-inch (24 cm) square cake pan, about 1½ inches (3½–4 cm) deep
- Brush with melted butter.
- Dust with flour.

BATTER

2⅔ ounces (75 g), or ¼ cup plus 2 tablespoons, superfine sugar

2 large eggs, separated, at room temperature

1 teaspoon (½ cl) vanilla extract

An 8¾-ounce (250 g) can *crème de marrons* (chestnut spread)

2 ounces (60 g), or 4 tablespoons, unsalted butter, barely melted

⅛ teaspoon (½ ml) cream of tartar (optional)

1½ ounces (45 g), or ¼ cup plus 3½ teaspoons, all-purpose flour

GLAZE

7 ounces (200 g) European bittersweet chocolate (such as Lindt Surfin)

1 teaspoon (½ cl) almond oil (preferably) or neutral vegetable oil

For 25 cookies

Preheat the oven to 425° F (220° C).

1. Set aside ⅓ ounce (10 g), or 2½ teaspoons, of the superfine sugar. Combine the remaining sugar with the egg yolks and vanilla in your electric mixer and beat with the wire whip, starting at low and gradually increasing to medium speed, until light, thick, and smooth. Beat in the chestnut spread, followed by the butter.

2. Whip the egg whites in an electric mixer at low speed until they start to froth. If you are not whipping the whites in a copper bowl, then add the cream of tartar at this point. Gradually increase the whipping speed to medium-high, and continue whipping until the whites are stiff but not dry. Add the reserved superfine sugar and whip at high speed for a few seconds longer to incorporate the sugar and tighten the meringue.

3. Sift the flour over the egg yolk mixture, add about a third of the meringue, and stir with a wooden spatula to mix quickly. Then gently fold in the remaining meringue.

4. Pour the batter into the cake pan, spread it evenly, and smooth the surface ①.

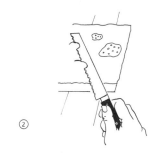

②

③

④

⑤

5. Bake until the top of the cake is lightly browned and springs back to the touch, about 16 to 20 minutes. Then unmold it onto a wire rack, turn it right side up onto a second rack, and let cool to room temperature.

6. When ready to glaze, trim any large bumps from the surface ② of the cake. Then invert it onto a cake cardboard so that you have a perfectly flat top surface to coat with chocolate.

7. Temper the chocolate with the almond oil as follows: Melt the chocolate ③ and stir in the almond oil. Dip the bottom of the pot of chocolate in a bowl of cold water and stir the chocolate until it begins to thicken. Immediately remove from the cold water and dip the bottom of the pot of chocolate in a bowl of hot water. Stir over the hot water just long enough to make the chocolate fluid again, then remove from the hot water.

8. Pour the chocolate over the top of the cake and spread it evenly with a palette knife ④, letting the excess flow down the sides. Then let the chocolate set.

9. Carefully trim the edges from the cake and cut the rest into 1⅝-inch (4 cm) squares ⑤. You can either saw through the chocolate glaze with a bread knife, or melt through it using a slicing knife with the blade warmed before each cut. In either case, work slowly so that you don't crack the chocolate. Do not separate the squares until ready to serve, and pack the trimmings against the sides of the cake to prevent them from drying out.

➤ **HOWS & WHYS:** In this recipe we have used a separated egg batter made by the traditional procedure. The whites are whipped only to the stiff-but-not-dry stage because they are meringued with very little sugar. If they were whipped to the slip-and-streak stage, the small amount of sugar would not make them cohesive enough and they would be difficult to incorporate into the batter. This is also true for French Brownies and Algerian Almond Squares, which are produced by a variant of the creamed butter method.

We advise against black steel cake pans because they make the bottom and sides of the cake cook too quickly.

STORAGE: In a covered cake platter for up to 3 or 4 days. Keep in a cool place—below 70° F (20° C)—to prevent fat bloom from forming on the chocolate glaze. If already cut, pack the trimmings against the sides of the cake to prevent the sides from drying out.

MATILDAS
MATHILDES

Here is a dense, moist bar cookie, rich with chopped glacé fruits and powdered almonds and flavored with rum. It is glazed with apricot jam and covered with chopped almonds and pistachios, completing a nice medley of colors, textures, and tastes.

EQUIPMENT

An 8-inch (20 cm) square cake pan, about 1½ inches (3½–4 cm) deep

- Brush with melted butter.
- Line the bottom with newsprint (preferably) or kitchen parchment.
- Brush the newsprint or parchment with melted butter.

BATTER

2 ounces (60 g), or 4 tablespoons, unsalted butter, softened

1 ounce (25 g), or 3 tablespoons, all-purpose flour

1 ounce (25 g), or 3 tablespoons, cornstarch

3 ounces (85 g), or ½ cup, glacé fruits

6 ounces (170 g), or 1¼ cups, almond and sugar powder

   Basic Preparation, page 482:

   3 ounces (85 g), or ½ cup plus 1 tablespoon, blanched almonds

   3 ounces (85 g), or ⅔ cup plus 2 teaspoons, confectioners' sugar

2 large eggs, at room temperature

4 teaspoons (2 cl) dark Jamaican rum

DECORATION

½ ounce (15 g), or 1 tablespoon plus 2 teaspoons, blanched almonds

½ ounce (15 g), or 1 tablespoon plus 2 teaspoons, unsalted, shelled pistachios

GLAZE

2 tablespoons (40 g) strained apricot jam
   [*Basic Preparation*, page 484]

For 28 cookies

Preheat the oven to 350° F (175° C).

1. Place the butter in a small stainless-teel bowl and beat with a wooden spatula, warming it over low heat as needed, to make it smooth, white, and creamy.

2. Sift the flour and cornstarch over the glacé fruits and chop them finely with your chef's knife.

3. Combine the almond and sugar powder with the eggs in your electric mixer and beat with the wire whip, starting at low and gradually increasing to medium speed, until cream-colored, thick, and light. Gently fold in the glacé fruits, flour, and cornstarch. When almost completely incorporated, add the rum and about ½ cup (1.2 dl) of the batter to the creamed butter, and stir with a wooden spatula to mix thoroughly. Then gently fold in the remaining batter.

4. Pour the batter into the cake pan, spread it evenly, and smooth the surface ①.

5. Bake until the top of the cake is a uniform beige and springs back to the touch, about 20 to 25 minutes.

6. Slide a palette knife around the sides ② of the pan to loosen the edges of the cake. Unmold the cake onto a wire rack and carefully peel off

①

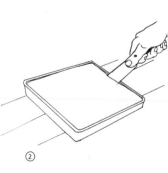

②

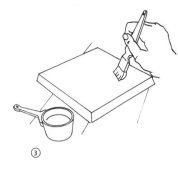

③

④

the newsprint. Lay the newsprint on the cake and turn it right side up onto another wire rack. Let the cake cool to room temperature.

7. Meanwhile, spread out the almonds on a baking sheet and roast them, stirring occasionally, until they are brown in the center, about 15 minutes. (Test by cutting one in half.) Transfer the almonds to your countertop and let them cool. Then chop the almonds and pistachios finely.

8. Warm the apricot jam over low heat, stirring occasionally, until melted. Brush the top of the cake ③ with the jam, then scatter the chopped almonds and pistachios over the cake ④. Let the jam dry for a couple of hours.

9. When ready to serve, trim off the edges of the cake and cut the rest into 1 by 1¾-inch (2½ by 4½ cm) rectangles ⑤ with your chef's knife.

➤ **HOWS & WHYS:** We advise against black steel cake pans because they make the bottom and sides of the cake cook too quickly.

STORAGE: In a covered cake platter for up to 3 days. If already cut, pack the trimmings against the sides of the cake to prevent the sides from drying out.

⑤

SUCCESS
RÉUSSIS

T*he name réussis, which translates literally as ''well made,'' suggests that the chef who created this bar cookie was very pleased with the result. Over a century later, so are we! The cake contains no butter but is enriched with powdered almonds, and after baking it is brushed with maraschino liqueur to flavor and moisten it. The top is then glazed with apricot jam and dusted with chopped almonds.*

EQUIPMENT
A 10-inch (25 cm) square cake pan, about 1½ inches (3½–4 cm) deep
- Brush with melted butter.
- Line the bottom with newsprint (preferably) or kitchen parchment.
- Brush the newsprint or parchment with melted butter.

BATTER
4½ ounces (130 g), or ¾ cup plus 3½ tablespoons, almond and sugar powder
Basic Preparation, page 482:
  2¼ ounces (65 g), or ¼ cup plus 3 tablespoons, blanched almonds
  2¼ ounces (65 g), or ½ cup plus 2 teaspoons, confectioners' sugar

For 54 cookies

3 large eggs, 2 of them separated, at room temperature
1 teaspoon (½ cl) vanilla extract
⅛ teaspoon (½ ml) cream of tartar (optional)
¾ ounce (20 g), or 1½ tablespoons, superfine sugar
1¾ ounces (50 g), or ⅓ cup plus 1 teaspoon, all-purpose flour

IMBIBAGE
1¾ ounces (50 g), or ¼ cup, sugar
2 tablespoons (3 cl) water
¼ cup (6 cl) maraschino liqueur

DECORATION
1½ ounces (45 g), or ¼ cup plus 1 tablespoon, blanched almonds

GLAZE
3 tablespoons (60 g) strained apricot jam
  [*Basic Preparation, page 484*]

Preheat the oven to 375° F (190° C).

1. Combine the almond and sugar powder, 1 whole egg, 2 egg yolks, and the vanilla in your electric mixer and beat with the wire whip, starting at low and gradually increasing to medium speed, until cream-colored, thick, and light.

2. Whip the egg whites in an electric mixer at low speed until they start to froth. If you are not whipping the whites in a copper bowl, then add the cream of tartar at this point. Gradually increase the whipping speed to medium-high, and continue whipping until the whites form very stiff peaks and just begin to slip and streak around the side of the bowl. Add the superfine sugar and whip at high speed for a few seconds longer to incorporate the sugar and tighten the meringue.

3. Sift the flour over the egg yolk mixture, add about a third of the meringue, and stir with a wooden spatula to mix quickly. Then gently fold in the remaining meringue.

4. Pour the batter into the cake pan, spread it evenly, and smooth the surface ①.

①

5. Bake until the top of the cake is a pale uniform beige and springs back to the touch, about 13 to 16 minutes.

6. Slide a palette knife around the sides ② of the pan to loosen the edges of the cake. Unmold the cake onto a wire rack and carefully peel off the newsprint. Lay the newsprint on the cake and turn it right side up onto another wire rack. Let the cake cool to room temperature.

②

7. For the *imbibage*, combine the sugar and water in a butter melter and bring to a boil, stirring as needed to dissolve all of the sugar. Immediately remove from the heat and let this heavy syrup cool. Stir together the maraschino liqueur and heavy syrup and brush the top of the cake ③ with it, using as much as you can without making the cake soggy.

③

8. Spread out the almonds on a baking sheet and roast them, stirring occasionally, until they are brown in the center, about 15 minutes. (Test by cutting one in half.) Transfer the almonds to your countertop and let them cool. Chop the almonds.

9. Warm the apricot jam over low heat, stirring occasionally, until melted. Brush the top of the cake with the jam, then scatter the chopped almonds over the cake ④. Let the jam dry for a couple of hours.

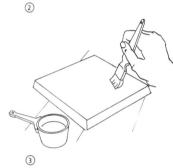

④

10. When ready to serve, trim off the edges of the cake and cut the rest into 1 by 1½-inch (2½ by 3¾ cm) rectangles ⑤ with your chef's knife.

➤ **HOWS & WHYS:** We advise against black steel cake pans because they make the bottom and sides of the cake cook too quickly.

STORAGE: In a covered cake platter for up to 4 days. If already cut, pack the trimmings against the sides of the cake to prevent the sides from drying out.

⑤

ALGERIAN ALMOND SQUARES
ALGÉRIENS

~~~~~~~
~~~~~~~

Following the conquest of Algeria in the mid-nineteenth century, the French adopted a policy of colonization and assimilation of their newly won territory. While assimilation never really worked politically, the French pastry chefs were, as ever, successful in enriching *pâtisserie* by absorbing the lessons of another culture. The moist, almond-rich cake squares called *algériens* are a striking example. While not as famous as *Blidas* (page 76), their moist, dense texture, subtle flavoring with orange juice, and heavy dusting with confectioners' sugar all point to their North African inspiration.

EQUIPMENT

An 8-inch (20 cm) square cake pan, about 1½ inches (3½–4 cm) deep

- Brush with melted butter.
- Line the bottom with newsprint (preferably) or kitchen parchment.
- Brush the newsprint or parchment with melted butter.

2 large eggs, separated, at room temperature
3 tablespoons (5 cl) fresh orange juice
1 teaspoon (½ cl) fresh lemon juice
⅛ teaspoon (½ ml) cream of tartar (optional)
⅓ ounce (10 g), or 2½ teaspoons, superfine sugar
1¼ ounces (35 g), or ¼ cup, cornstarch

DECORATION

Confectioners' sugar

BATTER

2½ ounces (70 g), or 5 tablespoons, unsalted butter, softened
6 ounces (170 g), or 1¼ cups, almond and sugar powder

{ *Basic Preparation, page 482:*
3 ounces (85 g), or ½ cup plus 1 tablespoon, blanched almonds
3 ounces (85 g), or ⅔ cup plus 2 teaspoons, confectioners' sugar

For 36 cookies

Preheat the oven to 425° F (220° C).

1. Place the butter in your electric mixer and beat with the flat beater until smooth, white, and creamy. Beat in the almond and sugar powder, and when smooth and light, beat in the egg yolks. Beat in the orange and lemon juices with the wire whip.

2. Whip the egg whites in an electric mixer at low speed until they start to froth. If you are not whipping the whites in a copper bowl, then add the cream of tartar at this point. Gradually increase the whipping speed to medium-high, and continue whipping until the whites are stiff but not dry. Add the superfine sugar and whip at high speed for a few seconds longer to incorporate the sugar and tighten the meringue.

3. Sift the cornstarch over the creamed butter mixture, add about a third of the meringue, and stir with a wooden spatula to mix quickly. Then gently fold in the remaining meringue.

4. Pour the batter into the cake pan, spread it evenly, and smooth the surface ①.

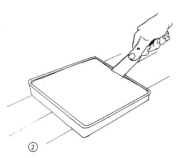

5. Bake until the top of the cake browns lightly and springs back to the touch, about 14 to 17 minutes.

6. Slide a palette knife around the sides ② of the pan to loosen the edges of the cake. Unmold the cake onto a wire rack and carefully peel off the newsprint. Lay the newsprint on the cake and turn it right side up onto another wire rack. Let the cake cool to room temperature.

7. When ready to serve, trim the edges of the cake and cut the rest into 1⅛-inch (3 cm) squares, without removing the edges or separating the squares. Dust the top of the cake ③ with confectioners' sugar, then separate the squares to serve them.

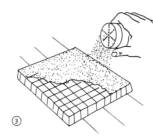

➤ **HOWS & WHYS:** We advise against black steel cake pans because they make the bottom and sides of the cake cook too quickly.

STORAGE: In a covered cake platter for up to 2 days. If already cut, pack the trimmings against the sides of the cake to prevent the sides from drying out.

CHAPTER 5
MISCELLANEOUS
NUT BATTERS

①

We call the recipes in this chapter "miscellaneous" because, unlike those in our other chapters, they are not based on a single general method. These cookies do, however, share several common characteristics: They all contain fairly large proportions of nuts and sugar and a low proportion of butter; they are all dry with a crisp, crunchy, or brittle texture; typically the mixing procedure amounts to little more than combining the ingredients in a bowl and stirring ①; and, for most of them, spooning the batter onto the baking sheet using a small ice cream scoop is a good alternative, if not the preferred procedure.

These cookies include some of the simplest in the French repertoire. They are also among the most distinctive and appealing. By far the largest group here is the *tuile* family ("tile" cookies). The traditional Almond Tiles are thin, crisp, round cookies that contain sliced almonds and are bent into arches to resemble Spanish roof tiles. There are many variations—for example, substituting hazelnuts for almonds (Hazelnut Tiles), flavoring with orange (Incredibles), and even leaving the cookies flat. The flat variations include Almond Tile Sandwiches (filled with meringue), Lemon Galettes and Citron Wafers (flavored with candied citrus fruits), and Marquises (orange-flavored fingers coated on the back with chocolate). There is also a butter-rich variation (Buttery Almond Tiles) that is based on the creamed butter and sugar method of preparation and is included in Chapter 1 (page 16). For all tiles, eggs (whether whole eggs or just the whites) supply the liquid in the batter.

A second group of cookies have some similarities to tiles but use cream instead of eggs as the liquid in the batter. Typically they have a brittle rather than crisp texture. Florentines are by far the most famous cookies of this type. They are thin caramelized disks studded with sliced almonds, glacé fruits, and candied orange peel and coated with chocolate on the back. While not really difficult to make, Florentines are much more time-consuming than the other cookies in this chapter. Simpler related cookies are Russian Lace and Orange Galettes.

The remaining cookies here are quite different from both tiles and Florentines. Lyon Croquets are thick, light, and crunchy nut cookies. On the other hand, Ribbons and Praliné Tongues are wafer-thin and crisp. The batters for these last two are very similar and contain almond and sugar powder but no chopped or sliced nuts. While Praliné Tongues have the familiar shape of Cats' Tongues (page 10), Ribbons are very striking three-dimensional spirals.

PREPARING THE BAKING SHEETS

Most of these cookies are piped on buttered baking sheets ② so that the batter will spread as it bakes and the finished cookies will be very thin. Naturally, there are exceptions. Florentines and Russian Lace are more caramelized than most of the others, and we prefer to bake them on baking sheets lined with kitchen parchment. And Marquises need to be baked on buttered and floured baking sheets to keep their nice oval shape.

②

ICE CREAM SCOOP OR
PASTRY BAG

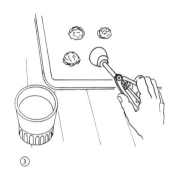

For most of the cookies in this chapter, the batter can be deposited on the baking sheets easily using a portion-control ice cream scoop ③. The sizes we use are #100 (1¾-teaspoon or 9 ml capacity) and #70 (2¾-teaspoon or 1.4-cl capacity), depending on the size of the cookies. (See the reference section on Equipment, page 418, for details and sources.) If too much batter sticks to the scoop, dip it in cold water after every 2 or 3 cookies. Lacking an ice cream scoop, you can drop the batter onto the baking sheets with a teaspoon or tablespoon, depending upon the size of the cookies. Scoop up a lump of batter. Then use a second spoon, or your fingertip (moistened in cold water as needed) to shape the batter into a ball, push it off the first spoon, and deposit it on the baking sheet ④ in a symmetrical mound.

③

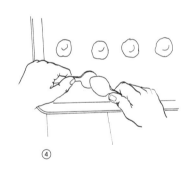

Piping the batter with a pastry bag also works very well provided the batter doesn't contain sliced almonds or diced candied fruit (which can clog the pastry tube) and isn't too runny. Three of the cookies in this chapter (Marquises, Ribbons, and Praliné Tongues) are shaped in fingers or strips, and must therefore be piped with the pastry bag in order to produce the required shapes. Piping techniques are explained in the reference section on "How to Use a Pastry Bag" (page 474).

④

For two cookies here—Florentines and Lyon Croquets—neither the ice cream scoop nor the pastry bag can be used to shape the batter. The batters for these cookies are very firm and must be cut with a knife.

STORAGE

Despite their diversity, the cookies in this chapter are similar in their storage limitations. All should be kept covered airtight in a tin cookie box or cookie jar, and most will last for up to one week. A few, such as Almond Tiles, will keep for only three or four days, and on the other hand Lyon Croquets are still good after two weeks.

As always, cookies that are glazed with chocolate must be kept cool—

below 70° F (20° C)—to prevent bloom from forming on the chocolate, and they should not be served in hot weather.

Many of these cookies are very fragile and break easily, so be careful not to crush or crack them when you put them in the cookie box or jar. For the arched tiles, it is best to arrange the cookies in neat overlapping rows in the cookie box so they don't take up too much space.

As with creamed butter and sugar cookies, all of our storage times assume that the cookies are not exposed to high humidity. If the weather is humid and the cookies become soft, any of the unglazed cookies can be dried and crisped by laying them out on a baking sheet in a low, 250° F (120° C) oven for a few minutes.

ALMOND TILES
TUILES AUX AMANDES

~~~~~~~~~

These thin, crisp cookies are among the most popular and enchanting of the French classics. Almond Tiles have an arched shape and are usually presented in neat, overlapping rows—like the Spanish roof tiles from which they take their name. The cookies are baked flat, then shaped when they come out of the oven.

Numerous books (including the distinguished Larousse Gastronomique) have recommended draping the baked cookies over a rolling pin to produce the requisite shape. In a professional pastry kitchen this procedure would be ridiculous because it is so tedious and the cookies are likely to fall off. After all, rolling pins are designed to roll. The standard professional method is to press the hot cookies upside down into a trough-shaped mold (such as a ring mold)—fast and foolproof.

EQUIPMENT

3 or 4 large, heavy baking sheets
• Brush with melted butter.
A #70 ice cream scoop, or a tablespoon
A narrow (about 2 inches or 5 cm wide) trough-shaped mold
• Either a special *tuiles* mold with multiple troughs
• Or a yule log mold, *pain de mie* mold, or ring mold

BATTER

4 ounces (115 g), or ½ cup plus 1 tablespoon, superfine sugar
4 ounces (115 g), or 1 cup plus 2½ tablespoons, sliced almonds
2 large eggs, at room temperature
½ teaspoon (¼ cl) vanilla extract
1¼ ounces (35 g), or ¼ cup, all-purpose flour
½ ounce (15 g), or 1 tablespoon, unsalted butter, melted

For about 25 to 30 cookies

Preheat the oven to 400° F (200° C).

1. Combine the sugar and almonds in a bowl, and stir in the eggs and vanilla with a wooden spatula. Sift the flour over the batter and stir it in, then stir in the butter.

2. Spoon the batter onto the baking sheets in 2½-teaspoon (1¼ cl) mounds using the ice cream scoop or tablespoon. Arrange the mounds in staggered rows and separate them by 1½ to 2 inches (4–5 cm).

3. Flatten each mound ① by pressing with the back of a fork (dipped in cold water as needed to prevent sticking).

①

4. Bake, 1 sheet at a time, until the batter has spread and the cookies are browned around the edges but still pale in the center, about 7 to 10 minutes.

5. Remove the baking sheet from the oven. Lift each cookie with a metal spatula and press it upside down into a trough-shaped mold ②. Once the cookies are cool enough to hold their shape, they can be unmolded and more cookies pressed into the mold.

STORAGE: Covered airtight in a cookie jar or tin cookie box for up to 3 or 4 days.

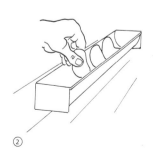

②

INCREDIBLES
INCROYABLES

This variation on Almond Tiles (page 257) contains chopped almonds and is flavored with orange juice and zest. The chef who originated the recipe obviously thought they were unbelievably good. Are they better than Almond Tiles? We'll let you be the judge.

EQUIPMENT

2 or 3 large, heavy baking sheets
• Brush heavily with melted butter.
A large pastry bag fitted with
• a ⅝-inch (16 mm) plain pastry tube (Ateco #8),
or a #70 ice cream scoop
A narrow (about 2 inches or 5 cm wide) trough-shaped mold
• Either a special *tuiles* mold with multiple troughs
• Or a yule log mold, *pain de mie* mold, or ring mold

BATTER

3 ounces (85 g), or ½ cup plus 1 tablespoon, blanched almonds, chopped
4 ounces (115 g), or ¾ cup plus 3 tablespoons, confectioners' sugar
2 large egg whites, at room temperature
2 teaspoons (1 cl) milk
1 tablespoon (1½ cl) fresh orange juice
1 teaspoon (½ cl) finely grated orange zest
Red food coloring
1¾ ounces (50 g), or ⅓ cup plus 1 tablespoon, all-purpose flour
1¾ ounces (50 g), or 3½ tablespoons, unsalted butter, melted

For about 25 to 30 cookies

Preheat the oven to 400° F (200° C).

1. Combine the almonds and sugar in a bowl, and stir in the egg whites, milk, orange juice and zest, and a drop of red food coloring with a wooden spatula. Sift the flour over the batter and stir it in, then stir in the butter.

2. Scoop the batter into the pastry bag, and pipe the batter ① onto the baking sheets in 2½-teaspoon (5 cl) mounds. Arrange the mounds in staggered rows and separate them by at least 2 inches (5 cm). Or, spoon the batter in 2½-teaspoon (1¼ cl) mounds using the ice cream scoop or a tablespoon.

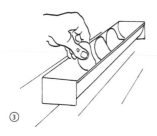

3. Flatten each mound ② by pressing with the back of a fork (dipped in cold water as needed to prevent sticking) to get an even distribution of almonds.

4. Bake, 1 sheet at a time, until the cookies are lighly browned around the edges but still pale pink in the center, about 6 to 9 minutes.

5. Remove the baking sheet from the oven. Lift each cookie with a metal spatula and press it upside down into a trough-shaped mold ③. Once the cookies are cool enough to hold their shape, they can be unmolded and more cookies pressed into the mold.

STORAGE: Covered airtight in a cookie jar or tin cookie box for up to 1 week.

HAZELNUT TILES
TUILES AUX NOISETTES

Chopped hazelnuts give these tile cookies a speckled appearance and a more intense flavor than Almond Tiles (page 257). Their assertive taste and crisp texture make Hazelnut Tiles a perfect companion to a dish of ice cream. The only difficulty is choosing between vanilla and chocolate—both pairings seem perfect.

EQUIPMENT

2 or 3 large, heavy baking sheets
• Brush with melted butter.
A large pastry bag fitted with
• a ⅝-inch (16 mm) plain pastry tube (Ateco #8),
or a #70 ice cream scoop
A narrow (about 2 inches or 5 cm wide) trough-shaped mold
• Either a special *tuiles* mold with multiple troughs
• Or a yule log mold, *pain de mie* mold, or ring mold

BATTER

3½ ounces (100 g), or ½ cup plus 3½ tablespoons, hazelnuts, chopped
3½ ounces (100 g), or ½ cup, superfine sugar
1 large egg, at room temperature
1 large egg white, at room temperature
1¼ ounces (35 g), or ¼ cup, all-purpose flour
½ ounce (15 g), or 1 tablespoon, unsalted butter, melted

For about 25 cookies

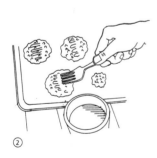
①

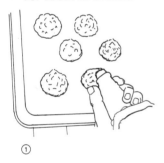
②

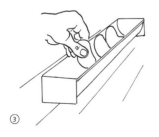
③

Preheat the oven to 400° F (200° C).

1. Combine the hazelnuts and sugar in a bowl and stir in the egg and egg white with a wooden spatula. Sift the flour over the batter and stir it in, then stir in the butter.

2. Scoop the batter into the pastry bag, and pipe the batter ① onto the baking sheets in 2½-teaspoon (1¼ cl) mounds. Arrange the mounds in staggered rows and separate them by at least 2 inches (5 cm). Or, spoon the batter in 2½-teaspoon (1¼ cl) mounds, using the ice cream scoop or a tablespoon.

3. Flatten each mound ② by pressing with the back of a fork (dipped in cold water as needed to prevent sticking) to get an even distribution of hazelnuts.

4. Bake, 1 sheet at a time, until the cookies are browned around the edges but still pale in the center, about 8 to 11 minutes.

5. Remove the baking sheet from the oven. Lift each cookie with a metal spatula and press it upside down into a trough-shaped mold ③. Once the cookies are cool enough to hold their shape, they can be unmolded and more cookies pressed into the mold.

STORAGE: Covered airtight in a cookie jar or tin cookie box for up to 1 week.

ALMOND TILE SANDWICHES
TUILES MIGNONS

This is a very thin, crisp type of tile cookie that is left flat rather than pressed into the usual roof-tile shape. The baked tiles are sandwiched with a vanilla meringue filling, and then baked a second time in a very low oven to dry the meringue. Thanks to the meringue filling, they are extraordinarily light and quite sweet, with an overwhelming flavor of vanilla.

EQUIPMENT

3 or 4 large, heavy baking sheets
• Brush heavily with melted butter.
A #100 ice cream scoop, or a tablespoon

BATTER

6 ounces (170 g), or 1 cup plus 2 tablespoons, sliced
    almonds
2½ ounces (70 g), or ½ cup plus 1 teaspoon, almond
    and sugar powder
Basic Preparation, page 482:
1¼ ounces (35 g), or 3 tablespoons plus
    2 teaspoons, blanched almonds
1¼ ounces (35 g), or ¼ cup plus 2 teaspoons,
    confectioners' sugar

5¼ ounces (150 g), or ¾ cup, superfine sugar
2 large eggs, at room temperature
2 large egg whites, at room temperature
1¼ ounces (35 g), or ¼ cup, all-purpose flour

FILLING

2 large egg whites, at room temperature
⅛ teaspoon (½ ml) cream of tartar (optional)
3½ ounces (100 g), or ½ cup, superfine sugar
1 teaspoon (½ cl) vanilla extract

For about 30 cookies

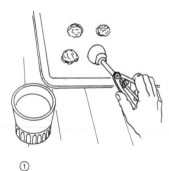

①

②

Preheat the oven to 375° F (190° C).

1. Chop the sliced almonds very coarsely and combine them with the almond and sugar powder and superfine sugar in a bowl. Stir in the eggs and egg whites with a wooden spatula. Sift the flour over the batter and stir it in.

2. Spoon the batter ① onto the baking sheets in 1½-teaspoon (¾ cl) mounds using the ice cream scoop or a tablespoon. Arrange the mounds in staggered rows and separate them by at least 2 inches (5 cm).

3. Flatten each mound ② by pressing with the back of a fork (dipped in cold water as needed to prevent sticking) to get an even distribution of almonds and make a thin round disk about 2 inches (5 cm) wide.

4. Bake, 1 sheet at a time, until the cookies are lightly browned around the edges but still pale in the centers, about 7 to 10 minutes.

5. Transfer the cookies to a wire rack with a metal spatula ③ and let cool to room temperature.

Reduce the oven temperature to 200° F (95° C). (To lower the oven temperature quickly, you can leave the oven door open temporarily.)

③

④

⑤

6. Prepare the filling as follows: Whip the egg whites in an electric mixer at low speed until they start to froth. If you are not whipping the whites in a copper bowl, then add the cream of tartar at this point. Gradually increase the whipping speed to medium-high, and continue whipping until the whites form very stiff peaks and just begin to slip and streak around the side of the bowl. Add the sugar ④ and whip at high speed for a few seconds longer to make the meringue smooth and shiny. Whip in the vanilla, then turn off the machine.

7. Using a palette knife, spread a layer of meringue ⅛- to ³⁄₁₆-inch (3–5 mm) thick on the back of one cookie ⑤ and sandwich it back to back with a second cookie. Gently press the 2 cookies together. Repeat with the remaining cookies. You may not need all of the meringue—use only enough to fill the space between the cookies.

8. Place the cookies on a wire rack and bake until the meringue is dry, about 1 to 1½ hours.

9. Remove from the oven and let the cookies cool on the wire rack.

➤ **HOWS & WHYS:** It is important that the oven temperature actually drop to 200° F (95° C) before you return the filled cookies to the oven. If the oven is much hotter than this, the cookies will darken and the meringue will turn beige rather than remaining white.

STORAGE: Covered airtight in a cookie jar or tin cookie box for up to 1 week.

OLD-FASHIONED TILES
TUILES ANCIENNES

These tile cookies contain almond and sugar powder as well as sliced almonds. They are a little thicker than Almond Tiles (page 257), making them less fragile and at the same time more old-fashioned. With an almond content of nearly 40 percent (and practically no flour), they are luxurious.

EQUIPMENT

2 or 3 large, heavy baking sheets
• Brush heavily with melted butter.
A #70 ice cream scoop, or a tablespoon
A narrow (about 2 inches or 5 cm wide) trough-shaped mold
• Either a special *tuiles* mold with multiple troughs
• Or a yule log mold, *pain de mie* mold, or ring mold

BATTER

3 ounces (90 g), or ⅔ cup, almond and sugar powder
} *Basic Preparation,* page 482:
{ 1½ ounces (45 g), or ¼ cup plus 1 tablespoon, blanched almonds
{ 1½ ounces (45 g), or ¼ cup plus 2 tablespoons, confectioners' sugar
}
1¼ ounces (35 g), or 3 tablespoons, superfine sugar
1½ ounces (45 g), or ¼ cup plus 3 tablespoons, sliced almonds
1 large egg, at room temperature
½ teaspoon (¼ cl) vanilla extract
⅓ ounce (10 g), or 1 tablespoon, all-purpose flour

For about 16 to 18 cookies

Preheat the oven to 375° F (190° C).

1. Combine the almond and sugar powder, superfine sugar, and sliced almonds in a small bowl, and stir in the egg and vanilla with a wooden spatula. Sift the flour over the batter and stir it in.

2. Spoon the batter onto the baking sheets in 2½-teaspoon (1¼ cl) mounds using the ice cream scoop or a tablespoon. Arrange the mounds in staggered rows and separate them by 1½ to 2 inches (4–5 cm).

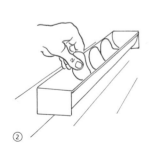
①

3. Flatten each mound ① by pressing with the back of a fork (dipped in cold water as needed to prevent sticking) to get an even distribution of almonds.

4. Bake, 1 sheet at a time, until the cookies are beige around the edges but still pale in the centers, about 10 to 14 minutes.

②

5. Remove the baking sheet from the oven. Lift each cookie with a metal spatula and press it upside down into a trough-shaped mold ②. Once the cookies are cool enough to hold their shape, they can be unmolded and more cookies pressed into the mold.

STORAGE: Covered airtight in a cookie jar or tin cookie box for up to 1 week.

LEMON GALETTES
GALETTES CITRON

Many pastries go by the name galette. *The one thing they have in common is that they are all round and flat. Lemon zest gives these thin almond cookies special pizzazz. We think they make a sensational partner to a dish of raspberry sorbet.*

EQUIPMENT

2 or 3 large, heavy baking sheets
• Brush lightly with melted butter.
A #100 ice cream scoop, or a tablespoon

BATTER

3½ ounces (100 g), or ⅔ cup, blanched almonds, chopped
3½ ounces (100 g), or ¾ cup plus 4 teaspoons, confectioners' sugar
Finely grated zest of ½ lemon

2 large egg whites, at room temperature
1½ ounces (40 g), or ¼ cup plus 1½ tablespoons, all-purpose flour
1½ ounces (40 g), or 3 tablespoons, unsalted butter, melted
Yellow food coloring

For about 40 cookies

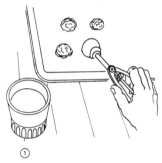

①

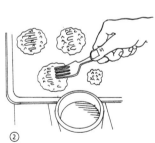

②

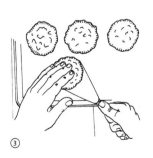

③

Preheat the oven to 375° F (190° C).

1. Combine the almonds, confectioners' sugar, and lemon zest in a bowl and stir in the egg whites with a wooden spatula. Sift the flour over the batter and stir it in. Then stir in the butter and tint the batter yellow with 2 drops of food coloring.

2. Spoon the batter onto the baking sheets ① in 1½-teaspoon (¾ cl) mounds using the ice cream scoop or tablespoon. Arrange the mounds in staggered rows and separate them by at least 2 inches (5 cm).

3. Flatten each mound ② by pressing with the back of a fork (dipped in cold water as needed to prevent sticking) to get an even distribution of almonds.

4. Bake, 1 sheet at a time, until the mounds have spread and flattened and are browned around the edges but still pale yellow in the centers, about 8 to 10 minutes.

5. Remove the baking sheet from the oven and let the cookies rest briefly on the baking sheet until they will hold their shape. Then lift each cookie with a metal spatula ③ and transfer it to a wire rack to cool.

STORAGE: Covered airtight in a cookie jar or tin cookie box for up to 1 week.

MARQUISES
MARQUISES

Orange zest and curaçao liqueur in these finger-shaped almond wafers are the perfect foil for the glaze of bittersweet chocolate on the backs. The subtle juxtaposition of orange and chocolate have made these exquisite cookies a bestseller for decades at Paul Bugat's pastry shop in Paris.

EQUIPMENT

2 or 3 large, heavy baking sheets
- Brush with melted butter.
- Dust with flour.

A large pastry bag fitted with
- a ⅜-inch (1 cm) plain pastry tube (Ateco #4)

BATTER

2½ ounces (70 g), or ½ cup plus 1 teaspoon, almond and sugar powder

{ *Basic Preparation, page 482:*
1¼ ounces (35 g), or 3 tablespoons plus 2 teaspoons, blanched almonds
1¼ ounces (35 g), or ¼ cup plus 2 teaspoons, confectioners' sugar

2¼ ounces (65 g), or ⅓ cup, superfine sugar

3 ounces (85 g), or ½ cup plus 1 tablespoon, blanched almonds, finely chopped

Finely grated zest of 1 orange

2 large egg whites, at room temperature

1 tablespoon (1½ cl) curaçao liqueur

1 ounce (25 g), or 3 tablespoons, all-purpose flour

1¼ ounces (35 g), or 2½ tablespoons, unsalted butter, melted

GLAZE

5¼ ounces (150 g) European bittersweet chocolate (such as Lindt Surfin)

¾ teaspoon (4 ml) almond oil (preferably) or neutral vegetable oil

For about 40 to 45 cookies

①

②

1. Mix the almond and sugar powder, superfine sugar, chopped almonds, and orange zest in a bowl. Stir in the egg whites and curaçao with a wooden spatula. Sift the flour over the batter and stir it in, then stir in the butter ①. Cover the batter airtight and refrigerate overnight, or for up to 1 week.

Preheat the oven to 350° F (175° C).

2. Scoop the batter into the pastry bag, and pipe the batter onto the baking sheets in diagonal fingers ② about 2½ inches (6 cm) long and ⅜ to ½ inch (10–12 mm) wide. Arrange the fingers in staggered rows and separate them by 1½ to 2 inches (4–5 cm).

3. Bake, 1 sheet at a time, until the cookies are lightly browned around the edges but still pale in the centers, about 9 to 13 minutes.

4. Remove from the oven, place the baking sheet on a wire rack, and let the cookies cool on the baking sheet.

5. Temper the chocolate with the almond oil as follows: Melt the chocolate ③ and stir in the almond oil. Dip the bottom of the pot of chocolate in a bowl of cold water and stir the chocolate until it begins to thicken. Immediately remove from the cold water and dip the bottom of the pot of chocolate in a bowl of hot water. Stir over the hot water just long enough to make the chocolate fluid again, then remove from the hot water.

6. Spread the back of each cookie with chocolate ④ and smooth it with a palette knife. Place the cookies chocolate side up on your countertop and let the chocolate set.

➤ **HOWS & WHYS:** If this batter is not refrigerated before it is baked, it is more difficult to pipe and spreads too much.

STORAGE: Covered airtight in a cookie jar or tin cookie box for up to 3 days in a cool place (below 70° F or 20° C).

CITRON WAFERS
PALAIS CÉDRAT

In French citron *means lemon, but in English it is the related citrus fruit that we usually encounter in candied form. Candied citron has a nicer texture and more subtle flavor than candied lemon peel.*

EQUIPMENT

2 or 3 large, heavy baking sheets
• Brush with melted butter.
A #100 ice cream scoop, or a tablespoon

BATTER

¾ ounce (20 g), or 2 tablespoons, diced candied citron
1 ounce (30 g), or about 3½ tablespoons, all-purpose flour
3 ounces (85 g), or ½ cup plus 1 tablespoon, blanched almonds, chopped

3 ounces (85 g), or ⅔ cup plus 2 teaspoons, confectioners' sugar
2 large egg whites, at room temperature
1¼ ounces (35 g), or 2½ tablespoons, unsalted butter, melted

For about 35 cookies

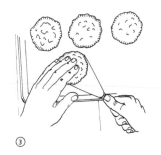
①

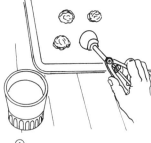
②

③

1. Combine the candied citron with about 2 teaspoons (5 g) of the flour and chop the citron with your chef's knife.

Preheat the oven to 375° F (190° C).

2. Combine the almonds, confectioners' sugar, and candied citron in a bowl and stir in the egg whites with a wooden spatula. Sift the remaining flour over the batter and stir it in. Then stir in the melted butter.

3. Spoon the batter onto the baking sheets ① in 1½-teaspoon (1¼ cl) mounds using the ice cream scoop or a tablespoon. Arrange the mounds in staggered rows and separate them by at least 2 inches (5 cm).

4. Flatten each mound ② by pressing with the back of a fork (dipped in cold water as needed to prevent sticking) to get an even distribution of almonds and candied citron.

5. Bake, 1 sheet at a time, until the mounds have spread and flattened and are browned around the edges but still pale in the centers, about 7 to 10 minutes.

6. Remove the baking sheet from the oven and let the cookies rest briefly on the baking sheet until they will hold their shape. Then lift each cookie with a metal spatula ③ and transfer it to a wire rack to cool.

STORAGE: Covered airtight in a cookie jar or tin cookie box for up to 3 days.

RUSSIAN LACE
DENTELLES RUSSES

These lacy cookies are similar in appearance and texture to Florentines (page 268), but not as thoroughly caramelized and without the chocolate on the back. They are much easier to make than Florentines, and their exquisite fragility belies the pungent accent provided by a hefty dose of dark Jamaican rum.

EQUIPMENT

2 or 3 large, heavy baking sheets
- Brush edges and diagonals with melted butter.
- Line with kitchen parchment.

A #70 ice cream scoop, or a tablespoon

BATTER

3 ounces (85 g), or ⅔ cup plus 2 teaspoons, confectioners' sugar

2 tablespoons (3 cl) crème fraîche (page 491)

2 tablespoons (3 cl) dark Jamaican rum

3 ounces (85 g), or ¾ cup plus 2½ tablespoons, sliced almonds

2 ounces (55 g), or ¼ cup plus ½ tablespoon, diced candied orange peel

1 ounce (25 g), or 3 tablespoons, all-purpose flour

For about 20 cookies

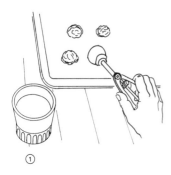

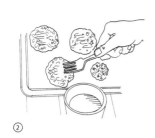

Preheat the oven to 375° F (190° C).

1. Combine the sugar, crème fraîche, and rum in a bowl, and stir with a wooden spatula until smooth. Toss together the almonds and candied orange peel and mix with the sugar, crème fraîche, and rum. Sift the flour over the batter and stir it in.

2. Spoon the batter onto the baking sheets ① in 2½-teaspoon (1¼ cl) mounds using the ice cream scoop or tablespoon. Arrange the mounds in staggered rows and separate them by 2 to 3 inches (5–7 cm).

3. Flatten each mound ② by pressing with the back of a fork (dipped in cold water as needed to prevent sticking) to get an even distribution of almonds and orange peel.

4. Bake, 1 sheet at a time, until the batter has spread and is browned around the edges but still pale in the centers, about 7 to 9 minutes.

5. Remove the baking sheet from the oven and place it on a wire rack. Let the cookies cool on the baking sheet. Then carefully peel the cookies off the parchment.

➤ **HOWS & WHYS:** Using crème fraîche in the batter offsets the sweetness of sugar and candied orange peel.

STORAGE: Covered airtight in a cookie jar or tin cookie box for up to 1 week.

FLORENTINES
FLORENTINS

Florentines are thin disks of brittle caramel studded with sliced almonds, glacé fruits, and candied orange peel, and glazed with chocolate on the back. To give them a nice shape they are baked in rings. While not technically difficult, the recipe is more time-consuming than the others in this chapter. Nonetheless, these very classic cookies are well worth the effort. They are substantial enough to be served alone as a dessert, and they are certain to dazzle your guests.

EQUIPMENT

1 large, heavy baking sheet
- Grease with neutral vegetable oil using a paper towel.

1 large, heavy baking sheet
- Brush edges and diagonals with melted butter.
- Line with kitchen parchment.

12 *tarte* rings, 3¼ inches (8 cm) in diameter (see Note)
- Melted butter
- Neutral vegetable oil

BATTER

7 ounces (200 g), or 1 cup, superfine sugar
¼ cup (6 dl) heavy cream
2 ounces (60 g), or 4 tablespoons, unsalted butter, melted

2⅔ ounces (75 g), or 3 tablespoons plus 2 teaspoons, honey
4 ounces (115 g), or 1 cup plus 2½ tablespoons, sliced almonds
2 ounces (60 g), or ⅓ cup, diced candied orange peel
3 ounces (85 g), or ½ cup, glacé cherries, cut into eighths
2 ounces (60 g), or ⅓ cup, glacé pineapple, cut into ¼-inch (6 mm) dice

COUNTERTOP DUSTING

Confectioners' sugar

GLAZE

10½ ounces (300 g) European bittersweet chocolate (such as Lindt Surfin)
1½ teaspoons (¾ cl) almond oil (preferably) or neutral vegetable oil

For 33 cookies

①

②

1. Combine the superfine sugar, cream, butter, and honey in a 2-quart (2 L) saucepan, stir to mix, and bring to a boil. Continue boiling until the syrup reaches the soft-ball stage or 237° F (114° C). Add the almonds, candied orange peel, and glacé cherries and pineapple ①. Stir to mix, then turn out onto the oiled baking sheet ②. Let cool to room temperature.

2. Brush the insides of eleven *tarte* rings with melted butter, and arrange them on the baking sheet. Grease another ring with vegetable oil using a paper towel.

3. Dust your countertop with confectioners' sugar. Place the caramel mixture on it. Dust with confectioners' sugar, gather it together, and divide it into 3 equal pieces (each about 8 ounces or 225 g). Roll each piece under your palms ③, dusting with confectioners' sugar as needed, to form a cylinder 11 inches (28 cm) long.

Preheat the oven to 375° (190° C).

4. Cut 1 of the caramel cylinders into eleven 1-inch- (2½ cm) long pieces ④. Dust each piece with confectioners' sugar and flatten it under

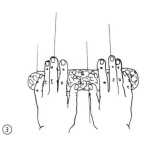

③

④

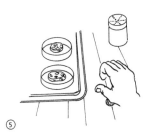

⑤

⑥

⑦

⑧

the heel of your hand to make a round disk. Place each disk in the center of a ring ⑤ on the parchment-lined baking sheet.

5. Bake until the caramel mixture melts and spreads to fill the rings, about 4 to 6 minutes. Then raise the oven temperature to 425° F (220° C) and continue baking until the cookies begin to brown, about 4 to 6 minutes longer.

6. Remove from the oven and lift off the rings. The disks of caramel will begin to spread. Use the oiled ring to pull in the edges of each disk ⑥ and keep it round. Place the baking sheet on a wire rack, and let the cookies cool on the baking sheet. Then carefully remove the cookies from the parchment. Leave the parchment on the baking sheet until all the batter is baked.

7. If you have not yet baked all of the batter, reduce the oven temperature to 375° F (190° C), clean the rings, and repeat steps 3 through 6.

8. Temper the chocolate with the almond oil as follows: Melt the chocolate and stir in the almond oil. Dip the bottom of the pot of chocolate in a bowl of cold water and stir the chocolate until it begins to thicken. Immediately remove from the cold water and dip the bottom of the pot of chocolate in a bowl of hot water. Stir over the hot water just long enough to make the chocolate fluid again, then remove from the hot water.

9. Spread the back of each cookie with chocolate ⑦ and wipe off the excess using a palette knife, then place the cookie chocolate side up on your countertop until the chocolate sets. Meanwhile, keep the pot of chocolate warm so that it doesn't set.

10. Spread the back of each cookie with chocolate a second time using the palette knife, and make a wavy pattern ⑧ across it with a scalloped bread knife or a cake decorating comb, then place the cookie on the counter chocolate side up until the chocolate sets.

NOTE: You can make a good substitute for the *tarte* rings by removing the tops and bottoms from empty fruit cans 3¼ inches (8 cm) in diameter and 2 inches (5 cm) deep, such as 8¼-ounce (234 g) pineapple cans.

STORAGE: Covered airtight in a cookie jar or tin cookie box for up to 1 week in a cool place (below 70° F or 20° C).

ORANGE GALETTES
GALETTES ORANGE

Our Orange Galettes are similar to Lemon Galettes (page 263), with candied orange peel replacing the lemon zest and crème fraîche instead of egg whites and butter. They have a crisp-crunchy texture, and the crème fraîche gives them an intriguing balance of sweet and sour.

EQUIPMENT

2 or 3 large, heavy baking sheets
- Brush with melted butter.

A large pastry bag fitted with
- a ½-inch (12 mm) plain pastry tube (Ateco #6),

or a #100 ice cream scoop

BATTER

3 ounces (85 g), or ¼ cup plus 3 tablespoons, candied orange peel

½ cup (1.2 dl) crème fraîche (page 491)

2 tablespoons (3 cl) milk

⅔ ounce (18 g), or 2 tablespoons, all-purpose flour

3 ounces (85 g), or ½ cup plus 1 tablespoon, blanched almonds, chopped

3 ounces (85 g), or ⅔ cup plus 2 teaspoons, confectioners' sugar

For about 35 to 40 cookies

①

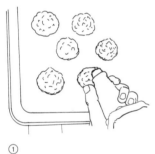

②

③

1. Puree the candied orange peel with the crème fraîche and milk in your electric blender. Strain through a fine sieve to eliminate any hard bits of candied orange peel.

Preheat the oven to 375° F (190° C).

2. Sift the flour and combine it with the almonds and confectioners' sugar in a bowl. Stir in the crème fraîche and candied orange peel mixture with a wooden spatula. Don't overmix.

3. Scoop the batter into the pastry bag, and pipe the batter onto the baking sheets in 1½-teaspoon (¾ cl) mounds ①. Arrange the mounds in staggered rows and separate them by at least 1½ inches (4 cm). Or, spoon the batter in 1½-teaspoon (¾ cl) mounds using the ice cream scoop or a tablespoon.

4. Flatten the mounds ② by pressing with the back of a fork (dipped in cold water as needed to prevent sticking) to get an even distribution of almonds and orange peel.

5. Bake, 1 sheet at a time, until the cookies are lightly browned around the edges but still pale in the centers, about 8 to 12 minutes.

6. Remove the baking sheet from the oven and let the cookies rest briefly on the baking sheet until they will hold their shape. Then lift each cookie with a metal spatula ③ and transfer it to a wire rack to cool.

➤ **HOWS & WHYS:** The candied orange peel is pureed with the crème fraîche and strained to prevent the cookies from being tough.

STORAGE: Covered airtight in a cookie jar or tin cookie box for up to 1 week.

RIBBONS
RUBANS

*T*hese crisp, corkscrew-shaped cookies are made by winding baked strips of batter around a metal tube or wooden dowel. Some chefs call them tortillons (twists) or copeaux (shavings), but whatever the name, the visual effect is a knockout. For a more intensely flavored variation, substitute hazelnuts for the almonds.

EQUIPMENT

3 or 4 large, heavy baking sheets
• Brush with melted butter.
A large pastry bag fitted with
• a 5/16-inch (8 mm) plain pastry tube (Ateco #3)
A wooden dowel or metal tube, 3/8 inch (1 cm) in diameter and about 12 inches (30 cm) long
(see Note)

BATTER

1¼ ounces (35 g), or ¼ cup, all-purpose flour
4½ ounces (130 g), or ¾ cup plus 3½ tablespoons, raw-almond and sugar powder
{ *Basic Preparation, page 482:*
2¼ ounces (65 g), or ¼ cup plus 3 tablespoons, raw almonds
2¼ ounces (65 g), or ½ cup plus 2 teaspoons, confectioners' sugar
1¼ ounces (35 g), or 3 tablespoons, superfine sugar
2 large egg whites, at room temperature

For about 20 to 25 cookies

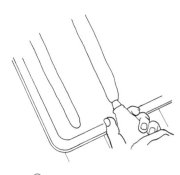

①

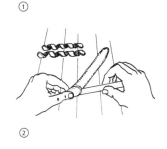

②

Preheat the oven to 400° F (200° C).

1. Sift the flour and mix it with the raw-almond and sugar powder and the superfine sugar in a bowl. Add the egg whites and stir with a wooden spatula until smooth.

2. Scoop the batter into the pastry bag, and pipe the batter onto the baking sheets in diagonal strips ① about 8 inches (20 cm) long and ¼ to 3/8 inch (6–10 mm) wide. Separate the strips by at least 1½ inches (4 cm). Do not pipe more than 6 to 8 strips per baking sheet.

3. Bake, 1 sheet at a time, until the strips of batter are browned around the edges but still pale in the centers, about 6 to 9 minutes.

4. Lift each cookie with a metal spatula, place it upside down on your countertop, and wrap it in a spiral ② around the wooden dowel or metal rod. Then slide the cookie off the rod onto the countertop. Work quickly because if the cookies cool they will become brittle. If they do cool and start to crack as you roll them, return the baking sheet to the oven briefly.

➤ **HOWS & WHYS:** Forming the spirals should be fairly easy. If the strips tear and fall apart as you try to roll them around the rod, then they are underbaked—return them to the oven to finish baking. On the other hand, if the strips crack as you form them, then either they are overbaked or they have cooled too much. If overbaked, leave them flat and transfer them to a wire rack to cool. They will taste every bit as good.

NOTE: Precut brass tubes of this size are available in hobby shops.

STORAGE: Covered airtight in a cookie jar or tin for up to 1 week.

PRALINÉ TONGUES
LANGUES PRALINÉ

*T*hese very light and crisp cookies are shaped like Cats' Tongues *(page 10), but the batter is very different—it contains no butter at all and has a high proportion of powdered raw almonds. In fact, the batter is very similar to that for Ribbons (page 271). While they do not contain any praliné, the baked cookies have a praliné-like flavor.*

EQUIPMENT

2 or 3 large, heavy baking sheets
- Brush with melted butter.

A large pastry bag fitted with
- a ⁵⁄₁₆-inch (8 mm) plain pastry tube (Ateco #3)

BATTER

1½ ounces (40 g), or ¼ cup plus 1½ tablespoons, all-purpose flour

3½ ounces (100 g), or ¾ cup, raw-almond and sugar powder

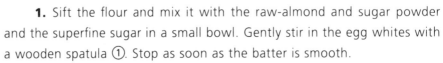

{ *Basic Preparation, page 482:*

1¾ ounces (50 g), or ⅓ cup, raw almonds

1¾ ounces (50 g), or ⅓ cup plus 4 teaspoons, confectioners' sugar

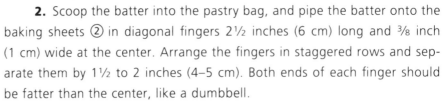

1¾ ounces (50 g), or ¼ cup, superfine sugar

2 large egg whites

For about 40 cookies

①

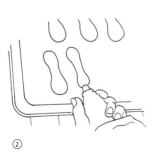

②

Preheat the oven to 400° F (200° C).

1. Sift the flour and mix it with the raw-almond and sugar powder and the superfine sugar in a small bowl. Gently stir in the egg whites with a wooden spatula ①. Stop as soon as the batter is smooth.

2. Scoop the batter into the pastry bag, and pipe the batter onto the baking sheets ② in diagonal fingers 2½ inches (6 cm) long and ⅜ inch (1 cm) wide at the center. Arrange the fingers in staggered rows and separate them by 1½ to 2 inches (4–5 cm). Both ends of each finger should be fatter than the center, like a dumbbell.

3. Bake, 1 sheet at a time, until the cookies are lightly browned around the edges but still pale in the centers, about 7 to 9 minutes.

4. Slide the cookies onto a wire rack using a metal spatula and let cool to room temperature.

➤ **HOWS & WHYS:** Since these cookies contain no egg yolks or butter to tenderize them, the batter must not be overworked or the cookies will be tough. This is why the whites are added last.

STORAGE: Covered airtight in a cookie jar or tin cookie box for up to 1 week.

LYON CROQUETS
CROQUETS DE LYON

Cookies named croquets *(the masculine form)* or croquettes *(the feminine form) are made as local specialties all over France. Most of them have little in common with each other except for their texture, which is always crunchy or crisp. For example,* croquets de lyon *are totally different from our* croquettes aux avelines *(page 330), an icebox cookie made from a sweet pastry dough.*

Lyon Croquets are thick, light, crunchy cookies that contain raw almonds and are flavored with orange flower water. The cookies spread and burst as they bake, giving them an irregular, rustic appearance. From the cook's point of view, their charm is enhanced by the offbeat (and easy) method of preparation.

A variation of Lyon Croquets with hazelnuts replacing half of the almonds and vanilla instead of orange flower water is called croquants aux noisettes *(Hazelnut Crunchies). The word* croquant, *which comes from the same verb* croquer *as* croquet *and* croquette, *means precisely ''crunchy'' or ''crisp.'' It is a fine example of the figure of speech called onomatopoeia (its sound reflects its meaning), and it characterizes perfectly the appealing brittle quality of these cookies.*

EQUIPMENT

2 large, heavy baking sheets
• Brush heavily with melted butter.

BATTER

4¾ ounces (135 g), or ⅔ cup, superfine sugar
1 large egg white, at room temperature
Orange flower water

2½ ounces (70 g), or ¼ cup plus 3½ tablespoons, raw almonds
2¼ ounces (65 g), or ¼ cup plus 3½ tablespoons, all-purpose flour

COUNTERTOP DUSTING AND DECORATION

Confectioners' sugar

GLAZE

Lightly beaten egg

For 28 cookies

①

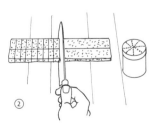

②

Preheat the oven to 350° F (175° C).

1. Combine the superfine sugar and egg white in a bowl, and beat with a wooden spatula until the mixture whitens. Beat in a few drops of orange flower water. Add the nuts, sift the flour over the batter, and stir to mix. Turn out the batter onto your countertop and chop with your chef's knife to coarsely chop the nuts. Gather the batter together into a rectangular pad.

2. Dust your countertop and the pad of batter with confectioners' sugar. Spread the batter into a rectangular sheet 4 inches (10 cm) wide, 10½ inches (28 cm) long, and about ⅜ inch (1 cm) thick, either by rolling with a rolling pin ① or by spreading it with your hands. Cut the rectangle lengthwise into two bands 2 inches (5 cm) wide and then crosswise ② into strips ¾ by 2 inches (2 by 5 cm).

3. Arrange the strips on the baking sheets, spacing them 1½ to 2 inches (4–5 cm) apart. Lightly brush the tops of the strips ③ with beaten egg.

(continued)

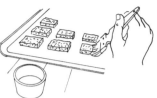

③

④

4. Bake, 1 sheet at a time, until the strips have turned beige on top, about 12 to 16 minutes.

5. Remove the baking sheet from the oven. Loosen each cookie with a metal spatula, then place the baking sheet on a wire rack and let the cookies cool on the baking sheet.

6. Before serving, lightly dust the tops of the cookies ④ with confectioners' sugar.

VARIATION: To make Hazelnut Crunchies, replace the orange flower water with ½ teaspoon (¼ cl) vanilla extract and substitute hazelnuts for half of the raw almonds.

STORAGE: Covered airtight in a cookie jar or tin cookie box for up to 2 weeks.

COOKIES MADE FROM PASTRY DOUGHS

CHAPTER 6
SWEET PASTRY
DOUGHS

①

②

Surprisingly, the pastry doughs in this chapter are a relatively modern innovation. At the beginning of the nineteenth century, Carême perfected a sweetened version of the basic short pastry dough, *pâte brisée,* in order to have a sweeter and more crumbly pastry dough to use for the bases of some of his creations. Soon, even sweeter versions of Carême's recipe evolved that were more fragile, crumbly, and melting in the mouth. Whereas these doughs had originally been baked in molds and *tarte* rings and used as components of more elaborate desserts, by the end of the nineteenth century they were also being made into small *galettes* ① (round disks) and eaten for their own sake. The *sablé* cookie was born.

Sweet pastry doughs are the easiest of all pastry doughs to prepare. You simply cream butter with sugar, stir in a little liquid, and then mix in flour. The ingredients used and the order of mixing them are identical to those employed in Chapter 1 for creamed butter and sugar batters, but here the liquid content is lower and the flour content higher. For pastry doughs it is essential that the ingredients be kept cool throughout the mixing process. For this reason the butter is creamed by a different method and to a less soft consistency than for batters, and the liquid is stirred rather than beaten into the creamed butter and sugar.

The high butter and sugar content of these doughs combined with the mixing method produces doughs that are fragile and not at all elastic, and cookies that are crisp, crumbly, and tender rather than flaky. The two factors that produce flakiness in French flaky pastry dough (*feuilletage*), and to a lesser extent in French short pastry dough (*pâte brisée*), are the development of a gluten fiber network in the dough and separation of the butter from the flour. In sweet pastry doughs, the creamed mixture is actually an emulsion, with the water molecules surrounded by fat molecules. When the flour is mixed in, the emulsion surrounds each flour particle, separating it from the water molecules. This inhibits the development of a gluten fiber network that would give the dough body and elasticity. The high sugar content enhances this effect by absorbing water in the emulsion, thus reducing its availability for moistening the flour. The method of mixing in the flour is also designed to avoid developing the gluten. Finally, the butter and flour are mixed intimately rather than being separated, thus producing a fine texture.

Sweet pastry doughs can be transformed into cookies in three ways. By far the most common is to chill the dough, roll it out into a thin sheet with a rolling pin, and then cut out rounds ②, ovals, squares, triangles, or more

elaborate shapes with a cookie cutter or chef's knife. Three out of four cookies in this chapter are made by this procedure.

The second alternative is the icebox method, in which the dough is formed into a cylinder ③ or log, chilled, and then sliced to make rounds or squares. The pastry doughs used for icebox cookies must be very dry so that the cylinder will be firm when chilled and will not lose its shape when sliced. Cookies produced by this method include Diamonds, Dutch Sablés, Ghent Almond Loaves, and Hazelnut Croquettes.

The third method is to divide the dough into small pieces, and then shape each piece by rolling it back and forth between your hands or under your hands on your countertop. This method is most often used to form tiny loaf shapes—for example, English Loaves. It can also be used to form thin batons of dough that are bent ④ into more complicated shapes, such as ears for Nero's Ears or pretzels.

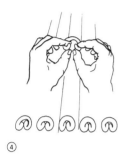

COMPOSITION OF THE DOUGH

However the cookies are formed, their texture after baking is determined by the character and proportions of the basic ingredients. The most versatile and widely used sweet pastry dough, called *pâte sucrée* (literally "sugared dough"), contains 4 ounces (115 g) each of butter and sugar, one large egg, and 8 ounces (230 g) of flour. The butter-sugar-flour ratio in this dough has not changed for over 100 years. Cookies made from it are crisp and slightly crumbly.

Cookies with a higher butter content than *pâte sucrée* are more crumbly and fragile and have a more porous, aerated texture. (The air is incorporated in the batter when it is creamed with the sugar.) The texture of these cookies is often described as sandy. Indeed, the French word for all sweet pastry dough cookies is *sablés,* which means "sandy." (Paradoxically, many cookies named *sablés* are made with much less butter and are not at all sandy.) The culinary use of this word originated in Normandy, where it was applied to a shortbread called *galette sablée,* or simply *sablé.* By comparison with modern *sablés* cookies, Norman *sablé* has a very high butter content and a very low sugar content.

Cookies with a higher sugar content than *pâte sucrée* require more liquid in the dough; they are harder and more brittle and have a less aerated, tighter texture. On the other hand, cookies with a much lower sugar content than *pâte sucrée* have a flakier texture. The sugar used is almost always confectioners' or superfine sugar. Confectioners' sugar makes the cookies crisper, whereas superfine sugar makes them lighter because the sharp edges of the sugar crystals incorporate more air into the batter during creaming. If coarser sugar were used it wouldn't dissolve completely in the small amount of liquid in the dough, and the undissolved sugar would caramelize when baked, producing dark spots in the finished cookies.

The liquid used in sweet pastry doughs is usually eggs, which facilitate the emulsion in the mixture, give flavor to the dough, and help bind it as the proteins in the egg coagulate during baking. In some doughs egg yolks (occasionally hard-boiled) are used instead of whole eggs to produce cookies with a finer, more crumbly texture. In warmer weather, yolks are sometimes substituted for whole eggs (two yolks for one egg) to make the dough drier and easier to work with. In doughs with a very high butter content, egg whites are sometimes used because they have a stronger coagulating ability than do whole eggs. Using cream, milk, or a liqueur rather than eggs produces a tighter and slightly finer texture.

In some recipes (such as Diamonds), no liquid other than a little vanilla extract is added to the dough. Such doughs are high in butter, which contains water and supplies the minimum liquid necessary to form a smooth, cohesive dough. These doughs are extremely dry and are too firm to roll out with a rolling pin, so they are used primarily for icebox cookies.

The proportion of flour in the dough is determined by the other ingredients. There must be enough flour to give the consistency of a dough rather than a batter (which would be much softer and moister), and to prevent the dough from being damp when it is rolled out. However, with too much flour the dough would be too dry, would crack excessively when rolled out, and would not have a smooth surface when baked.

For many cookies in this chapter part of the flour is replaced by powdered almonds or other nuts, always in the form of a nut and sugar powder. This powder usually includes all or at least most of the sugar in the recipe, and it is added to the butter at the beginning of the recipe. Cookies made with a large proportion of nuts tend to be more tender and crumbly than those made with flour alone.

Sweet pastry doughs are most often flavored with vanilla, liqueurs, or citrus zests. These flavorings are added at the same time as, or immediately after, the liquid in the recipe. Sometimes a tiny amount of salt is added at this point as a flavor enhancer. In recipes that call for whole nuts, raisins, or chopped glacé fruits, these solid ingredients are also added after the liquid. Occasionally, sweet pastry doughs are flavored with cocoa powder or coffee. Generally the French are not fond of spices in their desserts, but a few classic cookies are flavored with cinammon; and the distinguished nineteenth-century French pastry chef Jules Gouffé recommended flavoring *pâte sucrée* with ginger. Cocoa powder, instant coffee, or spices are sifted with the flour and added at the end of the recipe.

Sometimes it is desirable to add a chemical leavening to the dough to make the cookies lighter. This is most often done for cookies that contain milk or cream rather than eggs. Baking powder is not a good choice because it starts to work as soon as it comes into contact with water, and so loses some of its power while the dough is chilling. The best is usually ammonium carbonate, which doesn't start to react until heated. The ammonium carbonate is sifted with the flour.

ASSEMBLING THE DOUGH

Now let's take a closer look at the method of preparing sweet pastry doughs. First, be sure your kitchen is cool because the butter must not melt while you are preparing or working with the dough. If your kitchen is warmer than the melting point of butterfat, which is 68° F (20° C), then it will help to work on a marble pastry slab that has been cooled to between 50 and 55° F (10–13° C) in your refrigerator. When the kitchen temperature gets much above 75° F (about 25° C), making pastry doughs becomes an exercise in futility—even with a chilled marble slab.

⑤

⑥

Place the butter on your countertop (or marble slab) with the sugar (or almond and sugar) powder. If the recipe calls for confectioners' sugar, then sift it ⑤ over the butter. If you like, you can cut the butter into pieces with your dough scraper. Now cream the butter with the sugar (or almond and sugar powder) by repeatedly smearing it ⑥ across the countertop a little at a time, using the heel of your hand and then gathering it back together with a dough scraper. The object is to mix the butter uniformly with the sugar, producing a smooth mass without warming the butter any more than necessary. When you finish, the mixture should be soft but still plastic, not runny or greasy, and its temperature should be close to 60° F (15° C).

⑦

Gather the creamed butter and sugar together and add the liquid ⑦, all at once or a little at a time depending on the quantity. (If you like, form the creamed butter and sugar into a little well and put the liquid in the center.) Stir in the liquid with the fingertips of one hand, and use your dough scraper in the other hand to gather it back together when it starts to spread too much on the counter. Continue stirring until smooth. Then stir in any vanilla, liqueur, citrus zest, whole nuts, raisins, or glacé fruits called for in the recipe.

⑧

Sift the flour (with ammonium bicarbonate, cocoa powder, instant coffee, or spices if called for in the recipe) over the mixture and mix it in. The best way is to cut it in with a dough scraper. Or you can mix in the flour by stirring and tossing with your fingertips. Continue until you have a very loose, crumbly dough and there is no flour left unincorporated. Then finish mixing by smearing the dough across the countertop ⑧, a little at a time, with the heel of your hand. Gather the dough back together with your dough scraper and form it into a ball ⑨. With such a small quantity of dough it will probably

⑨

already be smooth. If not, repeat this smearing procedure once more and gather the dough together again into a ball.

Finishing the dough by the smearing method has two advantages. First, it gives the minimum body to the dough and doesn't warm it too much. Second, it ensures that there are no pieces of butter left in the dough that would melt, leaving holes, when baked.

If the dough is to be rolled out with a rolling pin, then press it into a square pad about 1 to 1½ inches (2½–4 cm) thick, depending on the quantity of dough. This will make it easier to roll out later. Dust the pad lightly with flour  on all sides, wrap it in wax paper, and chill it in the refrigerator for at least two hours and preferably overnight.

If the dough is destined for icebox cookies or some hand-shaped cookies, then form it before chilling.

USING AN ELECTRIC MIXER

For the small quantities in our recipes, we find it easiest to prepare the dough by hand. If you wish to prepare a much larger quantity of dough, then it will be easier to use an electric mixer. To do so, cream the butter with the sugar using the flat beater. Gradually stir in the liquid  with the flat beater. Then sift the flour over the batter, switch to the dough hook, and mix in the flour at low speed. If some of the flour cakes around the bottom and sides of the bowl, stop the machine and push the flour into the center with a rubber spatula. Then continue mixing with the dough hook until the dough is smooth. Do not mix any longer than necessary.

PREPARING THE BAKING SHEETS

For sweet pastry doughs that have a relatively low butter content, the baking sheet should be brushed lightly with melted butter ⑫ to prevent the cookies from sticking to the sheet when baked. Use only enough butter to coat the sheet with a thin film, since you don't want to make the bottoms of the cookies greasy.

Cookies high in butter can usually be baked on clean, unbuttered baking sheets. The butter in the dough is sufficient to make the baked cookies slide off the baking sheet easily. Note, however, that sticking is more likely to be a problem on aluminum or tinned steel baking sheets that cannot be seasoned as effectively as black steel baking sheets.

If the cookies will be brushed with egg wash before baking, then the baking sheet must be brushed with either melted butter or cold water ⑬ (just enough to moisten it) to prevent the cookies from moving around. Cold water is usually best for high-butter cookies, but it is not suitable for low-butter cookies.

ROLLING OUT THE DOUGH

When the dough will be rolled out with a rolling pin, it is essential that the dough be well chilled before you roll it out and that it remain cool throughout the rolling process. Unlike other pastry doughs, sweet pastry doughs have no body or elasticity supplied by the flour. When you roll them out, all that holds the sheet of dough together is the plasticity of the butter. If the butter gets too warm and starts to melt, the dough will fall apart when you try to lift it. So whenever the dough starts to soften during the rolling process, slide the sheet of dough onto a tray and chill it briefly in the freezer to make it cold and firm again (but don't let it freeze). If your kitchen is warm, then it also helps to work on a marble slab that has been cooled to between 50 and 55° F (10–13° C) in the refrigerator. Do not chill the marble slab to refrigerator temperature—that is, 35 to 40° F (2–4° C)—because the chilled slab would create condensation, making the dough stick to the slab.

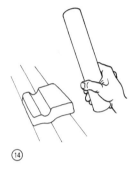

When you first take the pad of dough from the refrigerator it will be very firm. Place it on your countertop and strike it a couple of times with your rolling pin  to soften it a little without warming it and make it easier to roll. Lightly dust your countertop and the dough with flour. Then place your rolling pin on the dough and roll it ⑮ from the end nearest you to the far end, pressing firmly and evenly. Reverse direction and roll from the far end of the dough to the near end. Rotate the dough and roll your rolling pin over it again. Continue to roll your rolling pin over the dough, always pressing firmly and evenly, to thin it into a sheet of uniform thickness. Lightly dust the countertop and the dough with flour as needed to prevent the dough from sticking to the counter or rolling pin.

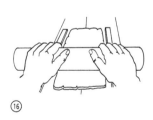

At the beginning of the rolling process the sides of the dough will probably crack in several places. Firmly press the sides in toward the center with your hands to seal the cracks back together. Some cracking is unavoidable, but you don't want large cracks extending into the center of the sheet. Also at the beginning of the rolling, fissures may appear on the top or bottom surface of the pad. These fissures should disappear as you repeatedly roll your rolling pin over them.

You want to end up with a sheet of dough ⅛ to ³⁄₁₆ inch (3–5 mm) thick. If the thickness is not uniform, some of the cookies will bake more quickly than others. To obtain an even thickness use spacers to control the thickness of the sheet. There are two ways to do this: either place a long narrow strip (for example, cardboard or neoprene) of the required thickness on each side of the dough ⑯ to support the ends of the rolling pin; or place a neoprene O-ring ⑰ of the required thickness on each end of the rolling pin.

When you get the dough close to the required thickness, it is essential to keep it cold. The thinner the dough, the more quickly it will warm up on your countertop. If the sheet of dough is warm when you finish rolling it out, then when you cut it with a cookie cutter the pieces of dough will deform and fall apart as you try to transfer them to a baking sheet. What's more, the sheet of dough will be too fragile to move onto a tray to chill it again. On the other hand, if the dough is cold, then the dough will be firm and will hold its shape when cut and transferred to the baking sheet.

CUTTING OUT COOKIES FROM A SHEET OF DOUGH

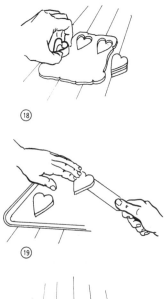

Use a cookie cutter, or occasionally (for triangles or squares) a chef's knife, to cut out cookies. Always cut by pressing straight down with the cutter ⑱ or knife. Don't use a twisting or sawing motion, which could deform the dough. For any small, simple shapes you can cut about three pieces of dough with the cookie cutter before removing them from the cutter.

Transfer the cut pieces of dough directly to the baking sheets ⑲ with a metal spatula. If you don't have enough sheets to hold all of the cookies at one time, you can stack the extras four to six high on a tray and keep them in the refrigerator until a baking sheet is available.

After cutting out the cookies, clean off any flour on the trimmings of dough and gather the trimmings together ⑳. Press the trimmings into a square pad. If the dough has warmed, chill it in the freezer for twenty to thirty minutes to make it cold and firm again (but don't let it freeze). You can then roll out this pad of dough a second time and cut more cookies from it. After that the quality of the dough deteriorates. You may be able to gather together the trimmings and roll them out once more if they haven't had too much flour dusting mixed in and become too dry or elastic. Or for many doughs you can save the trimmings from the second rolling and cutting for use in Vietnamese Hats (page 24).

ICEBOX COOKIES AND HAND-SHAPED COOKIES

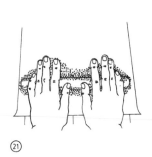

For icebox cookies, shape the dough into a cylinder or a square log right after preparing it. Dust the cylinder or log lightly with flour, or brush it with egg wash and roll it in crystal sugar ㉑ as required by the specific recipe. Wrap in wax paper and chill in the refrigerator for at least two hours and preferably overnight. The dough must be very firm so that it won't deform when cut. Mark the cylinder or log at regular intervals—usually ¼ to ⅜ inch (6 mm–1 cm)—as a guide for slicing. Then cut it into slices of uniform thickness with your chef's knife and transfer them to the baking sheets.

The methods for hand-shaped cookies are more specialized and are explained in the specific recipes.

FINAL REST AND GLAZING WITH EGG WASH

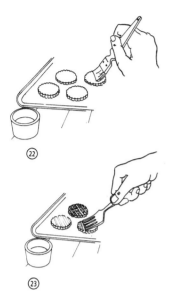

It is best to let the cookies rest in the refrigerator for twenty to thirty minutes before baking to firm the dough so the cookies will hold their shape when they first go into the oven. For icebox cookies, however, this step would be redundant.

When you arrange any *sablés* cookies on a baking sheet, press each one gently to make the dough stick to the baking sheet so that they won't slide around when you brush or score them.

Many *sablés* cookies are glazed with two coats of lightly beaten egg before baking in order to give them a rich color and golden sheen. The first coat of egg wash is applied before the final rest, and the second immediately before they go into the oven. Brush a light coating of egg wash on the top ㉒ surface of each cookie, just enough to make the surface glisten. After the second coat of egg wash, the tops of the cookies are sometimes scored in a decorative pattern ㉓ using a fork or the tip of a paring knife.

STORAGE

These cookies keep extremely well. The fresher the better, but if stored at room temperature, tightly covered in a cookie jar, a tin cookie box, or even a platic bag, most of them will last for a week or more.

Several cookies in this chapter are sandwiched with jam, jelly, honey, or *ganache* (chocolate cream filling). Before filling they can be kept for up to a week, just like the plain cookies. After filling those sandwiched with jam, jelly, or honey will keep from three days to a week, depending on how well reduced the jam is and how porous the texture of the cookie. If the cookies are dusted with confectioners' sugar they cannot be stacked, which makes storage cumbersome, so it is best to dust them shortly before serving. Cookies sandwiched with *ganache* can be kept in a cool place—below 65° F (18° C)—for up to one day. They should not be refrigerated or the cookies will soften.

Before baking, a pad or cylinder of sweet pastry dough can be kept in the refrigerator, wrapped in wax paper, for up to two or three days. For longer storage, let the dough rest in the refrigerator for one hour, then cover the wax paper with freezer wrap and freeze for up to one month. When ready to use, defrost overnight in the refrigerator.

The recipe for Vietnamese Hats (page 24) in Chapter 1 requires a small amount of sweet pastry dough. Trimmings leftover after rolling out and cutting many pastry doughs in this chapter can be used for that purpose. Gather the trimmings together into a ball and dust lightly with flour. Wrap the ball in wax paper and then in freezer wrap. Freeze for up to one month. Defrost overnight in the refrigerator before using.

TEA SABLÉS
SABLÉS POUR LE THÉ

～～～

*T*hese simple sablés *cookies are made from* pâte sucrée *(the basic sweet pastry dough) flavored with lemon zest. They can be cut in a wide variety of decorative shapes with cookie cutters. We often use cutters shaped as hearts, diamonds, spades, and clubs, like the suits of cards. Fluted round cookie cutters are another good choice and are classic. Whatever the shape, the cutters should be about 2 inches (5 cm) wide.*

The taste and texture of these cookies make them a natural with tea; and their decorative quality and ease of preparation also make them an ideal choice for a holiday cookie assortment.

EQUIPMENT

2 or 3 large, heavy baking sheets
• Brush lightly with melted butter.
Decorative cookie cutters about 2 inches (5 cm) wide
• such as hearts, diamonds, spades, and clubs

_____

PASTRY DOUGH

4 ounces (115 g), or ½ cup, unsalted butter, softened
4 ounces (115 g), or ¾ cup plus 3 tablespoons, confectioners' sugar

1 large egg, lightly beaten
¼ teaspoon (1 g) salt
Finely grated zest of ½ lemon
8 ounces (230 g), or 1½ cups plus 2 tablespoons, all-purpose flour

COUNTERTOP DUSTING

Flour

GLAZE

1 egg, lightly beaten

DECORATION

Candied orange peel, candied lemon peel, seedless raisins, or sliced almonds

For about 40 to 50 cookies

1. Place the butter on your countertop and sift the confectioners' sugar over it. Cream the butter with the sugar by repeatedly smearing it across the countertop with the heel of your hand and gathering it back together with a dough scraper. When smooth, mix in the egg, a little at a time, with your fingertips. Then mix in the salt and lemon zest. Work quickly so that you don't melt the butter. Sift the flour over the butter mixture. Mix in the flour, either by cutting it in with a dough scraper or by stirring and tossing with your fingertips, until you obtain a loose, crumbly dough. Gather the dough together and finish mixing by smearing it across the countertop, a little at a time, with the heel of your hand. Gather the dough together again. If it is not yet smooth, then repeat this smearing procedure.

2. Form the dough into a square pad about 1½ inches (4 cm) thick. Lightly dust the pad with flour, wrap it in wax paper, and refrigerate for at least 2 hours and preferably overnight.

3. Dust your countertop and the pad of dough with flour, and roll out the dough with a rolling pin into a sheet about ⅛ inch (3 mm) thick. Dust the counter and dough with flour as needed to prevent the dough from sticking to counter or rolling pin. Slide the dough onto a tray and chill it briefly in the freezer whenever it starts to warm and soften. If it is too

①

②

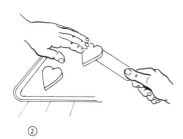

③

④

⑤

difficult to roll out the entire quantity in a single sheet, cut it in half and roll out each half separately.

4. Cut out decorative shapes ① with the cookie cutters. Carefully lift the shapes with a metal spatula ② and transfer them to the baking sheets. Separate them by at least ¾ inch (2 cm), and gently press each shape to make it stick to the baking sheet. Let rest in the refrigerator.

5. Gather together the remaining dough ③ and form it into a pad. If it is too soft to work with, chill it in the freezer for 20 to 30 minutes. Then roll it out into a sheet about ⅛ inch (3 mm) thick. Cut out more decorative shapes with your cookie cutters, arrange them on the baking sheets, and refrigerate. Repeat with the remaining scraps, or save them for use in Vietnamese Hats (page 24).

6. Lightly brush the tops of the cookies ④ with beaten egg. Let rest in the refrigerator until the egg wash dries, 20 to 30 minutes.

Preheat the oven to 350° F (175° C).

7. Lightly brush the tops of the cookies a second time with egg wash. Decorate by placing ⑤ a diamond of candied orange or lemon peel, or a raisin, or a couple of almond slices on the center of each.

8. Bake, 1 sheet at a time, until the cookies are lightly browned on the bottoms, the tops are golden and beginning to brown around the edges, and the egg wash has set to a satiny sheen, about 12 to 15 minutes.

9. Slide the cookies onto a wire rack using a metal spatula and let cool to room temperature.

STORAGE: Covered airtight in a tin cookie box or cookie jar for up to 1 week.

Before being rolled out, the dough can be kept in the refrigerator, wrapped in wax paper, for up to 2 or 3 days. Trimmings can be frozen, wrapped in wax paper and then in freezer wrap, for up to 1 month.

RUM PUNCH COOKIES
PUNCH-GÂTEAUX

~~~~~~

Punch *originated as a heated mixture of sugar and cane spirits that English sailors drank to keep their spirits up on the long ocean voyage home from the West Indies. In fact, the word* punch *is thought to derive from ''puncheon,'' which is a large cask used for rum in the West Indies. Today, we Americans refer to a wide variety of sweetened mixed alcoholic drinks as punches. However, to the French* punch *still has a Caribbean connotation, and pastries with the name* punch *are invariably flavored with rum.*

According to Alexandre Dumas in his Grand dictionnaire de cuisine, gâteaux *are a sort of pastry ''almost always round in shape, and usually made with flour, eggs, and butter. . . . Their name without doubt comes from the prodigality with which children are spoiled* (gâtés) *by having* gâteaux *given to them either as a reward, or as an encouragement of a gastronomic nature.''*

Punch-gâteaux are very crisp round cookies, rich in butter, sugar, and of course rum. With their alcoholic flavor, they are not really a children's cookie, but they certainly have the potential to spoil anyone you serve them to.

EQUIPMENT

2 or 3 large, heavy baking sheets
A fluted round cookie cutter 2 inches (5 cm) in diameter

PASTRY DOUGH

3½ ounces (100 g), or 7 tablespoons, unsalted
    butter, softened
3½ ounces (100 g), or ½ cup, superfine sugar
1 tablespoon (1½ cl) lightly beaten egg

1 tablespoon (1½ cl) dark Jamaican rum
4¾ ounces (135 g), or ¾ cup plus 3½ tablespoons,
    all-purpose flour

COUNTERTOP DUSTING

Flour

GLAZE

1 egg, lightly beaten
½ teaspoon (¼ cl) freeze-dried coffee, dissolved in
    ½ teaspoon (¼ cl) boiling water

For about 30 to 35 cookies

1. On your countertop, cream the butter with the sugar by repeatedly smearing it across the countertop with the heel of your hand and gathering it back together with a dough scraper. When smooth, mix in the egg and the rum with your fingertips. Work quickly so that you don't melt the butter. Sift the flour over the butter mixture. Mix in the flour, either by cutting it in with a dough scraper or by stirring and tossing with your fingertips, until you obtain a loose, crumbly dough. Gather the dough together and finish mixing by smearing it across the countertop, a little at a time, with the heel of your hand. Gather the dough together again. If it is not yet smooth, then repeat this smearing procedure.

2. Form the dough into a square pad about 1 inch (2½ cm) thick. Lightly dust the pad with flour, wrap it in wax paper, and refrigerate for at least 2 hours and preferably overnight.

3. Dust your countertop and the pad of dough with flour, and roll out the dough with a rolling pin into a sheet about ³/₁₆ inch (5 mm) thick. Dust

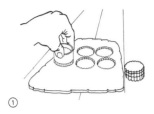

①

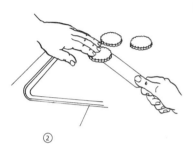

②

③

④

the counter and dough with flour as needed to prevent the dough from sticking to counter or rolling pin. Slide the dough onto a tray and chill it briefly in the freezer whenever it starts to warm and soften.

4. Moisten the baking sheets with cold water using a pastry brush.

5. Cut out 2-inch (5 cm) rounds ① using the cookie cutter. Carefully lift the rounds with a metal spatula ② and transfer them to the baking sheets. Separate the rounds by at least ¾ inch (2 cm), and gently press each round to make it stick to the baking sheet. Let rest in the refrigerator.

6. Gather together the remaining dough and form it into a pad. If it is too soft to work with, chill it in the freezer for 20 to 30 minutes. Then roll it out into a sheet about ³⁄₁₆ inch (5 mm) thick. Cut out more rounds, arrange them on the baking sheets, and refrigerate. Repeat with the remaining scraps, or save them for use in Vietnamese Hats (page 24).

7. Tint the beaten egg with the coffee and brush the tops of the rounds ③ with this egg wash. Let rest in the refrigerator until the egg wash dries, 20 to 30 minutes.

Preheat the oven to 350° F (175° C).

8. Brush each round a second time with egg wash. Draw the tines of a fork across the top of each cookie to make a set of parallel lines through the egg wash, then draw a second set of lines on the diagonal with respect to the first set, making a crisscross pattern ④.

9. Bake, 1 sheet at a time, until the cookies are lightly browned on the bottoms and the egg wash on the tops is a rich golden brown, about 14 to 16 minutes.

10. Slide the cookies onto a wire rack using a metal spatula and let cool to room temperature.

➤ **HOWS & WHYS:** Adding coffee to the egg wash gives the cookies a richer color. Professionals often use caramel food coloring to tint the egg wash, but at home instant coffee is easier. The amount of coffee used is minuscule and does not affect the taste of the cookies.

STORAGE: Covered airtight in a tin cookie box or cookie jar for up to 1 week.

Before being rolled out, the dough can be kept in the refrigerator, wrapped in wax paper, for up to 2 or 3 days. Trimmings can be frozen, wrapped in wax paper and then in freezer wrap, for up to 1 month.

ITALIAN CROWNS
COURONNES ITALIENNES

Here is another very crisp cookie, similar to Rum Punch Cookies *(page 288), but flavored with lemon zest instead of rum and shaped like a crown. A sprinkling of crystal sugar supplies the glittering "jewels" on top.*

EQUIPMENT

2 or 3 large, heavy baking sheets

A fluted round cookie cutter 2 inches (5 cm) in diameter

An apple corer or plain round cookie cutter ¾ inch (2 cm) in diameter

PASTRY DOUGH

3½ ounces (100 g), or 7 tablespoons, unsalted butter, softened

3½ ounces (100 g), or ½ cup, superfine sugar

2 tablespoons (3 cl) lightly beaten egg

Finely grated zest of ½ lemon

4¾ ounces (135 g), or ¾ cup plus 3½ tablespoons, all-purpose flour

COUNTERTOP DUSTING

Flour

GLAZE

1 egg, lightly beaten

DECORATION

Crystal sugar

For about 40 to 45 cookies

①

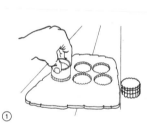
②

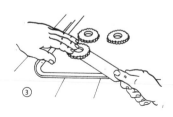
③

1. On your countertop, cream the butter with the sugar by repeatedly smearing it across the countertop with the heel of your hand and gathering it back together with a dough scraper. When smooth, mix in the egg with your fingertips. Then mix in the lemon zest. Work quickly so that you don't melt the butter. Sift the flour over the butter mixture. Mix in the flour, either by cutting it in with a dough scraper or by stirring and tossing with your fingertips, until you obtain a loose, crumbly dough. Gather the dough together and finish mixing by smearing it across the countertop, a little at a time, with the heel of your hand. Gather the dough together again. If it is not yet smooth, then repeat this smearing procedure.

2. Form the dough into a square pad about 1 inch (2½ cm) thick. Lightly dust the pad with flour, wrap it in wax paper, and refrigerate for at least 2 hours and preferably overnight.

3. Dust your countertop and the pad of dough with flour, and roll out the dough with a rolling pin into a sheet about ³/₁₆ inch (5 mm) thick. Dust the counter and dough with flour as needed to prevent the dough from sticking to counter or rolling pin. Slide the dough onto a tray and chill it briefly in the freezer whenever it starts to warm and soften.

4. Moisten the baking sheets with cold water using a pastry brush.

5. Cut out 2-inch (5 cm) rounds ① using the fluted cookie cutter. Cut out the center of each round ② using the apple corer or plain cookie cutter. Carefully lift the crowns with a metal spatula ③ and transfer them to the baking sheets. Separate the crowns by at least 1¼ inches (3 cm), and gently press each crown to make it stick to the baking sheet. Let rest in the refrigerator.

④

⑤

6. Gather together the remaining dough and form it into a pad. If it is too soft to work with, chill it in the freezer for 20 to 30 minutes. Then roll it out into a sheet about ³/₁₆ inch (5 mm) thick. Cut out more crowns, arrange them on the baking sheets, and refrigerate. Repeat with the remaining scraps, or save them for use in Vietnamese Hats (page 24).

7. Lightly brush the top of each crown ④ with beaten egg. Let rest in the refrigerator until the egg wash dries, 20 to 30 minutes.

Preheat the oven to 375° F (190° C).

8. Brush each crown a second time with egg wash. Sprinkle a little crystal sugar over the egg wash on top ⑤ of each crown.

9. Bake, 1 sheet at a time, until the cookies are lightly browned on the bottoms and edges, about 10 to 13 minutes.

10. Slide the cookies onto a wire rack using a metal spatula and let cool to room temperature.

STORAGE: Covered airtight in a tin cookie box or cookie jar for up to 1 week.

Before being rolled out, the dough can be kept in the refrigerator, wrapped in wax paper, for up to 2 or 3 days. Trimmings can be frozen, wrapped in wax paper and then in freezer wrap, for up to 1 month.

MILANESE SABLÉS
MILANAISES

~~~~~~~~~

The Milanese cake called panettone *is a sweet, egg-rich bread studded with raisins and candied citron and orange peel. The French cake called* milanais *is a variety of génoise flavored with anise and glazed with apricot jam and fondant. Borrowing a little from each of these classics, Milanese Sablés are rum-flavored sablés cookies, studded with the tiny raisins we call currants and glazed with a brushing of tart apricot jam followed by a mixture of rum and confectioners' sugar. The result is tender and enticing on the one hand, and thoroughly intoxicating on the other.*

EQUIPMENT

2 or 3 large, heavy baking sheets
• Brush lightly with melted butter.
A fluted round cookie cutter 2 inches (5 cm) in diameter

PASTRY DOUGH

3 ounces (85 g), or 6 tablespoons, unsalted butter, softened
4½ ounces (125 g), or 1 cup plus 2 teaspoons, confectioners' sugar
1 large egg, lightly beaten

1 tablespoon plus 1 teaspoon (2 cl) dark Jamaican rum
1½ ounces (40 g), or ¼ cup, currants
6 ounces (170 g), or 1 cup plus 3½ tablespoons, all-purpose flour

COUNTERTOP DUSTING

Flour

GLAZE

2½ tablespoons (50 g) strained apricot jam [*Basic Preparation*, page 484]
1¾ ounces (50 g), or ⅓ cup plus 4 teaspoons, confectioners' sugar
2 teaspoons (1 cl) dark Jamaican rum

For about 45 cookies

1. Place the butter on your countertop and sift the confectioners' sugar over it. Cream the butter with the sugar by repeatedly smearing it across the countertop with the heel of your hand and gathering it back together with a dough scraper. When smooth, mix in the egg, a little at a time, with your fingertips. Then mix in the rum, followed by the currants. Work quickly so that you don't melt the butter. Sift the flour over the butter mixture. Mix in the flour, either by cutting it in with a dough scraper or by stirring and tossing with your fingertips, until you obtain a loose, crumbly dough. Gather the dough together and finish mixing by smearing it across the countertop, a little at a time, with the heel of your hand. Gather the dough together again. If it is not yet smooth, then repeat this smearing procedure.

2. Form the dough into a square pad about 1½ inches (4 cm) thick. Lightly dust the pad with flour, wrap it in wax paper, and refrigerate for at least 2 hours and preferably overnight.

3. Dust your countertop and the pad of dough with flour, and roll out the dough with a rolling pin into a sheet about ³∕₁₆ inch (5 mm) thick. Dust the counter and dough with flour as needed to prevent the dough from sticking to counter or rolling pin. Slide the dough onto a tray and chill it briefly in the freezer whenever it starts to warm and soften.

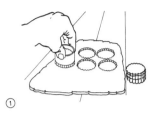

4. Cut out 2-inch (5 cm) rounds ① using the cookie cutter. Carefully lift the rounds with a metal spatula ② and transfer them to the baking sheets. Separate the rounds by at least ¾ inch (2 cm), and gently press each round to make it stick to the baking sheet. Let rest in the refrigerator.

5. Gather together the remaining dough and form it into a pad. If it is too soft to work with, chill it in the freezer for 20 to 30 minutes. Then roll it out into a sheet about ³⁄₁₆ inch (5 mm) thick. Cut out more rounds, arrange them on the baking sheets, and refrigerate. Repeat with the remaining scraps.

Preheat the oven to 400° F (200° C).

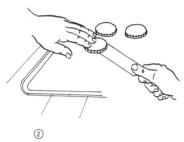

6. Bake, 1 sheet at a time, until the cookies are lightly browned on the bottoms and edges, about 10 to 13 minutes.

7. Meanwhile, warm the apricot jam over low heat, stirring ③ occasionally until melted. Sift the confectioners' sugar into a small bowl and stir in the rum. Then stir in enough cold water to make a smooth, creamy paste that is just fluid enough to spread easily with a pastry brush.

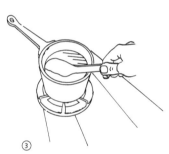

8. When the cookies are finished baking, brush each with jam ④ until lightly coated and glistening. Then lightly brush the confectioners' sugar and rum mixture over the jam on top of each cookie. The glaze will turn from opaque white to translucent.

9. Slide the cookies onto a wire rack using a metal spatula and let cool to room temperature.

➤ **HOWS & WHYS:** Since the cookies are glazed while they are hot out of the oven, they do not have to be returned to the oven to make the glaze set and turn translucent.

STORAGE: Covered airtight in a tin cookie box or cookie jar for up to 1 week.

Before being rolled out, the dough can be kept in the refrigerator, wrapped in wax paper, for up to 2 or 3 days.

IRISH WAFFLES
GAUFRES IRLANDAISES

~~~~~~~~~

For these cinnamon-flavored *sablés cookies the pastry dough is rolled out into a fairly thick sheet, and then the final rolling is done with a waffle or checkerboard rolling pin to make it appear that the cookies were baked in a waffle iron.*

EQUIPMENT

2 large, heavy baking sheets
• Brush lightly with melted butter.
Two ⅟₁₆-inch (1½ mm) thick spacers (see page 431)
A waffle or checkerboard rolling pin with knobs about ⅜ inch (1 cm) square and ³⁄₁₆ inch (5 mm) deep
A fluted or plain oval cookie cutter (see Note) 3¼ inches (8 cm) long and 2¼ inches (6 cm) wide

PASTRY DOUGH

4 ounces (115 g), or ½ cup, unsalted butter, softened
4½ ounces (125 g), or 1 cup plus 2 teaspoons, confectioners' sugar
2 tablespoons (3 cl) lightly beaten egg
1 tablespoon (1½ cl) milk
7 ounces (200 g), or 1¼ cups plus 3 tablespoons, all-purpose flour
¼ teaspoon (1 ml) ground cinnamon

COUNTERTOP DUSTING

Flour

For about 18 to 20 cookies

1. Place the butter on your countertop and sift the confectioners' sugar over it. Cream the butter with the sugar by repeatedly smearing it across the countertop with the heel of your hand and gathering it back together with a dough scraper. When smooth, mix in the egg with your fingertips. Work quickly so that you don't melt the butter. Sift the flour and cinnamon over the butter mixture. Mix in the flour, either by cutting it in with a dough scraper or by stirring and tossing with your fingertips, until you obtain a loose, crumbly dough. Gather the dough together and finish mixing by smearing it across the countertop, a little at a time, with the heel of your hand. Gather the dough together again. If it is not yet smooth, then repeat this smearing procedure.

2. Form the dough into a square pad about 1½ inches (4 cm) thick. Lightly dust the pad with flour, wrap it in wax paper, and refrigerate for at least 2 hours and preferably overnight.

①

3. Dust your countertop and the pad of dough with flour, and roll out the dough with a rolling pin ① into a sheet about ¼ inch (6 mm) thick. Dust the counter and dough with flour as needed to prevent the dough from sticking to counter or rolling pin. Slide the dough onto a tray and chill it briefly in the freezer whenever it starts to warm and soften. Be sure the sheet of dough is well chilled before proceeding to the next step.

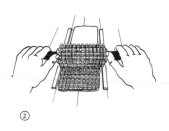

②

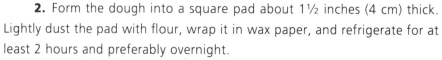

4. Place a spacer on your countertop on each side of the sheet of dough. Dust the top of the sheet of dough with flour. Slowly roll the waffle rolling pin over the sheet of dough ② to emboss the waffle design on top. If the dough sticks to the rolling pin, then slide your fingertips over the dough behind the rolling pin as you roll it to free the dough and keep it on the counter. After you finish rolling, brush any excess flour out of the waffle design with a pastry brush.

5. Cut out ovals ③ using the cookie cutter. Carefully lift the ovals with a metal spatula and transfer them to the baking sheets. Separate the ovals by at least 1 inch (2½ cm). Let rest in the refrigerator.

6. Gather together the remaining dough and form it into a pad. If it is too soft to work with, chill it in the freezer for 20 to 30 minutes. Then roll it out into a sheet about ¼ inch (6 mm) thick, and roll the waffle rolling pin over it. Cut out more ovals, arrange them on the baking sheets, and refrigerate. Repeat with the remaining scraps.

Preheat the oven to 375° F (190° C).

7. Bake, 1 sheet at a time, until the cookies are lightly browned on the bottoms and edges, about 13 to 16 minutes.

8. Slide the cookies onto a wire rack using a metal spatula and let cool to room temperature.

NOTE: You can make the oval cookie cutter from a round cutter 2¾ inches (7 cm) in diameter by carefully bending it into shape.

STORAGE: Covered airtight in a tin cookie box or cookie jar for up to 1 week.

Before being rolled out, the dough can be kept in the refrigerator, wrapped in wax paper, for up to 2 or 3 days.

CAEN-STYLE SABLÉS
SABLÉS DE CAEN

The Norman city Caen is the capital of the département of Calvados, and its most famous gastronomic specialty, tripe à la mode de caen, *is made with the renowned apple brandy of the region. Caen-Style Sablés don't contain any calvados, but they are distinctive for two reasons: they contain hard-boiled egg yolks, and they are cut in fluted squares. The hard-boiled yolks give the cookies a rich yellow color and an extraordinarily delicate texture, while their high butter content makes them quite flaky. If you have a surfeit of dyed hard-boiled eggs after Easter, here is a recipe where you can put them to good use.*

EQUIPMENT

2 or 3 large, heavy baking sheets
• Brush lightly with melted butter.
A fluted cookie cutter 3 inches (8 cm) square
(see Note)

PASTRY DOUGH

6 ounces (170 g), or ½ cup plus 4 tablespoons,
    unsalted butter, softened
3 ounces (85 g), or ⅔ cup plus 2 teaspoons,
    confectioners' sugar
Yolks of 2 large hard-boiled eggs, forced through a
    sieve or mashed with a fork

2 tablespoons (3 cl) milk
1½ teaspoons (¾ cl) vanilla extract
8 ounces (225 g), or 1½ cups plus 2 tablespoons,
    all-purpose flour

COUNTERTOP DUSTING

Flour

GLAZE

1 egg, lightly beaten

DECORATION

About 80 blanched almonds

For about 18 to 20 cookies

1. Place the butter on your countertop and sift the confectioners' sugar over it. Cream the butter with the sugar by repeatedly smearing it across the countertop with the heel of your hand and gathering it back together with a dough scraper. When smooth, mix in the egg yolks, milk, and vanilla with your fingertips. Work quickly so that you don't melt the butter. Sift the flour over the butter mixture. Mix in the flour, either by cutting it in with a dough scraper or by stirring and tossing with your fingertips, until you obtain a loose, crumbly dough. Gather the dough together and finish mixing by smearing it across the countertop, a little at a time, with the heel of your hand. Gather the dough together again. If it is not yet smooth, then repeat this smearing procedure.

2. Form the dough into a square pad about 1½ inches (4 cm) thick. Lightly dust the pad with flour, wrap it in wax paper, and refrigerate for at least 2 hours and preferably overnight.

①

3. Dust your countertop and the pad of dough with flour, and roll out the dough with a rolling pin ① into a sheet about ⅛ inch (3 mm) thick. Dust the counter and dough with flour as needed to prevent the dough

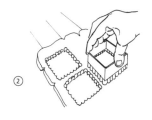

from sticking to the counter or rolling pin. Slide the dough onto a tray and chill it briefly in the freezer whenever it starts to warm and soften.

4. Cut out 3-inch (8 cm) squares ② using the cookie cutter. Carefully lift the squares with a metal spatula and transfer them to the baking sheets. Separate the squares by at least ¾ inch (2 cm), and gently press each square to make it stick to the baking sheet. Let rest in the refrigerator.

5. Gather together the remaining dough and form it into a pad. If it is too soft to work with, chill it in the freezer for 20 to 30 minutes. Then roll it out into a sheet about ⅛ inch (3 mm) thick. Cut out more squares, arrange them on the baking sheets, and refrigerate. Repeat with the remaining scraps.

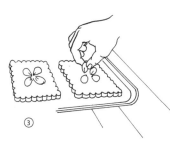

6. Brush the tops of the cookies with beaten egg. Let rest in the refrigerator until the egg wash dries, 20 to 30 minutes.

Preheat the oven to 350° F (175° C).

7. Brush the tops of the cookies a second time with egg wash. Decorate by arranging 4 blanched almonds on the center ③ of each square, pointing from the center to the corners.

8. Bake, 1 sheet at a time, until the cookies are browned on the bottoms and around the edges and the egg wash on the tops is golden, about 16 to 19 minutes.

9. Slide the cookies onto a wire rack using a metal spatula and let cool to room temperature.

NOTE: You can make the square cookie cutter from a large heart-shaped cookie cutter or a 4-inch (10 cm) round cookie cutter by carefully bending it into shape.

➤ **HOWS & WHYS:** The high butter and low sugar content of these cookies gives them a flaky rather than sandy texture. The hard-boiled yolks and milk make them very delicate.

STORAGE: Covered airtight in a tin cookie box or cookie jar for up to 1 week.

Before being rolled out, the dough can be kept in the refrigerator, wrapped in wax paper, for up to 2 or 3 days.

SWEET PASTRY DOUGHS

VENDÉE-STYLE SABLÉS
SABLÉS VENDÉENS

The *Vendée is a* département *in western France, which was the center of the royalist revolt of 1793 to 1795. Vendée-Style Sablés are made from a pastry dough similar to that for Caen-Style Sablés (page 296), containing hard-boiled egg yolks. They are flavored with lemon zest, cut into triangles, and imprinted with a design on the center using a cork. Like Caen-Style Sablés, they are buttery, delicate, and flaky, with a rich yellow color.*

EQUIPMENT

2 large, heavy baking sheets
• Brush lightly with melted butter.
A cork 1¼ inches (3 cm) in diameter

PASTRY DOUGH

3 ounces (85 g), or 6 tablespoons, unsalted butter, softened
2¼ ounces (65 g), or ½ cup plus 2 teaspoons, confectioners' sugar

Yolks of 2 large hard-boiled eggs, forced through a sieve or mashed with a fork
Finely grated zest of ½ lemon
¼ teaspoon (1 g) salt
4 ounces (115 g), or ¾ cup plus 1 tablespoon, all-purpose flour

COUNTERTOP DUSTING

Flour

For about 30 cookies

1. Place the butter on your countertop and sift the confectioners' sugar over it. Cream the butter with the sugar by repeatedly smearing it across the countertop with the heel of your hand and gathering it back together with a dough scraper. When smooth, mix in the egg yolks with your fingertips. Then mix in the lemon zest and the salt. Work quickly so that you don't melt the butter. Sift the flour over the butter mixture. Mix in the flour, either by cutting it in with a dough scraper or by stirring and tossing with your fingertips, until you obtain a loose, crumbly dough. Gather the dough together and finish mixing by smearing it across the countertop, a little at a time, with the heel of your hand. Gather the dough together again. If it is not yet smooth, then repeat this smearing procedure.

2. Form the dough into a square pad about 1 inch (2½ cm) thick. Lightly dust the pad with flour, wrap it in wax paper, and refrigerate for at least 2 hours and preferably overnight.

3. Cut a design in one end of the cork ① using a razor blade or X-Acto knife. The easiest is to make a star design by cutting 3 lines along diameters through the center of the face of the cork, dividing the face of the cork into 6 equal wedges. Cut the lines about ³⁄₃₂ inch (2 mm) wide and ⅛ inch (3 mm) deep.

①

4. Dust your countertop and the pad of dough with flour, and roll out the dough with a rolling pin into a sheet about ³⁄₁₆ inch (5 mm) thick. Dust the counter and dough with flour as needed to prevent the dough from

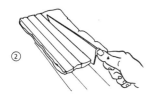

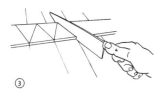

sticking to the counter or rolling pin. Slide the dough onto a tray and chill it briefly in the freezer whenever it starts to warm and soften.

5. Cut the sheet of dough ② into bands 2 inches (5¼ cm) wide, then cut each band ③ into triangles 2⅜ inches (6 cm) on a side. Carefully lift the triangles with a metal spatula and transfer them to the baking sheets. Separate the triangles by at least ¾ inch (2 cm), and gently press each triangle to make it stick to the baking sheet. Let rest in the refrigerator.

6. Gather together the remaining dough and form it into a pad. If it is too soft to work with, chill it in the freezer for 20 to 30 minutes. Then roll it out into a sheet about ³⁄₁₆ inch (5 mm) thick. Cut out more triangles, arrange them on the baking sheets, and refrigerate. Repeat with the remaining scraps.

7. Before the cookies have chilled and become firm, imprint a design on the center of each ④ by pressing with the cork. To prevent the dough from sticking to the cork, dip the face of the cork in flour and then tap it on the countertop to remove the excess flour before making each imprint.

8. Let the cookies rest in the refrigerator for 20 minutes.
Preheat the oven to 350° F (175° C).

9. Bake, 1 sheet at a time, until the cookies are browned on the bottoms and around the edges, about 13 to 15 minutes.

10. Slide the cookies onto a wire rack using a metal spatula and let cool to room temperature.

➤ **HOWS & WHYS:** The high butter and low sugar content of these cookies gives them a flaky rather than sandy texture. The hard-boiled yolks make them very delicate.

STORAGE: Covered airtight in a tin cookie box or cookie jar for up to 1 week.

Before being rolled out, the dough can be kept in the refrigerator, wrapped in wax paper, for up to 2 or 3 days.

NERO'S EARS
OREILLES DE NÉRON

When I first made Nero's Ears I thought the name was more fanciful than the unusual shape deserved and they would be a little too subtle for children. How wrong I was. My daughter Charlotte, who was two years old at the time I was perfecting the recipe, adored these fine-textured, delicate cookies from the first bite. And although I always used the French name for them, she would regularly wander into the kitchen to request (or rather demand) more ''ears,'' having coined that name on her own. Like Caen-Style Sablés (page 296) and Vendée-Style Sablés (page 298) Nero's Ears contain hard-boiled egg yolks.

EQUIPMENT
2 large, heavy baking sheets
• Brush lightly with melted butter.

PASTRY DOUGH
4¾ ounces (135 g), or ½ cup plus 1½ tablespoons, unsalted butter, softened
3½ ounces (100 g), or ¾ cup plus 4 teaspoons, confectioners' sugar

Yolks of 3 large hard-boiled eggs, forced through a sieve or mashed with a fork
1 teaspoon (½ cl) vanilla extract
6 ounces (170 g), or 1 cup plus 3½ tablespoons, all-purpose flour

COUNTERTOP DUSTING
Flour

GLAZE
1 egg, lightly beaten

For about 36 cookies

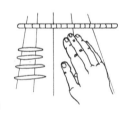

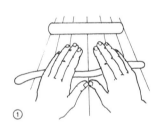

1. Place the butter on your countertop and sift the confectioners' sugar over it. Cream the butter with the sugar by repeatedly smearing it across the countertop with the heel of your hand and gathering it back together with a dough scraper. When smooth, mix in the egg yolks and vanilla with your fingertips. Work quickly so that you don't melt the butter. Sift the flour over the butter mixture. Mix in the flour, either by cutting it in with a dough scraper or by stirring and tossing with your fingertips, until you obtain a loose, crumbly dough. Gather the dough together and finish mixing by smearing it across the countertop, a little at a time, with the heel of your hand. Gather the dough together again. If it is not yet smooth, then repeat this smearing procedure.

2. Gather the dough into a ball and roll it back and forth on the countertop under your palms to form it into a cylinder and elongate it to about 8 inches (20 cm). Cut it in half crosswise (to make it more manageable) and roll each half back and forth under your palms to elongate it into a rope ① about 18 inches (45 cm) long. If necessary, dust the ropes very lightly with flour to prevent them from sticking to the countertop.

3. Cut each rope into 1-inch (2½ cm) lengths and roll each back and forth under your palms ② into a baton 5 inches (13 cm) long, with ends slightly thinner than the center. Bend the ends of each baton ③ around in 2 loops, with the ends meeting at the center of the baton; they will look like little ears. Carefully lift the ears with a metal spatula and transfer them to the baking sheets. Separate the ears by at least 1¼ inches (3 cm). Press your thumb on the center of each ear to make a small depression and make the ear stick to the baking sheet.

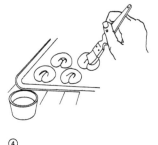

④

4. Lightly brush the tops and sides of the ears ④ with beaten egg. Let rest in the refrigerator until the egg wash dries, 20 to 30 minutes.

Preheat the oven to 350° F (175° C).

5. Lightly brush the tops and sides of the ears a second time with egg wash.

6. Bake, 1 sheet at a time, until the cookies are browned on the bottoms and the egg wash on the tops is a rich golden yellow and just beginning to brown lightly, about 17 to 20 minutes.

7. Slide the cookies onto a wire rack using a metal spatula and let cool to room temperature.

➤ **HOWS & WHYS:** This pastry dough is very fragile and must not be allowed to get warm while your are working with it. However, since it contains almost no liquid it becomes hard when cold, so the ears must be formed before the dough is chilled. If the ropes of dough become too warm and begin to sweat while your are working with them, refrigerate very briefly to cool the dough.

STORAGE: Covered airtight in a tin cookie box or cookie jar for up to 1 week.

DIAMONDS
DIAMANTS

These icebox cookies are made from a very dry dough containing only butter, sugar, flour, and a little vanilla, but no other liquid. The dough is formed into a cylinder that is coated with crystal sugar, chilled, and then sliced. When baked, the edge of the cookie browns lightly, setting off the crystal sugar "diamonds." The original name for these cookies was moques de Hollande, or Dutch Bull's-Eyes.

EQUIPMENT

1 or 2 large, heavy baking sheets
• Brush lightly with melted butter.

PASTRY DOUGH

4¾ ounces (135 g), or ½ cup plus 1½ tablespoons, unsalted butter, softened

2 ounces (60 g), or ½ cup, confectioners' sugar

1 teaspoon (½ cl) vanilla extract

6 ounces (170 g), or 1 cup plus 3½ tablespoons, all-purpose flour

COUNTERTOP DUSTING

Flour

DECORATION

1 egg, lightly beaten

1¾ ounces (50 g), or ¼ cup, crystal sugar

For about 40 cookies

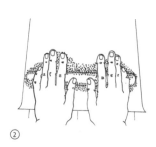

①

③

②

1. Place the butter on your countertop and sift the confectioners' sugar over it. Cream the butter with the sugar by repeatedly smearing it across the countertop with the heel of your hand and gathering it back together with a dough scraper. When smooth, mix in the vanilla with your fingertips. Work quickly so that you don't melt the butter. Sift the flour over the butter mixture. Mix in the flour, either by cutting it in with a dough scraper or by stirring and tossing with your fingertips, until you obtain a loose, crumbly dough. Gather the dough together and finish mixing by smearing it across the countertop, a little at a time, with the heel of your hand. Gather the dough together again. If it is not yet smooth, then repeat this smearing procedure.

2. Gather the dough into a ball and roll it back and forth on the countertop under your palms to form it into a cylinder and elongate it to about 10 inches (25 cm). Cut it in half crosswise (to make it more manageable) and roll each half back and forth under your palms to elongate it into a uniform cylinder about 8 inches (20 cm) long and 1¼ inches (3 cm) in diameter. If necessary, dust the cylinders very lightly with flour to prevent them from sticking to the countertop.

3. Brush each cylinder of dough ① with beaten egg. Place the crystal sugar on a sheet of wax paper and distribute it down the center. Roll each cylinder in the sugar ② to coat it evenly. Wrap each cylinder in wax paper and refrigerate for at least 2 hours and preferably overnight.

Preheat the oven to 375° F (190° C).

4. Cut each cylinder ③ into slices ⅜ inch (1 cm) thick with your chef's knife. Carefully lift the slices with a metal spatula and transfer them to the

④

baking sheets. Separate the slices by at least 1 inch (2½ cm). Press your thumb on the top ④ of each slice to make a slight depression in the center and make the slice stick to the baking sheet. Don't press too hard or the sides will crack.

5. Bake, 1 sheet at a time, until the bottoms of the cookies have browned and the edges have begun to brown but the centers are still pale, about 14 to 16 minutes.

6. Slide the cookies onto a wire rack using a metal spatula and let cool to room temperature.

➤ **HOWS & WHYS:** Because the batter contains so little liquid, it becomes very hard when cold. The cylinders must therefore be formed before chilling. The egg wash and crystal sugar can be applied before or after chilling. The sugar sticks better before chilling, but if the dough is too warm and soft to handle easily, it is better to chill them first and then coat them with egg wash and sugar.

STORAGE: Covered airtight in a tin cookie box or cookie jar for up to 1 week.

Before being coated with egg wash and crystal sugar, the cylinders of dough can be kept in the refrigerator, wrapped in wax paper, for up to 2 or 3 days.

DUTCH SABLÉS
SABLÉS HOLLANDAIS

~~~~~~~~

This is another icebox cookie made from the same dough as Diamonds (page 302). Here part of the dough is colored and flavored with cocoa powder, and then the cocoa dough and plain dough are formed into long strips and sheets that are pieced together in various ways in a cylinder or a square log. The cylinder or log is sliced crosswise, producing a visually striking bull's-eye or checkerboard pattern, depending on how it was put together.

The association of both Dutch Sablés and Diamonds (alias Dutch Bull's-Eyes) with Holland suggests that the French originally learned to make bar cookies with this type of dough from the Dutch. While Diamonds have been a French classic since the nineteenth century, Dutch Sablés are a more recent addition to the French repertoire and are really an international cookie. The English call them Dutch biscuits, the Germans Holländer, and they even turn up in lackluster form in commercial cookie assortments sold in the United States. Our crisp, buttery French version is the ultimate of the genre, and we think they are at their best with a glass of cold milk.

EQUIPMENT

1 or 2 large, heavy baking sheets
• Brush lightly with melted butter.

PASTRY DOUGH

4¾ ounces (135 g), or ½ cup plus 1½ tablespoons, unsalted butter, softened
2 ounces (60 g), or ½ cup, confectioners' sugar
1 teaspoon (½ cl) vanilla extract

6 ounces (170 g), or 1 cup plus 3½ tablespoons, all-purpose flour
1 tablespoon (6 g) unsweetened Dutch-processed cocoa powder for bull's-eyes

or

2 teaspoons (4 g) unsweetened Dutch-processed cocoa powder for checkerboards

COUNTERTOP DUSTING

Flour

For about 32 cookies

1. Place the butter on your countertop and sift the confectioners' sugar over it. Cream the butter with the sugar by repeatedly smearing it across the countertop with the heel of your hand and gathering it back together with a dough scraper. When smooth, mix in the vanilla with your fingertips. Work quickly so that you don't melt the butter. Sift the flour over the butter mixture. Mix in the flour, either by cutting it in with a dough scraper or by stirring and tossing with your fingertips, until you obtain a loose, crumbly dough. Set aside either 5½ ounces (150 g) of the dough for bull's-eyes or 3¼ ounces (90 g) of the dough for checkerboards. Gather together the remaining dough and finish mixing by smearing it across the countertop, a little at a time, with the heel of your hand. Gather the dough together again. If it is not yet smooth, then repeat this smearing procedure. Then form the dough into a ball. Next take the dough you set aside, sift the cocoa powder over it, and finish mixing it by the same smearing procedure, then form it into a ball.

2. FOR BULL'S-EYES: Roll the ball of cocoa dough back and forth on

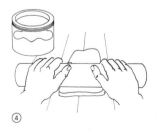

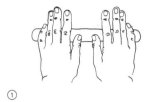

the countertop under your palms to form it into a cylinder ① and elongate it to about 8 inches (20 cm). If necessary, dust the cylinder very lightly with flour to prevent it from sticking to the countertop. Press on top of the cylinder to flatten it slightly, making it about ¾ inch (2 cm) thick. Then chill it so that it will be firm and hold its shape.

Lightly dust your countertop and the plain dough with flour, and form the dough into a rectangular pad about 1 inch (2½ cm) thick. Roll out the pad of dough with your rolling pin into a sheet 6 by 8 inches (15 by 20 cm). Trim the long edges of the sheet, and cut from one side a strip 1¼ inches (4 cm) wide and 8 inches (20 cm) long. Take the cocoa dough from the refrigerator and cut it in half lengthwise ②, through the thickest diameter of the flattened cylinder, to get 2 flattened half-cylinders. Lightly brush the 2 cut faces with cold water, and brush the top of the strip of plain dough with water. Place the strip of plain dough, moistened side down, on the cut face of one of the half cylinders, carefully lining up the edges, and press gently to seal the 2 together without deforming them. Now brush the top of the strip of plain dough with cold water, and place the second half cylinder on, top cut face down, lining up the edges carefully. Press gently once more to seal without deforming. You will now have an 8-inch- (20 cm) long cylinder of cocoa dough with a strip of plain dough down the center. Chill it in the freezer until firm.

Check to be sure that the remaining sheet of plain dough is wide enough to wrap all the way around the cylinder. If not, roll it out a little wider with your rolling pin. Lightly brush the top of the sheet with cold water. Moisten the cylinder as well. Place the cylinder on the center of the sheet and wrap the sheet around it ③. Trim the long edges of the sheet so they meet. Now you have a larger cylinder of dough. Gently roll it back and forth on your countertop to seal the outer layer of plain dough to the inner cylinder.

FOR CHECKERBOARDS: Take 4 ounces (115 g) of the plain dough. Lightly dust your countertop and this dough with flour, and form the dough into a rectangular pad about 1½ by 3 inches (4 by 8 cm) and 1¼ inches (3 cm) thick. Roll out the pad of dough with your rolling pin ④ into a band 1⅞ by 8 inches (5 by 20 cm) and ⅜ inch (1 cm) thick. Trim the long edges of the band and cut from one side 2 strips ⅜ inch (1 cm) wide and 8 inches (20 cm) long, leaving a band 1⅛ inches (3 cm) wide and 8 inches (20 cm) long. (If the strips and band of dough are too soft to handle easily, chill

(continued)

SWEET PASTRY DOUGHS

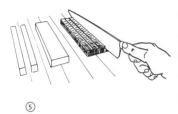

⑤

them in the refrigerator to make them more firm, being careful to lay them out straight on a tray.) Lightly dust your countertop and the cocoa dough with flour, and form the dough into a rectangular pad about 1½ by 3 inches (4 by 8 cm) and 1 inch (2½ cm) thick. Roll out the pad of dough with your rolling pin into a band 1½ by 8 inches (4 by 20 cm) and ⅜ inch (1 cm) thick. Trim the long edges of the band and cut it lengthwise ⑤ into four strips ⅜ inch (1 cm) wide and 8 inches (20 cm) long. (If the strips of dough are too soft to handle easily, chill them in the refrigerator to make them more firm, being careful to lay them out straight on a tray.)

Lightly brush one side of a cocoa strip and one side of a plain strip of dough with cold water and gently press the 2 moistened sides together to seal them. Moisten the side of the plain strip opposite the cocoa strip and one side of a second cocoa strip and gently press them together. Now you have a striped band 1⅛ inches (3 cm) wide and ⅜ inch (1 cm) thick, made of 3 strips of dough. Continuing to moisten all sides that will be sealed together, place the 1⅛-inch- (3 cm) wide band of plain dough on top of the striped band and gently press them together. Now the band is 1⅛ inches (3 cm) wide and ¾ inch (2 cm) thick. Finally seal the remaining 3 strips of dough on top of the plain band to form a square log with cocoa strips at all 4 corners. Chill it in the freezer until firm.

⑥

Lightly dust your countertop and the remaining plain dough with flour, and form the dough into a rectangular pad about 1 inch (2½ cm) thick. Roll out the pad of dough with your rolling pin into a sheet 5¼ by 8 inches (14 by 20 cm) and ³⁄₁₆ inch (5 mm) thick. Trim the long edges of the sheet and cut it lengthwise into 4 strips, two of them 1⅛ inches (3 cm) wide and the other two 1½ inches (4 cm) wide. Continuing to moisten all surfaces that will be sealed together, place the 2 narrow strips on opposite faces of the square log, carefully lining up the edges, and press gently. Finally place the 2 wide strips on the remaining 2 faces ⑥ of the log, again lining up the edges, and press gently. You now have a large log about 1½ inches (4 cm) square and 8 inches (20 cm) long, with plain dough on all 4 sides.

3. Wrap the cylinder or log in wax paper and refrigerate for at least 2 hours and preferably overnight.

Preheat the oven to 350° F (175° C).

4. Cut the cylinder or log into slices ¼ inch (6 mm) thick with your chef's knife. Carefully lift the slices with a metal spatula and transfer them to the baking sheets. Separate the slices by at least 1 inch (2½ cm), and gently press each slice to make it stick to the baking sheet.

5. Bake, 1 sheet at a time, until the cookies have browned lightly on the bottoms and edges, about 15 to 18 minutes.

6. Slide the cookies onto a wire rack using a metal spatula and let cool to room temperature.

➤ **HOWS & WHYS:** Because the batter contains so little liquid, it becomes very hard when cold. The cylinder or log must therefore be formed before chilling. It is very important that the cookies not be overbaked, otherwise the plain dough will brown, spoiling the contrast between the 2 doughs.

STORAGE: Covered airtight in a tin cookie box or cookie jar for up to 1 week.

Before being cut, the cylinders of dough can be kept in the refrigerator, wrapped in wax paper, for up to 2 or 3 days.

GHENT ALMOND LOAVES
PAINS D'AMANDES DE GAND

*T*his icebox cookie, based on a dough similar to pâte sucrée, contains whole raw almonds and is flavored with cinnamon. Cinnamon is an unusual flavoring in French desserts, and its presence almost invariably indicates a foreign origin. Ghent Almond Loaves is an adaptation of a Belgian classic, which the French have been enjoying for well over a hundred years. In the Middle Ages, Ghent was the seat of the counts of Flanders and was an important trade and manufacturing center noted especially for its textiles. Ghent is close to The Netherlands, and the use of cinnamon was probably borrowed from the Dutch, who had a virtual monopoly on the cinnamon trade for centuries.

EQUIPMENT

2 large, heavy baking sheets
• Brush lightly with melted butter.

PASTRY DOUGH

5¼ ounces (150 g), or ½ cup plus 3 tablespoons,
    unsalted butter, softened
4½ ounces (125 g), or ½ cup plus 2 tablespoons,
    superfine sugar

1 large egg, lightly beaten
3½ ounces (100 g), or ⅔ cup, raw almonds
9 ounces (250 g), or 1¾ cups plus ½ tablespoon,
    all-purpose flour
½ teaspoon (¼ cl) ground cinnamon
¼ teaspoon (1 ml) baking soda

COUNTERTOP DUSTING

Flour

For about 40 cookies

1. On your countertop, cream the butter with the sugar by repeatedly smearing it across the countertop with the heel of your hand and gathering it back together with a dough scraper. When smooth, mix in the egg, a little at a time, with your fingertips. Then mix in the almonds. Work quickly so that you don't melt the butter. Sift the flour, cinnamon, and baking soda over the butter mixture. Mix in the sifted flour, either by cutting it in with a dough scraper or by stirring and tossing with your fingertips, until you obtain a loose, crumbly dough. Gather the dough together and finish mixing by smearing it across the countertop, a little at a time, with the heel of your hand. Gather the dough together again. If it is not yet smooth, then repeat this smearing procedure.

2. Gather the dough into a ball and then press it into a rectangular block about 4 by 5 inches (10 by 12 cm) and 2 inches (5 cm) thick, with sides as straight as you can make them. If necessary, dust the dough very lightly with flour to prevent it from sticking to the countertop. Lightly dust the pad with flour, wrap it in wax paper, and refrigerate for at least 2 hours.

Preheat the oven to 375° F (190° C).

3. Trim the sides of the block of dough with your chef's knife to make the sides flat. Cut the block in half lengthwise ① to make 2 square logs about 2 by 2 inches (5 by 5 cm) and 5 inches (12 cm) long. Cut each log into slices ¼ inch (6 mm) thick with your chef's knife. Carefully lift the

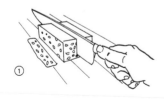

①

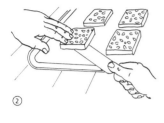

②

slices with a metal spatula and transfer them ② to the baking sheets. Separate the slices by at least 1¼ inches (3 cm), and gently press each slice to make it stick to the baking sheet.

4. Bake, 1 sheet at a time, until the cookies have browned on the bottoms and around the edges and the tops just begin to brown, about 13 to 17 minutes.

5. Slide the cookies onto a wire rack using a metal spatula and let cool to room temperature.

➤ **HOWS & WHYS:** Nineteenth-century recipes for Ghent Almond Loaves call for baking soda. At first we were puzzled by this, because there is no obvious acid in the recipe to interact with the baking soda and produce the desired leavening. In fact, the butter used in France is made from matured cream and is slightly sour; even American sweet cream butter has enough acidity to do the job. Without baking soda, the cookies are too dense.

VARIATIONS: Substitute English walnuts for the almonds and 2 teaspoons (3 g) instant coffee for the cinnamon. Or substitute hazelnuts for the almonds and 1 tablespoon plus 2 teaspoons (10 g) unsweetened cocoa powder for the cinnamon. For the hazelnut version, ignore the color of the dough and bake until the hazelnuts brown lightly in the centers.

Another alternative is to cut the dough in thinner slices—about ³⁄₃₂ inch (4 mm). It is very difficult to cut uniform slices this thin, and the thin slices burn very easily. But the result is worth the effort. When baked, there is a light caramelization, which enhances the flavor and crispiness, producing a supremely elegant cookie. If you want to try this, we suggest lightly chopping the nuts to make cutting the slices easier.

STORAGE: Covered airtight in a tin cookie box or cookie jar for up to 1 week.

Before being cut, the block of dough can be kept in the refrigerator, wrapped in wax paper, for up to 1 day. Longer storage is undesirable because the baking soda slowly interacts with the small amount of acid in the dough and loses its leavening power.

SPECTACLES
LUNETTES

~~~~~~~~~~~

These cookies are made from the same *pâte sucrée* as *Tea Sablés* (page 286). Here the dough is cut in large, pointed ovals or boat shapes, half of which have two round holes cut out like a mask. After baking, jam is spread on top of the plain ovals, and the ovals with the cutouts are placed on top. The relatively large size and striking yet easy presentation of these cookies make them ideal for serving to hungry teenagers (and, for that matter, college and graduate students). Thanks to their masklike shape, they would also be perfect for a costume party.

EQUIPMENT
2 large, heavy baking sheets
A fluted oval cookie cutter 3 inches (5½ cm) wide and 5 inches (7½ cm) long, with pointed ends—like a *barquette* or boat shape (see Note)
An apple corer or plain round cookie cutter ¾ to 1 inch (2–2½ cm) in diameter

PASTRY DOUGH
4 ounces (115 g), or ½ cup, unsalted butter, softened
4 ounces (115 g), or ¾ cup plus 3 tablespoons, confectioners' sugar

1 large egg, lightly beaten
¼ teaspoon (1 g) salt
8 ounces (230 g), or 1½ cups plus 2 tablespoons, all-purpose flour
COUNTERTOP DUSTING
Flour
FILLING
5 tablespoons (100 g) red currant jelly
DECORATION
Confectioners' sugar

For about 9 cookies

1. Place the butter on your countertop and sift the confectioners' sugar over it. Cream the butter with the sugar by repeatedly smearing it across the countertop with the heel of your hand and gathering it back together with a dough scraper. When smooth, mix in the egg, a little at a time, with your fingertips. Then mix in the salt. Work quickly so that you don't melt the butter. Sift the flour over the butter mixture. Mix in the flour, either by cutting it in with a dough scraper or by stirring and tossing with your fingertips, until you obtain a loose, crumbly dough. Gather the dough together and finish mixing by smearing it across the countertop, a little at a time, with the heel of your hand. Gather the dough together again. If it is not yet smooth, then repeat this smearing procedure.

2. Form the dough into a square pad about 1½ inches (4 cm) thick. Lightly dust the pad with flour, wrap it in wax paper, and refrigerate for at least 2 hours and preferably overnight.

3. Dust your countertop and the pad of dough with flour, and roll out the dough with a rolling pin ① into a sheet about ⅛ inch (3 mm) thick. Dust the counter and dough with flour as needed to prevent the dough from sticking to counter or rolling pin. Slide the dough onto a tray and chill it briefly in the freezer whenever it starts to warm and soften. If it is too

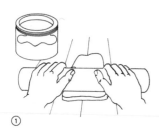

①

difficult to roll out the entire quantity in a single sheet, cut it in half and roll out each half separately.

4. Cut out ovals ② using the fluted cookie cutter. Cut out 2 ''eyes'' in half of the ovals ③ using the apple corer or plain round cookie cutter. Carefully lift the ovals with a metal spatula and transfer them to the baking sheets. Separate the ovals by at least ¾ inch (2 cm), and gently press each oval to make it stick to the baking sheet. Let rest in the refrigerator.

5. Gather together the remaining dough and form it into a pad. If it is too soft to work with, chill it in the freezer for 20 to 30 minutes. Then roll it out into a sheet about ⅛ inch (3 mm) thick. Cut out more ovals with your cookie cutter and cut out 2 ''eyes'' in half of them. Arrange the ovals on the baking sheets and refrigerate. Repeat with the remaining scraps, or save them for use in Vietnamese Hats (page 24).

Preheat the oven to 350° F (175° C).

6. Bake, 1 sheet at a time, until the cookies are lightly browned on the bottoms and edges but the tops are still pale, about 12 to 15 minutes.

7. Slide the cookies onto a wire rack using a metal spatula and let cool to room temperature.

8. Spoon 1½ teaspoons (¾ cl) of currant jelly on each of the plain pastry ovals and spread the jelly with your palette knife, leaving a ⅜-inch (1 cm) border uncovered on all sides. Dust the ovals with the eyes with confectioners' sugar ④ until they are white, then place one on each of the jelly-coated ovals.

NOTE: You can bend another fluted cutter (for example, a large round or heart-shaped cutter) into an oval cookie cutter.

VARIATION: In steps 4 and 5, use a 4-inch (10 cm) fluted round cookie cutter instead of the oval cookie cutter, and cut three ¾-inch (2 cm) round holes in the center of half of the pastry dough rounds. These aren't Spectacles, but they look and taste just as good.

STORAGE: It is best to fill these cookies and dust the tops with confectioners' sugar shortly before serving. Before filling and dusting, keep them covered airtight in a tin cookie box or cookie jar, for up to 1 week.

Before being rolled out, the dough can be kept in the refrigerator, wrapped in wax paper, for up to 2 or 3 days. Trimmings can be frozen, wrapped in wax paper and then in freezer wrap, for up to 1 month.

SOUVAROFFS
SOUVAROFFS

*T*hese are sablés *cookies flavored with kirsch and sandwiched with red currant jelly. If you prefer, they may be filled with apricot jam instead. The name is Russian, presumably that of a Russian aristocrat who had a French chef. In French cuisine there is also a method of preparing chicken or other fowl with foie gras and truffles, called* souvaroff.

EQUIPMENT
2 large, heavy baking sheets
A fluted or plain oval cookie cutter (see Note)
3¼ inches (8 cm) long and 2¼ inches (6 cm) wide

PASTRY DOUGH
4¾ ounces (135 g), or ½ cup plus 1½ tablespoons, unsalted butter, softened
2½ ounces (70 g), or ½ cup plus 4 teaspoons, confectioners' sugar

1 tablespoon plus 1 teaspoon (2 cl) kirsch
6 ounces (170 g), or 1 cup plus 3½ tablespoons, all-purpose flour

COUNTERTOP DUSTING
Flour

FILLING
4 tablespoons (80 g) red currant jelly

DECORATION
Confectioners' sugar

For about 12 cookies

1. Place the butter on your countertop and sift the confectioners' sugar over it. Cream the butter with sugar by repeatedly smearing it across the countertop with the heel of your hand and gathering it back together with a dough scraper. When smooth, mix in the kirsch with your fingertips. Work quickly so that you don't melt the butter. Sift the flour over the butter mixture. Mix in the flour, either by cutting it in with a dough scraper or by stirring and tossing with your fingertips, until you obtain a loose, crumbly dough. Gather the dough together and finish mixing by smearing it across the countertop, a little at a time, with the heel of your hand. Gather the dough together again. If it is not yet smooth, then repeat this smearing procedure.

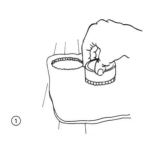

①

2. Form the dough into a square pad about 1 inch (2½ cm) thick. Lightly dust the pad with flour, wrap it in wax paper, and refrigerate for at least 2 hours and preferably overnight.

3. Dust your countertop and the pad of dough with flour, and roll out the dough with a rolling pin into a sheet about ⅛ inch (3 mm) thick. Dust the counter and dough with flour as needed to prevent the dough from sticking to counter or rolling pin. Slide the dough onto a tray and chill it briefly in the freezer whenever it starts to warm and soften.

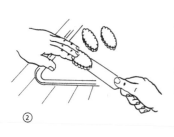

②

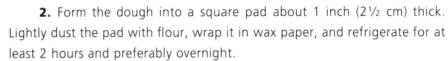

4. Cut out ovals ① using the cookie cutter. Carefully lift the ovals with a metal spatula and transfer them ② to the baking sheets. Separate

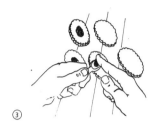

③

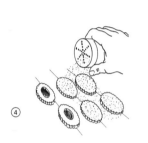

④

the ovals by at least ¾ inch (2 cm), and gently press each oval to make it stick to the baking sheet. Let rest in the refrigerator.

5. Gather together the remaining dough and form it into a pad. If it is too soft to work with, chill it in the freezer for 20 to 30 minutes. Then roll it out into a sheet about ⅛ inch (3 mm) thick. Cut out more ovals, arrange them on the baking sheets, and refrigerate. Repeat with the remaining scraps, or save them for use in Vietnamese Hats (page 24).

Preheat the oven to 400° F (200° C).

6. Bake, 1 sheet at a time, until the cookies are lightly browned on the bottoms and around the edges, about 9 to 11 minutes.

7. Slide the cookies onto a wire rack using a metal spatula and let cool to room temperature.

8. Spoon ½ teaspoon (¼ cl) of red currant jelly on top ③ of half of the pastry ovals. Dust the tops of the remaining ovals with confectioners' sugar ④ until they are white, then place 1 on each of the jelly-coated ovals.

NOTE: You can make the oval cookie cutter from a round cutter 2¾ inches (7 cm) in diameter by carefully bending it into shape.

STORAGE: It is best to fill these cookies and dust the tops with confectioners' sugar shortly before serving. Before filling and dusting, keep them covered airtight in a tin cookie box or cookie jar for up to 1 week.

Before being rolled out, the dough can be kept in the refrigerator, wrapped in wax paper, for up to 2 or 3 days. Trimmings can be frozen, wrapped in wax paper and then in freezer wrap, for up to 1 month.

HONEY-FILLED SABLÉS
FOURRÉS AU MIEL

Before refined sugar became widely available in Europe in the seventeenth century, honey was the standard sweetener in French pastry. Honey plays only a minor role in modern pastry, and today we would regard the use of honey alone to flavor a dessert as too much of a good thing. However, when used in moderation for its flavor rather than its sweetness, it is an ingredient of great subtlety and finesse.

These cookies are made from the same pâte sucrée as Tea Sablés (page 286) and Spectacles (page 310), but with the addition of finely chopped glacé fruits. The dough is cut in small rounds that are brushed with egg wash before baking and then sandwiched with honey after baking. The flecks of glacé fruit in the cookies give them a distinctive appearance, while the honey permeates them with its inimitable flavor.

EQUIPMENT

2 or 3 large, heavy baking sheets
• Brush lightly with melted butter.
A plain round cookie cutter 1½ inches (4 cm) in diameter

PASTRY DOUGH

3½ ounces (100 g), or ½ cup plus 1 tablespoon, glacé cherries and pineapple
8 ounces (230 g), or 1½ cups plus 2 tablespoons, all-purpose flour

4 ounces (115 g), or ½ cup, unsalted butter, softened
4 ounces (115 g), or ¾ cup plus 3 tablespoons, confectioners' sugar
1 large egg, lightly beaten
¼ teaspoon (1 g) salt

COUNTERTOP DUSTING

Flour

GLAZE

1 egg, lightly beaten

FILLING

¼ cup (75 g) honey

For about 45 cookies

1. Place the glacé fruits on your countertop and sift about ¼ cup (35 g) of the flour oven them. Chop the fruits finely with your chef's knife.

2. Place the butter on your countertop and sift the confectioners' sugar over it. Cream the butter with the sugar by repeatedly smearing it across the countertop with the heel of your hand and gathering it back together with a dough scraper. When smooth, mix in the egg, a little at a time, with your fingertips. Then mix in the salt, followed by the glacé fruits (along with the flour used in chopping them). Work quickly so that you don't melt the butter. Sift the remaining flour over the butter mixture. Mix in the flour, either by cutting it in with a dough scraper or by stirring and tossing with your fingertips, until you obtain a loose, crumbly dough. Gather the dough together and finish mixing by smearing it across the countertop, a little at a time, with the heel of your hand. Gather the dough together again. If it is not yet smooth, then repeat this smearing procedure.

3. Form the dough into a square pad about 1½ inches (4 cm) thick. Lightly dust the pad with flour, wrap it in wax paper, and refrigerate for at least 2 hours and preferably overnight.

4. Dust your countertop and the pad of dough with flour, and roll out the dough with a rolling pin into a sheet about ⅛ inch (3 mm) thick. Dust the counter and dough with flour as needed to prevent the dough from sticking to counter or rolling pin. Slide the dough onto a tray and chill it briefly in the freezer whenever it starts to warm and soften. If it is too difficult to roll out the entire quantity in a single sheet, cut it in half and roll out each half separately.

①

5. Cut out 1½-inch (4 cm) rounds ① with the cookie cutter. Carefully lift the rounds with a metal spatula and transfer them to the baking sheets. Separate the rounds by at least ¾ inch (2 cm), and gently press each round to make it stick to the baking sheet. Let rest in the refrigerator.

6. Gather together the remaining dough and form it into a pad. If it is too soft to work with, chill it in the freezer for 20 to 30 minutes. Then roll it out into a sheet about ⅛ inch (3 mm) thick. Cut out more rounds with your cookie cutter, arrange them on the baking sheets, and refrigerate. Repeat with the remaining scraps.

②

7. Lightly brush the tops of the rounds ② with beaten egg. Let rest in the refrigerator until the egg wash dries, 20 to 30 minutes.

Preheat the oven to 350° F (175° C).

8. Brush the rounds a second time with egg wash. Bake, 1 sheet at a time, until the cookies are lightly browned on the bottoms, beginning to brown around the edges, and the egg wash on the tops has set to a satiny sheen, about 11 to 14 minutes.

9. Slide the cookies onto a wire rack using a metal spatula and let cool to room temperature.

③

10. Turn half of the rounds upside down and spoon (or use a squeeze bottle) ¼ teaspoon (1 ml) of honey on the back of each. Place a second round right side up on top ③ of each honey-coated round.

➤ **HOWS & WHYS:** Chopping the glacé fruits with a little flour helps prevent them from sticking together.

STORAGE: Before filling, keep the baked rounds covered airtight in a tin cookie box or cookie jar for up to 1 week. After filling, the cookies can be kept for up to 3 to 5 days.

Before being rolled out, the dough can be kept in the refrigerator, wrapped in wax paper, for up to 2 or 3 days.

VALOIS
VALOIS

In 1328, Philip, count of Valois, became King Philip VI of France. For the next 250 years, France was ruled by members of the house of Valois. That dynasty ended in 1589, when the dying Henry III named his ally Henry of Navarre as his successor, transferring the throne to the house of Bourbon. Two centuries later, at the beginning of the Revolution, the monarchists met at the Café de Valois in the Palais Royal in Paris.

During the reign of the Valois kings, the gastronomy of France began to take shape. The most important of the early French cookbooks, today known as *Le Viandier*, was written in the late fourteenth century by Taillevent, the chef to Philip VI and Charles V. In 1533, Catherine de Médicis married the duke of Orléans. When the duke became King Henry II in 1547, Catherine brought Florentine refinement to the French court and installed her Florentine chefs in the royal kitchens. And the first French cookbook on confectionary, *Le Confiturier français*, was written in 1552 by Nostradamus, the personal physician and court astrologer to Charles IX.

The cookie called Valois was almost certainly created in the late nineteenth century, when sweet pastry doughs became fashionable for this purpose. It is made by sandwiching two butter-rich ovals of sweet pastry with the luxurious chocolate cream filling called ganache.

EQUIPMENT

2 or 3 large, heavy baking sheets
• Brush lightly with melted butter.
A fluted or plain oval cookie cutter (see Note) 2⅛ inches (5½ cm) long and 1⅜ inches (3½ cm) wide

PASTRY DOUGH

5 ounces (140 g), or ½ cup plus 2 tablespoons, unsalted butter, softened
3 ounces (85 g), or ⅔ cup plus 2 teaspoons, confectioners' sugar

For about 36 cookies

2 tablespoons (3 cl) lightly beaten egg
1½ teaspoons (¾ cl) vanilla extract
7½ ounces (215 g), or 1½ cups plus ½ tablespoon, all-purpose flour

COUNTERTOP DUSTING

Flour

GLAZE

1 large egg, lightly beaten

FILLING

4 ounces (115 g) European bittersweet chocolate (such as Lindt Excellence)
¼ cup plus 2 tablespoons (9 cl) heavy cream

1. Place the butter on your countertop and sift the confectioners' sugar over it. Cream the butter with the sugar by repeatedly smearing it across the countertop with the heel of your hand and gathering it back together with a dough scraper. When smooth, mix in the egg, a little at a time, with your fingertips. Then mix in the vanilla. Work quickly so that you don't melt the butter. Sift the flour over the butter mixture. Mix in the flour, either by cutting it in with a dough scraper or by stirring and tossing with your fingertips, until you obtain a loose, crumbly dough. Gather the dough together and finish mixing by smearing it across the countertop, a little at a time, with the heel of your hand. Gather the dough together again. If it is not yet smooth, then repeat this smearing procedure.

2. Form the dough into a square pad about 1½ inches (4 cm) thick. Lightly dust the pad with flour, wrap it in wax paper, and refrigerate for at least 2 hours and preferably overnight.

3. Dust your countertop and the pad of dough with flour, and roll out the dough with a rolling pin into a sheet about ⅛ inch (3 mm) thick. Dust the counter and dough with flour as needed to prevent the dough from sticking to counter or rolling pin. Slide the dough onto a tray and chill it briefly in the freezer whenever it starts to warm and soften. If it is too difficult to roll out the entire quantity in a single sheet, cut it in half and roll out each half separately.

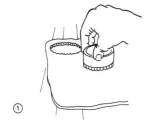

4. Cut out ovals ① using the cookie cutter. Carefully lift the ovals with a metal spatula and transfer them ② to the baking sheets. Separate the ovals by at least ¾ inch (2 cm), and gently press each oval to make it stick to the baking sheet. Let rest in the refrigerator.

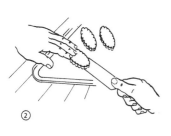

5. Gather together the remaining dough and form it into a pad. If it is too soft to work with, chill it in the freezer for 20 to 30 minutes. Then roll it out into a sheet about ⅛ inch (3 mm) thick. Cut out more ovals with your cookie cutter. Arrange the ovals on the baking sheets and refrigerate. Repeat with the remaining scraps, or save them for use in Vietnamese Hats (page 24).

6. Lightly brush the tops of the ovals with beaten egg. Let rest in the refrigerator until the egg wash dries, 20 to 30 minutes.

Preheat the oven to 400° F (200° C).

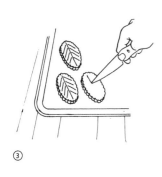

7. Brush the ovals a second time with egg wash. Score the top of each oval in a leaf design ③ by drawing a line lengthwise down the center with the tip of a paring knife and then drawing 4 parallel lines on the diagonal on each side of the center line and meeting at the center.

8. Bake, 1 sheet at a time, until the cookies are browned on the bottoms and edges and the egg wash on the tops is golden, about 8 to 10 minutes.

9. Slide the cookies onto a wire rack using a metal spatula and let cool to room temperature.

10. Prepare the *ganache* filling as follows: Chop the chocolate and put it in a small stainless-steel bowl. Bring the cream just to a boil, then reduce the heat and simmer for 2 minutes, stirring constantly with a wire whisk, to sterilize the cream. Gradually stir the cream into the chocolate ④

(continued)

with the whisk, and continue stirring until the chocolate is completely melted. (If some of the chocolate still doesn't melt, dip the bottom of the bowl of *ganache* in a bowl of hot water and stir a little longer.) Allow the *ganache* to cool, stirring occasionally with a wooden spatula, until it starts to thicken. Then fill the cookies right away, before the *ganache* sets. If the *ganache* does start to set before you finish using it, dip the bottom of the bowl of *ganache* in a bowl of hot water and stir it with a wooden spatula until it is soft and smooth (but not runny) again.

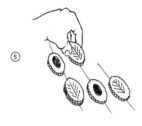

11. Turn half of the ovals upside down, and spread 1 teaspoon (½ cl) of *ganache* on the back of each. Then place a second oval right side up on top ⑤ of each and press gently to sandwich them together.

NOTE: You can make the oval cookie cutter from a round cutter 1¾ inches (4½ cm) in diameter by carefully bending it into shape.

STORAGE: Before filling, keep the baked ovals covered airtight in a tin cookie box or cookie jar for up to 1 week days. After filling, keep the cookies covered in a cool place—below 65° F (18° C)—for up to 1 day. Do not refrigerate them or the cookies will soften.

Before being rolled out, the dough can be kept in the refrigerator, wrapped in wax paper, for up to 2 or 3 days. Trimmings can be frozen, wrapped in wax paper and then in freezer wrap, for up to 1 month.

THREE-CORNERED HATS
CHAPEAUX FINS

~~~~~~

This is a delightful little cookie made by piping a tiny dome of raw almond paste on a round of pâte sucrée, then folding up three sides of the round to form a three-cornered hat. When baked, the outside of the cookie is crisp while the inside is soft.

EQUIPMENT

2 or 3 large, heavy baking sheets
• Brush lightly with melted butter.
A plain round cookie cutter 2 inches (5 cm) in diameter
A small or medium pastry bag fitted with
• a ⁷⁄₁₆-inch (11 mm) plain pastry tube (Ateco #5)

PASTRY DOUGH

4 ounces (115 g), or ½ cup, unsalted butter, softened
4 ounces (115 g), or ¾ cup plus 3 tablespoons, confectioners' sugar
1 large egg, lightly beaten
8 ounces (230 g), or 1½ cups plus 2 tablespoons, all-purpose flour

FILLING

1 large egg white
1 tablespoon (20 g) strained apricot jam
     [*Basic Preparation*, page 484]
6 ounces (170 g), or about 1¼ cups, almond and sugar powder
     Basic Preparation, page 482:
     85 g (3 ounces), or ½ cup plus 1 tablespoon, blanched almonds
     85 g (3 ounces), or about ⅔ cup plus 2 teaspoons, confectioners' sugar

COUNTERTOP DUSTING

Flour

GLAZE

1 egg, lightly beaten

DECORATION

Granulated sugar

For about 55 cookies

1. Place the butter on your countertop and sift the confectioners' sugar over it. Cream the butter with the sugar by repeatedly smearing it across the countertop with the heel of your hand and gathering it back together with a dough scraper. When smooth, mix in the egg, a little at a time, with your fingertips. Work quickly so that you don't melt the butter. Sift the flour over the butter mixture. Mix in the flour, either by cutting it in with a dough scraper or by stirring and tossing with your fingertips, until you obtain a loose, crumbly dough. Gather the dough together and finish mixing by smearing it across the countertop, a little at a time, with the heel of your hand. Gather the dough together again. If it is not yet smooth, then repeat this smearing procedure.

2. Form the dough into a square pad about 1½ inches (4 cm) thick. Lightly dust the pad with flour, wrap it in wax paper, and refrigerate for at least 2 hours and preferably overnight.

3. Stir the egg white into the apricot jam. Stir this mixture into the almond and sugar powder, using a wooden spatula or the flat beater of your electric mixer, to make an uncooked almond paste.

(continued)

4. Dust your countertop and the pad of dough with flour, and roll out the dough with a rolling pin into a sheet about ⅛ inch (3 mm) thick. Dust the counter and dough with flour as needed to prevent the dough from sticking to the counter or rolling pin. Slide the dough onto a tray and chill it briefly in the freezer whenever it starts to warm and soften. If it is too difficult to roll out the entire quantity in a single sheet, cut it in half and roll out each half separately.

5. Cut out 2-inch (5 cm) rounds using the cookie cutter ①. Carefully lift the rounds with a metal spatula, stack them 4 to 6 high on a tray, and refrigerate briefly. They must not be too cold or they will crack when you form the hats.

6. Gather together the remaining dough and form it into a pad. If it is too soft to work with, chill it in the freezer for 20 to 30 minutes. Then roll it out into a sheet about ⅛ inch (3 mm) thick. Cut out more rounds, arrange them in stacks on the tray, and refrigerate. Repeat with the remaining scraps, or save them for use in Vietnamese Hats (page 24).

7. Scoop the almond paste into the pastry bag. Lay out the pastry rounds on your countertop about a dozen at a time. Moisten a 1-inch- (2½ cm) wide border around the top ② of each round very lightly with cold water using a pastry brush, leaving the center unbrushed. Pipe a ⅝-inch (16 mm) dome of almond paste on the center ③ of each round of dough. Fold up 3 sides to enclose the almond paste, leaving center open so the top of the almond paste dome is exposed. Pinch the sides together ④ to seal them.

8. Carefully lift the hats with a metal spatula and transfer them to the baking sheets. Separate the hats by at least 1 inch (2½ cm).

9. Lightly brush the 3 sides of each hat with beaten egg. Let rest in the refrigerator until the egg wash dries, 20 to 30 minutes.

Preheat the oven to 400° F (200° C).

10. Lightly brush the sides of the hats a second time with egg wash. Drop a pinch of sugar on top ⑤ of the almond paste at the center of each hat.

11. Bake, 1 sheet at a time, until the cookies are browned on the bottoms, the almond paste is puffed up and browned on the tops, and the sides are golden yellow, about 10 to 13 minutes.

12. Slide the cookies onto a wire rack using a metal spatula and let cool to room temperature.

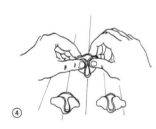

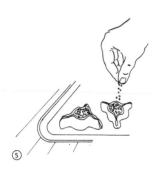

➤ **HOWS & WHYS:** The pinch of sugar on top of the almond paste makes the top brown better. The cookies must not be overbaked or the insides will be too dry and hard. If you like, you can bake the cookies at a higher temperature for a shorter time to keep the insides very soft—but be very careful not to burn the bottoms of the cookies.

STORAGE: Covered airtight in a tin cookie box or cookie jar for up to 2 or 3 days.

Before being rolled out, the dough can be kept in the refrigerator, wrapped in wax paper, for up to 2 or 3 days. Trimmings can be frozen, wrapped in wax paper and then in freezer wrap, for up to 1 month.

NANTES-STYLE GALETTES
GALETTES NANTAISES

~~~~~

These classic cookies, flavored with powdered almonds and vanilla, are dry, fragile, and tender. They are cut in large fluted rounds, brushed with egg wash, and scored with a fork to make a crisscross design on top. If you prefer to make small cookies, you can call them petits nantais.

Nantes is a seaport near the mouth of the Loire River in Brittany. The city dates from ancient Roman times, and it was here that, in 1598, Henry IV signed the Edict of Nantes granting religious freedom to his Protestant subjects, the Huguenots.

EQUIPMENT

2 or 3 large, heavy baking sheets
• Brush lightly with melted butter.
A fluted round cookie cutter, either 4 inches (10 cm) in diameter for large cookies or 2 inches (5 cm) in diameter for small cookies

PASTRY DOUGH

5½ ounces (150 g), or ½ cup plus 3 tablespoons, unsalted butter, softened
3½ ounces (100 g), or ¾ cup, almond and sugar powder
⎰ *Basic Preparation, page 482:*
⎱ *1¾ ounces (50 g), or ⅓ cup, blanched almonds*
⎱ *1¾ ounces (50 g), or ⅓ cup plus 4 teaspoons, confectioners' sugar*

2 tablespoons lightly beaten egg
1 teaspoon (½ cl) vanilla extract
6 ounces (170 g), or 1 cup plus 3½ tablespoons, all-purpose flour

COUNTERTOP DUSTING

Flour

GLAZE

1 egg, lightly beaten

For about 12 to 14 large or 55 to 60 small cookies

1. On your countertop, cream the butter with the almond and sugar powder by repeatedly smearing it across the countertop with the heel of your hand and gathering it back together with a dough scraper. When smooth, mix in the egg and the vanilla with your fingertips. Work quickly so that you don't melt the butter. Sift the flour over the butter mixture. Mix in the flour, either by cutting it in with a dough scraper or by stirring and tossing with your fingertips, until you obtain a loose, crumbly dough. Gather the dough together and finish mixing by smearing it across the countertop, a little at a time, with the heel of your hand. Gather the dough together again. If it is not yet smooth, then repeat this smearing procedure.

2. Form the dough into a square pad about 1½ inches (4 cm) thick. Lightly dust the pad with flour, wrap it in wax paper, and refrigerate for at least 2 hours and preferably overnight.

3. Dust your countertop and the pad of dough with flour, and roll out the dough with a rolling pin into a sheet about ⅛ inch (3 mm) thick. Dust

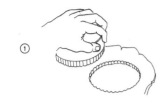

the counter and dough with flour as needed to prevent the dough from sticking to the counter or rolling pin. Slide the dough onto a tray and chill it briefly in the freezer whenever it starts to warm and soften.

4. Using the cookie cutter, cut out 4-inch (10 cm) rounds for large cookies ① or 2-inch (5 cm) rounds for small cookies. Carefully lift the rounds with a metal spatula and transfer them ② to the baking sheets. Separate the rounds by at least ¾ inch (2 cm) and gently press each round to make it stick to the baking sheet. Let rest in the refrigerator.

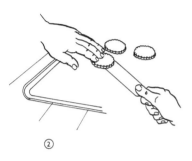

5. Gather together the remaining dough and form it into a pad. If it is too soft to work with, chill it in the freezer for 20 to 30 minutes. Then roll it out into a sheet about ⅛ inch (3 mm) thick. Cut out more rounds, arrange them on the baking sheets, and refrigerate. Repeat with the remaining scraps.

6. Lightly brush the tops of the rounds ③ with beaten egg. Let rest in the refrigerator until the egg wash dries, 20 to 30 minutes.

Preheat the oven to 350° F (175° C).

7. Brush each round a second time with egg wash. For small cookies, draw the tines of a fork across the top of each cookie to make a set of parallel lines through the egg wash; then draw a second set of lines on the diagonal ④ with respect to the first set, making a crisscross pattern. For large cookies, draw 2 parallel sets of lines, with a space between them across the top of each cookie with the tines of the fork; then draw 2 more sets of parallel lines ⑤ (also with a space between) on the diagonal with respect to the first 2 sets. The sets of line should crisscross 4 times, and there should be a diamond on the center of the cookie with no lines through it.

8. Bake, 1 sheet at a time, until the cookies are lightly browned on the bottoms and edges and the egg wash has set to a satiny sheet, about 11 to 14 minutes for small cookies or 13 to 16 minutes for large cookies.

9. Slide the cookies onto a wire rack using a metal spatula and let cool to room temperature.

STORAGE: Covered airtight in a tin cookie box or cookie jar for up to 1 week.

Before being rolled out, the dough can be kept in the refrigerator, wrapped in wax paper, for up to 2 or 3 days.

HALF-MOONS
SABLÉS DEMI-LUNES

*T*his almond-rich cookie, shaped like a half-moon, is light and almost flaky. If Galileo could believe that the moon's great dark plains were ''seas,'' perhaps it isn't too whimsical to suggest that the decorative scoring and sliced almonds on top of the cookie represent the lunar landscape.

EQUIPMENT

2 large, heavy baking sheets
• Brush lightly with melted butter.
A plain round cookie cutter 2½ inches (6 cm) in diameter

PASTRY DOUGH

3½ ounces (100 g), or 7 tablespoons, unsalted butter, softened
7 ounces (200 g), or 1½ cups, almond and sugar powder

} *Basic Preparation, page 482:*
3½ ounces (100 g), or ⅔ cup, blanched almonds
3½ ounces (100 g), or ¾ cup plus 4 teaspoons, confectioners' sugar

For about 45 to 50 cookies

1 tablespoon (1½ cl) crème fraîche (page 491)
1 teaspoon (½ cl) vanilla extract
4 ounces (115 g), or ¾ cup plus 1 tablespoon, all-purpose flour
¼ teaspoon (1 ml) ammonium carbonate

COUNTERTOP DUSTING

Flour

GLAZE

1 egg, lightly beaten

DECORATION

Sliced almonds

1. On your countertop, cream the butter with the almond and sugar powder by repeatedly smearing it across the countertop with the heel of your hand and gathering it back together with a dough scraper. When smooth, mix in the crème fraîche and the vanilla with your fingertips. Work quickly so that you don't melt the butter. Sift the flour and ammonium carbonate over the butter mixture. Mix in the flour, either by cutting it in with a dough scraper or by stirring and tossing with your fingertips, until you obtain a loose, crumbly dough. Gather the dough together and finish mixing by smearing it across the countertop, a little at a time, with the heel of your hand. Gather the dough together again. If it is not yet smooth, then repeat this smearing procedure.

2. Form the dough into a square pad about 1½ inches (4 cm) thick. Lightly dust the pad with flour, wrap it in wax paper, and refrigerate for at least 2 hours and preferably overnight.

3. Dust your countertop and the pad of dough with flour, and roll out the dough with a rolling pin into a sheet about ³⁄₁₆ inch (5 mm) thick. Dust the counter and dough with flour as needed to prevent the dough from sticking to the counter or rolling pin. Slide the dough onto a tray and chill it briefly in the freezer whenever it starts to warm and soften.

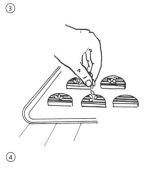

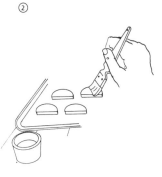

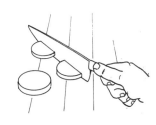

4. Cut out 2½-inch (6 cm) rounds ① with the cookie cutter. Cut each round in half ② with your chef's knife. Carefully lift the half-moons with a metal spatula and transfer them to the baking sheets. Separate the half-moons by at least ¾ inch (2 cm), and gently press each half-moon to make it stick to the baking sheet. Let rest in the refrigerator.

5. Gather together the remaining dough and form it into a pad. If it is too soft to work with, chill it in the freezer for 20 to 30 minutes. Then roll it out into a sheet about ³⁄₁₆ inch (5 mm) thick. Cut out more half-moons, arrange them on the baking sheets, and refrigerate. Repeat with the remaining scraps.

6. Lightly brush the tops of the half-moons ③ with beaten egg. Let rest in the refrigerator until the egg wash dries, 20 to 30 minutes.

Preheat the oven to 375° F (190° C).

7. Brush each half-moon a second time with egg wash. Draw the tines of a fork across the top of each cookie, parallel to the straight edge. Scatter a few almond slices ④ on top.

8. Bake, 1 sheet at a time, until the cookies are browned on the bottoms and the egg wash on the tops is golden, about 11 to 13 minutes.

9. Slide the cookies onto a wire rack using a metal spatula and let cool to room temperature.

➤ **HOWS & WHYS:** The ammonium carbonate, a cousin of baking powder, helps makes these cookies light. Unlike ordinary baking powder it does not start to break down and produce carbon dioxide until it is heated, so none of its leavening power is lost while the dough is resting.

STORAGE: Covered airtight in a tin cookie box or cookie jar for up to 1 week.

Before being rolled out, the dough can be kept in the refrigerator, wrapped in wax paper, for up to 2 or 3 days.

ENGLISH GALETTES
GALETTES ANGLAISES

~~~~~~~

Flavored with orange zest, studded with raisins, and coated with apricot jam and a sugar and orange liqueur glaze, this almond-rich cookie is a more luxurious version of Milanese Sablés (page 292).

EQUIPMENT

2 large, heavy baking sheets

A plain round cookie cutter 2 inches (5 cm) in diameter

PASTRY DOUGH

3½ ounces (100 g), or 7 tablespoons, unsalted butter, softened

7 ounces (200 g), or 1½ cups, almond and sugar powder

  Basic Preparation, page 482:
  3½ ounces (100 g), or ⅔ cup, blanched almonds
  3½ ounces (100 g), or about ¾ cup plus
      4 teaspoons, confectioners' sugar

2 large egg yolks

Finely grated zest of 1 orange

3½ ounces (100 g), or ½ cup plus 2 tablespoons, seedless raisins

4½ ounces (125 g), or ¾ cup plus 2 tablespoons, all-purpose flour

COUNTERTOP DUSTING

Flour

GLAZES

1 egg, lightly beaten

2½ tablespoons (50 g) strained apricot jam
      [*Basic Preparation*, page 484]

1¾ ounces (50 g), or ⅓ cup plus 4 teaspoons, confectioners' sugar

2 teaspoons (1 cl) curaçao liqueur

For about 40 cookies

1. On your countertop, cream the butter with the almond and sugar powder by repeatedly smearing it across the countertop with the heel of your hand and gathering it back together with a dough scraper. When smooth, mix in the egg yolks, 1 at a time, with your fingertips. Then mix in the orange zest and raisins. Work quickly so that you don't melt the butter. Sift the flour over the butter mixture. Mix in the flour, either by cutting it in with a dough scraper or by stirring and tossing with your fingertips, until you obtain a loose, crumbly dough. Gather the dough together and finish mixing by smearing it across the countertop, a little at a time, with the heel of your hand. Gather the dough together again. If it is not yet smooth, then repeat this smearing procedure.

2. Form the dough into a square pad about 1½ inches (4 cm) thick. Lightly dust the pad with flour, wrap it in wax paper, and refrigerate for at least 2 hours and preferably overnight.

3. Dust your countertop and the pad of dough with flour, and roll out the dough with a rolling pin into a sheet about ³⁄₁₆ inch (5 mm) thick. Dust the counter and dough with flour as needed to prevent the dough from sticking to the counter or rolling pin. Slide the dough onto a tray and chill it briefly in the freezer whenever it starts to warm and soften.

4. Moisten the baking sheets with cold water using a pastry brush.

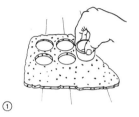

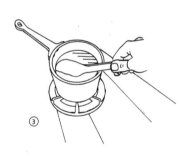

5. Cut out 2-inch (5 cm) rounds ① using the cookie cutter. Carefully lift the rounds with a metal spatula and transfer them to the baking sheets. Separate the rounds by at least ¾ inch (2 cm), and gently press each round to make it stick to the baking sheet. Let rest in the refrigerator.

6. Gather together the remaining dough and form it into a pad. If it is too soft to work with, chill it in the freezer for 20 to 30 minutes. Then roll it out into a sheet about ³⁄₁₆ inch (5 mm) thick. Cut out more rounds, arrange them on the baking sheets, and refrigerate. Repeat with the remaining scraps.

7. Brush the tops of the rounds ② with beaten egg. Let rest in the refrigerator until the egg wash dries, 20 to 30 minutes.

Preheat the oven to 375° F (190° C).

8. Brush each round a second time with egg wash.

9. Bake, 1 sheet at a time, until the cookies are browned on the bottoms and begin to brown around the edges, about 10 to 13 minutes.

10. Meanwhile, warm the apricot jam ③ over low heat, stirring occasionally until melted. Sift the confectioners' sugar into a small bowl and stir in the curaçao. Then stir in enough cold water to make a smooth, creamy paste that is just fluid enough to spread easily with a pastry brush.

11. When the cookies are finished baking, brush each with jam ④ until lightly coated and glistening. Then lightly brush the confectioners' sugar and curaçao mixture over the jam on top of each cookie. The glaze will turn from opaque white to translucent.

12. Slide the cookies onto a wire rack using a metal spatula and let cool to room temperature.

➤ **HOWS & WHYS:** Since the cookies are glazed while they are hot out of the oven, they do not have to be returned to the oven to make the glaze set and turn translucent.

STORAGE: Covered airtight in a tin cookie box or cookie jar for up to 1 week.

Before being rolled out, the dough can be kept in the refrigerator, wrapped in wax paper, for up to 2 or 3 days.

ENGLISH LOAVES
PAINS ANGLAIS

‾‾‾‾‾‾‾

These cookies, shaped like little loaves of bread, are very popular in France. Many pastry shops make them, but everyone uses a different recipe. The authors of one classic reference (Le Nouveau mémorial de la pâtisserie et des glaces) claimed to know fifteen recipes for English Loaves. Our recipe is rich in powdered almonds and has a fine texture. It is based on one developed by Louis Clichy about eighty years ago. Clichy was the founder of Pâtisserie Clichy, which Paul Bugat has owned for many years, and he was famous for his petits fours. Paul still uses Clichy's recipe for English Loaves.

EQUIPMENT

1 or 2 large, heavy baking sheets

A plain round cookie cutter 1¼ inches (3 cm) in diameter

PASTRY DOUGH

2½ ounces (70 g), or 5 tablespoons, unsalted butter, softened

4½ ounces (130 g), or ¾ cup plus 3½ tablespoons, almond and sugar powder

{ *Basic Preparation, page 482:*

2¼ ounces (65 g), or ¼ cup plus 3 tablespoons, blanched almonds

2¼ ounces (65 g), or ½ cup plus 2 teaspoons, confectioners' sugar

For about 40 cookies

¾ ounce (20 g), or 2 tablespoons plus 2 teaspoons, confectioners' sugar

2 large egg yolks

¾ teaspoon (4 ml) vanilla extract

3½ ounces (100 g), or ⅔ cup plus 1 tablespoon, all-purpose flour

COUNTERTOP DUSTING

Flour

GLAZE

1 egg, lightly beaten

½ teaspoon (¼ cl) freeze-dried coffee, dissolved in ½ teaspoon (¼ cl) boiling water

1. Place the butter on your countertop with the almond and sugar powder and sift the confectioners' sugar over it. Cream the butter with the almond and sugar powder and confectioners' sugar by repeatedly smearing it across the countertop with the heel of your hand and gathering it back together with a dough scraper. When smooth, mix in the egg yolks, 1 at a time, with your fingertips, then mix in the vanilla. Work quickly so that you don't melt the butter. Sift the flour over the butter mixture. Mix in the flour, either by cutting it in with a dough scraper or by stirring and tossing with your fingertips, until you obtain a loose, crumbly dough. Gather the dough together and finish mixing by smearing it across the countertop, a little at a time, with the heel of your hand. Gather the dough together again. If it is not yet smooth, then repeat this smearing procedure.

2. Form the dough into a square pad about 1 inch (2½ cm) thick. Lightly dust the pad with flour, wrap it in wax paper, and refrigerate for at least 2 hours and preferably overnight.

3. Dust your countertop and the pad of dough with flour, and roll out the dough with a rolling pin ① into a sheet about ⅜ inch (1 cm) thick. Dust

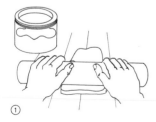
①

②

③

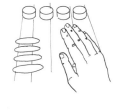

④

⑤

the counter and dough with flour as needed to prevent the dough from sticking to the counter or rolling pin. Cut out rounds 1¼ inches (3 cm) in diameter using the cookie cutter ②. Gather the trimmings into a pad, roll it out ⅜ inch (1 cm) thick, and cut out more rounds. Repeat to use up nearly all of the dough.

4. Roll each round back and forth under your palm to form it into a cigar ③ shape about 1½ inches (4 cm) long.

5. Moisten the baking sheets with cold water using a pastry brush. Arrange the cigars on the baking sheets, separating them by at least 1 inch (2½ cm). Press each gently to make it stick to the baking sheet.

6. Tint the beaten egg with the coffee, and brush the top and sides of each cigar ④ with this egg wash. Refrigerate until the egg wash has dried and the cigars are well chilled, 20 to 30 minutes.

Preheat the oven to 375° F (190° C).

7. Brush each cigar a second time with egg wash. Make 3 or 4 V-shaped depressions ⑤ lengthwise down the center of each cigar by pressing with the tip of a small, flexible paring knife held with the face of the blade against the top of the cigar. Dip the blade in cold water as needed to prevent sticking. (Or, you can make a groove lengthwise down the center of each cigar using the tip of the paring knife, with the face of the blade against the surface.)

8. Bake, 1 sheet at a time, until the cookies are puffed up and barely begin to brown on the bottoms, about 4 to 5 minutes. Then place an empty baking sheet underneath the sheet of cookies to protect the bottoms from burning, and continue baking until the cookies are richly browned on the bottoms, golden brown on the tops, and spring back when pressed gently with your fingertip, about 6 to 9 minutes longer.

9. Slide the cookies onto a wire rack using a metal spatula and let cool to room temperature.

➤ **HOWS & WHYS:** The dough is rolled out with a rolling pin in this recipe purely as a device for dividing it into pieces quickly and easily without working it too much. Since it is rolled out very thick, it shouldn't warm up much in the rolling process and you shouldn't find it necessary to chill the trimmings before rolling them out again.

Adding coffee to the egg wash gives the cookies a richer color, like the top of a loaf of bread. Professionals often use caramel food coloring

(continued)

to tint the egg wash, but at home instant coffee is easier. The amount of coffee used is minuscule and does not affect the taste of the cookies.

STORAGE: Covered airtight in a tin cookie box or cookie jar for up to 1 week.

Before being rolled out, the dough can be kept in the refrigerator, wrapped in wax paper, for up to 2 or 3 days.

HAZELNUT CROQUETTES
CROQUETTES AUX AVELINES

We most often think of croquettes in the context of oval balls of chopped meat or fish, mashed potatoes, or rice that have been dipped in egg and bread crumbs and then deep-fried. In pastry, croquettes is used for various cookies that have nothing in particular in common except that they are all crisp or crunchy. The word derives from the verb croquer, which means literally "to crunch" or "to munch," and more loosely "to gobble up."

Avelines is French for "filberts," which is really just another word for hazelnuts. Our croquettes aux avelines are a variation on Diamonds (page 302) made from a dough containing powdered hazelnuts. In addition to crystal sugar around the sides, the cookies are decorated with half of a blanched hazelnut on top. They are definitely crisp, crunchy, and very enjoyable to crunch, munch, and gobble up.

EQUIPMENT

1 or 2 large, heavy baking sheets
• Brush lightly with melted butter.

DECORATION

20 hazelnuts
1 egg, lightly beaten
1¾ ounces (50 g), or ¼ cup, crystal sugar

PASTRY DOUGH

3 ounces (85 g), or 6 tablespoons, unsalted butter, softened
4 ounces (120 g), or ¾ cup plus 2½ tablespoons, hazelnut and sugar powder
{ Basic Preparation, page 482:
2 ounces (60 g), or ¼ cup plus 3 tablespoons, hazelnuts
2 ounces (60 g), or ½ cup, confectioners' sugar

2 teaspoons (1 cl) heavy cream
¾ teaspoon (4 ml) vanilla extract
4 ounces (115 g), or ¾ cup plus 1 tablespoon, all-purpose flour

COUNTERTOP DUSTING

Flour

For about 40 cookies

Preheat the oven to 450° F (230° C).

1. Spread out the hazelnuts for decoration on a baking sheet and toast them in the hot oven, stirring once or twice to prevent the nuts nearest the edges of the sheet from burning, until their skins are dry and cracked and have darkened but not burned, about 4 to 6 minutes. (The hazelnuts should remain pale inside.) Transfer the hazelnuts to a large sieve, and rub the hot nuts against the mesh, using a towel to protect your hand, to remove most of their skins. Let the nuts cool. (You can toast these hazelnuts at the same time as the ones for the hazelnut and sugar powder if you wish.)

2. Cut the hazelnuts into halves and set them aside.

3. On your countertop, cream the butter with the hazelnut and sugar powder by repeatedly smearing it across the countertop with the heel of your hand and gathering it back together with a dough scraper. When smooth, mix in the cream and the vanilla with your fingertips. Work quickly so that you don't melt the butter. Sift the flour over the butter mixture. Mix in the flour, either by cutting it in with a dough scraper or by stirring and tossing with your fingertips, until you obtain a loose, crumbly dough. Gather the dough together and finish mixing by smearing it across the countertop, a little at a time, with the heel of your hand. Gather the dough together again. If it is not yet smooth, then repeat this smearing procedure.

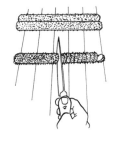

4. Gather the dough into a ball and roll it back and forth on the countertop under your palms to form it into a cylinder and elongate it to about 10 inches (25 cm). Cut it in half crosswise (to make it more manageable) and roll each half back and forth under your palms to elongate it into a uniform cylinder about 8 inches (20 cm) long and 1⅛ inches (3 cm) in diameter. If necessary, dust the cylinders very lightly with flour to prevent them from sticking to the countertop.

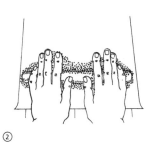

5. Brush each cylinder of dough ① with beaten egg. Place the crystal sugar on a sheet of wax paper and distribute it down the center. Roll each cylinder in the sugar ② to coat it evenly. Wrap each cylinder in wax paper and refrigerate them for at least 2 hours and preferably overnight.

Preheat the oven to 375° F (190° C).

6. Cut each cylinder ③ into slices ⅜ inch (1 cm) thick with your chef's knife. Carefully lift the slices with a metal spatula and transfer them to the baking sheets. Separate the slices by at least 1 inch (2½ cm). Place

(continued)

SWEET PASTRY DOUGHS

④

half of a blanched hazelnut on the center ④ of each slice and press it down into the dough slightly. Don't press too hard or the sides of the round will crack.

7. Bake, 1 sheet at a time, until the bottoms of the cookies have browned and the edges have begun to brown but the centers are still pale, about 14 to 16 minutes.

8. Slide the cookies onto a wire rack using a metal spatula and let cool to room temperature.

➤ **HOWS & WHYS:** Because the batter contains so little liquid, it becomes very hard when cold. The cylinders must therefore be formed before chilling. The egg wash and crystal sugar can be applied before or after chilling. The sugar sticks better before chilling, but if the dough is too warm and soft to handle easily it is better to chill them first and then coat them with egg wash and sugar.

STORAGE: Covered airtight in a tin cookie box or cookie jar for up to 1 week.

Before being coated with egg wash and crystal sugar, the cylinders of dough can be kept in the refrigerator, wrapped in wax paper, for up to 2 or 3 days.

TOMMIES
TOMMIES

~~~~~~~~

Yet another sandwiched cookie, this one is flavored with powdered hazelnuts and filled with apricot jam. The odd name reminds us of the nursery rhyme:

Pat a cake, pat a cake
Baker's man.
Make me a cake,
As fast as you can.

Pat it and prick it,
And mark it with a T,
And put it in the oven
For Tommy and me.

EQUIPMENT

2 or 3 large, heavy baking sheets
A fluted round cookie cutter 2 inches (5 cm) in diameter

PASTRY DOUGH

2¼ ounces (65 g), or ⅓ cup plus 2 tablespoons, hazelnuts
1¾ ounces (50 g), or ⅓ cup plus 4 teaspoons, confectioners' sugar
3½ ounces (100 g), or 7 tablespoons, unsalted butter, softened

1 tablespoon (1½ cl) milk
4½ ounces (125 g), or ¾ cup plus 2 tablespoons, all-purpose flour

COUNTERTOP DUSTING

Flour

FILLING

4 tablespoons (80 g) strained apricot jam
    [Basic Preparation, page 484]

DECORATION

Confectioners' sugar

For about 20 to 25 cookies

Preheat the oven to 450° F (230° C).

1. Spread out the hazelnuts on a baking sheet and toast them in the hot oven, stirring once or twice to prevent the nuts nearest the edges of the sheet from burning, until their skins are dry and cracked and have darkened but not burned, 4 to 6 minutes. (The hazelnuts should remain pale inside.) Transfer the hazelnuts to a large sieve, and rub the hot nuts against the mesh, using a towel to protect your hand, to remove most of their skins. Let the nuts cool.

2. Grind the hazelnuts with 1 ounce (30 g), or ¼ cup, of the confectioners' sugar in your food processor, stopping to break up any caking as needed, until finely ground but not at all oily. Sift through a medium sieve. Grind the hazelnuts that don't pass through the sieve with the remaining confectioners' sugar until reduced to a fine powder. Transfer all of the hazelnut and sugar powder to a bowl, break up any caking with your fingertips, and mix thoroughly.

(continued)

3. On your countertop, cream the butter with the hazelnut and sugar powder by repeatedly smearing it across the countertop with the heel of your hand and gathering it back together with a dough scraper. When smooth, mix in the milk with your fingertips. Work quickly so that you don't melt the butter. Sift the remaining flour over the butter mixture. Mix in the flour, either by cutting it in with a dough scraper or by stirring and tossing with your fingertips, until you obtain a loose, crumbly dough. Gather the dough together and finish mixing by smearing it across the countertop, a little at a time, with the heel of your hand. Gather the dough together again. If it is not yet smooth, then repeat this smearing procedure.

4. Form the dough into a square pad about 1 inch (2½ cm) thick. Lightly dust the pad with flour, wrap it in wax paper, and refrigerate for at least 2 hours and preferably overnight.

①

5. Dust your countertop and the pad of dough with flour, and roll out the dough with a rolling pin ① into a sheet about ⅛ inch (3 mm) thick. Dust the counter and dough with flour as needed to prevent the dough from sticking to counter or rolling pin. Slide the dough onto a tray and chill it briefly in the freezer whenever it starts to warm and soften.

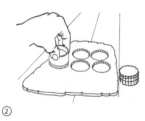
②

6. Cut out 2-inch (5 cm) rounds ② with the cookie cutter. Carefully lift the rounds with a metal spatula and transfer them ③ to the baking sheets. Separate the rounds by at least ¾ inch (2 cm), and gently press each round to make it stick to the baking sheet. Let rest in the refrigerator.

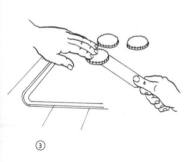
③

7. Gather together the remaining dough and form it into a pad. If it is too soft to work with, chill it in the freezer for 20 to 30 minutes. Then roll it out into a sheet about ⅛ inch (3 mm) thick. Cut out more rounds with your cookie cutter, arrange them on the baking sheets, and refrigerate. Repeat with the remaining scraps.

Preheat the oven to 400° F (200° C).

8. Bake, 1 sheet at a time, until the cookies are browned on the bottoms and begin to brown around the edges, about 7 to 9 minutes.

9. Slide the cookies onto a wire rack using a metal spatula and let cool to room temperature.

④

10. Spoon ½ teaspoon (¼ cl) of apricot jam on top of half the rounds. Dust the tops of the other half of the rounds with confectioners' sugar ④ until they are white, then place one on each of the jam-coated rounds.

➤ **HOWS & WHYS:** Since the amount of sugar in this recipe is less than the amount of hazelnuts, when grinding the nuts you must be especially careful not to let the powder become oily. This also precludes using the more common hazelnut and sugar powder made with equal weights of hazelnuts and sugar.

STORAGE: It is best to fill these cookies and dust the tops with confectioners' sugar shortly before serving. Before filling and dusting, keep them covered airtight in a tin cookie box or cookie jar for up to 1 week.

Before being rolled out, the dough can be kept in the refrigerator, wrapped in wax paper, for up to 2 or 3 days.

SMALL SANDWICH SABLÉS
PETITS SABLÉS

~~~~~~~

These small oval sablés, *flavored with powdered almonds and rum, are sandwiched with apricot jam. The understated name doesn't even hint at how good they are. Jams can have a very sensual quality, as the Roman poet Horace noted when he wrote in one of his epodes, ''Jam! Jam! I yield me to thy potent charm.'' Small Sandwich Sablés are a good example of how, even with a small addition of jam, that charm can transform a very simple cookie into something special.*

EQUIPMENT

2 large, heavy baking sheets
• Brush lightly with melted butter.
A fluted or plain oval cookie cutter (see Note)
2⅛ inches (5½ cm) long and 1⅜ inches (3½ cm) wide

_____

PASTRY DOUGH

3½ ounces (100 g), or 7 tablespoons, unsalted butter, softened
3½ ounces (100 g), or ¾ cup, almond and sugar powder
  Basic Preparation, page 482:
  1¾ ounces (50 g), or ⅓ cup, blanched almonds
  1¾ ounces (50 g), or ⅓ cup plus 4 teaspoons, confectioners' sugar

For 20 to 25 cookies

1 tablespoon (1½ cl) dark Jamaican rum
3½ ounces (100 g), or ⅔ cup plus 1 tablespoon, all-purpose flour

COUNTERTOP DUSTING

Flour

FILLING

2 tablespoons (40 g) strained apricot jam
  [*Basic Preparation*, page 484]

DECORATION

Confectioners' sugar

1. On your countertop, cream the butter with the almond and sugar powder by repeatedly smearing it across the countertop with the heel of your hand and gathering it back together with a dough scraper. When smooth, mix in the rum with your fingertips. Work quickly so that you don't melt the butter. Sift the flour over the butter mixture. Mix in the flour, either by cutting it in with a dough scraper or by stirring and tossing with your fingertips, until you obtain a loose, crumbly dough. Gather the dough together and finish mixing by smearing it across the countertop, a little at a time, with the heel of your hand. Gather the dough together again. If it is not yet smooth, then repeat this smearing procedure.

2. Form the dough into a square pad about 1 inch (2½ cm) thick. Lightly dust the pad with flour, wrap it in wax paper, and refrigerate for at least 2 hours and preferably overnight.

3. Dust your countertop and the pad of dough with flour, and roll out the dough with a rolling pin into a sheet about ⅛ inch (3 mm) thick. Dust

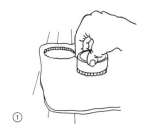

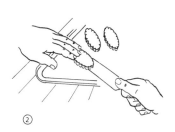

the counter and dough with flour as needed to prevent the dough from sticking to the counter or rolling pin. Slide the dough onto a tray and chill it briefly in the freezer whenever it starts to warm and soften.

4. Cut out ovals ① using the cookie cutter. Carefully lift the ovals with a metal spatula and transfer them ② to the baking sheets. Separate the ovals by at least ¾ inch (2 cm), and gently press each oval to make it stick to the baking sheet. Let rest in the refrigerator.

5. Gather together the remaining dough and form it into a pad. If it is too soft to work with, chill it in the freezer for 20 to 30 minutes. Then roll it out into a sheet about ⅛ inch (3 mm) thick. Cut out more ovals, arrange them on the baking sheets, and refrigerate. Repeat with the remaining scraps, or save them for use in Vietnamese Hats (page 24).

Preheat the oven to 325° F (160° C).

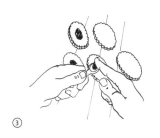

6. Bake, 1 sheet at a time, until the cookies are lightly browned on tops and bottoms, about 16 to 20 minutes.

7. Slide the cookies onto a wire rack using a metal spatula and let cool to room temperature.

8. Spoon ¼ teaspoon (1 ml) of apricot jam on top ③ of half of the pastry ovals. Dust the tops of the remaining ovals with confectioners' sugar ④ until they are white, then place one on each of the jam-coated ovals.

NOTE: You can make the oval cookier cutter from a round cutter 1¾ inches (4½ cm) in diameter by carefully bending it into shape.

STORAGE: It is best to fill these cookies and dust the tops with confectioners' sugar shortly before serving. Before filling and dusting, keep them covered airtight in a tin cookie box or cookie jar for up to 1 week.

Before being rolled out, the dough can be kept in the refrigerator, wrapped in wax paper, for up to 2 or 3 days. Trimmings can be frozen, wrapped in wax paper and then in freezer wrap, for up to 1 month.

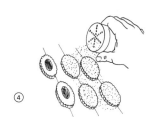

SIAMESE TWINS
SIAMOIS

Here is another small oval sablés cookie, this one flavored with powdered almonds and sandwiched with raspberry jam. The pastry dough is very similar to that for Nantes-Style Galettes (page 322), but contains egg white instead of whole eggs.

Except for an abortive attempt to establish diplomatic relations during the reign of Louis XIV, France had essentially no direct contact with Siam (now Thailand) until the twentieth century. The name of this cookie almost certainly derives from les Frères Siamois, Chang and Eng, the congenitally joined twins who were born in Siam in 1811 and lived to the ripe old age of sixty-three. Chang and Eng were minor celebrities during their lifetime, and it would have been very natural for a nineteenth-century pastry chef to name this sandwich cookie after them.

EQUIPMENT
2 or 3 large, heavy baking sheets
A fluted or plain oval cookie cutter (see Note)
2⅛ inches (5½ cm) long and 1⅜ inches (3½ cm) wide

PASTRY DOUGH
5¼ ounces (150 g), or ½ cup plus 3 tablespoons, unsalted butter, softened
4 ounces (120 g), or ¾ cup plus 2½ tablespoons, almond and sugar powder
  Basic Preparation, page 482:
  2 ounces (60 g), or ⅓ cup plus 1 tablespoon, blanched almonds
  2 ounces (60 g), or ½ cup, confectioners' sugar

For about 30 cookies

1 tablespoon (1½ cl) lightly beaten egg white
6 ounces (170 g), or 1 cup plus 3½ tablespoons, all-purpose flour

COUNTERTOP DUSTING
Flour

FILLING
2½ tablespoons (50 g) raspberry jam

DECORATION
Confectioners' sugar

1. On your countertop, cream the butter with the almond and sugar powder by repeatedly smearing it across the countertop with the heel of your hand and gathering it back together with a dough scraper. When smooth, mix in the egg white with your fingertips. Work quickly so that you don't melt the butter. Sift the flour over the butter mixture. Mix in the flour, either by cutting it in with a dough scraper or by stirring and tossing with your fingertips, until you obtain a loose, crumbly dough. Gather the dough together and finish mixing by smearing it across the countertop, a little at a time, with the heel of your hand. Gather the dough together again. If it is not yet smooth, then repeat this smearing procedure.

2. Form the dough into a square pad about 1 inch (2½ cm) thick. Lightly dust the pad with flour, wrap it in wax paper, and refrigerate for at least 2 hours and preferably overnight.

①

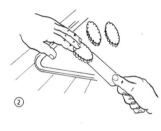

②

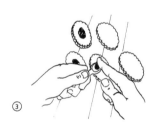

③

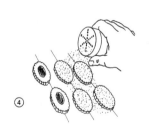

④

3. Dust your countertop and the pad of dough with flour, and roll out the dough with a rolling pin into a sheet about ⅛ inch (3 mm) thick. Dust the counter and dough with flour as needed to prevent the dough from sticking to the counter or rolling pin. Slide the dough onto a tray and chill it briefly in the freezer whenever it starts to warm and soften.

4. Cut out ovals ① using the cookie cutter. Carefully lift the ovals with a metal spatula and transfer them ② to the baking sheets. Separate the ovals by at least ¾ inch (2 cm), and gently press each oval to make it stick to the baking sheet. Let rest in the refrigerator.

5. Gather together the remaining dough and form it into a pad. If it is too soft to work with, chill it in the freezer for 20 to 30 minutes. Then roll it out into a sheet about ⅛ inch (3 mm) thick. Cut out more ovals, arrange them on the baking sheets, and refrigerate. Repeat with the remaining scraps, or save them for use in Vietnamese Hats (page 24).

Preheat the oven to 375° F (190° C).

6. Bake, 1 sheet at a time, until the cookies are lightly browned on the bottoms and edges, about 10 to 13 minutes.

7. Slide the cookies onto a wire rack using a metal spatula and let cool to room temperature.

8. If the raspberry jam is at all runny, simmer it gently to reduce the excess liquid and then cool before using. Spoon ¼ teaspoon (1 ml) of raspberry jam on top ③ of half of the pastry ovals. Dust the tops of the remaining ovals with confectioners' sugar ④ until they are white, then place one on each of the jam-coated ovals.

NOTE: You can make the oval cookie cutter from a round cutter 1¾ inches (4½ cm) in diameter by carefully bending it into shape.

STORAGE: It is best to fill these cookies and dust the tops with confectioners' sugar shortly before serving. Before filling and dusting, keep them covered airtight in a tin cookie box or cookie jar for up to 1 week.

Before being rolled out, the dough can be kept in the refrigerator, wrapped in wax paper, for up to 2 or 3 days. Trimmings can be frozen, wrapped in wax paper and then in freezer wrap, for up to 1 month.

LITTLE NEAPOLITAN CAKES
PETITS GÂTEAUX NAPOLITAINES

Gâteau napolitain *is a classic cake, famous many years ago, that was used as a display piece in elaborate buffets or at the ends of a table set for a large dinner party. It is made by layering several large rings of a baked sweet pastry dough with jam and adding a larger round of pastry on top and bottom. Then the outside is coated with apricot jam and decorated with piped royal icing or glacé fruits. The inside may be filled with pastry cream. The pastry dough used for this curiosity is called* pâte frolle *or* pâte à frol, *a name that obviously derives from that of the Italian sweet pastry dough,* pasta frolla. *The names of both the cake and the dough suggest an Italian origin, but probably* gâteau napolitain *was invented by the great nineteenth-century French chef Carême, who liked to give such names to his creations. And while* pasta frolla *is just a basic sweet pastry dough containing butter, sugar, eggs, flour, and flavorings, the French version includes a substantial amount of powdered almonds.*

Although gâteau napolitain *is now a historical curiosity, a cookie version of it is still made today. For Little Neapolitan Cakes, you cut out fluted rounds of* pâte frolle *and cut large holes in the centers of half of them to make rings. After baking, the rings are dusted with confectioners' sugar and sandwiched on top of the plain rounds with apricot jam. The jam shows through in the center in the same way as in Spectacles (page 310).*

EQUIPMENT
2 or 3 large, heavy baking sheets
A fluted round cookie cutter 3 inches (8 cm) in diameter
A plain round cookie cutter 1½ inches (4 cm) in diameter

PASTRY DOUGH
3½ ounces (100 g), or 7 tablespoons, unsalted butter, softened
7 ounces (200 g), or 1½ cups, almond and sugar powder
  Basic Preparation, page 482:
  3½ ounces (100 g), or ⅔ cup, blanched almonds
  3½ ounces (100 g), or ¾ cup plus 4 teaspoons, confectioners' sugar

For about 12 to 14 cookies

1 large egg, lightly beaten
Finely grated zest of 1 lemon
6 ounces (170 g), or 1 cup plus 3½ tablespoons, all-purpose flour

COUNTERTOP DUSTING
Flour

FILLING
¼ cup plus 3 tablespoons (140 g) strained apricot jam
  [*Basic Preparation*, page 484]

DECORATION
Confectioners' sugar

1. On your countertop, cream the butter with the almond and sugar powder by repeatedly smearing it across the countertop with the heel of your hand and gathering it back together with a dough scraper. When smooth, mix in the egg, a little at a time, with your fingertips. Then mix in the lemon zest. Work quickly so that you don't melt the butter. Sift the flour over the butter mixture. Mix in the flour, either by cutting it in with a dough scraper or by stirring and tossing with your fingertips, until you obtain a loose, crumbly dough. Gather the dough together and finish mixing

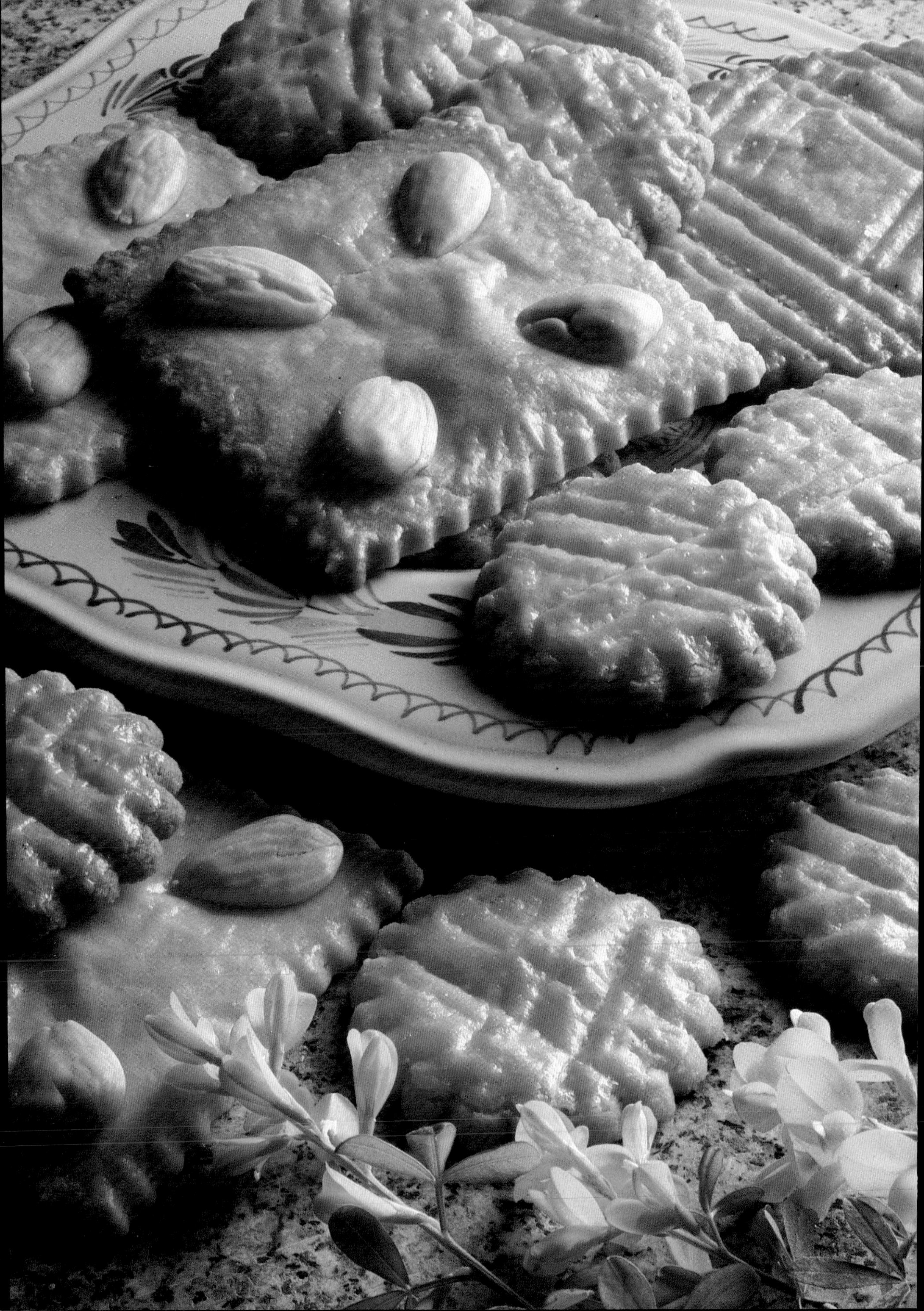

NANTES-STYLE GALETTES . 322 / CAEN-STYLE SABLÉS . 296

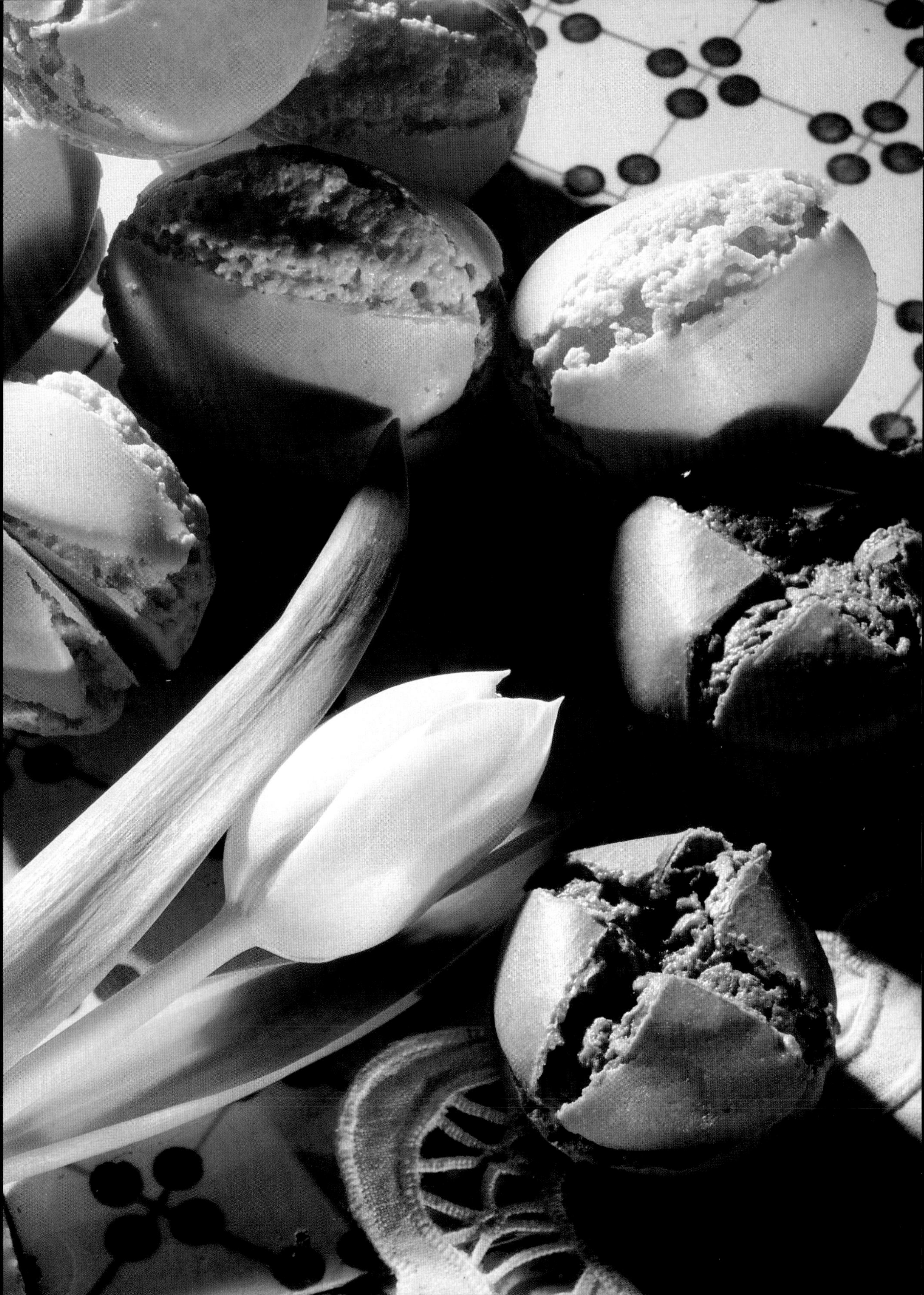

DUTCH MACAROONS . 178 / DUTCH CHOCOLATE MACAROONS . 180

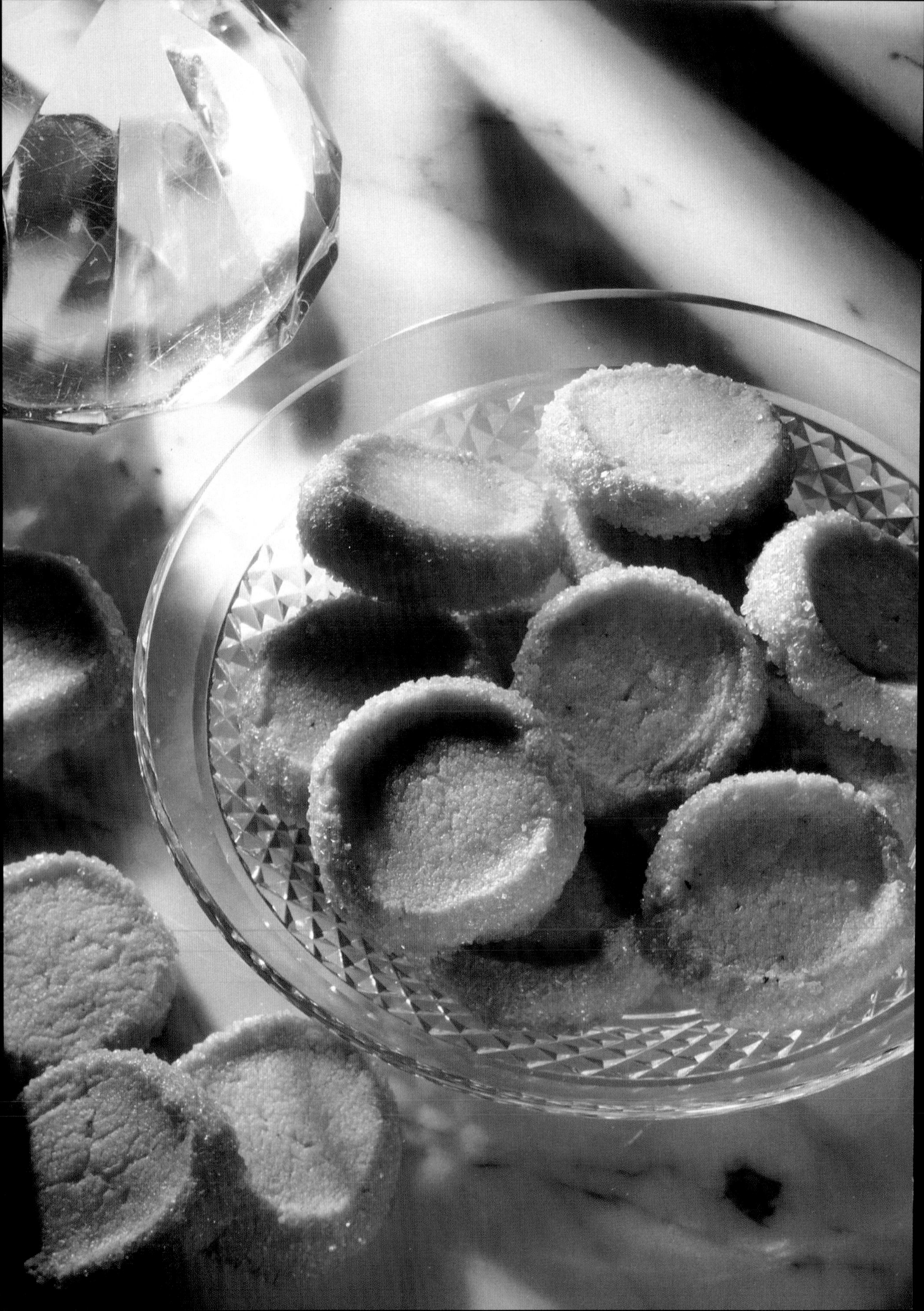

MARCEL PROUST

À LA RECHERCHE
DU TEMPS PERDU

1

DU CÔTÉ
DE CHEZ SWANN

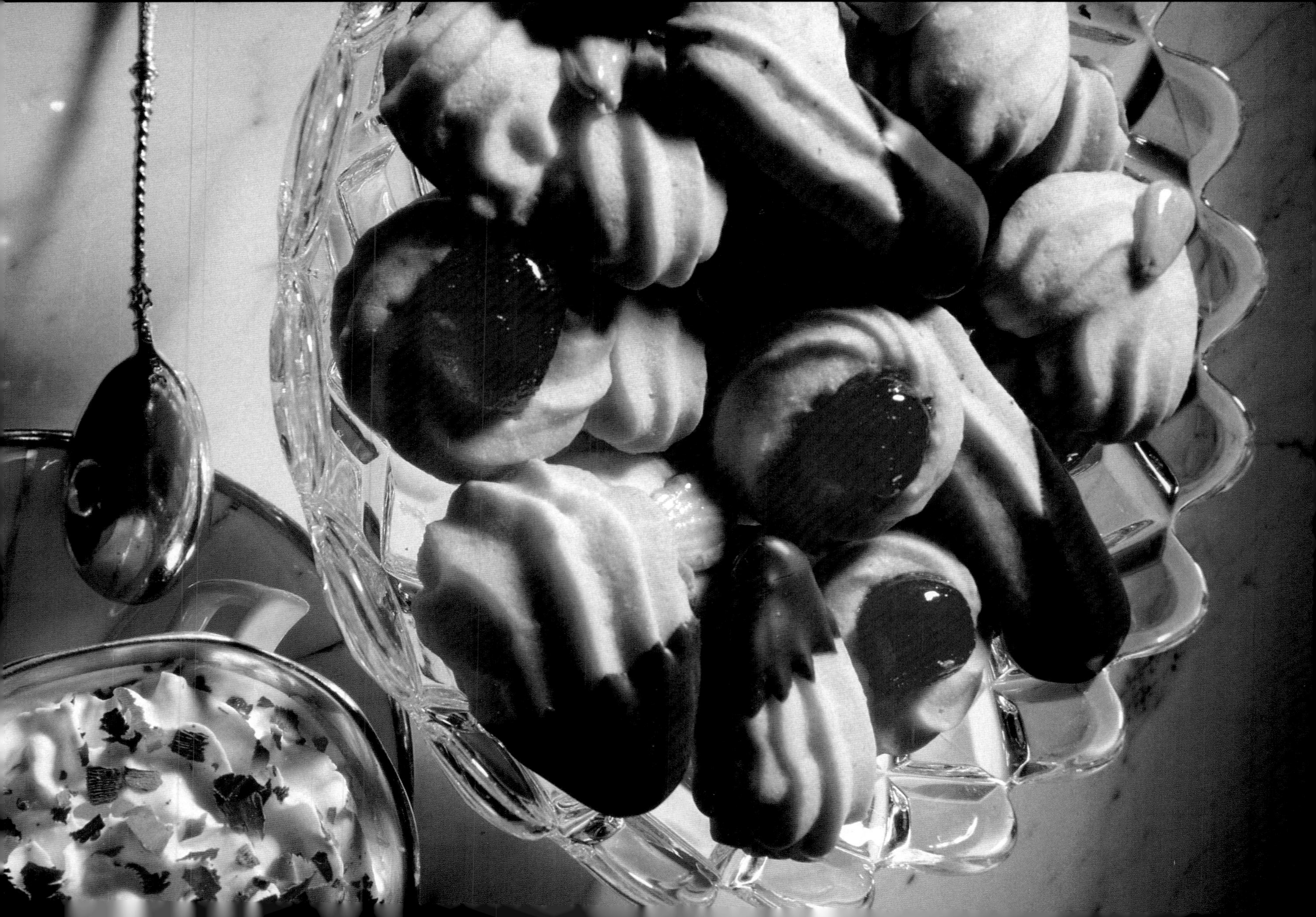

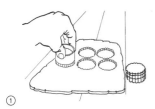

①

②

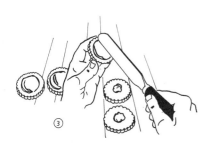

③

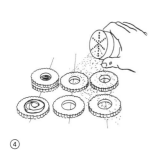

④

by smearing it across the countertop, a little at a time, with the heel of your hand. Gather the dough together again. If it is not yet smooth, then repeat this smearing procedure.

2. Form the dough into a square pad about 1½ inches (4 cm) thick. Lightly dust the pad with flour, wrap it in wax paper, and refrigerate for at least 2 hours and preferably overnight.

3. Dust your countertop and the pad of dough with flour, and roll out the dough with a rolling pin into a sheet about ⅛ inch (3 mm) thick. Dust the counter and dough with flour as needed to prevent the dough from sticking to counter or rolling pin. Slide the dough onto a tray and chill it briefly in the freezer whenever it starts to warm and soften.

4. Cut out 3-inch (8 cm) rounds ① using the fluted cookie cutter. Cut out the centers of half of the rounds ② to make rings using the plain round cookie cutter. Carefully lift the rounds and rings with a metal spatula and transfer them to the baking sheets. Separate the rounds and rings by at least ¾ inch (2 cm), and gently press each to make it stick to the baking sheet. Let rest in the refrigerator.

5. Gather together the remaining dough and form it into a pad. If it is too soft to work with, chill it in the freezer for 20 to 30 minutes. Then roll it out into a sheet about ⅛ inch (3 mm) thick. Cut out more rounds and rings, arrange them on the baking sheets, and refrigerate. Repeat with the remaining scraps, or save them for use in Vietnamese Hats (page 24).

Preheat the oven to 400° F (200° C).

6. Bake, 1 sheet at a time, until the cookies are browned on the bottoms and edges, about 9 to 11 minutes.

7. Slide the cookies onto a wire rack using a metal spatula and let cool to room temperature.

8. Spoon 1½ teaspoons (¾ cl) of apricot jam on each of the pastry rounds and spread the jam ③ with your palette knife, leaving a ⅜-inch (1 cm) border uncovered on all sides. Dust the rings with confectioners' sugar ④ until they are white, then place one on each of the jam-coated rounds.

STORAGE: It is best to fill these cookies and dust the tops with confectioners' sugar shortly before serving. Before filling and dusting, keep them covered airtight in a cookie box or cookie jar for up to 1 week.

Before being rolled out, the dough can be kept in the refrigerator, wrapped in wax paper, for up to 2 or 3 days. Trimmings can be frozen, wrapped in wax paper and then in freezer wrap, for up to 1 month.

CHAPTER 7
FLAKY PASTRY
DOUGHS

The flaky pastry dough that the French call *feuilletage* is one of the most elegant and versatile components in all of pastry making. It is used for desserts (such as the almond pastry cream filled *pithiviers*), to wrap savory preparations (as in beef Wellington), and cut into small decorative shapes for garnishes. In cookies, flaky pastry takes the widest range of forms. It can be rolled on flour or sugar; cut into small squares, circles, strips, or slices, or into long bands or large sheets for bar cookies; and shaped by folding, rolling, or twisting, or wrapped around a jam or almond filling. And this only begins to enumerate the possibilities.

Flaky pastry doughs of a crude sort had been made since ancient Roman times. The development of modern flaky pastry doughs began in the seventeenth century with the work of two pastry chefs. One was Claude Gellée, called *le Lorrain*, the celebrated landscape painter. Claude apprenticed as a pastry chef, and legend has it that he discovered the method of making flaky pastry by accident. The other was Feuillet, the pastry chef of Louis II de Bourbon, prince of Condé. Feuillet was one of the most outstanding pastry chefs of his time, and we suspect that his contribution was the more important one. At the beginning of the nineteenth century, Carême arrived on the scene and perfected the modern method of preparing flaky pastry. In *Le Pâtissier royal parisien*, he tells how he was inspired by the example of the great Feuillet.

Flaky pastry gets it distinctive flakiness from many layers of butter separated by layers of a flour and water dough called the *détrempe*. When the dough is baked, the water in the butter forms steam, pushing apart the layers of *détrempe*, and at the same time the butterfat melts into the layers of *détrempe*, inundating the *détrempe* with the flavor of sweet butter. It is one of the miracles of baking that this simple structure transforms flour, water, and butter into such flaky and tasty pastries. Over the years, pastry chefs have developed several methods for performing this miracle.

THE CLASSIC METHOD

In the classic procedure, the *détrempe* is wrapped around a block of butter, like an envelope, to form a pad of dough called a *pâton*. The *pâton* is rolled out into a long rectangle, simultaneously thinning both the *détrempe* and the butter. The rectangle is folded in three ① like a letter, making a *pâton* with three layers of butter separated and surrounded by layers of *détrempe*. This rolling and folding operation is called a turn. The *pâton* is rotated

①

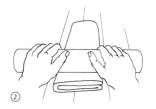

90° and rolled out 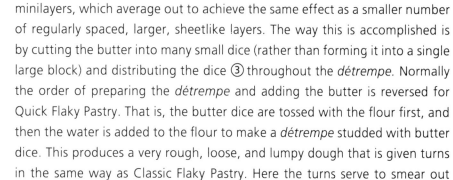 and folded again, making two turns and nine layers of butter. It is then allowed to rest in the refrigerator for an hour or two to relax the gluten in the flour. Next the *pâton* is given two more turns, always rotating it 90° between turns so that it is never given two successive turns in the same direction. This makes four turns and the *pâton* has eighty-one layers of butter. It is allowed to rest again, usually overnight, so that it will be well chilled and relaxed. This completes the basic preparation of the dough. Normally it is given two more turns (for a total of six turns and 729 layers of butter) as the first step in the recipe in which it is used.

When properly done, the classic method produces the lightest, flakiest flaky pastry. However, it is fairly difficult and time-consuming to do in a home kitchen, and only the most dedicated amateur cooks enjoy making it.

THE QUICK METHOD

Fortunately, there are easier methods for producing a flaky pastry dough that, while it may not be quite as flaky or rise quite as high as Classic Flaky Pastry, is still extraordinary. We have chosen the easiest of these methods, called *feuilletage rapide* (Quick Flaky Pastry), for use in our cookies, and we have refined the procedure to make the result as close to that produced by the classic method as possible. In addition we have developed a method for using the electric mixer to reduce the preparation time still further. With the mixer the actual work time required in the preparation is only fifteen to twenty minutes, and including rests between turns the total time required to produce a dough ready for use in any recipe is as little as 1½ hours.

The idea behind Quick Flaky Pastry is that a seemingly uniform layered structure can equally well be developed by making many randomly arranged minilayers, which average out to achieve the same effect as a smaller number of regularly spaced, larger, sheetlike layers. The way this is accomplished is by cutting the butter into many small dice (rather than forming it into a single large block) and distributing the dice ③ throughout the *détrempe*. Normally the order of preparing the *détrempe* and adding the butter is reversed for Quick Flaky Pastry. That is, the butter dice are tossed with the flour first, and then the water is added to the flour to make a *détrempe* studded with butter dice. This produces a very rough, loose, and lumpy dough that is given turns in the same way as Classic Flaky Pastry. Here the turns serve to smear out the butter dice, making many minilayers of butter embedded in the *détrempe*. The Quick Flaky Pastry is given only three turns during the basic preparation, compared with four turns for Classic Flaky Pastry, and the rest periods required between turns are shorter than for the classic method. Furthermore, compared with Classic Flaky Pastry, it is much easier to prepare Quick Flaky Pastry without overdeveloping the gluten strength of the dough.

As a result, the turns and subsequent rolling out of the dough require much less effort and the finished pastry is likely to be more tender.

As with the classic method, Quick Flaky Pastry is normally given two more turns as the first step in the recipe in which it is used. This division between the turns done in preparing the dough and those done as part of the cookie recipe is made for several reasons. First, the dough stores best before the last two turns are performed. Second, during the first three turns (or four turns for Classic Flaky Pastry) the countertop and dough are always dusted with flour to prevent the dough from sticking to the counter or rolling pin. We say the dough is rolled on flour. For many recipes the final two turns are also done on flour. However, for many classic cookies such as Palm Leaves the last two turns are done on sugar. Finally there are some recipes for which the last turns are not done in the standard way because some special effect is required. (For example, a half turn ④ is performed by rolling out the *pâton* and folding it in two; and in a double turn the ends of the rolled-out sheet of dough are folded in to meet in the center ⑤ and then the sheet is folded in half ⑥, making four layers.) By making the final turns as part of the cookie recipe we get the best storage and we keep our options open.

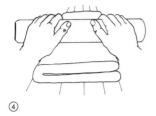

④

⑤

⑥

After the last two turns, the flaky pastry is allowed to rest for about thirty minutes before the final rolling. Since most home kitchens are warm, we recommend letting it rest in the freezer so that it will be very cold and will not soften too quickly when it is rolled out. (However, if you let the dough rest for much longer than thirty minutes, transfer it to the refrigerator so that it doesn't freeze.)

If you are one of those perfectionists who insists on Classic Flaky Pastry, recipes for it can be found in many books on French pastry (including our own *Mastering the Art of French Pastry*). Also, if there is a good French pastry shop in your area, they may be willing to sell you a *pâton* of their flaky pastry. You can use any classic "six turns" flaky pastry in our cookies, but remember to do only four of the turns before starting the cookie recipe.

CHOCOLATE FLAKY PASTRY

During the 1980s it became popular to make chocolate flaky pastry. This is accomplished by mixing cocoa powder with the butter for the dough before enveloping it in (or in the case of Quick Flaky Pastry, tossing it with) the *détrempe*.

KITCHEN TEMPERATURE AND MARBLE SLABS

Working with flaky pastry in a warm kitchen is an exasperating experience for even the most skilled professional, and for a beginner it is a guarantee of disaster. Don't even contemplate preparing flaky pastry (much less rolling it out) if your kitchen temperature is above 75° F (about 25° C). In a traditional French pastry kitchen, the *tours* "station" (where the pastry doughs are prepared) is in the basement and is kept at about 60° F (15° C), which is the temperature at which butter begins to soften. That is a bit cold for home cooks. As a realistic goal, we recommend keeping your kitchen below the melting point of butter—68° F (20° C)—whenever you are working with flaky pastry. In fact, we frequently suggest to our students that the first time they try making flaky pastry they do it in the winter with the windows open.

If your kitchen is warmer than 68° F (20° C), try to work on a marble pastry slab that has been cooled to between 50 and 55° F (10–13° C) in the refrigerator. This is especially valuable when rolling out dough in a thin sheet. Do not chill the marble slab to refrigerator temperature (35 to 40° F [2–4° C]), because this will create condensation, making the dough stick to the slab.

ROLLING OUT THE DOUGH

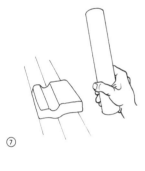

(7)

It is essential that the dough be well chilled before you roll it out and that it remain cool throughout the rolling process. When you first take the *pâton* of flaky pastry from the refrigerator it will be very firm. Place it on your countertop and strike it a couple of times with your rolling pin ⑦ to soften it a little without warming it and make it easier to roll. Lightly dust your countertop and the dough with flour. Then place your rolling pin on the dough and roll it from the end nearest you ⑧ to the far end, pressing firmly and evenly. Reverse direction and roll from the far end of the dough to the near end. Always begin rolling the dough in the direction perpendicular to the final turn. Continue rolling your rolling pin forward and backward over the dough in this direction until the *pâton* has reached one and one half to two times its initial length. Then you can roll it in the other direction as well. Continue rolling the dough, always pressing down as firmly and evenly as you can, to thin it into a sheet of uniform thickness. Lightly dust the countertop and the dough with flour as needed to prevent the dough from sticking.

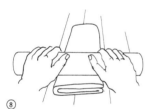

(8)

At the beginning of the rolling process the sides of the dough will probably crack in several places. Firmly press the sides in toward the center with your hands to seal the cracks back together. Some cracking is unavoidable, but you don't want large cracks extending into the center of the sheet.

For most recipes the flaky pastry must be rolled fairly thin—between ⅛ and ¼ inch (3–6 mm). This is the most physically demanding part of working with flaky pastry because as the dough is rolled progressively thinner it becomes progressively stronger. Also, as it gets thinner it warms up and softens very quickly, making it stretch and shrink back easily. If the dough starts to become elastic when you are rolling it, place it on a tray or baking sheet and chill it for at least 20 minutes. And whenever it starts to become soft and limp, chill it briefly in the freezer (being careful not to let it freeze solid) to make it cold and firm again. Whenever you lift the dough, fold it in halves or in quarters so that you can support it and prevent it from stretching under its own weight. Do not be impatient during the rolling out process. When the dough becomes elastic, every time you roll it out it will shrink back, and if you don't let it rest, eventually the gluten will become so strong that the dough will shrink excessively in the oven and the finished cookies will be tough. You can't beat the gluten, but you can outsmart it by using cold and rest periods to keep it under control.

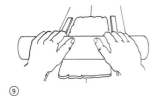

In order to roll the flaky pastry to a uniform thickness, we recommend using spacers to control the thickness of the sheet. There are two ways to do this: either place a long narrow strip ⑨ (for example, cardboard or neoprene) of the required thickness on each side of the dough to support the ends of the rolling pin; or place a neoprene O-ring of the required thickness on each end ⑩ of the rolling pin. If you are using an O-ring, be careful not to roll the O-ring over the sheet of dough.

DUSTING WITH FLOUR AND SUGAR

Throughout the turns and final rolling, you must lightly dust the countertop and dough with flour to prevent the dough from sticking to the counter or rolling pin. Use as little flour as possible, and at the end of each stage brush off any excess flour with a pastry brush. (See ''Flour'' in the reference section for a detailed explanation of the best method for dusting with flour.)

When a cookie recipe calls for doing the last two turns and the final rolling on sugar ⑪ instead of on flour, you do not have to be so light-handed with the dusting. Here the sugar dusting supplies most if not all of the sweetness in the cookies, and during baking the sugar caramelizes, giving the cookies a rich color. Use a dredge to sprinkle the sugar over the countertop and dough, dusting as much sugar as needed to prevent sticking and not worrying about a little excess sugar sticking to the dough. The one thing to keep in mind when dusting flaky pastry with sugar is that the sugar will extract moisture from the dough. If too much moisture comes to the surface, then when the cookies bake, sugar syrup will drip onto the baking sheet and caramelize (and possibly burn), making the cookies look sloppy. To avoid this, work quickly, use the freezer to keep the dough as cold as possible, and keep the rest periods to the minimum necessary to make the dough workable and prevent shrinking. Sugared flaky pastry cannot be stored in the refrigerator or freezer before forming the cookies. However, once you have formed the cookies, you can freeze them and then bake them later without first defrosting (see Storage in this section).

CUTTING AND SHAPING

Once you have finished rolling out the flaky pastry, lay it on a tray or baking sheet and let rest in the refrigerator or freezer for twenty to thirty minutes before cutting to prevent shrinking and deforming. Then cut and shape the dough quickly so that it doesn't soften too much.

Small circles are cut with a round pastry cutter. Place the cutter on the dough, press firmly straight down ⑫ to cut all the way through, and then give a slight twist to disengage the circle from the sheet of dough.

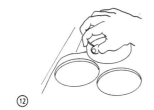
⑫

Cut other shapes with a chef's knife. Never drag the blade through the dough since that would stretch and deform it. Instead, place the tip of the blade on the counter and press the edge of the blade straight down ⑬ to cut through the dough. When making a series of long straight cuts on a large sheet of dough, fold the sheet in half and cut through both halves at once, then carefully unfold.

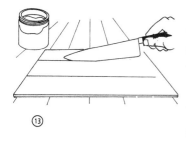
⑬

If you are cutting many small shapes from a very thin sheet of dough, they will probably already be soft by the time you finish cutting. In this case, stack them in piles of four to six on a tray or baking sheet and chill in the refrigerator or freezer until firm again. Then take them from the refrigerator a few at a time, keeping the remainder chilled, so that they will be easy to form or fill. When spreading filling on the flaky pastry, be especially careful not to stretch the dough.

WHAT TO DO WITH THE TRIMMINGS

Whenever you work with flaky pastry there will be trimmings left over from cutting the rolled-out dough into the required shapes. If the dough was rolled on flour, then the trimmings are saved and combined to form a pastry dough called *rognures* (literally ''trimmings'') in French. We refer to it as Flaky Trimmings Dough (see page 355). Flaky Trimmings Dough is used when you want a dough that is very flaky but doesn't rise as high as Quick Flaky Pastry or Classic Flaky Pastry. Unfortunately, when flaky pastry is rolled on sugar the trimmings cannot be saved because the sugar makes the dough sweat.

ARRANGING THE COOKIES ON THE BAKING SHEETS

⑭

If the flaky pastry has not been rolled on sugar, brush the baking sheet with a damp pastry brush ⑭ to moisten it lightly before arranging the cookies on it. The water makes the cookies stick to the baking sheet so they don't slide around or deform, and it helps minimize shrinkage during baking. This is particularly important with cookies for which large bands or sheets of dough are filled and assembled directly on the baking sheet.

On the other hand, cookies for which the flaky pastry has been rolled on sugar should be arranged on clean, dry baking sheets. Here the sheets are not brushed with water because the water would dissolve sugar on the surface of the dough, resulting in syrup on the baking sheet, which would burn in the oven.

Always space the cookies far enough apart on the baking sheets to allow for expansion and air circulation in the oven. A spacing of 1 to 1½ inches (2½–4 cm) is enough for some cookies, but for many of the sugared flaky pastry cookies the dough is sliced and laid on its side on the baking sheet, so it expands horizontally rather than vertically when baked. For these the spacing may need to be as much as 3 to 3½ inches (8–9½ cm).

If you do not have enough baking sheets to arrange all of the cookies at once, you can either lay them out on trays lined with wax paper and then transfer them to baking sheets as this becomes possible; or you can form only as many cookies as you can bake at one time, keeping the remaining dough in the refrigerator until you are ready for it. If you have enough baking sheets, then in order to fit several of them in your refrigerator (without removing everything else) you can place a small mold or glass at each corner of one baking sheet and stack another baking sheet on top.

FINAL REST AND GLAZING WITH EGG WASH

The cookies are now allowed to rest in the refrigerator for thirty to sixty minutes before baking, partly to relax them once more so they don't shrink unevenly in the oven and partly to be sure they are cold and firm so they hold their shape well rather than become limp when they first go into the oven.

Many of the flaky pastry cookies (but not the sugared ones) are glazed with egg wash. They are given two coats of lightly beaten egg. The first is applied before the final rest, and the second immediately before they go into the oven. Brush the egg wash on the top surface in a light coat, just enough to make it glisten. Do not allow any egg wash to get on the edges of the pastry. When the cookies bake, the egg wash coagulates very quickly and would glue the layers of flaky pastry together, preventing the edges from rising properly. After the second coat of egg wash, the top of the pastry is sometimes scored in a decorative pattern ⑮ with the tip of a paring knife.

BAKING

Flaky pastry requires a high initial oven temperature to make it rise properly and give the cookies a nice color. Usually the oven heat is reduced to moderate when the cookies begin to brown to prevent the bottoms from burning while the insides of the cookies are drying out. Most sugared flaky pastry cookies are turned upside down at the same time as the oven temperature is reduced so that the sugar caramelizes evenly on top and bottom. If the cookies are large, use a large metal spatula so that they don't break when you turn them.

When the cookies are finished baking, they should be removed from the baking sheet to cool on a wire rack or, for sugared flaky pastry, on the countertop to prevent sticking to the rack. Leaving the cookies on the baking sheet would make condensation form under the cookies and soften them.

When you turn sugared flaky pastry cookies or slide them off the baking sheet using a metal spatula, caramelized sugar sometimes sticks to the edge of the spatula. This can be removed easily by scraping the spatula with a dough scraper.

STORAGE

After baking, all of the flaky pastry cookies are best kept covered in a tin cookie box or a cookie jar for up to two or three days. Those filled with jam will lose their crispness more quickly than the others; on the other hand, most of the sugared flaky pastry cookies can even last a little longer than three days if kept very dry. But keep in mind that fresh butter is the essence of the flavor of all flaky pastry cookies, and while their texture may still be good even after a week if kept very dry, the butter taste will no longer be as appealing as when they have just been baked.

Before baking, all flaky pastry cookies can be frozen for up to one month. Arrange them on trays or baking sheets with a sheet of wax paper underneath and freeze after completing all steps preliminary to baking (including brushing with egg wash and scoring), then transfer them to a plastic bag. Or, for large bar cookies that cover an entire baking sheet and would be too fragile to remove from the sheet, simply cover the entire baking sheet in a large plastic bag. When ready to bake, arrange the frozen cookies on baking sheets and bake immediately in a preheated oven without first defrosting, following the same directions as if the cookies had never been frozen.

QUICK FLAKY PASTRY
FEUILLETAGE RAPIDE

We give the recipe for preparing Quick Flaky Pastry both by hand and using a heavy-duty electric mixer. In the hand method, the butter dice are tossed with the flour before adding the liquid to make the détrempe. However, in the mixer method, the liquid is added to the flour first and then the butter dice are tossed in.

Both methods are really quite easy, and the mixer method is unbelievably fast. If you have ever struggled with Classic Flaky Pastry, get ready for a pleasant surprise.

PASTRY DOUGH

1 pound (450 g) unsalted butter, chilled in the freezer until very firm but not frozen

1½ pounds (675 g), or 4¾ cups plus 1 tablespoon, all-purpose flour

1 cup (2.4 dl) cold water

2 teaspoons (12 g) salt

1 tablespoon (1½ cl) distilled white vinegar

2½ ounces (70 g), or 5 tablespoons, unsalted butter, barely melted

COUNTERTOP DUSTING

Flour

For 1 pâton weighing about 3¼ pounds (1,475 g)

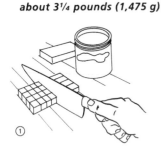

BY MACHINE

1. Put the butter on your countertop with ¼ cup (35 g) of the flour. Cut the butter into ½-inch (12 mm) dice ①, using the flour to keep the pieces from sticking together. Toss the dice with any flour remaining on the countertop, transfer to a bowl, and keep chilled in the refrigerator while you make the *détrempe*.

2. Mix ½ cup (1.2 dl) of the water with the salt and vinegar. Sift the flour into the bowl of your electric mixer. Attach the flat beater and turn on the machine at low speed to fluff the flour. Slowly pour in the water, salt, and vinegar mixture in a steady stream ②. Increase the mixer speed slightly and slowly pour in the melted butter in a steady stream. Increase the mixer speed again to between low and medium, and slowly pour in the remaining water in a steady stream. Stop the mixer as soon as you have finished adding the water.

3. Turn out the mixture onto your countertop. It will be very loose—like coarse meal rather than massed together like a dough. Gather together a little of the mixture and try to form it into a ball. If it holds together, it is ready. If not, then sprinkle a little more cold water, 1 teaspoon (½ cl) at a time, over the mixture, tossing to mix it in, until a small sample will hold together. This mixture is the *détrempe*. Add the butter dice to the *détrempe* and toss to distribute the dice evenly ③.

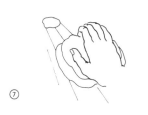

BY HAND

1. Put the butter on your countertop with ¼ cup (35 g) of the flour. Cut the butter into ½-inch (12 mm) dice, using the flour to keep the pieces from sticking together. Sift the remaining flour over the butter dice ④ and toss with the dice to distribute them evenly. Form the mixture into a mound.

2. Mix ½ cup (1.2 dl) of the water with the salt and vinegar. Toss the flour and butter dice with one hand while you slowly add the water, salt, and vinegar mixture ⑤ with the other, being sure to moisten the flour evenly so that none of it gets wet or forms lumps. Add the melted butter in the same way. Then gradually add the remaining water, continuing to toss the flour mixture so that it gets evenly moistened without gathering together in wet lumps.

3. The mixture will have a loose texture, like coarse meal, with the whole butter dice distributed ⑥ throughout. Gather together a little of the mixture and try to form it into a ball. If it holds together, it is ready. If not, then sprinkle a little more cold water, 1 teaspoon (½ cl) at a time, over the mixture, tossing to mix it in, until a small sample will hold together. You now have a *détrempe* mixed with butter dice.

BY EITHER METHOD

4. Gather the mixture and press it together to form a rough but cohesive mass of dough. The easiest way to do this is to first divide it into 4 or 5 portions and form each portion into a pad, pressing it firmly with your hands to make the dough hold together. Then press these pads one on top of the other ⑦ and form the dough into a single thick pad about 7½ to 8 inches (18–20 cm) square. This pad of dough is the *pâton*.

5. Dust your countertop with flour. Place the *pâton* on it and dust the *pâton* with flour. Roll out the *pâton* with your rolling pin ⑧ into a rough rectangle about 20 inches (50 cm) long, dusting with flour as needed to minimize sticking to counter or rolling pin. When the dough sticks to the countertop, lift it with your dough scraper, clean off the counter with the dough scraper, and dust more flour underneath. When finished rolling, fold the rectangle in thirds crosswise, like a letter ⑨. This is the first turn. Lightly dust with flour on top and bottom, wrap in wax paper, and let rest in the refrigerator for 30 minutes to 1 hour.

6. Dust your countertop and the *pâton* again with flour and roll out the *pâton* into a rectangle ⑩ about 20 inches (50 cm) long, in the direction perpendicular to the first turn. Fold it in thirds ⑪ like a letter. Rotate the *pâton* 90°, roll it out to about 18 inches (45 cm) long, and fold it in thirds again. This makes

(continued)

FLAKY PASTRY DOUGHS

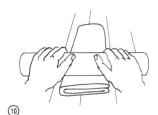

3 turns. Rotate the *pâton* 90° once more, roll it out to about 12 inches (30 cm) long, and cut it in half ⑫ crosswise. Dust each half *pâton* lightly with flour, wrap in wax paper, and let rest in the refrigerator for 30 minutes to 1 hour. The dough is now ready to use.

➤ **HOWS & WHYS:** The melted butter and vinegar are added to the *détrempe* to help prevent it from becoming too elastic. Salt is included because without it the flaky pastry would taste flat.

The size of the butter dice and the number of turns are chosen to make the flaky pastry rise as high as possible without baking unevenly. Cutting ⅜-inch (1 cm) rather than ½-inch (12 mm) butter dice would make the flaky pastry rise much less high. Keeping ½-inch (12 mm) butter dice but increasing the number of turns to 4 would have the same effect. Using larger butter dice would make the dough bake too unevenly.

At the end of the third turn, the dough should be fairly smooth but the smeared-out butter dice will still be distinctly visible. After the final 2 turns are completed at the beginning of the cookie recipe, the dough should be totally smooth and appear homogeneous, with all of the smeared butter dice distributed uniformly throughout the *détrempe* in layers so thin that they are almost invisible.

Classic Flaky Pastry is conventionally made in a *pâton* weighing approximately 3¼ pounds (1,475 g). This size is small enough to be easily manipulated and large enough to minimize edge effects from the turns. For Quick Flaky Pastry, the size of the *pâton* is not as standardized, since edge effects are less important for it. We have chosen to give the recipe for a 3¼-pound (1,475 g) *pâton* in order to keep our recipes compatible with Classic Flaky Pastry conventions and because it is much more efficient to make this size rather than a smaller *pâton*. All of our cookie recipes call for half a *pâton,* so we recommend cutting the *pâton* in half after the first 3 turns and freezing the half you aren't using right away. Or you can freeze both halves for later use.

STORAGE: Wrapped tightly in wax paper for up to 1 day in the refrigerator. For longer storage, let the dough rest in the refrigerator for 1 hour after the third turn, then cover the wax paper with freezer wrap and freeze for up to 1 month. When ready to use, defrost overnight in the refrigerator.

FLAKY TRIMMINGS DOUGH
ROGNURES

The most common pastry that uses Flaky Trimmings Dough is napoleons (mille-feuilles). In this book we use Flaky Trimmings Dough for three bar cookies—Little Champignys (page 402), Floréals (page 404), and Parisian Nougat (page 406).

PASTRY DOUGH
Trimmings from flaky pastry rolled on flour

COUNTERTOP DUSTING
Flour

For any quantity

of pastry dough

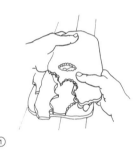

①

1. On your countertop, lay some flaky pastry trimmings edge to edge in a single layer, with any long pieces running parallel to each other in one direction. Arrange a second layer of trimmings on top of the first layer, with any long pieces running in the direction perpendicular to those in the first layer. Continue piling up layers of trimmings ① and then press the trimmings tightly together to form a square pad about ½ to 1 inch (12 mm–2½ cm) thick. The size and thickness will depend on the quantity of trimmings you have. You will need to consolidate the trimmings from 2 or more cookie recipes to get enough Flaky Trimmings Dough for 1 of our bar cookies recipes.

2. Lightly dust the dough with flour and wrap it in wax paper. Refrigerate for at least 2 hours and preferably overnight. Flaky Trimmings Dough can easily become very strong and elastic, so be especially careful when rolling it out to keep it well chilled and let it rest as often as necessary.

➤ **HOWS & WHYS:** The trimmings are arranged in layers to maintain as much of the structure of the original flaky pastry as possible. A less flaky but very usable Flaky Trimmings Dough can be made by simply gathering together the trimmings and forming them into a pad.

STORAGE: If the original flaky pastry was freshly made, the Flaky Trimmings Dough can be kept in the refrigerator, wrapped in wax paper, for up to 1 or 2 days. Or, after resting in the refrigerator for 2 hours, cover the wax paper with freezer wrap and freeze for up to 1 month. When ready to use, defrost overnight in the refrigerator.

If the original flaky pastry was not freshly made, reduce the storage times accordingly.

CHOCOLATE FLAKY PASTRY
FEUILLETAGE CHOCOLAT

Chocolate Flaky Pastry produces the most striking results when layered with ordinary flaky pastry to make a striped effect, and it has the best flavor when used in cookies that require rolling the dough on sugar. In order to prevent the butter layers from becoming too thin, we modify the last two turns when combining ordinary and chocolate flaky pastry doughs and layer the two on the final turn. The cookies that look best with striped flaky pastry are Bow Ties (page 360), Arlettes (page 368), and Flaky Wands (page 378), and we give special recipes for the striped versions, which we call zébrés.

PASTRY DOUGH

1 pound (450 g) unsalted butter

1¼ ounces (35 g), or ⅓ cup, unsweetened Dutch-processed cocoa powder

1½ pounds (675 g), or 4¾ cups plus 1 tablespoon, all-purpose flour

1 cup (2.4 dl) cold water

2 teaspoons (12 g) salt

1 tablespoon (1½ cl) distilled white vinegar

2½ ounces (70 g), or 5 tablespoons, unsalted butter, barely melted

COUNTERTOP DUSTING

Flour

For 1 pâton weighing about 3 pounds 5 ounces (1,500 g)

BY MACHINE

1. Cut the butter into pieces about 1 tablespoon (15 g) in size, place in your electric mixer, and beat with the flat beater. When the butter softens a little, add the cocoa powder and continue beating until smooth. Turn the butter out onto your countertop and form it into a rectangular block about 4½ inches (12 cm) long by 2¼ inches (6 cm) square. Dust lightly with flour, wrap in wax paper, and chill in the freezer until very firm but not frozen.

2. Put the butter on your countertop with 3 tablespoons (25 g) of the flour. Cut the butter into ½-inch (12 mm) dice ①, using the flour to keep the pieces from sticking together. Toss the dice with any flour remaining on the countertop, transfer to a bowl, and keep chilled in the refrigerator while you make the *détrempe*.

3. Mix ½ cup (1.2 dl) of the water with the salt and vinegar. Sift the flour into the bowl of your electric mixer. Attach the flat beater and turn on the machine at low speed to fluff the flour. Slowly pour in the water, salt, and vinegar mixture in a steady stream ②. Increase the mixer speed slightly and slowly pour in the melted butter in a steady stream. Increase the mixer speed again to between low and medium, and slowly pour in the remaining water in a steady stream. Stop the mixer as soon as you have finished adding the water.

4. Turn out the mixture onto your countertop. It will be very loose—like coarse meal rather than massed together like a dough. Gather together a little of the mixture and try to form it into a ball. If it holds together, it is ready. If not, then sprinkle a little more cold water, 1 teaspoon (½ cl) at a time, over the mixture, tossing to mix it in, until a small sample will hold together. This mixture is the *détrempe*. Add the butter dice to the *détrempe* and toss to distribute the dice evenly ③.

BY HAND

1. Place the butter on your countertop and soften it by smearing it across the countertop, a little at a time, with the heel of your hand. Add the cocoa powder and continue working with the heel of your hand until smooth and evenly mixed. Form the butter into a rectangular block about 4½ inches (12 cm) long by 2¼ inches (6 cm) square. Dust lightly with flour, wrap in wax paper, and chill in the freezer until very firm but not frozen.

2. Put the butter on your countertop with 3 tablespoons (25 g) of the flour. Cut the butter into ½-inch (12 mm) dice, using the flour to keep the pieces from sticking together. Sift the remaining flour over the butter dice ④ and toss with the dice to distribute them evenly. Form the mixture into a mound.

3. Mix ½ cup (1.2 dl) of the water with the salt and vinegar. Toss the flour and butter dice with one hand while you slowly add the water, salt, and vinegar mixture ⑤ with the other, being sure to moisten the flour evenly so that none of it gets wet or forms lumps. Add the melted butter in the same way. Then gradually add the remaining water, continuing to toss the flour mixture so that it gets evenly moistened without gathering together in wet lumps.

4. The mixture will have a loose texture, like coarse meal, with the whole butter dice distributed ⑥ throughout. Gather together a little of the mixture and try to form it into a ball. If it holds together, it is ready. If not, then sprinkle a little more cold water, 1 teaspoon (½ cl) at a time, over the mixture, tossing to mix it in, until a small sample will hold together. You now have a *détrempe* mixed with butter dice.

(continued)

(7)

(8)

(9)

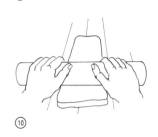

(10)

(11)

BY EITHER METHOD

5. Gather the mixture and press it together to form a rough but cohesive mass of dough. The easiest way to do this is to first divide it into 4 or 5 portions and form each portion into a pad, pressing it firmly with your hands to make the dough hold together. Then press these pads one on top of the other ⑦ and form the dough into a single thick pad about 7½ to 8 inches (18–20 cm) square. This pad of dough is the *pâton*.

6. Dust your countertop with flour. Place the *pâton* on it and dust the *pâton* with flour. Roll out the *pâton* with your rolling pin ⑧ into a rough rectangle about 20 inches (50 cm) long, dusting with flour as needed to minimize sticking to counter or rolling pin. When the dough sticks to the countertop, lift it with your dough scraper, clean off the counter with the dough scraper, and dust more flour underneath. When finished rolling, fold the rectangle in thirds crosswise, like a letter ⑨. This is the first turn. Lightly dust with flour on top and bottom, wrap in wax paper, and let rest in the refrigerator for 30 minutes to 1 hour.

7. Dust your countertop and the *pâton* again with flour and roll out the *pâton* into a rectangle ⑩ about 20 inches (50 cm) long, in the direction perpendicular to the first turn. Fold it in thirds ⑪ like a letter. Rotate the *pâton* 90°, roll it out to about 18 inches (45 cm) long, and fold it in thirds again. This makes 3 turns. Rotate the *pâton* 90° once more, roll it out to about 12 inches (30 cm) long, and cut it in half ⑫ crosswise. Dust each half *pâton* lightly with flour, wrap in wax paper, and let rest in the refrigerator for 30 minutes to 1 hour. The dough is now ready to use.

➤ **HOWS & WHYS:** The melted butter and vinegar are added to the *détrempe* to help prevent it from becoming too elastic.

The size of the butter dice and the number of turns are chosen to make the flaky pastry rise as high as possible without baking unevenly.

At the end of the third turn, the dough should be fairly smooth but the smeared-out butter dice will still be distinctly visible. After the final 2 turns are completed at the beginning of the cookie recipe, the dough should be totally smooth and appear homogeneous, with all of the smeared butter dice distributed uniformly throughout the *détrempe* in layers so thin that they are almost invisible.

Since our striped cookie recipes always call for half a *pâton* of Chocolate Flaky Pastry, we have included instructions for cutting the *pâton* in half following the third turn.

STORAGE: Wrapped tightly in wax paper for up to 1 day in the refrigerator. For longer storage, let the dough rest in the refrigerator for 1 hour after the third turn, then cover the wax paper with freezer wrap and freeze for up to 1 month. When ready to use, defrost overnight in the refrigerator.

BOW TIES
PAPILLONS

～～～～～

The name of this cookie is actually abbreviated from noeud papillon—literally, "butterfly knot"—which is what the French call a bow tie. It is one of the easiest flaky pastry cookies to make. The pastry dough is rolled very thick, trimmed, and sliced. Each slice is given a half twist, then laid on its side on the baking sheet. When baked, the centers are constrained by the twist and can't expand much, while the ends fan out horizontally to produce very dramatic Bow Ties.

EQUIPMENT
3 large, heavy baking sheets

PASTRY DOUGH
Half a *pâton* of Quick Flaky Pastry (page 352)
COUNTERTOP DUSTING
Granulated sugar

For about 18 to 20 cookies

1. Dust your countertop and the Quick Flaky Pastry with sugar, and give the *pâton* 2 final turns as follows: Roll out the flaky pastry perpendicular to the previous turn to about 18 inches (45 cm) long. Fold it in thirds like a letter. Rotate the *pâton* 90° and repeat this rolling and folding operation. Dust with sugar as needed to prevent the dough from sticking to counter or rolling pin. Let rest in the freezer 30 minutes.

①

2. Roll out the dough into a rectangle about 9 by 8 inches (22 by 20 cm) and ¾ inch (2 cm) thick. Dust both counter and dough with sugar as needed to prevent sticking. When finished rolling, let the dough rest in the freezer for 20 minutes to relax before cutting.

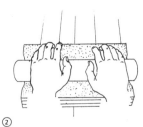

②

3. Using your chef's knife, trim the long sides of the rectangle to remove the rounded edges ① from the last turn, reducing it to a band about 6 inches (15 cm) wide. Lay your rolling pin lengthwise on the center of the band, and press firmly, rocking back and forth, to thin the center ② to about ⅜ inch (1 cm). Cut the band crosswise ③ into slices ⅜ inch (1 cm) thick, discarding the slices from the ends that aren't evenly layered. One at a time, grasp a slice on either side of the center with the fingertips of each hand, and give it a half twist ④. Lay the slices on their sides on the baking sheets, separating them by at least 3 inches (8 cm). Let rest in the refrigerator for 30 minutes.

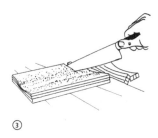

③

Preheat the oven to 425° F (220° C).

4. One at a time, place each baking sheet in the oven and reduce the temperature to 400° F (200° C). Bake until the cookies just begin to brown on the bottoms, about 7 to 10 minutes. Turn them upside down, reduce the temperature to 350° F (175° C), and continue baking until the cookies are golden brown on the tops and bottoms with no streaks of white in the centers, about 15 to 20 minutes longer.

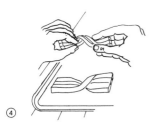

④

5. Slide the cookies onto your countertop using a metal spatula and let cool to room temperature.

➤ **HOWS & WHYS:** It is essential to eliminate all edge effects from the final turn; otherwise, the last fold will prevent the ends of the Bow Ties from expanding when they bake. The centers of the Bow Ties are rolled thinner than the ends in order to prevent them from becoming too thick during baking and making the cookies untwist. Since the centers are compressed, they require a longer baking time than would otherwise be necessary for this cookie. Be especially careful to turn the cookies and reduce the oven temperature as soon as the cookies begin to brown so that the ends don't burn before the centers are finished baking.

STORAGE: Covered airtight in a tin cookie box or cookie jar for up to 2 or 3 days.

Before baking, the cookies can be frozen for up to 1 month: form the cookies and freeze them on trays, then transfer them to plastic bags. When ready to bake, arrange the frozen cookies on baking sheets and bake immediately, without first defrosting.

STRIPED BOW TIES
PAPILLONS ZÉBRÉS

~~~~~~

This variation on Bow Ties (page 360) has two longitudinal stripes of Chocolate Flaky Pastry surrounded by stripes of Quick Flaky Pastry. The presentation looks as jazzy as the name sounds.

EQUIPMENT
5 or 6 large, heavy baking sheets

COUNTERTOP DUSTING
Granulated sugar

PASTRY DOUGH
Half a *pâton* of Quick Flaky Pastry (page 352)
Half a *pâton* of Chocolate Flaky Pastry (page 356)

For about 38 to 40 cookies

①

②

③

④

1. Dust your countertop and the Quick Flaky Pastry with sugar, and roll out this flaky pastry perpendicular to the previous turn to about 15 inches (38 cm) long. Do not fold it yet. Now roll it out in the other direction to make a sheet about 15 inches (38 cm) square. Dust with sugar as needed to prevent the dough from sticking to counter or rolling pin. Slide the sheet of Quick Flaky Pastry onto a tray and let rest in the freezer while you roll out the Chocolate Flaky Pastry.

2. Dust your countertop and the Chocolate Flaky Pastry with sugar, and roll out the Chocolate Flaky Pastry perpendicular to the previous turn to about 13 inches (33 cm) long. Fold it in half. This is a half turn. Rotate the *pâton* 90° and roll out the dough to about 14 inches (35 cm) long, but do not fold it. Dust with sugar as needed to prevent sticking. The band of Chocolate Flaky Pastry should be about 7 to 7½ inches (18–19 cm) wide. If necessary, roll it to widen it to this dimension.

3. Take the Quick Flaky Pastry from the freezer. Lay the band of Chocolate Flaky Pastry on top of the sheet of Quick Flaky Pastry ① so that it almost covers half of the plain sheet, with a long edge of the chocolate band centered on one edge of the plain sheet. Fold over the uncovered half of the plain sheet ② to enclose the chocolate band. Then fold in half crosswise ③ to make a pad of flaky pastry with 4 plain layers and 2 chocolate layers. This makes 1 full *pâton* of striped flaky pastry. Let it rest in the freezer for 30 minutes.

4. Roll out the dough, in the direction perpendicular to the last turn, into a rectangle about 18 by 8 inches (45 by 20 cm) and ¾ inch (2 cm) thick. Dust both counter and dough with sugar as needed to prevent sticking. When finished rolling, let the dough rest in the freezer for 20 minutes to relax before cutting.

5. Using your chef's knife, trim the long sides of the rectangle to

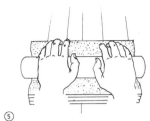

remove the rounded edges ④ from the last turn, reducing it to a band about 6 inches (15 cm) wide. Lay your rolling pin lengthwise on the center of the band and press firmly, rocking back and forth, to thin the center ⑤ to about ⅜ inch (1 cm). Cut the band crosswise ⑥ into slices ⅜ inch (1 cm) thick, discarding the slices from the ends that aren't evenly layered. One at a time, grasp a slice on either side of the center with the fingertips of each hand, and give it a half twist ⑦. Lay the slices on their sides on the baking sheets, separating them by at least 3 inches (8 cm). (Or freeze some for baking later.) Let rest in the refrigerator for 30 minutes.

Preheat the oven to 425° F (220° C).

6. One at a time, place each baking sheet in the oven and reduce the temperature to 400° F (200° C). Bake until the cookies just begin to brown on the bottoms, about 7 to 10 minutes. Turn them upside down, reduce the temperature to 350° F (175° C), and continue baking until the cookies are golden brown on the tops and bottoms with no streaks of white in the centers, about 15 to 20 minutes longer. (Judge the color of the plain flaky pastry, not the chocolate layers.)

7. Slide the cookies onto your countertop using a metal spatula and let cool to room temperature.

➤ **HOWS & WHYS:** It is essential to eliminate all edge effects from the final turn. Otherwise the last fold will prevent the ends of the Bow Ties from expanding when they bake. The centers of the Bow Ties are rolled thinner than the ends in order to prevent them from becoming too thick during baking and making the cookies untwist. Since the centers are compressed, they require a longer baking time than would otherwise be necessary for this cookie. Be especially careful to turn the cookies and reduce the oven temperature as soon as the cookies begin to brown so that the ends don't burn before the centers are finished baking.

NOTE: If you prefer not to make a full *pâton* of Striped Bow Ties, you can cut the *pâton* of striped flaky pastry in half after rolling it to 18 inches (45 cm) long. Then use one half in this recipe and the other half in Striped Flaky Wands (page 380).

STORAGE: Covered airtight in a cookie jar or tin for up to 2 or 3 days.

Before baking, the cookies can be frozen for up to 1 month: form the cookies and freeze them on trays, then transfer them to plastic bags. When ready to bake, arrange the frozen cookies on baking sheets and bake immediately, without first defrosting.

PALM LEAVES
PALMIERS

*O*f all the flaky pastry cookies, Palm Leaves are certainly the best known. Not only are they popular in France, they have long been a staple in bakeries in the United States under a variety of names, including butterflies and elephant ears as well as Palm Leaves. Unfortunately, most bakery Palm Leaves are a clumsy reflection of the real thing. Typically the flaky pastry is poor quality and the sugar isn't properly incorporated, so the cookies taste mediocre and the surfaces are too heavily caramelized. When you make our recipe at home, you will see why Palm Leaves deserve to be so famous.

EQUIPMENT
2 or 3 large, heavy baking sheets

PASTRY DOUGH
Half a *pâton* of Quick Flaky Pastry (page 352)

COUNTERTOP DUSTING
Granulated sugar
SEALING
1 egg, lightly beaten

For about 18 to 20 cookies

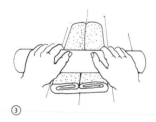
①

②

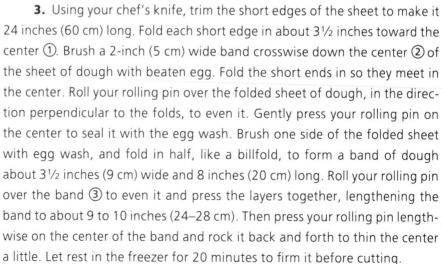
③

1. Dust your countertop and the Quick Flaky Pastry with sugar, and give the *pâton* 2 final turns as follows: Roll out the flaky pastry perpendicular to the previous turn to about 18 inches (45 cm) long. Fold it in thirds like a letter. Rotate the *pâton* 90° and repeat this rolling and folding operation. Dust with sugar as needed to prevent the dough from sticking to counter or rolling pin. Let rest in the freezer 30 minutes.

2. Roll out the dough into a rectangular sheet a little larger than 8 by 24 inches (20 by 60 cm) and about 3/16 inch (5 mm) thick. Dust both counter and dough with sugar as needed to prevent sticking. Chill the dough in the freezer whenever it starts to warm and become soft and limp. When finished rolling, let the dough rest in the freezer for 20 minutes to relax before cutting.

3. Using your chef's knife, trim the short edges of the sheet to make it 24 inches (60 cm) long. Fold each short edge in about 3½ inches toward the center ①. Brush a 2-inch (5 cm) wide band crosswise down the center ② of the sheet of dough with beaten egg. Fold the short ends in so they meet in the center. Roll your rolling pin over the folded sheet of dough, in the direction perpendicular to the folds, to even it. Gently press your rolling pin on the center to seal it with the egg wash. Brush one side of the folded sheet with egg wash, and fold in half, like a billfold, to form a band of dough about 3½ inches (9 cm) wide and 8 inches (20 cm) long. Roll your rolling pin over the band ③ to even it and press the layers together, lengthening the band to about 9 to 10 inches (24–28 cm). Then press your rolling pin lengthwise on the center of the band and rock it back and forth to thin the center a little. Let rest in the freezer for 20 minutes to firm it before cutting.

Preheat the oven to 425° F (220° C).

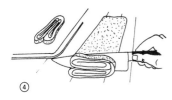

④

4. Cut the band ④ into slices ½ inch (12 mm) thick with your chef's knife, discarding the end slices that aren't evenly layered. Lay the slices on their sides on the baking sheets, separating them by at least 2½ inches (6 cm).

5. One at a time, place each baking sheet in the oven and reduce the temperature to 400° F (200° C). Bake until the cookies begin to brown on the bottoms, about 7 to 10 minutes. Turn the slices upside down, reduce the temperature to 350° F (175° C), and continue baking until the cookies are golden brown on the tops and bottoms with no streaks of white in the centers, about 15 to 20 minutes longer.

6. Slide the cookies onto your countertop using a metal spatula and let cool to room temperature.

➤ **HOWS & WHYS:** The precise shape of the Palm Leaves depends on the length and thickness of the sheet of dough. Our recipe produces an elegant, elongated shape. Rolling out a shorter and/or thicker sheet of dough would produce fatter, rounder cookies. In any case, it is best to make the folds loosely so that the cookies have room to expand at the centers.

STORAGE: Covered airtight in a tin cookie box or cookie jar for up to 2 or 3 days.

Before baking, the cookies can be frozen for up to 1 month: Form the cookies and freeze them on trays, then transfer them to plastic bags. When ready to bake, arrange the frozen cookies on baking sheets and bake immediately, without first defrosting.

PETITE PALM LEAVES
PETITS PALMIERS

Petite Palm Leaves are made in a slightly simpler shape, requiring fewer folds than standard Palm Leaves (page 364). While many of our flaky pastry cookies are fairly large (petits gâteaux size), our Petite Palm Leaves are a petits fours size, making them well suited for a buffet cookie assortment.

EQUIPMENT
3 large, heavy baking sheets

PASTRY DOUGH
Half a *pâton* of Quick Flaky Pastry (page 352)
COUNTERTOP DUSTING
Granulated sugar

For about 70 to 75 cookies

1. Dust your countertop and the Quick Flaky Pastry with sugar, and give the *pâton* 2 final turns as follows: Roll out the flaky pastry perpendicular to the previous turn to about 18 inches (45 cm) long. Fold it in thirds like a letter. Rotate the *pâton* 90° and repeat this rolling and folding operation. Dust with sugar as needed to prevent the dough from sticking to counter or rolling pin. Let rest in the freezer for 30 minutes.

2. Roll out the dough into a rectangular sheet a little larger than 16 by 11 inches (40 by 28 cm) and about 3/16 inch (5 mm) thick. Dust both counter and dough with sugar as needed to prevent sticking. Chill the dough in the freezer whenever it starts to warm and become soft and limp. When finished rolling, let the dough rest in the freezer for 20 minutes to relax before cutting.

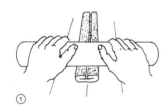

3. Using your chef's knife, trim the short edges of the sheet to make it 16 inches (40 cm) long, and cut it in half crosswise to make two sheets 8 inches (20 cm) wide. Fold the long edges of each sheet so they almost meet in the center, leaving a gap of about 1/4 inch (6 mm). Roll your rolling pin lengthwise over each folded sheet ① of dough to even it, and gently press your rolling pin on the center ② to thin it slightly. Fold each in half like a billfold to form a band of dough about 1 3/4 inches (4 cm) wide. Roll your rolling pin over each band to even it and press the layers together, lengthening the band to about 12 inches (30 cm). Let rest in the freezer for 20 minutes to firm it before cutting.

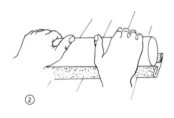

Preheat the oven to 425° F (220° C).

4. Cut the bands ③ into slices 5/16 inch (8 mm) thick with your chef's knife, discarding the end slices that aren't evenly layered. Lay the slices on their sides on the baking sheets, separating them by at least 2 inches (5 cm).

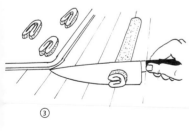

5. One at a time, place each baking sheet in the oven and reduce the temperature to 400° F (200° C). Bake until the cookies begin to brown on the bottoms, about 6 to 8 minutes. Turn the slices upside down, reduce the temperature to 350° F (175° C), and continue baking until the cookies are golden brown on the tops and bottoms with no streaks of white in the centers, about 7 to 10 minutes longer.

6. Slide the cookies onto your countertop using a metal spatula and let cool to room temperature.

➤ **HOWS & WHYS:** Since Petite Palm Leaves have fewer folds than the larger version, they don't require sealing with egg wash to prevent them from opening up too much when they bake.

STORAGE: Covered airtight in a tin cookie box or cookie jar for up to 2 or 3 days.

Before baking, the cookies can be frozen for up to 1 month: Form the cookies and freeze them on trays, then transfer them to plastic bags. When ready to bake, arrange the frozen cookies on baking sheets and bake immediately, without first defrosting.

ARLETTES
ARLETTES

Arlette *is a French girl's name, and we have always suspected that the chef who originated this recipe named it after a special woman in his life—perhaps his wife or daughter. The name is particularly apropos given the shape of these spirals of flaky pastry that, looked at from the right angle, resemble the lowercase letter* a.

EQUIPMENT
2 or 3 large, heavy baking sheets
A metal tube, ¾ inch (2 cm) in diameter and about 12 inches (30 cm) long (see Note)

PASTRY DOUGH
Half a *pâton* of Quick Flaky Pastry (page 352)
COUNTERTOP DUSTING
Granulated sugar

For about 25 cookies

1. Dust your countertop and the Quick Flaky Pastry with sugar, and give the *pâton* 2 final turns as follows: Roll out the flaky pastry perpendicular to the previous turn to about 18 inches (45 cm) long. Fold it in thirds like a letter. Rotate the *pâton* 90° and repeat this rolling and folding operation. Dust with sugar as needed to prevent the dough from sticking to counter or rolling pin. Let rest in the freezer for 30 minutes.

2. Roll out the dough into a sheet a little larger than 10 inches (25 cm) square and about ⅜ inch (1 cm) thick. Dust both counter and dough with sugar as needed to prevent sticking. Chill the dough in the freezer whenever it starts to warm and become soft and limp. When finished rolling, let the dough rest in the freezer for 20 minutes to relax before cutting.

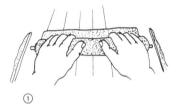
①

3. Using your chef's knife, trim 2 opposite edges of the square to make a sheet 10 inches (25 cm) wide. Loosely roll up this sheet around the metal tube to form a cylinder ①, with the untrimmed edges at the ends and the trimmed edges at the center and outside. Then remove the tube. Place the free end of the rolled sheet under the cylinder and gently roll your rolling pin down the length of the cylinder to flatten and elongate it slightly and press the free end tightly against it. Let rest in the freezer for 20 minutes to firm the dough before cutting.

Preheat the oven to 425° F (220° C).

4. Cut the cylinder ② into slices ⅜ inch (1 cm) thick with your chef's knife. Lay the slices on their sides on the baking sheets, separating them by at least 2 inches (5 cm).

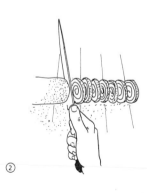
②

5. One at a time, place each baking sheet in the oven and reduce the temperature to 400° F (200° C). Bake until the cookies begin to brown on the bottoms, about 9 to 11 minutes. Turn the slices upside down, reduce the temperature to 350° F (175° C), and continue baking until the cookies are golden brown on the tops and bottoms with no streaks of white in the centers, about 10 to 20 minutes longer.

6. Slide the cookies onto your countertop using a metal spatula and let cool to room temperature.

NOTE: Precut brass tubes are available in hobby shops.

➤ **HOWS & WHYS:** Rolling the sheet of dough around a metal tube, then removing the tube gives the dough enough space to expand in the center. If this were not done, the centers of the cookies would buckle when baked and, not being able to expand, would be heavy and tough. A wooden dowel can't be used in place of the metal tube because the dough sticks to the wood.

STORAGE: Covered airtight in a tin cookie box or cookie jar for up to 2 or 3 days.

Before baking, the cookies can be frozen for up to 1 month: Form the cookies and freeze them on trays, then transfer them to plastic bags. When ready to bake, arrange the frozen cookies on baking sheets and bake immediately, without first defrosting.

STRIPED ARLETTES
ARLETTES ZÉBRÉES

Adding two bold stripes of Chocolate Flaky Pastry between layers of Quick Flaky Pastry emphasizes the vortexlike spiral of Arlettes and transforms this classic into a modern and dramatic cookie.

EQUIPMENT
4 to 6 large, heavy baking sheets
A metal tube, ¾ inch (2 cm) in diameter and about 12 inches (30 cm) long

PASTRY DOUGH
Half a *pâton* of Quick Flaky Pastry (page 352)
Half a *pâton* of Chocolate Flaky Pastry (page 356)
COUNTERTOP DUSTING
Granulated sugar

For about 50 cookies

1. Dust your countertop and the Quick Flaky Pastry with sugar, and roll out this flaky pastry perpendicular to the last turn to about 14 inches (35 cm) long. Fold it in half. This is a half turn. Rotate the *pâton* 90° and roll out the dough to about 14 inches (35 cm) long, but do not fold it. Dust with sugar as needed to prevent the dough from sticking to counter or rolling pin. Slide the Quick Flaky Pastry onto a tray and let rest in the freezer while you roll the Chocolate Flaky Pastry.

2. Dust your countertop and the Chocolate Flaky Pastry with sugar, and roll out the Chocolate Flaky Pastry perpendicular to the last turn to about 14 inches (35 cm) long. Fold it in half. Rotate the *pâton* 90° and roll out the dough to about 14 inches (35 cm) long, but do not fold it. Dust the counter and dough with sugar as need to prevent sticking.

①

3. Take the Quick Flaky Pastry from the freezer. The sheets of plain and Chocolate Flaky Pastry should be about the same size. Roll them with your rolling pin to make them as close to identical as possible. Lay the Quick Flaky Pastry flat on your countertop. Lay the Chocolate Flaky Pastry on the counter, with half of it overlapping the Quick Flaky Pastry and the side edges of the two sheets lined up. Fold the free end of the sheet of Quick Flaky Pastry over the Chocolate Flaky Pastry, then fold the free end of the Chocolate Flaky Pastry over the Quick Flaky Pastry ① making a pad of flaky pastry with 2 plain layers and 2 chocolate layers. This makes 1 full *pâton* of striped flaky pastry. Let it rest in the freezer for 30 minutes.

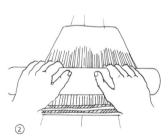

②

4. Roll out the dough into a rectangular sheet ② a little larger than 10 by 20 inches (25 by 50 cm) and about ⅜ inch (1 cm) thick. Dust both counter and dough with sugar as needed to prevent sticking. Chill the dough in the freezer whenever it starts to warm and become soft and limp. When finished rolling, let the dough rest in the freezer for 20 minutes to relax before cutting.

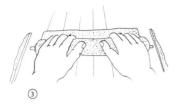

③

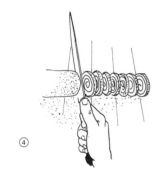

④

5. Using your chef's knife, trim the 2 long edges of the sheet to make a band 10 inches (25 cm) wide. Cut it in half crosswise. Loosely roll up each half around the metal tube ③ to form a cylinder, with the untrimmed edges at the ends and the trimmed edges at the center and outside. Then remove the tube. Place the free end of each rolled sheet under the cylinder and gently roll your rolling pin down the length of the cylinder to flatten and elongate it slightly and press the free end tightly against it. Let rest in the freezer for 20 minutes to firm the dough before cutting.

Preheat the oven to 425° F (220° C).

6. Cut the cylinders ④ into slices ⅜ inches (1 cm) thick with your chef's knife. Lay the slices on their sides on the baking sheets, separating them by at least 2 inches (5 cm). (Or freeze some to bake later.)

7. One at a time, place each baking sheet in the oven and reduce the temperature to 400° F (200° C). Bake until the cookies begin to brown on the bottoms, about 9 to 11 minutes. Turn the slices upside down, reduce the temperature to 350° F (175° C), and continue baking until the cookies are golden brown on the tops and bottoms with no streaks of white in the centers, about 10 to 20 minutes longer. (Judge the color of the plain flaky pastry, not the chocolate layers.)

8. Slide the cookies onto your countertop using a metal spatula and let cool to room temperature.

NOTE: Precut brass tubes are available in hobby shops.

➤ **HOWS & WHYS:** Rolling the sheet of dough around a metal tube, then removing the tube gives the dough enough space to expand in the center. If this were not done, the centers of the cookies would buckle when baked and, not being able to expand, would be heavy and tough. A wooden dowel can't be used in place of the metal tube because the dough sticks to the wood.

STORAGE: Covered airtight in a tin cookie box or cookie jar for up to 2 or 3 days.

Before baking, the cookies can be frozen for up to 1 month: Form the cookies and freeze them on trays, then transfer them to plastic bags. When ready to bake, arrange the frozen cookies on baking sheets and bake immediately, without first defrosting.

FANS
ÉVENTAILS

These are the most elaborate, and probably the least well known, of the cookies made from sugared flaky pastry. They are similar to Palm Leaves (page 364), but they have an additional folded band of flaky pastry inserted in the center. When baked they spread out like fans.

EQUIPMENT
2 or 3 large, heavy baking sheets

PASTRY DOUGH
Half a *pâton* of Quick Flaky Pastry (page 352)
COUNTERTOP DUSTING
Granulated sugar

For about 20 cookies

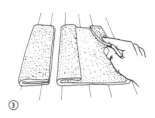

1. Dust your countertop and the Quick Flaky Pastry with sugar, and give the *pâton* 2 final turns as follows: Roll out the flaky pastry perpendicular to the previous turn to about 18 inches (45 cm) long. Fold it in thirds like a letter. Rotate the *pâton* 90° and repeat this rolling and folding operation. Dust with sugar as needed to prevent the dough from sticking to counter or rolling pin. Let rest in the freezer 30 minutes.

2. Roll out the dough into a rectangular sheet a little larger than 10 by 19 inches (25 by 48 cm) and about ³/₁₆ inch (5 mm) thick. Dust both counter and dough with sugar as needed to prevent sticking. Chill the dough in the freezer whenever it starts to warm and become soft and limp. When finished rolling, let the dough rest in the freezer for 20 minutes to relax before cutting.

3. Using your chef's knife, trim the short edges of the sheet to make it 19 inches (48 cm) long. Cut the sheet crosswise ① into 2 rectangles, one 7 by 10 inches (18 by 25 cm) and the other 12 by 10 inches (30 by 25 cm). Fold the small rectangle ② in half lengthwise, making a 3½ by 10-inch (9 by 25 cm) band. Fold the 2 short sides of the large rectangle ③ in 2½ inches (6 cm) toward the center, making a 7 by 10-inch (18 by 25 cm) band. Lay the narrow band on one side of the wide band, with the folded edge of the narrow band extending about ½ inch (12 mm) beyond the folded edge of the wide band. Then fold the wide band in half to enclose the narrow band ④, with the folded edge of the narrow band extending ½ inch (12 mm) beyond both folded edges of the wide band. Gently roll your rolling pin lengthwise over the band ⑤ to even it and press the layers together, elongating it slightly. Chill the band in the freezer for 20 minutes to firm it before cutting.

Preheat the oven to 425° F (220° C).

4. Cut the band into slices ½ inch (12 mm) thick with your chef's

⑤

knife. Lay the slices on their sides on the baking sheets, separating them by at least 2½ inches (6 cm).

5. One at a time, place each baking sheet in the oven and reduce the temperature to 400° F (200° C). Bake until the cookies begin to brown on the bottoms, about 8 to 10 minutes. Turn the slices upside down, reduce the temperature to 350° F (175° C), and continue baking until the cookies are golden brown on the tops and bottoms with no streaks of white in the centers, about 8 to 15 minutes longer.

6. Slide the cookies onto your countertop using a metal spatula and let cool to room temperature.

STORAGE: Covered airtight in a tin cookie box or cookie jar for up to 2 or 3 days.

Before baking, the cookies can be frozen for up to 1 month: Form the cookies and freeze them on trays, then transfer them to plastic bags. When ready to bake, arrange the frozen cookies on baking sheets and bake immediately, without first defrosting.

JAM TARTINES
TARTINES À LA CONFITURE

A tartine *is a buttered slice of bread, and a tartine de confiture is a slice of bread with jam. The latter combination can range from the mundane to the sublime, depending on the quality of the bread and the jam. In our recipe, slices of flaky pastry substitute for the bread, adding an entirely different textural dimension.*

As with Bow Ties (page 360), the flaky pastry is rolled out quite thick for Jam Tartines, so this cookie is also relatively easy to prepare.

EQUIPMENT
2 large, heavy baking sheets

PASTRY DOUGH
Half a *pâton* of Quick Flaky Pastry (page 352)
COUNTERTOP DUSTING
Granulated sugar

FILLING
6 to 8 tablespoons (120 to 160 g) raspberry jam
DECORATION
Confectioners' sugar

For about 20 cookies

1. Dust your countertop and the Quick Flaky Pastry with sugar, and give the *pâton* 2 final turns as follows: Roll out the flaky pastry perpendicular to the previous turn to about 18 inches (45 cm) long. Fold it in thirds like a letter. Rotate the *pâton* 90° and repeat this rolling and folding operation. Dust with sugar as needed to prevent the dough from sticking to counter or rolling pin. Let rest in the freezer for 30 minutes.

2. Roll out the dough about 8 inches (20 cm) square and ¾ inch (2 cm) thick. Dust both counter and dough with sugar as needed to prevent sticking. When finished rolling, let the dough rest in the freezer for 20 minutes to relax before cutting.

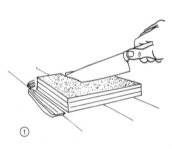
①

3. Using your chef's knife, trim 2 opposite sides of the square to remove the rounded edges from the last turn, reducing it to a band about 6 inches (16 cm) wide. Cut it in half lengthwise ① to make two bands 3 inches (8 cm) wide. Cut these bands crosswise into slices ⅜ inch (1 cm) thick with your chef's knife. Lay the slices on their sides on the baking sheets, separating them by 3 to 3½ inches (8 cm). Let rest in the refrigerator for 30 minutes.

Preheat the oven to 425° F (220° C).

4. One at a time, place each baking sheet in the oven and reduce the temperature to 400° F (200° C). Bake until the cookies begin to brown on the bottoms, about 9 to 12 minutes. Turn them upside down, reduce the temperature to 350° F (175° C), and continue baking until the cookies are golden brown on the tops and bottoms with no streaks of white in the centers, about 8 to 10 minutes longer.

5. Slide the cookies onto your countertop using a metal spatula and let cool to room temperature.

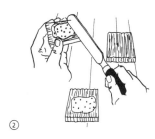

②

6. If the raspberry jam is at all runny, simmer it gently to reduce the excess liquid and then cool before using. One at a time, spread a baked slice of flaky pastry with raspberry jam ② and sandwich it with a second slice of flaky pastry. The slices will have bent slightly while baking. Be sure that both slices are concave side down so that you don't have to use too much jam to fill them.

7. Cut a strip of paper ¾ inch (2 cm) wide and about 12 to 18 inches (30 to 45 cm) long. Arrange several cookies on your counter, with the top and bottom edges adjacent to each other and the side edges lined up. Lay the strip of paper down the center of the cookies. Dust heavily with confectioners' sugar ③. Then carefully remove the strip of paper, leaving a bare strip down the center of each cookie. Repeat with the remaining cookies.

③

➤ **HOWS & WHYS:** It is essential to eliminate all edge effects from the final turn; otherwise, the last fold will prevent the ends of the cookies from expanding when they bake. Before filling with jam these cookies are extremely fragile. Sandwiching two slices with jam makes them reinforce each other.

STORAGE: Covered airtight in a tin cookie box or cookie jar for up to 2 or 3 days.

Before baking, the cookies can be frozen for up to 1 month: Form the cookies and freeze them on trays, then transfer them to plastic bags. When ready to bake, arrange the frozen cookies on baking sheets and bake immediately, without first defrosting.

CHOCOLATE TARTINES
TARTINES CHOCOLAT

I n this variation on the tartines *theme, small slices of flaky pastry have one end dipped in covering chocolate. We think they are an especially nice accompaniment to a dish of coffee ice cream, and like Petite Palm Leaves (page 366), they are a good size for including in a buffet cookie assortment.*

EQUIPMENT
3 large, heavy baking sheets

PASTRY DOUGH
Half a *pâton* of Quick Flaky Pastry (page 352)
COUNTERTOP DUSTING
Granulated sugar

For about 72 cookies

GLAZE
10½ ounces (300 g) European bittersweet chocolate
    (such as Lindt Surfin)
1½ teaspoons (¾ cl) almond oil (preferably) or
    neutral vegetable oil

1. Dust your countertop and the Quick Flaky Pastry with sugar, and give the *pâton* 2 final turns as follows: Roll out the flaky pastry perpendicular to the previous turn to about 18 inches (45 cm) long. Fold it in thirds like a letter. Rotate the *pâton* 90° and repeat this rolling and folding operation. Dust with sugar as needed to prevent the dough from sticking to counter or rolling pin. Let rest in the freezer for 30 minutes.

2. Roll out the dough into a sheet a little larger than 9 inches (24 cm) square and about ⅜ inch (1 cm) thick. Dust both counter and dough with sugar as needed to prevent sticking. When finished rolling, let the dough rest in the freezer for 20 minutes to relax before cutting.

3. Using your chef's knife, trim the sides of the sheet and cut it ① into three bands 3 inches (8 cm) wide. Cut these bands crosswise into slices ⅜ inch (1 cm) thick. Arrange the slices on their sides on the baking sheets, separating them by at least 2 inches (5 cm). Let rest in the refrigerator for 30 minutes.

Preheat the oven to 425° F (220° C).

4. One at a time, place each baking sheet in the oven and reduce the temperature to 400° F (200° C). Bake until the cookies begin to brown on the bottoms, about 9 to 11 minutes. Turn them upside down, reduce the temperature to 350° F (175° C), and continue baking until the cookies are golden brown on the tops and bottoms with no streaks of white in the centers, about 9 to 11 minutes longer.

5. Slide the cookies onto your countertop using a metal spatula and let cool to room temperature.

6. Temper the chocolate with the almond oil as follows: Melt the chocolate ② and stir in the almond oil. Dip the bottom of the pot of choc-

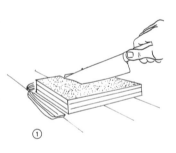

①

②

olate in a bowl of cold water and stir the chocolate until it begins to thicken. Immediately remove from the cold water and dip the bottom of the pot of chocolate in a bowl of hot water. Stir over the hot water just long enough to make the chocolate fluid again, then remove from the hot water.

7. Dip one end of each cookie ③ in the chocolate, clean off the excess on the edge of the pot, and place the cookies on a sheet of wax paper. Let the chocolate set.

➤ **HOWS & WHYS:** As with Jam Tartines, the baked slices of flaky pastry are very fragile. Here the chocolate coating on one end stabilizes the layers.

STORAGE: Covered airtight in a tin cookie box or cookie jar for up to 2 or 3 days in a cool place—below 70° F (20° C).

Before baking, the cookies can be frozen for up to 1 month: Form the cookies and freeze them on trays, then transfer them to plastic bags. When ready to bake, arrange the frozen cookies on baking sheets and bake immediately, without first defrosting.

FLAKY WANDS
ARLÉSIENNES

An Arlésienne *is a woman from the city of Arles in Provence. The cookie is probably named after Alphonse Daudet's* L'Arlésienne, *for which Georges Bizet wrote the incidental music. In this drama, everyone talks about the woman, but she is never seen.*

These cookies are formed by twisting long strips of sugared flaky pastry into corkscrew shapes. Some chefs prefer to call them baguettes feuilletées, *which, while not as musical as* arlésiennes, *provides our more descriptive English translation.*

EQUIPMENT
2 or 3 large, heavy baking sheets

PASTRY DOUGH
Half a *pâton* of Quick Flaky Pastry (page 352)
COUNTERTOP DUSTING
Granulated sugar

For about 35 cookies

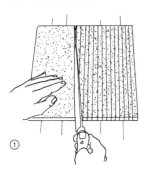
①

1. Dust your countertop and the Quick Flaky Pastry with sugar, and give the *pâton* 2 final turns as follows: Roll out the flaky pastry perpendicular to the previous turn to about 18 inches (45 cm) long. Fold it in thirds like a letter. Rotate the *pâton* 90° and repeat this rolling and folding operation. Dust with sugar as needed to prevent the dough from sticking to counter or rolling pin. Let rest in the freezer for 30 minutes.

2. Roll out the dough into a rectangular sheet a little larger than 8 by 14 inches (20 by 35 cm) and about 5/16 inch (8 mm) thick. Dust both counter and dough with sugar as needed to prevent sticking. Chill the dough in the freezer whenever it starts to warm and become soft and limp. When finished rolling, let the dough rest in the freezer for 20 minutes to relax before cutting.

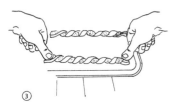
②

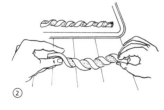
③

3. Using your chef's knife, trim the long edges of the sheet to make a band 8 inches (20 cm) wide. Cut the band crosswise ① into strips 3/8 inch (1 cm) wide and 8 inches (20 cm) long. Take the ends of each strip and give it 3 full twists ② to make a long corkscrew shape. Arrange the corkscrews on the baking sheets, separating them by about 1 inch (2½ cm). Gently press the ends of the corkscrews on the baking sheet ③ to anchor them. Let rest in the refrigerator for 30 minutes.

Preheat the oven to 425° F (220° C).

4. One at a time, place each baking sheet in the oven and reduce the temperature to 400° F (200° C). Bake until the cookies begin to brown on the bottoms, about 6 to 9 minutes. Turn the corkscrews upside down, reduce the temperature to 350° F (175° C), and continue baking until the cookies are golden brown on the tops and bottoms and the centers are lightly colored with no streaks of white, about 10 to 20 minutes longer.

5. Slide the cookies onto your countertop using a metal spatula and let cool to room temperature.

➤ **HOWS & WHYS:** Twisted flaky pastry has a tendency to untwist when baked. Slightly overtwisting, pressing the ends of the strips on the baking sheet, and letting the twisted strips rest before baking all help counter this tendency. But these cookies have enough twists that even if they do untwist a little it isn't a problem.

STORAGE: Covered airtight in a tin cookie box or cookie jar for up to 2 or 3 days.

Before baking, the cookies can be frozen for up to 1 month: Form the cookies and freeze them on trays, then transfer them to plastic bags. When ready to bake, arrange the frozen cookies on baking sheets and bake immediately, without first defrosting.

STRIPED FLAKY WANDS
ARLÉSIENNES ZÉBRÉES

Two stripes of Chocolate Flaky Pastry surrounded by stripes of Quick Flaky Pastry emphasize the rhythmic twists of these wands. This is a cookie that, while not exceptionally difficult, looks like it must have been made by a professional.

EQUIPMENT

4 to 6 large, heavy baking sheets

COUNTERTOP DUSTING

Granulated sugar

PASTRY DOUGH

Half a *pâton* of Quick Flaky Pastry (page 352)
Half a *pâton* of Chocolate Flaky Pastry (page 356)

For about 70 cookies

1. Dust your countertop and the Quick Flaky Pastry with sugar, and roll out this flaky pastry perpendicular to the previous turn to about 15 inches (38 cm) long. Do not fold it yet. Now roll it out in the other direction to make a sheet about 15 inches (38 cm) square. Dust with sugar as needed to prevent the dough from sticking to counter or rolling pin. Slide the sheet of Quick Flaky Pastry onto a tray and let rest in the freezer while you roll out the Chocolate Flaky Pastry.

2. Dust your countertop and the Chocolate Flaky Pastry with sugar, and roll out the Chocolate Flaky Pastry perpendicular to the previous turn to about 13 inches (33 cm) long. Fold it in half. This is a half turn. Rotate the *pâton* 90° and roll out the dough to about 14 inches (35 cm) long, but do not fold it. Dust with sugar as needed to prevent sticking. The band of Chocolate Flaky Pastry should be about 7 to 7½ inches (18 to 19 cm) wide. If necessary, roll it to widen it to this dimension.

3. Take the Quick Flaky Pastry from the freezer. Lay the band of Chocolate Flaky Pastry on top of the sheet of Quick Flaky Pastry ① so that it almost covers half the plain sheet, with a long edge of the chocolate band centered on one edge of the plain sheet. Fold over the uncovered half of the plain sheet ② to enclose the chocolate band. Then fold in half crosswise ③ to make a pad of flaky pastry with 4 plain layers and 2 chocolate layers. This makes 1 full *pâton* of striped flaky pastry. Let it rest in the freezer for 30 minutes.

4. Roll out the dough into a rectangular sheet a little larger than 16 by 14 inches (40 by 35 cm) and about 5/16 inch (8 mm) thick. Dust both counter and dough with sugar as needed to prevent sticking. Chill the dough in the freezer whenever it starts to warm and become soft and limp. When finished rolling, let the dough rest in the freezer for 20 minutes to relax before cutting.

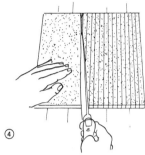

5. Using your chef's knife, trim the long edges of the sheet, and cut it in half lengthwise to make 2 bands, each about 8 by 14 inches (20 by 35 cm). Cut each band crosswise ④ into strips ⅜ inch (1 cm) wide and 8 inches (20 cm) long. Take the ends of each strip and give it 3 full twists ⑤ to make a long corkscrew shape. Arrange the corkscrews on the baking sheets, separating them by about 1 inch (2½ cm). Gently press the ends of the corkscrews on the baking sheet ⑥ to anchor them. Let rest in the refrigerator for 30 minutes. (Or freeze some to bake later.)

Preheat the oven to 425° F (220° C).

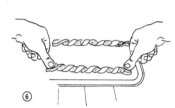

6. One at a time, place each baking sheet in the oven and reduce the temperature to 400° F (200° C). Bake until the cookies begin to brown on the bottoms, about 6 to 9 minutes. Turn the corkscrews upside down, reduce the temperature to 350° F (175° C), and continue baking until the cookies are golden brown on the tops and bottoms and the centers are lightly colored with no streaks of white, about 10 to 20 minutes longer. (Judge the color of the plain flaky pastry, not the chocolate layers.)

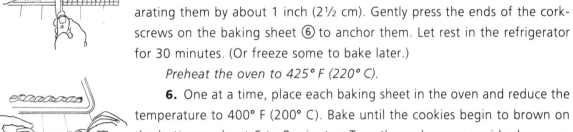

7. Slide the cookies onto your countertop using a metal spatula and let cool to room temperature.

➤ **HOWS & WHYS:** Twisted flaky pastry has a tendency to untwist when baked. Slightly overtwisting, pressing the ends of the strips on the baking sheet, and letting the twisted strips rest before baking all help counter this tendency. But these cookies have enough twists that even if they do untwist a little it isn't a problem.

NOTE: If you prefer not to make a full *pâton* of Striped Flaky Wands, you can roll out the *pâton* of striped flaky pastry perpendicular to the last turn to about 8 by 16 inches. Then cut it in half crosswise and use one half in this recipe (rolling it out to one 8 by 14-inch, or 20 by 35 cm, band to make about 35 cookies) and the other half in Striped Bow Ties (page 362).

STORAGE: Covered airtight in a tin cookie box or cookie jar for up to 2 or 3 days.

Before baking, the cookies can be frozen for up to 1 month: Form the cookies and freeze them on trays, then transfer them to plastic bags. When ready to bake, arrange the frozen cookies on baking sheets and bake immediately, without first defrosting.

SACRISTANS
SACRISTAINS

~~~~~~~

These corkscrew-shaped cookies, coated with crunchy chopped almonds and sparkling crystal sugar, are named for the official in charge of the sacred vessels in the Roman Catholic church. In contrast to Flaky Wands (page 378), the flaky pastry is rolled on flour rather than sugar for the last two turns and final rolling, so that sweetness is provided only by the crystal sugar on the surface. Sacristans are also shorter than Flaky Wands, and their size and striking appearance make them ideal for a buffet cookie assortment or as an accompaniment to serve with tea.

EQUIPMENT

2 or 3 large, heavy baking sheets

PASTRY DOUGH

Half a *pâton* of Quick Flaky Pastry (page 352)

COUNTERTOP DUSTING

Flour

DECORATION

1 large egg, lightly beaten

5¼ ounces (150 g), or 1 cup, blanched almonds, finely chopped

5¼ ounces (150 g), or ¾ cup, crystal sugar

For about 80 cookies

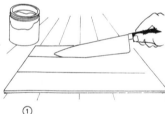

①

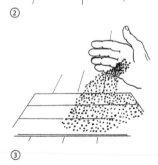

②

③

1. Dust your countertop and the Quick Flaky Pastry with flour, and give the *pâton* 2 final turns as follows: Roll out the flaky pastry perpendicular to the previous turn to about 18 inches (45 cm) long. Fold it in thirds like a letter. Rotate the *pâton* 90° and repeat this rolling and folding operation. Dust with flour as needed to prevent the dough from sticking to counter or rolling pin. Let rest in the freezer for 30 minutes.

2. Roll out the dough into a rectangular sheet a little larger than 12 by 16 inches (30 by 40 cm) and about ³⁄₁₆ inch (5 mm) thick. Dust both counter and dough with flour as needed to prevent sticking. Chill the dough in the freezer whenever it starts to warm and become soft and limp. When finished rolling, let the dough rest in the freezer for 20 minutes to relax before cutting.

3. Using your chef's knife, trim the sides of the sheet and cut it lengthwise ① into three 4 by 16-inch (10 by 40 cm) bands, leaving the bands adjacent to each other. Brush the bands well ② with beaten egg. Mix the chopped almonds and crystal sugar and dust a little more than half of it over the bands ③. Gently roll your rolling pin lengthwise over the bands to make the almonds and sugar adhere. Turn the bands upside down, placing them adjacent to each other again and collecting the almonds and sugar that fall off. Brush the second sides of the bands with egg wash and dust them with all of the remaining almonds and sugar. Roll the rolling pin lengthwise over the 3 bands.

4. Cut the bands crosswise into strips ⅝ inch (1½ cm) wide. Take the ends of each strip and give it 3 half twists ④ to make a short corkscrew shape. Arrange the corkscrews on the baking sheets, separating them by about 1 inch (2½ cm). Gently press the ends of the corkscrews on the baking sheet to anchor them. Let rest in the refrigerator for 30 minutes.

Preheat the oven to 425° F (220° C).

5. One at a time, place each baking sheet in the oven and reduce the temperature to 400° F (200° C). Bake until the cookies begin to brown on the bottoms, about 8 to 12 minutes. Turn the corkscrews upside down, reduce the temperature to 350° F (175° C), and continue baking until the cookies are golden brown on the tops and bottoms with no streaks of white in the centers, about 10 to 20 minutes longer.

6. Slide the cookies onto your countertop using a metal spatula and let cool to room temperature.

➤ **HOWS & WHYS:** The twisted strips of flaky pastry have a tendency to untwist a little when they bake. Since these cookies have only 1½ twists, it is important to minimize this tendency. To do so, overtwist each strip slightly, press both ends of each cookie onto the baking sheet (but not so firmly as to tear the dough), and be sure to respect the 30-minute rest period before baking.

STORAGE: Covered airtight in a tin cookie box or cookie jar for up to 2 or 3 days.

Before baking, the cookies can be frozen for up to 1 month: Form the cookies and freeze them on trays, then transfer them to plastic bags. When ready to bake, arrange the frozen cookies on baking sheets and bake immediately, without first defrosting.

MATCHSTICKS
ALLUMETTES

These are strips of flaky pastry glazed with royal icing. The dough is rolled on flour, and the only sugar comes from the crisp icing on top. We particularly enjoy their delicate flakiness and understated sweetness with a bowl of fresh berries.

EQUIPMENT

4 or 5 large, heavy baking sheets
Two ⅛-inch- (3 mm) thick spacers (see page 431)

PASTRY DOUGH

Half a *pâton* of Quick Flaky Pastry (page 352)
COUNTERTOP DUSTING
Flour

ROYAL ICING

3 tablespoons (4½ cl) lightly beaten egg white, at room temperature
6 ounces (170 g), or 1¼ cups plus 3 tablespoons, confectioners' sugar
¼ teaspoon (1 ml) distilled white vinegar

For about 45 to 50 cookies

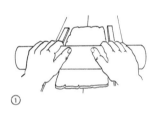

①

1. Dust your countertop and the Quick Flaky Pastry with flour, and give the *pâton* 2 final turns as follows: Roll out the flaky pastry perpendicular to the previous turn to about 18 inches (45 cm) long. Fold it in thirds like a letter. Rotate the *pâton* 90° and repeat this rolling and folding operation. Dust with flour as needed to prevent the dough from sticking to counter or rolling pin. Let rest in the freezer for 30 minutes.

2. Roll out the dough into a rectangular sheet a little larger than 20 by 16 inches (50 by 40 cm) and about ⅛ inch (3 mm) thick. Dust both counter and dough with flour as needed to prevent sticking. The dough must have a uniform thickness, so use spacers ①. Chill the dough in the freezer whenever it starts to warm and become soft and limp. When finished rolling, let the dough rest in the freezer for 20 minutes to relax before cutting.

3. Using your chef's knife, trim the sides of the sheet and cut it in fourths lengthwise to make four bands 4 inches (10 cm) wide. Gather together the trimmings and save them for Flaky Trimmings Dough (page 355). Lay the bands of flaky pastry flat on a baking sheet or tray and chill them in the freezer (but do not let them freeze).

4. Place the egg white in your electric mixer. Sift the confectioners' sugar and gradually stir it into the egg white. When all of the sugar has been added, beat at medium speed with the flat beater for 15 minutes to make the mixture light and thick, like a meringue. It will form soft peaks when you lift the beater. Add the vinegar and continue beating a little longer. This is royal icing.

5. Lightly brush the baking sheets with cold water.

6. One at a time, take each band of flaky pastry from the freezer and lay it on your countertop. Brush the band to remove any flour. Spread the

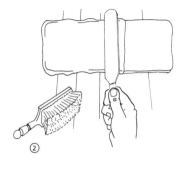

top with a thin layer of royal icing. Smooth it with your palette knife by sweeping in one long, even motion ② down the length of the band, slowly rotating the blade as you go to remove the excess icing. Trim the edges with your chef's knife, dipping it in flour between cuts to prevent sticking. Then cut the band ③ into strips 1½ inches (4 cm) wide, dipping your chef's knife in flour between each cut. Carefully lift the strips, one at a time, with a metal spatula, and arrange them on the baking sheets, separating them by at least 1 inch (2½ cm). Let rest in the refrigerator until the royal icing forms a crust on top, at least 30 minutes.

Preheat the oven to 425° F (220° C).

7. One at a time, place each baking sheet in the oven on the bottom rack, reduce the temperature to 400° F (200° C), and bake until the tops of the strips barely begin to brown around the edges, about 4 to 6 minutes. Reduce the temperature to 350° F (175° C) and continue baking until the tops are beige and there are no streaks of white left on the edges, about 20 to 25 minutes longer.

8. Slide the strips onto a wire rack using a metal spatula and let them cool to room temperature.

➤ **HOWS & WHYS:** The bands of flaky pastry must be thoroughly chilled before spreading the royal icing or they will soften and stretch while you are spreading it. All flour must be brushed off so that the icing does not separate from the pastry when it bakes. Allowing the royal icing to form a crust on top before baking gives it a nice shiny appearance when baked. It is especially important to reduce the oven temperature as soon as the tops of the cookies show the slightest bit of browning because the icing caramelizes and burns very easily.

VARIATIONS: Matchsticks are identical to Condés (page 386), except for the glaze. You can use half a *pâton* of flaky pastry to make half a recipe of each. As a variation for Matchsticks or Condés, slit the cookies in half horizontally after baking and fill them with a little raspberry jam.

STORAGE: Covered airtight in a tin cookie box or cookie jar for up to 2 or 3 days. The tops are very fragile.

Before baking, the cookies can be frozen for up to 1 month: Form the cookies and freeze them on trays, then transfer them to plastic bags. When ready to bake, arrange the frozen cookies on baking sheets and bake immediately, without first defrosting.

CONDÉS

CONDÉS

~~~~~

The princes of Condé *were descended from a branch of the French royal family and owned the castle of Chantilly. The most illustrious prince of this line was Louis II de Bourbon, called* Le Grand Condé. *He was a formidable general and military strategist who in 1643, at the age of twenty-two, commanded the French Army against the Spanish forces in northern France, and in his victory at Rocroy began the long period of French military supremacy in Western Europe. In his later years he became devoted to literature and surrounded himself with a brilliant circle, including Molière, Racine, and La Fontaine. Condé entertained on a lavish scale, and King Louis XIV was the guest of honor at one of his more famous banquets. His maître d'hôtel was Vatel, who invented crème chantilly (sweetened whipped cream), and his pastry chef was Feuillet, one of the principal innovators in the development of flaky pastry doughs.*

The cookies called Condés may well have been created by Feuillet for his employer. They are identical to Matchsticks (page 384) except that they have finely chopped almonds added to the royal icing on top and are dusted with confectioners' sugar. The texture of almonds is not apparent, but they make the glaze thicker and give the cookies a subtle yet distinctive almond taste.

EQUIPMENT
4 or 5 large, heavy baking sheets
Two ⅛-inch- (3 mm) thick spacers (see page 431)

PASTRY DOUGH
Half a *pâton* of Quick Flaky Pastry (page 352)
COUNTERTOP DUSTING
Flour

ROYAL ICING
2 large egg whites, at room temperature
8 ounces (225 g), or 1¾ cups plus 3 tablespoons,
   confectioners' sugar
¼ teaspoon (1 ml) distilled white vinegar
1 ounce (30 g), or 3 tablespoons plus 1 teaspoon,
   blanched almonds, very finely chopped
DECORATION
Confectioners' sugar for dusting

For about 45 to 50 cookies

1. Dust your countertop and the Quick Flaky Pastry with flour, and give the *pâton* 2 final turns as follows: Roll out the flaky pastry perpendicular to the previous turn to about 18 inches (45 cm) long. Fold it in thirds like a letter. Rotate the *pâton* 90° and repeat this rolling and folding operation. Dust with flour as needed to prevent the dough from sticking to counter or rolling pin. Let rest in the freezer for 30 minutes.

2. Roll out the dough into a rectangular sheet a little larger than 20 by 16 inches (50 by 40 cm) and about ⅛ inch (3 mm) thick. Dust both counter and dough with flour as needed to prevent sticking. The dough must have a uniform thickness, so use spacers ①. Chill the dough in the freezer whenever it starts to warm and become soft and limp. When finished rolling, let the dough rest in the freezer for 20 minutes to relax before cutting.

3. Using your chef's knife, trim the sides of the sheet and cut it in

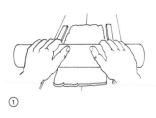

①

fourths lengthwise to make four bands 4 inches (10 cm) wide. Gather together the trimmings and save them for Flaky Trimmings Dough (page 355). Lay the bands of flaky pastry flat on a baking sheet or tray and chill them in the freezer (but do not let them freeze).

4. Place the egg whites in your electric mixer. Sift the confectioners' sugar and gradually stir it into the egg whites. When all of the sugar has been added, beat at medium speed with the flat beater for 15 minutes to make the mixture light and thick, like a meringue. It will form soft peaks when you lift the beater. Add the vinegar and continue beating a little longer. This is royal icing. Stir in the chopped almonds with the flat beater.

5. Lightly brush the baking sheets with cold water.

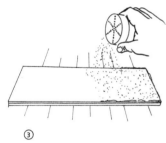

6. One at a time, take each band of flaky pastry from the freezer and lay it on your countertop. Brush the band to remove any flour. Spread the top with a layer of royal icing. Smooth it with your palette knife by sweeping in a long, even motion ② down the length of the band, slowly rotating the blade as you go to remove the excess icing. Dust the band heavily ③ with confectioners' sugar. Trim the edges with your chef's knife, dipping it in flour between cuts to prevent sticking. Then cut the band ④ into strips 1½ inches (4 cm) wide, dipping your chef's knife in flour between each cut. Carefully lift the strips, 1 at a time, with a metal spatula, and arrange them on the baking sheets, separating them by at least 1 inch (2½ cm). Let rest in the refrigerator for 30 minutes.

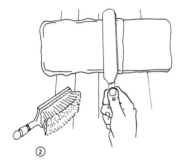

Preheat the oven to 425° F (220° C).

7. One at a time, place each baking sheet in the oven on the bottom shelf, reduce the temperature to 400° F (200° C), and bake until the tops of the strips barely begin to brown around the edges, about 4 to 6 minutes. Reduce the temperature to 350° F (175° C) and continue baking until the tops are beige and there are no streaks of white left on the edges, about 20 to 25 minutes longer.

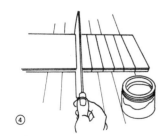

8. Slide the strips onto a wire rack using a metal spatula and let them cool to room temperature.

➤ **HOWS & WHYS:** The bands of flaky pastry must be thoroughly chilled before spreading the royal icing or they will soften and stretch while you are spreading it. All flour must be brushed off so that the icing does not separate from the pastry when it bakes. It is especially important to reduce the oven temperature as soon as the tops of the cookies show the slightest

(continued)

bit of browning because the icing caramelizes and burns very easily. Note that the royal icing on this pastry is thicker than that for Matchsticks because here it contains chopped almonds.

VARIATIONS: You can use half a *pâton* of flaky pastry to make half a recipe of Condés and half a recipe of Matchsticks (page 384). As a variation for both Matchsticks and Condés, you can slit the cookies in half horizontally after baking and fill them with a little raspberry jam.

STORAGE: Covered airtight in a tin cookie box or cookie jar for up to 2 or 3 days. The tops are very fragile.

Before baking, the cookies can be frozen for up to 1 month: Form the cookies and freeze them on trays, then transfer them to plastic bags. When ready to bake, arrange the frozen cookies on baking sheets and bake immediately, without first defrosting.

SUGARED MATCHSTICKS
ALLUMETTES SUCRÉES

For this variation on Matchsticks (page 384), the flaky pastry is given the last two turns and final rolling on sugar, and the royal icing is omitted. Sugared Matchsticks are less subtle than classic Matchsticks, but they are also easier to make and their more overt sweetness and crunch make them a favorite with children.

EQUIPMENT
2 large, heavy baking sheets

PASTRY DOUGH
Half a *pâton* of Quick Flaky Pastry (page 352)

For 66 cookies

COUNTERTOP DUSTING
Granulated sugar
TOPPING
1 egg, lightly beaten
3½ ounces (100 g), or ½ cup, granulated sugar

1. Dust your countertop and the Quick Flaky Pastry with sugar, and give the *pâton* 2 final turns as follows: Roll out the flaky pastry perpendicular to the previous turn to about 18 inches (45 cm) long. Fold it in thirds like a letter. Rotate the *pâton* 90° and repeat this rolling and folding operation. Dust with sugar as needed to prevent the dough from sticking to counter or rolling pin. Let rest in the freezer for 30 minutes.

2. Roll out the dough into a rectangular sheet ① a little larger than 13 by 21 inches (33 by 54 cm) and about ⅛ inch (3 mm) thick. Dust both

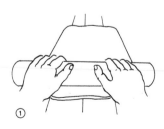
①

counter and dough with sugar as needed to prevent sticking. Chill the dough in the freezer whenever it starts to warm and become soft and limp.

3. Cut the sheet in half crosswise using your chef's knife. Lay each rectangle on one of the baking sheets. Brush each rectangle with beaten egg ②. Dust the top of each evenly with granulated sugar ③. Let rest in the refrigerator for 30 minutes.

Preheat the oven to 425° F (220° C).

4. Using your chef's knife, trim (but do not remove) the edges of each sheet to get a rectangle 13 inches (33 cm) long and 10½ inches (27 cm) wide. Cut each rectangle lengthwise into three bands 3½ inches (9 cm) wide, and then crosswise ④ into 1⅛-inch (3 cm) strips, without separating them.

5. One at a time, place each baking sheet in the oven and reduce the temperature to 400° F (200° C). Bake until the cookies puff up and the tops crack, about 5 to 8 minutes. Then, before the bottoms of the cookies start to brown, reduce the oven to 350° F (175° C). Continue baking until the cookies are light brown and crusty on the tops, a rich golden brown on the bottoms, and lightly colored on the edges, about 18 to 24 minutes longer.

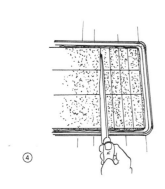

6. Separate the cookies and slide them onto your countertop using a metal spatula, then let cool to room temperature.

➤ **HOWS & WHYS:** Unlike the other cookies for which the flaky pastry is rolled on sugar, these are not turned upside down part way through the baking. To avoid excess browning or burning of the bottoms, it is therefore essential that the oven temperature be reduced before the bottoms begin to brown.

STORAGE: Covered airtight in a tin cookie box or cookie jar for up to 2 or 3 days.

Before baking, the cookies can be frozen for up to 1 month: After cutting, freeze directly on the baking sheets, and then cover in large plastic bags. Do not defrost before baking.

FLAKY TURNOVERS
CHAUSSONS FEUILLETÉS

We use apricot jam to fill these small turnovers, but you could equally well substitute another fruit. The jam keeps the insides of Flaky Turnovers moist and makes them more luscious than the plain flaky pastry cookies. Chausson *is the French word for slipper and refers to the turnover's shape.*

EQUIPMENT
2 large, heavy baking sheets

PASTRY DOUGH
Half a *pâton* of Quick Flaky Pastry (page 352)
COUNTERTOP DUSTING
Flour

FILLING
½ cup to ½ cup plus 1 tablespoon (160 to 180 g)
     apricot jam

SEALING AND GLAZE
1 large egg, lightly beaten
Confectioners' sugar

For about 25 cookies

1. Dust your countertop and the Quick Flaky Pastry with flour, and give the *pâton* 2 final turns as follows: Roll out the flaky pastry perpendicular to the previous turn to about 18 inches (45 cm) long. Fold it in thirds like a letter. Rotate the *pâton* 90° and repeat this rolling and folding operation. Dust with flour as needed to prevent the dough from sticking to counter or rolling pin. Let rest in the freezer for 30 minutes.

2. Roll out the dough into a sheet a little larger than 18 inches (45 cm) square and about ⅛ inch (3 mm) thick. Dust both counter and dough with flour as needed to prevent sticking. Chill the dough in the freezer whenever it starts to warm and become soft and limp. When finished rolling, let the dough rest in the freezer for 20 minutes to relax before cutting.

3. Using a plain round pastry cutter, cut from the sheet about 25 circles ①, each 3½ inches (9 cm) in diameter. Gather together the trimmings and save them for Flaky Trimmings Dough (page 355).

4. Stack the circles on a tray in piles of 4 to 6, and chill them briefly in the freezer so they will not be limp and will be easy to handle.

5. If there are large pieces of fruit in the jam, cut them up with a knife. Brush a band ½ inch (12 mm) wide around the outside of each circle with beaten egg ②. Spoon about 1 teaspoon (½ cl) of jam in the center of each, and fold over the pastry to enclose the jam. Press the edges with your fingertips to seal with egg wash, and firmly press the rim of a glass or the rolled top edge of a small round pastry cutter on the dough just outside of the jam filling ③ to reinforce the seal.

6. Lightly brush the baking sheets with cold water. Turn the filled pastry rounds upside down and arrange them on the sheets, separating them by about 1 inch (2½ cm). Lightly brush the tops of the pastries with

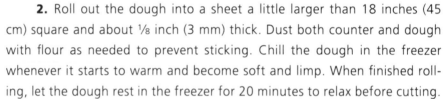

④

beaten egg, being careful not to get any egg wash on the sealed edges. Let rest in the refrigerator for 30 minutes.

Preheat the oven to 450° F (230° C).

7. Lightly brush the tops of the pastries a second time with egg wash. Use the tip of your paring knife to score the top of each pastry ④ in a sunburst pattern, drawing 5 lines radiating out from the center of the straight, folded edge to the round edge. Hold the blade of the paring knife at a sharp angle in order to cut deeply into the top layer of pastry without cutting through to the jam inside.

8. Bake, 1 sheet at a time, until the bottoms of the cookies begin to brown, about 10 to 12 minutes. Reduce the temperature to 375° F (190° C), and continue baking until the cookies are golden brown on the tops with no streaks of white in the edges, about 10 to 15 minutes longer.

9. Remove the cookies from the oven and turn on the broiler.

10. Dust the tops of the cookies with confectioners' sugar until they are white. Return them to the oven, on the top or second from top shelf, until the sugar melts and turns golden brown. Rotate the baking sheet as needed to prevent burning, and transfer the cookies to a wire rack using a metal spatula as they are finished.

11. Let the cookies cool on the wire rack.

➤ **HOWS & WHYS:** The confectioners' sugar glaze is not absolutely necessary, but it gives the cookies a more attractive, shiny surface. Another alternative is to glaze them by brushing with 30° Be heavy syrup when they come out of the oven (see the recipe for Almond Turnovers, page 394, for details).

STORAGE: Covered airtight in a tin cookie box or cookie jar for up to 2 or 3 days.

Before baking, the cookies can be frozen for up to 1 month: Form the cookies, brush twice with egg wash, and score the tops. Freeze them on trays, then transfer to plastic bags. When ready to bake, arrange the frozen cookies on baking sheets and bake immediately, without first defrosting.

KALISYS

KALISYS

These cookies are formed by spreading an almond filling on squares of flaky pastry and folding the corners to the center. When baked the corners stand up, revealing a cross of almond filling. The cross is then enhanced with a glaze of red currant jelly. The name kalisys is not French, and its origin is obscure. Whatever its history, the red cross on top suggests that this was originally an Easter pastry.

EQUIPMENT
2 large, heavy baking sheets

PASTRY DOUGH
Half a *pâton* of Quick Flaky Pastry (page 352)
COUNTERTOP DUSTING
Flour
FILLING
2 ounces (60 g), or 4 tablespoons, unsalted butter, softened
1 large egg
1 tablespoon (1½ cl) lightly beaten egg white

4½ ounces (130 g), or ¾ cup plus 3½ tablespoons, almond and sugar powder
Basic Preparation, page 482:
2¼ ounces (65 g), or ¼ cup plus 3 tablespoons, blanched almonds
2¼ ounces (65 g), or ½ cup plus 2 teaspoons, confectioners' sugar
½ ounce (15 g), or 1 tablespoon plus 2 teaspoons, all-purpose flour
GLAZE AND DECORATION
1 egg, lightly beaten
3 to 3½ tablespoons (40 g) crystal sugar
3 tablespoons (60 g) red currant jelly

For about 25 cookies

①

②

1. Dust your countertop and the Quick Flaky Pastry with flour, and give the *pâton* 2 final turns as follows: Roll out the flaky pastry perpendicular to the previous turn to about 18 inches (45 cm) long. Fold it in thirds like a letter. Rotate the *pâton* 90° and repeat this rolling and folding operation. Dust with flour as needed to prevent the dough from sticking to counter or rolling pin. Let rest in the freezer for 30 minutes.

2. Place the butter in a small stainless-steel bowl and beat with a wooden spatula, warming it over low heat as needed, until smooth, white, and creamy. Stir the egg and egg white into the almond and sugar powder ① with a wooden spatula. Sift the flour and mix it in. Then stir in the butter. Do not beat or the filling will separate.

3. Roll out the dough into a sheet a little larger than 16 inches (40 cm) square and about ⁵⁄₃₂ inch (4 mm) thick. Dust both counter and dough with flour as needed to prevent sticking. Chill the dough in the freezer whenever it starts to warm and become soft and limp. When you have finished rolling the dough, prick it all over with a fork and then let it rest in the freezer for 20 minutes to relax before cutting.

4. Using your chef's knife, trim the sheet to a 16-inch (40 cm) square. Gather together the trimmings and save them for Flaky Trimmings Dough (page 355). Fold the square in half and cut it ② perpendicular to the fold into five bands 3¼ inches (8 cm) wide. Unfold the bands and cut them into 3¼-inch (8 cm) squares.

5. Stack the squares on trays in piles of 4 to 6, and chill them briefly in the freezer so they will not be limp and will be easy to handle.

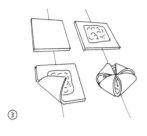

6. Spread 2 teaspoons (1 cl) of almond filling on each square. Fold all 4 corners to the center ③, with the edges meeting. Firmly press the center with your fingertip ④. Arrange the filled squares next to each other, 5 by 5 in a square. Lay a sheet of wax paper on top and gently roll your rolling pin over them ⑤ to flatten slightly.

7. Lightly brush the baking sheets with cold water. Arrange the squares on the baking sheets, separating them by about 1 inch (2½ cm). Lightly brush the tops of the pastries with beaten egg. Let rest in the refrigerator for 30 minutes.

Preheat the oven to 400° F (200° C).

8. Lightly brush the tops of the pastries a second time with egg wash. Dust the tops of the folded corners ⑥ with crystal sugar, trying not to allow much of the sugar to get in the cracks.

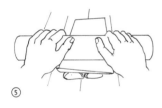

9. Bake, 1 sheet at a time, until the bottoms of the cookies are browned, the corners have opened and turned golden brown, there are no streaks of yellow left on the edges, and the almond filling on the tops is a uniform beige, about 25 to 30 minutes.

10. Slide the cookies onto a wire rack using a metal spatula and let them cool to room temperature.

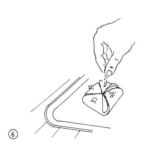

11. Force the currant jelly through a fine sieve. Brush the almond filling on each cookie with jelly to form a cross. The almond filling will absorb some jelly; if necessary, brush it a second time so the cross glistens.

➤ **HOWS & WHYS:** The folded corners of this pastry must open up to reveal the almond filling, but at the same time they must contain the filling so that it doesn't spill out onto the baking sheet. Pressing the corners with your fingertip and then rolling over the top with a rolling pin accomplishes the desired result.

STORAGE: Covered airtight in a tin cookie box or cookie jar for up to 2 or 3 days.

Before baking, the cookies can be frozen for up to 1 month: Form the cookies, brush twice with egg wash, and sprinkle with crystal sugar. Freeze them on trays, then transfer to plastic bags. When ready to bake, arrange the frozen cookies on baking sheets and bake immediately, without first defrosting.

ALMOND TURNOVERS
DENTELLES AUX AMANDES

These are related to Flaky Turnovers (page 390), but here the pastry dough is cut in squares instead of circles and filled with raw almond paste rather than jam. The edge of each cookie is cut at closely spaced intervals to produce a toothlike effect, which is the origin of the name. In modern French, dentelle means ''lace,'' but it derives from dent, the French word for ''tooth.''

EQUIPMENT
2 large, heavy baking sheets

PASTRY DOUGH
Half a *pâton* of Quick Flaky Pastry (page 352)
COUNTERTOP DUSTINGS
Flour
Confectioners' sugar
FILLING
1 large egg white
1 tablespoon (20 g) strained apricot jam
   [*Basic Preparation*, page 484]

7 ounces (200 g), or 1½ cups, almond and sugar powder
{ *Basic Preparation*, page 482:
   3½ ounces (100 g), or ⅔ cup, blanched almonds
   3½ ounces (100 g), or ¾ cup plus 4 teaspoons, confectioners' sugar
SEALING AND GLAZE
1 large egg, lightly beaten
1 ounce (25 g), or 2 tablespoons, sugar
1 tablespoon (1½ cl) water

For about 30 cookies

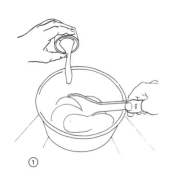
①

②

1. Dust your countertop and the Quick Flaky Pastry with flour, and give the *pâton* 2 final turns as follows: Roll out the flaky pastry perpendicular to the previous turn to about 18 inches (45 cm) long. Fold it in thirds like a letter. Rotate the *pâton* 90° and repeat this rolling and folding operation. Dust with flour as needed to prevent the dough from sticking to counter or rolling pin. Let rest in the freezer for 30 minutes.

2. Mix the egg white and apricot jam into the almond and sugar powder ① to make an uncooked almond paste for the filling.

3. Roll out the dough into a rectangular sheet a little larger than 16 by 19 inches (40 by 48 cm) and about ⅛ inch (3 mm) thick. Dust both counter and dough with flour as needed to prevent sticking. Chill the dough in the freezer whenever it starts to warm and become soft and limp. When finished rolling, let the dough rest in the freezer for 20 minutes to relax before cutting.

4. Using your chef's knife, trim the sheet to a rectangle 16 by 19 inches (40 by 48 cm). Gather together the trimmings and save them for Flaky Trimmings Dough (page 355). Fold the rectangle in half crosswise and cut it ② perpendicular to the fold into five bands 3¼ inches (8 cm) wide. Cut the bands into 3¼-inch (8 cm) squares. Separate the 2 layers and, for the squares with the folds, unfold and cut in half.

5. Stack the squares on a tray in piles of 4 to 6 and chill them briefly in the freezer so they will not be limp and will be easy to handle.

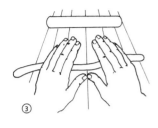

③

④

⑤

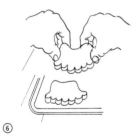

⑥

6. Dust your countertop and the almond paste with confectioners' sugar, and roll the almond paste under your palms to make a long even cylinder. Cut the cylinder into 3 equal pieces. Roll each piece under your palms ③, dusting with confectioners' sugar as needed, to elongate it to about 25 inches (60 cm). Cut each piece into ten pieces 2½ inches (6 cm) long.

7. Brush a band ½ inch (12 mm) wide around the outside of each flaky pastry square with beaten egg. Lay a piece of almond paste down the center ④ of each and fold over the pastry to enclose the filling. Press the edges with your fingertips to seal with the egg wash. Cut slits ¼ inch (6 mm) long through the long sealed edges ⑤ at ⅜-inch (1 cm) intervals using your paring knife.

8. Lightly brush the baking sheets with cold water. Gently bend each pastry ⑥ to open up the slits, and arrange them on the baking sheets, separating them by about 1 inch (2½ cm). Lightly brush the tops of the pastries with beaten egg, being careful not to get any egg wash on the sealed edges. Let rest in the refrigerator for 30 minutes.

Preheat the oven to 450° F (230° C).

9. Lightly brush the tops of the pastries a second time with egg wash.

10. Bake, 1 sheet at a time, until the bottoms of the cookies begin to brown, about 10 to 12 minutes. Reduce the temperature to 375° F (190° C), and continue baking until the cookies are golden brown with no streaks of white in the edges, about 10 to 15 minutes longer.

11. While the cookies are baking, combine the sugar and water in a butter melter and bring to a boil, stirring occasionally to dissolve the sugar. Then remove from the heat.

12. Brush the tops of the hot cookies with this syrup until they are shiny, using only as much syrup as necessary. Slide the cookies onto a wire rack using a metal spatula and let them cool to room temperature.

➤ **HOWS & WHYS:** Instead of glazing with syrup, Almond Turnovers can be glazed in the same way as Flaky Turnovers (page 390) by dusting the tops with confectioners' sugar and then running them under the broiler. With the confectioners' sugar method, it is more difficult to get them evenly glazed, but when done well the result is superior. A simpler alternative is to omit the sugar glaze entirely.

(continued)

VARIATION: A larger version of this pastry can be made by filling long bands (rather than squares) of flaky pastry with raw almond paste. After slitting the edge, the bands are bent into semicircular arcs. These resemble the lace collars that women once wore on their dresses and are called *collerettes*. They are cut into several pieces after baking.

STORAGE: Covered airtight in a tin cookie box or cookie jar for up to 2 or 3 days.

Before baking, the cookies can be frozen for up to 1 month: Form the cookies and brush twice with egg wash. Freeze them on trays, then transfer to plastic bags. When ready to bake, arrange the frozen cookies on baking sheets and bake immediately, without first defrosting.

DARTOIS
DARTOIS

Here is a bar cookie made by sandwiching an almond cream filling between two bands of flaky pastry. The name is an abbreviation of gâteau d'artois. Artois is the northernmost region of France, bordering on the English Channel and Belgium.

The subtle sweetness and rich almond and butter flavor of Dartois make it an ideal choice to serve with a bottle of fine Sauternes or Barsac.

EQUIPMENT
1 large, heavy baking sheet

PASTRY DOUGH
Half a *pâton* of Quick Flaky Pastry (page 352)
COUNTERTOP DUSTING
Flour
FILLING
2 large egg yolks
1½ ounces (40 g), or 3 tablespoons, unsalted butter, barely melted
1½ tablespoons (2 cl) dark Jamaican rum

7 ounces (200 g), or 1½ cups, almond and sugar powder
 ⎱ Basic Preparation, page 482:
 ⎰ 3½ ounces (100 g), or ⅔ cup, blanched almonds
 ⎱ 3½ ounces (100 g), or ¾ cup plus 4 teaspoons, confectioners' sugar
SEALING AND GLAZE
1 egg, lightly beaten
2 tablespoons (25 g) sugar
1 tablespoon (1½ cl) water

For 20 cookies

1. Dust your countertop and the Quick Flaky Pastry with flour, and give the *pâton* 2 final turns as follows: Roll out the flaky pastry perpendicular to the previous turn to about 18 inches (45 cm) long. Fold it in thirds like a letter. Rotate the *pâton* 90° and repeat this rolling and folding operation. Dust with flour as needed to prevent the dough from sticking to counter or rolling pin. Let rest in the freezer for 30 minutes.

2. Roll out the dough into a rectangular sheet a little larger than 20 by 16 inches (50 by 40 cm) and about ⅛ inch (3 mm) thick. Dust both counter and dough with flour as needed to prevent sticking. Chill the dough in the freezer whenever it starts to warm and become soft and limp. When finished rolling, let the dough rest in the freezer for 20 minutes to relax before cutting.

3. Combine the egg yolks, butter, and rum in a bowl and gradually stir in the almond and sugar powder with a wooden spatula ① to make the almond cream filling.

4. Using your chef's knife, trim the long edges of the sheet and cut it in fourths lengthwise to make four bands 4 inches (10 cm) wide. Cut the ends to the length of your baking sheet (preferably about 18 inches or 45 cm). Gather together the trimmings and save them for Flaky Trimmings Dough (page 355).

①

(continued)

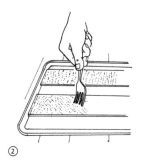

②

③

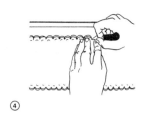

④

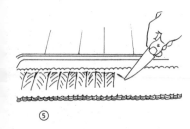

⑤

⑥

5. Lightly brush the baking sheet with cold water. Arrange 2 of the bands on the baking sheet about 2 inches (5 cm) apart. (Keep the other 2 bands chilled in the refrigerator until you are ready to use them.) Prick the bands on the baking sheet all over with a fork ②. Brush a border of beaten egg ¾ inch (2 cm) wide around all 4 sides of each band. Spread the almond cream filling evenly within the egg wash borders ③ using a palette knife. One at a time, take each of the remaining 2 bands from the refrigerator and drape it over one of the bands on the baking sheet, carefully lining up the edges. Press the borders all the way around with your fingertips to seal with the egg wash. Trim the edges with your chef's knife to make them straight.

6. Make toothlike indentations at ⅜-inch (1 cm) intervals along both long edges of each band ④ by pressing the back edge of a paring knife against the edge of the pastry at the same time as you press 2 fingers of your other hand on the border on either side of the knife to hold the pastry in place. Lightly brush the tops of the 2 bands with beaten egg. Let rest in the refrigerator for 30 minutes.

Preheat the oven to 450° F (230° C).

7. Lightly brush the tops of the 2 bands a second time with egg wash. Lightly score the tops of the bands crosswise with the tip of your paring knife, starting about 1¼ inches (3 cm) in from each end and then dividing the remainder into 10 equal strips, each about 1⅝ inches (4 cm) wide. Make a couple of slits through each score mark to let steam escape. Next, decorate the top of each strip with a chevron pattern ⑤ by scoring it with the tip of the paring knife. Hold the blade at a sharp angle and cut deeply into the top layer of pastry without piercing it through to the filling.

8. Place the baking sheet in the oven, reduce the temperature to 425° F (220° C), and bake until the tops of the bands brown lightly, about 10 to 13 minutes. Reduce the temperature to 350° F (175° C) and continue baking until the tops are a uniform golden brown and there are no streaks of white left on the edges, about 25 to 30 minutes longer.

9. While the bands are baking, combine the sugar and water in a butter melter and bring to a boil, stirring occasionally to dissolve the sugar. Then remove from the heat.

10. Brush the tops of the hot bands with this syrup ⑥ until they are shiny, using only as much syrup as necessary. Slide the bands onto a wire rack using a metal spatula and let them cool to room temperature.

THE FRENCH COOKIE BOOK

11. Cut off the ends of both bands, and cut the remainder of the bands crosswise into 10 equal strips at the score marks. To make each cut, first saw through the top layer of pastry with a bread knife, then cut through the bottom layer with your chef's knife.

➤ **HOWS & WHYS:** Instead of glazing with syrup, Dartois can be glazed in the same way as Flaky Turnovers (page 390) by dusting the tops with confectioners' sugar and running them under the broiler. However, it is difficult to get them evenly glazed and there is always unmelted sugar left in the deep score marks, so glazing with syrup is easier. The syrup used is the standard 30° Be heavy syrup.

STORAGE: Covered airtight in a tin cookie box or cookie jar for up to 2 or 3 days.

Before baking, the cookies can be frozen for up to 1 month: After brushing the second time with egg wash and decorating the top layer, freeze directly on the baking sheet, then take the bands off the baking sheet and seal in plastic bags. When ready to bake, arrange the frozen bands on baking sheets and bake immediately, without first defrosting.

VENETIAN BLINDS
JALOUSIES

For this bar cookie, apricot jam is sandwiched between two bands of flaky pastry. The top layer is slit crosswise at closely spaced intervals, and the slits open during baking to resemble venetian blinds.

EQUIPMENT
1 large, heavy baking sheet

PASTRY DOUGH
Half a *pâton* of Quick Flaky Pastry (page 352)
COUNTERTOP DUSTING
Flour

FILLING
¾ cup (240 g) apricot jam
SEALING AND GLAZE
1 egg, lightly beaten
DECORATION
2 tablespoons (40 g) strained apricot jam
    [*Basic Preparation,* page 484]
2 tablespoons (25 g) crystal sugar

For 20 cookies

1. Dust your countertop and the Quick Flaky Pastry with flour, and give the *pâton* 2 final turns as follows: Roll out the flaky pastry perpendicular to the previous turn to about 18 inches (45 cm) long. Fold it in thirds like a letter. Rotate the *pâton* 90° and repeat this rolling and folding operation. Dust with flour as needed to prevent the dough from sticking to counter or rolling pin. Let rest in the freezer for 30 minutes.

2. Roll out the dough into a rectangular sheet a little larger than 20 by 16 inches (50 by 40 cm) and about ⅛ inch (3 mm) thick. Dust both counter and dough with flour as needed to prevent sticking. Chill the dough in the freezer whenever it starts to warm and become soft and limp. When finished rolling, let the dough rest in the freezer for 20 minutes to relax before cutting.

3. Using your chef's knife, trim the long edges of the sheet and cut it in fourths lengthwise to make four bands 4 inches (10 cm) wide. Cut the ends to the length of your baking sheet (preferably about 18 inches or 45 cm). Gather together the trimmings and save them for Flaky Trimmings Dough (page 355).

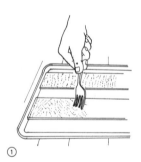

4. Lightly brush the baking sheet with cold water. Arrange 2 of the bands on the baking sheet about 2 inches (5 cm) apart. (Keep the other 2 bands chilled in the refrigerator until you are ready to use them.) Prick the bands on the baking sheet all over with a fork ①. Brush a border of beaten egg ¾ inch (2 cm) wide around all 4 sides of each band. Spread the apricot jam evenly within the egg wash borders ② using a palette knife. One at a time, take each of the remaining 2 bands from the refrigerator and drape it over one of the bands on the baking sheet, carefully lining up the edges. Press the borders all the way around with your fingertips to seal with egg wash. Trim the edges with your chef's knife to make them straight.

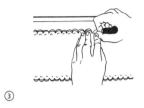

③

5. Make toothlike indentations at ⅜-inch (1 cm) intervals along both long edges of each band by pressing the back edge of a paring knife against the edge of the pastry ③ at the same time as you press 2 fingers of your other hand on the border on either side of the knife to hold the pastry in place. Lightly brush the tops of the 2 bands with beaten egg. Let rest in the refrigerator for 30 minutes.

Preheat the oven to 450° F (230° C).

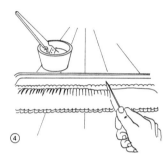

④

6. Lightly brush the tops of the 2 bands a second time with egg wash. Using your paring knife, make crosswise slits through the pastry ④ covering the jam at ⅜-inch (1 cm) intervals, leaving a ¾-inch (2 cm) border uncut on all 4 sides.

7. Place the baking sheet in the oven, reduce the temperature to 425° F (220° C), and bake until the tops of the bands brown lightly, about 9 to 11 minutes. Reduce the temperature to 350° F (175° C) and continue baking until the tops are a uniform golden brown and there are no streaks of white left on the edges, about 25 to 30 minutes longer.

8. Slide the bands onto a wire rack using a metal spatula and let them cool to room temperature.

⑤

9. Warm the strained apricot jam over low heat, stirring occasionally, until melted. Lightly brush the tops of the bands with the jam. Dust a border ½ inch (12 mm) wide on both long edges of each band with crystal sugar ⑤.

10. Cut off the ends of both bands, and cut the remainder of the bands crosswise into 10 equal strips, each about 1½ inches (3½–4 cm) wide. To make each cut, first saw through the top layer of pastry with a bread knife, then cut through the bottom layer with your chef's knife.

➤ **HOWS & WHYS:** In addition to being decorative, the slits in the top layer of pastry allow steam to escape so that the pastry bakes evenly, without a large hollow air space above the jam.

STORAGE: Covered airtight in a tin cookie box or cookie jar for up to 2 or 3 days.

Before baking, the cookies can be frozen for up to 1 month: After brushing the second time with egg wash and slitting the top layer, freeze directly on the baking sheet, then take the bands off the baking sheet and seal in plastic bags. When ready to bake, arrange the frozen bands on baking sheets and bake immediately, without first defrosting.

LITTLE CHAMPIGNYS
PETITS CHAMPIGNYS

Champigny is a small city on the Marne River about 20 kilometers east of Paris. This bar cookie sandwiches raspberry jam between two sheets of Flaky Trimmings Dough, the pastry dough made from flaky pastry trimmings. After baking it is cut into squares.

EQUIPMENT
1 large, heavy baking sheet

PASTRY DOUGH
1¾ pounds (800 g) Flaky Trimmings Dough (page 355)

COUNTERTOP DUSTING
Flour

FILLING
7 ounces (200 g) raspberry jam
SEALING AND GLAZE
1 egg, lightly beaten
Confectioners' sugar

For 24 cookies

①

②

③

1. Dust your countertop and the Flaky Trimmings Dough with flour, and roll out the dough into a rectangular sheet a little larger than 16 by 24 inches (40 by 60 cm) and about ⅛ inch (3 mm) thick. Dust the counter and dough with flour as needed to prevent the dough from sticking to counter or rolling pin. Chill the dough in the freezer whenever it starts to warm and become soft and limp. When finished rolling, let the dough rest in the freezer for 20 minutes to relax before cutting.

2. Using your chef's knife, trim the edges of the sheet of dough and cut it in half crosswise to make two 12 by 16-inch (30 by 40 cm) rectangles.

3. Lightly brush the baking sheet with cold water. Place one rectangle of dough on the baking sheet. (Keep the other one chilled in the refrigerator until you are ready to use it.) Prick the dough on the baking sheet all over with a fork ①. Brush a border ② of beaten egg ¾ inch (2 cm) wide around all 4 sides of the dough. Spread the raspberry jam evenly within the egg wash border ③ using a palette knife. Take the remaining rectangle from the refrigerator and drape it over the rectangle ④ on the baking sheet, carefully lining up the edges. Press the border all the way around with your fingertips ⑤ to seal with the egg wash. Lightly brush the top with beaten egg. Let rest in the refrigerator for 30 minutes.

Preheat the oven to 425° F (220° C).

4. Lightly brush the top a second time with egg wash. Prick the top all over with a fork in closely spaced, even rows. Make small slits all over the top ⑥ with the tip of a paring knife to let steam escape.

5. Place the baking sheet in the oven, reduce the temperature to 400° F (200° C), and bake until the top of the pastry is a rich, uniform golden brown, with no streaks of white on the edges, about 40 to 45 minutes.

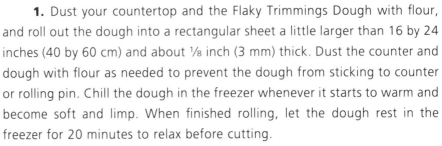
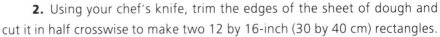
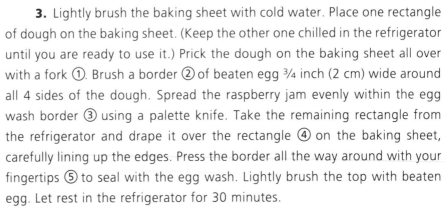
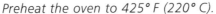

④

⑤

⑥

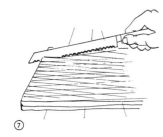

⑦

6. Remove the baking sheet from the oven and turn on the broiler.

7. Dust the top of the pastry with confectioners' sugar until it is white. Return it to the oven, on the top or second from top shelf, until the sugar melts and turns golden brown. Rotate the baking sheet as needed to prevent burning.

8. Slide the pastry onto a wire rack using a metal spatula and let cool to room temperature.

9. Cut off all 4 sides of the pastry, and cut the remainder into 24 squares, each about 2 inches (5 cm) on a side. To make each cut, first saw through the top layer of pastry ⑦ with a bread knife, then cut through the bottom layer with your chef's knife.

➤ **HOWS & WHYS:** If the top layer of pastry is not pricked and slit thoroughly, the pastry will puff up in a dome and will not bake evenly.

This recipe requires a large quantity of Flaky Trimmings Dough. If you don't have enough, you could cut the recipe in half, rolling out the dough to 12 by 16 inches (30 by 40 cm) to make one filled sheet 8 by 12 inches (20 by 30 cm). After baking, trim the sheet and cut it into 12 equal squares.

STORAGE: Covered airtight in a tin cookie box or cookie jar for up to 2 or 3 days.

Before baking, the cookies can be frozen for up to 1 month: After brushing a second time with egg wash and pricking and slitting the top, freeze directly on the baking sheet, and then cover in a large plastic bag. Do not defrost before baking.

FLORÉALS
FLORÉALS

During the French Revolution, the Gregorian calendar was replaced with a newly devised Republican calendar. The eighth month of this calendar, from April 20–21 to May 19–20, was called Floréal, the month of flowers. While the Republican calendar was not a great success (the Gregorian calendar was restored in 1806), several enduring gastronomic creations have been named for its months (another is Thermidor).

The cookies called Floréals are similar to Little Champignys (page 402), but they have an almond cream filling. They are thicker than Little Champignys and therefore are cut into smaller squares.

EQUIPMENT
1 large, heavy baking sheet

PASTRY DOUGH
1¾ pounds (800 g) Flaky Trimmings Dough (page 355)

COUNTERTOP DUSTING
Flour

FILLING
2 large egg yolks
1½ ounces (40 g), or 3 tablespoons, unsalted butter, barely melted
1½ teaspoons (¾ cl) vanilla extract

7 ounces (200 g), or 1½ cups, almond and sugar powder
    Basic Preparation, page 482:
    3½ ounces (100 g), or ⅔ cup, blanched almonds
    3½ ounces (100 g), or ¾ cup plus 4 teaspoons, confectioners' sugar

SEALING
1 egg, lightly beaten

GLAZE
3 tablespoons (60 g) strained apricot jam [*Basic Preparation*, page 484]

DECORATION
1 ounce (25 g), or 3 tablespoons, unsalted pistachios, finely chopped
2 tablespoons (25 g) crystal sugar

For 35 cookies

①

②

1. Dust your countertop and the Flaky Trimmings Dough with flour, and roll out the dough into a rectangular sheet a little larger than 16 by 24 inches (40 by 60 cm) and about ⅛ inch (3 mm) thick. Dust the counter and dough with flour as needed to prevent the dough from sticking to counter or rolling pin. Chill the dough in the freezer whenever it starts to warm and become soft and limp. When finished rolling, let the dough rest in the freezer for 20 minutes to relax before cutting.

2. Combine the egg yolks, butter, and vanilla in a bowl and gradually stir in the almond and sugar powder with a wooden spatula to make the almond cream filling. If the filling is too thick to spread evenly, stir in a little more egg yolk or a little water.

3. Using your chef's knife, trim the edges of the sheet of dough and cut it in half crosswise to make two 12 by 16-inch (30 by 40 cm) rectangles.

4. Lightly brush the baking sheet with cold water. Place one rectangle of dough on the baking sheet. (Keep the other one chilled in the refrigerator until you are ready to use it.) Prick the dough on the baking sheet all over

③

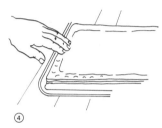

④

⑤

⑥

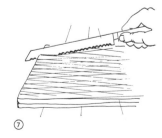

⑦

with a fork. Brush a border ① of beaten egg ¾ inch (2 cm) wide around all 4 sides. Spread the almond cream filling evenly within the egg wash border ② using a palette knife. Take the other rectangle from the refrigerator and drape it ③ over the one on the baking sheet, carefully lining up the edges. Press the border all the way around with your fingertips ④ to seal with the egg wash. Let rest in the refrigerator for 30 minutes.

Preheat the oven to 425° F (220° C).

5. Prick the top all over with a fork in closely spaced, even rows. Make small slits all over the top ⑤ with the tip of a paring knife to let steam escape.

6. Place the baking sheet in the oven, reduce the temperature to 400° F (200° C), and bake until the top of the pastry is a rich, uniform golden brown, with no streaks of white on the edges, about 35 to 40 minutes.

7. Slide the pastry onto a wire rack using a metal spatula and let cool to room temperature.

8. Warm the apricot jam over low heat, stirring occasionally, until melted. Brush the top of the pastry with the jam.

9. Mix the pistachios and crystal sugar. Dust them ⑥ evenly over the top of the pastry.

10. Cut off all 4 sides of the pastry, and cut the remainder into 35 squares, each about 1½ inches (4 cm) on a side. To make each cut, first saw through the top layer of pastry ⑦ with a bread knife, then cut through the bottom layer with your chef's knife.

➤ **HOWS & WHYS:** Since this cookie is glazed with jam, it does not need to be brushed with egg wash before baking.

This recipe requires a large quantity of Flaky Trimmings Dough. If you don't have enough, you could cut the recipe in half, rolling out the dough to 12 by 16 inches (30 by 40 cm) to make 1 filled sheet 8 by 12 inches (20 by 30 cm). After baking and decorating, trim the sheet and cut it into 15 equal squares.

STORAGE: Covered airtight in a tin cookie box or cookie jar for up to 2 or 3 days.

Before baking, the cookies can be frozen for up to 1 month: After brushing a second time with egg wash and pricking and slitting the top, freeze directly on the baking sheet, and then cover in a large plastic bag. Do not defrost before baking.

PARISIAN NOUGAT
NOUGAT PARISIEN

This bar cookie is totally different from the other cookies in this chapter. A band of Flaky Trimmings Dough, with edges formed into a rim, is filled with apricot jam and covered with sliced almonds. When it is baked, the jam bubbles up and the almonds sink into it, producing a chewy nougat. The word nougat was taken into French from the Provençal language and ultimately derives from the Latin word nux for "nut."

EQUIPMENT
1 large, heavy baking sheet

PASTRY DOUGH
9 ounces (250 g) Flaky Trimmings Dough (page 355)
COUNTERTOP DUSTING
Flour

For about 8 cookies

①

②

③

FILLING, SEALING, AND GLAZES
6 tablespoons (120 g) strained apricot jam
[*Basic Preparation*, page 484]
2 ounces (60 g), or ½ cup plus 2 tablespoons, sliced almonds
1 egg, lightly beaten

1. Dust your countertop and the Flaky Trimmings Dough with flour, and roll out the dough into a rectangular sheet a little larger than 5 by 17 inches (13 by 43 cm) and about ⅛ inch (3 mm) thick. Dust the counter and dough with flour as needed to prevent the dough from sticking to counter or rolling pin. Chill the dough in the freezer whenever it starts to warm and become soft and limp. When finished rolling, let the dough rest in the freezer for 20 minutes to relax before trimming.

2. Using your chef's knife, trim the edges of the sheet to make a band 5 by 17 inches (13 by 43 cm). Brush a border 1 inch (2½ cm) wide around the edge of the band with beaten egg. Fold over the edge to form a rim (the technique is called *videler*) as follows: Start at one corner and take the border of the band between the thumb and index finger of your right hand. Fold over a segment of the border about ⅝ inch (16 mm) long and ⅝ inch (16 mm) wide, twisting it ① slightly clockwise, and press it firmly onto the band. Hold this segment down with the index finger of your left hand. Moving about ⅝ inch (16 mm) to the right, take the next segment of border between thumb and index and fold it over, twisting it slightly clockwise to make a diagonal pleat on the left. Press this segment firmly onto the band, with the pleat overlapping the previous fold. Continue all the way around the edge ② of the band. Press the entire border down firmly with your fingertips to be sure it is folded and sealed securely. The band of pastry will now have a diagonally pleated rim ⅝ inch (16 mm) wide.

3. Prick the bottom of the band inside the rim all over with a fork, and place it on the baking sheet. Spread 5 tablespoons (100 g) of the apricot jam evenly inside the rim ③ using a palette knife. Cover the jam with the almonds ④. Lightly brush the rim with beaten egg.

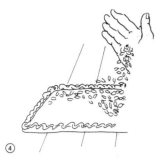

4. Let rest in the refrigerator for 30 minutes.

Preheat the oven to 400° F (200° C).

5. Lightly brush the rim of pastry a second time with egg wash.

6. Place the baking sheet in the oven, reduce the temperature to 350° F (175° C), and bake until the almonds sink into the jam and brown lightly on top, the jam bubbles up and begins to darken very slightly, and the rim is golden brown, about 40 to 45 minutes.

7. Slide the pastry onto a wire rack using a metal spatula and let cool to room temperature.

8. Warm the remaining apricot jam over low heat, stirring occasionally, until melted. Lightly brush the tops of the almonds with the jam.

9. Cut off the ends of the band, and cut the remainder of the band crosswise into strips 1⅝ inches (4 cm) wide. To make each cut, first saw through the almonds with a bread knife, then cut through the pastry below with your chef's knife.

➤ **HOWS & WHYS:** When you scatter the almonds over the jam, there will be more almonds than would adhere at this point. But they will sink into the jam, and after baking there will be several layers of almonds embedded in the jam. The diagonal pleats in the rim give it a twisted, ropelike appearance after baking.

STORAGE: Covered airtight in a tin cookie box or cookie jar for up to 2 or 3 days.

REFERENCE

EQUIPMENT

Knowing *your equipment and how to use it will make cookie baking easier and more enjoyable. This chapter presents a fairly comprehensive guide to the cookie makers' arsenal. Most of the equipment we recommend is sold at cookware shops throughout the country. We have provided mail order sources for any items that might be difficult to locate if you don't have a good cookware shop in your vicinity.*

BAKING SHEETS AND COOKIE SHEETS. Good baking sheets are essential for successful cookie making. They should be large to accommodate as many cookies as possible, heavy gauge (thick) to conduct heat well and promote even baking, and have a low rim to allow easy removal of baked cookies.

The maximum size of your baking sheets is determined by the size of your oven. For proper air circulation in the oven, there must be at least 1 to 1½ inches (2½–4 cm) between the baking sheet and the oven wall on all sides. Standard home ovens should accommodate at least a 12 by 16-inch (30 by 40 cm) baking sheet.

The best baking sheets are about ¹/₁₆ inch (1½ mm) thick and are made from either black steel or aluminum. Tinned steel is not good for baking sheets because the tin has a low melting point—about 450° F (230° C).

French black steel baking sheets are our favorite. All four sides and corners of these baking sheets are enclosed by a gently sloping rim about ¼ inch (6 mm) high. They are available in two sizes suitable for home ovens: 12 by 16 inches (30 by 40 cm) and 13 by 20 inches (33 by 50 cm). At the factory they are coated with oil to protect the surface during shipping. Before using a baking sheet for the first time, wipe off this oil and season the sheet with a neutral vegetable oil as follows: Coat the entire surface of the baking sheet with oil using a paper towel. Heat it in a 350° F (175° C) oven until the oil just begins to smoke. Then let it cool, and wipe off the excess oil with a paper towel. These baking sheets should never be washed because they can rust easily. There should always be a thin film of oil on the surface to protect it and to help prevent cookies from sticking. After each use, scrape the baking sheet clean with a dough scraper. If food still sticks to the surface, remove it by using coarse kosher salt as an abrasive and rubbing it with a paper towel dipped in vegetable oil. Occasionally, the baking sheets should be seasoned again, following the same procedure as for a new baking sheet, to maintain a thin film of oil on the surface.

We also like the polished aluminum Toroware cookie sheets made by Leyse.

These have low sloping rims on the two short ends but are open on the two long ends, making it very easy to slide cookies off. They are available in two sizes: 12 by 15 inches (30 by 38 cm) and 14 by 17 inches (35 by 43 cm).

Whichever baking sheets you choose, you should have several of them. Few recipes are so small that all of the cookies can be baked on one sheet. Also, some cookies require double sheeting, or placing an empty baking sheet underneath the sheet of cookies in order to protect the bottoms of the cookies. If you don't have enough baking sheets for an entire recipe, then fill as many baking sheets as you have available; after baking the first batch, cool and clean them before proceeding to bake the remaining cookies.

Sources: La Cuisine, Dean & DeLuca, The Peppercorn.

BAKING SHEET PREPARATION. The baking sheets can be prepared in several ways, depending on the cookies you are baking. Cookies made from pastry doughs are baked on clean (seasoned, but not buttered or otherwise prepared) baking sheets if the butter content in the dough is high enough to prevent sticking after baking. For pastry doughs with lower butter content, the baking sheets should be brushed with melted butter to prevent sticking. Before baking, on the other hand, you don't want the cookies sliding around on the baking sheet. With a buttered baking sheet this is not a problem. However, with a clean baking sheet it can be, particularly if the cookies will be brushed with egg wash before baking. In this case, the problem can often be eliminated by brushing the baking sheet lightly with cold water—just enough to make the unbaked cookies stick to it.

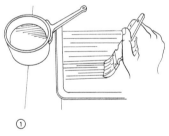
①

For cookies made from batters, there are more possibilities for preparing the baking sheets. These cookies will stick to an ungreased baking sheet after baking, so baking on a clean (unprepared) baking sheet is not an option. To avoid sticking, brush the baking sheets ① with melted butter. Using a pastry brush allows you to coat the baking sheets evenly and gives you the best control over how heavily the butter is applied. (However, if you don't have a pastry brush, you can always coat the baking sheet with softened butter using a paper towel.) The more likely a particular cookie is to stick to the baking sheet, the more heavily you should coat the baking sheet in order to avoid this unfortunate result. On the other hand, when you pipe some very thick batters on a buttered baking sheet, you want only a very light film of butter on the baking sheet so that the batter will not slip around as you pipe it. To produce this film of butter, first brush a very light coating of butter on the baking sheet, and then wipe the baking sheet with a clean paper towel to remove all but the barest trace of butter.

Many cookie batters have a tendency to spread and lose their shape if they

are baked on buttered baking sheets. This problem can be overcome by dusting the buttered baking sheets with flour ②. In addition to preventing the cookies from spreading too much, the flour and butter form a light crust on the bottoms of the cookies. First brush a uniform coating of melted butter over the surface of the baking sheet. Spoon flour over the butter, adding more than will be needed to coat it. Then tilt, shake, and tap the baking sheet to distribute the flour and coat the butter evenly. Once a thin layer of flour covers the butter, no more will adhere. Invert the baking sheet and tap the bottom sharply with a wooden spoon ③ to dislodge the excess flour.

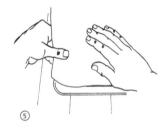

Another method of preparing the baking sheets is to line them with kitchen parchment. In most cases, a parchment lined baking sheet is more or less equivalent to a buttered and floured baking sheet, and the two can be used interchangeably. The parchment is less work, but more costly than butter and flour. We often prefer it for cookies that are brushed after baking (while still on the baking sheet) with apricot jam followed by a confectioners' sugar and water glaze, for cookies dusted with almonds or crystal sugar, for some particularly fragile cookies that cool on the baking sheets, and for a number of cookies (notably those based on almond paste) that contain no flour and for which a butter and sugar crust on the bottom would be undesirable. To line a baking sheet with parchment, first brush the edges and diagonals of the baking sheet with melted butter ④. Cut the sheet of parchment to size. Then place it on the baking sheet and press it on the butter to hold it in place ⑤. Alternatively, if you have French black steel baking sheets with a low turned up lip around the edges, then you can place the uncut sheet of parchment directly on the baking sheet, press it on the butter to hold it in place, and trim off the excess by running the back edge of your chef's knife over the paper around the edge of the baking sheet.

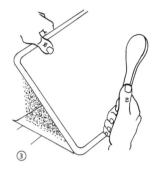

Finally, for macaroons and many other cookies made from almond paste batters, the baking sheets are lined with newsprint and the cookies are steamed off the newsprint after baking. These techniques are explained in detail in Chapter 3 (see page 126).

BONBON CUPS. Pleated paper cups are made in a variety of sizes for use as liners in molds (most frequently cupcake and gem pans), for baking without molds, and for presenting chocolates and other candies. They are available in prints, solid colors, and foils. The smallest size, called bonbon cups ⑥, are ⅝ inch (16 mm) deep and about 1 inch (2½ cm) wide across the bottom. They are perfect for baking several different cookies in the meringue and almond paste chapters. Gem pan liners (or "minicups") are ¾ inch (2 cm) deep and 1⅜ inches (3½ cm) across the bottom; we use them for baking miniature fruitcakes.

Source: Maid of Scandinavia.

BOWLS. We recommend stainless-steel mixing bowls for nearly all purposes in cookie making. They are durable, don't react with foods, and transfer heat quickly. They are available in every size you could possibly need, from 1 cup (2½ dl) up. For whipping egg whites, a copper bowl is best, but not a necessity (see **COPPER BOWLS** in this section, and Chapter 2, page 56).

BOWL SCRAPERS. These are similar to rubber spatulas, but they don't have handles. The only ones worth buying are made of nylon; they are roughly rectangular, with two short straight edges, one long straight edge, and one long, convex curved edge. Nylon bowl scrapers ⑦ are superior to spatulas for scooping up ingredients and batters, for scraping out bowls, and for smoothing batters in a cake pan. The best size is about 4½ inches (12 cm) wide by 3½ inches (9 cm) high.

⑦

Sources: La Cuisine, Dean & DeLuca, J.B. Prince.

BREAD KNIVES. See **KNIVES**.

CAKE PANS. We use square cake pans ⑧ for baking sponge cake bar cookies. The pan should be about 1½ inches (3½–4 cm) deep and made of tinned steel or aluminum. The sizes called for in our recipes are 8 inches (20 cm), 9 inches (24 cm), and 10 inches (26 cm) square. Do not use black steel cake pans or aluminum cake pans with a dark annodized finish, since a dark cake pan would make the bottom and sides of the cake cook too quickly and brown excessively.

⑧

CARAMEL POT. This is an unlined copper saucepan with a pouring spout, made specifically for cooking sugar. Clean it in the same way as copper mixing bowls (see **COPPER BOWLS**).

Sources: La Cuisine, Dean & DeLuca, Kitchen Glamor, The Peppercorn, J.B. Prince.

COOKIE CUTTERS. Two sets of round cutters ⑨, one plain and one fluted and ranging in diameter from 1¼ to 4 inches (3–10 cm), are indispensable for cutting cookies from a rolled out sheet of sweet pastry dough or flaky pastry dough. Occasionally we also use oval cookie cutters, but since these are difficult to find and quite expensive, we recommend making your own from inexpensive (and not very rigid) round cutters by carefully bending them into the required shape. Cookie cutters can also be used to make guide marks for piping on a buttered and floured baking sheet. Decoratively shaped cutters are fun for some special cookies.

⑨

Sources: La Cuisine, Dean & DeLuca, J.B. Prince, Maid of Scandinavia, The Peppercorn, Kitchen Glamor.

COOKIE JARS AND TIN COOKIE BOXES. One or the other is essential to keep cookies fresh as long as possible, and to prevent them from being crushed. They should have tight-fitting lids to keep moisture in or out, depending on the cookie. Tin (actually tinned steel) cookie boxes are especially nice because, being relatively wide and shallow, they often make it easier to arrange the cookies neatly without damage and their lids allow easy access.

COOKIE PRESS. This is an alternative to the pastry bag for very thick batters that aren't too sticky. It consists of a metal cylinder fitted with a plunger at one end and a metal template at the other. The template has a design cut out in the center for shaping the cookie dough. Each model comes with a large selection of templates. The plunger may be operated by a ratchet mechanism or a crank. The ratchet models have a trigger like a caulk gun and are called cookie guns.

COOLING RACKS. One or more large wire cooling racks ⑩ are essential for cooling cookies quickly when they come out of the oven. Most cookies are transferred directly from the baking sheet to the wire rack immediately after baking to prevent condensation from forming under them and to avoid the possibility of the cookies sticking to the baking sheet. For cookies that are too fragile to remove from the baking sheet while hot, the cookies are left on the baking sheet and the baking sheet is placed on a wire rack to speed cooling. Since cookies are small, it is best to have cooling racks with closely spaced wires. Wire racks designed for candy making are ideal because they have a grid of wires running in both directions that prevents cookies from falling through.

⑩

COPPER BOWLS. Copper bowls are the best choice for whipping egg whites. Bowls designed for whipping whites with a wire whisk have a hemispherical shape ⑪, which allows you to incorporate air most efficiently. If you have one of KitchenAid's heavy-duty electric mixers, we strongly recommend the optional copper liner bowl made for these machines by Atlas Metal Spinning.

To clean a copper bowl, first wash it thoroughly with hot water. Clean the surface with a mixture of coarse kosher salt and distilled white vinegar, which removes oxidation. Rinse out the bowl with cold water, and leave it upside down to drain and air dry.

⑪

Sources: La Cuisine, Dean & DeLuca, The Peppercorn, Maid of Scandinavia.

DOUGH SCRAPER. This is a flat, rectangular piece of steel—typically about 3 by 6 inches (7½ by 15 cm)—with a thick handle along one long edge. It is used as a mixing tool for pastry doughs, for moving ingredients and doughs, and for scraping your countertop and black steel baking sheets clean. It is also referred to as a pastry scraper or block scraper.

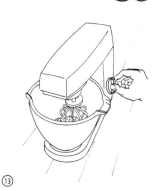

DREDGE. For dusting confectioners' sugar and cocoa powder, this cylindrical metal container with a perforated lid is the ideal tool. It can also be used for granulated sugar when you are rolling out flaky pastry dough on sugar. To dust with a dredge, flick it forward horizontally ⑫ at the same time as you tilt it forward, throwing a sprinkling of powder onto cookies or your countertop. This gives you better control than turning it upside down and shaking it.

Sources: La Cuisine, Dean & Deluca, The Peppercorn.

⑫

ELECTRIC MIXER. Many cookies can be made quite easily without an electric mixer. For others, the mixer is an indispensable labor-saving device. The best, and most versatile electric mixers available are the heavy-duty, planetary-action stand mixers ⑬ made by KitchenAid and Kenwood. These mixers have a single beater rotating on a vertical axis at the same time as the axis itself (mounted on the perimeter of a wheel) revolves around the bowl. They have three types of beaters: a wire whip for whisking, a flat beater ⑭ for mixing batters and creaming butter, and a dough hook for mixing pastry doughs. The planetary-action mechanism ensures that the beater constantly moves around the entire interior of the bowl. All of these mixers are large. KitchenAid has two models, the 4½-quart (4½ L) K45 and the 5-quart (5 L) K5; and Kenwood also makes two models, the 5-quart (5 L) Chef and the 7-quart (7 L) Major. However, they all have a deep, beehive-shaped bowl with a dimple in the bottom that makes them equally effective with both small and large quantities.

⑬

Most of the other electric mixers on the market employ the eggbeater mechanism. The eggbeater has two beaters that rotate on fixed axes in opposite directions. When beating a liquid, this mechanism sets up two whirlpools that circulate the liquid around the bowl and draw it between the beaters. However, if the liquid becomes too viscous (as it does when you whip egg whites or heavy cream), then the circulation breaks down and the beaters reach only part of the mixture in the bowl. For thick batters that aren't fluid to start with, the eggbeater simply is not appropriate. Despite the basic design flaw, an eggbeater-type electric mixer can be used to do the early phase of the whipping for cream or egg whites; then when the liquid starts to become too viscous, the whipping should

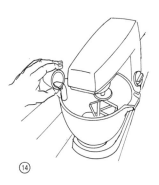

⑭

be finished by hand with a wire whisk. Used in this way, a hand-held electric eggbeater can be particularly advantageous in situations (such as whipping a batter in a double boiler) where a stand mixer is impractical.

FOIL PAPER WRAPPERS. These are squares of confectioners' foil designed for wrapping individual pieces of chocolate and other candies. Available in 3¼-inch (8 cm), 5-inch (13 cm), and 11-inch (28 cm) squares. We use the 5-inch (13 cm) squares for Amiens Macaroons (page 160).

Source: Maid of Scandinavia.

FOOD PROCESSOR. The primary purpose of the food processor in our cookie recipes is for preparing nut powders and pastes. In most recipes the quantities required demand a full-size, direct-drive food processor ⑮ with a work bowl capacity of at least 7 cups (1¾ L). We use the French food processors manufactured by Robot Coupe. Another excellent brand is Cuisinart.

⑮

GRATERS. Grated orange and lemon zests are frequent flavorings in French cookies. There are two types of graters that are excellent for grating the zest directly off the fruit. A two-piece round cheese grater has a large, slightly domed grating surface over a stainless-steel bowl. The best ones have two interchangeable grating surfaces. The other option is a box grater. The "box" is open at top and bottom, with a handle at the top. Each of the four sides has a different grating surface.

For grating chocolate, the Mouli rotary grater is preferable to the round cheese grater or the box grater. The advantage of the Mouli is that you don't have to hold the chocolate with your warm hands while grating. In addition, the handle on the drum of the rotary grater gives you a mechanical advantage that is a big plus for grating any hard food substance. The Mouli can also be used for grating nuts, but we find it much faster and easier to grind nuts with sugar in the food processor.

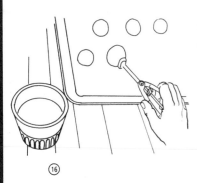

ICE CREAM SCOOPS. Small stainless-steel ice cream scoops are an excellent alternative to the pastry bag for spooning some cookie batters onto baking sheets or into molds. These are referred to as "portion-control" scoops ⑯ because they are used in restaurants to serve ice creams and other foods in precisely measured portions. They are operated by squeezing the spring-loaded handle that, by means of a ratchet wheel, sweeps a semicircular scraper around the inside of the bowl to release the contents. These scoops are sized according to the approximate number of scoops per quart or liter of ice cream, ranging from one hundred down to eight scoops. Italian-made scoops are usually sized to the liter

⑯

and are therefore slightly larger (about 5 percent) than scoops manufactured in the Far East for the American market and sized to the quart.

As a rule, the ice cream scoop works best for cookie batters that are not too sticky and that spread during baking or are baked in molds. For spooning batter onto baking sheets, the size we use most often is the #100 (1¾ to 2-teaspoon, or 9 to 10 ml, capacity). Two others that are occasionally valuable are the #70 (2¾-teaspoon, or 1.4 cl, capacity) and a special "midget" scoop (1-teaspoon, or ½ cl, capacity). Scooping batter into molds works best when a larger scoop is appropriate. We find the #50 (4-teaspoon or 2 cl), #40 (5-teaspoon or 2½ cl), and #30 (2-tablespoon or 3 cl) scoops most useful for this purpose.

Whenever you use an ice cream scoop in one of our cookie recipes, fill the scoop level with the rim. To do this, first scoop up the batter to fill it above the rim. Then remove the excess by sweeping the top of the scoop across the rim of the bowl of batter or by sweeping a small palette knife over the top of the scoop. Turn the scoop upside down over the baking sheet or mold and squeeze the handle to release the batter. When dropping the batter onto a baking sheet, adjust the angle at which you hold the scoop so that the batter falls flat side down onto the baking sheet and the top of the batter retains the domed shape of the scoop.

Sources: La Cuisine, Maid of Scandinavia, Dean & DeLuca, The Peppercorn, J.B. Prince.

~~~~~~~~~~

KITCHEN PARCHMENT. This strong, stiff, greaseproof paper is used for lining baking sheets and for making parchment decorating cones. For lining baking sheets, it is roughly equivalent to brushing the sheet with butter and then dusting it with flour. However, parchment is normally used only when the cookies will be cooled on the baking sheet. Parchment is particularly advantageous when the cookies will be brushed with jam and a confectioners' sugar and water glaze after baking or when you want to minimize browning and forming a crust on the bottoms of the cookies.

To line a baking sheet with parchment, first brush the edges and diagonals of the baking sheet with melted butter. Place the sheet of parchment on the baking sheet, and smooth it with your hands to eliminate any wrinkles and make it stick to the butter. If the parchment was not cut exactly to size, then trim off the excess by running the back edge of your chef's knife over the paper on the edge of the baking sheet so that the edge of the baking sheet cuts the paper.

KNIVES. The only important knives for cookie making are the chef's knife, paring knife, and bread knife. The chef's knife is often used for making long, straight cuts in sheets of pastry dough ⑰, so a long blade is advantageous. We find a 10-inch (25 cm) chef's knife ideal. The paring knife should have a blade 3 to 3½ inches (7½–9 cm) long.

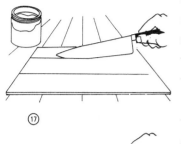

⑰

The best knife for slicing bread and for sawing through many fragile pastries without shattering is a bread knife with a scalloped (rather than serrated) edge ⑱. This knife can also be used for making a decorative pattern in the chocolate coating on the back of a cookie.

⑱

We especially recommend the high-carbon stainless-steel knives manufactured in Solingen, Germany, by F. Dick and by Wusthof-Trident.

Sources: Dean & Deluca, La Cuisine, J.B. Prince, Williams-Sonoma, The Peppercorn, Kitchen Glamor.

MARBLE PASTRY SLAB. It is essential to keep pastry doughs cool when you are preparing them and rolling them out. A marble pastry slab or countertop is very helpful, as marble does not warm up quickly while you are working on it. Instead, it absorbs the heat generated by rolling out the dough, so both the marble and pastry dough remain cool. Marble has a high thermal mass and requires a lot of heat to warm it. When you touch marble, it absorbs heat from your hand without warming and therefore feels cool to the touch.

It is not true, as some authors have claimed, that the temperature of the marble is below the ambient temperature of the room, unless of course you have chilled the marble in the refrigerator. If the marble were able to maintain a temperature below that of its surroundings, it would be a violation of the Second Law of Thermodynamics and would permit the construction of a perpetual-motion machine—to be technical, a perpetual-motion machine of the second kind. We know that is impossible.

If you don't have a marble countertop, then you want a marble slab that is as large as possible without being unwieldy. It should be ¾ to 1 inch (2–2½ cm) thick. We think an 18 by 24-inch (45 by 60 cm) slab is a good size. Chilling the slab before using can be helpful in a warm kitchen, so get one that will fit in your refrigerator. The marble must not be too cold or it can produce condensation, making the pastry dough stick to the marble. For best results, we recommend chilling it to between 15 and 20° F (8–12° C) below room temperature.

Source: Ranier Devido Stone & Marble Company.

MEASURING CUPS AND SPOONS. There are two types of measuring cups—one for liquids and the other for dry ingredients. The difference between the two is demanded by the fact that liquids have a surface tension that makes the surface of the liquid curved rather than flat.

When you measure dry ingredients, you fill the measuring cup above the rim and then sweep off the excess using a metal spatula or other implement with a straight edge so that the cup is filled level with the rim. Measuring spoons are generally designed for dry ingredients and are used in the same way. Dry-measure cups and spoons are almost always made of metal or opaque plastic, since there is no reason to see through the side of the measuring implement.

Liquid-measure cups are transparent and have graduations marked on the side. The curved surface of the liquid in the cup is called the meniscus. For water and for most other liquids found in the kitchen, the meniscus is concave. Liquid measure cups are designed to measure the volume based on the level of liquid at the bottom (center) of the meniscus.

Measuring liquid in a dry-measure cup or spoon is more tricky. If you underfill the cup slightly, then the liquid will reach the top of the cup at the rim, but the surface will form the same concave meniscus as in a liquid-measure cup. However, it is also possible to overfill the cup without spilling the liquid. In this case the surface tension of the liquid makes its surface become convex (just as it does with water droplets on a flat surface) and the liquid domes above the rim of the cup.

For both liquid- and dry-measure cups and spoons, we advise against purchasing cheap tools. Poor-quality measuring utensils are sometimes calibrated inaccurately, rendering them worse than useless.

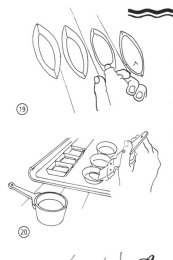

MOLDS. With the exception of Chapter 4, on sponge cake batters, molds do not play an extensive role in this book. Most of the molds we do use are French, and they give each cookie its characteristic traditional shape. Typically the molds are tinned steel, and a few are aluminum. In some cases, black steel molds are available in the same shapes as the tinned steel ones. However, we do not recommend using the black steel molds because they would produce excessive browning with our recipes. Molds can be produced individually or they can be made in a plaque, with several or many molds' stamped in a single sheet of metal.

The molds we use most often are:

- **Barquettes** ⑲ are boat-shaped, with a pointed bow and stern. Available in many sizes. We use 3½ inches (9 cm) long, 1½ inches (4 cm) wide, and ½ inch (12 mm) deep.

- **Round and square *petits fours*** ⑳ are 1½-inch (4 cm) rounds or 1⅝-inch (3½ cm) squares, both about ⅜ inch (1 cm) deep.

- **Rectangular *petits fours*** ㉑ are 2 inches (5 cm) long, 1 inch (2½ cm)

(22)

wide, and ⅜ inch (1 cm) deep. You can substitute *barquette* molds 2½ inches (6½ cm) long and ⅜ inch (1 cm) deep.

■ **Royal ovals** (22) are like very small, oval cake pans. The size we use is 2¾ inches (7 cm) long, 1¾ inches (4½ cm) wide, and ¹¹⁄₁₆ inch (18 mm) deep.

■ *Tartelettes* (23) are shallow round molds with gently sloping sides; many sizes available. We use 2¾ inches (7 cm) wide and ½ inch (12 mm) deep.

■ *Madeleines* **plaques** (24) are elongated shell shapes, typically 12 depressions per plaque, each 3 inches (8 cm) high. Other sizes exist but are less common.

■ *Coques* **plaques** (25) are shaped like scallop shells, 8 depressions per plaque, each 2½ inches (6½ cm) wide. Can be used interchangeably with *madeleine* plaques.

■ **Champagne biscuit plaques** (26) are rectangular baton-shaped molds, 20 depressions per plaque, each 4¼ inches (11 cm) long and 1 inch (2½ cm) wide.

(23)

(24)

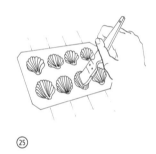

(25)

(26)

■ *Langues de chat* **plaques** (27) are dumbbell-shaped fingers, 10 depressions per plaque, each 3¾ inches (9½ cm) long and ⅝ inch (16 mm) wide at the center.

■ *Visitandines* **plaques** (28) are turban-shaped molds, 8 depressions per plaque, each 2⅝ inches (6 cm) wide. Can be used interchangeably with *madeleines* plaques.

■ **Gem pans** (29) are miniature cupcake pans, 12 cups per plaque, each 1¾ inches (4½ cm) wide. An American mold, ideal for baking individual fruitcakes.

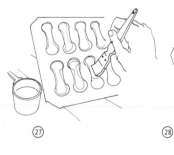

(27)

(28)

(29)

(30)

- **_Tarte_ rings** ㉚ are rings with no bottom, also called flan rings. Many sizes are available. They are intended for making _tartes,_ quiches, etc. We use 3¼-inch (8 cm) _tarte_ rings for shaping Florentines. You can make a substitute by removing the tops and bottoms from empty fruit cans 3¼ inches (8 cm) in diameter and 2 inches (5 cm) deep (such as 8¼-ounce, or 234 g, pineapple cans).

- **_Tuiles_** ㉛ are multiple troughs made from a single sheet of steel for shaping Almond Tiles (_tuiles_). Any other narrow (about 2 inches, or 5 cm, wide) trough-shaped mold can be substituted—for example, ring molds, _pain de mie_ molds, or yule log molds.

Sources: La Cuisine, Dean & DeLuca, The Peppercorn, J.B. Prince.

㉛

NEWSPRINT. This is the type of paper that newspapers are printed on. It is used to line baking sheets for many cookies, particularly those in the macaroon family. After baking, these cookies are steamed off the paper by pouring water between the hot baking sheet and the newsprint. The steam keeps the insides and bottoms of the cookies soft. Kitchen parchment is not an alternative here because it blocks the steam from reaching the cookies. Some other cookies (particularly bar cookies made from sponge cake batters) are baked on buttered newsprint. In this case, the newsprint absorbs and holds the butter better than does parchment, but the parchment is an acceptable substitute.

Many local newspapers sell their end-rolls of newsprint at nominal charge, and they are the most economical source for this paper. You can also purchase newsprint in pads of 50 or 100 sheets from art supply stores. Artists' newsprint is higher quality than most printers' newsprint, and the pads are available in several sizes—including 12 by 18 inches (30 by 45 cm), 14 by 17 inches (35 by 42 cm), and 18 by 24 inches (45 by 60 cm). While more expensive than newspaper end-rolls, these pads are still considerably less expensive than kitchen parchment, and they are more convenient than the end-rolls.

OVENS. There are many types of ovens, but in home kitchens the most common by far is an electric or gas _roasting_ oven. In a roasting oven, the heat is generated by a heating element just above (for electric) or below (for gas) the oven floor, and food is cooked on racks that can be positioned at three or four different heights inside the oven cavity. Our cookie recipes are designed for use in a roasting oven. Other ovens, such as convection ovens and deck ovens, have very different baking characteristics. If you are using a different type of oven, follow the manufacturer's guidelines for adapting the recipes.

Within the cavity of your roasting oven, heat is circulated by radiation (infrared light waves emitted by the oven floor, walls, and—for electric ovens—the heating element) and by natural convection (air circulation produced by differences in pressure between air masses at different temperatures). Heat flows predominantly from the bottom of the oven to the top because the heating element is at the bottom of the cavity and because hotter air is lighter than cooler air. The hottest air is at the top of the oven, and the greatest amount of radiant heat is at the bottom of the oven. The higher the oven temperature, the more radiant heat is generated by the heating element, and the greater the differential between the heat at the bottom and top of the oven.

Most home ovens have two racks, but it is usually best to bake on only one rack at a time. The vertical position of the oven rack is a major determining factor in how the cookies bake. Choosing a lower rack position will make the bottoms of the cookies cook more quickly and the tops more slowly. Conversely, a higher rack position will make the bottoms cook more slowly and the tops more quickly. Generally it is best to bake on one of the middle rack positions to make the cookies bake evenly. There are, however, situations that require relatively more top heat or more bottom heat. When this is necessary, we specify baking on the top or bottom oven rack. When we do not specify the rack position in the recipe, you should bake on a middle rack position.

Regardless of rack position, always allow at least 1 to 1½ inches (2½–4 cm) between your baking sheet and the oven walls on all sides. If you position your baking sheet too close to the oven wall, air currents are forced to travel between the oven wall and the edge of the baking sheet too quickly, producing greater heat transfer and excessive browning of cookies near the edge of the baking sheet.

Horizontal heat circulation in a roasting oven is very poor. When you bake on two oven racks simultaneously, you disrupt the flow of heat in the space between the baking sheets. As a result, the bottoms of the cookies on the upper baking sheet and the tops of the cookies on the lower baking sheet will cook slowly, while the tops of the cookies on the upper baking sheet and the bottoms of the cookies on the lower baking sheet will cook quickly. In a medium or hot oven, where the differential between bottom heat and top heat is an important factor, this is a disaster. On the other hand, in a low oven the heat is much more uniform and the baking is slower. So the problems created by baking on two racks simultaneously are less serious in a low oven and can be compensated for by switching the baking sheets between top and bottom rack positions partway through the baking period. This situation is relevant primarily for meringues, and we discuss it more fully in the introduction to Chapter 2 (page 66).

The oven temperature determines not only how long the cookies will bake but also their characteristics and quality. Baking cookies accomplishes several things. It melts butter, makes air bubbles in the batter expand and water evaporate, coagulates proteins and gelatinizes starches making the batter set, and finally caramelizes sugar, giving the cookies an appealing brown, beige, or golden color. For each cookie recipe, the oven temperature is chosen to balance these and many other factors so that the cookies have the proper texture and appearance after baking.

Preheating the oven is essential. For some cookies, the initial oven heat sets the batter quickly, preventing the cookies from spreading too much. For others, it makes the cookies rise quickly before they start to set, making them lighter. How long the oven needs to preheat depends partly on the oven temperature and partly on the characteristics of your particular oven. As a rule of thumb, always let it preheat for a minimum of fifteen minutes. Most ovens will preheat to even a high temperature within this time. For a hot oven, thirty minutes of preheating is even better. The oven thermostat cycles the heating element off and on, as the oven temperature rises and falls around the temperature you select. It can take one or two full cycles for the oven to reach the point where this pattern is established and the oven temperature is not overshooting the range it is designed to operate within.

You should expect the oven temperature to fluctuate within a range of about 25° F (15° C) around the temperature you set, provided the thermostat is properly calibrated. Unfortunately, oven thermostats drift over time, so even if properly calibrated at first they can eventually become inaccurate. It is a good idea to check your oven thermostat regularly with an oven thermometer. Position the thermometer at the center of the oven cavity, and read it several times over the course of at least one cycle. If you find that the thermostat is inaccurate, then have it corrected (you may be able to do this yourself, following the manufacturer's instructions) or compensate for the inaccuracy by adjusting the oven temperature you set accordingly.

PALETTE KNIVES. Many American cooks refer to these as icing spatulas. They have a flat, narrow blade with straight, parallel edges and rounded end. Palette knives are extremely useful for spreading glazes ㉜ (particularly chocolate and royal icing) and fillings on cookies and for moving cookies on and off baking sheets. The sizes we use most often have 4-inch (10 cm), 6-inch (15 cm), and 8-inch (20 cm) blades. Occasionally a 10-inch (25 cm) blade is valuable for spreading royal icing on a sheet of dough or batter before cutting.

Sources: La Cuisine, Dean & DeLuca, Maid of Scandinavia, The Peppercorn, J.B. Prince.

PARCHMENT DECORATING CONE. This is used for writing and fine decorative work when even a small pastry bag with a decorating tube is too large. The French call it a *cornet,* and it was invented in 1808 by a pastry chef in Bordeaux named Lorsa.

It is easiest to make four decorating cones at a time. Cut a rectangle of parchment 10 inches (25 cm) long from a roll 15 inches (38 cm) wide. Cut each rectangle in half crosswise to make two 7½ by 10-inch (19 by 25 cm) rectangles, and cut each of these in half along the diagonal to get four right triangles, one for each cone. Lay one triangle on your countertop with the 10-inch (25 cm) side on the bottom and the 7½-inch (19 cm) side on the right. Turn your right hand palm up and grasp the upper right corner of the triangle between the thumb and index finger of your right hand ㉝, with your thumb under the corner of the parchment. Rotate your right hand toward you to roll up the upper half of the triangle into a tight cone ㉞, with the point of the cone near the center of the hypotenuse of the triangle and the corner of the parchment on top of the center of the long side. Grasp the corner and the center of the long side between your right thumb on the inside of the cone and the index and middle fingers of your right hand on the outside of the cone. Lift the cone, point up, and wrap the free corner of the triangle around the outside of the cone with your left hand. The corner of the parchment on the outside of the cone should overlap the inside corner slightly, with a single layer of parchment in between. Grasp the corners between both thumbs inside the cone and your index and middle fingers outside the cone ㉟, and slide them in opposite directions to tighten the cone and give it a sharp point. The corners of the parchment triangle will extend below the base of the cone. Fold the corners up inside the cone ㊱ to secure the finished decorating cone.

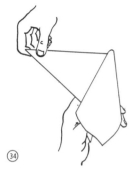

To use the decorating cone, spoon about 1 tablespoon (1½ cl) or less of the ingredient to be piped into the cone ㊲. Press the open end of the cone flat to enclose the contents. Fold over the corners, and then fold over the center in the opposite direction as the corners to secure the closure. Holding the decorating cone tip up, cut off the tip to make a tiny hole. (The hole must be just large enough to allow the contents to flow easily but not run out the tip.) Grasp the folded end of the decorating cone between the thumb and the index and middle fingers of one hand, turn it tip down, and press gently with your fingertips to make the contents flow through the hole and drop onto the top of the cookie you are decorating. When you want to stop the flow, release the pressure and turn the cone upside down.

PASTRY BAGS. The fastest and easiest way to shape batters into cookies is almost always by piping with a pastry bag. The shape of the cookie is determined both by the pastry tube used and by the piping method. The pastry bag can be made of canvas with a plastic-coated interior or of nylon. We prefer the canvas because, unlike nylon, it isn't slippery when it gets wet. The advantage of nylon bags is that they dry quickly after washing.

Large pastry bags are advantageous for making cookies because they allow you to pipe an entire batch of batter without refilling the bag. For piping the batters in most of our recipes, we recommend a pastry bag 16 inches (40 cm) or 18 inches (45 cm) long. For smaller quantities of batter, a 14-inch (35 cm) pastry bag is a good size.

It is also handy to have a small pastry bag for piping fillings in cookies. A 12-inch (30 cm) pastry bag is most versatile; but when you are piping, say, ½ cup (1.2 dl) of buttercream, you may prefer a 10-inch (25 cm) bag.

Sources: Maid of Scandinavia, La Cuisine, Dean & Deluca, McGuckin Hardware, The Peppercorn, Kitchen Glamor.

PASTRY TUBES. Pastry tubes used for cookie batters (as well as other types of batter) are large—typically about 2 inches (5 cm) long. They are distinguished from decorating tubes, which are much smaller and are used for decorative piping on cakes and other desserts. To our knowledge, Ateco is the only American manufacturer that produces a complete range of pastry tubes. We use their numbering system in our recipes, in addition to the size and shape of each tube. Most of the tubes we use for cookies have plain or fluted round openings.

The plain tubes are numbered from 0 to 9, with openings ranging from 5/32 to 11/16 inch (4–18 mm) in diameter. We use all but the two smallest sizes in this book, but most cookies can be piped with tubes in the range between #4 and #7. In addition to shaping cookies on baking sheets, we use the plain pastry tubes for piping batter into molds.

There are two sets of fluted pastry tubes, depending on the number and size of the teeth. The basic fluted tubes, numbered from 0 to 9 in increasing size, have wide, deep teeth. We use these for nearly all cookies that require a fluted tube because they produce very pronounced fluting in the cookies. The relevant sizes here are #3 and #5.

B-series, "French-style" fluted pastry tubes are numbered from 0B to 9B and have short, narrow teeth. We use them occasionally (in particular, the #4B for Cornmeal Cookies in Chapter 1), but for most cookie batters they produce fluting that becomes too indistinct after baking.

The only other pastry tube we use for cookies is a ¾-inch (2 cm) ribbon tube (Ateco #47). This tube has a narrow rectangular opening, plain on one side and fluted on the other. It can be used teeth up or down to pipe fluted or plain ribbons of batter.

French-made pastry tubes differ from most of those made by Ateco (as well as other American manufacturers) in that they have a rolled rim at the back end of the tube. The French supplier Matfer produces pastry tubes in an even larger range of shapes and sizes than does Ateco, but the numbering system is completely different.

Couplers are made to permit changing the pastry tube without emptying the pastry bag. Unfortunately, the largest coupler on the market will not accommodate any pastry tubes larger than an Ateco #5.

Sources: Maid of Scandinavia, La Cuisine, Dean & DeLuca, J.B. Prince, The Peppercorn, Kitchen Glamor.

PASTRY BRUSHES. These are indispensable for coating baking sheets and molds with melted butter, for brushing egg wash, jam, and sugar-and-water glazes on cookies, and for removing excess flour from sheets of pastry dough and your countertop. The brush should have natural boar bristles (called Chinese bristles) rather than nylon, which melts if it gets hot. The shape can be flat or round. Flat brushes are more versatile. For brushing egg wash and glazes on cookies, a flat brush ¾ inch (2 cm) or 1 inch (2½ cm) wide is usually ideal. For buttering molds one of these or a larger flat brush 1½ inches (4 cm) wide can be used, depending on the size of the mold. A round brush ½ to ⅝ inch (12–16 mm) wide can also be good for this purpose. For buttering baking sheets and cake pans, a flat brush 1½ to 2 inches (4–5 cm) wide ㊳ works best.

㊳

To clean a pastry brush, wash it thoroughly by hand with detergent and hot water, working the detergent in between the bristles with your fingers. Then rinse thoroughly. (A dishwasher will ruin the wooden handle.) Shake out the excess water, then press the bristles between towels to remove as much moisture as possible. Hang the brush bristles down to finish drying.

Sources: La Cuisine, Dean & DeLuca, J.B. Prince, Maid of Scandinavia, The Peppercorn, McGuckin Hardware, Kitchen Glamor.

㊴

ROLLING PINS. Smooth, cylindrical rolling pins are used extensively for rolling out pastry doughs and occasionally for very firm, dry almond paste batters. There are two basic styles and they are available in several materials, including hardwoods (boxwood or beechwood), marble, stainless steel, and plastic.

The most versatile style is the French rolling pin, a simple cylinder of hardwood ㊴ about 20 inches (50 cm) long and 2 inches (5 cm) in diameter. This is easy to maneuver and gives you a good feeling for the thickness of the dough you are rolling. We are very fond of a stainless-steel version of this rolling pin, which is actually just a length of stainless-steel pipe. The stainless steel is heavier, and so does more of the work for you; and it has a higher thermal mass than does the wood, so it stays cooler when you are working with it.

The American-style rolling pin is a cylinder of wood mounted on a handle at each end. Good ones have large cylinders, preferably 15 to 18 inches (38–45 cm) long and 3 to 3½ inches (7½–9 cm) in diameter; and they spin smoothly on ball bearings around the center shaft that connects the handles. While more clumsy than the French style, they are quite efficient for rolling out large sheets of dough. Rolling pins with marble cylinders are also made in this style, but unfortunately most of them are too small and are poorly engineered so that they don't spin smoothly.

There are also a few special-purpose rolling pins worth mentioning. The Tutové looks like an American rolling pin, but has a longitudinally ribbed plastic cylinder. It is designed for performing the turns on flaky pastry doughs.

Other plastic and wood rolling pins with textured surfaces are designed to produce a textured surface on a sheet of pastry dough or almond paste. Ribbed, checkerboard, and basket-weave patterns are the most common. The textures range from very fine to quite large and deep. We use a checkerboard rolling pin to produce a waffle texture ④⓪ on the surface of a sweet pastry dough cookie called Irish Waffles.

Sources: La Cuisine, Maid of Scandinavia, Dean & DeLuca, Kitchen Glamor, Williams-Sonoma, The Peppercorn, J.B. Prince.

④⓪

RULERS. These are indispensable both for measuring the sizes of cookies and for using as a guide for making long, straight cuts in sheets of pastry dough. Stainless-steel or aluminum rulers are best for durability, and it is convenient to have two lengths: 18 inches (45 cm) and 24 inches (60 cm).

SCALES. For anyone who does much baking, a kitchen scale is invaluable. Generally, the most accurate way to measure dry ingredients is by weight. This is particularly important for powders (such as flour and confectioners' sugar) and for ingredients in large pieces (such as nuts). Granulated sugars can be measured fairly accurately by volume, but this can be more cumbersome than weighing the sugar when fractional cup amounts are required. Measuring by volume is the superior method only for very small quantities that are below the level of sensitivity of the kitchen scales, typically ¼ ounce (7 g) and for some metric scales as low as 1 or 2 g.

Of course, an inaccurate kitchen scale is no advantage. Many of the spring balances made for kitchen use are very unreliable. Our preference is for a beam balance. A single-beam balance has two platforms—one for the ingredients and one for the balance weights—and one balance beam with a sliding weight for small increments. Even better is a double-beam balance, which has one platform on top for the ingredients and two balance beams with sliding weights for small and large weight increments, respectively. More cumbersome but just as reliable is a traditional equal-arm balance, with two platforms but no balance beam.

Digital kitchen scales can also be a good choice. While more fragile than beam balances, they can be quite accurate and they are very easy to use.

While all of our recipes give both avoirdupois and metric weights, we urge you to get a metric scale and to use the metric system. No one likes to think in fractions of an ounce less than ¼, and we have never seen a kitchen scale calibrated in avoirdupois units with gradations finer than this. But metric scales calibrated in increments of 1 g are quite common, and the sensitivity they provide makes them much more desirable. We particularly recommend the metric double-beam balance made by Teraillon.

Source: La Cuisine, The Peppercorn.

SIEVES AND SIFTERS. These are devices for sifting dry ingredients and for straining liquids. Sieves can have a bowl-shaped mesh set into a metal or plastic frame with a handle, a cone-shaped mesh in a metal frame with a handle (the French call this a *chinois* because it is shaped like a Chinese hat), or a large flat mesh set in a cylindrical frame ㊶ with no handle (this is a drum sieve or *tamis*). An American flour sifter is just a sieve with a cylindrical metal frame, a flat or bowl-shaped mesh, and an agitator of some type.

More important than the style of the sieve is the fineness of the mesh. The mesh is graded according to the distance between two adjacent wires, measured center to center.

A fine mesh (less than ¹⁄₁₆ inch or 1½ mm) is best for straining liquids. There are wonderful stainless-steel strainers imported from Italy (and less expensive knock-offs from the Far East) that have a very fine, bowl-shaped mesh ㊷, about ³⁄₆₄ inch (1 mm). A bouillon strainer (which the French call an *étamine* because it is as fine as muslin) has the finest mesh of all, about ³⁄₁₂₈ inch (½ mm). Except for the bouillon strainer, which is usually cone shaped, fine-mesh strainers are typically bowl-shaped sieves or drum sieves.

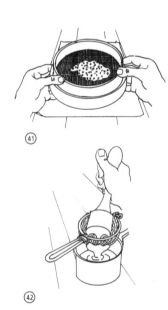

For sifting flour, confectioners' sugar, and most other powdered ingredients (including almond and sugar powder), you should choose a sieve with a medium mesh, ¹⁄₁₆ to ³⁄₃₂ inch (1½–2 mm). This is most likely to be a flour sifter ㊸ or a drum sieve. The flour sifters with multiple screens sift slowly and are difficult to clean. We prefer ones with a wire rotor agitator operated by a crank and a single bowl-shaped screen contoured to the rotor. For sifting almond and sugar powder and for large quantities of other dry ingredients, a 12-inch (30 cm) drum sieve is the most convenient and efficient.

Sieves with meshes much coarser than ³⁄₃₂ inch (2 mm) are used primarily for sifting chopped nuts. These are most likely to be drum sieves.

A drum sieve we find particularly versatile is a stainless-steel garden sieve with interchangeable meshes. The one we use has three meshes: ³⁄₃₂ inch (2 mm), ³⁄₁₆ inch (4 mm), and ⁵⁄₁₆ inch (7 mm).

Sources: La Cuisine, Dean & Deluca, Maid of Scandinavia, McGuckin Hardware, The Peppercorn, J.B. Prince.

SPACERS. When you roll out pastry doughs into sheets, it is advantageous to use spacers in order to get sheets of uniform thickness. One way to do this is to place a long, narrow strip of the required thickness on each side of the sheet of dough ㊽ to support the ends of the rolling pin. The strips can be cardboard, neoprene, or a metal such as brass. Cardboard is inexpensive but not very durable. Neoprene, available in sheets of various thickness from hardware stores, is durable and convenient. We recommend cutting the neoprene into strips 1 inch (2½ cm) wide and at least 12 inches (30 cm) long. (The strips can be stacked or placed end to end to provide a variety of thicknesses or accommodate larger sheets of dough.) Keep in mind that the neoprene will compress slightly when you press the rolling pin down on it, so the thickness of the spacer must actually be a little greater than the required thickness of the dough. Brass strips are sold by hobby shops in several thicknesses; they are somewhat more cumbersome than neoprene, but they don't compress.

Another method is to place a neoprene O-ring of the required thickness on each end ㊺ of the rolling pin. Hardware stores sell them in a range of standard sizes and can also custom make them to fit any size rolling pin. This is the most elegant solution to the problem, but you must be careful not to roll the ends of the rolling pin across the sheet of dough or the O-rings will make grooves in the dough.

Source: McGuckin Hardware.

SPATULAS. We use three types of spatulas—rubber, metal, and wooden—for different purposes.

Rubber spatulas are excellent for folding batters and for scraping out bowls. In our opinion, the rubber spatulas made by Rubbermaid Professional are by far the best on the market. They make two styles. Both have a heavy rubber blade with a long, rigid handle. In the traditional style, the blade is rectangular and flat, tapering from the thick, rigid center to thinner, more flexible edges. In the newer "spoonula" style, the blade is similar but concave so that it can be used for scooping up batters more effectively.

A metal spatula or pancake turner (called an offset spatula) is excellent for moving cookies and particularly for removing them from baking sheets when they come out of the oven. Some people refer to palette knives as icing spatulas, but these have narrow blades and are not really spatulas at all. By definition, a spatula has a wide blade.

Wooden spatulas or paddles are discussed under **WOODEN SPATULAS**.

Sources: La Cuisine, Dean & DeLuca, Maid of Scandinavia, Williams-Sonoma, The Peppercorn, McGuckin Hardware.

THERMOMETERS. Temperature plays an important role in many aspects of cookie making, so accurate thermometers are great assets. Three thermometers are of particular importance.

As mentioned in **OVENS**, you should monitor your oven thermostat by checking the oven temperature regularly with an oven thermometer. Extreme precision isn't necessary, since recipes are conventionally given with oven temperatures in 25° F (10 to 15° C) intervals, and this is also about the range of fluctuation in oven temperature permitted by most oven thermostats. Taylor makes mercury oven thermometers with stainless-steel stands that do the job.

For cooking sugar syrups, you can check the degree of cooking either by assessing its consistency or by measuring the temperature of the syrup. Candy thermometers are made for this purpose. Here again we recommend mercury thermometers. Since the consistency of the sugar syrup changes quite rapidly with increasing temperature, the thermometer should be calibrated in 2° F (1° C) gradations. It should be designed in such a way that it can give an accurate reading for even a small volume of syrup. The sugar syrup must cover the bulb of the thermometer, so always choose the pot for cooking sugar syrups accordingly. Two candy thermometers we especially like are the extremely accurate Cordon Rose glass candy thermometer and Taylor's confectionary–deep-fry thermometer, which has a glass thermometer mounted on a stainless-steel backing.

When you temper chocolate, you must accurately gauge the temperature at each stage of the process. You can do this by assessing the viscosity of the chocolate or by using a chocolate thermometer. We especially like the convenience of Taylor's instant-reading Bi-Therm thermometer, with a 5-inch (13 cm) stem and a 1-inch (2½ cm) dial that measures from 25 to 125° F (−4 to 52° C) in 2° F (1° C) gradations. Even more accurate is the Cordon Rose chocolate thermometer, a glass thermometer containing a long, slender column of mercury.

Since the whole point of using a thermometer is to get accurate temperature measurements, we suggest testing any new thermometer. The easiest way to do this is by measuring the temperature of ice water or boiling water. They should be 32° F (0° C) and 212° F (100° C)—at sea level—respectively. This test doesn't guarantee the accuracy for all temperatures, but it gives a good indication of the care taken by the manufacturer. If you buy a thermometer that can't pass this basic test, return it for another one.

Sources: Maid of Scandinavia, La Cuisine, The Peppercorn, J.B. Prince.

TIMERS. The baking times for many cookies are short, and the difference between perfect cookies and overbaked ones is often just a minute or so in the oven. For accuracy and convenience, we recommend using a modern electronic kitchen timer with an unrelenting alarm that refuses to be ignored. Oven timers are less accurate, but they still beat looking at the clock and depending on your memory to determine when to check the cookies.

WAX PAPER. We find wax paper invaluable for two purposes in cookie making. First, we like to measure out dry ingredients on a sheet of wax paper. To pour the ingredients, we lift two opposite edges of the sheet of paper and use it like a funnel ⑯. Second, wax paper is ideal for wrapping pastry doughs to store in the refrigerator. Plastic wrap is not good for this purpose because it seals the dough airtight and can cause condensation.

(46)

WHISKS. There are two distinct types of wire whisks: the batter whisk for mixing and beating batters, butter, and other heavy materials; and the balloon whisk for whipping cream and eggs. Both are available in a wide range of sizes for handling different volumes of ingredients.

The batter whisk ㊼ has relatively stiff wires enclosing an area that tapers gently from the widest part down to the handle. For making cookies at home, two convenient sizes are about 8 inches (20 cm) and 12 inches (30 cm) long.

(47)

The balloon whisk has very flexible wires and a more bulbous shape than the batter whisk. The larger the number of wires, the finer and more flexible they are, and the larger the volume they enclose, the more efficient the whisk will be for whipping air into the cream or eggs. If you plan to do much whipping by hand, we advise you to invest in the best balloon whisk you can find, preferably about 12 inches (30 cm) long.

Sources: La Cuisine, Dean & DeLuca, The Peppercorn, Kitchen Glamor.

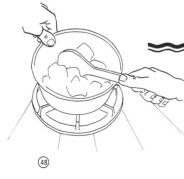

WOODEN SPATULAS. Shaped like a paddle, these flat spatulas are wonderful for mixing batters and creaming butter ㊽. They won't scratch your bowls or scrape the tin lining off the inside of a copper pot. And unlike rubber spatulas

(48)

they can be used to stir hot ingredients without damaging the spatula. Wooden spatulas are usually made of boxwood (the best) or beechwood. The sizes of interest for cookie making range from 8 to 14 inches (20–35 cm) long.

Sources: La Cuisine, Dean & DeLuca, The Peppercorn.

INGREDIENTS

An understanding of your ingredients is more valuable in baking that in any other area of cooking, with the possible exception of sauce making. As for equipment, we provide a thorough summary of the ingredients used for French cookies in glossary form. The majority of ingredients used in French cookies are supermarket items, and the remainder are available at gourmet food or wine shops. We provide mail order sources for the few items that may be difficult to find in some areas of the country.

〜〜〜〜〜

ALMONDS. Almonds are the kernel of a stone fruit closely related to the peach. They are one of the most important ingredients in French cookies; and they are used in some form—whole, sliced, chopped, or powdered—in more than half of the recipes in this book. Sometimes they supply only a decoration, but more often they provide both flavor and texture and give the cookies much of their richness and interest.

Two distinct types of almonds—sweet and bitter—can be used in baking. Bitter almonds contain a sugar-cyanide complex that, when acted on by an enzyme, reacts with water to produce prussic acid and benzaldehyde. Since prussic (hydrocyanic) acid is extremely poisonous, bitter almonds are a potentially deadly taste treat. However, a small amount of bitter almonds can be eaten without ill effect, and furthermore the prussic acid evaporates when heated, leaving only the benzaldehyde which, in small quantity, contributes a distinctive and appealing bitter note to some almond cookies. The problem is rather academic in the United States, since bitter almonds cannot legally be sold as food here. We have therefore omitted from this book a few classic cookies for which the bitter almond taste is an essential feature.

The sweet almond is by far the more important one in baking, and it poses no health risks. It contains a high percentage of oil (typically about 54 percent) as well as proteins (19 percent) and carbohydrates (20 percent). The almond is covered with a thin, papery skin that can be removed by blanching (plunging the almonds first in boiling water, then in cold water). Almonds with the skins intact are called raw (or sometimes ''natural''), those with the skins removed are called blanched. Raw almonds have a more robust, and less sweet, flavor than blanched almonds. The choice of whether to use raw or blanched almonds is dictated partly by flavor and partly by visual aesthetics, since in most cookies the two will produce very different appearances.

Commercially, almonds are sold in a variety of forms, including whole raw almonds, whole blanched almonds, blanched slivered almonds, and sliced almonds. The sliced almonds may be raw or blanched, and blanched sliced almonds are preferable when available because they are more attractive in most cookies.

Almonds frequently must be chopped or powdered in cookie making; and they are sometimes roasted to brown them, reduce their moisture content, and intensify their flavor. See **NUTS** in this section and "Nut and Sugar Powders" on page 482 in the Basic Preparations and Procedures section for details. Almonds are also an ingredient in the roasted nut and caramel paste called praliné; see **PRALINÉ** in this section and page 485 in the Basic Preparations and Procedures section.

〰〰〰

ALMOND OIL. We use almond oil to thin chocolate for glazing cookies. American almond oil is sold in supermarkets and natural food stores. It has a relatively neutral taste. Two good brands are Spectrum Naturals and Hain. French almond oil has a more pronounced almond flavor and is very expensive. You can use either the American or the French almond oil in our recipes. The quantity required is quite small, so the difference is insignificant. If you want to use almond oil to flavor a salad dressing, then the French one is the better choice.

〰〰〰

AMMONIUM CARBONATE. This white crystalline solid was widely used as a chemical leavening before the invention of modern baking powder. It was commonly referred to as hartshorn because it was originally produced from the antlers of deer. The technically correct name is ammonium bicarbonate, but ammonium carbonate is the more standard kitchen usage. Ammonium carbonate has a noticeable ammonia smell, is water soluble, and breaks down into carbon dioxide, ammonia, and water when heated to 140° F (60° C). When used properly, all of the ammonium carbonate decomposes and the ammonia gas is driven off during baking, leaving no residue. It is still used today in some crackers and pastry doughs. The advantage of ammonium carbonate in a pastry dough is that, since it does not decompose until heated, it does not reduce the storage possibilities of the dough. It is sold in pharmacies.

〰〰〰

BAKING POWDER. This is a chemical leavening composed of an alkali (almost always baking soda) and one or more acid salts, plus a starch (such as cornstarch) to absorb moisture and give the powder more volume. Most modern baking powders contain two acid salts and are called "double acting." One of these acid salts (such as cream of tartar or calcium acid phosphate) begins interacting with the baking soda to produce carbon dioxide gas as soon as the baking powder is mixed into the batter and moistened. This first interaction produces many small bubbles of carbon dioxide in the batter. The other acid salt (usually sodium aluminum sulphate) interacts with the baking soda when the batter is heated. This second interaction expands the gas bubbles produced by the first interaction. Since it occurs after the batter has begun to set, the second phase of the double action helps reduce the opportunity for the walls between gas bubbles to break down or for the gas to escape before the final structure of the cookie is established.

~~~~~~~~

BAKING SODA. The common name for bicarbonate of soda, baking soda is alkaline, and it interacts with acids to produce carbon dioxide gas. This interaction is the most common method for producing chemical leavening in baking. The acid may be supplied by an ingredient in the cookie batter—for example, crème fraîche, fruits, honey, or molasses (which is also present in brown sugar). Or, if there is insufficient acid in the batter, then an acid must be added along with the baking soda—usually in the form of baking powder.

Batters containing baking soda should be baked soon after they are prepared in order not to lose the leavening power by allowing the carbon dioxide gas to dissipate. The quantity of baking soda must not be too great because, if there is insufficient acid to neutralize it, the baking soda will produce an unpleasant, soapy taste. To ensure that the baking soda is mixed well with the batter, it is usually sifted with flour before adding it to the other ingredients.

~~~~~~~~

BUTTER. The only fat used to any significant extent in French cookies is *unsalted butter*. For many cookies—particularly those made from creamed butter and sugar batters and from pastry doughs—it is one of the central ingredients, contributing both flavor and texture. On the other hand, there are many cookies—including nearly all of the meringues and almond paste cookies—that contain no butter at all. In sponge cake batters, butter may play an important or incidental role, or it may be absent altogether. In addition to its role as an ingredient in many batters, butter can be used in fillings for some cookies and for brushing baking sheets and molds to prevent sticking.

Nearly all butter sold in the United States is made from sweet cream. This gives it a delicate, slightly sweet taste. By law it must contain at least 80 percent butterfat; the remainder consists of water (about 18 percent) and milk solids (proteins, salts, and lactose).

French butters are made from matured cream, producing a rich nutty aroma and a fuller but less sweet flavor than American sweet cream butters. Typically, they have a higher butterfat content (82 to 86 percent) and contain less water than do American butters.

A large proportion of American butter is salted to extend its shelf life. Most

French cookies contain no salt, and using salted butter in them produces an undesirable saltiness. Do not use salted butter in our recipes.

The USDA grades butter based on several characteristics, including aroma, taste, texture, body, and uniformity of color. Only grades AA and A are sold in most supermarkets. Land O' Lakes makes excellent Grade AA unsalted butter that is widely distributed.

When you are preparing a cookie batter or dough, the temperature of the butter is important. Butter is very firm at refrigerator temperatures and begins to soften at about 60° F (15° C). Butterfat begins to melt at about 68° F (20° C). When butter melts, the emulsion that holds the butterfat and water together starts to break down and the milk solids begin to separate.

When butter is used as an ingredient in a batter or pastry dough, it must be either creamed or melted in order to mix it uniformly with the other ingredients in the recipe. When you are going to cream butter for a batter, first soften it by letting it warm at room temperature to between 60 and 63° F (15–17° C). (The butter will soften more quickly and uniformly if it is cut into small pieces.) Then place it in a stainless-steel bowl and beat it with a wooden spatula to make it soft and smooth. While you beat the butter, gently warm it over low direct heat as needed to soften it, but do not let it become runny and liquid. The butter must not get warmer than 68° F (20° C). Continue beating the butter vigorously until it is white and creamy. When creamed in this way, the French call it butter *en pommade*. For large quantities of butter, the creaming can be done in a heavy-duty electric mixer using the flat beater. In that case, there is no need to warm the butter while creaming it, since the mixer will warm it as it works.

When butter is used as an ingredient in a sweet pastry dough, it must be creamed by a different method (and to a different degree) than that used for batters. Here the butter must stay cooler, so it is best to start with cold butter. Place the butter on your countertop with the sugar called for in the recipe, and cut the butter into pieces with your dough scraper. Cream the butter with the sugar by repeatedly smearing it across the countertop, a little at a time, using the heel of your hand and then gathering it back together with a dough scraper. The object is to mix the butter uniformly with the sugar, producing a smooth mass without warming the butter any more than necessary. When you finish, the mixture should be soft but still plastic, not runny or greasy, and its temperature should be close to 60° F (15° C). For large quantities of butter, you can cream the butter with the sugar using a heavy-duty electric mixer. Cut the cold butter into small pieces and place it in the mixer with the sugar. Then work it with the flat beater until the mixture is smooth and creamy.

If the butter is to be melted for mixing into a batter, then warm it gently over low heat and stir it to keep it from separating. The butter should be warmed only enough just to melt it.

When butter is to be used for coating molds or baking sheets, it is usually melted and applied with a brush. This is the easiest and fastest method, and gives you more control over the thickness and uniformity of the butter than you would get by rubbing the mold or baking sheet with a piece of softened butter. The butter will coat the metal best when it is liquid but not hot. For buttering molds, it is best to clarify the butter, since otherwise the milk solids can cause sticking. To clarify butter, warm it gently without stirring. When the butter is melted, skim off the foam (which contains the whey proteins) on top. Then pour the clear yellow liquid—the clarified butter—through a fine strainer, leaving the milky residue (the milk protein casein and various salts) in the bottom of the pan.

If you melt butter and continue to heat it, the milk solids in the butter will brown. This imparts a nutty flavor to the butter and changes its color from yellow to brown. The result is called browned butter. See page 490 in the Basic Preparations and Procedures section for details.

Unsalted butter stores quite well provided it is kept cold and airtight to prevent it from picking up off odors. In the refrigerator it will keep for two to three weeks (provided it was fresh to begin with), and in the freezer it can last for two or three months. If frozen, defrost the butter overnight in the refrigerator before using.

CANDIED CITRON, LEMON PEEL, AND ORANGE PEEL. The candied peels of these citrus fruits are frequently used in French cookies for both flavor and decoration. They are preserved against bacteria by virtue of being cooked in sugar syrup, but candied fruits are still somewhat perishable, especially the fine-quality ones that contain a minimum of artificial preservatives. They can be kept in the refrigerator, covered airtight, for two or three months, or frozen for up to six months. After that they can dry and harden, or part of their sugar content can crystallize on the surface.

Good candied citrus peels should be firm but tender, with an appealing taste of citrus zest. Unfortunately, most of those sold in supermarkets are hard and taste too much of artificial preservatives. For exceptional-quality candied citrus peels look for ones imported from France or Switzerland.

Often the citrus zest must be finely chopped when it is used in a cookie batter or dough. To prevent the bits of chopped zest from sticking together, mix a little flour with them before chopping.

Sources: La Cuisine, Balducci's, Dean & DeLuca.

CHESTNUTS. Unlike other nuts, chestnuts contain little oil and have a high starch content. They play a limited, but special role in French pastry in general, and they are rarely used in cookies. In fact, the only chestnut cookie we are familiar with is *carrés aux marrons*. (Chestnut Squares) The batter for these chestnut brownies is made with a very rich, sweet chestnut puree called *crème de marrons* (chestnut cream), which is imported from France. *Crème de marrons* is packaged in 8¾-ounce (250 g) and 17½-ounce (500 g) cans and sold in supermarkets and specialty stores.

Sources: La Cuisine, Balducci's, Dean & DeLuca.

CHOCOLATE. All types of chocolate are derived from a dark brown paste called chocolate liquor, which is produced by milling the kernels (called nibs) of roasted cocoa beans. A little more than half of the weight of the chocolate liquor is a fat called cocoa butter. The other constituents (proteins, carbohydrates, etc.) of the chocolate are suspended in the cocoa butter. Cocoa butter is unusual among natural fats in that it has a sharp melting point and it does not go rancid quickly.

Unsweetened chocolate (also called baking chocolate) is the pure chocolate liquor. It has a strong, bitter taste; and it is always melted and mixed with other ingredients—for example, in cookie batters—to flavor them. The quality of the chocolate is determined by the beans from which it is made and how they are processed, particularly the roasting (which brings out their aroma) and how finely the nibs are milled.

Bittersweet and semisweet chocolate are produced by adding sugar and extra cocoa butter to the chocolate liquor and then kneading the mixture mechanically (a process called conching) to give it a smooth texture, evaporate volatile acids, and make the flavor more mellow. Vanilla (or the artificial substitute vanillin) is often added to enhance the chocolate flavor and lecithin (an emulsifier) is used to keep the cocoa solids evenly distributed in the cocoa butter. In principle, semisweet chocolate should be sweeter than bittersweet, but in practice the distinction is blurred and the two terms are often used interchangeably. Typically, bittersweet chocolate contains about 40 percent sugar and 33 percent cocoa butter.

Covering chocolates (also referred to by their French name, *couvertures*) are bittersweet chocolates with a higher cocoa butter content, usually 36 to 40 percent. The extra cocoa butter gives the chocolate more sheen and a firmer snap. It also makes the chocolate more fluid when melted, permitting a thinner coating on a cookie or other dessert.

With the exception of meringues, chocolate is used to flavor French cookie batters and doughs only occasionally. When chocolate is included in a batter or dough, most often it is either unsweetened chocolate or cocoa powder (see following entry). Since these forms have nothing added to the chocolate, they give the maximum chocolate flavor for a given amount of chocolate and don't alter the sugar content of the batter.

The primary uses for chocolate in French cookies are as a glaze or a filling. For these purposes we use bittersweet chocolate. Milk chocolate and sweet chocolate are never used in French cookies because they are too sweet, the chocolate flavor is too diluted, and in the case of milk chocolate the color is too washed out.

For glazing cookies the chocolate must be quite fluid when melted in order to coat the cookies thinly. If the glaze were thick, it would look clumsy and the taste and texture of the chocolate would overwhelm the cookie. A thin, dark, shiny glaze, on the other hand, makes the cookies look elegant and nicely balances the textures and flavors of chocolate and cookie. In order for the melted chocolate to have sufficient fluidity, it must have a high fat content. This can be achieved either by using a high-quality covering chocolate or by adding a little oil to bittersweet chocolate. Since bittersweet chocolates are more widely available than covering chocolates, we recommend the latter. The oil can be any neutral vegetable oil, but we prefer to use almond oil since almonds are a natural and frequently used cookie ingredient, whereas safflower seeds and corn are not. Use about 1 teaspoon (½ cl) of almond oil for each 7 ounces (200 g) of European bittersweet chocolate.

The most common chocolate filling for French cookies is a rich chocolate cream called *ganache*. (See page 488 in the Basic Preparations and Procedures section.) We also use bittersweet chocolate for *ganache,* but since the chocolate is diluted with cream here, ideally we prefer a bittersweet chocolate with a higher chocolate liquor content, and correspondingly lower sugar and cocoa butter contents, than we would use for glazing.

Chocolate should never be melted over direct heat because it scorches easily. There are many ways to melt chocolate, but basically any procedure that warms the chocolate gently and evenly is suitable. For example, you can melt chocolate in a double boiler ① over hot (not boiling) water, under an infrared heat lamp (with the distance between the lamp and the chocolate adjusted to avoid overheating), in a microwave oven, or by putting the bowl of chocolate in a warm place (such as a gas oven with only the pilot light on). Whatever method you choose, first chop the chocolate and then warm it gently, stirring occasionally to make it melt more quickly and evenly. Ideally the temperature of the melted chocolate should be between 113 and 118° F (45–48° C), and it should never exceed 120° F (49° C).

Do not allow any water to get into melted chocolate. The addition of a tiny amount of water (even a little steam) can make the chocolate become thick and granular rather than fluid and smooth. We say the water makes the chocolate "seize." Unsweetened chocolate is particularly susceptible to this problem because, unlike most bittersweet chocolates, it contains no emulsifier. Once chocolate has seized, the only way to make it smooth again is to add more liquid, either water or oil. Depending on how the chocolate is being used, this may or may not be feasible.

When chocolate is melted, the cocoa solids suspended in the cocoa butter have a tendency to separate. The cocoa solids sink and some cocoa butter comes to the surface; then the cocoa butter on the surface crystallizes as the chocolate cools. The crystals of cocoa butter form dull gray streaks called fat bloom, and the texture of the cooled chocolate is no longer smooth and velvety. This poses a potential problem for glazing, since in that situation the chocolate is not mixed with other ingredients and can't be stirred as it sets to prevent separation. The problem is avoided by a process called tempering, which places the chocolate just above the melting point so that it will set quickly and not have time to separate. See page 486 in the Basic Preparations and Procedures section for details.

When properly stored, chocolate (both unsweetened and bittersweet) will last for over a year. The chocolate should be kept in a cool place—60 to 75° F (15–24° C)—and covered airtight to prevent it from absorbing odors. If the temperature is warmer, cocoa butter will migrate to the surface and form fat bloom. Chocolate should not be stored in the refrigerator because refrigeration can cause drops of water to condense on the surface of the chocolate. The water dissolves sugar in the chocolate, then evaporates, leaving sugar crystals on the surface. This is called sugar bloom.

Chocolates vary enormously from one brand to another. In general, European chocolates are milled more finely and conched for a longer time (up to four days) than American chocolates, which are usually conched for only a few hours. As a result, European chocolates are appreciably smoother and richer than their American counterparts. Each brand has its own blends of beans and roasting procedures, and combines different proportions of chocolate liquor, cocoa butter, sugar, and other ingredients in its bittersweet chocolates. We feel that the finest chocolates are those made by Valrhona in France and Lindt in Switzerland. Lindt makes two bittersweet chocolates, called Excellence and Surfin, that are sold in 3-ounce (85 g) bars at supermarkets and gourmet stores throughout the United States. Of the two, Excellence has a slightly higher cocoa liquor content and lower sugar content, whereas Surfin has more cocoa butter. Lindt also markets three covering chocolates—called Excellence, Surfin Vanille, and Courante Speciale—in 4.4-pound (2 kg) blocks through professional sources. The first two are similar to Lindt's bittersweet chocolate bars, but higher in cocoa butter. The Courante

Speciale is an extra-bittersweet couverture, so it has a very low sugar content as well as a high cocoa butter content. Valrhona makes an even wider array of chocolates, also sold in large blocks through professional sources and broken down into smaller quantities by some suppliers. Since the Lindt bittersweet bars are widely available and sold in a size convenient for our recipes, we have chosen them as the standard bittersweet chocolates for our cookie recipes. We use Excellence bittersweet chocolate for *ganache* and whenever a bittersweet chocolate is required to flavor a batter. We use Surfin bittersweet chocolate for glazing because it has more sheen and is more fluid when melted. Substituting other European bittersweet chocolates for these will produce slight differences in flavor and texture, but should not affect the success of the recipes.

European unsweetened chocolates are more difficult to come by than the bittersweets. Of the standard American brands, we prefer Baker's unsweetened chocolate, and this is what we used in developing our recipes. If you can get a European one, such as the Valrhona, so much the better.

One other form of chocolate we occasionally use for cookies is sprinkles, which the Europeans call chocolate vermicelli. The ones on the supermarket shelf are artificially flavored, but real chocolate sprinkles, glazed with sugar, are available from gourmet shops.

Sources: La Cuisine, Dean & DeLuca, Maid of Scandinavia, Williams-Sonoma.

━━━━━

COCOA POWDER. Much of the cocoa butter can be removed from chocolate liquor by means of a hydraulic press. The remainder is formed into cakes, dried, pulverized, and sifted to make cocoa powder. The cocoa powder still contains between 10 and 25 percent cocoa butter. Since it has a higher percentage of cocoa solids than does unsweetened chocolate, cocoa powder produces a stronger flavor and darker color when used to flavor a cookie batter or dough. Generally when cocoa powder is used in a batter or dough it is sifted with the flour called for in the recipe.

In Europe cocoa powder is Dutch processed by first treating either the beans or the chocolate liquor with alkaline carbonates or ammonia. This process makes the cocoa powder less bitter, gives it a deeper reddish-brown color, and makes it more soluble in water. Our recipes are designed to use Dutch-processed cocoa powder. Some of the best brands are Lindt from Switzerland, Valrhona and Poulain from France, and Pernigotti from Italy. Droste cocoa powder from The Netherlands is also quite good and is widely distributed in supermarkets.

American cocoa powders, which are not Dutch processed, have different baking characteristics from the European ones. They are mildly acidic, and the acidity needs to be compensated for by an alkaline ingredient such as baking soda in order to bring out the color and flavor of the cocoa. For this reason American cocoa powders cannot be used interchangeably with European Dutch-processed ones. Sweetened cocoa powders are suitable only for making hot cocoa, not for baking.

Sources: La Cuisine, Dean & DeLuca, Maid of Scandinavia, Williams-Sonoma.

COFFEE. Several cookie batters, doughs, and fillings are flavored with coffee. The coffee flavoring must be very concentrated in order to produce a rich coffee taste in the cookies. The easiest way to do this is to use instant coffee. Professional French pastry books often call for Nescafé, which is ubiquitous in France and has become almost a generic name for instant coffee there. The type of instant coffee we prefer is freeze dried. Usually the coffee should be mixed with a tiny amount of boiling water—just enough to dissolve it so that you don't add any more liquid than necessary and alter the consistency of the batter, dough, or filling. Occasionally the instant coffee is added directly to a batter or dough, and is then dissolved by the water in the batter or dough as it cooks and the water turns to steam.

CORNSTARCH. Used frequently in sauces but only occasionally in cookies, cornstarch is almost pure starch. It has twice the thickening power of flour.

CORNMEAL. This flour, made from corn, is rarely used in France except in the Bresse region where corn is an important crop. Unlike wheat flour, the proteins in cornmeal do not form gluten. We use cornmeal in one cookie, called *maïs,* which is the French word for "corn."

CREAM AND CRÈME FRAÎCHE. Cream is very important in other areas of French pastry, but its role in cookies is rather limited. It is an ingredient in a few batters and in the chocolate cream filling called *ganache.*

Cream is classified from light to heavy in direct proportion to its butterfat content. The higher the butterfat content, the thicker the cream. However, since butterfat is lighter than water, heavy cream actually weighs less than light cream. In batters, we always use cream with a high butterfat content, either heavy cream (by law at least 36 percent butterfat) or, if heavy cream is unavailable, then whipping cream (legal minimum 30 percent butterfat, which is considered the minimum for whipping). Heavy cream is sometimes labeled "heavy whipping cream."

Crème fraîche is a heavy cream that has been matured by culturing with special bacteria. It has a nutty and slightly sour taste, and it is much thicker than ordinary (sweet) heavy cream. Crème fraîche is the standard heavy cream in France. It has become popular in the United States only recently, but it is now marketed nationally. The butterfat content is not standardized. Some producers, such as Alta-Dena, market crème fraîche with a butterfat content comparable to ordinary heavy cream. Others, such as Vermont Butter & Cheese and Sante, have a higher butterfat content of about 40 percent and are correspondingly more expensive. You can make a substitute for crème fraîche at home by culturing ordinary heavy cream with a little buttermilk. (See page 491 in the Basic Preparations and Procedures section.)

When our recipes call for crème fraîche, we assume a butterfat content close to that of ordinary heavy cream or whipping cream. If you are using a deluxe, high-butterfat crème fraîche, then dilute it with cold milk accordingly (about 1 part milk for 6 parts crème fraîche) before measuring out the amount required in the recipe.

Like milk, cream is almost always pasteurized to kill harmful bacteria. Pasteurized heavy cream will last for about one week in the refrigerator. Crème fraîche will last even longer—at least ten days, and up to several weeks if it was cultured commercially.

To make cream less perishable, the dairy industry came up with the process of ultrapasteurization, a high-temperature sterilization process. Unfortunately, ultrapastuerized cream is devoid of the wonderful fresh, sweet taste of real pasteurized cream, and it has artificial emulsifiers added to restore the whipping properties of the cream, which are destroyed by the ultrapastueurization. If pasteurized heavy cream is unavailable, you can substitute two parts half-and-half (a light cream with about 12 percent butterfat) plus one part melted butter for the heavy cream in cookie batters. Or you can use crème fraîche in place of the heavy cream, provided the crème fraîche has a butterfat content comparable to that of heavy cream. In *ganache,* you can substitute either half-and-half or crème fraîche for heavy cream, since here the exact butterfat content is not crucial.

CREAM OF TARTAR. The potassium salt of tartaric acid, cream of tartar, can supply the acid needed in several baking situations, among them inhibiting crystallization in sugar syrups and providing one of the acid components in baking powder. When you are whipping egg whites, adding a little cream of tartar is the next best thing to whipping the whites in a copper bowl to reduce the risk of overbeating (see Chapter 2, page 56).

CURAÇAO LIQUEUR. This sweet, orange-flavored liqueur of medium proof is extracted from orange peels by steeping them in alcohol. Originally it was produced by the Dutch from the skins of the green oranges grown on the island of

Curaçao, off the coast of Venezuela. This liqueur has an intense orange flavor with a slight edge of bitterness, making it ideal for flavoring cookies.

Grand Marnier is a proprietary curaçao-type liqueur made by the cognac house Marnier-Lapostelle in France. It has a cognac base and is the most elegant of the orange liqueurs, but it is less bitter and intense than curaçao and so is less suitable as a cookie flavoring.

DÉCORS NON-PAREILS. These multicolored sprinkles are tiny beads of sugar and cornstarch, with a little food coloring. Some manufacturers call them mixed décors or assorted non-pareils.

EGGS. Eggs are the most versatile ingredient in cookie making. For some cookies they are used simply as a flavorful liquid or a glaze, but for others they give the cookies structure through their coagulating or foaming abilities.

Eggs contain proteins, both saturated and unsaturated fats, all essential amino acids and vitamins (except C), and most essential minerals. They are low in carbohydrates and contain only about 80 to 100 calories per large egg. About 11 percent of the egg's weight is in the shell, which has uses in cooking but not for cookies. Of the remainder, a little more than one-third is in the yolk and slightly less than two-thirds is in the white.

The yolk contains about 51 percent water, 16 percent protein, and 30 to 33 percent lipids (fats and related compounds, including the emulsifiers lecithin and cholesterol). Water and fat are not soluble in each other. In the yolk, microscopic globules of fat are surrounded by molecules of lecithin that, in turn, bond loosely with water molecules, keeping the fat globules suspended in the water. The mixture is called an emulsion. The yolk contains more lecithin than it needs to keep itself emulsified, so it can stabilize other fat-in-water emulsions. This emulsifying ability is particularly important in sauces, but it also helps keep the butterfat distributed in some batters. Cholesterol, on the other hand, is particularly effective in stabilizing water-in-fat emulsions. (Cholesterol is a long, fatty molecule and most of its length associates with the fat phase of the system, with only the end sticking up into the emulsified water droplets. Most other emulsifiers, including lecithin, tend to have nearly their entire length in the water phase and so are more effective for fat-in-water emulsions.) Butter is an example of a water-in-fat emulsion stabilized, in part, by cholesterol; and cholesterol probably also plays a minor roll in stabilizing the emulsion in some sweet pastry doughs that contain eggs but very little water.

The white consists almost entirely of water (about 88 percent) and proteins (about 11 percent), and is called the albumen. It is made up of four layers, alternating thick and thin. The first layer of albumen contains two thin, twisted, opaque white filaments—the chalazas—that connect the yolk to the inner membrane of the egg shell and keep the yolk anchored near the center of the egg. There are six major albumen proteins as well as several minor ones, and even the minor ones can play a significant role in the nature of the egg. But in terms of quantity, about 85 percent of the albumen proteins are made up by ovalbumin, conalbumin, and the globulins.

Overall, the egg is 70 to 75 percent water. When used in place of water as the liquid in cookies, eggs give a richer taste and color. This is especially noticeable in sweet pastry doughs.

Perhaps the most important property of eggs for cooking generally, and for baking in particular, is the ability of egg proteins to coagulate, turning from liquid to solid. The proteins are long chains of amino acids. In the egg they are folded up into compact little balls. Physical hydrogen bonds between amino acids on the same chain hold the folds in place. Each molecule has negative charge, so the protein molecules repel each other and bonds do not form between different protein molecules. However, if the intramolecular bonds are broken and molecular motion is increased sufficiently to overcome the electrical repulsion between molecules, then bonding between protein molecules becomes possible. When a mixture containing egg whites and/or yolks is heated, increased vibration of the molecules can break the intramolecular bonds. The initially compact proteins become stretched out, or denatured. The heat eventually increases the molecular motion to the point where strong chemical, covalent bonds can form between molecules—that is, they coagulate. As more intermolecular covalent bonds form, the molecules form an interlocking network with water molecules bound in the spaces between proteins by relatively weak hydrogen bonds to the amino acids in the proteins. This structure is called a gel. The bonds between protein molecules are stronger than the hydrogen bonds that hold the water in the gel. So as time goes on, the heat disrupts protein-water bonds and more covalent protein-protein bonds form. The structure becomes more rigid, and at the same time fewer sites are available for protein-water bonds. Eventually this squeezes out water, and the gel becomes harder and drier.

The process of coagulation has direct application to thickening sauces and to baking cookies. In sauces, coagulation first produces thickening. But if the proteins coagulate too much and squeeze water out of the gel, then the sauce curdles. In baking, on the other hand, coagulation gives the cookies a rigid structure and water evaporates as it is squeezed out of the gel. A soft, moist batter develops into a cookie that is, at least relatively, firm and dry.

The mechanical action of whipping eggs produces extensional forces on protein molecules that can result in breaking intramolecular bonds and unfolding the molecules, denaturing them just as heat does. At room temperature, the proteins cross-link by forming hydrogen bonds between denatured protein molecules. In an egg foam, whipping traps air bubbles in the liquid eggs, and the cross-linked and denatured proteins stabilize the bubbles. (We discuss whipping egg whites and the mechanism of foam production in detail in the introduction to Chapter 2 on Meringues. Whipping eggs for sponge cake batters is explained in the introduction to Chapter 4.)

Acids (such as cream of tartar and lemon juice) can promote or inhibit coagulation. Adding acid to a liquid lowers its pH. If the initial pH is alkaline (as it is in egg whites), lowering the pH reduces the charge on protein molecules and thus their mutual repulsion. As a result, bonds between protein molecules can form more easily. On the other hand, if the initial pH is neutral or acidic, lowering the pH increases the charge on protein molecules, increasing their mutual repulsion and inhibiting coagulation. (The latter effect is important in emulsified sauces.)

Egg whites begin to coagulate at about 145° F (60–65° C). Heating whites above 160° F (71° C) toughens them. Yolks coagulate at about 155° F (70° C). The coagulation temperature can be raised by diluting the eggs with water or adding sugar; both slow coagulation by separating the protein molecules so that they must move more in order to bump into each other. In custard sauces, which contain both liquid and sugar, the temperature must reach 175 to 185° F (80–85° C) before coagulation occurs.

Eggs are graded by the USDA according to both quality and size. The higher the quality grade, the thicker and more viscous the white and the firmer and plumper the yolk. Only the highest grades—AA and A—are sold in most retail markets.

Sizes are graded from *small* to *jumbo*, corresponding to a minimum weight of from 18 ounces (510 g) to 30 ounces (850 g) per dozen. We always use *large* eggs, which weigh about 2 ounces (57 g) each (in the shell).

Fresh eggs have thicker whites, firmer yolks, and better flavor than old eggs. Starting from the moment the egg is laid, its pH increases. The yolk starts off slightly acidic, with a pH of about 6. Within a few days it has risen to about 6.6, which is nearly neutral. The white begins with a slightly alkaline pH of about 7.7 and rises to a very alkaline level over 9. The higher pH increases the repulsion between protein molecules in both white and yolk. At the same time the yolk membrane weakens because it is stretched as the yolk absorbs water from the white. Also the proportion of thick albumen in the white decreases, and the white becomes more runny. Eggs can be kept for up to one month in the refrigerator before they actually spoil. However, their quality declines so much that we recommend using them within one week. Store the eggs upright (that is, large end up) in the coldest part of the refrigerator. Keep them in their carton to minimize absorption of odors and escape of moisture through the shell.

It is easiest to separate eggs when they are cold because the whites and yolks have greater viscosity and surface tension. Fresh eggs are easiest because they have stronger membranes around their yolks. Always crack the side of the egg shell on the countertop rather than on the edge of a bowl, which can force a sharp edge of the cracked shell to puncture the yolk. Hold the egg vertically over a bowl, insert the tips of your thumbs in the crack, and pry the shell open. Let the white drop into the bowl, then pour the yolk back and forth between the halves of the shell until all of the white has separated from the yolk. Separate the chalazas from the yolk by running your fingertip over the edge of the shell. Add the chalazas to the rest of the white. If a speck of yolk gets in the white, remove it with the edge of the shell or blot it up with the corner of a paper towel. After separating each egg, pour the white into another bowl. That way if you puncture a yolk and too much drops into the bowl with the white, you will loose only one white. After separating, you can store the whites in an airtight container for up to four or five days in the refrigerator, but the sooner you can use them, the better.

For most purposes it is best to bring the eggs to room temperature, and this is particularly important if they are to be whipped. Remove the eggs from the refrigerator and take them out of their carton at least forty-five minutes in advance. If you forget to take out the eggs in advance, you can warm them quickly by immersing them in warm water for five to ten minutes, then drying the shells thoroughly before cracking.

Many cookies made from pastry doughs are brushed with egg wash before baking to give them a rich color and sheen. The egg wash is prepared by beating a whole egg with a fork until homogeneous, and then applied sparingly with a pastry brush to avoid producing a thick crust.

~~~~~~~

EAU-DE-VIE. This is the French term for brandy. Literally translated, it means "water of life." It is most frequently encountered in connection with the *alcools blancs,* which are clear, colorless brandies distilled from fresh fruits such as cherries (*kirsch*), raspberries (*framboise*) and pears (*poire*). These brandies are aged in glass or pottery. They are dry, high in alcohol (80 to 90 proof), and very aromatic. The best examples are produced in France, Switzerland, and Germany. We especially like the French ones, which tend to have more of the perfume of the fresh fruit. See also **FRAMBOISE** and **KIRSCH**.

Brandies made from grapes (such as cognac and Armagnac) and apples (calvados) are aged in wood, which gives them a caramel color. They are very different from the *alcools blancs,* and they are not often used in cookies.

~~~~~~~~

FILBERTS. See **HAZELNUTS.**

~~~~~~~~

FLOUR. Only white flour is suitable for use in French cookies. The particular white flour that we used in developing our recipes is Gold Medal *unbleached all-purpose flour.* Whole-wheat and bran flours, which contain all or part of the germ and/or bran of the wheat and are therefore higher in natural vitamins, minerals, and proteins, have textures totally incompatible with our cookies.

White flour contains primarily starch, proteins, and water. The proportions depend on the type of wheat from which it was made and how the flour was milled.

Starch makes up the largest share (typically 73 percent to 78 percent) of the flour. There are two types of starch molecules (amylose and amylopectin), and they are distributed in the flour in the form of granules. Starch is particularly important in batters (as well as in sauces), and to a lesser extent in cookie doughs, because of its ability to absorb water. If the granules are damaged, they can absorb cold water, but intact granules do not absorb water until the temperature of the batter reaches 140° F (60° C). At that temperature, the starch granules absorb water and swell up all at once. This makes the batter thicker and more viscous, and we say the starch has "gelatinized." In addition, since the starch molecules do not actually dissolve in the water, they contribute a solid component and help give structure to the cookies.

The protein content of white flours ranges from about 7 percent for cake flour to 12 percent or 13 percent for bread flour, with all-purpose flour in the middle at around 10 percent. About 85 percent of the protein is made up of two types of protein molecules, gliadin and glutenin. These two proteins are not soluble in water, but they can absorb up to twice their weight of water. Furthermore, when mixed with water they form a complex called gluten, which is essential to the structure of both flaky pastry doughs and breads. The gliadin and glutenin proteins are very large and complex molecules, made of long chains of atoms with many side groups of atoms attached. The chains are coiled up and folded onto themselves. Side groups adjacent to each other, whether on the same or different molecules, bond with each other. When the flour is mixed with water to make a dough and the dough is kneaded, the protein molecules unfold and become more stretched out so that more side groups become exposed to side groups on other molecules. This enables the proteins to form an extended intertwined network, with water molecules held within it by hydrogen bonds with side groups on the protein chains. Eventually the molecules tend to line up side by side and form progressively more cross-linking bonds that make the structure more stable and difficult to deform.

Nonetheless, each protein molecule still has many kinks and folds, maintained by bonds between side groups on the molecule. When the dough is stretched, these bonds resist and then break as the stress increases. Then when the stress is released, the bonds re-form, making the molecules kink and fold again and at the same time pulling back neighboring molecules that are cross-linked to them. This makes the dough shrink back.

Some minor constituents of flour also play a role in the development of gluten. Fats, present in flour in very small quantity, play an essential role in the development of gluten by bonding to both gliadin and glutenin molecules on the one hand and by promoting slippage between large sheets of gluten on the other. Fats also bind gluten to the surfaces of starch granules.

Groups of one sulphur and one hydrogen atom (called thiol groups) are present on molecules in freshly milled flour. These thiol groups can bond with side groups on gluten proteins, blocking formation or reestablishment of sulphur to sulphur bonds that make the kinks and cross-linkings in the gluten network. This inhibits the development of an elastic gluten fiber network and makes the flour unsuitable for flaky pastry doughs and breads. Aging the flour reduces the thiol content by oxidation and thus improves the quality of the gluten. Aging also permits oxidation of yellow pigments in the flour, thus making the flour whiter. The same effects can be produced by chemical bleaching. Flours that have been aged naturally are called unbleached, those that have been bleached chemically are called bleached.

The relative importance of starch and gluten in a cookie batter or dough is determined in large part by the proportions of other ingredients. In a batter that contains a large amount of liquid, the flour proteins are dispersed in the liquid and their concentration is too low to form a strong gluten fiber network. Also, the flour is usually folded in gently at the end of the mixing process to avoid activating the gluten so that the cookies will be tender. Thus the structural role of the flour comes primarily from gelatinization of the starch.

In contrast, in a flaky pastry dough the gluten fiber network is the dominant structural element. The water content is low, and most of it is held by the gluten. When the dough bakes, the gluten proteins coagulate and form rigid bonds. The gluten releases water that is absorbed by the starch, but since the amount of water is relatively small, the starch is only partly gelatinized and its structural role is secondary.

Yet another situation occurs in sweet pastry doughs and many creamed butter and sugar batters. These contain large proportions of butter and sugar and a small proportion of water. The starch granules and gluten fibers are surrounded by the butter-sugar mixture and isolated from each other. Furthermore, since sugar is hygroscopic, it absorbs most of the available water, preventing formation of the gluten complex and severely limiting gelatization of the starch. As with other batters, the flour is gently folded in at the end of the mixing, which also limits gluten development. So in these doughs and batters, the structural contributions of both starch and gluten are greatly reduced, and as a result the cookies are tender and crumbly.

Four basic types of white flour are widely available in the United States—namely, unbleached all-purpose flour, bleached all-purpose flour, cake flour, and bread flour. Some brands, such as Gold Medal and Pillsbury, are marketed nationally, while others are available regionally. The packaged flour on your supermarket shelf is labeled with the approximate contents of carbohydrate (mostly starch), protein, fat, and sodium. The remainder is primarily water and a small amount of ash (natural minerals from the wheat). The water content varies slightly as the flour loses moisture by evaporation during storage; in cookie doughs containing a high percentage of flour it is occasionally necessary to compensate for this by adjusting the amount of flour or liquid in the recipe. By law, white flours must be enriched to replenish vitamins and minerals removed in milling and in aging or bleaching.

We use Gold Medal unbleached all-purpose flour for nearly all cookies. It contains about 10 percent protein and 77 percent carbohydrate. The bleached all-purpose flours from Gold Medal and Pillsbury have the same proportions of protein and carbohydrate, and so can be used interchangeably with the Gold Medal unbleached. If you use another all-purpose flour with different proportions of protein and carbohydrate, you may have to alter our recipes to compensate for their different baking characteristics. (For accurate protein and carbohydrate percentages, telephone the manufacturer. Do not rely on the vague package label.)

Cake flour is a very fine textured, soft (low-gluten) flour that has been bleached with chlorine. Unlike the bleaches used for all-purpose flours, the chlorine bleach does not help improve the gluten, and in fact inhibits development of the gluten by raising the acidity of the flour. Cake flour is suitable only for cakes. In principle it could be used in any of our sponge cake cookies, but we have chosen to use it only in our recipe for Madeleines. Substituting cake flour for all-purpose flour in other cookies would require adjusting the recipe because of the cake flour's very different characteristics. For a complete guide to baking cakes with cake flour, see Rose Beranbaum's *The Cake Bible*.

Bread flour is a very high protein (12 to 13 percent) flour made from hard wheats. It is usually bleached and treated with potassium bromate to improve the gluten's elasticity. Suitable only for breads, we never use it for cookies.

Whenever you roll out a pastry dough it is necessary to dust the countertop and the dough with flour to prevent the dough from sticking to countertop or rolling pin. Use as little flour as possible in order to avoid altering the proportion of flour in the dough. Unless the dough is particularly sticky,

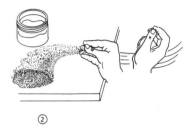

②

a light film of flour is sufficient. The dusting can be done with a fine sieve by putting some flour in the sieve and then tapping it gently to release a light, uniform dusting. However, most flour sifters are too coarse for this purpose and produce a heavy, blotchy dusting. The best method is to throw out the flour onto your countertop by hand. Here's how: Take a little flour between your thumb and fingertips. Slowly draw back your hand, then without releasing your fingertips, throw your hand horizontally over the front half of your countertop ② as though you were skimming a rock across a pond. There will be enough loose flour around your fingers to make a light film float down over the counter. Always keep your hand about four to six inches (10–15 cm) above the countertop, and repeat as many times as necessary. Place the dough on the flour-dusted countertop and dust the dough with flour by the same method. This technique takes a little practice, but once mastered it is quick, easy, and effective.

FOOD COLORINGS. These are used to enhance the natural colors of ingredients in some cookies and occasionally to provide decorative accent colors. Red is frequently used in batters flavored with raspberry or orange to produce a pink or orange color and in chocolate batters to enrich the brown color of the chocolate. Yellow can be used with pineapple, and also combined with green food coloring to enhance the natural green of pistachios.

FRAMBOISE. This is just the French word for raspberry. It is often used as an abbreviation for *eau-de-vie de framboise,* the clear, colorless brandy (an *alcool blanc*) distilled from fresh raspberries. In German it is called *Himbeergeist.* Framboise is dry and has a heady perfume of fresh raspberries. About 9 pounds (4 kg) of raspberries are required to produce one bottle of brandy, so it is very expensive. Sweet raspberry liqueurs are considerably cheaper (though still not inexpensive), but they are insipid compared with the *eau-de-vie.* See also **EAU-DE-VIE**.

FRUITS. Citrus zests and juices are frequently used to flavor cookie batters and doughs. Candied and glacé fruits can be used in the batter or dough for flavor and texture, or they can be used as decoration. Jams are used as fillings and as an ingredient in batters to help keep the cookies fresh longer. Fruits appear in other forms in cookie recipes (such as chopped pineapple in Pineapple Soufflés) only occasionally.

GLACÉ FRUITS. Fruits that are preserved by cooking in sugar syrup and then glazed with syrup are referred to as glacé (from the French word for *glazed*) or, less precisely, candied. The ones we see most often in the United States are cherries, pineapple slices, and apricots. Glacé pears and peaches are also available, and in the luxury food shops of Paris you can find everything from plums and citron to whole glacé melons and pineapple. Glacé fruits are sold primarily in the fall and winter, especially around the holidays.

We use glacé cherries and pineapple primarily as decoration for cookies, and occasionally chopped to add texture and flavor. Unfortunately, the candied fruits sold in supermarkets in the United States taste too much of artificial preservatives and not enough of fruit. On the other hand, the fine-quality glacé fruits imported from France and Switzerland are luxurious delicacies, and excellent glacé fruits are also available from Australia. Like candied citrus peels, they can be kept in the refrigerator, wrapped airtight, for two or three months, or frozen for up to six months. If stored longer they dry out and harden, and part of the sugar content can crystallize on the surface.

Sources: La Cuisine, Balducci's, Dean & DeLuca.

HAZELNUTS. What is the difference between hazelnuts and filberts? Some authors state that filberts are cultivated hazelnuts; others that hazelnuts grow on bushes, filberts on trees; still others that filberts are elongated in shape while hazelnuts are globular. *Larousse Gastronomique* gives *hazelnut* as the translation for the French *noisette, filbert* for *aveline* (which, at least originally, was the large, cultivated St. John filbert from Avella in Campania); it also states that *filbert* is another name for hazelnut. Despite all the attempts to distinguish the two, hazelnuts and filberts have become two words for the same nut. Those wishing to identify the two by shape will be disappointed to learn that the same tree (or bush) can produce elongated nuts one year and globular ones the next, and sometimes one shape on one branch and the other on another branch in the same year. This suggests that at least part of the confusion derives from the fact that many cultivated varieties are hybrids, and some "wild" species may in fact be descended from varieties that were once cultivated. The hazelnut has, after all, been cultivated for thousands of years. Having said all that, we cease making any distinction between hazelnuts and filberts. We prefer the sound and associations of the word *hazelnut,* but we use both words almost indiscriminantly.

The flavor of the hazelnut is unique—more assertive than the almond but not as aggressive as the walnut. It is a distinctive flavoring in numerous desserts (including many cookies), it marries well with chocolate, and it can be accented to advantage with vanilla or cinnamon.

Native American hazelnuts are undistinguished for eating compared with their European counterparts. European varieties have been planted extensively in Oregon and Washington State, and most of the hazelnuts marketed in the United States are grown in those areas and in Europe.

Like almonds, hazelnuts have a thin, papery skin that can be removed by blanching, although the method is different from that used for almonds. However, unlike almonds, hazelnuts are almost always marketed raw (that is, with skins on). The producers tell us that the reason they don't market blanched hazelnuts is that sometimes the skins come off easily, but sometimes they don't and no one knows why. While we can't provide an explanation, we can offer a diagnostic: In our experience, globular hazelnuts can be blanched easily while elongated ones cannot. So we recommend selecting globular hazelnuts whenever you have the choice.

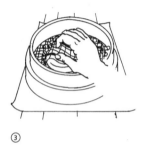

③

To blanch hazelnuts, spread out the nuts on a baking sheet and heat them in a preheated 450° F (230° C) oven, stirring once or twice to prevent the nuts nearest the edge of the sheet from burning, until their skins are dry and cracked and have darkened but not burned, about four to six minutes. (The hazelnuts should remain pale inside.) Transfer the hazelnuts to a sieve and rub the hot nuts against the mesh ③, using a towel to protect your hand, to remove most of the skins. Then let the nuts cool.

In cookies, hazelnuts are often used whole or chopped as a garnish. When powdered hazelnuts are included in a cookie batter or dough, they can provide a primary flavoring and textural element. Sometimes the hazelnuts are roasted to brown them and enhance their flavor (see **NUTS**). After roasting, the skins are also removed by rubbing the hot nuts against the mesh of a sieve.

HONEY. Honey contains the two simple sugars dextrose and fructose. It was the predominant sweetener in French pastry before refined cane sugar became widely available in Europe in the seventeenth century, but today it is used only when its unique flavor is desired.

JAMS AND JELLIES. Many cookies are filled with jam or jelly. The ones we use most often are apricot and raspberry jam and red currant jelly.

Jams are also used as ingredients in batters, partly for flavor and sweetening but more importantly because they contain invert sugar, which helps keep soft cookies moist and fresh. The standard jam for this purpose is apricot, but occasionally other jams (such as pineapple) are used depending on the flavor of the particular cookie.

For either purpose, apricot jam (as well as any other jam that contains solid pieces of fruit) should be forced through a strainer to puree the pieces of fruit. See page 484 in the Basic Preparations and Procedures section for details.

The best jams and jellies to choose have a firm, not runny, texture and taste like sweetened fruit. Cheap, poor quality jams taste more of citric acid and sugar than they do of fruit, and should be avoided. Among the standard brands sold in supermarkets, we particularly like the Bonne Mamman line from France. Knotts Berry Farm and Smucker's are also quite acceptable.

If your jam is runny rather than well set and firm, then it is too liquid to use for a filling and would add too much moisture to a batter. In this case, the jam should be cooked over low heat, stirring occasionally, to reduce its moisture content. Do not reduce it too much or it will become rubbery when cool.

~~~~~

KIRSCH. A clear, colorless brandy distilled from cherries. Also called Kirschwasser, this is the most famous and widely available of the *alcools blancs* (see also **EAU-DE-VIE**). It gives a subtle cherry flavor to several cookies.

The kirsch brandies produced in the United States are a pale reflection of the elegant and very expensive originals from France, Switzerland, and Germany. The only less expensive kirsch brandy that we recommend for use in cookies is the kirsch distilled in The Netherlands by Bols.

~~~~~

LEMONS. This citrus fruit supplies two distinct flavoring elements—the juice and the zest. The juice with its high acid content gives piquancy to some cookies. On the other hand, the zest—which is the thin outer surface of the skin—is oily and aromatic and provides a more subtle and seductive flavor. The zest is usually required in finely grated form, which is most easily obtained by rubbing the whole lemon across a grater. The white, inner part of the skin is the pith, which is bitter and is not used except when the peel is candied (see **CANDIED CITRON, LEMON PEEL, AND ORANGE PEEL**). A few recipes require lemon extract, which is produced by combining oil pressed from lemon skins with alcohol.

~~~~~

LIQUEURS. Many of these sweet, flavorful alcoholic liquors can be used to flavor cookies. The most common are the orange liqueurs, particularly curaçao (see **CURAÇAO LIQUEUR**). Two others we use occasionally are maraschino and anisette.

Maraschino liqueur is distilled from fermented Marasca sour cherries. At one time, these cherries grew only in Dalmatia and the liqueur was produced in the city of Zadar. Today maraschino is produced in Italy as well as Croatia. In contrast to kirsch, the stones of the cherries are crushed for maraschino. This, and the fact that maraschino is sweet, makes it very different from kirsch.

Anisette is flavored with aniseed.

MILK. Milk contains primarily water (about 87 percent), with the remainder butterfat (about 3½ percent), proteins, and carbohydrates (including the sugar lactose). It is used as the liquid in a few cookie batters.

NUTS. Botanically, a nut is a fruit with one seed and a dry, hard fruit layer. However in common English usage the word *nut* is applied to any edible kernel surrounded by a hard shell. Of the five nuts—almonds, hazelnuts, pistachios, walnuts, and chestnuts—we use in this book, only the hazelnut and chestnut qualify as true nuts. Almonds, pistachios, and walnuts are the seeds of drupes, which, like the peach, apricot, and plum (also drupes), have both soft and hard layers surrounding the seed. The only other nut that has been used to any extent in French pastry is the pine nut, which grows in the pinecone with no covering. Historically, when almonds have been too expensive in France, pine nuts have sometimes been used in cookies that traditionally call for almonds. Today pine nuts are used occasionally in cookies from Provence, but their taste is not particularly popular in most of France.

Nuts are always expensive, but prices for small packages (1½ to 2 ounces or 40 to 60 g) sold in supermarkets are much higher than for nuts sold in large packages (6 to 8 ounces or 170 to 225 g) or in bulk. Sometimes the convenience of small vacuum-packed bags of nuts with a long shelf life is worth the expense, but if you are using large quantities of nuts, it is advisable to shop for more economical alternatives. If your supermarket does not have large packages or bulk nuts, try a natural foods market or specialty store.

Almonds, hazelnuts, pistachios, and walnuts are to some extent interchangeable and are often handled by the same methods. In particular, these four nuts are frequently chopped, powdered, or roasted. Chestnuts are in a class by themselves because of their low fat and high carbohydrate content.

You can chop nuts with a chef's knife on a cutting board, in a wooden chopping bowl, or in a food processor. The food processor is extremely fast, but it chops the nuts unevenly and is difficult to control. We prefer to chop the nuts by hand; even then, it is impossible to get bits of uniform size, and some of the nuts will be reduced almost to a powder. The only way to get a more uniform size is to sift out the nuts that are chopped too fine. We feel that it is almost always sufficient to sift out the very fine powdery bits using a medium sieve (1/16 to 3/32 inch, or 1½ to 2 mm, mesh), regardless of how fine the nuts are chopped. While chopped nuts are occasionally an ingredient in batters, they are used more often to decorate the tops of cookies; powdered bits of nuts detract from the desired effect.

Powdered nuts, particularly almonds, are required in close to half of all French cookies. The food processor is by far the most efficient tool for producing the substantial quantities often needed. Most nuts have a high oil content—typically between half and two-thirds of their weight. Some of the oil is released when the nuts are ground. We invariably grind the nuts with sugar to absorb this oil and prevent it from transforming the powdered nuts into a paste. The standard proportion is equal weights of nuts and sugar. The procedure is described in detail under "Nut and Sugar Powders" on page 482 in the Basic Preparations and Procedures section. Naturally the nuts with higher oil content (particularly walnuts) require the most care.

Nuts can be roasted to enhance their flavor, brown them, and reduce their moisture content. To do this, spread out the nuts on a baking sheet and cook them in a preheated 350° F (175° C) oven, stirring occasionally to prevent uneven cooking or burning of the nuts near the edge of the baking sheet. Chopped or sliced almonds should be roasted until lightly browned, about ten to twelve minutes. Whole nuts should be roasted until light brown in the center, about fifteen to twenty-five minutes (depending on the type and size of the nuts); test one by cutting it in half. Be careful not to overcook the nuts or they will burn. When the nuts are sufficiently browned, transfer them to your countertop and allow them to cool. Or, for hazelnuts, transfer them to a large sieve and rub them against the mesh, using a towel to protect your hands ④, to remove most of their skins, then allow them to cool. Roasted nuts are most often used for decoration or in fillings. Pistachios are not roasted because it is desirable to preserve their green color.

④

ORANGES. Like lemons, oranges provide flavor from both their juice and zest. Orange juice lacks the piquancy of lemon juice and doesn't have enough intensity to be used alone, but in combination with the zest it sometimes gives a more balanced flavor than does the zest alone. The zest is the thin outer surface of the peel. It is oily and aromatic, with the strong scent characteristic of oranges. When grated zest is required for a cookie, the whole orange should be rubbed across a fine grater to remove the zest but not the bitter white pith beneath it.

The orange peel can be used in candied form (see **CANDIED CITRON, LEMON PEEL, AND ORANGE PEEL**). And orange liqueurs (see **CURAÇAO LIQUEUR**), which derive their flavor from orange peels, are frequently used in cookies as well.

ORANGE FLOWER WATER. This fragrant liquid is distilled from neroli, an oil obtained from orange blossoms. It is the classic flavoring for Ladyfingers.

PINEAPPLE. Glacé pineapple (see **GLACÉ FRUITS**) is frequently used in cookies, particularly for decoration. A few cookie batters are flavored with pineapple, either pineapple jam or pineapple preserved in heavy syrup. When using pineapple in heavy syrup, care must be taken to squeeze as much moisture as possible out of the fruit in order not to soften the batter excessively.

PISTACHIOS. This nut is native to central Asia and is most closely associated with Middle Eastern cooking. Pistachios are quite popular in France, where they are used in desserts as well as in savory dishes such as pâtés.

Nutritionally, pistachios are almost identical to almonds, and they are sometimes referred to as green almonds. But the pastel green color and subtle yet seductive flavor of pistachios give them a unique appeal. Pistachios are quite expensive, so they are reserved for use in cookies where their color and/or flavor have special impact. They can be outstanding in cookies made from a nut paste. Unfortunately, their color is often too weak in a cookie batter and is usually enhanced with a little food coloring.

Only unsalted pistachios should be used in desserts. They are available both in the shell and shelled from specialty food stores. Obviously, buying shelled pistachios saves a lot of effort.

Source: La Cuisine.

RAISINS AND CURRANTS. While the flavor and texture of the large muscat or Malaga raisins make them wonderful for eating out of hand, they are too large for most French cookies. The raisins we use most often are sun-dried seedless rasins (which the French call *raisins de Smyrne* and the English sultanas) and currants (*raisins de Corinthe* in French). In the United States, seedless raisins are made from Thompson seedless grapes. If the same grapes are treated with sulphur dioxide to preserve their color and then dried artificially, they are called golden raisins. Currants are made from a smaller seedless grape. They are especially useful in batters that are piped, since they are less likely to clog the pastry tube than are larger raisins.

RUM. Rum is distilled from molasses and from sugarcane juice, as a by-product of refining sugarcane. It originated in the Caribbean Islands. The rich, heavy, pungent rums from Jamaica (as well as Haiti, Martinique, and Guadeloupe) are frequently used to flavor cookies. The dry, light-bodied Puerto Rican rums are not used in desserts because their flavor is too weak.

SALT. For some cookies (primarily those made from flaky pastry doughs), a tiny amount of salt is included in the batter or dough to enhance the flavor of butter or eggs. This must be done carefully, since too much salt conflicts with sweet flavors. Furthermore, as we reduce the quantity of salt in our diets, our sensitivity to salt increases. Many recipes that were designed one or two generations ago now seem oppressively salty. We include salt in recipes only where it produces noticeable flavor enhancement without discernible saltiness. We never use salted butter.

~~~~~~

SPICES. With the exception of cinnamon, spices are extremely rare as flavorings in French cookies. A few old cookies were flavored with ginger, but on the whole the French tend to regard spices as savory flavorings.

~~~~~~

SUGARS. Sugars are a large class of carbohydrates, but only a few of them are of interest in cooking. The most basic structurally are the simple sugars, or monosaccharides, composed of one sugar unit, $C_6H_{12}O_6$. These include dextrose (also called glucose) and fructose.

The double sugars, or disaccharides, are composed of two simple sugar units joined together. A water molecule is dropped in the process, so the formula for the common double sugars sucrose, lactose, and maltose is $C_{12}H_{22}O_{11}$.

Only simple and double sugars taste sweet. Starches are polysaccharides, consisting of many simple sugar units joined together.

Ordinary sugar is 99.8 percent pure sucrose, refined from sugarcane and from sugar beets. It is by far the most common sweetener used in baking, and sucrose is an essential ingredient in every cookie. Sucrose is a hard, white, crystalline solid that is very soluble in water but insoluble in alcohol. In baking it has several important properties. The simplest are its ability to enhance other flavors and contribute a rich color via caramelization. Cookies that are too low in sugar look pale and taste bland.

At a deeper level, sugar raises the coagulation temperature of eggs, giving batters more time to rise or spread before setting. It is hygroscopic, meaning that it absorbs water from its environment. This permits moist cookies without sogginess, and is particularly important in sponge cakes, almond paste cookies, and some meringues. Since the sugar retains moisture after baking, it retards drying and helps keep the cookies fresh. Also, since the sugar competes with starch and gluten for available moisture, it reduces starch gelatinization and gluten formation and thus makes the cookie's structure less rigid and more tender.

In whipped eggs the sugar becomes part of the cell walls of the foam. It gives strength and rigidity to the structure by absorbing moisture from the foam and thus firming the eggs. This is especially apparent in meringues where, added at the end of the whipping, sugar prevents graininess and smoothes and stabilizes the meringue.

The simple sugars dextrose and fructose are not nearly as important as sucrose in cookies, but they are used occasionally in small amounts (usually in jam, brown sugar, or honey) because of their special properties. Dextrose is the sugar that is used as fuel by the cells in our bodies. It is the predominant sugar in sweet corn and is also an important constituent in honey. Like sucrose, dextrose is very soluble in water, but it is less than half as sweet as sucrose. On the other hand, fructose, which is found in ripe fruits and in honey, is about 50 percent sweeter than sucrose and more soluble in water than is sucrose. It is very difficult to crystallize because of its high solubility. Both of these simple sugars are more hygroscopic than sucrose.

When sucrose is dissolved in acidulated water and boiled, some of the sucrose is transformed into a mixture of equal parts dextrose and fructose, called invert sugar. This process is important in the preparation of jams because invert sugar inhibits crystallization of sucrose from solutions. When the jam cools, the invert sugar prevents the sugar from crystallizing and making the jam grainy. Because invert sugar is made up of dextrose and fructose, it is even better than sucrose in its ability to absorb water from its environment. So adding jam to cookie batters keeps the cookies fresher longer than if they were prepared with sucrose alone. Honey and brown sugar also contain invert sugar and are sometimes added to batters for this same reason.

Lactose is the sugar in milk and contributes to cookies only incidentally through the small percentage in milk and milk products. Maltose plays no significant role in cookies, and its importance in baking is primarily limited to products leavened with yeast.

Sucrose melts at 320° F (160° C), forming a clear, nearly colorless liquid. As the temperature increases it takes on a yellowish cast, and at 335 to 338° F (168–170° C) it begins to break down and caramelize, turning pale amber and developing a richer and less sweet flavor. This light caramel stage is used for praliné and *nougatine*. The caramel gradually turns a deeper shade of amber as the temperature increases. At 355° F (180° C) the sugar looses one-sixth of its weight by evaporation of water in the sugar molecules themselves and begins to boil. The caramel will be a medium amber and have a very rich caramel taste. Like sugar itself, caramel is water soluble, but unlike plain sucrose it is noncrystalline. At higher temperatures, the caramel darkens and gives off a faint burnt odor, then at around 375° F (190° C) it begins to smoke and turns dark brown, almost black. At this point it is very bitter and suitable only as a brown food coloring. At 410° F (210° C) the sugar decomposes completely, leaving only carbon.

Sugar syrups are prepared by moistening sugar with water, heating to completely dissolve the sugar and then gradually boiling off the water and raising the concentration of sugar in the syrup. Sugar syrups play a limited role in cookies, almost exclusively through Italian meringue. This is discussed in detail in the introduction to Chapter 2, Meringue Batters. We also use this method of cooking sugar for praliné (see page 485 in the Basic Preparations and Procedures section). Note that when sugar syrups are cooked at high altitude, the syrup reaches a given concentration at a lower temperature than it would at sea level. The reason is that the boiling point of water is reduced by the lower atmospheric pressure at high altitude. This affects the correlation between the temperature and density of the sugar syrup from the boiling point of water—212° F (100° C) at sea level—up to 293° F (145° C), at which point all of the water in the syrup has evaporated. Within this range, the temperature required to reach any given concentration of sugar is reduced by 1.8° F (1° C) for each 1,000 feet (300 meters) above sea level. Above 293° F (145° C) altitude has no effect on cooking sugar syrups.

COMMERCIAL FORMS OF SUCROSE

- **Granulated sugar.** Relatively large crystal size makes this too coarse for most batters and doughs. It doesn't dissolve quickly enough and can produce a grainy texture. We use granulated sugar for making syrups—for example, in the recipe for Italian meringue. Extra-fine granulated sugar has crystals between granulated and superfine in size.

- **Superfine sugar.** Sold in 1-pound (454 g) boxes, this sugar has the smallest crystals of any granulated sugar. As a result, it dissolves more quickly than ordinary granulated sugar. Also, the smaller crystals are better for aerating creamed butter and egg foams. This is the best sugar to use for many cookie batters and doughs.

- **Confectioners' sugar.** This powdered sugar is produced by milling granulated sugar. A tiny amount of cornstarch is added to prevent caking. Confectioners' sugar dissolves more quickly than superfine. However, it doesn't have crystals with sharp edges, so it is less good for aerating creamed butter and egg foams. It gives a crisper texture to some cookies when used in the batter or dough. It is also used to dust cookies for decoration.

- **Crystal sugar.** This is a sugar with very large crystals—about $\frac{1}{16}$ inch (1½ mm). Used for decoration, it gives a sparkling, jewel-like appearance. It is also available colored. A mixture of crystal sugars of different colors is sometimes called party sugar.

- **Sanding sugar.** With crystals about $\frac{1}{32}$ inch (1 mm) in size, this sugar stands between crystal sugar and granulated. It is used for decorating when crystal sugar would be too coarse and crunchy.

- **Brown sugar.** Originally brown sugars were partly refined cane sugars, with some of the molasses retained. Today they are made by dissolving refined sugar in a molasses syrup and then recrystallizing it. As a result, the crystals of sucrose in brown sugar are coated with molasses. Brown sugars contain more moisture than pure sugar because, in molasses, some of the sucrose is broken down into glucose and fructose, which are more hygroscopic. Used in cookie batters, brown sugar gives a rich color and taste. We use only *light brown sugar* in this book. Dark brown sugar contains more molasses than light brown sugar and is too strong for most French cookies. Turbinado sugar is similar to light brown, but is produced by refining the sugar less thoroughly. The crystal size of turbinado sugar is usually too large for cookie batters.

Source (crystal sugars and sanding sugar): Maid of Scandinavia.

~~~~~~

COMMERCIAL SUGAR SYRUPS

■ **Corn syrup.** This syrup, produced by incomplete hydrolysis of cornstarch, contains glucose plus some maltose as well as more complex carbohydrates (particular a gummy substance called dextrin). When corn syrup is added to sucrose syrups, the larger carbohydrate molecules inhibit crystallization by surrounding the sucrose molecules and preventing them from joining together. We use it in cooked almond paste (marzipan) to prevent graininess.

■ **Molasses.** This is the syrup left after most of the sucrose has been crystallized out of the juice of the sugarcane. It contains sucrose, fructose, and glucose, plus a small amount of vitamins and minerals. Molasses is rarely used directly in French desserts, but contributes occasionally via brown sugar.

~~~~~~

VANILLA. Vanilla is the most frequently used flavor in French cookies. For some cookies it is the dominant flavor, while for others it is an accent flavor.

The vanilla bean is derived from the pod fruit of a climbing vine in the orchid family. Originally found in Mexico, today it is grown in tropical regions around the world. There are about seventy species of vanilla, but the one of culinary interest is *Vanilla planifolia*. The best beans for pastry making come from Mexico, the east coast of Madagascar, and the island of Réunion in the Indian Ocean. Madagascar is by far the world's largest producer. Vanilla beans from Réunion, Madagascar, and other neighboring islands are called Bourbon vanilla beans because the French first planted vanilla on the Ile de Bourbon (the old name for Réunion), and then later transplanted the vanilla to France's other tropical islands.

The vanilla pods must be harvested underripe, before they open and release the seeds and pulp inside. Initially the beans are yellow and have no vanilla taste because their principal flavor component, vanillin, is linked to glucose in the pulp.

The beans must be cured in a fermentation process that lasts for three to six months. During fermentation, enzymes in the pod release the vanillin from the interfering glucose linkage, and the color of the pod changes to a very dark brown. The beans are then aged for up to two years to produce a fuller, richer vanilla flavor.

While vanillin is the dominant component of the vanilla flavor, by itself it is rather monochromatic and boring. There are many secondary flavor components that contribute to the complexity and subtlety of the full vanilla flavor. The most important of these secondary components is piperonal, which has a scent of heliotrope.

Good vanilla beans are shiny, almost black, thin, and typically about 8 inches (20 cm) long. Some classic references give a length of 8 to 12 inches (20–30 cm), but beans near 12 inches (30 cm) in length are in fact extremely rare. The very best beans are covered with a "frost" of white vanillin crystals, indicating that they were well cured and aged.

Tahitian vanilla, which is currently enjoying a certain vogue, is not actually true *Vanilla planifolia*. In fact it is a different species, *Vanilla tahitiensis,* which is descended from the Bourbon vanilla vines that the French planted in Tahiti in the nineteenth century. Tahitian vanilla beans are plumper and wetter than Bourbon or Mexican beans, and they have an overwhelming fragrance more strongly scented of heliotrope. Traditionally they have been regarded as inferior for use in desserts and primarily suited for making perfumes.

Vanilla extracts are produced by steeping vanilla beans in a mixture of alcohol and water. The intensity of the extract is determined by the amount of vanilla. The standard intensity, called one-fold vanilla extract, uses 13.35 ounces of vanilla beans per gallon of liquid. A two-fold extract is twice as strong, and so on. Nearly all of the vanilla extracts sold for the retail market are one-fold. We particularly like Nielsen-Massey's Bourbon vanilla extract.

To get the full complexity of the vanilla flavor it is best to use vanilla beans. This works very well when you are flavoring a liquid—for example, a custard. The bean should be slit in half lengthwise, the aromatic pulp and seeds scraped out, and the pod, pulp, and seeds added to the liquid before cooking. After cooking, the liquid is strained to remove the pod. The pod is thoroughly rinsed and dried, then covered with sugar in an airtight container. The sugar takes on the vanilla flavor and is called vanilla sugar.

It is not convenient to use whole vanilla beans to flavor most cookies, but there are several alternatives. The most convenient is to use vanilla extract, and this is the method we use in nearly all our cookie recipes. The disadvantage of using vanilla extract is that it can lose some of its intensity as the cookies bake and the extract evaporates. To partly remedy this disadvantage and for the sake of economy, many professionals like to powder the dried vanilla beans they have preserved after flavoring a liquid, and add this powder to their batters. This procedure is more difficult to standardize in home baking, but if you want to try it you should grind the dried beans to a powder in a coffee grinder, then sift the powder through a fine strainer. Powdered vanilla is also available now in some specialty food stores, and can be substituted for vanilla extract following the manufacturer's instructions. Yet another alternative is to substitute vanilla sugar for part or all of the ordinary sugar called for in the recipe. Again, this is difficult to standardize in home baking, since the intensity of the vanilla sugar depends on how the beans were first used, the ratio of beans to the sugar in which they were stored, and how long the beans were stored in the sugar.

Imitation vanilla extracts are produced from vanillin derived from sources other than vanilla beans, such as cloves or the lignin in wood wastes. They lack the subtlety and complexity of pure vanilla extract, and they are not acceptable substitutes.

Sources: La Cuisine, Dean & DeLuca, Balducci's, Williams-Sonoma, Maid of Scandinavia.

~~~~~~~

VASELINE. Petroleum jelly is occasionally used to lubricate molds—in particular for Classic Champagne Biscuits. It gives the cookies a smoother, less porous surface than they would have if the molds were lubricated with butter.

~~~~~~~

VINEGAR. We use this acetic acid solution for cleaning copper (see the **COPPER BOWLS** entry in the Equipment section) and as an ingredient in royal icing. The vinegar should be inexpensive and neutral in flavor for these purposes, so use distilled white vinegar.

~~~~~~~

WALNUTS. Walnuts have been eaten in Europe for thousands of years, and during the Middle Ages they were a very important food in France. Today, however, walnuts play a limited role in French cooking.

Two varieties of walnut are generally available—the English walnut and the black walnut, although only the English walnut is used in French desserts. Also called the Persian walnut, it is native to the region from southeastern Europe and Asia Minor to the Himalayas. It probably was first planted in England in the fifteenth or sixteenth century, and was subsequently planted by the English in their American colonies. Today some of the largest producers of English walnuts are California, Oregon, and the region of France around Grenoble.

English walnuts have a higher oil content—about 64 percent—than do almonds. As a result, special care should be exercised when grinding them with sugar to make a walnut and sugar powder.

SOURCES FOR EQUIPMENT AND SPECIALTY INGREDIENTS

Most, *if not all, of the equipment and ingredients needed for making our cookies should be available at local cookware, grocery, gourmet food, and wine shops. If you can't find an item locally, then we recommend these mail order sources.*

Balducci's, 424 Avenue of the Americas, New York, NY 10011. Telephone: 212-673-2600. Ingredients including French glacé fruits and candied citrus peels, *crème de marrons* (chestnut cream), and vanilla beans and extracts. Catalog available on request.

Dean & DeLuca, 560 Broadway, New York, NY 10012. Telephone: 800-221-7714 and 212-431-1691. European and American bakeware and cooking equipment. Ingredients including glacé fruits, Lindt and Valrhona chocolates, cocoa powders, vanilla beans and extracts, and *crème de marrons* (chestnut cream). Catalog available on request.

J.B. Prince Company, 29 West 38th Street, New York, NY 10018. Telephone: 212-302-8611. European bakeware and cooking equipment. Catalog available.

Kitchen Glamor, 26770 Grand River Avenue, Redford Township, MI 48240. Telephone: 313-537-1300. European and American bakeware and cooking equipment.

La Cuisine, 323 Cameron Street, Alexandria, VA 22314. Telephone: 800-521-1176 or 703-836-4435. Vast selection of French bakeware and European cooking utensils. Ingredients including Valrhona chocolates and cocoa powder, cocoa butter, vanilla beans and extracts, Swiss glacé fruits and candied citrus peels, shelled pistachios, and *crème de marrons* (chestnut cream). Catalog available at nominal charge.

Maid of Scandinavia, 3244 Raleigh Avenue, Minneapolis, MN 55416. Telephone: 800-328-6722 or 612-927-7966. Kitchen machines and gadgets. American and some European baking equipment and supplies (foil paper wrappers and bonbon cups). Ingredients including Lindt chocolates and cocoa powder, cocoa butter, sanding and crystal sugars, and vanilla beans and extracts. Catalog available at nominal charge.

McGuckin Hardware, 2525 Arapahoe Avenue, Boulder, CO 80302. Telephone: 303-443-1822. Hardware supplies including neoprene sheets and O-rings, brass tubes and strips, and metal rulers. Kitchen machines and gadgets. American and European bakeware and cooking equipment.

The Peppercorn, 1235 Pearl Street, Boulder, CO 80302. Telephone: 800-447-6905 or 303-444-9621. Extensive selection of European and American bakeware and cooking equipment.

Ranier Devido Stone & Marble Company, 2619 New Butler Road, New Castle, PA 16101. Telephone: 412-658-8518. Marble pastry slabs.

Williams-Sonoma, P.O. Box 7456, San Francisco, CA 94120-7456. Telephone: 415-421-4242. Kitchen machines and gadgets, American and European bakeware and cooking equipment. Ingredients including vanilla beans, Nielsen-Massey vanilla extract, Valrhona chocolates, and Pernigotti cocoa powder. Catalog available on request.

MEASUREMENT AND EQUIVALENCES

Like other areas of baking, cookie making requires accurate measurement of ingredients for dependable results. The tools of measurement—namely measuring cups and spoons and kitchen scales—are discussed in the Equipment section. Here we focus on equivalences between weight and volume methods of measurement and on the peculiarities inherent in measuring particular ingredients. We also include a conversion table for American, metric, and British units of measurement.

It is usually most accurate and convenient to measure dry ingredients by weight and liquid ingredients by volume. Nonetheless, we realize that not all home cooks have a kitchen scale, never mind an accurate one. Furthermore, there are exceptions to this general guideline (for example, when the quantity is too small to weigh on a kitchen scale). We therefore give approximate volume equivalences to the weights of dry ingredients in our recipes whenever possible. And we give weight equivalences for the volume measurements of some very viscous liquids.

DRY INGREDIENTS

Dry ingredients consisting of powders (such as flour and confectioners' sugar) or large pieces (such as nuts) are particularly difficult to measure accurately by volume because the amount of air included with the ingredients in a measuring cup is hard to control. On the other hand, most granulated forms of sugar have a density that does not vary significantly and can therefore be measured quite well by volume. Also, the tiny amounts of some dry ingredients (particularly baking powder, ammonium carbonate, baking soda, and cream of tartar) called for in recipes are often too small to measure with a kitchen scale; in this case, a measuring spoon is preferable.

Particularly for powders, the method used to measure dry ingredients by volume can have a major effect on their density. We use the dip-and-sweep method for all dry ingredients except brown sugar and nuts. The ingredients are measured before sifting. Scoop the dry ingredient directly into a dry measure cup or measuring spoon, without packing it down. Then level the top by sweeping the straight edge of a metal spatula, a bowl scraper, or a ruler across the rim of the cup. Other methods (such as sifting powders into a measuring cup) give very different equivalences for powdered ingredients. However, most granulated sugars (except brown sugars) are not sensitive to the measurement method; for example, the equivalence will be the same if the granulated sugar is poured into the measuring cup and then swept level with the rim as it would be with the dip-and-sweep method.

Brown sugar must be packed into the measuring cup to get an accurate measurement by volume. Otherwise air pockets are trapped between masses of adhering sugar crystals. Fill the dry measure cup above the rim, and remove the excess using the straight edge of a metal spatula, a bowl scraper, or a ruler.

We use nuts in a variety of forms in our recipes. The difficulty in measuring nuts by volume is that the size of the pieces is often large relative to that of the measuring cup. So the way the nuts are packed around the sides, bottom, and top of the cup affects the amount of nuts in the cup. If you must measure nuts by volume, we suggest filling the cup above the rim, shaking it to redistribute the nuts and eliminate any large air spaces, and then removing the nuts above the rim of the cup. We emphasize that measuring nuts by volume is extremely unreliable, particularly for whole nuts and sliced almonds. Chopped nuts and slivered almonds are less of a problem because they are smaller and tend to pack more regularly. Nut and sugar powders, like other powdered dry ingredients, should be measured by the dip-and-sweep method.

LIQUIDS

Most liquids are easy to measure by volume using a liquid-measure cup. You need only know that you must measure the level of the liquid at the bottom of the meniscus—its curved top surface. This is discussed in detail in the Equipment section under **MEASURING CUPS AND SPOONS**. For very viscous liquids, such as honey, measuring by volume is perfectly accurate but potentially messy. If you have a kitchen scale, you may prefer to weigh such liquids directly into the mixing bowl with the other ingredients in the recipe.

EGGS

In home baking we normally measure eggs in integral units of whole eggs, whites, or yolks. All of our recipes call for large eggs—which weigh about 2 ounces (57 g) each—in the shell. Volume and weight equivalences are useful when a fraction of an egg is required or when eggs of different sizes are being substituted. In terms of volume, there are 5 large eggs or 8 large whites or 14 large yolks per cup (2.4 dl). Additional volume and weight equivalences are tabulated below. If you are using eggs other than large in size, then convert the number of eggs in our recipe to volume or weight using these equivalences and then measure the required volume or weight of eggs.

VOLUME AND WEIGHT EQUIVALENCES

Ingredient	Volume	Weight
Granulated sugars (Including superfine, crystal, and sanding)	1 cup	7 ounces (200 g)
Confectioners' sugar	1 cup	4¼ ounces (120 g)
Light brown sugar	1 cup	7½ ounces (215 g)
All-purpose flour	1 cup	5 ounces (140 g)
Cake flour	1 cup	4½ ounces (125 g)
Cornstarch	1 cup	4¾ ounces (135 g)
Yellow cornmeal	1 cup	4⅔ ounces (130 g)
Cocoa powder	1 cup	3¾ ounces (105 g)
Ammonium carbonate	2 tablespoons	.2 ounce (6 g)
Baking powder	1 tablespoon	.4 ounce (12 g)
Baking soda	1 tablespoon	.6 ounce (16 g)
Cream of tartar	1 tablespoon	.3 ounce (9 g)
Salt	1 tablespoon	.7 ounce (19 g)
Butter	1 cup	8 ounces (225 g)
Honey	1 tablespoon	¾ ounce (20 g)
Corn syrup	1 tablespoon	¾ ounce (20 g)
Jams	1 tablespoon	¾ ounce (20 g)
Almonds (whole)	1 cup	5¼ ounces (150 g)
Almonds (slivered)	1 cup	4½ ounces (130 g)
Almonds (sliced)	1 cup	3½ ounces (100 g)
Hazelnuts (whole)	1 cup	5 ounces (140 g)
Pistachios (whole)	1 cup	5 ounces (140 g)
Walnuts (halves)	1 cup	3½–4 ounces (100–115 g)
Nut and sugar powders	1 cup	4¾ ounces (135 g)
1 large egg (in shell)	—	2 ounces (57 g)
1 large egg (no shell)	3 tablespoons plus ½ teaspoon	1¾ ounces (51 g)
1 large egg white	2 tablespoons	1⅛ ounces (32 g)
1 large egg yolk	1 tablespoon plus ½ teaspoon	⅔ ounce (19 g)

AMERICAN-METRIC-BRITISH CONVERSIONS

NOTE: We give all measurements of ingredients, temperatures, and lengths in our recipes in both American and metric units, using the standard conventions for each system. British units are identical to the American ones except for the volume measures, for which the conversions are included here. We also include a list of abbreviations for metric units.

VOLUME

1 quart
= 4 cups
= 0.95 liter
= 33 British fluid ounces
= 32 American fluid ounces

1 cup
= 16 tablespoons
= 2.4 deciliters
= 8.3 British fluid ounces
= 8 American fluid ounces

1 tablespoon
= 3 teaspoons
= 4.5 centiliters
= 0.52 British fluid ounce
= 0.5 American fluid ounce

1 teaspoon
= 0.5 centiliter
= 0.17 British fluid ounce

1 liter
= 10 deciliters
= 1.06 quarts

1 deciliter
= 10 centiliters
= 6.8 tablespoons

1 centiliter
= 10 milliliters
= 2 teaspoons

LENGTH

1 inch
= 2.54 centimeters

1 centimeter
= 10 millimeters
= 3/8 inch

WEIGHT

1 pound
= 16 ounces
= 454 grams

1 ounce
= 28.4 grams

1 kilogram
= 1,000 grams
= 2.2 pounds

TEMPERATURE

°F= °C × 9/5 + 32°

32° F= 0° C
212° F= 100° C

METRIC ABBREVIATIONS

g = gram
kg = kilogram
l = liter
dl = deciliter
cl = centiliter
ml = milliliter
cm = centimeter
mm = millimeter

HOW TO
USE A
PASTRY BAG

The pastry bag is the cookie baker's secret weapon. It is just a funnel of canvas, with an opening at the tip to accommodate a variety of pastry tubes. Nonetheless, this remarkably simple device, which wasn't even invented until the nineteenth century, makes it possible to form batters and fillings into a mind-boggling array of shapes with ease and speed. Few machines can match its power and versatility; yet it costs only a few dollars and requires just a little practice to use with facility. The effort you invest to master it will be repaid a hundredfold in time saved, not just in cookie making but in many other areas of baking and culinary decoration—from cake decorating to shaping cream puffs and eclairs to filling deviled eggs.

TRIMMING THE TIP OF THE PASTRY BAG

When you purchase a new canvas pastry bag, the opening at the tip will be quite small and will need to be enlarged to accommodate all but the smallest pastry tubes. Take the largest pastry tube you expect to use with this pastry bag and drop it into the tip, pressing the tube firmly in place. Using a pencil, mark a circle on the bag about ¼ inch (6 mm) up from the tip of the pastry tube. Then remove the pastry tube and cut off the tip of the pastry bag at this line.

For nylon pastry bags, the opening at the tip of the bag is hemmed and should not be cut. The opening is scaled to the size of the bag and should be large enough to accommodate almost any tube you might use with it.

SELECTING THE PASTRY TUBE

The size of the pastry tube for each cookie is chosen according to the shape to be piped and the consistency of the batter. If the opening is too large, the batter will be difficult to control; if the opening is too small, the batter will require too much effort to pipe and may soften and deflate from too much pressure. For each cookie we specify the pastry tube that we find ideal, but they are partly a matter of preference. In most cases using a pastry tube of the next size up or down makes only a small difference.

FITTING THE PASTRY TUBE

Fold over the wide end of the pastry bag to form a large cuff ①. The length of the cuff should be about one-third of the total length of the pastry bag, or 4½ to 6 inches (12–15 cm) for a 14- to 18-inch (35–45 cm) bag.

①

Drop the pastry tube, tip down, into the pastry bag and slide it tightly into the opening at the tip ② of the bag. Twist the bag just behind the pastry tube, and press the twisted fabric inside the tube. This blocks the tube so that the batter won't run out through the tube while you are filling the pastry bag. It also gives the bag a firmer grip on the tube.

FILLING THE PASTRY BAG

Hold the pastry bag tip down with one hand, draping the cuff over your thumb and fingers to hold the bag open like a funnel and support it. Alternatively, you can place the pastry bag inside a large plastic drinking cup, draping the cuff over the rim of the cup to hold it open. (The size of the cup required will depend on the size of the pastry bag and the quantity of batter. In most of our cookie recipes you can use a 1-quart (1 L) cup with a top diameter of about 4 inches (10 cm).

Scoop up some batter from your mixing bowl and drop it ③ into the bag. This is easiest with a bowl scraper; a large rubber spatula will also work. Scrape off the bowl scraper or spatula on the inside rim ④ of the cuff, and repeat until all the batter is in the bag.

Unfold the cuff and press the batter down to the end of the bag ⑤. You can do this either by pinching the bag between your fingers and sliding them down the bag or by laying the bag on your countertop and sliding the handle of a dough scraper or the side of your hand down the bag behind the batter. Twist the bag immediately behind the batter ⑥ to enclose it securely. Then wrap the thumb and index finger of one hand around the twisted fabric to hold it closed. You will apply pressure to the bag with your palm

③   ④   ⑤   ⑥

and fingers; as the batter is piped out, you will gradually twist the fabric behind the batter tighter to push the batter down toward the tube.

Hold the pastry tube in the fingertips of your free hand. When you are piping, you will guide the tube with this hand. Now pull the pastry tube and untwist the fabric behind it. Gently press on the batter with your other hand until it reaches the tip of the tube. You are ready to pipe.

Whenever you want to stop the flow of batter, release the pressure on

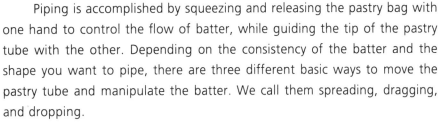

the bag and turn the pastry bag tip up so it won't drip. Support the weight of the bag with the hand wrapped around the wide end. If the batter is runny, cover the tip of the tube with the tip of your index finger ⑦ immediately after releasing the pressure on the bag. Once the bag is upside down, you can remove your fingertip.

GENERAL PIPING TECHNIQUES

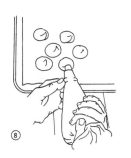

Piping is accomplished by squeezing and releasing the pastry bag with one hand to control the flow of batter, while guiding the tip of the pastry tube with the other. Depending on the consistency of the batter and the shape you want to pipe, there are three different basic ways to move the pastry tube and manipulate the batter. We call them spreading, dragging, and dropping.

Spreading is the method used for piping domes with a plain pastry tube and rosettes with a fluted pastry tube. Hold the tip of the pastry tube just above the baking sheet, with the pastry bag at an angle of about 60° with respect to the surface. Press on the bag, and when the batter starts to spread around the tip of the tube, gradually raise the tip of the tube without lifting it out of the mound of batter. To make a simple dome ⑧, raise the tube straight up, allowing the batter to spread around the tip in a dome of increasing height and width. The tip of the tube remains inserted in the batter so that you are inflating the dome from the inside rather than dropping batter on top of it. To make a rosette ⑨ (which is just a fluted dome), move the tip of the tube in a small, tight circle at the same time as you lift it.

The *dragging* method can be used to produce many shapes, including fingers, batons, ovals, teardrops, *S*s, and spirals. It is also used to make wreaths and long strips with firm batters. Place the tip of the pastry tube on or just above the baking sheet and draw the tip of the pastry tube across the baking sheet as you press on the bag. This produces a ribbon of batter. If you hold the pastry bag close to vertical, the ribbon will be relatively flat, whereas if you hold the bag close to horizontal, the ribbon will be more cylindrical and rope shaped. For most cookies the pastry bag should be held at an angle of about 60° with respect to the baking sheet. Then by varying the pressure on the bag and the speed at which you move the tube, you can vary the width of the ribbon. For example, to make a baton ⑩, the pressure and speed should be constant to get a uniform width. The same is true for *S*s, spirals, wreaths, and long strips ⑪. For ovals ⑫, the width increases from the beginning to the middle, and then decreases to the end. Fingers and teardrops are more complicated and require special instructions (see page 478).

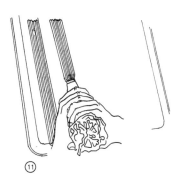

Dropping is used to pipe wreaths and long strips of soft batter. Hold

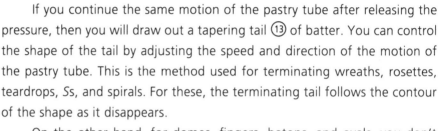

the pastry bag at a 60° angle with respect to the baking sheet and keep the tip of the pastry tube ¾ to 1½ inches (2–4 cm) above the surface. Press on the pastry bag and let the batter drop onto the baking sheet, moving the tip of the tube to trace out the shape you want to pipe. Adjust the pressure on the bag and the speed at which you move the tube to get a uniform rope.

TERMINATING

The piping motion can be terminated in one of two ways, depending on shape. Always release the pressure on the pastry bag a little before you reach the size and shape you want, since the batter will continue flowing briefly.

If you continue the same motion of the pastry tube after releasing the pressure, then you will draw out a tapering tail ⑬ of batter. You can control the shape of the tail by adjusting the speed and direction of the motion of the pastry tube. This is the method used for terminating wreaths, rosettes, teardrops, *S*s, and spirals. For these, the terminating tail follows the contour of the shape as it disappears.

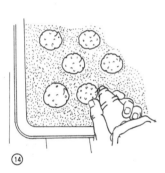

On the other hand, for domes, fingers, batons, and ovals, you don't want a tail and the termination should be almost invisible. The trick is to make a quick lateral motion with the tip of the pastry tube so that the edge of the tube severs the connection between the piped shape and the batter in the tube. For domes, you accomplish this by a semicircular flick with the tip ⑭ of the pastry tube. For fingers and batons, you stop the piping motion and flick the tip of the tube in the reverse direction ⑮. In both cases the tip of the tube must just skim the surface of the piped batter. If the tube is too low it will drag the batter on the baking sheet, damaging the piped shape; if it is too high it can draw out an unwanted tail. To keep a fluid rhythm to the piping motion you should make the terminating flick take you to the position where you will pipe the next shape. This is easiest if you pipe the batter in regularly spaced rows.

For piping long strips of batter, the terminating procedure isn't so important since the strips are cut into lengths after baking and the ends are eliminated. You can use either of the methods described above.

FINGERS, BATONS, AND TEARDROPS

We differentiate between a baton and a finger. While a baton has uniform thickness, a finger is thinner at the center than at the ends. For some finger-shaped cookies (particularly those piped with a fluted pastry tube), the variation in thickness between ends and center is slight. It just turns out to be easier to pipe this shape than a baton of uniform thickness. But for other cookies, such as Cats' Tongues, the shape is more exaggerated, almost like a dumbbell. The technique is slightly different depending on whether you are using a plain or a fluted pastry tube.

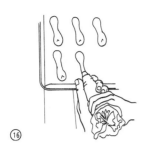

If you are using a plain pastry tube, start each finger as though you were piping a dome. Hold the tip of the tube just above the baking sheet, and press on the bag until the batter spreads around the tip. Then draw the tip toward you, adjusting the pressure on the bag to get a center section of uniform thickness ⑯. When you reach the end of the finger, stop moving the tip and let the batter spread around the tip again to make this end the same size as the first end. Release the pressure on the bag, and flick the tip across the surface of the batter in the reverse direction to terminate it with no tail. For some long, thin cookies like Cats' Tongues, there is a special variation on this technique to make it easier to get the center section straight. For these, rather than pipe the center section directly onto the baking sheet, lift the tip of the pastry tube in an arc from one end of the dumbbell to the other, drawing out the center section of the dumbbell and letting it drop onto the baking sheet. This technique requires a little more practice than the basic method, but it produces beautiful, straight dumbbell-shaped fingers.

If you are using a fluted pastry tube, place the tip of the tube just above the baking sheet and start by pressing firmly on the pastry bag and moving the tip of the tube away from you. Quickly reverse direction, moving the tip of the tube in a small loop—up, toward you, and back down—as you press firmly on the bag to establish the width of the finger. Draw the pastry tube toward you in a straight line, making the center section almost as wide as the beginning of the finger. When you reach the end of the finger, stop moving the tube momentarily to make the finger symmetrical. Release the pressure on the bag and reverse direction once again, flicking the tip of the pastry tube across the surface of the batter ⑰ to avoid producing a vertical tail.

Teardrops are almost always piped with a fluted pastry tube. You start in the same way as for a finger piped with a fluted tube. Press firmly on the bag and move the tip of the pastry tube away from you. Quickly reverse direction, moving the tip of the tube in a small loop—up, toward you, and back down—as you press firmly on the bag to make the batter spread and form the wide end of the teardrop. Draw the tube toward you, gradually decreasing the pressure on the bag to get a teardrop ⑱ of decreasing width. As you near the end of the teardrop, release the pressure on the bag and quickly pull the tube toward you to draw out the tip of the teardrop.

REFILLING

When you want to refill the pastry bag, first squeeze out any batter remaining in the tube. Then twist the bag just behind the tube and press the twisted fabric into the back of the tube just as you did at the start. Scrape down the batter on the inside of the bag with a bowl scraper or rubber spatula, then fill the bag in the way described above.

BASIC PREPARATIONS AND PROCEDURES

Here are a few basic preparations and procedures that are used in a wide variety of cookies. Some of these (ganache, tempered chocolate, royal icing, and browned butter) are included as an integral part of each recipe where they are required. Others (nut and sugar powders, strained apricot jam, and praliné) are listed as ingredients in each cookie recipe, with a cross reference to the basic preparation recipe in this chapter. Almond and sugar powder and strained apricot jam are used so frequently that, to minimize work, we recommend preparing them in large batches to have on hand when needed. With praliné there is no choice; the minimum quantity you can make is much larger than you need for a single batch of cookies.

Crème fraîche is sold commercially. We have included here the recipe for the standard crème fraîche substitute in the event that the commercial product is unavailable or out of stock in your local market.

For convenience, the most frequently used basic preparation recipes are printed on the endpapers in an abbreviated, easy-to-use form. To locate recipes that require a particular basic preparation, see the Cross-Index of Basic Preparations (page 494).

NUT AND SUGAR POWDERS

Many recipes in this book require a powder made by grinding together equal weights of nuts and confectioners' sugar. Almonds and hazelnuts are called for most often, but occasionally other nuts are used. For each recipe, you can prepare just the amount of nut and sugar powder you need. Or, if you bake cookies often, you can prepare the most frequently used nut and sugar powders in larger batches to keep on hand in your pantry.

If the nut specified in a particular cookie is used very rarely (for example, pistachios or walnuts), or if some of the confectioners' sugar is replaced by light brown sugar (as in Tender Macaroons and Gerbet Macaroons) or granulated sugar (for Cossack Biscuits), then we include the instructions for preparing the nut and sugar powder in the cookie recipe. Otherwise, we list the quantity of nut and sugar powder as an ingredient in each cookie recipe, along with the quantities of nuts and confectioners' sugar needed to make it.

Blanched almonds are used much more often than any other nuts, so we refer to the powder made with blanched almonds simply as ''almond and sugar powder.'' When raw almonds are required, we specify ''raw-almond and sugar powder.'' Hazelnuts should always be blanched as the first step in preparing hazelnut and sugar powder for our cookie recipes.

Some cookies call for a powder containing both almonds and hazelnuts. If you are preparing nut and sugar powders in advance, it is best to grind the almonds and hazelnuts separately so that you aren't restricted to using them for a particular cookie. But if you are preparing the nut and sugar powder for a single cookie recipe, then grind them together.

The following recipe can be prepared in a standard 7-cup (1¾ L) food processor. If you have a much larger food processor, you may be able to prepare up to 24 ounces (700 g) of nut and sugar powder in one batch.

INGREDIENTS

6 ounces (170 g) nuts
(1 cup plus 2 tablespoons for almonds,
      or 1 cup plus 3½ tablespoons for hazelnuts)
6 ounces (170 g), or 1¼ cups plus 3 tablespoons,
      confectioners' sugar

> *Or use the quantities specified in each cookie recipe*

For 12 ounces (340 g), or 2½ cups

1. *For hazelnuts only:* Spread out the hazelnuts on a baking sheet and toast them in a preheated 450° F (230° C) oven, stirring once or twice to prevent the nuts nearest the edges of the sheet from burning, until their skins are dry and cracked and have darkened but not burned, about 4 to 6 minutes. (The hazelnuts should remain pale inside.) Transfer the hazelnuts to a large sieve, and rub the hot nuts against the mesh, using a towel to protect your hand, to remove most of their skins. Let the nuts cool.

2. Grind the nuts with half the confectioners' sugar in your food processor, stopping to scrape down the sides of the processor bowl ① and

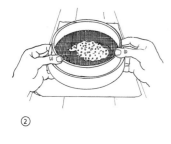

②

break up any caking as needed. Process until the nuts are finely ground butnot so long that the mixture becomes oily.

3. Sift through a medium sieve ② (¹⁄₁₆ to ³⁄₃₂ inch, or 1½ to 2 mm, mesh). Grind the nuts that don't pass through the sieve with the remaining confectioners' sugar until the nuts have been reduced to a fine powder.

4. Transfer all of the nut and sugar powder to a bowl, break up any caking with your fingertips, and mix thoroughly.

➤ **HOWS & WHYS:** This method is designed to produce the finest possible texture while extracting the minimum amount of oil from the nuts. The food processor fluffs up the mixture as it grinds the nuts, minimizing compression and heat, which would extract more oil. The sugar in the powder absorbs the oil, helping to keep the powder from caking and turning into a paste.

A few of our cookie recipes require a very small quantity of nut and sugar powder. If you are grinding less than about 1½ ounces (40 g) of nuts, then processing with only half of the sugar at a time (and sifting in between) has no advantage. In this case, combine the nuts with all of the confectioners' sugar in step 2, delete step 3, and proceed to step 4.

STORAGE: Covered airtight for up to 1 month at room temperature.

STRAINED APRICOT JAM

Strained apricot jam is used in many cookies as an ingredient or as a glaze, and it is also used to glaze fruit tartes. We recommend straining an entire jar at a time so that you will always have it on hand. But if you prefer, you can strain just the amount you need for each recipe, remembering that some volume is lost in the process so you must start with more jam than the recipe requires.

INGREDIENT

Apricot jam or preserves

For any quantity

①

1. Melt the apricot jam over low heat in a small saucepan, stirring occasionally with a wooden spatula.

2. Force the jam through a fine sieve with a wooden pestle ① to puree the pieces of fruit. Work as much of the fruit through the sieve as you can. Then discard any dry fibrous bits that won't go through the sieve.

3. Return the jam to the saucepan and stir to make it homogeneous. Simmer it gently to reduce any excess liquid, then let it cool. The finished jam should be thick and not runny, but still soft and spreadable.

➤ **PRECAUTIONS:** To avoid introducing air bubbles into the jam, stir only occasionally with a wooden spatula (never a wire whisk) while heating it.

STORAGE: Covered airtight for up to several months in the refrigerator.

PRALINÉ

This fine, creamy paste, made by pureeing almond brittle (roasted nuts embedded in caramel), is exquisitely aromatic and sensual. The original pralines (without the accent on the letter e) were caramel coated almonds. They were invented by the chef of Marshal du Plessis-Praslin in the middle of the seventeenth century. The marshal was a French soldier and diplomat who rose to prominence under Louis XIII and became a minister of state under Louis XIV. He liked to offer these candies to the ladies in his circle, and the ladies christened them praslines. They became very popular at the French Court in the eighteenth century, and chefs began to pulverize them to make what we now call praliné.

Today, praliné is used extensively in chocolates and to flavor ice creams and fillings for cakes and pastries. We mix it with creamed butter to make a deliciously unctuous cookie filling called praliné butter. There are several methods for making praliné. The one given here is the simplest and allows preparation of a fairly small quantity. If you prefer a more strongly flavored praliné, substitute hazelnuts for half of the almonds in the recipe.

EQUIPMENT
1 large baking sheet
• Grease lightly with vegetable oil using a paper towel.

INGREDIENTS
7 ounces (200 g), or 1 cup, sugar
¼ cup (6 cl) cold water
7 ounces (200 g), or 1⅓ cups, raw almonds

For 12 ounces (340 g), or

1 cup plus 3 tablespoons

①

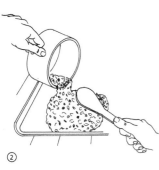

②

1. Combine the sugar and water in a small, heavy saucepan or copper caramel pot and stir to moisten the sugar thoroughly. Bring to a boil over medium heat. Wash down the walls of the pot with a moistened pastry brush to dissolve any sugar crystals that form there. Then continue boiling until the sugar reaches the thread stage, or about 230° F (110° C).

2. Add the almonds to the sugar syrup ①. Continue cooking, stirring constantly. The syrup will gradually thicken, forming progressively larger bubbles. Then it will become white and sandy as the sugar crystallizes.

3. Reduce the heat to low and continue cooking to melt the sugar and roast the almonds. The sugar will turn pale amber as it melts. Test the almonds by cutting one in half. They are ready when they are light brown in the center. There will still be a thin coating of white crystallized sugar on the almonds. Pour the almond and caramel mixture onto the oiled baking sheet ② and allow it to cool.

4. Break up the almond brittle and grind it in your food processor. Continue processing until it becomes a smooth, creamy paste with just a slight grittiness. This will take some time and the praliné will become hot.

5. Transfer the praliné to a bowl and let cool to room temperature.

STORAGE: Covered airtight for up to 3 months at room temperature or in the refrigerator. If some oil separates on top of the praliné, stir it back in before using.

TEMPERED CHOCOLATE

When bittersweet chocolate is to be used for glazing, it must be tempered in order to prevent the cocoa solids and cocoa butter from separating and producing bloom when the chocolate cools. In the process of tempering, the chocolate is first melted and then cooled to a temperature that is actually below the melting point of the cocoa butter (though the chocolate is still fluid), and finally warmed back to just above the melting point. In this state it will set very quickly. Also, tempering creates many small "seed" crystals of stable cocoa butter and distributes them uniformly throughout the chocolate; then as the chocolate sets, these seed crystals serve as centers for crystallization of the remaining cocoa butter, keeping the cocoa butter evenly distributed and preventing separation. Finally, tempering gives the chocolate the ideal working consistency—just fluid enough to spread easily and coat thinly.

For glazing we recommend tempering bittersweet chocolate with a little almond oil or neutral vegetable oil—about 1 teaspoon (½ cl) of oil for each 7 ounces (200 g) of chocolate—to make it more fluid. This addition is not needed for good covering chocolates (couvertures), which have already been thinned with extra cocoa butter.

Here is the method we recommend for tempering small quantities—less than about 1 pound (450 g)—of chocolate.

INGREDIENTS

European bittersweet chocolate (such as Lindt Surfin)

1 teaspoon (½ cl) almond oil (preferably) or neutral vegetable oil for each 7 ounces (200 g) of chocolate

For any quantity

①

②

1. Melt the chocolate ①. Unless you are using a good *couverture*, stir in the almond oil.

2. Dip the bottom of the pot of chocolate in a bowl of cold water and stir the chocolate constantly ② until it begins to thicken. At this point, the cocoa butter is beginning to solidify and the temperature is between 80 and 84° F (27–29° C). The chocolate must not be allowed to set. Immediately remove it from the cold water.

3. Dip the bottom of the pot of chocolate in a bowl of hot water and stir over the hot water ③ just long enough to make the chocolate fluid again. Then remove it from the hot water. The temperature of the chocolate will now be 86 to 90° F (30–32° C), and the chocolate is ready to use for glazing. The temperature must not get above 90° F (32° C), or you will have to repeat the tempering—cooling the chocolate until it starts to thicken, then warming it until just fluid again.

➤ **PRECAUTIONS:** The small amount of almond oil used to thin the chocolate makes it more susceptible to forming fat bloom than is pure bittersweet chocolate. For this reason, cookies glazed with the thinned choc-

③

olate should be kept in a cool place—below 70° F (20° C)—both while the chocolate is setting and during storage.

STORAGE: If all the tempered chocolate is not used, lay a sheet of wax paper on a marble slab (preferably) or your countertop. Pour the excess chocolate onto the wax paper and spread it in a thin layer with a metal spatula, then let it set. Peel the paper away from the chocolate, place the chocolate in an airtight container, and keep it in a cool place—below 70° F (20° C).

When you are ready to glaze more cookies, simply substitute this chocolate for part of the chocolate (and the corresponding amount of almond oil) in the recipe, and temper it with the rest of the chocolate.

GANACHE

The rich chocolate cream filling called ganache *is used in many classic French* gâteaux (cakes) and cookies. *Ganache* is made from bittersweet chocolate and heavy cream. It is very rich, dark, and chocolaty. By comparison, chocolate buttercream is much less intense in flavor and much lighter in both color and texture. Crème fraîche or half-and-half can be substituted for the heavy cream to make the *ganache* either less sweet or less rich, respectively. Ideally the chocolate should have a relatively high cocoa liquor content and low sugar content.

The recipe for ganache *is so simple that we have incorporated it in our cookie recipes whenever it is needed. If you are making several cookies that require a* ganache *filling or want to use* ganache *for another purpose (such as filling a cake) as well, then we recommend preparing a larger quantity. The recipe that follows can be scaled up or down, depending on how much* ganache *you want to make.*

INGREDIENTS

4 ounces (115 g) European bittersweet chocolate
   (such as Lindt Excellence)

6 tablespoons (9 cl) heavy cream

For about ¾ cup (190 g)

①

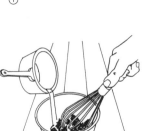

②

1. Chop the chocolate and put it in a small bowl.

2. Bring the cream just to a boil. Then reduce the heat and simmer it for 2 minutes, stirring constantly ① with a wire whisk, to sterilize the cream.

3. Gradually stir the hot cream into the chocolate ② with the wire whisk, and continue stirring until the chocolate is completely melted. (If some of the chocolate still doesn't melt, dip the bottom of the bowl of *ganache* in a bowl of hot water and stir a little longer.) Then allow the *ganache* to cool, stirring occasionally with a wooden spatula, until it starts to thicken.

4. Use the *ganache* right away, before it sets. If the *ganache* does start to set before you finish using it, dip the bottom of the bowl of *ganache* in a bowl of hot water and stir with a wooden spatula until it is soft and smooth (but not runny) again.

Or, if you don't use the *ganache* right away, refrigerate it until needed. Let it soften at room temperature for 1 hour. Then place it in a stainless-steel bowl over hot water and beat it vigorously with a wooden spatula until it is smooth.

STORAGE: Covered airtight for up to 1 week in the refrigerator. After cookies are filled with *ganache* they must be allowed to rest in a cool place until the *ganache* sets. Then they must be stored in either a cool place or the refrigerator. The refrigerator is better for the *ganache,* since it keeps the cream longer without spoiling. But crisp cookies can soften quickly in the refrigerator; if the cookies will not be kept too long (less than 1 day), it is better to store them in a cool place.

ROYAL ICING

Royal icing is a sort of meringue made by whipping egg white with confectioners' sugar until white and thick. In principle the whipping can be done by hand with a wooden spatula, but in practice this is extremely tedious and the whipping should be done with an electric mixer using the flat beater. A little acid (vinegar is most convenient, and sometimes lemon juice is used) is added at the end of the whipping to whiten the royal icing and make it drier.

We use royal icing as a glaze on some cookies made from flaky pastry dough and from almond paste batter. For these cookies the pastry dough or almond paste is rolled out into a sheet and the royal icing is spread on top using a palette knife before baking. The sheet is cut into pieces immediately, before the icing forms a crust on top, using a knife dipped in flour (or in cold water) to prevent the icing from sticking to it. Then the icing is allowed to dry and set before baking.

INGREDIENTS

1 large egg white, at room temperature
4 ounces (115 g), or ¾ cup plus 3 tablespoons,
    confectioners' sugar

⅛ teaspoon (½ ml) distilled white vinegar

For about ½ cup (1.2 dl)

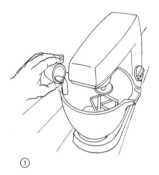

①

1. Place the egg white in the bowl of your electric mixer ①. Sift the confectioners' sugar and gradually stir it into the egg white.

2. When all the sugar has been added, beat at medium speed with the flat beater for 15 minutes to make the mixture light and thick, like a meringue. It will form soft peaks when you lift the beater.

3. Add the vinegar and continue beating a little longer.

PRECAUTIONS: Because royal icing has a very high sugar content, it browns quickly and can burn easily. After baking, the color of the icing should be pale beige on flaky pastry cookies and nearly white on cookies made from almond paste batter, so the baking must be monitored carefully.

STORAGE: Royal icing should be used right away or the surface will begin to dry and form a crust. If necessary, cover the surface with a damp cloth to keep it from drying out; then cover airtight with plastic wrap and keep for up to a few hours. Beat with a wooden spatula before using.

BROWNED BUTTER

Cooking melted butter browns the milk solids, imparting a nutty flavor to the butter and changing its color from yellow to brown. The browning must be done carefully in order to prevent the milk solids from burning and producing a bitter flavor. The French name for browned butter is beurre noisette, or hazelnut butter. It is used to give a very distinctive taste to some cookies, including Commercy Madeleines, Friands, and Visitandines. For some recipes the browned butter must be used while hot, but for others it can be made in advance.

INGREDIENT
Unsalted butter

For any quantity

①

②

1. Melt the butter in a heavy saucepan, and boil it. Foam will come to the top. When the foam collapses, stir to mix.

2. Continue to boil. Soon bubbles will start to form on the surface— at first large bubbles and then progressively smaller ones. When the surface is covered with an opaque foam of tiny bubbles and the foam mounts in the saucepan, stir ① to deflate it.

3. Boil the butter until a new layer of tiny bubbles forms on top, then stir to deflate it again. Pour through a fine strainer ② into a bowl. This is the browned butter.

STORAGE: Covered airtight for up to 1 week in the refrigerator.

CRÈME FRAÎCHE

You can make a substitute for crème fraîche at home by culturing ordinary heavy cream with a little buttermilk. The taste is not identical to real crème fraîche, since the bacteria in the cultures are not the same. However, as an ingredient in a cookie batter the two are almost indistinguishable. If you have some commercial crème fraîche, you can use it in the same way as buttermilk to culture your heavy cream and the result will have the authentic crème fraîche taste.

INGREDIENTS
1 cup (2.4 dl) pasteurized heavy or whipping cream
1 teaspoon (½ cl) cultured pasteurized buttermilk
    (see Note)

For about 1 cup (2.4 dl)

1. Stir together the cream and buttermilk. Gently heat to between 85 and 90° F (30–32° C). Do not overheat or you will kill the culture.

2. Pour the cream into a glass or earthenware container, cover loosely, and let stand undisturbed at room temperature—65 to 85° F (18–30° C)—until thickened. Thickening will take from 6 to 30 hours, depending on the temperature of the room.

3. When thick, cover the crème fraîche airtight and chill it in the refrigerator.

NOTE: It is essential to use cultured pasteurized buttermilk rather than pasteurized cultured buttermilk, since pasteurization after culturing kills the essential bacteria.

STORAGE: Covered airtight for up to 10 days in the refrigerator.

BIBLIOGRAPHY

Bellouet, Gérard Joël. *La Pâtisserie: Tradition et Évolution.* Fontenay-le-Fleury, France: G. J. Bellouet, 1987.

Beranbaum, Rose Levy. *The Cake Bible.* New York: William Morrow and Company, 1988.

Bianchini, F., and F. Corbetta. *The Complete Book of Fruits and Vegetables.* (English translation by Maurice Messegue). New York: Crown Publishers, 1976.

Bilheux, Roland, and Alain Escoffier. *Traité de Pâtisserie Artisanale.* Paris: Éditions St. Honoré, 1984–87.

Carême, Marie Antonin. *Le Pâtissier Royal.* Paris: J. G. Dentu, 1815. 3rd ed. Paris: Chez MM, 1841.

Chaboissier, D. *Le Compagnon Pâtissier,* 2nd ed. Paris: Éditions Jerome Villete, 1984.

Cuny, Jean-Marie. *La Cuisine Lorraine.* Saint-Nicolas-de-Port: Imprimerie Star, 1977.

Curnonsky. *Cuisine et Vins de France.* Paris: Librairie Larousse, 1953.

Darenne, Émile, and Émile Duval. *Traité de Pâtisserie Moderne.* Nouvelle éd. Paris: Éditions L. Lambert, 1961. Originally published in 1909.

Dubois, Marguerite-Marie et al. *Larousse Dictionnaire Moderne.* Paris: Librairie Larousse, 1960.

Dumas, Alexandre. *Le Grand Dictionnaire de Cuisine.* Paris: Alphonse Lemerre, 1873. Selections translated as *Dumas on Food* by Alan and Jane Davidson. London: The Folio Society, 1978.

Encyclopedia Britannica, 11th ed. London: The Encyclopedia Britannica Company, Ltd., 1910.

Fance, Wilfred J. *The New International Confectioner,* 5th ed. London: Virtue & Company Limited, 1981.

Fitzgibbon, Theodora. *Food of the Western World.* New York: Quadrangle/New York Times Book Co., 1976.

Flammarion (editors). *L'Art Culinaire Français.* Paris: Flammarion, 1976.

Franchiolo, P.-J. *L'Art Chez le Pâtissier, Confiseur, Glacier.* Paris: 1958. Reprinted, Paris: Éditions Steff, 1979.

Good Cook, The: Cookies & Crackers. Alexandria, Va.: Time-Life Books, 1982.

Gouffé, Jules. *Le Livre de Pâtisserie,* (1873). Reprinted, Paris: Éditions Henri Veyrier, 1988.

Healy, Bruce, and Paul Bugat. *Mastering the Art of French Pastry.* Woodbury, N.Y.: Barron's, 1984.

Lacam, Pierre. *Le Nouveau Mémorial de la Pâtisserie et des Glaces,* 8th ed. Crosnes, France: Chez Seurre-Lacam, 1949. Originally published as *Mémorial Historique de la Pâtisserie,* 1888.

McGee, Harold. *On Food and Cooking.* New York: Charles Scribner's Sons, 1984.

Minifie, Bernard W. *Chocolate, Cocoa, and Confectionary: Science and Technology,* 2nd ed. Westport, Conn. AVI Publishing Company, 1980.

Montagné, Prosper. *Larousse Gastronomique.* Paris: Augé, Gillon, Hollier-Larousse, Moreau, et Cie (Librairie Larousse), 1938. English translation by Nina Froud, Patience Gray, Maud Murdoch, and Barbara Macrae Taylor. New York: Crown Publishers, 1961.

Page, Edward, and P. W. Kingsford. *The Master Chefs.* New York: St. Martin's Press, 1971.

Pasquet, Ernest. *La Pâtisserie Familiale.* Paris: Flammarion, 1974.

Pellaprat, Henri-Paul. *L'Art Culinaire Moderne.* Paris: Jacques Kramer, 1936.

Proust, Marcel. *À la Recherche du Temps Perdu.* Translated as *Remembrance of Things Past* by C. K. Scott-Moncrieff. London: Chatto & Windus, Ltd., 1928.

Sekelli, Z. *L'Art Culinaire à Travers l'Algérie.* Algiers: Société Nationale d'Édition de Diffusion, 1973.

Simon, Andre L., and Robin Howe. *A Dictionary of Gastronomy.* Woodstock, N.Y. The Overlook Press, 1978.

Stein, Jess, and Laurence Urdang, eds. *The Random House Dictionary of the English Language.* New York: Random House, 1967, 1966.

Stobart, Tom. *The Cook's Encyclopedia.* New York: Harper & Row, 1981.

Tante Line. *La Bonne Pâtisserie Française.* Paris: Guy Le Prat Éditeur, 1948.

Tante Marie's French Pastry. (English translation by Charlotte Turgeon). New York: Oxford University Press, 1954.

Thuries, Yves. *Le Livre de Recettes d'un Compagnon du Tour de France.*

   Tome I, *Pâtisserie Française.* Cordes-sur-Ciel, France: Sociétés Éditar, 1980.

   Tome II, *Glaces, Petits Fours, Chocolats, Confiserie.* Cordes-sur-Ciel, France: Sociétés Éditar, 1982.

   Tome III, *Nouvelle Pâtisserie, Pièces Montées, Travail du Sucre.* Gaillac, France: Sociétés Éditar, 1979.

CROSS-INDEX
of
BASIC PREPARATIONS

The purpose of this index is to help you utilize basic preparations that can be kept on hand for use in a variety of cookies. We include here the flaky pastry doughs, which are used repeatedly throughout Chapter 7, as well as basic preparations for which recipes appear in the reference section on Basic Preparations and Procedures.

Each basic preparation is followed by the page numbers of the recipes in which it is required, with the recipe for the basic preparation itself listed first in **boldface** type. Note that for hazelnut, almond, and sugar powder and for hazelnut, raw almond, and sugar powder, you can mix hazelnut and sugar powder with the appropriate almond and sugar powder, in the proportions indicated in each recipe.

GENERAL INDEX

Page numbers in **boldface** type indicate the locations of recipes and of entries in the reference sections on Equipment and Ingredients.

Cookies for which there are color photos are indicated by a bullet (•) at the left. The location of the photo is listed in brackets, with the first number indicating which color insert it is in (1 or 2) and the second number the page within that color insert.

bowls, **415**
   copper, 56, **416**
bowl scrapers, **415**
• Bow Ties, [1:2], 356, **360**, 362, 374
• Bow Ties, Striped, [1:2], **362**
brandy, 450
   cookies flavored with, 140
Bresse, region of Burgundy, 44
brown sugar, 463
browned butter, 440, **490**
   cookies flavored with, 220, 234, 236
brownies, 184, 185
   French, **242**
Brussels Rum Cookies, **11**
bruxellois, **11**
butter, **438**
   browned, 220, 234, 236, 440, **490**
   to clarify, 440
   to cream, 5, 6, 189, 281, 439
   en pommade, 5, 439
buttercream, cookies filled with, 96, 102
Buttery Almond Tiles, **16**, 17, 254

C

Caen, city in Normandy, 296
• Caen-Style Sablés, [2:2], **296**, 298, 300
Café de Valois, 316
café filtré, cookies to serve with, 198
cake, le, 226
cake pans, **415**
   cookies baked in, 242, 244, 246, 248, 250
candied citron, lemon peel, and orange peel, **440**
Caracas Wafers, 58, **84**

caramel pot, **415**
Carême, 194, 278, 340, 344
carrés chocolat, 185, **242**
carrés aux marrons, **244**
Catherine de Médicis, 123, 316
Cats' Tongues, 4, **10**, 26, 254, 272, 478
champagne, cookies to serve with, 202, 204, 206, 214
champagne biscuit plaques, 422
   cookies baked in, 202, 204, 206, 208, 210
champagne biscuits, 184, 192, 193
   Alicante Biscuits, 184, 188, **216**
   Almond Champagne Biscuits, 203
• Classic Champagne Biscuits [1:1], 184, 188, **202**
   Cossack Biscuits 184, **210**
   Labbé Biscuits 184, **208**
   Langres Biscuits 184, **206**
   Mexican Biscuits 184, **212**
   Palma Biscuits 184, **214**
• Strawberry Champagne Biscuits [1:1], 184, **204**
Champigny, city on the Marne River, **402**
Champigny, Little, 355, **402**, 404
champigny, petits, **402**
Chang and Eng, 338
Chantilly, castle of, 386
chantilly, crème, 386
chapeaux fins, **319**
Charles V, King, 316
Charles IX, King, 316
charlotte russe, 194
Chartres, 96
chaussons feuilletés, **390**
chemins de fer, **42**
Cherry Balls, **140**
Cherry Rosettes, 121, **128**, 132
chestnut cream, 441
   cookies made with, 244
Chestnut Squares, 185, 186, **244**

N

O

W

V